RANGEMASTER

Law Enforcement
RANGEMASTER

A Foundational Guide

Paul Wood
Benjamin Kurata
Jason Wuestenberg

ACKNOWLEDGEMENTS

by Paul Wood

First, thanks to my amazing and talented wife, Tina, for sharing her knowledge and expertise with me and for being patient with my many requests and questions. Anything I know about writing, design, or photography (as well as many other topics) I owe to you. Thank you for your always constructive criticism and for supporting me even in my most ludicrous endeavors. I am very glad *you* are my eternal companion.

Thanks to JL Webber for teaching me how to be a rangemaster. You took me under your wing from the start and showed me by example what it takes to be a great instructor. Your insights into how to run a firearms program, conduct courses of instruction and so many other things were the bedrock that has supported whatever I may have accomplished in my career. Thank you for being my friend and mentor.

Thanks to Kyle Caffey for sharing your passion and humor as an instructor and a law enforcement officer. Thanks for showing me the ropes in my first assignment as a deputy and as a new firearms instructor. You proved that someone can actually hit *Charlie* at 100 yards, with a pistol, one handed. You have been missed; rest in peace brother.

Thank you to Steve Bebell for the painstaking work laying the foundation of the glossary. Your meticulous research of firearms terms will undoubtedly be a valuable resource for many generations of instructors yet to come.

To my friend Dan Murphy, thanks for sharing your in-depth knowledge of tactics with me. You have made me a better cop, supervisor, and instructor not to mention giving me a chance to work a fire hose! *Can I get an Amen?*

To my brother and amazing teaching partner, Al Brown. You brought so many good ideas to us making our skills programs infinitely better. Thanks for the passion you have shared, and let me be a part of, for the last 25 years.

To my good friends and co-authors, Jason Wuestenberg and Ben Kurata. It has been a long and arduous journey but totally worth it. It has been my honor to rub elbows with two such dedicated and knowledgeable rangemasters.

Lastly, to the dedicated firearms instructors of the Larimer County Sheriff's Office and Fort Collins Police Firearms Training Units that I have had the honor and privilege to teach with during the last 30 years. You have made a difference and undoubtedly saved people's lives.

by Ben Kurata

I have to admit, when I first tried to write an acknowledgement for this text, the famous words kept running through my head:

"But lately it occurs to me, what a long, strange trip it's been."
- The Grateful Dead.

It has been a long, strange trip, punctuated by moments of panic, but ultimately, worth every moment.

The first group of people I'd like to thank are my past, recent, current and future students. What good is someone who calls himself an "Instructor" without students? I have had the privilege of standing on ranges with intelligent, motivated, talented, curious students who brought open minds to class and were unafraid to ask questions and make (minor) mistakes while expanding their abilities as operators and as instructors. Without the students I have been blessed to have, I would not be an instructor. For every "Oh, S_ _t!" moment I've had on the range over the past 30 + years (just a handful), I've had countless moments of "Oh, Wow!" when a student pushed through their previous conception of what they were, and became better.

I can't remember all of the names of instructors, rangemasters, and peer students that have helped me along the way. For that I blame the 30 + year thing. But some people who I can distinctly remember are:

- Ray Chapman, for pushing my mental envelope of what a "shake, rattle and roll" 1911A1 with fixed iron sights is capable of with a good shooting platform and knowing how to refine a sight picture. (100% hits on a standard pepper popper at 300 yards, once I got my elevation dialed in.)
- Bank Miller, Director of the original SIGARMS Academy, for bringing his real-world experience of gunfights, first under Lt. Col. Hal Moore in a little valley in Viet Nam called Ia Drang, and later in every area of the world that the DEA had operations in.
- George Harris, Assistant Director of the original SIGARMS Academy, and USAR Camp Perry Double Distinguished, Service Rifle and Service Pistol. Mr. Harris is probably the most knowledgeable shooter / Instructor that I've ever known, and started

my current understanding of eye dominance and the effects of high stress on eye dominance in dynamic, low light engagements.

- Ken Good, Director of the original SureFire Institute. Probably the most challenging Instructor Certification I ever earned; I learned that the only thing worse than two 5th Group SF NCOs stalking you in the dark is a former SEAL with the latest night vision. I blame him for my lifelong fascination with night vision.
- Ken Murray, the co-inventor of FX dye marking cartridges and the father of force-on-force training. I still would not want to live inside his head!
- Clint Smith, the Founder and Director of Thunder Ranch, for pushing his students and their gear to the breaking point and pushing them beyond their previous self - imposed level of performance. In my case, it was a timely, "Suck it up! Nobody cares about your problems!" (More on that later.)
- Lt. Col. Dave Grossman, for doing the research and finding a way for good people to forgive themselves when they have to take another human's life.
- Jeff Hoffman, Owner of Black Hills Ammo, for our deep conversations as to what is on the event horizon to be looking for, often having nothing to do with firearms and ammunition.
- Dr. Bill Lewinski, Director of Force Science Institute, for doing the hard science that has saved and will save countless cops. (And for taking my advice on 1911s.)
- Billy Stojack, who was never here and I never saw, for befriending me for no good reason.

And finally, I would like to acknowledge my co-authors, Jason Wuestenberg and Paul Wood. When Jason first surfaced the idea of writing this book, I had a silent "Oh S _ _ t!" moment, as I have been presenting Rangemaster in all of its incarnations and permutations for about 20 years, going back when we created it at the SIGARMS Academy in 2001 - 2002ish. I have to admit, I have had many previous offers to collaborate on various texts, and all of those projects ended in disappointment. Not so in this case. Jason and Paul brought their A game, day in, day out, week after week until we arrived at what you hold in your hands (subject to future revision). It's rare when you're doing a group project that your colleagues bring as much, if not more, to the project than you do, but that has certainly been the case with this book. Thank you, Jason and Paul, for letting me tag along on this project.

by Jason Wuestenberg

There are a number of people who have helped me get to where I am today. First and foremost, I thank my wife Melissa for her unwavering support throughout our life together. She supported every decision I made in my career and with NLEFIA. She has made my life journey easier and enjoyable to say the least. Thank you and I love you!

Next, I want to thank my co-authors, Paul and Ben. It has taken nearly a year, from idea to print, for this dream to be realized. Not only are these guys my top instructors for the NLEFIA Rangemaster Development course, they are my humble friends as well. It has been an honor to work with both of them to produce this valuable book. Thank you for letting me be a part of it!

While there are several instructors that I have received training from and have influenced me over the years, there are a few that deserve special recognition. First and foremost, Mark Fricke. Mark was the first firearms instructor I received training from outside my agency before I became a firearms instructor. He was the epitome of a great instructor providing great training at a great price. I took all of his courses within the first five years of becoming a police officer. Our business relationship became a personal friendship over time. After being a firearms instructor for several years, Mark encouraged me to enter the national training arena to pass on my knowledge and experience to other instructors across the nation. I'm grateful for all that he has done for me…and I'm honored to call him my friend.

Next, I want to thank the firearms staff I worked with when I became a full-time firearms instructor at the Training Bureau for my agency. They all mentored me in one way or another: Sgt Bill Hawk, Arnie Stallman, Morris Jacoby, Ray Anderson, Murray Williams, Fred Musser, and Bill Collins. These guys not only molded me as an instructor but also taught me how to navigate the behind-the-scenes politics that are associated with both firearms instructor and rangemaster positions within a large agency.

Lastly, I want to thank two groups of awesome instructors. The first group is my instructor staff when I was a Rangemaster at my agency; a hard-working crew that only cared about putting on the best training possible for our officers. Thank you to Mark Nelson, Jack Villa, Patrick Crouse, Stacie Merrin, Steve White, and the numerous adjunct instructors that assisted us in our training. You guys are the reason we had a kick-ass training program that other agencies envied and emulated.

The second group is my instructor staff at NLEFIA. Again, an experienced crew that only cares about putting on the best training possible to help firearms instructors improve their training programs. You guys are the reason NLEFIA is successful…thank you!

by The Authors

To M. Escobar, CSP, MS, for her assistance with various technical, industrial safety information and keeping us honest. The value of a professional safety and risk management partner cannot be overstated and she has made an unforgettable contribution to safety in her workplace as well as volunteering her practical expertise for this book.

To Hannah Wood (hannahwoodcreates.com) for sharing her marvelous talents in the creation of the cover and various illustrations for this work and for all the edits we made you do.

Thank you to Dale Krupinski, owner of On Target Safety Academy (ontargetsafetyacademy.com) and member of the NLEFIA Board of Advisors (National Industrial Hygienist Advisor) for reviewing Chapter 11 for accuracy, contributing his wealth of knowledge and expertise on hazards and exposures and for the very quick turn-around.

Thanks to John Krupa, III for taking the time to read our various musings and write the forward for our work.

Thank you to Alex Babcock, owner of On Point Steel Targets (optargets.com), for technical information regarding steel targets.

Sincere thanks to the members of NLEFIA for embracing our informal expectation of "check your ego at the door" so that as a profession our collective OODA loop continues to improve.

And finally, we want to thank all of the instructors and hard-core trigger pressers (too numerous to name) that went out of their way to share their knowledge and skill, thus making us better instructors.

DEDICATION

This book is dedicated to law enforcement professionals of the past, present, and future that risk their lives every day to protect their communities and their fellow officers. In addition, this book is dedicated to the rangemasters and firearms instructors that provide life-saving training to law enforcement officers.

CONTENTS

Contents

Contents

Contents

FORWARD

by John Krupa III

W hen the authors invited me to review *Rangemaster: A Foundational Guide* and write the forward for this book, I realized that I was about to take on a task that required me to analyze the transitional aspects of firearms instructors who are preparing to work as rangemaster or director of training, and some of the logistical duties associated with those jobs. I was selected to write this forward because my successful evolution from firearms instructor to rangemaster and finally to CEO and Director of Training for a nationally-recognized training company is somewhat unique. It is a self-made success story nearly 28 years in the making, inspired by a single incident and fueled entirely by a passion to share my skills and knowledge with law enforcement professionals everywhere with the hope that they remain safe and effective throughout their tours of duty.

I, myself, am a proud third generation police officer. I joined law enforcement in 1991, working first for the Cicero Police Department (IL.) and shortly thereafter, joining the Chicago Police Department. At the time, I was an avid shooter, competitor, and firearms operator. But on March 8, 1995, my best friend that joined the Chicago Police Department with me, Police Officer Daniel Doffyn, was killed in the line of duty while responding to a burglary in progress. It was a sobering day that led me to realize just how undertrained we were as police officers, especially with respect to firearms and tactics. This incident would inspire my life-long mission to become a conduit for firearms and tactical training information that could be shared with other law enforcement officers with the ultimate goal of minimizing line-of duty injuries and deaths. (See Daniel J. Doffyn at www.ODMP.org)

I understood very well that I would be unable to develop training programs and deliver this information the way it needed to be delivered through my role as a Chicago Police Officer, so I took it upon myself to start a private training company. I started out very simple by researching information that could be used to fill in the gaps where I recognized that training was lacking. I attended training courses with some of the biggest names in the firearms training industry at the time: Jeff Cooper, Ray Chapman, Clint Smith, Bill Rogers, Chuck Taylor, John Farnam, Jim Cirillo, Massad Ayoob, Dave Lauck, Louis Awerbuck, John Shaw, and Rob Leatham. I studied their respective shooting techniques and teaching styles, and I read all of their books.

I continued training, specifically working on refining my instructor credentials. I completed my State of Illinois Firearms Instructor Certification and Master Firearms Instructor Certification, which opened doors for me to attend firearms instructor certification programs with the FBI, DEA, FLETC and the Secret Service Academy, among others. With the wealth of knowledge I was accumulating, I developed my own curriculum for a variety of training courses for handgun, rifle, shotgun and sub-machinegun. I taught those courses both through my own training company and as an adjunct master firearms instructor with the University of Illinois Police Training Institute.

In 1996, I learned first-hand as the result of my own police-involved shooting, that although my shooting skills were strong, my tactical acuity was not. I looked to the expertise of Brian McKenna and, in particular, his after-action reviews of police shooting incidents published in The Police Marksman Magazine. I found McKenna's analyses were on point and indispensable to learn tactical strategies in real-life situations. I integrated many of the ideas I learned from his articles into my own practices and training programs alike.

I realized quickly that I owe much of my success in this industry to other thriving professionals who so graciously share their knowledge and expertise. Early on, I developed strong instructor networking resources as a member of the American Society for Law Enforcement Trainers (ASLET) and the International Association of Law Enforcement Firearms Instructors (IALEFI). Additionally, I became a charter member of the International Law Enforcement Educators and Trainers Association (ILEETA) and a charter life member with the National Law Enforcement Firearms Instructors Association (NLEFIA). I maintain active membership with these organizations to this day.

By 2000, I started recruiting, training, and mentoring range safety officers, adjunct instructors, and lead instructors to help me run training programs that were offered through my company. In doing so, I discovered that managing range operations and staff employees was uniquely complex and required an entirely different set of skills beyond my instructor skill-sets. Much of what I had learned to this point was simply by observing others and replicating the best practices of professional firearms instructors who were successful in managing their own ranges, academies, and training programs. But in 2002, I was fortunate to attend the 40-hour Rangemaster Certification Course at the Sigarms Academy and learn professional range management strategies. Taught by industry training experts; Bank Miller, George Harris, and co-author of this book, Ben Kurata, this course offered invaluable information and detailed the intricacies of range operations management required of a rangemaster.

The rangemaster's responsibilities are vast. A successful rangemaster must recruit, vet, and train personnel for range safety officer, assistant firearms instructor, lead firearms instructor, and armorer positions. The rangemaster must keep all training curriculum current and verify that the lead instructors are qualified to teach their respective programs. The rangemaster must maintain archived records of instructor and range safety officer certifications, student training records, certificates of insurance, copies of lesson plans, course syllabi, itineraries, and reference source materials, all of which may be subpoenaed as part of discovery for criminal and civil litigation cases. Additionally, the rangemaster must ensure that range operations are in compliance with OSHA and EPA regulations, develop emergency medical action plans for indoor and outdoor training sites, maintain range equipment, and control firearms, ammunition, and training equipment inventory.

The authors of *Rangemaster: A Foundational Guide* have unique backgrounds in law enforcement training and the firearms training industry, and they unanimously acknowledged that there was a training gap that needed to be filled defining the role of the rangemaster position. To address this issue, the authors came together as members of the National Law Enforcement Firearms Instructors Association (NLEFIA) and developed one of the most comprehensive and up-to-date rangemaster training courses currently available in the firearms training industry. They streamlined the traditional 40-hour rangemaster program into a 3-day Rangemaster Development Course and established a national training standard model for rangemaster training.

Rangemaster: A Foundational Guide is an independent extension of NLEFIA's Rangemaster Development Course that includes 17 chapters detailing the duties, liabilities, goals and responsibilities of the rangemaster.

Whether you are working as a range safety officer, assistant firearms instructor, lead firearms instructor, rangemaster or director of training, *Rangemaster: A Foundational Guide* is a valuable training resource that will contribute to the knowledge, health and safety for all of these positions.

NLEFIA's motto is *"Advancing the knowledge and skills of professional firearms instructors"*. *Rangemaster* delivers to this standard at all levels!

Find what drives *your* passion in training and make it contagious. Enjoy the book and train safe!

Respectfully,

John Krupa III
Police Officer
CEO / Director of Training
Certified Firearm Specialist (IFSA)
Master Firearms Instructor (ILETSB)
Distinguished Weapons Expert (DHS)
Spartan Tactical Training Group, LLC

John Krupa, III has over 30 years of experience in law enforcement and has served as a patrol officer, FTO and firearms instructor. He is a recipient of the Award of Valor, Silver Star for Bravery, Distinguished Service Award and numerous department commendations and awards for his actions in the line of duty, including Police Officer of the Year Award for 1998 and 2005. John is founder, president and Director of Training for Spartan Tactical Training Group, LLC and has presented as a guest instructor at training conferences for ASLET, GTOA, IALEFI, ILEETA, ISOA, Action Target LETC, MidTOA, MTOA, NTOA and TTPOA. John can be reached at jkrupa@teamspartan.com

PREFACE

No basic police academy that we know of covers subjects such as government purchasing procedures, risk management, workplace safety, environmental protection regulations, inventory and record keeping, and product testing. Law enforcement is somewhat unique in that we hire new, sworn employees as officers or deputies and train them to do those duties. Then, at some point in their career, some are chosen to fill positions for which they often have little or no formal training or background, and in many cases are not provided resources to gain that knowledge.

Becoming a rangemaster is no exception to this phenomenon. While a person appointed to be rangemaster may have formal training as a firearms instructor, basic instructor certification courses do not cover most of these topics, and it is rare for them to have a background or extensive training in the topics listed above, or others they may face in the job. They are often left to navigate these difficult subjects on their own. Many, like the authors, learn on the job from their own experience and mistakes or from those willing to mentor them.

This book is intended as a resource for new or existing rangemasters to help fill the gap in at least some of the knowledge base required for this position. It is written as a guide for law enforcement and corrections firearms instructors that are responsible for the research, development, approval, administration, and defense of their agency's firearms training program. Additionally, it contains information about the design and operation of both indoor and outdoor, live-fire ranges.

While this book was written by the three authors who served as rangemasters with both similar and different experiences, the information within this book is the culmination of input from several rangemasters, who serve as staff instructors for the National Law Enforcement Firearms Instructors Association (NLEFIA), while developing the 3-day Rangemaster Development course.

Although this book is packed with information, it is not all-inclusive and only serves as a foundational guide for agency rangemasters. Various information may change over time as local and national trends change. This book, while not a replacement for, is an excellent supplement to the NLEFIA Rangemaster Development course.

Chapter 1: RANGEMASTER OVERVIEW & RESPONSIBILITIES

While training around the United States, we routinely hear some variation of the following when students introduce themselves in the Rangemaster Development course, "I was just handed the firearms program last week." Often these students feel completely overwhelmed by the task and responsibility in front of them. Sometimes, they are supervisors and other times line level personnel that were delegated the responsibility by someone above them. Not infrequently they are thrust into this role because a previous rangemaster left the agency; often this person has left nothing behind by way of written guidance for the next person.

Perhaps you are one of these individuals who has, without warning, had a major use of force program or oversight of a training facility thrust upon you. Maybe you have been a rangemaster for a number of years but have received little in the way of formalized training. Or, it might be that you are an experienced rangemaster that is looking to refresh or invigorate your training program or improve your range facility. Whatever your situation, we are confident that you will find useful information relevant to your position and

Photo by author

responsibilities within these pages. We are also confident that this book will be helpful in taking your program or facility to the next level and beyond.

The use of firearms in modern law enforcement has never been more controversial or scrutinized as it is today. At the same time, officers are still required to make split-second decisions in quickly evolving, highly volatile, and violent encounters. Against this backdrop, the law enforcement rangemaster is responsible for providing safe, effective, relevant training and/or managing training facility operations. This book will provide the new or experienced rangemaster with information, tools and resources to fulfill this mission.

The role and responsibilities of a rangemaster can be varied. In some agencies they may manage the range facility. In others, the rangemaster may coordinate the firearms training program. In yet another segment of agencies, the rangemaster may have both of these responsibilities and others. The following chapters will explore the different responsibilities that may fall within the position, and provide the rangemaster with guidance on how to manage these responsibilities and run a facility, training program, or both, successfully.

What is a rangemaster? The National Law Enforcement Firearms Instructor Association defines a rangemaster as:

> *A person of authority or seniority that manages an agency's firearms program and oversees the daily operations of a shooting range. Typically, a supervisory position or position of leadership. Ideally a certified firearms instructor with notable experience.*

Certification as a firearms instructor and significant experience in that role is often beneficial to becoming a rangemaster but may, or may not be requisite within a particular agency. Additionally, for agencies that use a third party's range, a rangemaster may be a person of authority or seniority that oversees a training program but has limited responsibility for range facility operations.

Regardless of whether a particular rangemaster has responsibility for a facility, a training program, or both, the position is one of formal leadership and the responsibilities are often far reaching. The position may be occupied by someone of rank (e.g., sergeant or lieutenant), it may be occupied by a line level officer or deputy, or it may be occupied by a civilian (retired officer / firearms instructor), depending on the size and configuration of the agency. In either case, the rangemaster responsibilities dictate that a certain amount of authority is provided in order to function in the job. As we discuss the various duties of the position, it will become clear that a rangemaster *is* a supervisory role, regardless of whether it is recognized by rank or not. This concept has relevance to the selection of personnel which will be discussed in a later chapter.

The supervisory obligations of a rangemaster vary from one organization to the next. A rangemaster may have a direct supervisory role, meaning they have subordinates that report to them within the formal organizational structure. They may also have an indirect supervisory role, such as adjunct instructors that take direction from the rangemaster but only within the limits of range or training operations.

Examples of individuals that a rangemaster may supervise often include but are not limited to:

- Firearms Instructors (FI): Certified to safely run a shooting range and train individuals in the use of firearms. Firearms instructors may need to have additional certifications for specific types of firearms training.
- Range Safety Officers (RSO): Certified to safely run a firing line, however NOT certified to train individuals in the use of firearms.
- Armorers: Certified to conduct manufacturer level inspections and repairs on various weapon systems.
- Administrative Staff: Individuals tasked with various office and support duties necessary for range or program operations.

Photo by author

Some agencies have started moving toward many of the above positions being non-sworn rather than sworn personnel. In the case of firearms instructors, non-sworn staff must have significant previous experience in sworn operations and firearms instruction to enable them to competently provide instruction on the use of deadly force to serving officers from a position of authority and experience.

One advantage of non-sworn personnel in these positions is that they are freed from other duties and on-going training responsibilities necessary to maintain regulatory entity requirements, such as a state Peace Officer Standards and Training (POST), or other required certifications. Thus, providing more time for these staff members to focus on training, armorer, or administrative responsibilities. Additionally, these positions often cost the agency less in salary and/or benefits.

The most significant disadvantage to non-sworn firearms instructors is likely that it is more difficult for them to maintain relevant work experience. As their experience becomes dated, it may be problematic to authoritatively instruct sworn personnel on current trends, tactics, or challenges related to law enforcement field work. While this is somewhat dependent on individual circumstances, it can be mitigated with ongoing contact and study of street situations by the non-sworn instructor. Nevertheless, it is likely that these personnel will have a "shelf-life" of relevance which should not be ignored by the agency.

Notwithstanding the composition or organizational structure of a particular agency, the rangemaster will often be intimately involved in the selection of the various range personnel mentioned above. Such selections frequently have a significant impact on the direction, quality, and character of the entire firearms program.

In addition to supervising staff, either directly or indirectly, rangemasters also have a responsibility to protect the agency, range staff, and firearms training programs from liability. They must be continuously looking at trends and cases and adjusting program operations accordingly. Individuals in this position often oversee the development, implementation, and revision of firearms training programs. This helps keep the training current with regional and national trends and legal updates. It also ensures that the most current and relevant training is being provided to officers and that training is integrated with other force and tactics instruction within the agency.

Rangemasters usually oversee the inventory of firearms and ammunition within an agency. They may also have budgetary responsibility for spare parts, weapon accessories, range supplies, and other equipment associated with the firearms program or range. This may include the selection of practice and duty ammunition and other equipment needed by the agency within the firearms program.

Rangemasters must be aware of and ensure that safety standards are implemented and followed by range personnel, students, and range guests. The rangemaster may have significant input or accountability for hearing conservation, selection and purchase of personal protective equipment, mitigation of lead or other hazardous materials, and selection and disposal of chemicals and other substances used within range facilities. Rangemasters should work closely with risk management, industrial hygienists, or similar personnel within their organizational structure to ensure that required or industry recommended workplace safety standards are being met.

If the agency operates its own range or contracts with a private facility, the rangemaster frequently has an obligation to ensure proper range maintenance is completed. This may include everything from daily cleaning and maintenance of bullet traps to ventilation or target system upgrades and nearly everything in between. The individual in this position may also be called upon for input in refurbishing, adding on to existing facilities, or development of new range facilities.

Finally, the rangemaster may have responsibility or input into development or modification of agency policy as a subject matter expert. Input may include either use of force or firearms possession and training depending on the experience and expertise of the rangemaster. They may also be called upon to conduct or advise on investigations regarding use of force review, firearms-related violations such as unintentional discharges, or other alleged policy violations.

In reviewing the various requirements and obligations of the rangemaster position, the significance of this position becomes clear. The magnitude of responsibilities is typically far above the duties of the average line level officer, deputy, trooper, or agent. Many of the tasks assigned to rangemasters have clear and distinct supervisory functions regardless of whether the position is assigned formal rank within the agency or not.

Whether you are new to the position of rangemaster or have been running a program or range for years, the following chapters will provide detailed insight into each of the responsibilities discussed above. The authors will provide examples, effective practices, and resources to help guide you in building or improving your firearms training program, range facility or both.

In discussing the position of rangemaster, we would be remiss not to mention several things that can be exceptionally detrimental to a firearms program or to facility management. Those include: big egos, stagnation, and kingdom building. You likely recognize one or more of these problems either from areas within your own agency or others with which you are familiar. These characteristics are often connected and tend to feed off each other. Unfortunately, they are all too common in many fields, including policing.

It is difficult, if not impossible, to advance a program or improve a facility if the person in the position of power possesses a big ego. Individuals in this situation are often more concerned about self-advancement or appearance over substance. Often, if the person in control is egotistical, it is exceptionally challenging to change anything about the program unless it is that person's idea or they believe it is. This is also a source of contention, stress, and high turnover of staff within a program. It also often leads to the siloing of skills, meaning that one skill, such as firearms, operates in a vacuum; completely independent of other skills such as patrol tactics or arrest control rather than being cohesive, correlative disciplines.

Stagnation is also prevalent within policing. Organizationally, we find it difficult to change and it is easy to "do it the way it has always been done." This problem may exist because the person in charge is reluctant to change, is overwhelmed with other duties and lacks time to focus on rangemaster responsibilities, or refuses to allow others to propose or implement change (kingdom building). Whatever the case, an agency's training and/or facilities can become quickly out of date unless the person in charge, the rangemaster, is constantly seeking input for the program and pursuing regular maintenance, improvement, or replacement of the range and equipment. Hosting outside training courses, encouraging junior instructors to present new ideas for consideration, and working with budget personnel on capital replacement programs are a few ways the rangemaster can avoid stagnation.

Finally, kingdom building is routinely prevalent within facilities and programs and is often ego driven and frequently leads to stagnation. The term 'kingdom building' is, of course, referring to a single person being in charge of a facility or program and exercising draconian control over all aspects of their position. These individuals will rarely share information nor will they encourage or provide professional development for their staff, often out of fear of losing their position and/or power. Whether they have developed the program or inherited it from someone else, they are typically not interested in entertaining any type of change.

As a result, details about a facility and necessary maintenance or access are often hidden. Similarly, programs under these individuals are usually dogmatic, with 'always' and 'never' policies that are rarely written down. Questions regarding why a particular practice or technique is used are summarily dismissed or discouraged. If curriculum is in a written format, the kingdom building rangemaster will typically be the only one with access to the material. In addition to being out of date and lacking progress and innovation, when the rangemaster finally does vacate their position, the next person often has nothing to start with and has to build everything from scratch again. We regularly hear statements along these lines from attendees in the NLEFIA Rangemaster course. We hope that the course and this book will provide a necessary starting place for rangemasters in this situation as well as those functioning under well organized, positive leadership.

Photo by author

As you read the following sections, we hope that you will recognize that we are not advocates or practitioners of haughty egos, program or position stagnation, or kingdom building. On the contrary, NLEFIA is an organization that values recognition of varied experience, advocates for innovation, and promotes knowledge sharing. As a rangemaster, these qualities and values can elevate your program or the operation of your facility to an entirely new level, as many have shown throughout our profession. To accomplish this takes hard work, cooperation, and the strong desire to pass on the knowledge we gain through our experience to the next generation of rangemasters. In short, that is why this book has been written.

Chapter 2: SAFETY

Safety must be established as the foundation of any firearms training program or range operations protocol. However, safety does not have to stifle quality, relevant, dynamic range training if instructors have the proper knowledge base, understand, and practice risk mitigation in their coaching tactics. As one of the Association instructors said, "firearms training is dangerous, but it should *not* be reckless." - *V. Rosado, NLEFIA Instructor*

Firearms and Range Rules

Firearms training often begins with a discussion about safety which is completely appropriate. This discussion often includes sets of rules to be followed by participants in the training. We will separate these rules into two categories and discuss each separately and how they interact. The first is firearms safety rules and the second is range safety rules.

Firearms safety rules are usually taught as applying in any environment whether on or off the range. These are generally taught as four firearms safety rules and are derivatives of rules standardized and made popular by the late Colonel Jeff Cooper, a noted firearms trainer who started Gunsite, a well-known firearms training school in Paulden, Arizona. Most POST organizations and law enforcement agencies around the United States have adopted some version of these four rules into their firearms training programs.

The rules have been re-written and altered by many organizations to fit their needs since they were originally introduced. When NLEFIA was starting, the Executive Director, Jason Wuestenberg, approached several members of the Board of Advisors to develop a set of firearms safety rules that were practical for the next generation of firearms instructors. Being a national organization, the intent was to develop a set of rules that could serve as a template for organizations throughout the U.S. and beyond to guide the safe handling and operation of firearms in a law enforcement setting. The following rules were introduced by the Association during their first classes and remain a key part of the training today:

1. **Know the status of your firearms at all times.** This version of the first rule was first heard by one of the authors in 2012 from national trainer Pat McNamara (Pat Mac) of TMACS. Anytime you handle a firearm, or carry one on your person, you must know the status of the weapon system at any given time. Is there a magazine inserted and seated properly? Is there a round in the chamber? Is the hammer de-cocked? Is the external, mechanical safety in the proper position? Rather than statements about the condition of a firearm or how it should be treated, this rule makes clear that it is the operator's responsibility to know, without a doubt, what condition their firearm is in. A common version of the first firearms safety rule is, "all guns are always loaded," which is a lie. All guns are *not* always loaded. How many officers on duty are walking around with an empty chamber because they have been indoctrinated with *all guns are always loaded.* Shooters should not make assumptions that firearms are always loaded. They should know the condition, or they should verify the condition so that they *do* know.

2. **Never point your firearm at anything you are not willing to shoot.** This rule is self-explanatory and addresses specifically how to handle firearms. It is commonly referred to as the "laser rule", meaning if there were a laser emitted from the muzzle/barrel of your firearm, you should not allow it to touch anything you are not willing to shoot. Once again, this rule is simply stated and places accountability on the operator of the firearm to determine what they are willing to point their firearm at or not including if that means holding a suspect at gunpoint in the case of law enforcement. Secondly, many re-written versions of these rules use the word "destroy" or similar inflammatory language to emphasize the importance of this rule. While pistol rounds are capable of causing damage, they rarely *destroy* the objects they impact. Another version of this rule uses reverse language, "Always point your firearm in a safe direction." This verbiage is not appropriate for law enforcement as officers are often required to hold a suspect at gunpoint. Pointing a firearm at a body would not be considered a safe direction but it may be appropriate in a deadly force encounter. NLEFIA opted for simple, clear rules that were true in all circumstances.

3. **Keep your trigger finger straight along the frame / receiver until you are on target and have decided to fire.** This rule is also self-explanatory. Before you can touch the trigger, your firearm must be pointed at your intended target and you must have made the decision to fire. Both conditions must exist before touching the trigger. Anything less than that and the trigger finger should be straight along the frame or receiver, above the trigger guard. Therefore, this rule applies to both training and operational environments equally. Many versions of this rule use the phrase "ready to fire" instead of "decided to fire". There is a clear distinction between the two. Law enforcement officers should always be ready to fire, but that should not give them permission to touch the trigger. Generally speaking, the use of external mechanical safeties typically follows the same rule. Safeties should remain on or in the "safe" position, until you are on target and have decided to fire. When you come off the sights and trigger, then the safety goes back on.

4. **Identify the threat and environment before firing.** "Identify the threat," is all encompassing and means whether the intended target is friendly or hostile and if the target is armed or not. "Identify the environment," is also all encompassing and means knowing the surrounding area and situation. For example, know what is behind the target (backstop) in case of an over-penetration or miss. Know what is left and right of the target to ensure no one can step into your line of fire. Know what is in front of the target (e.g., hostage, type of cover, etc.) Know where the other "good guys" are in relation to the threat. This rule is also intended to be applicable to both training and operational conditions within the law enforcement realm.

Some advocate for keeping the original, or their version of the original, rules in place because of tradition or purity or whatever other reason. NLEFIA's goal is not to tell individuals or agencies how to run their programs or their ranges. Rather, it is to offer suggestions and ideas on how agencies or rangemasters might move their programs forward, be innovative, and adapt to an ever-changing world. The above rules are not the only way to do it but rather *a way* to do it that is simply stated and backed by carefully thought-out reasoning and intention.

Many rangemasters are confined to particular verbiage of these rules by a higher regulatory entity like a Peace Officer Standards and Training (POST) organization. Whatever the case, rangemasters should be intimately familiar with these rules and the "why" behind each one. They should ensure that all instructors enforce them as intended. As much as possible, rangemasters should establish a pattern of teaching these rules to all officers along with an understanding of how to practically apply them on the range as well as in the field, at home, or in any other environment.

Range safety rules, on the contrary, are typically designed and implemented for a specific training venue. These rules routinely include specifics for the layout of the range, equipment present, ammunition allowed, actions allowed or not allowed by shooters, etc. Some common range safety rules are: eye and ear protection must be worn at all times during live fire; loading and unloading may only take place in certain areas or under specific direction; the condition firearms must be in when not on the 'firing line'; etc. Some rules are appropriate and necessary such as the use of eye, ear and other safety equipment relative to the use of the range. Others are less relevant.

Common Range Safety Rules:
- Eye and ear protection must be worn at all times on the range
- No food or drink allowed on the range
- Loading and unloading may only be done in designated areas
- Shooting only allowed from firing line
- Only discharge firearms from approved shooting stations
- No one may go forward of the firing line until the range is declared safe
- Do not handle firearms when others are down range.
- Shooters may not pick up items from the ground until instructed by rangemaster
- Always keep your firearm pointed in a safe direction

Rules such as those prohibiting shooters from picking anything up off the ground without specific direction or not allowing anyone forward of the firing line during live fire, can inhibit conducting practical law enforcement training. That is not to say that some of these rules do not have a place in modern law enforcement training. For example, initial recruit training may be conducted in a far more restrictive manner with some of the above safety protocols in place. However, as shooter skills progress, rangemasters and instructors should have the ability to modify or lift some range safety rules to allow for practical training.

One of the tenets of NLEFIA's training is that if you expect an officer to perform a skill in the field environment, they should be able to practice that skill on the range, at least in some fashion. For example, if the range has a rule that does not allow anyone forward of the designated firing line during live fire, how can officers practice bounding movement drills which are a widely accepted tactic in law enforcement today? This example shows how too many restrictive range safety rules can reduce the practicality and effectiveness of the training that instructors are able to provide.

One of the author's previously worked for an agency that has practiced live-fire, officer/citizen down rescues, using a live person on the range as the 'victim' since the early 2000's. Another of the authors' works for an agency that recently performed similar training in an indoor range using patrol vehicles to practice the rescues. This type of training can be done safely and responsibly with the appropriate instructor knowledge, preparation and coaching. Further, it is invaluable for law enforcement officers to learn these techniques and tactics in a controlled environment in which they have a coach with them to ensure that any mistakes are minor rather than fatal.

To conduct practical training, some *range* safety rules may need to be suspended; however, *firearms* safety rules are always followed.

Rangemasters should regularly discuss the efficacy of the range safety rules they have in place with their staff and give critical thought to the necessity of each one and what they may be giving up by having too many restrictive rules in place. A different approach would be to have range safety rules that were relevant depending on the group being trained. For example, new recruit officers with unknown firearms experience versus officers returning to the range for in-service or advanced officer training (AOT). Some of the rules enforced for the former may be able to be suspended for the latter to conduct more practical, advanced, field-relevant training.

Both firearms safety rules and range safety rules should be conspicuously posted as a reminder to all using the range or classroom of a training facility. At a minimum, the firearms safety rules should be reviewed at the beginning of every training session either as part of or in addition to the safety plan (see Appendix A for an example of a site safety plan).

Classroom Safety

September, 2005: A 23-year-old Georgia police recruit is killed when a firearms instructor unintentionally shoots her during a training demonstration[1].

August, 2011: A 24-year-old Georgia probation officer is killed during in-service training when she was unintentionally shot by a firearms trainer in the classroom[2].

September, 2014: A 26-year-old Pennsylvania State Trooper is killed when a firearms instructor unintentionally shoots him during a classroom demonstration[3].

August, 2016: A 73-year-old retired librarian is shot and killed by an instructor during a citizen's academy shoot / don't shoot demonstration[4].

April, 2022: A civilian role-player is shot in the abdomen by a police auxiliary officer when a live firearm was introduced into a traffic stop scenario training.[5]

Many agencies have suffered tragic, yet completely avoidable, injuries or deaths during training, even within the classroom environment. Most, if not all, of these horrific incidents could have been avoided by following the firearms safety rules listed above. The classroom may be an environment that warrants some additional rules or protocols regarding safety.

If available, the best option for classroom demonstration is an inert training firearm that is clearly marked as such. However, if one is not available, functioning firearms are sometimes necessary in classroom settings to train officers on the operation, cycle of function, disassembly, maintenance, and reassembly of the firearms they may be handling. Nevertheless, some basic protocols can be enacted to prevent unintentional discharges, injuries, or deaths in this environment.

First and foremost, all personnel, including and perhaps especially instructors, must follow the Firearms Safety Rules at all times. No functioning firearm should ever be pointed at a student or instructor for any reason, period. This behavior is reckless, negligent and a violation of basic firearms safety. If the demonstration requires the simulation of pointing a firearm at a suspect, ONLY a totally inert training firearm (blue gun) should be used.

Photo by author

When live firearms are used in classroom instruction, safety rules must be strictly followed at all times.

Second, ammunition should be strictly prohibited from the classroom environment when firearms will be handled by any person. Ammunition from students AND instructors should be downloaded and secured in a separate designated location before commencing classroom instruction with firearms. This can be a clearing barrel or station, or the range as long as it is a known and established process. There should also be thorough checks of students and instructors prior to beginning classroom instruction.

Another common safety practice that *must* be thoroughly ingrained in all instructional staff is to have at least one other person (preferably more than one) physically verify the empty condition of any firearm and associated ammunition devices (magazines, clips, speed loaders, etc.) prior to beginning any demonstration. Similarly, confirming that any cartridges used for demonstration are fluorescent, inert, training ammunition ONLY - commonly referred to as dummy rounds. Even with these practices, the firearm should always be pointed in a safe direction; a direction in which if the gun were to discharge, no one would be injured. Finally, the instructor should always verify the firearm is unloaded *each time* before pulling the trigger, if that is necessary for the demonstration.

If students are to be handling firearms, instructors must individually and personally verify that the following is observed:

- None of the firearms are loaded.
- No student has any live ammunition on their person or in the classroom.
- Enough space exists for students to point the firearm in a safe direction while handling, disassembling, reassembling or function testing it.
- Instructors should indicate what is a safe direction for students to point their firearm.
- All Firearms Safety Rules are adhered to at all times with no tolerance for carelessness.

These rules and procedures *cannot* be handled nonchalantly by instructors. They must be observed and adhered to with the utmost awareness and attention to detail. This is not to say that the classroom environment has to be totally rigid and unpleasant but when it comes to the safe handling of firearms, there is no room for callous behavior and rangemasters and instructors cannot condone it.

Along with the rules and protocols above, instructors should always be striving to exemplify safe and proper handling of firearms regardless of the activity or environment. The responsibility of the rangemaster is to impress this behavioral expectation upon the instructor staff and ensure it is carried out in daily activities until it becomes part of the culture of the program.

As discussed above, range safety must begin with the Firearms Safety Rules reviewed as part of training, conspicuously posted, and strictly observed by students and instructors alike. Additional range safety rules may be created for the facility; however, range safety rules should not interfere with training objectives as long as the Firearms Safety Rules are being followed. Range safety rules will not be universal but rather specific to each individual training venue. Equipment, layout, and limitations of each range will dictate the range safety rules needed.

Personal Protective Equipment (PPE)

Eye protection is a basic, mandatory requirement for live-fire shooting ranges. Rangemasters must ensure that this is rigorously enforced on the ranges and during the training for which they are responsible. The question becomes, what type of eye protection is appropriate for shooting activities?

Eye protection for shooting should be "wrap around" or be constructed to include side protection. The glasses should be 100% UVA and UVB rated, regardless of shading, if used outdoors. Anti-fog is another good feature to consider providing the shooter with the clearest view possible. The glasses should also be rated for high impact as defined by the American National Standards Institute (ANSI). How do you tell if glasses have this rating? To be qualified for standard or high impact rating through ANSI, glasses must be stamped on the frame or more commonly on the ear piece with "Z87" for standard impact or "Z87+" or "Z87.1" for high impact[6]. Additionally, most vendors that sell safety glasses list the rating in the description on web-based shopping sites or in catalogs.

Rangemasters and instructors should be wary about allowing shooters with standard prescription glasses to use those for range activities. Impact resistance varies greatly on standard prescription eyewear and most day-to-day wear glasses lack any type of wrap around protection.

For prescription eyeglass wearers, safety and risk management departments of most governmental agencies will offer a program to provide prescription safety eyewear for employees. Rangemasters may need to educate risk management personnel on the potential hazards of range activities to show the justification for higher (Z87+) impact rating. Discussing hazards such as fragmentation of projectiles off metal targets or target frames, ejected brass, defective rounds causing a catastrophic malfunction of the firearm, or flying debris from shooting in prone, around actual or simulated cover or other positions are examples of hazards that are common on law enforcement ranges. If shooters are on SWAT there may be additional hazards if they practice explosive breaching techniques.

If safety glasses are used in combination with over the ear hearing protection, the glasses should have thin profile ear pieces so as not to interfere with the effectiveness of the hearing protection.

Photo by author

Proper hearing protection is another absolute requirement of live-fire training. Typical law enforcement firearms generate impulse noise around 140 to 160 decibels (dB) sound pressure level (SPL). SPL changes with distance from the source. Another consideration is the duration that an individual is exposed to the noise. Effective hearing protection must be able to protect the wearer sufficiently from the impulse noise generated on the range for the span of time during which they are likely to be exposed. Comfort should not be overlooked when determining appropriate hearing protection to ensure the users can wear it for the expected duration.

Agencies should supply sufficient hearing protection for anyone working on or around the range including observers. Depending on regulatory agencies for the state or locality, agencies may be required by law to provide this equipment. Regardless of this, providing adequate hearing protection for firearms ranges is a standard practice throughout the industry and should be observed. Rangemasters should keep additional hearing protection at the range available for use by anyone who does not have a personal set. This can be disposable foam ear plugs, quality over-the-ear muffs or a combination of the two. Rangemasters and instructors should also verify that the noise reduction rating (NRR) of the hearing protection being used on the range is sufficient for the noise generated and the duration individuals will be exposed. For more information on hearing protection see *Chapter 11: Hazards and Exposures.*

Brimmed hats have become a commonly required PPE item on many ranges. The concept is that hats with a brim such as baseball hats, or "boonie" hats prevent hot brass from lodging in the safety glasses of shooters, avoiding potential eye injuries. While this is a legitimate safety concern, there is another issue that must be addressed in using brimmed hats on the range.

One of the authors recently engaged in the testing of a variety of hearing protection options for a new indoor range. When the muffs were worn over a standard baseball cap, the hat broke the seal of the muff around the wearer's ear. During testing, NRR was reduced up to 11 dB. This meant that an earmuff with a 29 NRR was only operating with an 18 dB NRR which would be insufficient for use on an indoor range.

Rangemasters must be aware of such "trade-offs" in the combination of safety equipment and adjust their equipment selection accordingly. Similar to the above problem, some safety glasses can cause a break in the seal of over the ear hearing protection resulting in the same problem. Glasses, hearing protection, and hats should be evaluated together. No PPE should ever create an additional safety hazard for the user.

Ballistic vests are also commonly required for use on many law enforcement ranges. This requirement is not without merit but may also have some limitations that rangemasters should take into account. Rangemasters must be able to logically evaluate when a procedure or item of equipment is increasing safety or may compromise safety. We must be willing to question and think through the pros and cons of the "always done it that way" practices.

Standard body armor is effective against most pistol rounds, depending on the rating, and provides an additional layer of safety for range operations in many cases. Wearing body armor during training may prevent a serious or even fatal injury to an instructor or student should there be an unintentional discharge. However, unless specifically rated plates are used, body armor will be largely ineffective for typical 5.56 or .223 caliber rifle rounds used in law enforcement rifle programs.

Additionally, if range rules require the use of body armor during on-body covert or concealed carry pistol training, the armor could actually create a higher likelihood of an unintentional discharge or injury. The bulk of the armor in combination with tighter fitting concealment holsters may cause the firearm to hang up on the armor during the draw or holstering of the pistol. Further, the student may have to holster at an awkward angle due to the armor and cover themselves with the muzzle of the pistol.

Another consideration of the use of body armor during training is environmental. If officers are training outside in extreme heat, the addition of required body armor for every drill could exacerbate the occurrence of heat related injuries.

There is no doubt that training in the gear and uniform officers will wear on the job is important. "Shaking out" or testing various pieces of equipment during range exercises can be invaluable to determine performance or adjustments needed for field operation. Nevertheless, rangemasters should exercise reasonable discretion in determining when "full kit" is necessary for range exercises and when it is not. If the addition of equipment such as body armor is going to increase the likelihood of an injury on the range, the instructor or rangemaster should seriously consider adjustments such as allowing shooters to practice without the armor.

Other range personal protective equipment may include the type of clothing worn by shooters, gloves, cold weather gear, protection against sun exposure, knee and elbow pads or other items as determined by range staff. Any hazards that reasonably exist should be addressed by staff.

Most law enforcement ranges properly require personnel to wear long pants to avoid brass burns and other unnecessary injury to the legs. Long pants can also prevent insect bites, sunburn, or other hazards that are not directly related to shooting activities.

Depending on the environment, gloves may be recommended to avoid burns, thorns or injury to the hands from rocky ground or other hazards. Learning weapon manipulation with gloves may be necessary if gloves are part of the standard uniform. Similarly, cold weather gear may be necessary to protect students from the elements or the training may be specific to working in that gear.

Sun exposure can be dangerous and cause long-term health risks. Providing or recommending protection such as sunscreen, long sleeve SPF rated clothing, neck scarves and hats is appropriate for outdoor range operations.

When range staff expect to work on position shooting as part of training, recommending knee and elbow pads to be worn by students can prevent unnecessary injury leading to loss of duty time or career shortening damage to joints.

One of the greatest limitations of any type of PPE is the proper use. Many people misuse, don't use, or don't know how to use PPE properly. It is up to rangemasters and instructor staff to provide adequate training on the use of all range PPE and enforce its use during training until it becomes ingrained in the culture of the organization.

Site Safety Plans

Each range facility should have a site safety plan. The safety plan includes items such as the address and possibly the longitude and latitude coordinates of the range, if helicopter medical assistance will be summoned. The site safety plan should include the date and time of training, the instructor in charge, other roles such as safety officer, location of a trauma kit and AED if available, location of a fire extinguisher, and locations and/or directions to the nearest emergency room, fire station, and/or trauma center.

Specific hazards for the range facility should be briefed as well. These may include animal hazards such as snakes, alligators, stinging insects for those who may be allergic, and so on. Environmental hazards should be addressed as well. These may include use of sunscreen, hydration, frostbite, trip hazards, rodent holes, and shelters available for wind, hail, or lightning. In short, any reasonably common hazard which may cause injury to personnel should be noted and discussed in the briefing.

The site safety plan should also include information on procedures for reporting and treating minor injuries and procedures in case of serious injury such as a gunshot wound. If there are specific instructors or students present with advanced medical training such as EMTs or paramedics, the site safety plan should identify those individuals. Time should be given for them to familiarize themselves with the medical equipment available.

Information regarding procedures for contacting emergency medical assistance should be provided in the site safety plan. It should answer questions such as:

- Who is responsible for summoning medical assistance?
- What is the primary and back-up method of communication with EMS? (e.g., radio then cell phone)
- Who determines if a patient will be treated in place or transported to meet the ambulance or directly to the hospital?

- If it is possible a patient will be transported, what is the transportation plan? What vehicles, drivers and back-up drivers, route, etc.?

It is suggested that the site safety plan also include chain of command notification procedures, identify who will be in charge of securing the scene of the injury for investigation, any follow up that must be completed before training resumes, or other reporting requirements. Finally, the site safety plan may include the Firearms Safety Rules and any proactive steps that should be taken to create and maintain a safe training environment.

The site safety plan should be reviewed and briefed to all instructors and students who are attending training. If specific responsibilities are assigned such as driving the transport car or communicating with a dispatch center, the instructor can conduct a "brief back" in which they ask the group, "who is the driver of the transport car," and so on to ensure the group understands the plan. It is also suggested that the plan be rehearsed, at least with the instructors, on a semi-regular basis to adequately prepare them for what is, hopefully, a very rare event.

If agencies utilize a commercial range for training while members of the public are present, part of the briefing of the site safety plan should include consideration of implementing the plan for an individual or group outside the officers' present for training. If emergency vehicles are parked at a particular range and a serious injury occurs on another range, it is not unlikely that someone will come to where the first responders are to summon help.

An example of a Site Safety Plan may be found in *Appendix 1: Forms*. For a downloadable copy of the site safety plan template and other forms go to *www.rangemasterforms.com*.

Range Staffing

As part of planning training, consideration must be given to the staffing necessary to operate the range. This is typically done by established ratios of instructors to students. Regulatory agencies such as state POST organizations may have mandatory instructor to student ratios for recruit training, in-service or advanced officer training, low light training, live-fire scenario training or a combination of these.

Rangemasters should carefully consider the appropriate staffing level for the training they are undertaking. Almost every agency we have interacted with across the U.S. is understaffed in some way. Lack of agency staffing *should not* influence conducting safe range operations with adequate instructor student ratios. This may require that smaller relays are conducted due to fewer instructors which may result in more down time for students. Nevertheless, safety CANNOT be compromised for the sake of getting more people through training.

Photo by author

Most agencies range between 1:4 and 1:6 for daylight, line drills with no forward or backward movement. These ratios *may* be different for recruit training or advanced officer training. Usually, agencies will have lower ratios for low light training; typically, 1:3. For live-fire scenario training or dynamic solo or team drills the ratios may drop to 1:1 or 1:2 depending upon what the drill is, the experience and competency of the students, and so on.

Generally, rangemasters should error on the side of lower ratios and higher safety. The higher the ratio, the less control each line instructor will have over their designated group of shooters. This will also impact their ability to effectively coach the shooters.

Use of Non-reactive Stationary Steel Targets

Steel targets are excellent training tools when used properly; however, they have several safety considerations which must be taken into account when they are used for range training. The type of targets, design considerations, minimum shooting distances, type of ammunition used, and angling of targets should be intentionally and thoughtfully addressed.

Before using steel targets, rangemasters should first consider their training objectives. They can be great training aids for practical shooting; however, if working on marksmanship skills, the instructors may be better served by utilizing paper targets. Advantages to using steel targets include reducing down time checking and marking paper targets in between reps or shooters through a drill.

The construction of steel targets is important for the safety of the shooters and instructors. Rangemasters should have a solid understanding of steel targets. First, the steel plate should have a rating of AR500 or AR550. Abrasion resistant (AR) steel with a Brinell hardness rating of 500 is what most steel targets are made from. AR500 steel is often referred to as being "through hardened", meaning a high velocity rifle round will not penetrate through the steel plate. However, depending on the projectile velocity at the time of impact, it could cause pitting in the surface of the steel plate. As a general rule, projectile velocity should be less than 2800 feet per second (ft/sec) at the time of impact to prevent any pitting. This generally means typical rifle rounds used in law enforcement should be fired from 100 yards or greater.

AR550 steel plates, with a Brinell hardness rating of 550, are often referred to as "surface hardened", meaning the surface is less likely to pit from high velocity rifle projectiles. Again, this depends on the projectile velocity at the time of impact. As a general rule, projectile velocity should be less than 3000 ft/sec at the time of impact to prevent pitting on an AR550 plate. This generally means typical rifle rounds used in law enforcement can be fired from as close as 25 yards without causing pitting. It is always best to check with the steel target vendor if the steel rating was certified by a third party.

The next consideration is the thickness of the steel plate. Steel plates are commonly cut in 1/4-inch, 3/8-inch, and 1/2-inch thickness. 1/4-inch plates are okay for smaller pistol calibers but not the best for pistol calibers used for law enforcement. 3/8-inch is the most common thickness; however, it is susceptible to warping over time, even with an AR550 rating. The warping affect can be countered by reversing the plate as soon as any warping is observed, if the plate is designed to do so. A thickness of 1/2-inch is the most rugged and durable plate for training, but it weighs more than a 3/8-inch plate of equal size.

The next feature to take into account is the target design. The steel target should be designed so the strike plate has a 15 to 20-degree downward deflection angle. This allows most of the projectile fragmentation to be deflected downward. The strike plate should also allow for some movement when hit. This offers the instructor and/or shooter a visual indicator of a successful hit, and also reduces the energy transfer from the projectile which helps preserve the life of the steel plate.

The minimum safe distance for shooting at steel targets will depend on the AR rating, the condition of the steel plate surface, and the specific projectile being fired. As a general rule, the minimum distance for handgun training should be 10 yards. If the steel plate surface is mildly pitted, then the minimum distance should be increased. As a general rule for rifle rounds, the minimum safe distance is 25 yards. If the plate surface is mildly pitted or it's rated as AR500, then the minimum distance should be increased. If training requires the shooter to engage a steel target inside of recommended minimum safe distances, then frangible ammunition should be used.

Rangemasters must monitor the condition of the steel targets used to ensure safety for shooters. Steel targets that are pitted or showing early signs of warping can be reversed (if the bracket system allows) as mentioned above. Alternatively, if they are badly pitted, warped, or otherwise damaged, they should be taken out of service and replaced. Likewise, the stands, brackets and posts should be regularly checked for damage and repaired or replaced as necessary.

It is advisable to have range staff wear heavy work gloves when moving or working with steel targets. When shot, the metal can become deformed around the edges and result in sharp surfaces that can cause injury. Target systems with 2x4 or other wooden supports can become embedded with metal fragments from projectiles deflected off of the steel target into the wood. Handling the wood posts can be hazardous without proper protective gloves.

For more in-depth information about using steel targets, download the free *Steel Target Guide for Law Enforcement Firearms Instructors* from the NLEFIA website (nlefia.org).

Low Light Range Operations

Training in low light conditions is exceptionally important for law enforcement and required by case law. See *Chapter 13: Case Law* for more information about training requirements. It also presents some unique challenges for instructional staff and warrants additional safety protocols to ensure a safe training environment.

The most obvious challenges are that it is difficult for instructors to see students, for students to see each other, and for everyone to see hazards or personnel down range. Therefore, it is necessary for rangemasters to develop specific and clearly stated protocols for low light range operations. Below are some suggested practices; however, specific practices should be developed for each unique venue. For example, low light training at an indoor range where

Photo by author

Lights (red) on the shoulder of each instructor allow the lead to quickly locate his or her adjuncts.

lighting can be turned on between exercises may be very different from low light training at an outdoor range where the only light sources are flashlights and/or vehicles. Therefore, each rangemaster should work with his or her staff to develop safety protocols that are effective for their given range facility. If they operate at more than one facility, the staff may need to modify protocols to fit the unique features of each venue.

The below list of suggested protocols is by no means exhaustive. It is intended to provide examples and create additional discussion among rangemasters and their staff to determine the best procedures for their range.

1. Use chem lights or LED safety lights to mark instructors and students. Some type of low intensity light on the front, back, shoulder or hat of each student and instructor can help keep track of people on the range.
2. Use of headlamps by instructors. Some agencies use headlamps for instructors so they can be seen while down range and these can be used for marking targets, checking student firearm conditions, or other activities which might require the use of both hands.
3. Darkness and silence protocol: the idea is that darkness and silence indicate the line is ready, safe, or other affirmative response to the lead instructor. For example, if the Lead says, "Shooters ready?" if a shooter is *not* ready, they should indicate by light on or verbally responding "no" or "not ready".
4. Instructor staff can also use lights on as a status indication. For example, "when everyone is in the holster, shine a flashlight at your feet." The Lead can then see when the line is safe.
5. Downrange clear. A common safety protocol that is highly suggested is after checking targets and returning to the firing line, one instructor is designated to be the last person back and to check down range by a slow sweep of a flashlight to ensure all students and instructors are back at the firing line. The instructor then verbally indicates to the lead, "Downrange Clear." This clear verbal communication also affords the opportunity for someone who is downrange to respond, "cease fire" or similar.
6. Range lighting between drills. If the range is equipped, low intensity lighting can be turned on between drills to help students navigate the range, mark targets, load magazines and instructors to complete paperwork or other administrative functions. Lighting may be overhead, on target carriers, etc.
7. Lower instructor to student ratios. As previously mentioned, changing instructor to student ratios is advisable for low light range operations. A ratio of 1:3 is fairly standard. This better allows instructors to see the students they are responsible for in low light conditions. It also allows them to be closer to the student if they need to physically prevent a safety violation.
8. Restricted staging areas and headcounts. Students may be more restricted to where they are able to move on the range during low light

so instructors can better account for students when it is difficult to see. Instructors may do headcounts before starting a drill and students may be required to advise a specific instructor if they need to leave the range for some reason.

These are just a few examples of protocols that many agencies use for low light range operations. Additional restrictions may be necessary to maintain safety on the range during this type of training. Any protocols used should be briefed at the beginning of a training session.

Instructor Certification and Competency

Details concerning instructor certification, experience, and competency will be discussed in more detail in a later chapter; however, as a safety issue, instructors must be certified and/or have the requisite experience and competency to safely instruct specific topics on the range.

Most basic firearms instructor programs teach instructors how to run recruit level training. That is, basic training in line drills for beginning students. Additional certification or experience is necessary for instructors to conduct dynamic drills, live-fire scenarios, force-on-force training, or shoot house training. These are examples of specific types of training that require additional instructor development, practice and experience for instructors to run safely. Rangemasters must ensure that their staff is properly certified and trained to run whatever training courses are assigned.

Casualty Care Program

A casualty care program is an important part of instructor development that a rangemaster should consider essential. All instructors should be currently certified in first aid and CPR as well as being familiar with the use of an AED (automatic external defibrillator). Additionally, instructors should be competent in the initial treatment of traumatic wounds, particularly gunshot injuries.

Obviously, no one wants a serious injury to occur, but the reality is that firearms training is dangerous; individuals are handling live, loaded firearms. Additionally, for law enforcement training, officers are moving, turning, drawing and holstering dynamically under various conditions. Rangemasters must have contingencies in place for the eventuality of a serious injury on the range. That includes a casualty care program that incorporates treatment of gunshot wounds.

A variety of programs exist; however, rangemasters should consider hosting or obtaining certification for their instructor staff on the level with a tactical combat casualty care or TCCC program. These are typically courses on combat medical care (traumatic injuries) for non-medical personnel. It should include the application of hemostatic agents or bandages such as QuikClot® and the proper application of tourniquets.

If possible, the program should include dry and live fire scenarios in which instructors have to identify simulated injuries, apply casualty care techniques, control the scene and other shooters, take control or secure live firearms that may have been dropped, and so on. Competent instructors can coach student instructors through these scenarios to give them practical experience at handling a serious incident on a live-fire range. This will enable them to be far better prepared for the rare incident of a serious injury or gunshot wound during training.

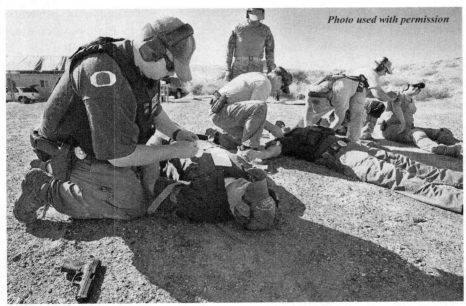

Photo used with permission

One of the most common gunshot wounds on a law enforcement range occurs when a student holsters while their finger is on the trigger. While these can occur with any group, they happen with some regularity during recruit training with new shooters who have not yet developed the motor memory of indexing their finger along the frame while holstering. These errors can happen in fractions of seconds and even if proper instructor student ratios are observed, it may not be possible for an instructor to intervene. Therefore, programs need to support the ability and certification to provide emergency care for these types of injuries.

If an agency SWAT team supports a TEMS program (Tactical Emergency Medical Service), which typically includes professional medical personnel as members, they may be able to provide initial or ongoing refreshers for firearms instructors. Some POST organizations have begun including some type of tactical casualty care for police recruits and may have resources for certified trainers that can assist in providing instruction for a firearms program staff.

Safety Off the Range

Firearms training programs should include information regarding safe handling and storage of firearms away from the range. A number of tragic and avoidable accidental shootings have occurred in the homes of law enforcement officers. During initial and ongoing safety training, instructors should provide guidance and options for officers on how to properly store firearms in their homes.

Providing locking mechanisms for issued firearms may be worth consideration for the agency. Most firearms are sold with some type of lock included or they can be obtained at little cost from a variety of sources. Additionally, rangemasters should be aware of any local or state laws regarding safe storage of firearms and ensure that students are made aware of these during training.

Lastly, agencies should include in their policy or procedures appropriate notification and actions if an officer's firearm is lost or stolen, or in the case of an unintentional discharge on or off the range. See *Chapter 14: Firearms Policies* for more information.

Lead Exposure Mitigation

Safety training programs must include information on lead exposure for firearms students. Basic procedures for avoiding exposure during training and how to properly clean up afterwards are essential. Instructors should, of course, lead by example. An important aspect of lead exposure mitigation that must not be overlooked is avoiding exposure of pregnant women to the lead range environment. Lead exposure can have severe impacts on unborn fetuses and young children. Rangemasters should consult with their organization's human resources and risk management departments to determine proper advice and safety measures for pregnant women who may be exposed to the range. More information about lead mitigation will be covered in *Chapter 11: Hazards and Exposures.*

In short, rangemasters and their staff should work to anticipate and mitigate whatever hazards may exist in the training environment. Hazards should be eliminated if possible. If not, they should be mitigated to the lowest risk reasonably achievable. Finally, personal protective equipment should be used to protect students from injury. There will always be some risk involved in live-fire range operations; however, the rangemaster's job is to ensure that students are as well protected from that risk as reasonably possible, while still achieving the training goals.

---

[1] Associated Press. (2005). *Police trainee accidentally shot, killed by instructor.* AccessWDUN.com: Gainsville, GA. https://accesswdun.com

[2] Police1 staff. (2011). *Accidental discharge kills Ga. probation officer.* Police1. https://www.police1.com

[3] Associated Press. (2014). *Pennsylvania trooper shot dead during gun training.* USAtoday.com. https://www.usatoday.com

[4] Associated Press. (2016). *Former librarian, 73, accidentally killed when Florida police officer uses live ammo in community exercise.* Jacksonville.com: Jacksonville, FL. https://www.jacksonville.com

[5] Dupnack, Amiri, Nissen. (2022). *Role player shot in stomach after friendly fire incident during Taylor Auxiliary Police training exercise.* Fox 2 Detroit News. www.fox2detroit.com

[6] International Safety Equipment Association. (2010). *American national standard for occupational and educational personal eye and face protection devices.* ISEA: Arlington, VA. https://safetyequipment.org

Chapter 3: VARIOUS TRAINING PROGRAMS

The rangemaster may supervise a multitude of training curriculums within their overall firearms program. These may include handgun, carbine rifle, shotgun, precision rifle, or select fire weapon systems or any combination of these. Additionally, rangemasters may be tasked with supervision of force-on-force simulations programs, video simulator systems, or a variety of non-lethal or less lethal weapons such as PepperBall®, baton launchers, or shotgun stun bag systems. Each of these programs will require unique instructor certifications or qualifications, lesson plans, equipment management, safety protocols, minimum operator performance standards, and other elements managed by the rangemaster.

All of these programs can and should have crossover regarding tactics, communication, terminology, and structure or implementation. Nevertheless, they should each be treated as a stand-alone program when considering instructor or operator certification and qualification. For example, a competent handgun instructor may be completely out of their depth as a carbine rifle instructor if they lack the experience and certification to teach that system. Similarly, force-on-force simulations training or live fire shoot house training requires specific instructor training and certification to avoid potential serious student or instructor injuries or deaths during training. These types of advanced training programs should only be conducted by qualified and trained personnel.

Rangemasters should evaluate their entire firearms training program, as well as each component program separately, on an annual basis to ensure it is up-to-date. All programs should reflect the latest changes in statutory and case law. They should also reflect national trends that could reasonably impact the individual jurisdiction. If the program content and/or standards are prescribed by a higher authority (i.e., state level Peace Officer Standards and Training, or POST), the rangemaster must ensure that their individual program meets or exceeds those standards. When this is done, it provides another layer of liability protection for the rangemaster, their staff, and the agency.

One way for rangemasters to instill a practice of following the curriculum is to assign one instructor to follow along in the training plan or manual as another teaches a topic. At the end of the topic, the instructor presenting should ask the other instructor, "did I miss anything?" This will provide the second instructor with an opportunity to suggest areas in which the presenter should provide more detail, or an item or topic that the presenter missed. Once solidified as a practice, it will be a normal expectation for new instructors to follow the lesson plan and for other instructors to follow along and ensure nothing is left out or deviates too far from the agency program.

This practice also affords an opportunity for senior instructors to review the program as it is being taught. They should be making notes about suggested changes that can later be reviewed with the rangemaster. As the lesson is being taught, these experienced instructors can be on the lookout for outdated information, new techniques that should be added, areas in which the information does not flow well, or other changes that may be needed. By making regular (annual) small changes in the program, a rangemaster can avoid having to take on massive program revisions every few years after parts of the program have become completely obsolete.

If rangemasters or instructors choose to deviate from the minimum required content or standards suggested or prescribed by the higher authority, they may place the agency at much greater risk of civil liability. These actions may also risk sanctions from the higher authority such as the forced shutdown of academy or in-service training programs, or suspension of instructor or peace officer certifications until the program is brought into line with the requirements of the higher authority.

Once the training program content meets or exceeds the standards of the higher authority, the rangemaster(s) must ensure that the program is consistently delivered as written by their subordinate instructors. Staff instructors must have the self-discipline and larger understanding that if they go "off script" in their presentation, they expose the agency to greater liability or sanctions. Rangemasters should educate instructors on the danger of deviating from program content and provide clear expectations for teaching the agency approved program.

If the training program is NOT dictated by a higher authority, it is incumbent upon the rangemaster to do their research and make certain the agency program follows the most current guidelines and practices within the law enforcement industry. Sources to benchmark a given program against can include:

- State police academy.
- Other well-established programs in the geographic region.

- Federal Bureau of Investigation (FBI), Quantico, Virginia.
- Federal Law Enforcement Training Center (FLETC), Glynco, Georgia.
- Nationally recognized organizations and trainers.

Note: FLETC actually administers firearms training for over 140+ federal agencies. If the rangemaster is going to benchmark with FLETC, they should be looking at FLETC's Firearms Instructor Program, required if an individual is going to become an instructor at FLETC[1].

The following represent examples of typical firearms training programs an agency may conduct. This is not an all-inclusive, exhaustive list of possible programs a rangemaster may supervise; however, similarities in the types of training and standard practices can be seen throughout the common programs operated by many agencies.

Recruit Training

If you are responsible for training academy recruits, the firearms training program is usually dictated by a higher authority (POST). As previously mentioned, the rangemaster has to continuously monitor the delivery of this program to ensure that it meets the standards set by POST or a similar entity. Instructors who consistently depart from the content or who vehemently disagree with portions of the content should not deliver this type of training. In fact, the rangemaster may need to reconsider their positions as

Photo by author

instructors entirely in that case. Some POST organizations regularly audit recruit academy training to ensure it is meeting the minimum standards. This should incentivize rangemasters and instructors to have their curriculum in line with established rules and guidelines.

If the recruit training is NOT dictated by a higher authority, the rangemaster should have their program reviewed by a peer, accredited academy or a nationally recognized organization. This review should be repeated any time the agency makes significant changes in the training curriculum.

Some agencies run pre-service training for officers who have a current certification from an academy or previous agency within the same state or from a different state. Training requirements for these new employees vary greatly from state to state. Onboarding of these officers may involve state POST or other entity testing in various areas for the officer to become certified with a new agency. If the agency conducts pre-service firearms training in addition to what is required for certification, the rangemaster should ensure this training meets or exceeds minimum required standards. Some agencies will provide training content beyond what is required by a governing entity. This practice is common and not an issue IF the training is clearly documented and is NOT contradictory to the standards established by the governing authority. This content often includes tactics and expectations unique to the agency, community, and environment in which the officers will be working.

In-service / Advanced Officer Training

In-service training for each weapons system can vary greatly from agency to agency. In general, higher frequency, shorter duration, continuing training is more effective than low frequency, longer duration training. For example, quarterly sessions of in-service or advanced officer training (AOT) of two hours on each weapon system is more effective than one 8-hour session per year covering all weapons systems.

Often the areas in which officers struggle are manipulation and shooting fundamentals. Handling and shooting their firearms *more* frequently can improve overall performance far better than only shooting once per year. Further if the shooting the officers are doing once per year is only a weapon qualification, then NO training is taking place which may result in significant risk of liability for the agency. *See Chapter 5: Firearms Qualification.*

Photo by author

Whatever frequency, rangemasters should make use of all of the training time provided. Unfortunately, it is rare for agencies to afford officers the time necessary to maintain proficiency in various weapon systems. It is therefore the responsibility of the rangemaster and their staff to ensure the time provided is not wasted.

Some states or governing entities may have minimum requirements for ongoing officer training. Whether they do or not, court decisions such as *Oklahoma City v. Tuttle* clearly indicate a court-imposed need for agencies to provide continuing training to officers. As with all training, AOT should be documented with training plans, attendance sheets and so on. These should indicate the time, date, location, content, duration, attendance and any changes that may have been made such as adding or omitting a drill or topic.

Remedial / Skill Builder Training

Remedial and skill builder programs are generally in place to correct skills that are deemed to be deficient. They may also provide additional training to specifically identified individuals or those who are voluntarily seeking to improve their abilities. Often officers are assigned to remedial training because they have failed to pass a weapon qualification; however, progressive rangemasters may offer skill builder programs to those officers who are struggling before they are designated a remedial shooter due to a failure to qualify.

If an officer fails to qualify after the allowed number of attempts, remedial training should be provided before any additional attempts at qualification. Failure to qualify resulting in required remedial training should be clearly outlined in agency policy. At a minimum, the policy should outline the following:

- Number of allowed attempts at qualification prior to requiring remedial training.
- Required minimum or maximum time of remedial training.
- Time period, if any, between remediation and the officer's next attempt to qualify.
- Timeframe in which the remedial training must be completed.
- The officer's work status while designated a remedial shooter.
- Consequences for failing to meet minimum performance standards after remedial training (e.g., discipline up to and including termination, etc.)
- Whom the matter is referred to if the remediation is unsuccessful.
- Possession status of the officer's firearm (e.g., may not carry in an official capacity, surrendered to the supervisor/rangemaster, etc.)
- How the remedial training is documented and who it is submitted to.

Photo by author

Some agencies may have a written program for conducting remediation. Others may have a form or other documentation that allows the instructor to simply document their diagnosis of the shooter's problems and efforts to correct them. Whatever method your agency chooses, all remedial or skill builder training should be documented and conducted according to policy. Retention of these documents is essential to show a pattern of behavior over time or that the issue never repeated itself. This documentation serves to protect both the officer and the agency.

No matter how the remedial program is structured, it is highly inadvisable to allow an officer to return to regular duties after a failure to qualify. Agencies that allow this likely place themselves at extreme risk of civil liability. Additionally, it is a serious disservice to the officer. If we, as instructors, have just proven to someone they are not up to standard to operate a firearm, then sent them back to their normal job, it stands to reason they will be psychologically compromised when responding to calls or performing their duties. Their confidence in their ability to defend themselves or others will likely be diminished, leaving them vulnerable to hesitation and uncertainty.

Another reason for these procedures to be clearly outlined in policy, is to avoid undue pressure from unit supervisors to return their officer to work in order to maintain minimum staffing, even though the employee is in a remedial status. Having the procedure in policy, requiring reassignment and remedial training before resuming duties, provides cover for the instructor and rangemaster who can point to the requirements of policy, approved by the agency.

How long should the remedial training be? The outcome depends on many variables such as the motivation of the individual, the diagnostic and coaching skills of the remedial training instructor(s) assigned, etc. The remedial training policy should require a minimum amount of time and a maximum number of sessions or hours before the matter is referred to the chain of command or other administrative action is taken such as termination.

Example:

1. *The rangemaster will ensure that a minimum of 4 hours of remedial training is conducted with the individual prior to allowing an attempt to re-qualify.*

2. *During the time that the officer is designated a remedial shooter, they are not allowed to carry the firearm, with which they failed to qualify, in an enforcement capacity.*

3. *The remedial training must take place within three working days of the initial failure to qualify unless a delay is authorized by the Training Lieutenant.*

4. *The officer in question will be assigned to administrative functions only while they are designated as a remedial shooter.*

5. *If, after 12 hours of remedial training, the instructor and/or rangemaster feel that little or no progress has been made for the officer to meet minimum performance requirements, they will submit the remedial training documentation to the chain of command for consideration of discipline, up to and including termination. The remedial documentation must include a diagnosis of the skill deficiencies and all efforts to remediate the shooter as well as the results of such remediation. The documentation may also include recommendations, if any, from the instructor conducting the training and/or the rangemaster.*

This is only a brief sample of the types of information which the remedial program policy may include. There are many variations and different methods of addressing a failure to qualify and the resulting remedial program. Each policy and program must be tailored to the individual needs of the agency. An agency with five or ten sworn officers may have a very different policy and program than a 3000-officer department. The key is for every agency to (1) *have* a policy and (2) *follow* that policy when it comes to training deficiencies and remedial training. As can be noted in *Chapter 13: Case Law*, courts rarely dictate the details of these issues such as hours, standards, or number of attempts, but they do look closely at whether the agency had a standard or policy and if they followed that policy.

It is important for rangemasters and agency administrators alike to understand the concept of *negligent retention*. An article from the publication *Law and Order*, explains that negligent retention can be claimed when an employer knows or should have known, that an employee was unqualified to do the job they were performing at the time of the damaging action.[2] In most civil lawsuits it is also necessary for the plaintiff to demonstrate that the deficiency in question was a proximate cause to the damage caused by the employee. For this topic, that means an officer who has repeatedly shown below minimum skills with a firearm, using the firearm in a situation which results in the injury of a person outside of the justifiable use of force. Negligent retention on the part of an agency can lead to costly legal action and damages against the agency as well as the supervisory chain of command, including instructors and rangemasters in the case of a firearms incident.

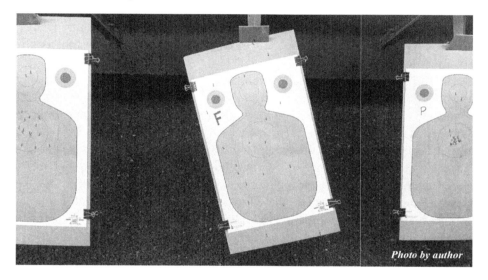

Photo by author

According to the article, this does not mean that agencies or supervisors must monitor every action that an employee takes. Rather, they should have reasonable and appropriate policies and training practices in place. Additionally, they should have clearly spelled out remedial and disciplinary procedures to correct deficiencies in employee performance including what issues may lead to dismissal if not corrected. No qualified trainer wants a student to fail; however, instructors and rangemasters have a duty to ensure that all officers meet minimum standards of performance to protect the community, fellow officers, and the agency.

So, how many times does an employee have to fail, and receive remedial training, before an agency should consider termination or reassignment? There is no hard and fast rule, but again, the number of remedial attempts should be clearly spelled out in policy. Agencies put a great deal of time, money and effort into selecting and training personnel. Therefore, it is reasonable that an agency should make at least one, and perhaps several, good faith efforts to remediate an otherwise good employee. However, if after multiple, well documented remedial training attempts, the individual is unable to perform at a minimum level, retaining that employee in an armed position poses too great a liability to the agency. The officer should be terminated or reassigned to a position that does not involve the use of firearms. As stated previously, the number of qualification attempts and the amount of remedial training prior to an employment decision, should be part of the agency's firearms training policy and not left up to the subjective impressions of the instructors or supervision involved.

When conducting remedial training and/or the last qualification attempt prior to disciplinary action, it is advisable to have more than one instructor present. This is not possible for some small agencies where there may only be one instructor. In those cases, a supervisor or even another officer being present can help preserve the integrity of the process for both the officer and the instructor. Assigning an instructor who was not involved in the officer's initial failure to qualify can sometimes be helpful to the student. It also demonstrates impartiality on the part of the program and, although not required, another step the agency has taken to help the officer be successful.

If possible, rangemasters should allow for individuals to seek voluntary improvement of their skills (i.e., skill builder programs). As trainers and teachers, we should not stifle individual motivation to improve if we have the ability to provide assistance. As with remedial, it is a good idea to document the time spent with an individual, particularly at their request. If you are providing instruction, it is considered training and should be tracked as such. Also, it serves as a record of what instruction has been provided to an individual that may be later built upon by other instructors. Finally, it can be provided to supervisors for performance evaluations of the officer to demonstrate positive, self-motivation on the part of the officer to improve their skills.

Rifle & Shotgun Programs

Many agencies have some type of program for officers, deputies or agents to carry and deploy an auxiliary, shoulder-fired weapon system. This may be a carbine rifle or pistol caliber carbine, shotgun, sub-machine gun, personal defense weapon (PDW), or some combination of weapon systems. The most common systems in U.S. law enforcement are the carbine rifle and shotgun. We will primarily focus on those two systems for this section; however, regardless of what the agency authorizes, there should be a separate training and certification course for each weapon system carried by enforcement personnel.

A key rangemaster responsibility mentioned previously is instructor development. Before presenting training on one of these systems to recruits or serving officers, instructors should receive certification to provide instruction for the individual weapon system (e.g., rifle instructor, shotgun instructor, etc.) Ideally, this certification is conducted by a higher authority such as a POST organization or by a nationally recognized training association. However, if budgeting is tight for an agency *and* there is a qualified person within the agency to provide instructor level training, the certifications may be done "in house." If this is done, the training should be well documented with a detailed lesson plan, credentials of the person providing the training, and certificates issued to the participants that successfully complete the course.

Some agencies issue rifles or shotguns and others allow officers to carry personally owned weapons. Some allow modifications or additional equipment to be added to the weapons by officers and some do not allow modifications. Other agencies have combinations of these program components. For example, an agency might issue rifles but allow an officer to carry their own rifle if they so choose. While none of these is necessarily right

Photo by author

or wrong, each has distinct advantages and disadvantages that the rangemaster should weigh for their own program.

A primary advantage to issued weapon systems is the control over the weapons by the agency to determine what equipment can be added to the rifle or shotgun, the specific features of the system, and the ability to remove the weapon from the officer's possession if needed. This lends itself to consistency for training and familiarity by instructors. If six or seven optical sights are allowed for rifles, the instructors will have to be familiar with all of those to give competent instruction. However, if only one optic is authorized and issued by the agency, the instructors can become more intimately familiar with the use and adjustment of that equipment.

Disadvantages of issued systems include the cost to the agency and some inability to customize the system for the individual shooter. If weapons are issued, the budget for the agency has to bear the costs of the weapons, any ancillary equipment, and ongoing repair and replacement of the systems. Additionally, someone has to manage and track that inventory. Further, there is less opportunity to allow officers to set the rifle or shotgun up for their personal preference or need.

Conversely, agencies who allow the use of personally owned weapons do not have the budgetary obligations of issued firearms. While inspections and qualification records may be required, there is less administrative work to track inventory, equipment and purchasing for weapon systems. Depending on agency restrictions, officers likely have some ability to set up the rifle or shotgun to their personal preference.

If the agency issues weapon systems and allows the officer to customize it, they may not always get the weapon back in the same condition it was issued. It may be missing the stock, handguard, or other parts if officers are allowed to replace them with personally purchased equipment. This can be a significant inventory hassle for the rangemaster.

Many agencies use a so-called "pool" program to ensure there are plenty of shotguns or rifles during every patrol shift. A pool program is where shotguns or rifles are signed out of storage daily by different officers and then returned to storage at the end of shift. Another way to run a pool program is to have the shotgun or rifle stored in each patrol vehicle which is then signed out by a different officer every shift. There are many problems with this type of disbursement program. First, it gives the illusion that shotguns or rifles are always available during a patrol shift. In reality, if an officer doesn't like shotguns or rifles, or feels uncomfortable using them, or isn't confident in their ability with them, they won't deploy them. Supervisors who are concerned about not having a shotgun or rifle available during a shift should consider that if you have to order an officer to deploy the weapon system because they won't do it on their own...is that really the person you want behind a shotgun or rifle on your scene?

In a pool program, one person, usually a firearms instructor, has to zero each shotgun or rifle meaning they are not zeroed to the individual officer. Due to the possibility of impact shift, the variance of the point of impact with a given firearm being used by different shooters, that may occur from one officer to another, many agencies implement a policy that states the shotgun or rifle shall not be deployed beyond 50-100 yards. This policy artificially limits the capability of the weapon. There are also maintenance issues associated with this type of program due to the fact that officers typically don't have a feeling of responsibility to the weapon system because it's not assigned to them like their pistol. A better option is to assign the shotguns and rifles to individual officers who want to carry and deploy them. This also gives the agency an opportunity to choose officers with better decision making, tactical or other skills that would be desirable for deploying these systems. The weapons will be zeroed to the individual officer assigned which gives them greater capability. There are also fewer maintenance issues and the agency will save time and money by not requiring every officer to qualify with a shotgun or rifle to use a pool weapon system.

Regardless of how the agency chooses to issue equipment, there should be clear guidelines in a policy, standard operating procedure (SOP) or other written document, outlining specifically what weapons, calibers, features, modifications, ammunition, and so on are authorized for carry while on-duty. Rangemasters may also want to consider including how or if weapons can be used off-duty for practice or recreation. For example, an agency may want to prohibit the use of reloaded ammunition in agency owned firearms if it voids the warranty.

If carrying a shotgun or rifle is mandatory, there should be a remedial training program available for those who fail the shotgun or rifle qualification. As with the handgun remedial training, the policy should clearly spell out what happens to an officer or the weapon system in the event of a failure to qualify. It should specifically outline the process for remedial training and consequences if the officer is unsuccessful after remediation.

If the shotgun or rifle program is voluntary, then no remedial program is necessary. The shooter can be removed from the program and advised (in writing) they are no longer allowed to carry the weapon in the case of a personally owned firearm. Or, in the case of an agency owned firearm, the officer can be required to surrender the weapon. The agency may allow the officer to retake the certification training; however, there should be a limit on how many times an officer can attempt or complete that training.

Specialized Firearms Instructor Training

A basic law enforcement handgun instructor certification does not qualify a new instructor to conduct specialty firearms training such as live-fire shoot house exercises or force-on-force scenarios. Allowing an instructor with only an initial law enforcement handgun instructor certification to conduct these types of advanced programs greatly increases the possibility of having students seriously injured or even killed during training. Specific instructor development training and certification is needed to ensure such programs can be provided safely and competently to recruits or tenured officers.

Team Tactics Training

Conducting live-fire, tactical drills or scenarios involving multiple officers working together is not typically covered during basic firearms instructor certification. Examples of these drills include: live-fire, person-down, rescues (with or without vehicles) with a live person down range (rather than a dummy), active shooter scenario drills in which officers can respond on the range with little or no restriction on their movement, or triangulation drills

Photo by author

which involve shooters identifying and creating their own shooting lanes for a single target or set of targets. These advanced drills require specific set up and design to be conducted safely.

The advantage of running these drills is they incorporate more realistic movement and response to threats than most drills. They allow the shooters dynamic freedom of movement that more closely resembles field application of tactics. If instructors do not understand the principles of properly setting up the range and instructor control of the drills, they can risk serious injury to students. Rangemasters and instructors for these drills must understand proper target placement, starting positions and avenues of movement, as well as instructor position and ratios for a given drill.

As with the above topics, these drills should only be conducted by instructors with specific certifications for this type of instructor or extensive experience running tactical ranges with multiple officers. An example of a certification course is NLEFIA's Tactical Firearms Instructor course. Additionally, it is good practice to run through drills with instructors in advance of training to determine where problems could arise and mitigate them.

Shoot House Training

Live-fire shoot house training involves significant, inherent risks. These risks can be mitigated and minimized by proper instructor control which only comes from quality instructor training and certification. This type of training can also be exceptionally beneficial by allowing officers to conduct live-fire training in a truly three-dimensional environment in which the threats can be located in a variety of places. This training provides some of the most realistic experience under live-fire conditions that law enforcement officers can receive. The officers must learn to work with and around each other, in sometimes confined spaces, using live weapons. Firearms instructors conducting this training should receive a separate live-fire, shoot house *instructor* certification before conducting this training with students. Instructor training should be from a reputable organization and involve significant time acting in the role of an instructor while other course participants act in the role of students.

As a rangemaster, if you manage a live-fire or non-lethal marking cartridge shoot house, any instructor conducting training should have a shoot house instructor certification. If you allow outside agencies to use the shoot house, you should require the agency instructor to produce a current shoot house instructor certificate from a reputable organization before a reservation is confirmed. You may even consider vetting one or more courses that instructors must have completed before conducting training in your agency's shoot house facility. It is also advisable to keep a copy of their certification on file.

Photo by author

The rangemaster or a certified shoot house instructor should do a walk-through of the facility with the visiting agency's instructor prior to training. Features, limitations, specific rules and safety protocols of the shoot house (i.e., frangible pistol cartridges only) should be discussed and documented. Written acknowledgement of rules and regulations for a shoot-house, or any range used by another entity, is a good standard operating procedure. The first time another agency uses your shoot house, consider having your certified instructor present for the first session to monitor their training and instructors. While this may be a small, extra expense, it is worth it to ensure the safety of participants and instructors.

Rangemasters should not make exceptions for specialty units or tactical teams regardless of their real or imagined reputation or status. All instructors and students utilizing the shoot house facility should be held to the same standard. The truly elite units will respect professional requirements and have no problem meeting them. If a team cannot produce the proper certification credentials they may not be as "special" as their acronym implies.

Force-on-Force / Reality Based Training

Force-on-Force (FoF) or Reality Based Training (RBT) is training involving simulated weapons that fire some non-lethal projectile. Live role players act as suspects, bystanders, victims, or other officers. Often conducted as scenarios, this training offers recruits or experienced officer's opportunities to react to live-persons, interacting both verbally and physically in real time. When conducted correctly, this type of training can be highly valuable in educating officers in reaction time, decision making and tactics.

If it is not conducted properly, like the shoot house training, it can be dangerous and even fatal. During the last two decades, several officer or student deaths in the United States have been attributed to training related accidents in which a live weapon was introduced into training[3]. This includes two of the deaths listed in *Chapter 2: Safety*. In some cases, live weapons were used that were thought to have been unloaded. In other cases, officers had switched out simulated weapons for live weapons during a break and forgot to switch back.

How does such an avoidable tragedy occur? If each incident was carefully examined, it is likely that several shortcomings could be found that ultimately led to an officer's injury or death. These may include using live weapons in scenario training that will involve pointing the weapons at another person; a highly dangerous and irresponsible practice, not to mention a violation of the Firearm Safety Rules. Another likely cause is improper, lax, or non-existent safety protocols. Finally, an instructor was likely in charge of each of these training sessions during which an accident occurred. Although there may be a number of contributing factors to such deadly incidents, the instructors in charge of the training cannot be totally absolved of responsibility. Rangemasters and instructors have a critical duty to ensure the training environment and activities are conducted in a safe manner following reasonable safety protocols.

FoF/RBT can be completed on an open range, in a shoot house, a parking lot, or dedicated FoF facility. Regardless of setting, there has to be a multi-layer, redundant safety procedure in place that ensures that no live weapons or ammunition enter the training area. This is not something to be casually talked about or lackadaisically implemented. These procedures must be approached with deadly seriousness every time training is presented. This starts with ensuring the training area is sanitized and cordoned off. Multiple checks are completed of every participant entering the area. Instructors maintain complete control over any simulated weapons to be used. These and other procedures are strictly adhered to for the safety of everyone involved in the training.

Photo by K. Valdez

Just as with shoot house training, firearms instructors conducting force-on-force exercises should first attend and successfully complete a separate FoF/RBT instructor certification course. The rangemaster in charge of a dedicated FoF facility should require outside agency instructors to provide a current FoF/RBT instructor certificate from a reputable organization. As with shoot house training, rangemasters may decide to require certification through a certain course(s) prior to use. Receiving a written acknowledgement of rules for the use of the facility and management of training is also a wise practice. Finally, where possible having a certified FoF/RBT instructor from the owner agency observe the first training session to ensure safety protocols are followed is prudent.

If you have dedicated FoF weapons available for loan to visiting agencies, there should be a process for inspecting them and signing them out. They should also be visually and physically inspected before signing them back into your agency's inventory. This ensures that all pistols, magazines, and other equipment are returned, and in the same condition they were loaned. Additionally, it verifies that no live rounds or firearms have been introduced into the case containing simulated weapons. While this may sound unlikely, an incident occurred in a facility operated by one of the author's home agencies in which a live pistol was left in a case of simulated guns loaned out to another agency for training. A simulated pistol was missing, inferring that an officer was carrying a simulated pistol instead of their live one when they left training.

If an outside agency violates safety protocols for the facility, the rangemaster should consider suspending their use of that facility. If the suspension is lifted, after discussions with the visiting agency supervision, it is advisable to require supervision of a home agency certified instructor for a period of time. If appropriate, the home agency may decide to require the visiting agency to bear all or part of the expense of personnel costs for such supervision.

Video Simulation

Video simulation training can range from "homemade" or professionally produced videos projected onto paper or a sheet at an indoor or outdoor range using live firearms, to systems with multi-directional screens that can be set up in a classroom using simulated firearms and alternate weapons systems like pepper spray or conducted energy weapons (CEW). Many instructors have set up this training with what they have on hand while other agencies have purchased professional systems ranging in cost from several hundred to many thousands of dollars. Whatever the individual situation, the rangemaster should understand a few basic concepts for utilizing a video simulator for training.

First, the primary use of a video simulator is to provide decision making training. Should the officer shoot, should they not shoot, should they transition to another weapon system or take some other action? Using video scenarios

Photo by author

System using modified weapons with lasers and CO_2 cartridges to identify hits or misses and simulate recoil.

can provide opportunities to expose officers to several different situations in different "locations" in a short period of time and without complicated set up and multiple role players. In only a few short minutes, an officer can be presented with half a dozen or more decision-making problems to address.

Additionally, these systems can be used to test previously trained decision-making skills. Some agencies use these systems on an annual or other regular basis to test officers' decision making for advanced officer training (AOT) also known as in-service training. If there are deficiencies in an officer's decisions, these can then be remediated or corrected so the officer is better prepared to react to a variety of problems on the street.

Some professionally produced systems may use live firearms on a projected image in a range environment while others use simulated firearms that emit a beam or some other mechanism to record "marksmanship" during an exercise. Systems using simulated firearms have a limited application for remedial marksmanship training. Using a simulated firearm, matching the officer's issued sidearm, instructors can work on basic marksmanship principles in an environment in which the noise, and potentially the recoil, can be reduced or eliminated. Laser or light emitting devices in the simulated pistol mark the shots on the screen so the instructor and student can see their marksmanship results and make adjustments before heading back to the live-fire range.

Video simulation on a projected, static target using a simulated firearm can be useful in diagnosing a shooter's problem(s) as a part of a remedial training program. If the shooter is performing well on a simulator static target, then they understand sight alignment and trigger control. If that doesn't translate to the live-fire range, the instructor can look at possible causes for the disconnect such as recoil control, anticipation of the shot, and other related issues.

Although occasionally suggested by administrators, non-live fire video simulation should NOT be considered a replacement for live-fire firearms training. While some simulators use compressed air or CO_2 cartridges to simulate the firing of a live weapon, no simulator approximates the full muzzle blast and recoil of a live firearm. Those who have been involved in firearms training even for a short time have seen an undeniable correlation to range practice and proficiency with firearms. While non-live fire video systems can augment live-fire training and improve decision making, they are not a substitute for firing and manipulating a live firearm. Excessive dependence on these simulators in place of live-fire training may lead to a degradation in skills such as recoil management, sight picture recovery, multiple threat acquisition and engagement, and so on.[4]

Video simulation training is often provided by the product manufacturer as part of the installation. This training is most often focused on how to set up and run the system rather than how to train, diagnose, and coach students using the simulator. This is certainly important training but should be considered *operator* training rather than *instructor* training.

It is important for the rangemaster to create an instructor development class for those providing training using the simulator. Depending upon the complexity of the system and the intended use(s), a typical instructor development course might be two to four hours. The training should cover the following at a minimum:

- How to set up and run the system.
- How to select scenarios or features for specific training needs.
- What instructors should look for in a student's performance.
- How to coach and critique a student including reviewing and repeating failed scenarios to result in a positive training outcome for the student.
- Review standards for testing protocols if used for that purpose.
- Evaluation of whether instructors being trained view particular situations as lethal force, other use of force, or a different outcome – instructors must be consistent in their direction to personnel.

What constitutes a pass or fail? Marksmanship is only one of several outcomes. If an agency is using the simulator for decision-making testing, they will need to ensure that pre-recorded or instructor-made scenarios result in the desired outcome. The rangemaster also needs to ensure that the expected performance from students is compliant with agency policy and law. Expected performance should be written down so it can be evaluated the same by all instructors. It is important for instructors to be in complete consensus with the scenarios being presented. If there is a questionable scenario that instructors can't agree is a shoot or no shoot, how can they expect a student to get the "right" answer?

Purchase of a commercial virtual simulator can be quite expensive depending on the features chosen. The rangemaster must be involved in the purchasing process and review requests for proposal (RFP) and contracts carefully. For example, determining if continuing maintenance of the system is covered in a service agreement and for how long or weather the service agreement includes the ability to receive updated videos from the manufacturer. Some systems allow the agency to record new videos which allows the training to remain fresh and relevant to the jurisdiction at a lower cost. Other simulator manufacturers will shoot custom videos to your specifications or come to your agency and shoot videos in your locale but this may be an extra expense. Simply put, the agency needs to know what it is getting for its expenditure and what will cost extra.

Photo by author

Some systems have "branches" allowing instructors to choose subject actions

The simulator should not be open for unsupervised use. Virtual simulator use should be supervised by a trained instructor just as live fire or force-on-force equipment. Without instructor input, it is easy for the simulator to become a 'video game' and encourage poor habits and decision making. Additionally, commercial systems usually represent a sizable investment in training for the agency. The investment won't pay off if the system is broken due to unauthorized use by untrained personnel.

The programs above are examples of common training courses utilized by many agencies. The rangemaster will likely be responsible for some or all of these and others. These examples provide evidence of the importance for individual instructor training and certification to train various topics and in conditions beyond those incorporated in a basic firearms instructor certification. While not all of these require sending instructors to paid outside training, it is exceptionally important for the rangemaster to ensure that staff members are adequately trained to provide instruction in the topics assigned to them. Failure to do so can lead to deadly consequences and costly liability.

---

[1] FLETC. (2022). *Firearms instructor training program*. Federal Law Enforcement Training Centers. Glynco, GA. https://www.fletc.gov/firearms-instructor-training-program

[2] Sharp, K. (2009). Negligent retention. *Law and Order*, volume: 57, issue 12, https://www.ojp.gov/ncjrs/virtual-library/abstracts/negligent-retention

[3] *Officer down memorial page*. (2022). Fairfax, VA. https://www.odmp.org

[4] Dees, T. & Zoch, R. Can simulation replace live-fire training? PoliceOne.com and LaserShot Simulations. *https://media.cdn.lexipol.com/custom-images/Can-simulation-replace-live-fire-training-eBook.pdf*

Chapter 4: IDENTIFYING TRAINING NEEDS

Why do many law enforcement firearms programs (and likely other programs also) suffer from stagnation? "We need to maintain the purity of the training." "The incidents we've had have turned out okay." "It's the way we've always done it." If you have been an instructor very long, you have probably heard variations of these statements justifying a resistance to changing your training programs. The fact is, evaluating current training and updating training content and delivery takes significant effort, and is time consuming. As a result, programs remain the same for years at a time. In this chapter we will explore how you can identify training needs and choose what new methods and materials should be implemented to keep your training current and relevant.

Current Program Evaluation

Any effort to update a training program must start with an honest and critical evaluation of the material currently being presented. This is one of many areas in which instructor networking can be a powerful benefit for the rangemaster. Initiating discussions with other instructors about their training philosophy, drills they conduct, frequency of training, details of weapon qualifications, how they choose their content, recent changes they have made, and other topics can be enlightening and spark ideas we otherwise would not have considered. Selection of personnel for a firearms program is another critical area (discussed more fully in a later chapter.) Anyone can run the same three line drills every time officers come to training, but an instructor with passion and talent will push officers of every level to constantly improve. These are also the people that will be able to look at the program and see what can be improved.

When evaluating your program, begin with how things are going now. It may help to make a list of topics and skills you are training and what is missing. If you are not sure, start with the basics such as marksmanship and weapon manipulations, such as reloading and malfunction clearance. How would you rate your officer's skill level in these areas? Another area to consider is whether you are training topics that have been deemed necessary by previous case law decisions. These include deadly force decision making, low light shooting, moving targets or at least officer movement, training with all weapons, off-duty action, and knowledge of law and policy, and the application to actual situations. We also recommend including de-escalation and weapon transitions as part of your ongoing training in light of recent, high-profile use of force cases.

Post Incident Debriefs

The next area to consider are the types of incidents occurring in your own geographical region and that your agency responds to with some frequency. Which of those are likely to, or have resulted in shootings? For example, one local agency might respond to high numbers of suicidal subjects. Therefore, they have a need to train more frequently on de-escalation, less-lethal contact team tactics, distance, use of cover and communication. A federal agency may be primarily in charge of responding to anti-government extremists targeting federal offices or courthouses. They may need to practice responding to threats in crowded areas, solo or team response to armed subjects, and so on. Each agency will have some uniqueness to the calls they respond to, the environment they work in, and therefore, the type of training they need.

Rangemasters from medium to large agencies should be part of post-incident use of force review panels, particularly regarding officer involved shootings. This will allow them to both answer questions that may come up in the review about training, tactics, and actions of the officer as well as provide insight into how the incident unfolded and why. They are likely in the best position to determine if the officer complied with policy and training as they will be most intimately familiar with both. Involvement on such panels, whether or not there is "fault" to be found, the rangemaster can identify potential areas of deficiency within a training program. Those in charge of training for smaller agencies in which critical incidents are far less frequent may have to "widen their net" to review critical incidents of similarly sized and situated jurisdictions. Once again, becoming part of a network of instructors from all types and sizes of agencies, can be of benefit in this regard.

Taking part in other post-incident debriefs, critical incidents that were resolved without the use of deadly force, can also be useful to extrapolate additional training needs and determine what is working well for officers. Trainers of all disciplines should be wary of the "it all turned out okay" mentality that we can sometimes fall into. Was the result luck, or the culmination of well thought out tactics and training? Even though no one was hurt, should we handle a similar situation differently next time? Sometimes called a "hotwash" these debriefings, if conducted critically but without overzealous finger pointing, can be tremendously useful to improving the quality of training provided.

National Trends

Finally, rangemasters and instructors must at least be aware of and consider national trends of officer involved, deadly force incidents. Access to video and details of police involved critical incidents around the nation has never been more available. It may be tempting for us to sit in the comfort of our home or office and evaluate the actions or performance of officers during, perhaps, the most terrifying moments of their career or even their lives. However, we believe there is a better way to utilize information publicly available surrounding these events.

Asking ourselves, "what is the likelihood that a similar incident could occur in my jurisdiction?" is a good way to determine if the material is worth analyzing for training purposes or just interesting news. While a multiple member terror cell planning an attack may be a reality for officers in New York City or Los Angeles, it is far less likely to be the case for a 5-person agency in rural Wyoming. However, a lone active shooter could be a reality for all of those jurisdictions. We have to be realistic about the types of incidents that our officers may face, and do our best to prepare them for those situations. Spending valuable training time preparing for incredibly rare events that are highly unlikely, only takes time away from preparation for what an officer is more likely to face a day or a week after training takes place.

If we see incidents that are occurring nationally that may have an impact in our agency, the next question may be, "how would we handle this situation if it occurred in our jurisdiction?" Or, in the case of negative public or industry views of a particular police response, "would we react the same way as [name the agency] in this situation?" For example, a number of tragic, yet likely preventable, instances have occurred in which officers have mistaken their firearm for their conducted energy weapon (CEW)[1]. Obviously, unacceptable performance that we want to avoid for our officers. First, you may ask, "are we doing any transition training on the range?" If the answer is 'no', that is a significant red flag that your agency may be the next to suffer this error. In this example, we may also be considering where the CEW is carried, what hand is used to deploy it, how many repetitions are we providing officers in transitions, whether we are providing any stress-based scenarios, and so on. This, of course, is just one example of many ways to identify training needs from national trends and police involved incidents.

The above examples illustrate a few ways that we can use this widely available information to assess our own training needs. We can do this without trying to "armchair quarterback" what another agency did or didn't do, without knowing critical details about the call, the officer's training, or other important details that are, frankly, not necessary for us to do our job.

Training Needs Committee

As mentioned above, training time is a limited commodity for the vast majority of agencies. Rangemasters must constantly evaluate how they are utilizing that time and attempt to make the most of it. The training must be relevant. Trying to train on too many topics because they are the latest, high-speed techniques used by tier one military operators on YouTube, will likely result in officers who aren't really proficient in any area. Instead, identifying the likely tasks and problems that officers will face, and structuring training to meet those needs will better allow rangemasters to continually advance their program and grow the mastery of their officer's skills.

Depending on the size of the agency, another good option is forming a training needs committee. This can be structured in whatever way best suits the individual agency; however, it will typically involve skills-based trainers in firearms, arrest control, driving, tactics, and so on. Together, this committee can plan out a calendar for in-service or advanced officer training that will provide complimentary work in each of these areas.

Another advantage of the training needs committee is for the skills experts to work out common terminology and agree on overlapping skills. For example, consistent training in firearms and arrest control regarding holding suspects at gunpoint and approaching them for arrest. Too many agencies train their skills in individual silos with contradictory information being given to students. The result can be the use of poor tactics by officers in the field and it is totally preventable. Instead, we should be striving for integrated, consistent skills, terminology, and tactics regardless of the specialized discipline. This may require regular cross-training of instructors which can all start with a training needs committee.

Photo by K. Valdez

If your agency is too small to have such a committee, seeking the assistance of a nearby, larger agency to assist with training expertise may be an option. If you are a trainer in a larger agency, sharing ideas, training, and mentoring instructors in surrounding smaller agencies is a worthy undertaking. Collaboration doesn't mean having to do things the same way another agency does; we all have unique environments and training needs. However, it often leads to better ideas than we can create on our own. It also affords insight into how our neighboring agencies work so when officers from different agencies are together during a critical incident, their understanding of each other's training will likely lead to a better outcome.

Assessing training needs once per year or once every two years is likely sufficient. This can be done in conjunction with annual or biyearly planning for training. Some instances may occur locally or nationally that require an adjustment to training sooner. An example might be a change in state use of force laws or the above-mentioned mistaken weapon system incidents. No matter how a rangemaster decides to address it, assessing training needs should be something that is scheduled and prioritized to be completed on a regular basis.

[1] Feuer, A. & Zaveri, M. (2021). *At least 15 officers in the US have mistaken guns for tasers. Three were convicted.* New York Times: New York, NY. https://www.baltimoresun.com

Chapter 5: FIREARMS QUALIFICATION

One of the many duties of a rangemaster is to conduct firearms qualifications, or oversee the firearms instructors who administer the qualification. A firearm qualification is a shooting skills test and, potentially, a test of firearm manipulation.

The purpose of having a firearms qualification is to reduce liability for the agency by showing that an officer can operate and shoot a specific firearm at a minimum level of proficiency. How a shooter performs during a firearms qualification is not an indicator of how they will perform in a deadly force confrontation as there are too many factors that cannot be replicated in a qualification. For instance, a deadly force confrontation will likely involve a dynamically moving attacker in a three-dimensional environment rather than a static, two-dimensional paper target used for qualification. Another difference is during a qualification, instructions are given to shoot a prescribed number of rounds, usually from a stationary position. Contrast that with an officer having to constantly evaluate the effectiveness of their shots under extreme adrenaline stress, typically while their life is in jeopardy, in a deadly force confrontation.

What a rangemaster must keep in mind is that firearms qualification is, as previously stated, a test. It is not training. It cannot be considered training because firearms instructors cannot coach a shooter during the qualification. A firearms instructor is acting as an evaluator, not as a coach. Their function during a qualification is to determine if the shooter can meet the minimum standards outlined in the course of fire.

A qualification course of fire is often dictated by a higher authority such as a state level peace officer council. In some cases, the state level authority dictates a specific course for academy recruit training but not for on-going qualifications for sworn officers. If the course of fire is not dictated by a higher authority, then it is often left up to the individual agencies to create and administer their own firearms qualification.

There is no formal standard (nationally) or case law that dictates what skills should be tested, how many rounds should be fired, what distances they should be fired from, or what targets should be used in a firearms qualification. For that reason, there are literally thousands of different firearms qualifications across the country. And while a qualification course of fire must be reasonable and defensible, they are rarely challenged in court.

If the agency is responsible for creating and administering their own firearms qualification then the rangemaster should ensure that the course of fire is reasonable and only test skills directly related to the operation of the firearm. Oftentimes, agencies try to add too many skills to the qualification or try to replicate a combat course of fire. The rangemaster should remember that the firearms qualification is not training, nor a representation of how an officer will perform in a deadly force confrontation. It is merely a test of the officer's ability to operate a tool, the firearm, to a minimum standard. Keeping the qualification course of fire to the minimum round count necessary to accomplish the above stated purpose, will reduce the amount of time spent on administering the qualification. This will, in turn, allow firearms instructors to dedicate more time and ammunition to productive firearms training.

When administering the firearms qualification, whether state-level or agency-level, the rangemaster must ensure the firearms instructors involved understand their role as evaluators. The course of fire is administered the same way every time, the targets are scored the same way every time, and every shooter is treated the same. The integrity of the rangemaster, firearms instructors, and agency firearms program will be questioned if it is discovered that the firearms qualification is not administered equitably. While there is no case law that addresses required standards in a firearms qualification, there is case law that requires agencies to administer the firearms qualification equally to all employees (see *Griffin v. City of Omaha*, in *Chapter 13: Case Law*).

What to Test in a Firearms Qualification

A firearms qualification is designed to test the officer's ability to operate the firearm…that's it. The biggest mistake firearms instructors and agencies make is to create or revise a qualification to test other skills that don't need to be tested. Some agencies design courses with tasks such as shooting on the move, shooting from cover, or shooting at two targets (multiple target engagement) as part of their firearms qualification. If the agency does not train those skills every year, why are they being tested? What do those tasks have to do with the officer's ability to operate the firearm? Those skills are tactics-oriented and better suited to be exercised during training, not the qualification. The instructors designing these courses will often reason that they are making the qualification "realistic" to a street situation; however, as previously stated, that is not the purpose of a qualification. Further, qualifications are intended to be objective evaluations and therefore have narrow rules such as specific round counts, target areas, and virtually no decision making on the part of the officer. That is not "realistic" to a street situation.

Photo by author

While a firearms qualification is not considered training, it does provide repetition of skills. Accordingly, if an agency is responsible for establishing a firearms qualification, then the rangemaster must ensure the tasks do not conflict with how they want officers to perform on the street; these conflicts are commonly referred to as "training scars". For example, if an agency is conducting a rifle qualification where the officers perform an empty gun reload at fifteen yards, that would be in conflict with good training practices in which officers would transition to their pistol if they run out of rifle ammo at that distance. Empty gun reloads should be conducted at or beyond twenty-five yards; therefore, that is the distance they should be incorporated into a qualification as well as training.

An agency responsible for establishing their own qualification standards, will first need to decide what skills they want to test, and at what distance. While the particular type of firearm will have some influence on these decisions, the following skills are baseline abilities that should be tested with any firearm.

Marksmanship is obviously the primary task to evaluate; however, there are two aspects of marksmanship to test. One is precision marksmanship and the other is practical marksmanship. Precision marksmanship is the ability to consistently place hits in the same (designated) target zone thus demonstrating the ability to apply marksmanship fundamentals. The only way to test precision marksmanship accuracy is by incorporating distance or using a reduced target zone at closer distances. For example, firing five rounds into a four-inch circle at ten yards with a rifle. Conversely, practical marksmanship is the ability to hit a reasonable "center mass" zone under various conditions. These may include time pressure or marksmanship in combination with other tasks, such as presenting the firearm to the target. Practical marksmanship is tested throughout the rest of the course while testing other skills such as position shooting or weapon manipulation.

Testing the officer's ability to present the firearm is important. It demonstrates the officer's ability to acquire an appropriate sight picture in a limited amount of time and then hit the designated target with one or more rounds. For pistols, this means starting from the holster (all retention devices in place) for most stages of the course of fire. Shoulder-fired firearms should start most frequently from a low ready or high ready position (no cheek weld established). There may be exceptions to this depending on the task being tested.

Testing an officer's ability to manipulate the firearm is also important to evaluate the officer's ability to keep the firearm in operational condition. A reload should be included in the qualification to observe the officer's ability to quickly and efficiently replenish the ammunition in the firearm. There should also be a malfunction clearance in the qualification to evaluate the officer's ability to correct a stoppage in the weapon system.

Testing an officer's ability to manage and control recoil during rapid fire is important because it assesses the officer's shooting platform (stance and grip). Many officer-involved shootings have resulted in officers firing multiple rounds in rapid succession. Having a good shooting platform to manage and control the recoil will improve the likelihood of accurate multiple shots. With this in mind, there should be a course of fire involving at least five rounds in an extremely short time frame at relatively close distances (depending on the specific firearm being tested). Although this can be related to a practical field situation, it is a quantifiable test of a particular skill; the ability to demonstrate a good shooting platform to control recoil during rapid, multiple shots. It is not a demonstration of tactics.

Various shooting positions can also be tested, depending on the weapon system. These require the shooter to adapt their marksmanship fundamentals to a position other than standing, potentially under time pressure depending on the course of fire.

Other than the skills listed above, no other firearm skills need to be tested during a qualification. Leave all of the other skills to training. A reasonable evaluation of an officer's basic firearm skills can be accomplished with 20 to 25 rounds and in 15 minutes or less on a well-designed course of fire. There are even a few qualifications out there that are conducted with 10 rounds. Both the National Law Enforcement Firearms Instructors Association (NLEFIA) and the National Rifle Association (NRA) Law Enforcement Division have conducted 20-round firearms qualifications for instructor development courses. The point is, it is unnecessary to conduct a 50-round qualification in which some skills are tested multiple times. Such courses are a waste of valuable ammunition and training time. Any agency that demands a firearms qualification with a higher round count typically only wants it so they can use the qualification as "training". There is no other logical explanation. Unfortunately, agencies that pretend an annual qualification amounts to adequate firearms training are fooling themselves and likely taking on significant civil liability.

Typical passing percentages for firearms qualification ranges between 70 - 90% for a passing minimum standard. Some precision rifle / sniper qualifications may require a 100% to pass. Once again, these standards are somewhat ambiguous due to the wide variety of targets used, tasks required, and methods utilized for scoring the targets. Nevertheless, allowing a standard below 70% would likely be considered unreasonable by most subject matter experts (SME) for virtually any course of fire.

Firearms qualifications are a necessary task that should be conducted with the highest integrity…but, they should also get very little attention when it comes to range time. Conduct them when needed and then move on to better training that demands more from the shooters than the qualification.

Practicing Qualifications

Agencies should avoid practicing a specific firearms qualification as part of their training or remediation session. If an instructor wants to practice the qualification, they should leave off one task or stage (typically the easiest task / stage) so the qualification is not administered completely. Another option is to practice the stages that the officer is struggling with. By practicing one or more stages multiple times, or leaving out easier stages, you have deviated from the formal qualification course.

If a firearms qualification course of fire is administered completely and according to standards, then there is no difference between a "practice" run and a "formal" attempt. This means if an officer fails the qualification when it was intended for practice, then the officer should be placed on administrative status until they pass the qualification. If the officer is allowed to return to regular work duties, then gets involved in a deadly force confrontation using their firearm, and it's discovered they had failed their most recent firearms qualification, there could be some liability for the agency.

There is a case where an officer failed all of their firearms qualification attempts. They attended extensive remedial training. The day before their final attempt at the qualification, the firearms instructor administered the complete qualification to the officer for practice. The officer passed the qualification. However, the next day the officer failed the final qualification. During the investigation for terminating the officer (policy violation for failing to pass the firearms qualification / negligent retention), the investigators found out the officer had passed the qualification the previous day. When consulting with the legal unit about the issue, the legal unit stated the officer should have never been administered the final qualification because the officer had passed the qualification the day before. They believed if the officer contested the termination through the civil service board, they would likely receive their job back. As a result, the officer was not terminated at that time.

To avoid any undue liability or administrative issues regarding conducting the firearms qualification, it is best to avoid practicing the qualification in its entirety. Omit a stage or change some aspect of the qualification course so that it is not the complete, formal qualification.

Firearms Qualification Frequency

Qualifying on a specific firearm once a year is an acceptable standard from a legal standpoint. Many agencies across the nation do so without legal repercussions. This standard has been cited as part of the factual circumstances in numerous cases without questioning by the courts (see *Chapter 13: Case Law* for examples.) Agencies that choose to conduct multiple firearms qualifications within a calendar year need to realize that it will NOT offer additional liability protection. There is a case where an officer qualified earlier in a year, then failed to attend another firearms qualification later in the same year, and was later involved in a deadly force confrontation with the firearm. The agency's legal advisors indicated there was no liability to the agency or officer for not attending the latest qualification because the officer already had a passing qualification on file for that calendar year.

Conducting multiple firearms qualifications each year exposes the officers to more opportunities to fail the qualification, resulting in being placed on administrative status until they pass. Additionally, this possibility can also induce unnecessary stress to many officers. Lastly, as indicated previously, the unnecessary, additional qualifications consume time and ammunition that could be better utilized for practical training to further develop officers' skills and decision making.

Ammunition Used for Qualifications

There is an ongoing debate among instructors as to whether it is necessary to shoot qualifications with duty ammunition or not. To the best of our knowledge, there is no legal requirement to do so. Most federal agencies fire their qualifications with duty ammo simply because they only issue duty ammunition to regional offices for carry, practice, and qualification.

Duty ammunition should be replaced on a regular basis. One way to do so is to have officers use their existing duty ammunition during their annual qualification and the remainder for any training presented. At the end of the session, issue all new duty ammo. As part of issuing new ammunition, the rangemaster may want to record the lot number(s) of the issued ammunition for tracking purposes if there are problems with a particular lot later on.

Since most departments qualify once per year, this practice ensures that the officers are issued fresh duty ammunition at least that frequently. Secondly, it is an opportunity to ensure officer's firearms are functioning properly with the issued duty ammunition.

Low Light Firearms Qualifications

There is no case law that indicates agencies are required to conduct low light firearms *qualifications*. There is, however, case law that requires agencies to provide low light *training* (see *Chapter 13: Case Law* for examples.) Obviously, if a nighttime qualification is required by a higher authority, then you must conduct it. But, if not, then an agency should not impose a nighttime qualification.

While conducting low light training and qualifications are typically not a problem for agencies that have access to an indoor range facility, agencies that only have access to an outdoor range have a greater logistical problem. Conducting low light training on an outdoor range facility can typically only occur for a six-month period (fall/winter months). Consequently, conducting a nighttime qualification that is not needed only wastes valuable training time.

Many states do not require an annual nighttime qualification for law enforcement officers to maintain their peace officer certification. Failure to conduct such a qualification has never been an issue with any officer-involved shooting incident occurring at night in those states. Therefore, if a nighttime qualification is not mandated by a higher authority in your jurisdiction, there is no need to have one for any of your authorized firearms. Save that time for low light training instead.

Qualifications are an essential part of a legitimate, well-run firearms program; however, they are only a *small part* of such a program. They serve to hold officers accountable for maintaining a minimum level of basic firearms skills and provide some liability protection for the agency in that area. They should be administered with a high standard of integrity and complete consistency for all officers. All of that said, they should take up as little time and ammunition as absolutely necessary to meet the requirement of a higher authority or hold the agencies officers to a reasonable, minimum standard. All other time and resources should be devoted to providing quality training with higher expectations of performance than the minimum standard required for the qualification.

Chapter 6: DOCUMENTATION

Policing agencies have a duty to train their officers and maintain their training at a competent level for various skills and knowledge-based topics. Failure to properly train officers may lead to significant civil liability for agencies and has in the past on numerous occasions. Several examples can be found in *Chapter 13: Case Law*. In order for agencies to insulate themselves from this liability, they not only need to provide the training but they should also be documenting what training was provided. Rangemasters must also document several other types of information. Examples include injuries and exposures, damage to property, inventory, discipline, and maintenance. This chapter will explore different types of documentation for various responsibilities in the realm of the rangemaster.

Training

Training is information that is passed on to the officer from the agency through its representative – the instructor or rangemaster. Officers are expected to use this information, whether knowledge or skills, in the course of their duties. Therefore, documenting *what* information was provided is of the utmost importance. ALL training should be documented. Even informal training such as "roll call" training should be documented in some way. This includes individual assistance at the request of an officer, to overcome a problem or improve their skills. The instructor should document what they worked on with the shooter and guidance provided. In addition to being a record for the agency, it may provide insight to other instructors who assist the same student.

Training may be documented in many different ways. Some training will be documented in more than one way, but all training should be documented using at least one of the following records:

- Lesson plans – a detailed outline of the topic and information provided in training.
- Syllabus – an overview outline of training topics, usually not as detailed as a lesson plan.
- Attendance roster – provides a record of date/time, place, attendees, topic(s), instructors, and injury checks depending on the format.

- Training plan – a synopsis of the training, and details about how it should be set up and conducted, may be a separate document or included as part of a lesson plan, may also be connected to drill sheets.
- Drill sheet – a description of a drill(s) conducted that provide details of how the information from the lesson plan was put into practical application.
- Written tests – documents the student's understanding of training provided to a minimum level, it is recommended to document that a review of the test results was completed after testing.
- Training certificates – verifies attendance and/or certification for a particular topic including the date and instructor certifying the training.
- Remedial form(s) – form or checklist specific to remediation in a given topic such as firearms.
- Written memorandum – may be used to document a wide variety of training but often used to document a particular issue, remediation, or disciplinary action connected with training.

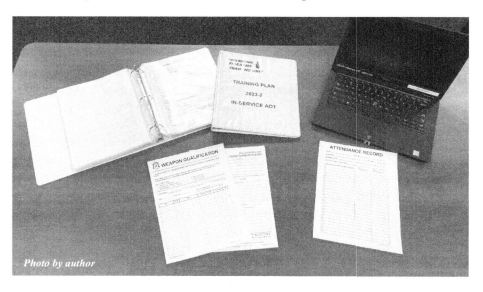

Photo by author

Typically, several of these documents will be used to document recruit or advanced officer training. However, for impromptu shift or unit training or one-on-one coaching, an attendance sheet with topics listed and corresponding drill sheets would be sufficient. The bottom line is that if instructors provide training to individuals or groups, the rangemaster must ensure that training is documented and on file.

Working with a remedial shooter is *training* and should be documented that way. Although the documentation might be different or include additional details, it can and should be documented using one or more of the methods listed above. Instructors should clearly document identification of the specific problems encountered and methods used to correct them. These details will be key if the employee is subjected to discipline or termination as a result of the remedial training.

Lesson Plans

Of all of the documentation listed above, lesson plans or training outlines are the most detailed regarding the specific information provided to students. Lesson plans serve a number of important purposes. They are used to present information in a logical order, preventing omissions, and standardizing classes from one presentation to the next. They can provide a direct connection with policy where officers are required to act "in accordance with agency training" by a given policy or standard operating procedure. Lesson plans help substitute instructors ensure that they cover all relevant material. They also serve as a ready reference for questions about the program and what is being taught for administrators or investigators during an incident review. Finally, they provide for program supervision and accountability by furnishing a method for supervisors to review and approve training content.

A training syllabus and lesson plan should be completed for any formalized training course, including in-service or AOT, provided to agency personnel. The lesson plan can refer back to a more detailed manual or other program document to avoid redundancy if appropriate.

The syllabus should be brief and contain a list of topics that will be addressed during the training.

The lesson plan or training outline should contain much more detail with definitions, bulleted teaching points, or more particularized explanations of topics, techniques, or examples. Each lesson plan should have a cover sheet with information about the course including the following:

- Course title
- Training hours or duration of the course
- Performance objectives – these should describe the major points of what the student is expected to learn from the class

- Date prepared
- Author
- Date(s) revised
- Revision author(s)
- Content sources (e.g., POST training, national training organization, specific publication or trainer, etc.)
- Approving supervisor/authority signature
- Materials needed (classroom, range or both)
- Minimum or maximum class attendance
- Location requirements
- Method of instruction (lecture, demonstration, practical exercise, etc.)
- Testing
- Other specific instructor or student needs

The cover sheet of a lesson plan or training outline should provide the instructor with a checklist to prepare for the course. The body of the lesson plan then includes the details of *what* is being trained.

Qualifications

Obviously, any standard(s) that an officer is required to meet through testing should be clearly documented. As discussed in *Chapter 5,* firearms qualifications are a test of the officer's ability to perform basic functions with their firearm. Documentation should include the specific course of fire, standards and rules, scoring, and whether the specific officer met the standard or not with the weapon being used.

Any course of fire being used for qualification should be clearly outlined with the standards and how those standards are to be measured and administered. This includes specifics on the target used, distances, time allowed, starting position of the shooter (holstered, ready position, etc.), number of rounds to be fired, positions used, manipulation or other required tasks. The qualification should be detailed enough that all instructors can administer the course to officers the same way.

The rules for scoring, make-up shots, actions, and/or consequences by and for the shooter should be clearly outlined. These may include how to deal with shots after time expires, if the shooter fires too many or too few rounds, misses off the silhouette, failure to perform a required action, how the shooter should address an unexpected malfunction, and so on. The rules should be reviewed before commencing the qualification and the students should have an opportunity to ask questions.

There is much debate over whether to record scores as a pass or fail, percentage, or point score and the "liability" attached to one method or another. In reality it doesn't matter, as long as the standard is reasonable and applied consistently to all shooters. There is no greater liability to one method or the other; there is liability in not applying the standards equally to all personnel. See *Chapter 13: Case Law* for more information regarding qualification liability and equality in applying standards.

Qualification records should include:

- Date and time
- Qualification type
- Qualification number or name if applicable
- Instructors administering the qualification
- Instructor scoring the target
- Student name
- Badge or employee number
- Weapon make and model
- Weapon serial number
- Number of attempts (should be a limit to allowed attempts)
- Pass, fail, or score

If an officer fails to qualify and is not allowed to carry their firearm in an official capacity, that action should be documented separately from, but in addition to the qualification record. For example, if policy requires that an officer who fails qualification may not deploy their rifle until completing remedial training, they should be advised of such in writing. This could be done via hard copy or electronically. It is recommended that their immediate supervisor be advised of the failure to qualify as well. (See *Chapter 5: Firearms Qualifications* for more information)

Weapon Inspections & Maintenance

Documentation of weapon inspections and maintenance provides a record of compliance with policies regarding frequency, and issues with specific firearms. It also helps track what parts are being used most frequently for inventory management. Finally, it can show the last time the firearm was known to be fully operational if there is a problem later.

In addition to the usual date, time, and specific weapon information including serial number, it is important to record the individual armorer providing the maintenance. Documenting the specific details of any problem encountered and parts replaced to repair the firearm is important to show a pattern of issues with a particular weapon. If one part is breaking with more frequency on one firearm than other weapons of the same make and model, it may warrant further investigation or return to the factory. Similarly, documenting unusual wear to a specific area of the firearm can help identify chronic problems that need to be addressed.

Documenting maintenance is key to identifying weapon system problems.

Not only can this documentation assist in identifying issues with specific firearms but also with entire weapon systems. If a particular make and model of issued pistol is having frequent maintenance issues, the agency may decide to replace them with more reliable systems. The documentation will be the evidence to show a pattern of problematic performance.

Injuries and Damage

Most government organizations will have specific documentation procedures for reporting injuries to employees and documenting damage to property. The rangemaster should be familiar with these, and have reports, whether paper or electronic, readily available.

It is important to impress upon instructors the need to document any injury or exposure that occurs on the range. A seemingly small injury can develop into a serious condition and if it is a result of a work-related accident, it should be documented for the officer and agency's protection. Even if no immediate medical attention is needed, documenting a minor injury is important. Instructors should always err on the side of obtaining medical treatment or examination for employees *including* themselves when necessary. Law enforcement officers are notorious for not seeking medical attention when they should. Instructors should have permission and authority from the rangemaster and agency to require an officer to be examined for work related injuries.

Similarly, damage that occurs to personal or organizational property should be documented. First, documentation is important to ensure that the damage is repaired, such as damage to a target system, so it is available for future training. Secondly, the incident causing the damage can be reviewed for any necessary changes in protocols for the facility or training. Finally, it provides accountability if the damage was caused by undue carelessness or negligence.

Other Documentation Considerations

While digital records are used heavily by agencies, keeping a hard copy of the training outline (what was trained) and roster (who was trained) is recommended. A hard copy of an outline can show minor adjustments that were made for a particular group of students that are listed on the roster for that training session. Government agencies, including law enforcement, are not immune from attempted cyber intrusion. As such, the rangemaster should be diligent about keeping backup copies of any digital records, databases, training documentation, and other items on a drive stored securely and separately from the agency server. These should obviously be synced regularly to ensure current versions are saved. This is another advantage of keeping hard copies of important documents, even if temporarily.

When documenting technical information (i.e., factory armorer manuals, ammunition specifications, policy / procedure numbers, etc.) be specific, detailed and thorough. However, when describing shooting drills, be more generalized. This allows for changes if certain training aids are not available, the instructor is using a different range than planned, or other variables occur. It also allows for slight modifications based on the skill level of the shooters. For example, rather than a drill with a stated shooter start position of 21-feet from the target, it might be better to say the start position is "6 to 10 yards from the target," to allow the instructor to adjust as needed. Similar generalities may be used for the target style (silhouette target vs. specific target number), standards (instructor discretion on line breaks in or out), or complexity of the drill (number of tasks involved.) If an instructor modifies a shooting drill beyond the generalized description, they should hand write the changes on the hard copy of the outline or attached drill sheet.

It can also be useful to record the general range conditions if the training is held on an outdoor range. Instructors can document temperature, wind and precipitation on the training outline. Alternatively, screen shots from a weather application on your smart phone can be printed out and attached to the training record. This can help document that you trained under various inclement weather conditions if that is relevant to the training conducted.

If your training session starts in late afternoon and goes into hours of darkness, a screen shot at the start of the training and at the end can establish the local conditions you trained under. Similarly, if you have to pause or terminate the training session because of weather (i.e., lightning strikes), screen shots of local weather alerts and warnings can support the justification for terminating planned training.

Sometimes the author of the outline and the instructor presenting the information to the students are not the same person. If you are called to testify in court or give a legal deposition concerning the training, only the outline author(s) should testify to the contents of the outline. The instructor(s) should only testify as to what they taught from the outline and how they taught it. If an attorney asks an instructor about the *content* of the training outline the instructor did not write, the instructor should refer them to the outline author. If an attorney asks an outline author about *how* the training was presented to a specific group of officers, the author should refer them to the specific instructors that presented the training to those officers. Once again, this is if the author of the outline and the instructor for the class in which the outline was presented are not the same person.

Documentation will be key if an agency is under scrutiny regarding the training of employees. If training is not documented, it will be exceptionally difficult to show evidence that it occurred. Consider that you may be called to testify to specific training months, or even years after the training occurred. This can be in the form of a written, video recorded, or in-person deposition or in-person court testimony. As much as we prefer to think it can't happen to us, it can and has happened to a number of firearms instructors.

Consider the following two scenarios in which you are being questioned by a plaintiff's counsel during a deposition or law suit involving training you have written, planned, supervised or instructed:

1. You and your agency have on file and have submitted copies of the lesson plan, drill sheet(s), attendance roster, qualification record and other documentation outlining what took place with specifics of the date, time, persons present and what was presented with any alterations for a specific group. You are asked questions about specific details and can refer to those in your answer or present them as evidence; or

2. You don't have any of the above documentation to refer back to and must rely solely on your memory as to what the specific training was about, who attended, their performance, and so on.

Detailed memory would be relatively easy to discredit or at least introduce skepticism into a jury or court's mind if asked simple questions by the plaintiff's attorney such as, "Were you in uniform that day or not?" or "Describe the target scores that Officer Jones, whom you say attended this training, shot on that day." Obviously being questioned under oath to recall details of a training that happened months or years earlier is much more difficult to defend and easier to be discredited for than signed and dated training records. In these situations, proper documentation may provide a shield for rangemasters and instructors, and save their agencies millions of dollars in civil penalties.

It is a good idea for rangemasters and instructors to keep a curriculum vitae (CV). A CV is different from a resume in that is a listing of certifications, documented professional development, and previous positions, usually in reverse chronological order. It is often far more detailed than a resume. If kept on file electronically, you may include scanned copies of all certificates of completion or attendance in the same order. This can be valuable if called to testify, whether as a witness in an action against your agency or as an expert witness in various types of hearings.

One of the authors previously worked for a major firearms industry manufacturer and in that position was presented with many more deposition requests than when employed as an instructor in public sector law enforcement. The manufacturer's retained counsel responded to such requests with the author's CV and scanned certifications, which resulted in him not providing a deposition in the decade he worked in the industry. While you may not be able to avoid providing testimony, well documented credentials and training records can make the testimony you provide considerably more credible in the eyes of the court or the jury.

Proper documentation is necessary to provide an accounting of officer training. This information can serve to aid in professional development of the officer, protect the agency, instructor, and officer during civil litigation, and hold officers accountable to the expectations of the agency. Quality documentation of weapon maintenance and inventory can help identify problems and shortages. Finally, documenting injuries or damage will ensure that employees get proper treatment and benefits, indicate to rangemasters where changes need to be made, or ensure that property is repaired and those responsible for negligent damage are held accountable. Appropriate documentation in all of the above categories is a key role for the agency rangemaster.

Chapter 7: INVENTORY & RECORD KEEPING

Inventory and record keeping for the firearms program or range facility is another duty that generally falls to the rangemaster. Whether they delegate some of this work to other employees or function as the sole person responsible, it is important they ensure accuracy in this area. Inventory can include a wide range of items and methods of tracking. It is up to each agency to determine the level of detail, and system used to track property within the firearms program. Here are a few considerations and suggestions for documentation of inventory and other records that may assist in making those decisions.

Inventory records help to minimize the possibility of running out of supplies. They also assist in projecting budget needs for the next fiscal cycle and amounts of supplies to be ordered. Good record keeping can identify trends or problems within the program or facility. For example, if the rangemaster notices an increased frequency of a particular weapon part being replaced it may indicate a weapon problem or a defective part in a weapon system. Similarly, if a rangemaster determines more ammunition is missing from storage than has been used for training, it may indicate theft or a documentation problem that needs to be rectified.

Inventory systems can be widely varied as well. Some may use paper forms or an excel spreadsheet. Others may use a customized system created by the organization's information technology department, and still others may purchase a commercial program for tracking inventory of some or all of the following items. It is challenging to find one system that "does it all" for tracking the variety of items required for the typical rangemaster. A combination of these systems may be necessary. Some items, such as office supplies, can be done visually from a supply cabinet – when only one box of pens is left, order more. Other items such as firearms and expensive equipment will likely require a more formalized and sophisticated system to ensure accountability.

Firearms

Obviously, firearms should be tracked meticulously. Every agency owned firearm should have a record indicating when it was obtained, who it has been issued to, its current location, when it was disposed of and the details of the disposition. If a firearm is returned to the factory for repair or replacement, the inventory should indicate when it was shipped, the carrier and any unique tracking number for the shipment. These records should be as detailed as possible concerning the make, model, serial number and any unique equipment or features of the firearm. If a firearm is lost or stolen, the agency should be able to quickly retrieve this information for a report. Routine audits of the weapon inventory are highly recommended.

Photo by author

If an agency uses restricted weapons such as select fire rifles, submachine guns, or suppressors, the rangemaster should check with the regional office of the Bureau of Alcohol, Tobacco, Firearms, and Explosives (BATFE) for any specific requirements regarding the disposition of such weapons. As regulations change from time to time, the best practice is to verify that the disposition is being conducted appropriately and within legal requirements.

Less Lethal Weapon Systems

If the rangemaster is responsible for less lethal weapon systems, they should be tracked the same as firearms whether they are classified as such or not. If the agency uses shotguns as a less lethal system, it is important to remember they are still firearms even if they have a green or orange stock and you only shoot stun bags. The federal government still identifies them as firearms and they should be listed in the inventory with all other firearms used regardless of their specific purpose.

Other systems may not be legally classified as firearms but should nevertheless be tracked as carefully as they are weapon systems and sometimes restricted to law enforcement use only. Examples of other weapon systems are:

- Conducted energy weapons (e.g., TASER®)
- Less lethal baton launchers
- Pava / oleoresin capsicum powder ball launchers

Another system with specific training and record keeping requirements is noise flash diversionary devices, commonly referred to as flashbangs. These are strictly regulated by the BATFE and have specific storage, training, and inventory tracking requirements.[1]

Ammunition:

Agencies track ammunition in many different ways. Some will track purchases and use by cases of 200, 500 or 1000 rounds depending on type, and others will track ammunition by the individual cartridge. Whatever the agency policy or SOP for ammunition inventory, the rangemaster should strive to be accurate and conscientious about the use of ammunition as a valuable training resource. Documentation and tracking of use are also helpful in future budgeting for specific training. See *Chapter 8: Budgeting* for more details.

Different types of ammunition will have different purposes for practice and duty and should, therefore, be tracked appropriately. Practice ammunition for pistol, rifle, or shotgun will likely account for the lion's share of ammunition inventory. Duty ammunition should be replaced on a regular basis as determined by the rangemaster and agency. Therefore, a sufficient supply should be stocked for this replacement and reordered as it is issued. Specialty munitions, such as frangible rounds and shotgun breeching ammunition, have specific purposes and should be restricted to those uses due to their higher cost. Amounts needed should be determined by annual training plans.

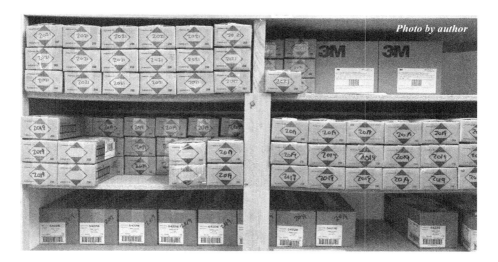

Agencies differ in policies on using duty ammunition for qualifications and practice. Some use duty ammunition for all live-fire qualifications and training, but others only shoot duty ammunition occasionally and use less expensive "ball ammo" for practice and training. Whatever the situation for a specific agency, the rangemaster must ensure there is enough in stock for upcoming training activities and duty issue. They must understand order to delivery timing to avoid shortages and disrupted training.

Over the last two decades or more, ammunition shortages have occurred on a regular basis. Military and federal government contracts have interrupted supply for state and local agencies. Panic buying of ammunition by the public due to political changes, national or world crises has impacted production and delivery for police agencies. Rangemasters must understand these trends and work with administrators and budget managers to develop a strategy for enduring them. The alternative is being caught short without practice or duty ammunition and being unable to complete critical training or required qualifications.

One of the authors was contacted by a distressed state police rangemaster who stated that all of the pistol ammunition the agency had was on the trooper's belts: 16 cartridges in the pistol and 30 cartridges in the magazine pouch. Rangemasters must not allow inventory to dwindle to this critical level. Alert your management well ahead of time of the possible consequences of ammunition supplies becoming unavailable.

Subscribing to shooting industry newsletters such as The Shooting Wire, The Tactical Wire, The National Shooting Sports Foundation (NSSF), and others will alert a rangemaster to impending, sizeable contracts being awarded. Subscriptions to industry emails also provides notification of ammunition safety and firearm recalls.

It is essential for agency administrators and rangemasters to consider that lack of budget will likely not be seen as a viable excuse for inadequate police training by a court during civil litigation. In *City of Canton Ohio v. Harris[2]*, the United State Supreme Court included in their opinion that, *"The inadequacy of police training may serve as the basis for § 1983 liability only where the failure to train in a relevant respect amounts to deliberate indifference to the constitutional rights of persons with whom the police come into contact."* Using this decision, the general counsel for the California Police Chief's Association stated in a client alert memorandum[3], *"The lack of funding from outside sources does not, in any way, relieve a department of its obligation to train its officers."* They further warned their clientele that discontinuing training due to lack of funds would likely be seen by a court as "deliberate indifference" to a person's rights.

In today's climate, it is advisable for rangemasters to prioritize budget for the acquisition of ammunition to supply eighteen months to two years of training, qualification, open range practice, and rotation of duty ammunition. Additionally, rangemasters should impress on instructors the value of ammunition as a resource and the need to ensure every round fired is with an identified training purpose. That is not to suggest a return to the days of firing only two rounds every time the pistol is drawn. If the training content and objectives call for multiple rounds to be fired then so be it. Ammunition consumption must be balanced appropriately with training needs. Simply put…don't waste it. See *Chapter 8: Budgeting* for more information on determining the appropriate budget for ammunition.

Firearm Parts and Accessories

Tracking and maintaining an inventory of replacement parts for firearms is another important task for the rangemaster. Depending on the weapon system, the parts inventory may not represent a significant budgetary item, perhaps only a few hundred dollars; however, knowing what parts are used most frequently can ensure the rangemaster has these on hand to avoid having weapons out of service for an unnecessarily long time. Additionally, a good inventory system will help range personnel know when it is time to order these parts.

Holsters, duty belts, magazine pouches, spare magazines and similar items may fall under the rangemasters purview or under the umbrella of general supply within an agency. If the latter is true, it is important for the rangemaster to communicate with the supply officer regarding the brand, type, retention and other features of holsters and magazine pouches as well as other items which have an impact on firearms related training. Sufficient supplies of these items should be kept on hand to replace damaged gear or gear contaminated by blood or other hazardous materials that officers may encounter. Further, gear wears out. Officers should not have to carry a holster with sub-standard retention due to the agency's negligence in stocking replacement equipment.

Today, law enforcement organizations are quickly transitioning to optical sights for pistols, often referred to as red dot sights or RDS. As individual agencies authorize or purchase this equipment for issue, rangemasters will have a new item on their list of inventory responsibilities. Instructors can help brainstorm all of the additional parts that will be necessary to install and maintain these systems. Items may include: mounting plates, suppressor height sights, spare mounting screws (for the plate and RDS), thread locker, tools for installation and proper torque adjustment, batteries, sealing plates, spare RDS systems, and sight adjustment tools, just to name a few.

Other Inventory Items

Personal protective equipment is another important inventory item to be maintained by the rangemaster. This should include clear eye protection, ear plugs, and spare ear muffs, as well as standard first aid supplies and a trauma kit(s). It is highly recommended that every agency firearms instructor be issued an individual first aid kit (IFAK) in an easily recognizable pouch, containing the recommended tools and materials from a tactical combat casualty care or similar program. Spare kits should be available at the range if needed for impromptu sessions or visiting instructors.

Any number of other items will need to be tracked as necessary by the rangemaster to ensure a fully functioning range and sufficiently stocked armory. These can include filters for range ventilation systems, weapon cleaning supplies, targets and backers, tape and staples, sunblock, insect repellant, batteries, tools, office supplies, and others as determined by the rangemaster.

---

[1] Bureau of Alcohol, Tobacco, Firearms and Explosives. (2012). *Federal explosives law and regulations.* U.S. Department of Justice: Washington, D.C. https://www.atf.gov

[2] *City of Canton Ohio v. Harris,* 489 U.S. 378 (1989). https://supreme.justia.com

[3] Mayer, M. (2009). *The duty to train officers is unaffected by the lack of reimbursement resources.* Client Alert Memorandum, Vol. 24, No. 2. https://www.jones-mayer.com

Chapter 8: BUDGETING

Budgeting, while not as exciting as range training, is a crucial responsibility for the rangemaster. The only way range training is accomplished is if sufficient resources exist to conduct it. Those resources require proper budget planning and execution. Fiscal budgeting is somewhat unique to the particular organization or agency in which the rangemaster is employed; however, in this chapter we will discuss some general budgeting concepts and suggestions to help the rangemaster obtain and/or justify the resources to successfully operate their facility or program.

Creating a Budget

Even if you are in the position of being a newly appointed rangemaster, it is likely some budget has already been established by your agency or organization. All the same, we have encountered individuals in this position for which there is no established budget and the chief, sheriff, commander or some other individual, moves or authorizes money from a general "training" budget as needed for the firearms program. Although it may take a number of conversations and significant time, it is worth working to convince those in charge that a firearms program and/or range facility needs its own dedicated budget.

One item for this discussion, that we have alluded to already, is the necessity for ongoing firearms training. Numerous court decisions have pointed out the requirement for police agencies to provide on-going training to officers in the use of deadly force and particularly practical decision-making exercises. See *Chapter 13: Case Law* for specific case examples. Ongoing training requires an ongoing budget to provide the resources to operate the program. Furthermore, any facility will require an annual budget just to keep it in operational condition to say nothing of capital replacement of systems, equipment, or structures that have finite lifespans. See *Chapter 9: Outdoor Ranges* and *Chapter 10: Indoor Ranges* for information on specific infrastructure.

The next step in creating a budget is to ask for help. Make a connection with the organization finance manager. Depending on the size of the organization, this may be a person within the police department or sheriff's office, or it may be at the larger city, county, or state level finance department.

Regardless, it is worth the rangemaster's time and effort to meet with this person and become educated on budgeting. This should, of course, be done with the knowledge and approval of the agency's supervision. Rather than telling the finance manager what "you need", ask them for assistance in creating a realistic budget for the program or facility. Invite them to visit the range or attend a session of training. It is rare for individuals in these positions to receive that type of personal investment from a program manager. If done sincerely, it will likely go a long way to getting you the help and information you need to be successful.

Photo by author

Another advantage of inviting the finance manager to learn more about the range or firearms program is that they can suggest categories to divide your budget into. Ammunition and firearms would be two obvious categories, but they may be able to provide good suggestions on how to divide armory supplies, range supplies, maintenance, repairs and so on. By asking questions with an "outsider perspective" they may also prompt you to consider budget items you would otherwise overlook.

Find out how the finance manager prefers to get your projected budget numbers. They may very well have a template for you to follow. If you need additional methods of tracking various budget items, they probably have the knowledge to help you set up a spreadsheet or some other tracking method. It is likely the agency and/or larger organization has some proprietary software you will need to learn for purchase orders, submitting quotes, reviewing invoices and the like. The finance manager will be the subject matter expert to train you on these systems.

For creating a firearms program budget, here are some possible items and categories to consider as line items within the larger overall budget.

1. Firearm purchases – consider how frequently the issued firearms will need to be replaced and how that will best be done by your agency.
2. Weapon parts – what do you need to keep on hand and how many parts do you go through in a budget cycle?
3. Holsters and related gear – how often do these need to be replaced? How many do you need on hand for new employees and replacement if broken or damaged?
4. Weapon accessories – in addition to weapon parts, do you have sufficient weapon mounted lights, optical sighting systems, slings, spare magazines, etc.?
5. Tools – what general tools and weapon specific tools do you need for the armory? How often do they need to be replaced?
6. Training – what instructor development and/or armorer training do you need for range personnel and how often do they need to recertify?
7. Computer hardware and software – you should have a budget for periodic replacement of hardware and purchasing new programs or annual subscriptions for general and program specific software.
8. Office equipment and supplies – similarly you should have a budget for replacement of printers, copiers, and other equipment as well as pens, paper, staples, and so on.
9. Dues and subscriptions – this would cover membership in professional organizations for the rangemaster and/or instructors as needed, along with subscriptions to professional publications (hard copy or electronic) for industry updates in training, case law, etc.
10. Protective supplies – this might be items for instructors worn on the range such as instructor vest carriers, safety vests, marker lights for low light training, IFAKs, or similar equipment.
11. Other – there will usually be a catchall "other supplies" category for those items that don't fit the above.

For the range facility you may have a separate budget or it may be combined with the firearms program budget subcategories listed above. In either case, there will be several other line items necessary for the range budget:

1. Paper targets, backers, tape, staples, stencils, paint, etc.
2. Health and safety supplies such as hearing protection, eye protection, and other safety gear.
3. Tools and related supplies.
4. Disposal of hazardous materials – lead mining (outdoor or indoor range).
5. Repair and maintenance services – any type of service upkeep for the facility.
6. Rental services – if you rent range space or any ongoing rental equipment such as storage containers, trash removal, port-o-let services.
7. Sound and lead mitigation – air filters for indoor range, lead cleaning supplies, replacement sound absorbing panels for walls, etc.
8. Classroom supplies – markers, audio visual equipment, copier supplies, or other items for classroom operations.

Photo by author

Inviting the budget manager to visit the range or attend training can increase understanding of needs and help forge a beneficial relationship.

Facility Purchases and Improvements

The rangemaster should consider and plan for capital replacement items for the range facility such as flooring and paint upgrades, target system replacement, bullet trap replacement, and other expensive items that will need to be upgraded or repaired over time.

If the rangemaster is charged with purchasing a new backstop or target system for the range they will not likely be able to get a T&E model to try out. The next best thing is for the agency to invest in sending the rangemaster or range staff member to another agency that has the equipment being considered. A site visit with someone who has used the equipment for several years can be exceptionally valuable in determining any otherwise unforeseen issues to be addressed before the purchase. Seeing the equipment in operation can provide insight into additional questions or specifications to include in the bid specifications.

The same type of review can and should be done by phone for facilities that may be too far or too expensive to travel to. Range design and equipment companies should be able to provide a list of previous projects for references of their work.

Asking for a copy of the operator's manual up front may also provide some insight on how the system works or what is involved in maintenance. The range staff should collectively create a list of questions for companies bidding on the project to ensure the agency is getting the equipment that will work best for them. Knowing up front what maintenance will be required and at what frequency, any infrastructure changes that are necessary such as electrical improvements, and performance expectations are key to getting the most value for the budget expended.

Bid specifications for these larger projects should be specific and include any optional considerations that companies can bid on. The specifications should include standard warranty and performance guarantees, timelines for production and installation, and so forth. The organization purchasing department should be involved in these projects and will have other good suggestions to ensure a quality product is selected.

Budget Increases

It can be challenging for the rangemaster to obtain needed budget increases to maintain a program or facility as costs rise. All too frequently training suffers the first cut of the budget axe within many agencies. While some agencies value and support training efforts, others do not, making it much more difficult for rangemasters to provide quality training to officers. Below are a few suggestions for timing budget requests, configuring budgets to grow with the agency, and providing administrators with options.

It is the rangemasters responsibility to identify gaps in agency training and bring those concerns to staff members along with proposed solutions. It is wise to temper these solutions with options that address some problems without a significant budget increase (e.g., a new training topic that can be accomplished within the existing budget). This signals the staff that you are responsible and do not request increases unless necessary. When you do ask for an increase, it is more likely to be considered seriously.

Unfortunately, it often requires tragedy to spur action for some administrators. Whether the incident occurs in our jurisdiction or another, many times staff is motivated by these events to act. The rangemaster should be prepared and respond to requests quickly, even if they have requested the equipment or change previously and been turned down. When administration is prepared to increase your budget is not the time to be beating the "I told you so" drum.

An example, is an agency in which the rangemaster had proposed a magnified rifle optics program for patrol several times and had been turned down. When an officer was shot and killed by a suspect with a scoped rifle, the rangemaster was asked how quickly he could put the program together and told that essentially, "money was no object." It may be infuriating to receive such a request when you feel that previous inaction has led to someone being injured or even killed; however, to provide better training, equipment and preparation to avoid future harm, we may have to put our frustration aside. The rangemaster in this situation was able to do that and put forth a quality magnified optics program with good equipment and training which bettered their officer's ability to respond to such threats.

When budgeting for equipment such as issued firearms, or supplies such as ammunition, it is often beneficial to present these to the decision makers as "per officer" costs instead a total number budget request. For example, the cost of providing issued pistols is $600 per officer versus stating it as $30,000 for the agency. The reason to break it down this way is to show that anytime there is a personnel increase, the cost of a firearm needs to be included. Therefore, the budget for replacement weapons also increases. Similarly, if ammunition is budgeted per officer, when the agency size increases, it is easier to identify the need for an increase in the ammunition budget.

If the instructor cadre identifies a need for a new piece of equipment or a training need, budget should always be considered in the proposal. Being creative about budget options is an intelligent approach. Providing decision makers with two or three well thought out options, can be very advantageous. These options should outline advantages and disadvantages of both. What will you gain by the more expensive approach that will be of value to the agency? What will you give up by the cheaper approach that will still be of value but not to the extent or level of the more expensive options? All options should be acceptable to meet the training or facility goals of the instructor team. Sometimes moving forward with a basic version is better than not moving forward at all.

Fiscal Year Budgeting

If you are new to budgeting as a rangemaster, don't expect to budget like you might for your household. Most governmental budgets are within a fiscal year (e.g., January to December, July to June, etc.) Whatever budget is allocated for that year must be spent, or encumbered (described below), within that year or it will, in most cases, be forfeited back to the governmental entity (city, county, state, etc.) Often this results in budgets being shuffled around an organization in the middle of the fiscal year to cover unexpected costs or a frenzied rush to spend left-over money at the end of the budget period.

As a rangemaster in charge of a budget for the range facility, firearms program or both, it is important to understand these concepts and plan your spending throughout the financial year. It is generally unwise to wait until the end of a year to spend the bulk of your budget. This often results in having money taken from your budget to spend on other items throughout the agency. In most cases it is best to spend the bulk of your budgeted funds by about the ninth month of the fiscal year. This allows the rangemaster to ensure they have sufficient supplies to last until the next budget cycle and that "budget raiders" will pass them by. Leaving a small amount in the budget for unforeseen and incidental expenses is prudent.

Depending on the purchasing practices of the individual organization, larger expenses like ammunition orders and weapons purchasing should be done early in the financial year. These are typically done by purchase order which encumbers the funds or "earmarks" money in your budget as reserved for these purchases. Although the money will not be actually spent until the items are received and you are invoiced by the vendor, it typically cannot be spent or moved to another part of the organization because it is reserved for something already on order. Many times, funds for purchase order expenditures are allowed to be carried over from one financial year to the next. For example, you may order ammunition in one fiscal year but not receive it until the following year. A purchase order, encumbering the funds, ensures that it is paid for out of the same budget year in which it was ordered. This is highly beneficial for any purchase for which delivery may be significantly delayed.

Another feature which seems unique to government budgeting is if a manager doesn't spend all of the money in their budget in one year, the budget is reduced in the next year. It is somewhat counter intuitive in that it seems to punish the manager for not spending money rather than reward them for being responsible or frugal. While we don't suggest spending government (citizen's) money unwisely, if you have a budget for training and equipping police officers, you should spend it for those purposes. Additionally, you should find ways to get the most value possible out of the funds that you are provided for training and equipment. For example, before sending several new instructors to a training class, it may be a good idea to send one, experienced instructor first to vet the class and ensure it will be a good investment for future instructors to attend.

Recycling or Trade-in Credit

Another source of funding for the rangemaster can be recycling of lead and brass or trade-in of old equipment. Both of these sources can be returned as cash to the agency or firearms program; however, when returned in the form of cash, the agency or larger organization (e.g., city, county, etc.) often deposits the money in a "general fund" rather than back into the firearms budget. If allowed, the rangemaster can usually request funds from recycling or trade-in of equipment as credit. This offers some different advantages to the rangemaster.

Depending on the company used, recycling credit can be used to purchase other supplies or services. If the agency uses a range service-oriented company, they may be able to trade recycled brass or lead for paper targets, steel targets, backers, filters for indoor ranges, rubber or sound materials, range services or any number of other items. Similarly, if the agency completes a trade-in of firearms or other equipment being taken out of service with a law enforcement distributor, they can often use the credit to buy new weapons, holsters, weapon accessories or other items.

Photo by author

If the rangemaster receives cash back into their budget for recycling or trade-in, it usually has to be used within the same fiscal year. On the other hand, if they receive credit instead, it can usually be carried over from one year to another. This way the rangemaster is not forced to buy additional items just to spend the money. They can wait until needs arise, and use the credit to purchase needed equipment or services. Some companies even offer an incentive for receiving funds as credit instead of cash (e.g., the company would pay market value for recycled lead but 10% more if taken in credit with the vendor). This can make the rangemaster's budget for items available through the vendor to go even further.

Taking returns in credit instead of cash may have limitations depending on the company you are working with. With some recycling contracts, the money must be spent on items available from that particular vendor. For other companies, the material to be recycled is weighed for value and the rangemaster is allowed to choose products from any vendor. The orders are sent to the recycling collection company who orders the items for shipment to the agency using the agency's credit. Similarly, if the company returns the recycling value in cash to the agency, it can be used to purchase whatever is needed for the program. Nevertheless, even if the rangemaster must use credit for vendor specific products such as targets, the budget line item for targets could then be reallocated for other range supplies or equipment.

Budget Documentation

It is common for managers to use spreadsheet programs to track budgeting. While it is often unusual for government organizations to do detailed reviews of past budgets, it is still a good idea for rangemasters to keep copies of past budgets for reference. This can be used by the current rangemaster or the next person in the job to understand what has been allocated in the past for various purchases.

The current rangemaster may need to refer back to budgets over the last several years to determine if a particular budget has kept up with rising supply costs. This may help justify an increase in budget if there has not been one and/or if there has been an increased demand or expense in a particular area. Rangemasters can also show what has been spent previously in various areas to justify future expenditures, especially to a new manager in the chain of command or a new budget manager.

Having good budget records will also benefit a new rangemaster in learning the job and understanding how budgeting has been done in the past. A budget spreadsheet along with an electronic file of receipts can help the new rangemaster determine vendors used for particular items and the volume and frequency of necessary supply purchases. These can also be helpful if there is an error in accounting at the larger organization level to show an accurate listing of what has been purchased from the firearms or range budget.

It is highly recommended that you keep paper copies of all proposed and approved budgets or store back-up copies on a separate hard drive kept in a secure location. Hackers routinely target local and state government infrastructure, and cloud storage suffer intrusions from time to time as well. In August of 2021, the Port Authority of Houston successfully defeated a hacking attack[1]. The 25-mile-long port complex handles approximately 247 million tons of cargo per year. A successful hack of their systems could have had devastating impacts. If you think your small to mid-sized agency is too small to get a hacker's notice, keep in mind that at some level your systems are tied into NCIC and other sensitive investigative systems.

---

[1] Coble, S. (2021). *Port of Houston quells cyber-attack.* Infosecurity magazine. https://www.infosecurity-magazine.com

Chapter 9: OUTDOOR RANGES

Outdoor ranges are the most common facilities for conducting firearms training. An outdoor range may be as primitive as portable target stands placed against a hill or gravel pit with yard lines marked with paint or sport cones. Alternatively, they may be expensive, lush facilities with multiple ranges, high-end steel backstops, grass covered range decks with concrete yard markers, range lights, a tower with a PA system, and adjacent, air-conditioned classrooms. Some agencies don't have their own range and must use another agency's range or a privately-owned facility. In all of these situations, the rangemaster must know the ins and outs of outdoor range operations.

This chapter will cover various considerations for operating, designing, and/or constructing an outdoor range. If you are a rangemaster responsible for a currently operating outdoor range, planning to build a new outdoor firearms range, or seeking ways to improve your existing outdoor range facility, this chapter will be particularly informative for you.

All facilities have advantages and disadvantages for conducting law enforcement training and outdoor ranges are no exception. Some of these considerations may be relevant to your specific region or range while others are not. However, these are some common pros and cons to consider when operating or building an outdoor firearms training facility.

Outdoor shooting ranges frequently offer larger spaces for training, particularly longer ranges. If land is available, an outdoor range can include as much distance for shooters as desired. This may also afford an agency the opportunity to construct multiple ranges for different purposes at the same facility location. This allows for additional training opportunities and reduces conflicts. Adding a second range to an indoor facility is far more costly and involved. Further, these larger spaces allow for more freedom of movement including the use of vehicles on the range which is far less available with indoor ranges.

Outdoor range typically involve less shooting noise issues for those using the facility than indoor ranges. Because outdoor ranges are not typically enclosed with walls and a roof, shooting noise dissipates more readily and is not reverberated back to the shooter. An exception to this can be using a steel trap on an outdoor range which will be discussed later in the chapter. This lower noise level, coupled with good hearing protection provides for better hearing conservation for officers and instructors.

Another advantage of outdoor ranges is the ability to use steel targets. These are often not allowed or usable at indoor ranges due to damage that can be caused to the facility by fragmenting rounds. In addition to instant feedback for the shooter, steel targets can improve training efficiency by providing marksmanship accountability while not having to spend time walking down range to check and mark hits. This is a particular advantage when working with shoulder fired weapons at distances of 50 or 100 yards.

Finally, most outdoor ranges boast significantly less operation and maintenance (O&M) costs than indoor ranges of the same size or even smaller. Due to the fact that there is generally no need for ventilation or range building maintenance makes an outdoor range attractive for agencies with limited budgets. Depending on construction, backstops or bullet traps can be similar to indoor ranges or cost far less. However, overall cost of construction and operation of outdoor facilities is likely to be much less expensive for an agency that an indoor shooting facility.

Two of the most significant drawbacks of outdoor ranges are weather and encroachment. First, staff and students are at the mercy of weather conditions at an outdoor range. This can be good on some days and miserable on others. Depending on the region, this can also mean that for part of the year, the range is unusable due to extreme heat, extreme cold, inaccessibility in areas with heavy snow or rain, and so on. This can mean a facility is only usable eight or nine months out of the year, leaving a quarter of the year or more that it is unavailable for firearms training.

Encroachment of housing and businesses is a significant issue for many outdoor range facilities, including law enforcement ranges. Regardless of how long a range has been present in an area, the political reality for chiefs and sheriffs is that if housing is encroaching on the range, some compromise of limited hours and days of shooting is likely to be reached. Limited hours often negatively impact low light training, which is essential to a well-rounded firearms program.

This leads to the next disadvantage of outdoor ranges which is that low light training is limited to times when it is dark outside. A frequent result of this drawback is that many officers receive little if any low light training. In colder climates, this training is often conducted during winter months, particularly if there are restrictions that only allow shooting until a specific time. Cold and dark conditions can be miserable for students and instructors alike and lead to a lack of focus resulting in safety concerns. With the addition of heavier clothing and gloves, the chance of an unintentional discharge may increase.

Lastly, for many outdoor ranges, the proximity to a classroom facility is not convenient for breaks during training, transitioning from classroom training to range, or shelter during inclement weather. While some outdoor ranges may have a fully furnished and operational classroom near the range with restroom facilities, many other ranges have no permanent structures at all. Some have only rudimentary shelter with no electricity or running water. This can create additional challenges for rangemasters and instructors, particularly running full-day classes.

Photo by author

This range features a shelter and storage but no running water or electricity. The sign between the ranges includes the safety rules and GPS location.

Range Amenities

The features of an outdoor range can make the difference between an optimal training experience and one that is difficult for both students and instructors. Ideally, a range will have most or all of the following amenities to support training operations:

- The Firearms Safety Rules (not range rules) posted conspicuously.

- A designated safe location to load, unload, and disassemble a firearm.
- Yard line markers at common distances from the bullet trap/backstop.
- A covered area with tables and chairs for officers to store their gear and rest during breaks.
- Running water to wash hands.
- Restrooms for both genders.
- A classroom facility with basic seating, electricity and so on within a few minutes' walk or drive from the range.

Simple signage can mark common distances and safe weapon loading areas.

Some trainers might cling to such axioms as, "if it ain't raining, it ain't training," or perhaps worse, "if they are going to work in these conditions, they should train in them." The reality is, student comfort can directly impact learning and safety. Providing the above basic amenities for training can improve training value, reduce instructor set up time, and increase safety for both instructors and students. If a range does not have the features listed above, the rangemaster should try to find a reasonable substitute. Below are some examples that will help improve the usability of more primitive ranges that lack some useful facilities:

- Portable sign with the firearms safety rules listed. At a minimum, the rules are covered during the briefing for the training.
- A side berm can be used as a safe location to load or unload. Be sure to advise the shooters.
- Yard line markers can be created with spray paint on the ground or small sport cones.

- Pop-up covers, folding tables, and folding chairs can be brought out to the range for breaks.
- A 5-gallon jug of water and soap or hand wipes for officers and instructors to clean their hands.
- Porta-potties can be positioned near the range for restroom breaks.

If using another department's range or a private range, the agency rangemaster may consider negotiating with the owner of the facility for space to place a storage container or shed for their range supplies. This storage container can also be stocked with some of the above supplies to be used during training days if not already present on the range (e.g., pop up shelters, etc.) Another option is to invest in a training trailer that can be transported to the range and has the necessary equipment for the training to be accomplished.

The target system for an outdoor range may be a high-end turning target system with a moving "running man" target, or stationary target stands or frames situated behind a protective knee wall. The range may have no set target system requiring the use of portable target stands and frames. The more mechanically involved the target system is, the more maintenance it will require. Quality training can be accomplished with any of these target systems; however, frequent breakdowns of more "technologically advanced" systems can be detrimental to training time and value.

Regardless of the specific features or target system of an outdoor range, the rangemaster must be aware of the capabilities and limitations of the range they use. Being prepared to adapt and improve the range to include at least the above features will provide a safer, more comfortable training experience for instructors and students alike.

Square Ranges

A typical outdoor range is often called a "square range" and usually consists of an impact area, bullet trap or dirt berm, and two side impact barriers. While many ranges in rural or undeveloped locations may not have side berms, the purpose of having side berms is to contain fired rounds to a specific area. If an agency is conducting dynamic, tactically-oriented, live-fire drills, where firearms may be pointed in directions other than directly toward the main impact area, having side berms should be considered.

50-yard range with steel bullet trap and concrete side walls

We recommend the minimum dimensions for a law enforcement shooting range as follows:

Range Length: A 50-yard range will provide a satisfactory, usable working area for all weapon systems commonly used by law enforcement. The extended distance of a 100-yard range would provide greater flexibility for training with shoulder-fired weapons than a 50-yard range.

Range Width: A wide range has more flexibility for training than a narrow range. We recommend a minimum width of 10 shooting lanes, five to six feet per lane. This allows a range width of 50 to 60 feet. Slightly wider outside lanes are a nice feature but not required.

Designing an outdoor range with dimensions smaller than listed above will work, but will also limit your training capabilities. Other considerations to take into account for the width of an outdoor range include expected capacity. If you currently have attendance at the recruit level of 12 officers, and it is within the budget to do so, building a range that will accommodate this capacity is recommended. Ideally, building a range for expected capacity 10 to 15 years into the future would be best, as it would allow for agency growth. If the range capacity is smaller than the typical class size, additional relays must be used for line drills and fewer stations may be set up for solo drills. Both of these factors will limit the repetitions that can be completed within the given training time.

Cost and space are obvious limiting factors to the above "ideal" conditions that must be taken into account. Nevertheless, within those limitations, the rangemaster should advocate for the appropriate space with an eye toward expected agency growth several years into the future.

No Blue Sky Ranges

A variation of a typical square range is called a "no blue sky" range in which overhead baffles are placed across the range to prevent fired projectiles from traveling over the backstop. From the shooter's perspective on the range facing the bullet trap, the baffles are placed in such a way that the shooter cannot see "blue sky," thus the reason for the name. As shooters walk down range, depending on the style of baffles, there is an open view to the sky looking straight up or up range toward the shooting lines. These overhead baffles should be considered if there is any concern of errant projectiles flying over the backstop and striking nearby structures or travel ways.

Use of overhead baffles may cause reverberation and/or increased noise levels on the range. This should be taken into consideration for this type of range and may necessitate the installation of sound dampening materials installed on the baffles. Refer to *Chapter 11: Hazards & Exposures* for more information on sound mitigation.

If the overhead baffles are evenly spaced for the full length of the range, then the range is designed to allow individuals to shoot from any distance. If the baffles are close together up range and then spread further apart as you walk downrange, the range has been designed for individuals to shoot from one location up range (specific yard line). This baffle layout should be avoided for law enforcement purposes. The baffles should be evenly spaced for the full length of the range to allow training to be conducted from any distance including movement in various directions on the range.

There are two common styles of overhead baffles: angled and venetian blind. As the name implies, angled baffles are installed at an angle so if a shooter lifts the muzzle upward it will be pointed at the face of the baffle. Any fired rounds deflecting off the baffle will be directed toward the bullet trap. The venetian blind baffles are installed vertically and block the view but do not direct projectiles toward the backstop. They simply stop the round from leaving the shooting area.

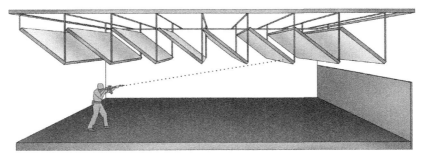

Angled baffles allowing for shooting from any distance.

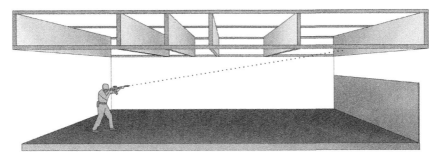

Vertical (Venetian blind) baffles allowing for shooting only from fixed distances.

The three most common construction materials for overhead baffles are wood and pea gravel, concrete, and steel. Wood and pea gravel is typically used for venetian blind style designs. The baffle is made with wood boards (typically 1x6-inch) built in a U-shape and filled with pea gravel. This baffle is the least expensive to build but maintenance and repair are problematic. Baffles with multiple holes may have to be replaced rather than repaired. Concrete baffles are usually used in an angled design. These require minimal maintenance but may become chipped and worn over time requiring replacement or more expensive repair. Steel baffles are typically used in an angled design and, although they are the most expensive material, they require the least maintenance and can take many bullet strikes over many years without needing repair or replacement.

360 Degree / Tactical Ranges

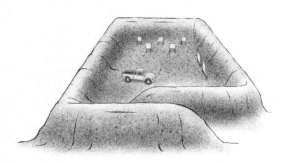

Another range design is called a 360-degree range, or a "tactical" range. It is a range that allows officers to shoot in virtually any direction safely. The range is designed so the opening to the range overlaps a side barrier so if any rounds are fired toward the entrance, they will not leave the range. However, it is common practice not to allow shooters to fire rounds towards the range entrance. Although the name implies 360-degree use, the practical, allowable zone of fire is closer to 300 degrees.

The range design should allow two to three vehicles to drive on to the range for drills and exercises. The recommended minimum usable range dimensions are 50-yards by 50-yards, measured from the base of the impact berms. The

This unique 360-degree range layout also includes the Agency's shoot house

impact surface (berm) must be the same height all the way around the range allowing for 300-degree firing.

360-degree ranges are outstanding for incorporating multiple targets, multiple officers, and vehicles in training exercises. It forces shooters to get out of the typical "square range" mentality incorporated into much law enforcement training. They must keep their head "on a swivel" to maintain situational awareness. Instructors must be extremely aware of the drill design and their positioning when running complex or advanced, tactical, live-fire drills on a 360-degree range.

A 360-degree range is also a great training venue for conducting force-on-force training. The entry point and safety check area can be easily controlled, ensuring a safe training area. This eliminates the danger of an uninvolved person walking into the training area that is a hazard when using areas such as parking lots. Additionally, it allows actors and students to move freely and shoot in all directions, creating a more realistic experience for participants.

Shoot Houses

Most agencies do not have access to a live-fire shoot house. Those that do, typically have a shoot house built as part of their outdoor range facility. A live-fire shoot house is a great training environment for law enforcement, but they are expensive to build. Many agencies will elect to use non-ballistic materials to build a shoot house used only for force-on-force training in which no live-fire is allowed. While this option is better than no shoot house at all, it falls short of the training capabilities of a live-fire ballistic shoot house that can be used for both live-fire and force-on-force training. In this section, we will discuss considerations for those currently operating a live-fire shoot house and those considering building one in the future.

A live-fire shoot house is typically considered a 360-degree "close quarter battle" (CQB) training environment, and as such, it presents unique training challenges. As mentioned previously in *Chapter 3: Various Training Programs*, firearms instructors should attend a reputable shoot house instructor certification course before conducting any live-fire training inside of a shoot house facility. These courses will typically cover training methodology, how to set up drills, proper instructor positioning, proper instructor-student ratio, how to conduct low light training in a shoot house, etc. Rangemasters should require copies of shoot house instructor certificates

Photo by author

Students in this NLEFIA Shoot House Instructor Course prepare for entry into a steel shoot house while other students observe from the catwalk.

for instructors from other agencies that are allowed to use the shoot house. NLEFIA provides one of the most comprehensive shoot house instructor courses in the country.

Just as with standard range construction, it is important for rangemasters to understand proper shoot house construction. Each construction method has limitations, advantages, and drawbacks. The following is a brief overview of some common shoot house construction methods.

Tires (AKA Tire-house)

This is one of the first methods used to construct shoot houses. Two rows of sand-filled tires stacked in an offset pattern prevents projectiles from exiting the shoot house. Often a large pole is placed in the center of some or in every stack of tires to prevent the stacks from falling over. While a fairly economical way to build a shoot house, because you can use old donated tires, the configuration lacks the realism and training capabilities that are desired in a shoot house today. The thickness of the two-row walls and rounded shape of the tires does not simulate the interior configuration of buildings well. These shoot houses are acceptable for use with rifles; however, there have been cases of pistol rounds (slower and larger diameter) bouncing off tires that have become weathered and hardened potentially causing injury to training participants or instructors. Over time, stacks of tires can begin to lean and must be reinforced or reconstructed.

Railroad Ties

This is a similar concept to the tire shoot house, except construction is done by stacking two columns of railroad ties and filling the gap between with pea gravel. Like tire construction, this is another economical way to build a shoot house, and like the tire facility, it also lacks the modern-day realism and training capability that most agencies desire in a shoot house. Maintenance of these types of shoot houses can also be challenging. The railroad ties deteriorate as projectiles strike them and replacement means disassembly of the wall.

Concrete-filled Block

Just as the title implies, construction uses standard hollow concrete blocks filled with concrete during construction to create a solid ballistic wall. This construction is similar to homes made of concrete block, so there is more realism with use of doors and the ability to add windows to the shoot house. The interior of these structures is often lined with sheets of plywood to prevent splash back from any projectiles that impact the block wall. Allowing too many projectiles to strike the same location(s) in such a shoot house can cause structural damage which can be costly and difficult to repair.

Steel

These shoot houses are constructed of steel plates that are ballistically rated for handgun or rifle ammunition. The interior is typically lined with plywood sheets or rubber composite blocks to prevent splash back of any projectiles that impact the steel wall. Steel shoot houses are among the most expensive to build, but they offer the most realism and training capability, require the least amount of maintenance, and last longer than other construction types.

Shoot House Design

There are certain features a rangemaster should try to have incorporated into a shoot house design. First, multiple entry points into the shoot house will help keep the training challenging and provide a different look for students as they move through the floorplan. Second, adding a few windows will allow officers to practice tactics that involve window breaching. Simply hang black plastic over the window so officers cannot see inside the shoot house until the window is breached. Include a large room, a hallway, and three to four small rooms at a minimum. The large room can serve as a living room of a house or main lobby to a business while the small rooms can serve as bedrooms or offices. The hallway provides an opportunity for multiple officers to move within confined quarters. Finally, consider installing a catwalk to give a top-down perspective on the training.

Photo by author

Covered steel shoot house with exterior staging area

Catwalks provide a valuable opportunity for instructors to evaluate student movement and tactics within a shoot house; however, they are *not* the best way to control shooters in a shoot house as the instructor has verbal control only. When using a catwalk, there are two main rules:

1. Don't use the catwalk during live-fire training if the entry team uses muzzle-up techniques.
2. Never be forward of the entry team's direction of movement. Observers should be standing over the top of the entry team or trailing the entry team, but never forward of the entry team where they are in the team's field of view.

Considering these rules for its use, how a catwalk is installed is critical to its successful and safe use for training. As a general rule, it should be

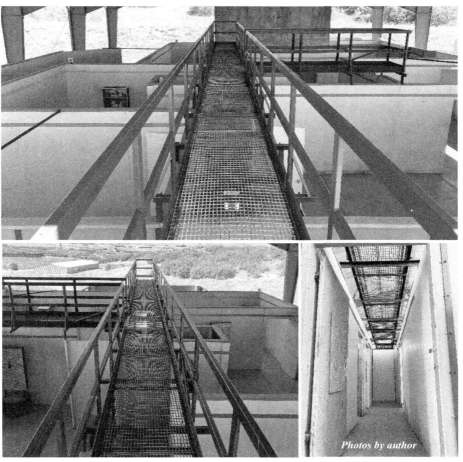

Photos by author

The catwalk extends nearly the length of this shoot house above the center hallway with an extension to one side allowing instructors to observe safely.

positioned over the hallway and run down the center of the shoot house. Avoid putting a catwalk around the perimeter of the shoot house.

When considering the construction of a shoot house, rangemasters should incorporate the expertise of building engineers, SWAT team trainers, and experienced shoot house instructors to ensure the shoot house is built to meet the safety and training needs of the agency. It is also helpful to involve these different individuals to enable the design to replicate as many different construction features officers will likely encounter during field deployments as possible.

Range Construction

Constructing a new outdoor range or expansion of an existing range is a great opportunity for the rangemaster. In doing so, the rangemaster has the ability to plan the features most needed and desirable for the expected use and within the provided budget. Several construction methods may be used for the impact area and side barriers for outdoor ranges. In the following paragraphs we will discuss the most common types of construction as well as advantages and drawbacks of each.

Dirt Impact Surfaces

Dirt construction is the most common method of building outdoor range impact areas. One reason it is so common is that dirt construction is the least expensive method available to create a shooting range backstop. Often times, local governments have the equipment necessary to do the work, further reducing cost for construction of the impact and side berms. Many outdoor ranges, such as the one shown on page 97, include natural barriers behind/above the constructed backstop to help contain errant projectiles. As long as it is constructed properly, it is a very safe and relatively easy range to maintain.

One of the most significant downsides to dirt berms is they consume a lot of ground space. If the total property size for the range is relatively small, other construction options for the primary impact area or side impact areas may be more beneficial to provide the proper usable range size for the agency.

The National Rifle Association (NRA) suggests a specific dimension in their Range Operations and Development course[1]. While they insist that their suggestion is not a recommended standard, many ranges have been built to the specifications in their suggestion, thereby making it a common standard. This is what the NRA suggests for backstop berms:

- 60 feet deep at the base from front to back
- 20 feet high
- 4-10 feet wide cap at the top of the berm
- Slope angle is 1.5:1 or 2:1* to reduce excessive erosion
- Inner core can be made of hard packed dirt and rocks
- Outer 24 inches should be soft soil with no rocks

* This means the berm is sloped to extend 1 ½ to 2 feet horizontally for every 1 foot of vertical height.

If the side berms are intended for projectile impacts (180-degree tactical range), then the side berms should be the same height as the backstop berm. If the side berms are only intended for occasional, unintentional errant projectiles, then the berm dimensions can be smaller. Here is what the NRA suggests for unintentional, side impact berms:

- 24 feet deep base from the inside of the range to the outside
- 8 feet high
- 2-4 feet wide cap at the top of the berm
- Slope angle is 1.5:1 or 2:1 to reduce excessive erosion
- Inner core can be made of hard packed dirt and rocks
- Outer 24 inches should be soft soil with no rocks

If ground space is limited, then a concrete-filled cinder block wall, or similar solid material, can be used in place of dirt side berms. However, the wall should be embedded into the backstop berm so there is no gap for ricochet projectiles to escape. Depending on the size of the range and other factors, this type of wall may increase noise and necessitate some type of sound dampening material to be attached to the inside of the wall for proper hearing conservation.

Dirt berms will need to be mined for lead (lead reclamation) and reconstructed from time to time. Lead reclamation should be done by a professional lead removal company, such as MT2 Firing Range Services (mt2.com), because there are specific lead reclamation protocols outlined by the Occupational Health and Safety Administration (OSHA). How often a range should be mined for lead depends on the volume of use. A very active range should consider lead reclamation approximately every 5 years. Depending on the amount of lead pulled from the berms, it can be recycled to defray or cover the cost of the service. Before engaging the services of a lead removal company, the contract should be carefully reviewed by an organization's legal counsel.

Rubber Impact Surfaces

Rubber construction is a viable alternative to dirt construction, particularly if dust control or lack of ground space is a concern. Rubber construction usually involves either granulated rubber berms or compressed rubber blocks. While generally more expensive than dirt construction, it can solve some problems for the rangemaster such as those mentioned above.

Photos by K. Gillette

Range with granulated rubber berm inside a concrete structure

Granulated rubber is rubber that has been cut into small chunks to create a sloping berm like a dirt berm. It is typically placed on a steel support / dispensing structure. The steel structure needs to be capable of withstanding an impact from fired projectiles that over penetrate the rubber granules. They require additional, regular maintenance such as raking the rubber to even out cavities created from multiple projectile strikes in the same area. Rubber berms can also be a fire hazard. No incendiary devices of any kind should be used on a range that uses rubber impact surfaces.

Rubber berms also have to be mined for lead like dirt berms. The equipment necessary for this operation requires specialized electrical outlets. If the range does not have electricity available, a granulated rubber berm will likely not be a feasible option. When exploring backstop options, follow up maintenance should be discussed in detail with vendors to ensure the agency gets the most value for the money spent on construction. See *Chapter 10: Indoor Ranges* for more information on granulated rubber berms.

Compressed rubber blocks are similar to concrete-filled cinder blocks but typically constructed of high-density rubber composite material. The blocks capture and encapsulate the fired projectiles. These blocks can be stacked on top of each other against a steel wall to create a ballistic backstop or placed on a sloping steel frame to give a sloping berm appearance. Like the granulated rubber berms, the steel wall or frame needs to be capable of withstanding an impact from fired projectiles that over penetrate the rubber blocks. Additional blocks can be stacked in front and used for target placement.

The rubber blocks typically have self-healing properties to seal the projectile's path and encapsulate the bullet within. The blocks can typically handle several thousand rounds before needing replacing. Instead of having to mine for lead like dirt berms and granulated rubber, these blocks can be replaced and disposed of as needed.

A significant advantage of compressed rubber blocks is the ability to save space. By being able to stack the blocks against a flat barrier creating an impact wall, the space needed is only several feet instead of the 60-foot base needed for a dirt berm. Like granulated rubber, block construction also has the advantage of reducing dust in the air which can be a problem for some dirt ranges.

Building a range utilizing rubber block construction is also more expensive and maintenance intensive than dirt construction. Initial construction typically requires some sub-structure or wall to be built to stack the blocks against. Further, the blocks must be rotated and replaced from time to time which may require equipment to assist in lifting and moving the blocks as they will contain several thousand projectiles as mentioned above. Please see *Chapter 10: Indoor Ranges* for more information about rubber block usage.

Steel Impact Surfaces

Steel backstops, or bullet traps, are the most expensive of the backstop construction types. The advantage of steel backstops over dirt and rubber traps is that the fired projectiles are captured in a decelerator and then emptied into buckets or a barrel automatically for easy recycling. They are also durable and long lasting, requiring little maintenance beyond the emptying of lead*. This does not mean that they are maintenance free. Steel backstops must be inspected periodically, depending on volume of use, and if repairs are needed, they can be expensive.

Photo by author

Additionally, the design typically creates an echo, projecting noise back toward the shooter, like a band shell in an auditorium, which can be problematic for nearby residences or businesses. One of the ranges which we teach at regularly has encountered such a problem. Their steel backstop directs noise toward nearby houses and, as a result, has limited the hours in which the range can operate by agreement between the agency and homeowners. If an agency is considering a steel backstop for their outdoor range, placement of the backstop on the property and the direction it faces should be considered carefully for noise control.

The backstop is designed with upper and lower steel baffles angled at 20 degrees or less to keep projectiles from fragmenting on contact. The overlapping baffles force the projectiles into a circular decelerator chamber where they spin around the interior of the decelerator until the velocity drops enough for the spent round to fall into a collection chamber. The collection chamber is then cleaned out periodically. That is the extent of lead reclamation for these bullet trap systems.

The ease of lead collection for these types of bullet traps allows rangemasters to use the lead as a source of funding for range operations. The captured lead can be sold for recycling or collected by vendors that will provide credit to the agency for various range supplies. An added benefit is that the collection can be done by range personnel using simple personal protective equipment and does not require specialized collection by a range services company. This means that more of the money from recycling can go back into the range budget.

> * There is a caveat to decreased maintenance for systems with automated, motorized augers. The auger spins below the deceleration chamber and pushes the lead to a large collection drum. On outdoor ranges, these systems are vulnerable to varying weather conditions, animals chewing through electrical wiring, and so forth creating additional maintenance issues.

Other Construction Types

Other types of materials exist beyond those mentioned in detail above for range side wall and berm construction. These construction methods may not be as common in law enforcement, but they are just as effective to create impact barriers on ranges. Products such as SACON® (*Shock Absorbing CONcrete*) blocks, stackable concrete barriers, and Hesco® (dirt-filled) barriers are simple ways to form side berms. Each of these have their own advantages and disadvantages. Using the concepts discussed above will help the rangemaster to quickly identify the advantages and drawbacks of virtually any construction material. The rangemaster should do extensive research to determine what solution will best fit their budget and the range situation.

Range Grading

Range grading is a topic that is often overlooked by rangemasters and firearms instructors when developing ranges or trying to improve an outdoor range. Proper range grading is needed to prevent a range from becoming flooded during, and after a passing rain storm. If a range is not properly graded, the flooding can impact range training for many days after a storm has passed.

Proper grading allows water runoff to drain up range and to one side of the range. A two to three percent grade slope should be adequate to drain water from a range. Rangemasters should consult with their local property inspectors for proper grading.

An important aspect to consider when establishing the range grade is *where* the runoff will drain. Water coming off the berms and ground will likely contain lead and other contaminants. It's imperative that the water runoff does not reach a local water source such as a stream, lake, or water reservoir. Again, working with local property inspectors will ensure the water runoff is drained properly.

Ground Composition

The ground of a range can be made of several types of material such as dirt, gravel, grass, concrete, asphalt, and so on. There are advantages and disadvantages to all of them not to mention some surfaces are simply not available in some parts of the country. If the range is dirt, gravel, or grass then it is important to keep the range landscape properly manicured. Tall grass, weeds, and large rocks can become home for various critters that can injure shooters on the range. Rodents that burrow holes in the range can cause trip and fall hazards for students and instructors.

Outdoor ranges can be excellent training areas when properly constructed and equipped with some basic facilities. These spaces offer great flexibility for practical training and typically remove some of the hearing conservation concerns of indoor ranges. Constructing a new range or adding to an existing one creates many opportunities for a rangemaster and many considerations to weigh carefully. Properly surveying the site for the range, brainstorming with the instructor team, soliciting input from other rangemasters and thoroughly exploring various options will help the rangemaster make good decisions regarding the best facility options within the agency's budget.

---

[1] National Rifle Association. (2013). *NRA range development and operations course.* National Rifle Association of America, General Operations: Fairfax, VA.

Chapter 10: INDOOR RANGES

An indoor range presents a variety of advantages and challenges differing from an outdoor range. It is important for the rangemaster running or planning the development of an indoor range to be aware of the various unique design, operation, and ongoing maintenance traits of such a facility. Training can and must be tailored to the space available to an agency. The particular attributes of an indoor range can be leveraged to offer many valuable training opportunities; however, they present limitations in other areas that rangemasters must consider. In this chapter, we will examine the benefits and drawbacks of indoor ranges and how the rangemaster can maximize the effectiveness of this training space.

Perhaps one of the most noteworthy advantages of indoor ranges is that training is not affected by weather conditions. An agency using an outdoor range in southern Arizona will experience times of the year during which the extreme heat will limit the time or amount of training they can conduct. Similarly, an agency in Calgary, Alberta will experience times during which an outdoor range may be inaccessible let alone suitable for training. Conversely, indoor ranges are typically operational regardless of the weather conditions. We have likely all heard instructors who say "if we have to work in these conditions, we should train in them." While there is some truth to that, conducting training in extreme weather conditions should be done as a specialized class focusing specifically on that topic. Attempting to teach a recruit class the fundamentals of pistol or rifle marksmanship in below freezing weather will likely be ineffective. When the student is thinking about how miserable they feel, they will not be focused on the essential lessons being taught. Indoor ranges eliminate these distractions and allow students and instructors to focus on the training at hand in a comfortable environment.

Another distinct advantage to indoor ranges is that nearly any lighting situation can be simulated. It is difficult to simulate the full light of an outdoor range on a cloudless summer day; however, most ranges can offer everything from a brightly lit interior to pitch black darkness at any time of the day or night. Many agencies are unable to accomplish the amount of low light training that they should on outdoor ranges with restricted hours. Additionally, their low light training must be done when it is actually dark out, so scheduling training becomes an additional issue. Indoor ranges offer the opportunity to conduct drills in full light and low light within the same 4-hour training block for each shift that comes in during a day of training. This opens up significant training opportunities for agencies with access to an indoor range.

A third benefit of indoor ranges is that they are generally not subject to noise complaints or abatement from encroachment. Numerous agencies that have used or operated outdoor ranges have encountered vehement protests from encroaching residential developments. Even when the range is on government owned property, is well established prior to other development, and is known to those who develop and purchase property, many ranges have had to drastically restrict training hours and activities due to expansion of residential construction around them. One of the authors is aware of two ranges in neighboring jurisdictions facing these issues. One range has been completely shut down despite being established on a government owned site and in service for more than three decades. Another has had to cut hours so that low light training is virtually impossible. Indoor ranges, even those located in busy metropolitan areas, are often immune to such complaints if constructed properly to mitigate shooting noise. This is something to be seriously considered for any rangemaster or administrator looking to build a new training facility in an area that is well populated or growing quickly.

Photo by author

Other, less impactful advantages of indoor ranges include the ability to recover 100% of brass fired for recycling, no loss of dummy rounds, and the like. If the indoor range uses a turning or retriever target system, it is not affected by weather whereas mechanical target systems for outdoor range are more difficult to maintain in varying weather conditions. Indoor ranges are often built with classroom facilities within the same building or closely adjacent making transition from classroom to range more convenient and less time consuming.

Indoor ranges are, of course, not without their drawbacks. From a range development perspective, the most obvious drawback is cost. Indoor ranges are expensive to build and to maintain. Whether you operate a lead-free range or one that allows the use of lead ammunition or primers, there must be a bullet trap and some type of ventilation system. Depending on the size of the range, these can run into hundreds of thousands or millions of dollars. Treating the interior walls with some type of sound absorbent material is also an expensive but necessary cost of construction. Finally, while you can use static target stands, most indoor ranges have some type of turning or moving target system which is an additional expense, usually in the range of $10,000 to $12,000 per lane (2021 costs).

Ongoing maintenance for indoor ranges can also be expensive. Depending on the type of range and backstop, mining lead or copper and proper disposal of materials used to clean contaminated surfaces can be costly; however, recycling programs for lead and non-toxic frangible materials can recoup some or most of the costs of these services. Cleaning requires specialized equipment such as an explosion resistant vacuum which prevents unspent gunpowder

Photo by author

from igniting inside the vacuum. These vacuums can cost thousands of dollars and the collected waste must be disposed of through a hazardous materials program if it contains lead, which is an additional expense. Additional ongoing costs for indoor ranges include lighting and ventilation. Due to the size and performance needs of specialty ventilation systems, used in traditional indoor ranges that allow lead ammunition, these systems use a significant amount of energy to operate. Even using lead free ammunition, it is necessary to have ventilation throughout the space. Moving air through such large spaces, not to mention heating or cooling it, can be costly.

Indoor ranges are very finite, defined spaces with specific shooting distances and widths. Expanding an indoor range means embarking on a major construction project. Conversely, expanding an outdoor range, depending on the land available, is much less costly and typically involves far fewer infrastructure changes. Although some can, many indoor ranges cannot be accessed by vehicles, thus limiting the training that is often available on outdoor ranges.

Other drawbacks of indoor ranges include that, due to the confined space, they are often louder with more actual or perceived reverberation of sound for shooters than outdoor ranges. This greatly depends on mitigation efforts and sound absorbing materials used in construction. These ranges also may limit the types and placement of targets. For example, many metal targets are not suitable for indoor range due to damage created by fragmentation of projectiles, including frangible ammunition. Range personnel may also be limited on where targets and target stands may be placed on an indoor range for safety or to avoid damage to the range. Outdoor ranges often have more latitude in these areas allowing the instructor staff to vary training conditions to a wider extent.

Indoor Range Design and Construction

Being assigned to lead or serve as part of a team for the construction of a new indoor range can be a daunting task. Indoor ranges involve the use of numerous, highly technical systems which must function together and ultimately must safely meet the training needs of the personnel that will use the range. The following information is in no way comprehensive enough to address all aspects of the construction of an indoor range; however, it will provide the assigned rangemaster with several key points to consider during planning and construction.

Perhaps even before a budget is determined, the rangemaster should consider what the training needs are and how the range will be used. This might be determined based on current or past training or by identifying known deficiencies. For example, if the range currently being utilized does not allow for vehicles to be used, it may be important to include vehicle access to the range. Another example may be, if the current range does not allow for shooting moving targets, a target system that includes at least one moving target may be desirable.

Two other considerations are distance and number of shooting lanes. Both of these will be limited by the final budget; however, the rangemaster should propose the number of shooting lanes based on current class size, expected changes in training schedules that would impact class attendance, and expected growth of the agency in the foreseeable future. For example, if the current class size is 15 officers and the jurisdiction is expecting moderate growth, requesting a range with 20 shooting lanes would not be out of order. If the budget only allows for a 12-lane shooting range, then planning adequate space for staging a second relay and alterations to training time will become necessary. Planning for distance is much the same. If the range will only be used for handgun shooting, a maximum distance of 25 yards may be adequate; however, if it will be used for rifle, the rangemaster should push for a minimum of 50 yards of shooting distance. Many agencies train and qualify with rifles at 100 yards and that is a reasonable standard for the rifle, even within a metropolitan jurisdiction.

Ultimately, compromises may need to be made for distance and number of shooting lanes but the rangemaster should propose what is needed. These needs can be supported by an assessment of current training, anticipated future training needs, and training required or supported by case law or common national trends.

Other considerations when tackling a new range construction project that should be thoroughly discussed prior to the design stage include:

- What weapon systems and types of ammunition will be supported?
- What is the cost of constructing a stand-alone range versus a range with classrooms attached?

- What is the proposed site location, cost of land and who owns it if it is being leased?
- What is the travel time from the main station to the range and back and how will this affect the current training schedule?
- What is the life expectancy of the range based on current residential / commercial construction trends?
- Is there space for future expansion as the agency grows or training needs change?

Many of the above issues apply to both indoor and outdoor ranges being constructed by the agency. Building a new range from the ground up can be an exciting project to be part of; however, the rangemaster will need to educate themselves on a variety of topics as they prepare to participate in the process. We hope the following pages will provide some insight into planning and preparation for such a project.

Protection of Building Infrastructure

When considering indoor range construction, it is necessary to remember that the construction must be completed with the purpose of total containment of fired projectiles. In most instances this will require poured or precast concrete floors, walls and ceiling, a filled concrete block design or something similarly bullet resistant for the type of weapons and ammunition intended to be used inside the facility.

Seams in precast concrete sections must be properly sealed and protected from bullet impacts. For walls this may mean using ballistic steel deflectors, strips or lining to protect the walls and seams. These may be covered by ballistic rubber tiles or BRT, which is a compressed rubber tile meant to absorb the impact of projectiles without fragmentation or deflection.

To protect the ceiling usually requires a baffle system. If the range consists of established shooting points (e.g., 25 yards, 15 yards, 10 yards, etc.) the baffles may be suspended in such a way to avoid rounds being fired into the ceiling from those points but not to cover the entire ceiling from any vantage point. The baffles are designed to deflect any projectiles that hit them into the bullet trap. This type of baffle system will be less costly and require less engineering support from the ceiling to hold the weight. Using such a baffle system does not eliminate an agency's ability to move, or shoot from areas

Wall of range at the bottom edge of bullet trap. Notice the severe decay from deflected rounds. Photo used with permission of facility.

other than the designated firing points; however, doing so risks projectile strikes to the ceiling of the structure, ventilation systems, lighting equipment, or electrical conduit.

The other ceiling baffle system option is referred to as a "tactical range" setup within the range architectural industry. With this system the ceiling is entirely covered from any shooting point by overlapping baffles of ballistic steel, usually covered by plywood and BRT or a sound absorbent material depending on the proximity of the baffles to the bullet trap. The closer baffles (10 yards or less) are typically covered with BRT to absorb errant projectiles fired at the trap whereas the baffles farther from the bullet trap are covered with sound absorbing material to aid in reducing noise and concussion reverberation. The downside to this system is that it adds significant weight, which must be supported by the ceiling. This in turn adds materials cost to the range design for the structure and the baffles themselves. The span of the ceiling that is able to support the weight of the baffle system will often dictate the number of lanes allowed in the design.

When deciding on the materials used to cover the walls and ceiling baffles, rangemasters and others should consider the type of target system being used. If a system of hanging or turning targets is stationary at the bullet trap, it is far less likely that a significant number of bullet strikes will occur on the walls or ceiling, except very close to, or inside the bullet trap area. However, if a target retriever system is used and the agency allows cross lane shooting, that is allowing the shooter on one lane to shoot a target on a different lane, it is much more likely that the walls and ceiling will sustain bullet strikes. These systems typically keep the shooter at a fixed distance from the bullet trap and move the target to adjust distance. As the targets are closer to the shooter, shots to different target areas such as the head may strike the ceiling. Using command targets (targets with multiple colored or numbered shapes) may result in strikes on the walls particularly for the outer lanes on each side of the range.

As in other areas, compromises must be decided upon for the materials used to cover the walls and ceiling. Target placement and instructor control can mitigate some of the damage caused by bullet strikes to surfaces other than the bullet trap. Even so, if a target retriever system is used, the agency should expect more bullet strikes to the walls, floor and ceiling of the range than if the targets are statically located near the bullet trap. Materials that are effective at dampening noise are typically not designed to take repeated bullet strikes and materials such as BRT, that are designed to absorb bullet strikes are not designed to dampen sound. The rangemaster and others involved in designing the range must consider these factors, and the possible monetary and workplace safety impacts they may have for shooters.

Bullet Traps

Another major design consideration is the type of bullet trap that will be used in the facility. Many types of bullet traps have been used in the past. We will discuss the advantages and disadvantages of three systems that are widely used in law enforcement indoor ranges today. Those systems are the steel bullet trap, the granulated rubber trap, and the compressed rubber block trap.

Steel Bullet Traps

Steel bullet traps are not new to indoor ranges but the design of these traps has improved dramatically. Today's steel traps are deeper from the front or mouth of the trap to the collection point, making the angle of the steel plates more parallel to the path of the projectile. This is typically an angle of 20 degrees or less. An advantage to this design is that bullets are more intact when entering the collection point of the trap. This results in less pulverization of projectiles which in turn reduces the amount of lead or other contaminants in the air which must be filtered out by the ventilation system. Previous steel traps, with more perpendicular plates, cause projectiles to be fragmented and pulverized into dust-like particles. This often resulted in splash back on the shooter potentially causing injury or lead contaminants in the air and on range surfaces posing a health risk to shooters and instructors.

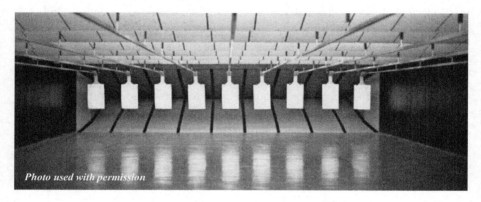

Photo used with permission

Many steel traps today feature a deceleration chamber which allows the projectile to enter at speed and control the deceleration within a round tube resulting in less impact and a more intact projectile. Projectiles ultimately fall to the bottom of the chamber where they drop through into a series of buckets attached to the deceleration chamber or into an auger system designed to push expended projectiles to a single collection point at the end of the chamber. This system is cleaner and more efficient for the collection of fired projectiles than steel traps of the past.

Steel traps require less overall ongoing maintenance than other systems. The newer designs result in longer lasting steel plates due to the shallower angle of impact than earlier systems. This design also drastically reduces fragmentation splash back on the shooter making them safer than systems of the past. Expended projectiles can be collected and recycled by range staff, providing a return income that can be used for range supplies, maintenance, or upgrades.

Steel traps do have a few disadvantages as well. They are typically more expensive on the front-end during construction than other systems. They also require a much larger footprint (space on the floor) than the other systems discussed here. If retrofitting an existing range, this can mean losing available maximum distance from the target to the shooter. Some require access to the back of the trap, requiring additional floor space and a door or access portal behind the bullet trap. Steel traps often reflect more noise which can be problematic for an indoor range. Finally, they do not completely eliminate the risk of splash back on the shooter or pulverization of lead into the air. This is most prominent if targets are located at the backstop and the shooter is very close to the trap.

Granulated Rubber Bullet Traps

Granulated rubber bullet traps offer a variety of their own advantages over other systems. These traps have an underlying steel structure built at approximately a 45-degree angle from the floor to the back wall of the range. A rubber medium made from shredded airplane tires is then used to cover the base and make a "berm" of rubber to shoot into. Baffles overhead ensure that high shots are deflected into the trap. These traps capture fired projectiles with very little or no deformation thus eliminating splash back or deflection even at extremely close range. Further, because the rounds are captured whole, there are no lead contaminants added to the air, creating a safer environment for officers and longer periods between air filter replacement.

Granulated rubber traps have other advantages as well. They reduce the amount of noise and concussion reflected back on the shooter due to the loose rubber surface of the trap. These traps can be mined to remove and recycle the lead or copper projectiles which may drastically off-set or eliminate the cost of the service. These traps have a smaller footprint than modern steel traps making them useful for retrofitting existing ranges. They are also less expensive and do not require access to the back side of the trap reducing construction or retrofitting costs further.

Granulated rubber bullet traps require more maintenance than steel traps. As shooters use individual shooting lanes, cavities or trenches are formed in the rubber berm behind the center of the targets. In order to maintain sufficient depth in the rubber medium to avoid projectiles striking the metal frame, the rubber must be smoothed regularly using an asphalt rake or similar implement. Also, as the range is used, individual rubber chunks are flung onto the floor in front of the trap by the impact of the bullets. These must be regularly pushed back to the trap. Similarly, the rubber will slide down the berm toward the floor as multiple impacts occur. Part of the regular maintenance will involve shoveling rubber from the floor back onto the top of the berm to keep the depth and angle of the impact area consistent. If this is done routinely after each shooting session, it only takes minutes to complete; however, if it is not done regularly it can lead to damage and serious, costly maintenance issues.

Photo by author

These traps must also be mined at certain intervals depending on usage. The mining requires specialty equipment and must be contracted to a vendor. These traps can absorb tens of thousands of rounds before mining is needed; however, if the trap is not mined when needed, the projectiles will begin impacting others already in the trap. Due to the heat generated by fired projectiles the metal will start to fuse together into larger chunks. When this happens, fragmentation can occur causing a hazard to shooters. A commercial range that is used every day, may need to be mined once per year; whereas, a law enforcement range that is used regularly but does not have the same volume of use may be able to go three years between mining. If planned properly, the recycling revenue from the reclaimed projectiles will pay for the service.

Lastly, a disadvantage to rubber bullet traps is the fire hazard. If rubber berms are not serviced properly to remove projectiles, unspent gunpowder and paper fragments from targets, the heat generated by projectiles impacting fused chunks of lead in the backstop can cause a fire. The rubber will burn and is difficult to extinguish. Also, incendiary rounds or devices, such as hot burning gas canisters, used too close to a rubber bullet trap can ignite it. It is wise to ban these types of devices or ammunition on any range with rubber impact panels or a rubber bullet trap. Fire retardant can be applied to granulated rubber berms to greatly reduce the risk of combustion.

Rubber Block Bullet Traps

Finally, rubber block bullet traps provide features that neither the steel bullet trap or granulated rubber traps offer. Most notably, is the minimal footprint. These traps are formed of rectangular, compressed rubber composite blocks stacked on one another. These are usually placed against a precast or concrete block wall lined with AR500 steel and two-inch BRT panels. The rubber blocks absorb incoming projectiles and capture them whole, eliminating fragmentation or deflection. Several thousand rounds can be fired into these blocks before replacement is needed. These are often used in smaller ranges where limited space is a significant issue.

Rubber block traps are one of the least expensive bullet traps available. They offer the same advantage of granulated rubber in reducing lead dust from

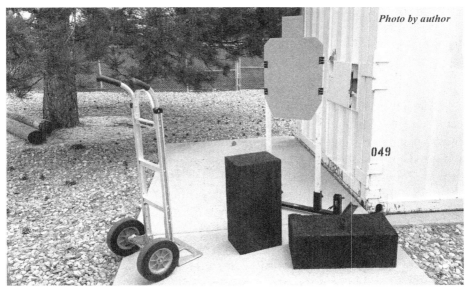

Photo by author

Compressed rubber blocks used for portable or range bullet traps

bullets and saving on filtration costs. The lead is recyclable although the entire block must be sent out for recycling and replaced with new blocks on a rotating basis. These traps are built directly to the rear wall of the range and do not require access to the rear of the trap making installation simple and inexpensive. Block traps can also be set up on a stair-step frame allowing for easier replacement of blocks as they are not stacked on top of one another.

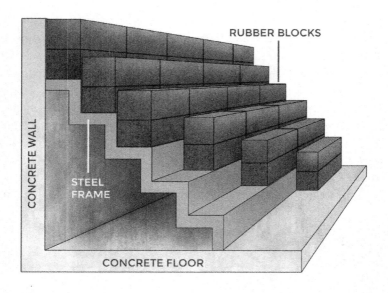

Drawbacks of the rubber block trap included maintenance and block replacement. While they do not require frequent maintenance, replacing blocks can be an arduous process. The blocks themselves are heavy but when thousands of rounds of projectiles are added they become difficult to manage requiring multiple people and potentially mechanical assistance to move. As the blocks fill with projectiles, they also begin to bulge. This makes stacks of blocks less stable and opens gaps between blocks through which projectiles may pass.

The blocks used in these traps are compressed and hard on the surface so they do not offer much sound dampening effect. They may be slightly better than a steel surface but individual testing should be done to determine the noise reverberation created from these traps. Rubber block traps have the same vulnerability to fire so similar precautions should be taken. Like granulated traps, they can be treated with fire retardant to reduce those hazards.

Other Bullet Traps

Another type of trap used in a variety of private and public indoor ranges is sand. The range has a concrete exterior and the sand is placed in the end forming a berm similar to that used for an outdoor range. To control dust, Linatex® (a self-sealing material) or similar curtains are placed in front of the trap. The footprint of the trap would be roughly equivalent to a granulated rubber trap. A sand trap would also need to be mined for lead at regular intervals. After many thousands of rounds, the curtains must be replaced as well. Nevertheless, this may be another inexpensive alternative for an indoor range bullet trap.

Photo by author

Indoor range sand bullet trap with Linatex® curtains in front to control dust.

If your range is older, you may have a bullet trap similar to or vastly different than those described above. As an example, for a period of time, some steel traps used constantly running water or oil, flowing over the trap to reduce the amount of lead dust created. The liquid was recycled like an artificial waterfall. This system created other logistical issues and expenses such as disposal of the lead contaminated liquid. These traps have become obsolete due to advancements in steel trap technology, the environmental issues with liquid disposal, and ongoing maintenance issues with corrosion, leakage and so on.

Older steel bullet traps can be problematic as well. Previous designs included steel plates at a much more vertical angle. Projectiles striking these plates would frequently disintegrate creating additional lead dust in the air and, consequently, an additional exposure hazard. Agencies with older, technologically outdated bullet traps like the two examples presented here should consider replacing the trap with one of the options described above that suit their needs.

Ultimately, the rangemaster and staff designing the agency's range must determine what is the best bullet trap option for their project. Cost, available space, level of expected usage, the type of weapons and ammunition used, noise concerns and other factors should be considered carefully when choosing the appropriate bullet trap for the range.

Ventilation

Proper ventilation is a key component of any indoor firing range design. Even ranges designated as "lead free" still need proper ventilation to remove contaminants from the air after firearms are discharged. Adequate ventilation is not a matter of getting air to move faster or using more powerful fans; rather it requires equipment designed specifically to move air steadily through the entire range space. As most law enforcement ranges are designed to shoot lead ammunition, we will primarily discuss ventilation from the standpoint of avoiding excessive lead exposure. Differences between standard and lead-free ranges will be discussed later in the chapter.

Ventilation in an indoor range establishes a laminar air flow from up range, the farthest point from the bullet trap, to down range or inside the bullet trap. Laminar flow is a principle of fluid dynamics that simply means that particles,

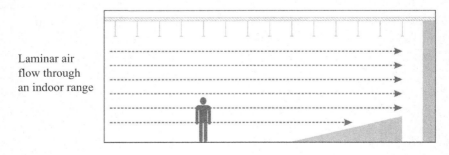

Laminar air flow through an indoor range

in this case air, flow smoothly in even layers without turbulence[1]. The air at ceiling level should flow at the same speed and in the same direction as air at floor level across all shooting lanes. The recommended speed of this air flow is 75 feet per minute[2].

If turbulence occurs because of a blockage or poor design, the air will flow in various directions creating a risk of contaminants being circulated at the shooter's position. Indoor range ventilation should be designed and installed only by professionals who specialize in range ventilation systems. The design needed for these spaces is drastically different from typical HVAC systems.

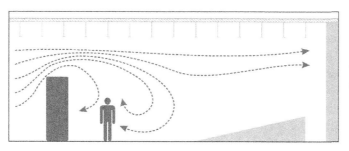

Turbulence caused by obstruction on range

The purpose of a range ventilation system is to remove contaminants from the air which result from the firing of a weapon. The flow of air through the range keeps the range at a negative pressure in relation to other rooms in the building. This prevents the escape of contaminates into the rest of the building space, avoiding exposure for those who are not inside the range[3].

Ventilation systems for indoor ranges which allow the use of lead ammunition, must have specific filtration for the air to pass through before it is expelled into the atmosphere outside of the range to avoid lead pollution. Usually, air will pass through two filters: the first stage is a standard bag filter which removes most large particles; the second stage is a high efficiency particulate air (HEPA) filter to remove the remaining dangerous contaminants before the air is evacuated to the outside.

The frequency in which these filters need to be changed depends greatly on the range design. Bullet traps which capture individual projectiles whole, without striking hard surfaces resulting in lead pulverization, result in far fewer particulates in the air than ranges with steel traps which cause fragmentation of projectiles. The stage one filters or bag filters are intended to capture the bulk of airborne particulates. They are less expensive and therefore can be changed more frequently adding life to the more expensive HEPA filters. Nevertheless, replacement filters are an ongoing expense that must be planned for by the rangemaster as well as storage space for replacement filters.

Indoor ranges that use lead ammunition must dispose of used air filters as hazardous waste. This requires specialized handling and packaging of the filters, proper transportation and documentation, and disposal at an approved HAZMAT landfill. The rangemaster should avail themselves of the expertise of knowledgeable waste management personnel within their governmental organization if available. If the organization is too small for such a person, contacting such a person in a larger, nearby organization may be helpful in obtaining information about the process. Several range maintenance companies specialize in replacement and disposal of filters and other range waste; however, proper disposal of hazardous waste is the responsibility of the 'generator' or in this case, the owner agency of the range. Therefore, ensuring proper handling and disposal of hazardous materials in accordance with state and federal law, is ultimately the responsibility of the *rangemaster and their organization*.

Some indoor ranges use a plenum wall, essentially a wall at the back of the range which air flows from, to provide the laminar flow. Other ranges use radial diffusers to create the laminar flow of air through the range. These are cylindrical diffusers, typically located near the ceiling at the back of the range. A common error committed by rangemasters is to allow objects to be stored along the back wall of the range. Many times, tables, seating, range props such as barricades and other large objects are stored in this area. When this is allowed to happen, it almost undoubtedly interferes with the laminar flow of air through the range regardless of which system is used. Blockage often causes turbulence in these areas which circulates contaminated air in the same area for significant time, allowing it to be inhaled by range occupants.

The back wall of an indoor range should be kept as totally clear of objects as possible. Carts with ammunition and targets should allow air to pass through horizontally (e.g., steel wire carts) rather than blocking horizontally moving air. These carts should be placed along the sides of the range or away from the back wall to avoid blocking air flowing down to the floor from diffusers. Other objects such as barricades should be placed so that they present the most minimal profile available to air moving from the back of the range to the bullet trap. Generally, shooters should be between the diffusers or plenum wall and any objects placed on the range such as barricades or vehicles. The air on the bullet trap side of these objects will likely be disturbed and not flow as intended. Brief movement between the objects and the bullet trap is okay for the purposes of a drill but rangemasters should not allow sustained firing forward of an object that is blocking the proper flow of air through the range.

Range doors and any other openings must be sealed properly for most range specific ventilation systems to function properly. The ventilation system creates a negative pressurized air condition in the range which must be maintained for proper function. Negative pressure is created by having a greater exhaust than supply of air within the range. Usually, these systems are designed to shut down if a certain pressure level is not maintained. It is ideal to have a vestibule system for entrance with multiple (at least two) doors. Typically, if the system shuts down due to an inability to maintain appropriate pressure, it cannot be restarted for a period of time, delaying training.

While these ventilation systems are complex and the initial cost can be expensive, they are not complicated for range staff to operate. Most have a one-button or switch start/stop function and simple control panel to regulate heat or cooling. They typically have an integrated or computer-based monitoring method for determining problems, adjusting settings, or providing warnings and notifications of impending maintenance needs such as filter replacement. If the range has internet access, several companies offer remote access to diagnose and even make adjustments to solve problems or restart the system. When proper maintenance schedules are followed, the costs are not overly burdensome and can easily be planned and budgeted for.

Hearing Conservation and Communication

If you are considering building a new range or performing a major overhaul of an existing range, involve the experts from the beginning. We particularly recommend experts for two areas: ventilation as mentioned above, and sound control. General commercial construction contractors typically lack the expertise to properly design systems in these areas. As with ventilation, the agency should consult experts in sound control specific to indoor ranges. Some materials are suitable for indoor range use and others are not.

Several range construction companies will have appropriate options for sound control. They should be able to provide specifications for the materials they use. If you have an industrial hygienist in your organization, they will be qualified to review this data and provide recommendations. If a qualified person is not available in your area, you may check with a nearby university with an industrial hygienist program to see if the professor would be willing to review the material with you.

The importance of proper sound control cannot be overstated. The last thing that you want to do is build an expensive indoor range only to find out the noise levels are too high to be safe for use regardless of hearing protection. The below case study known to one of the authors is a cautionary tale on this topic.

A Tier One Special Operations unit had an indoor range built that was considered state of the art. Everything but the bullet trap was poured concrete, including the overhead baffles. The bullet trap was designed to take a high / rapid volume of military, M855 rifle projectiles. The first unit to use the new range fired several select fire and continuous fire stages. When they came off the range all of the shooters had severe ringing in the ears and headaches.

A Department of Defense industrial hygienist was called in, and conducted various sound measurements with startling results. In order to conserve the operator's hearing with double hearing protection on, the maximum rounds fired would have to be reduced to one shooter at a time and seven rounds of rifle ammunition during a 24-hour period. Also, the shots would have to be fired no less than 5-seconds apart.

The hygienist found that the combination of a steel trap and concrete surfaces resulted in extreme reverberation of sound which exceeded the maximum allowable exposure to the shooter. Ultimately, the range was salvageable by the proper application of acoustical materials by a company specializing in sound mitigation for ranges. Subsequent testing confirmed the unit could resume their typical training regimen without permanently damaging the operator's hearing[4]. See *Chapter 11: Exposures and Hazards* for more information on hearing conservation.

Another consideration for indoor ranges is the background noise associated with air handling systems that can make communication difficult. The rangemaster and firearms instructors should consider wearing electronic amplifying ear muffs so they can hear normal conversation on the range. The rangemaster must ensure that this hearing protection is sufficient for the environment as electronic ear muffs often have a lower noise reduction rating than passive muffs or ear plugs.

If the range is large and instructors shouting at the top of their lungs still results in commands not heard on the firing line, consider a portable or permanently installed loudspeaker system. Another option is multi-band capable headsets. One setting is for issuing range commands over the headset communication with the students; the other is for communicating with other instructors and range staff present. Be certain to verify which channel you're on and turn off your microphone when giving corrective feedback to an individual shooter.

The ultimate goal is to allow everyone to hear the range commands without having to remove their hearing protection and allowing for effective communication with range staff if there is a problem or emergency.

Standard versus Lead Free Ranges

Although some agencies operate lead free ranges, there is no mandate for them on the horizon. Standard lead ammunition and primers may be used safely with a proper backstop and air filtration. There are many government regulations on exposure to lead and air quality and some local and state governments may be required to comply with these while others are not. Nevertheless, most government organizations comply voluntarily if not mandatorily so the rangemaster should be familiar with these regulations. See *Chapter 11: Hazards & Exposures* for more information about workplace exposure regulations. Lead free ranges make it easier to meet government regulations; however, they significantly restrict an agency's flexibility for range use.

Operating a lead-free range means that only ammunition completely devoid of lead is ever used inside the range. The purpose is to improve employee health by eliminating the hazard of exposure to lead. Lead-free ammunition is not necessarily the same as frangible ammunition. Some ranges use frangible ammunition, generally with older steel bullet traps, as a safety measure to prevent lead fragmentation injuring shooters. Frangible ammunition breaks into powder when hitting a hard surface like steel to prevent fragmentation injury; however, some frangible ammunition contains lead in the primer and/or powder. These rounds may not be used on a lead-free range without contaminating the facility. As indicated above, lead-free ammunition is totally devoid of any lead in the cartridge.

Ammunition costs vary significantly between standard lead, frangible, and lead-free. Standard lead practice ammunition is typically the least expensive for government purchase while lead-free practice ammo is the most expensive. Ammunition pricing can vary greatly depending on demand, political environment, and so on; however, the author's experience has been that lead-free training ammunition has historically cost approximately twice what standard lead practice ammunition is sold for on state contracts[5].

NON-TOXIC FRANGIBLE AMMUNITION ONLY

Use of Ammunition Containing Lead PROHIBITED

In addition to lead-free ranges requiring increased ammunition costs, another critical consideration for rangemasters is that duty ammunition may *not* be fired on a lead-free range for testing firearms, qualification or training. This can significantly impact the usefulness of the range and require access to a second facility for using standard lead duty ammunition.

Laminar air flow from shooting line to bullet trap is essential as noted above for both standard and lead-free ranges. Copper dust from frangible or lead-free ammunition is similar to lead danger but requires far greater quantities to reach copper toxicity. Appropriate air filtration ensures good air quality and prevention of exposure to heavy metals such as lead and copper; however, due to the less-toxic nature of lead-free ammunition, ventilation filtration requirements may not be as stringent. Coupled with no requirement to dispose of filters as hazardous materials, this can reduce costs for range ventilation to some degree.

The quality of the bullet trap and the air flow system can help an agency determine the balance between maintaining good health and safety with the ability to maximize ammunition budgeting and training value. Rangemasters must weigh the advantages offered by use of lead-free ammunition to improve overall workplace exposure safety against the financial and practical advantages of using lead practice and duty ammunition inside their range. Regardless of the decision, rangemasters have a duty to provide a safe training environment for their shooters and take steps to minimize or eliminate exposure to hazards such as lead.

Maintenance

Unburned gunpowder expelled from firearms can present a flashover hazard in an indoor range. The authors have been present for multiple fires on ranges from this hazard. Ranges must be regularly vacuumed using an OSHA approved, explosion-proof, HEPA vacuum. A standard shop vacuum is NOT a suitable replacement. The spark of the electric motor of a standard vacuum can ignite unburned gun powder resulting in an explosion and injuries to range personnel. According to OSHA guidelines, shoveling, dry or wet sweeping, and brushing may be used only where vacuuming or other methods have been found not to be effective[6]. No compressed air should be used inside the range due to the risk of creating an airborne lead hazard.

When performing any cleaning maintenance inside an indoor range, it is recommended that personnel have the ventilation system operating and wear an N-95 or half-face respirator *at a minimum* to avoid breathing any contaminated air agitated by the cleaning. The respirators should be supplied by the organization and tested for fit. This can often be done through the safety and risk management department of the organization.

Brass may be collected using a hard edge implement such as a floor squeegee or a "brass picker" collection device made for indoor ranges. Use of brooms without proper respiratory protection for everyone in the range is hazardous and may be prohibited by state or federal regulations.

As described above, the ventilation system must maintain a consistent laminar air flow from floor to ceiling at a specific rate while maintaining negative air pressure. Filters must be changed regularly depending on the use of the range and other factors. Most current range ventilation systems have internal monitors to notify the rangemaster when filters need to be ordered and replaced. In addition to the use of the range, another factor that can drastically impact filter replacement is the type of bullet trap. Ranges that utilize a trap that captures projectiles whole, without fragmentation, will likely require less frequent filter replacement. If there is less contamination in the air, the filters will last longer.

Other ongoing maintenance of ventilation systems should be planned for on a scheduled basis, in accordance with manufacturer recommendations. These include:

- Ventilation motor maintenance and lubrication
- Changing drive belts
- Seasonal heating and cooling system checks
- Checks of any exposed ductwork for damage from projectiles

The bullet trap will also need ongoing maintenance and repair. As noted above in this chapter, granulated rubber berms require that projectiles and debris be removed from the trap by trained personnel and rubber replaced as needed to maintain the integrity of the trap. These also require that the rubber be raked to prevent cavities forming in the berm and damage to the metal support system. Similarly, rubber block traps require the replacement and rotation of blocks from time to time for the same reasons. Steel traps must have lead collected from buckets or drums, maintenance to motorized augers if applicable and so on. All of these systems will eventually wear out and require upgrade or replacement, although for modern traps this will generally be after millions of rounds have been fired.

The target system for the indoor range will also need ongoing maintenance. The maintenance required will greatly depend on the system being used. Because the system is down range, it is reasonable to expect that, over time, it will suffer damage from projectiles. Working with the target company to determine parts to keep on hand and routine maintenance procedures will extend the life of the system. One author recently worked on replacing a target system for an indoor range and the companies involved in bidding rated the life span of their systems between 10 and 15 years. Depending on the level of use of the range and the quality of on-going maintenance, the rangemaster should anticipate replacement or upgrades to these systems in that time frame.

Range Upgrades and Capital Replacement

The three systems mentioned above (ventilation, bullet trap, and target system) will all require funding for periodic upgrade or capital replacement. Good monitoring of these systems and their functionality will help the rangemaster predict replacement timing. As maintenance costs on a system begin to rise due to more frequent breakdowns, it may be time to start working with the budget manager to determine the proper approach to fund replacement.

The ventilation and bullet trap are systems that have workplace safety considerations. This should be taken into account by the rangemaster and the agency when proposing funding for upgrade or replacement. The target system typically doesn't have workplace safety considerations, but a non-functioning target system can affect the quality of training. For example, non-functioning lanes may allow for fewer shooters to participate, reducing the amount of training during a given period. Similarly, non-functioning systems that may have been used for decision-making drills may mean that training is no longer available, or not available at the level the agency is accustomed to. These issues may be able to be leveraged to justify the replacement of a failing system. See *Chapter 8: Budgeting* for more information on budgeting for replacement items.

Outside Agency Use

Do you plan to lease your range to other qualified agencies? If so, several important questions will need to be considered. Allowing outside agency use of a facility can impact maintenance, training time, agency relationships, and funding for various facility needs. Each of the following issues should be discussed thoughtfully with range staff and agency supervision before extending invitations for other agencies to utilize a range facility.

- How will the additional use impact maintenance? More shooters using the range equates to more projectiles and more maintenance.
- Will you charge a fee for other agencies to use the range to off-set maintenance?
- How will you prioritize scheduling of the range and who will be responsible for this task?

- If there is a scheduling conflict, how will it be resolved?
- Who will be responsible to repair damage caused by an outside agency?
- How will you ensure outside agency instructors are properly trained to use the range equipment?
- Who is responsible for various range maintenance tasks after another agency uses the range?
- What supplies will be provided by the home agency and which will be supplied by the outside agency? Targets, backers, etc.
- Will outside agencies be required to leave their brass at the range to fund maintenance, supplies, etc.?

These are some of the questions the rangemaster and agency should answer before allowing other agencies to schedule time on the range. Regardless of how the owner agency manages it, a contract or memorandum-of-understanding (MOU) should be agreed upon and signed by any outside users clearly outlining expectations. These should be reviewed by each agency's legal counsel.

Any visiting agency should be provided with a written copy of range facility SOPs which clearly outline expectations and safety rules. They should also include contact information if there is a problem with the range, if the agency is allowed to use the facility unsupervised. It is wise to provide a semi-formalized orientation for outside agency instructors so they are familiar with the equipment and procedures. This orientation should be documented so the home agency knows who has attended the orientation and is allowed to operate the range. It is not unreasonable for the home agency to require proof of certification of firearms instructors that will be running the range.

Allowing outside use of a facility can be beneficial for inter-agency relationships. Just the opportunity to work together with other agencies can bridge gaps in communication and understanding of how neighboring agencies perform their duties. Opportunities may present themselves for joint training or hosting courses that can be attended by more than one agency.

One of the most significant drawbacks of allowing outside agency use is available time for home agency use is reduced. If too much time is booked for outside agencies, conflicts for home agency use can lead to less flexibility for unscheduled training or needs that arise unexpectedly. Rangemasters should consider reserving some time on their range that cannot be booked by outside agencies so it is available for these needs.

[1] Editors of Britannica. (2006). *Laminar flow.* Britannica. https://www.britannica.com

[2] Provencher, B. (2017). *Understanding government range ventilation criteria.* National Shooting Sports Foundation. https://www.nssf.org/articles

[3] AT. (2014). *The 411 on shooting range ventilation.* Action Target: Provo, UT. https://actiontarget.com/why-range-ventilation-is-important/

[4] Bergiadis, B. (2019). *Shooting range acoustics.* Troy Acoustics. Presented at 2019 NSSF Shot Show.

[5] Colorado State Price Agreements. (2022). *Ammunition – law enforcement.* Colorado office of the state controller: Denver, CO. https://osc.colorado.gov/spco/state-price-agreements

[6] OSHA. (2022). *Standard 1910.1025 - Toxic and hazardous substances - lead.* Occupational Safety and Health Administration: Washington, D.C. https://www.osha.gov/laws-regs/regulations

Chapter 11: HAZARDS & EXPOSURES

Firearms training can be dangerous. It presents a variety of potential hazards to the students (officers), instructors, and observers. These hazards range from the firearm itself, being capable of causing serious injury or death, to the sound and toxic exposures one may encounter by its use without proper precautions. The rangemaster must both, be aware of the hazards present in their facility and/or training program, *and* how to properly mitigate those hazards in order to provide the safest training environment possible.

Hierarchy of Hazard Controls

Within the safety and risk management industry, most organizations follow the Hierarchy of Hazard Controls developed by the National Institute for Occupational Safety and Health (a research and advisory agency described below). This hierarchy approaches hazards and exposures for workers (in our case, instructors and students) in the following order:

HEIRARCHY OF CONTROLS

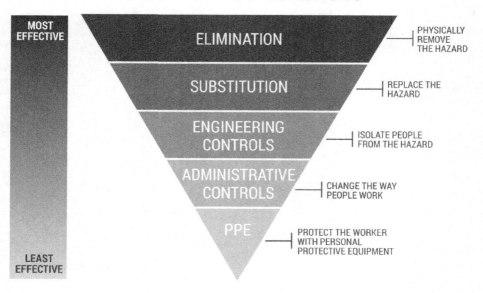

As indicated above, the first choice is to eliminate the hazard. If we are looking at the hazards of noise and lead exposure, a radical example of eliminating the hazard posed by live-fire training would be to mandate simulator training only. We are certainly not suggesting that agencies do so for all the reasons mentioned in *Chapter 3: Various Training Programs*. We merely use it here as an example of removing a hazard.

An example of substitution might be using lead-free ammunition only or training only with simulated systems typically used for force-on-force training. Lead-free ammunition may be used to eliminate exposure to lead but not eliminate exposure to excessive noise. Using only simulated weapon systems may address noise exposure hazards or the danger posed by the use of live firearms. However, use of simulated weapon systems does not always accurately mimic the use of live firearms; therefore, it may not be a true equal substitution for training purposes.

Engineering controls (isolating the worker from the hazard), are design features that help prevent exposure or excessive exposure to individuals. The primary goal of law enforcement firearms training is to improve the individual officer's skill with a very specific tool, the firearm. Therefore, officers are necessarily exposed to noise and potentially toxic substances (lead) while completing this training. Engineering controls such as ventilation in an indoor range and sound absorption materials for an indoor or outdoor range help reduce the individual's exposure to these hazards.

Administrative controls are best described as *how* employees are asked to perform a task in a safe manner. One example is limiting an individual's duration or frequency of exposure to the hazard. The Occupational Safety and Health Administration (OSHA) uses standard for sound exposure based on an 8-hour time weighted average (discussed further below). This is a standard for determining how long a person can be exposed to a particular hazard, in this case sound or lead, based on an 8-hour work period. These standards are particularly relevant to rangemasters regardless of personal protective equipment. Other examples of administrative controls are limiting the number of shooters firing at one time, hand washing after training, and use of gun cleaning mats to prevent contamination of classroom surfaces. These are all ways an agency can require officers to perform certain tasks in order to reduce individual exposure to various hazards.

Finally, if none of the above are available or can be implemented, or if additional mitigation is necessary, personal protective equipment (PPE) is the LAST control option. This includes hearing protection, eye protection, and other protective equipment that depends on proper fit and use to be effective. PPE is typically recommended as a supplement to the other control strategies and should not be relied upon as the sole means of protection. It is considered to be the least effective control available.

Rangemasters not only need to be familiar with the hazards to which personnel under their supervision will be exposed, but the best options for control of those hazards. In this chapter we will discuss various hazards, control measures for each, and the regulatory and advisory agencies that have authority over and provide information to agencies in relation to these hazards and exposures.

Agencies Related to Hazards & Exposures

Before we discuss particular hazards the rangemaster must deal with, we will identify the agencies that may have a direct or indirect impact on the range facility and/or firearms training program. These agencies fall into three basic categories:

1. Regulatory agencies – those that have enforcement authority as well as advisory roles.
2. Advisory and research agencies – those that have advisory or research functions only and no enforcement authority.
3. Non-governmental organizations – those that may recommend industry standards but are not government agencies and generally do not have any compliance authority.

Below are several agencies and organizations that have information beneficial to the rangemaster to ensure that their programs and facilities are safe and in compliance with industry standards as well as government regulations and laws.

The Environmental Protection Agency (EPA)

The EPA is a stand-alone agency focused on the protection of the environment. Essentially, anything associated with your range facility that may be deposited into the atmosphere, the ground, ground water or waterways, or transported off your range for disposal (e.g., waste contaminated with lead). The EPA does not regulate individual worker safety.

The EPA was established in 1970 to consolidate a variety of federal research, monitoring, standards setting, and enforcement activities geared to reducing environmental risk to people where they live, learn, and work.[1] The EPA both sets and enforces standards. Some of the issues the EPA may monitor or regulate relative to a firearms range are:

- Lead dust emissions to the atmosphere (not exposure to persons) such as exhaust from an indoor range ventilation system.
- Contaminated solvent disposal (e.g., rags, cleaning patches, etc.)
- Contaminated waste from a range (e.g., used filters, lead contaminated mop solution, or other waste from range cleaning.)
- Lead contamination from water run off or retention at ranges.

If an agency is moving off of a site such as an outdoor range, the EPA may inspect the site to determine what clean-up is required. Similarly, the EPA might respond to a report of improper hazardous waste disposal or other pollution emanating from an improperly operated range. It is unlikely that a law enforcement rangemaster will have a random inspection by the EPA that is not the result of a complaint or an action, such as the repurposing of land to other use.

An example of this is an outdoor range, used by an agency, in an area being considered by the state for use as a reservoir for drinking water. Such is the case for an agency near one of the authors. If this plan proceeds, it is likely the agency will have to spend money on cleanup of the range site and work with the EPA to ensure it is done to an acceptable standard. As mentioned in *Chapter 9: Outdoor Ranges,* water runoff and collection are significant concerns when choosing a site and building an outdoor range.

The Occupational Safety and Health Administration (OSHA)

OSHA's focus, as the name implies, is on individual worker safety. For the purposes of our discussion, "worker" can include:

- Staff personnel assigned to the range;

- All officers that use the range for training, qualification, etc.
- Range maintenance personnel

Note: observers and guests at a facility, while not workers, may have access to civil claims if there is evidence of below standard safety practices that are the proximate cause of an injury.

OSHA is part of the U.S. Department of Labor, and is a regulatory agency. It was established as part of the Occupational Safety and Health Act of 1970. It sets and enforces standards for worker safety, as well as provides training, education, and assistance.[2] They can be a resource or asset as they have funding specifically designated for workplace safety training, safety education, and assistance. For those in flagrant violation of workplace safety, they are also an enforcement agency empowered to fine workplaces for non-compliance.

The federal Occupational Health Safety Act covers most private sector workers; however, it does not automatically cover state and local government workers. If a state has an OSHA-approved state plan, it may cover private sector and government workers or it may only be applicable to state and local government workers. At the writing of this book, 22 states have OSHA-approved state plans that cover private, as well as state and local government workers. An additional five states and one U.S. territory have OSHA-approved state plans that cover state and local government workers only. In other states, OSHA has no authority over state and local governments for workplace safety standards. However, many local governments comply with OSHA standards voluntarily, and use them as a guide for workplace safety policies and practices. If a range, under state or federal regulatory authority, is found to be out of compliance with state and/or federal OSHA standards, hefty fines can be levied against the employer. Prolonged non-compliance can result in the range being closed as a workplace hazard until it is brought into compliance.

The rangemaster must educate themselves on regulatory standards and ensure conformity to those standards. The best resource for this is the organization's safety and risk management department. Ideally, the governmental unit will have an industrial hygienist within their safety and risk management department that can counsel with the rangemaster to ensure compliance with programs and facilities. If not, the agency may be able to consult with a contractor who provides similar services. These contractors should have certified safety professionals or certified industrial hygienists.

Whether or not your governmental unit falls under OSHA authority, a state occupational health and safety plan, or chooses to voluntarily comply with OSHA regulations or not, the below serve as industry standard guidelines for workplace safety. The rangemaster should be familiar with these standards and be aware of how any hazards to employees are being mitigated.

- Occupational noise exposure - 1910.95
- Eye and face protection - 1910.133
- Toxic and hazardous substances: lead - 1910.1025
- Portable fire extinguishers - 1910.157
- Hazard communication: safety data sheets - 1910.1200
- Bloodborne pathogens – 1910.1030

These and other workplace safety standards may be found on OSHA's website. Additionally, OSHA offers a variety of training materials online that outline training requirements for organizations under their regulatory authority. These can be helpful resources even if your organization is in a state that does not require OSHA compliance.

Bureau of Alcohol, Tobacco, Firearms, and Explosives (BATFE)

The BATFE, or ATF for short, is a federal law enforcement agency charged with the investigation and enforcement of federal statutes having to do with illegal trafficking and use of firearms, illegal use and storage of explosives, acts of arson and bombings, acts of terrorism and the illegal diversion of alcohol and tobacco products.[3] The ATF also regulates federal firearms licensing for firearm dealers.

Firearms ammunition is considered an "explosive" for shipping purposes because of the smokeless powder and primers.[4] However, 18 USC § 845 generally exempts small arms ammunition (calibers up to .50 BMG) from the provisions of 18 USC, Chapter 40 (explosive materials). This is limited to traditional ammunition containing smokeless powder propellants and primers. The exemption does not include ammunition that has additional pyrotechnic properties.

A BATFE approved magazine (bunker for storage of explosives) is not required for the storage of small arms ammunition. However, other items that may be classified as "explosives" may require storage in a magazine as defined by BATFE.[5] If explosives (e.g., C4 or detonating cord) are stored at the range for use in explosive breaching or bomb squad training, they should be stored in an approved magazine. This requirement also covers the storage of noise flash diversionary devices (flashbangs). The rangemaster can contact the regional BATFE office or check their online resources for more information on requirements.

The ATF is also a valuable resource for information regarding the purchase, issue and disposition of select fire weapons, short barreled rifles or shotguns, suppressors and so on. Before purchasing or disposing of such items, the rangemaster should familiarize themselves with the relevant regulations. Once again, contacting an agent that specializes in regulation at a regional office of the BATFE will be invaluable to ensuring these weapons are handled properly.

A few resources that may be valuable for firearm, ammunition, and explosive regulations are listed below. The most current versions of these can be found online.

- Gun Control Act – 18 USC Chapter 44
- National Firearms Act – 26 USC Chapter 53
- Storage (magazines) – 27 CFR § 555

National Institute for Occupational Safety & Health (NIOSH)

NIOSH was also established as part of the Occupational Safety and Health Act of 1970 and is part of the U.S. Centers for Disease Control & Prevention (CDC) within the U.S. Department of Health and Human Services. NIOSH's primary focus is research that is centered on chronic, on-the-job health issues, and providing recommended standards.[6] It is a "watch dog" for worker health and safety, but is NOT an enforcement agency. Once NIOSH has detected a problem and identified a solution (new standard), they work with OSHA to implement and enforce the new standard.

Several agencies (including an agency one of the authors works for) have participated in NIOSH research projects to improve employee safety. The results of this research are available on NIOSH's website in a searchable format (https://www.cdc.gov/niosh/pubs/). The rangemaster can find valuable information through NIOSH on the following topics as well as many others:

- Hearing protection
- Eye protection
- Lead exposure
- N95 Particulate Filtering Facepiece Respirator (mask)
- Hazards pertaining to indoor ranges

American National Standards Institute (ANSI)

ANSI was founded in 1918 as a not-for-profit organization. It is the voice of the U.S. voluntary standards and conformity assessment system. It is also the official U.S. representative to the International Organization for Standardization (ISO).[7] It is not an enforcement agency; however, they create uniform testing standards and guidelines.

ANSI has valuable information for the rangemaster evaluating eye and ear protection. They provide uniform testing standards for shatter resistant eyewear. Eye protection that meets these standards will usually be marked on the arm of the glasses with "Z87+" or "Z87.1" to indicate impact resistant safety glasses suitable for eye protection on the range. ANSI also provides a standard (ANSI S3.19) for hearing protection performance. This is important for the rangemaster when selecting hearing protection with the appropriate noise reduction rating for whatever range conditions they may have.

Often times, other regulatory agencies, such as OSHA, will incorporate ANSI standards into their various regulations. As a neutral, standards organization, they provide research, standards of testing, and recommendations for the best practices available in work place safety.

American Conference of Governmental Industrial Hygienists (ACGIH)

Industrial Hygiene is the science of protecting and enhancing the health and safety of people at work and in their communities from hazards that include chemical, biological, physical, and ergonomic stressors. ACGIH started as the National Conference of Governmental Industrial Hygienists (NCGIH) in 1938. In 1946 the name was changed to the American Conference of Governmental Industrial Hygienists or ACGIH.[8] As a private organization, ACGIH functions in a research and advisory role only and is not a regulatory agency. Nevertheless, the standards they recommend are followed by many industrial hygienists working within various governmental organizations. Their standards and recommendations are, in some cases, more stringent than OSHA but often align with NIOSH.

The association has created alliances with other organizations within the occupational health and safety industry such as the American Industrial Hygiene Association (AIHA) and the Foundation for Occupational Health & Safety (FOHS). These associations work together to accomplish aligned purposes to include:

- Sponsoring research, education, and the publication of scientific information.
- Providing a vehicle for financial support of the improvement and enhancement of occupational and environmental health and safety and the general public.
- Disseminating the results of valuable research findings and assuring a heightened quality of continuing education in occupational safety and health.

Many city, county, and state agencies employ industrial hygienists; persons certified through education and experience in the area of industrial hygiene. Their responsibilities often include ensuring OSHA and EPA regulations are implemented and followed throughout the organization. They are an excellent resource in assisting the rangemaster with mandatory safety training, obtaining safety or personal protective equipment (PPE), industry standardized noise level testing, work surface contamination and air quality sampling. Similar to the budget managers discussed in *Chapter 8: Budgeting,* the industrial hygienist will often go out of their way to help the rangemaster who sincerely desires to make the range facility and firearms program safe for all participants. However, in the end, their job is to ensure compliance with standards throughout the organization, with or without the rangemaster's cooperation.

Industrial hygienists can often make forward progress on projects such as the replacement of range ventilation systems, where the rangemaster receives rejection or hesitant support. In the realm of occupational health, once a workplace hazard is identified, the organization has an obligation to address it. Therefore, when an industrial hygienist says something must be fixed, installed, replaced, or upgraded, administrators tend to listen. Partnering with an industrial hygienist can lead to many improvements in safety and health for a facility or program overseen by the rangemaster.

It is important for the rangemaster to have a trained industrial hygienist assess the noise levels and airborne lead levels of a range. Their education and training make them qualified to conduct the testing properly and interpret the results in order to ensure compliance with OSHA, NIOSH or ACGIH standards. If you are a rangemaster for a small, rural agency, your organization may not employ an industrial hygienist; however, there is likely someone assigned at the state level who can come to your range and conduct the necessary testing. Once that is performed, ask for assistance in bringing whatever is below standard into compliance as quickly as possible. The industrial hygienist may know of state funds or even federal grant funds specifically earmarked for worker safety.

The rangemaster should obtain written results from the industrial hygienist and make written recommendations to their administration to bring their program or facility into compliance where there are gaps. Once the industrial hygienist conducts their measurements on your range, if changes are necessary to comply with required standards, the agency is "on the clock" to make those changes. Agencies who ignore official documentation of conditions that fall below required standards may be considered deliberately indifferent in a work injury related lawsuit. Further, they may (depending on the state regulations) be subject to sanctions by the regulating authority. The rangemaster should never ignore official reports of unacceptable conditions on their range. Any such information should be passed along to agency administrators with recommendations for corrective action without delay.

Other State & Local Agencies

State-level occupational safety & health (OSH) agencies, may have regulatory authority over local government workplace safety, including law enforcement agencies, as previously discussed. An example of such organizations is in Arizona where NLEFIA is headquartered. Arizona has an OSHA-approved state plan covering most private sector and all state and local government workers. The Arizona Division of Occupational Safety & Health (ADOSH), a component of the Industrial Commission of Arizona (ICA), is the regulating authority. They have the ability to regulate workplace safety issues for state and local government entities.

Conversely, states such as Colorado, Texas, Wisconsin, and a variety of others, are under federal OSHA jurisdiction covering most private sector and federal workers but not state and local government workers.

Nearly every state has an agency which regulates environmental protection in some way. The rangemaster should be aware of the agency with respective jurisdiction and the state-level regulations that are relevant to their range.

Many local fire departments or fire authorities have the ability to conduct regular inspections of private business and government buildings regarding compliance with fire code and safety measures. These measures include ingress and egress accessibility, sprinkler systems, fire doors, and the condition and location of fire extinguishers.

As ranges are being built, the agency will likely have to work with local planning and zoning agencies as well as building inspectors to ensure compliance with a variety of building regulations. One of the authors was recently involved in the construction of a new, two-agency, joint training facility including an indoor range, which was built on local airport property. The agencies had to work with the airport authority (which both city governments are part of) to ensure Federal Aviation Administration regulations were followed as well as other airport regulations for maximum structure height, fencing, and other safety standards.

Specific Hazards and Exposures

The law enforcement rangemaster has several responsibilities regarding workplace hazards and exposures. First is to identify and be aware of potential hazards. Some may be obvious such as noise on the range or lead exposure. Others may be overlooked, such as an armorer's exposure to chemical cleaning solvents or lack of adequate ventilation in the armory. A good relationship with an industrial hygienist can help identify and prioritize hazards and exposures that need to be addressed.

Second, the rangemaster must determine the best way of mitigating these hazards using the hierarchy of hazard controls discussed previously. Again, it is important to keep in mind that personal protective equipment is the least effective and least desirable solution to address hazards. While sometimes unavoidable, other options should be considered first. An example would be eliminating toxic, oil-based cleaning solvents and substituting water-based, non-toxic cleaning agents; thus, reducing or eliminating exposure in confined or poorly ventilated armories.

Finally, the rangemaster is responsible for awareness of regulatory requirements established by the government or national organizations described above. Even if the standards are not legally mandated in your area, understanding and complying with industry standards for worker safety is wise on the part of the agency.

In the next sections, we will discuss specific hazards, some technical information useful to the rangemaster, and considerations for mitigation. The information contained in these sections DOES NOT provide a replacement for consultation with a certified industrial hygienist or other professional in the workplace safety industry. These sections merely provide additional information for the rangemaster to have a better understanding of some of the hazards and exposures they may be responsible for in their respective position overseeing a facility or training program.

Occupational Noise Exposure

Noise Exposure Details

Firearms are loud. Continued, unprotected exposure to gunfire can result in permanent hearing loss. The noise is typically measured as sound pressure level (SPL) using the decibel scale (dB). The science of SPL measurement and the use of the decibel scale is somewhat complicated. For the rangemaster, a functional understanding is sufficient since we are not preparing for a physics exam.

The decibel (dB), is a logarithmic unit used to measure sound pressure. In acoustics, the decibel is used to quantify sound pressure level that people hear.[9] In the case of firearms, SPL is the measurement of the difference between the pressure of a sound wave (gunshot) and the ambient air pressure the sound wave is traveling through. For our purposes we will use the terms "noise" and "sound pressure level" synonymously. The decibel level is expressed in a logarithmic progression, not a mathematic progression, which means that a small increase or decrease in decibel measurement can be a significant increase or decrease in noise for the person exposed. See

Determining Noise Exposure below for an example of this logarithmic progression regarding the recommended "exchange rate" for noise exposure.

The following chart indicates common sounds and their relative decibel level according to OSHA[10]:

Noise	Decibels
Gunshot	140
Snowmobile	120
Threshold of pain	120
Chain saw	110
Wood shop	100
Belt sander	90
OSHA permissible exposure limit	90
OSHA / ACGIH / NIOSH recommended maximum exposure	85
Noisy cafeteria	80
Normal conversation	60
Whisper	30
Threshold of unimpaired hearing	0

In a NIOSH report specific to firearms use, researchers noted that impulsive noise, such as gunfire, is more damaging to the ear than continuous sounds. Unprotected exposure to high intensity impulsive noise can cause acute acoustic trauma. This may result in symptoms such as ringing in the ears (tinnitus) and temporary or permanent hearing loss.[11]

When it comes to noise exposure, there is a difference between age-related hearing loss and noise-induced hearing loss (NIHL). Age-related hearing loss is a natural, progressive weakness of the "sensory hairs" within the inner ear (cochlea). Noise-induced hearing loss may be temporary or permanent. Exposure to a high level of noise, whether constant like a loud concert, or impulse noise like gunfire, can cause a temporary threshold shift (TTS). A TTS results in temporary hearing loss. Time spent in a quiet environment can result in a return to normal hearing levels. Continued exposure to high levels of noise can result in a permanent threshold shift (PTS) from which humans cannot recover. Some short-term exposure to high levels of noise or continued exposure to high levels of noise (constant or impulse) may result in the destruction of sensory hairs within the ear. Once damaged, they do not regenerate, resulting in permanent hearing loss.[12] Rangemasters should be aware that the risk of hearing loss is increased while working in environments in which ototoxins, like lead, are present. See *Lead Exposure* below for additional details on ototoxins.

Tinnitus is a potential side effect of both TTS and PTS. Tinnitus is a continuous ringing or buzzing in the ear. When the sensory hairs mentioned above are damaged or broken due to exposure, they sometimes begin "leaking" random electrical impulses to the brain, causing the constant phantom ringing or buzzing. People may develop tinnitus as a result of temporary or long-term exposure to high levels of noise. While there are other causes of tinnitus, if it is the result of long-term exposure to noise, it is often unable to be cured. Some treatments can help reduce symptoms but it is unlikely to go away all together. Tinnitus is a serious health condition that can lead to depression and anxiety due to the constancy of the noise perceived in the patient's ears.[13]

Determining Noise Exposure

OSHA requires a 90 dB permissible exposure limit. This is calculated on an 8-hour time weighted average (TWA). This means that a student or instructor should not be exposed to noise that results in 90 dB average over the course of an 8-hour shift. OSHA regulations currently require a 5 dB exchange rate (see table below). This means that for every 5 dB increase over the maximum permissible limit, the worker should reduce their exposure by half.

Noise Level	Exposure Limit
90 dBA	8.0 hours
92 dBA	6.0 hours
95 dBA	4.0 hours
97 dBA	3.0 hours
100 dBA	2.0 hours
102 dBA	1.5 hours
105 dBA	1.0 hour
110 dBA	30 minutes
115 dBA	15 minutes
OSHA Permissible Noise Exposure Limits for 8-hour work period[14]	

Both NIOSH and ACGIH *recommend* an 85 dB, 8-hour TWA maximum exposure and a 3 dB exchange rate. If an instructor is exposed to an 8-hour TWA of 88 dB, they should only be exposed for 4 hours instead of 8 hours at 85 dB. Both NIOSH and ACGIH tend to be more conservative and make recommendations developed from current research.

Personal noise dosimetry (measuring noise exposure to individual employees) is required by OSHA and is necessary to ensure that the appropriate hearing protection is selected. If rangemasters are looking to measure the noise exposure to individuals on their range, they should seek the assistance of a certified safety professional or industrial hygienist. High speed digital sampling equipment is desirable to obtain more accurate readings over traditional analog equipment.

Other critical factors are the placement of recording equipment and the number of shooters sampled. Noise sampling equipment should be placed as high on the shoulder of the shooter or instructor as possible and away from the neck and clothing to accurately capture the exposure. Further, if the typical range day includes 10, 15 or 20 shooters, the testing should include the "worst case" exposure level. Enough samples should be collected to produce a 90% confidence level that the top 10% of exposure levels have been sampled. Only by taking the most accurate measurements and correct sampling can rangemasters determine the proper hearing protection needed for personnel on the range.

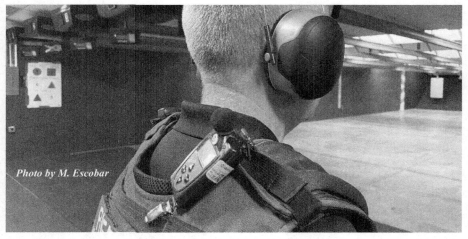

Photo by M. Escobar

Use of personal dosimeter to measure individual noise exposure.

The maximum allowable peak pressure a worker should be exposed to is 140 dB, even if wearing properly fitted and worn hearing protection.[15] This means that peak impulse noise, the maximum SPL that a gunshot registers, in the work environment should not exceed that amount. Measurement of sound exposure should be done using personal dosimetry (dosimeters worn on individuals in the environment) with properly calibrated devices that have the ability to measure the appropriate decibel range for gunfire.

The industrial hygienist will use the readings from the dosimeter and the noise reduction rating (NRR) of any hearing protection worn, to calculate the employee's exposure. This is a significantly technical process and should only be done by qualified professionals.

As noted above, a factor that can impact exposure is the proper fit and use of hearing protection. Hearing PPE must be worn as directed to maximize the NRR. If the seal of a shooter's ear muffs is compromised by safety glasses or hats being worn, or if hearing plugs are improperly inserted, the noise attenuation may be significantly less. For this and other reasons, only a certified safety professional should measure and calculate exposure for the purposes of making decisions about PPE or other mitigation efforts.

Another factor in measuring occupational exposure to sound is reverberation time (RT60) or the duration of the sound before it drops to a safe level. The longer the peak pressure lasts, the more damaging it is for anyone exposed to the gunfire regardless of PPE. Reverberation time is measured as the amount of time it takes for the pressure curve to drop to 60 dB.[16]

Reverberation can be measured using specialized sound mapping instrumentation on the range. This will provide the rangemaster with information on where the sound is loudest and any specific areas that need mitigation as well as an overall evaluation of range noise. As with the dosimetry above, this should only be done by trained hygienists with the appropriate equipment. The goal of noise mitigation at the range is to bring the peak level below 140 dB and reduce the reverberation time as much as possible. This will allow for the safest shooting environment available.

Mitigation and Hearing Protection

Due to the necessity of live-fire firearms training for law enforcement officers, eliminating the hazard and substituting the hazard are usually not feasible when considering noise exposure. We will discuss engineering controls, administrative controls, and PPE that can be used to reduce exposure for officers and range staff. We will also discuss conservation programs and on-going testing which can contribute to a well-rounded hearing safety program.

Regardless of whether you operate an indoor or outdoor range, some engineering controls may be beneficial to reducing noise for the instructors and shooters. As discussed in *Chapter 9: Outdoor Ranges,* side barriers and overhead baffles on some outdoor ranges can have hard surfaces that reflect noise to the shooter. This noise can be mitigated by the application of acoustical materials. Similarly, indoor ranges frequently must have some acoustical material in order to reduce the SPL reverberation to acceptable levels as noted in the example in *Chapter 10: Indoor Ranges* of the Department of Defense range that was unusable after construction due to the lack of proper acoustic mitigation. Even with good acoustic materials on range surfaces, there will still be peak SPL from the muzzle blast of a firearm. However, quality acoustic materials can drastically reduce the reverberation of the noise from the muzzle, thereby reducing the overall exposure for the officer.

Only specific materials should be used for reducing noise on a range. A number of range design and acoustical surface companies offer solutions for the rangemaster. When considering these products, it is important for the rangemaster to obtain detailed specifications from the various manufacturers. It is also wise to ask some particular questions during the selection process. Acoustic materials for ranges should be durable, washable, and resist the collection of lead particles. If used on an outdoor or no-blue-sky range, they should stand up to inclement weather well, and resist bacteria and fungi growth. Materials used in the range should be Class A fire rated; a rating by the American Society for Testing and Materials indicating superior fire protection. Finally, and perhaps most importantly, they should be effective at reducing reverberation noise from firearm discharges.

This is yet another area in which a well-trained safety professional or industrial hygienist will be of assistance. They can help interpret the specifications from the various manufacturers, looking at the different frequencies of noise reduced by the product to help the rangemaster pick the most effective material for their needs.

Rangemasters should avoid products made for other uses such as foam "sound proofing" designed for sound studio applications. These products often lack the features needed for the range. If they are excessively porous, they can collect lead and gunpowder particles. Depending on the material, they may not lend themselves to cleaning. They are also sometimes not fire rated or are rated lower than materials needed for a range, creating a serious fire hazard.

Vinyl wrapped fiberglass or standard fiberglass insulation is not a particularly good choice. It is often not very durable and when exposed to water, supports fungi growth.[17] This equates to mold and mildew potentially creating additional health concerns.

Some polypropylene materials, such as porous expanded polypropylene or P.E.P.P., are widely used in ranges and have features that make them appropriate for those spaces. Other polypropylene materials can be a fire hazard and release toxic fumes if set on fire. Once again, obtaining detailed specifications on the product will assist the rangemaster in choosing the correct material.

Photo by author

Ballistic rubber tile (BRT) is not an acoustic material. These tiles are made of highly compressed rubber medium and are designed primarily to prevent the fragmentation or deflection of projectiles. They reflect sound significantly and should not be used for acoustic treatment of range surfaces. Typically, these tiles can be used on baffles close to the bullet trap and the side walls of the trap itself to capture errant projectiles that may hit those areas. Depending on the range design, it is rarely necessary to have the tiles extend out of the bullet trap. BRT is typically not fire rated and may need to be treated with a fire retardant.

Photo by author

One of the authors is currently working on a project to replace BRT that was installed on a significant portion of a new range. Unfortunately, the person in charge of the project didn't understand sound mitigation and didn't ask for specifications for the product (there are no sound specifications available for BRT because it is not an acoustic product). The reverberation from these panels is similar to bare concrete. When measured by a trained industrial hygienist, the sound readings were far higher than allowable by OSHA standards for an 8-hour TWA. Much of this had to do with instructors and students being exposed to multiple, peak level impulse noises, caused by the reverberation of sound off the BRT.

One material that is widely used for noise mitigation for indoor ranges is a combination wood, concrete fiber board panel. Several companies make these types of panels in different sizes and thicknesses under different trade names. Most of these products are exceptional at reducing reverberation noise within a range across a broad frequency spectrum. When combined with various types of insulation behind them, they can be even more effective. However, they can also be brittle and break easily if something is pushed against them. Therefore, the rangemaster should consider appropriate placement of these materials if used within their range.

Another consideration of range acoustic treatment is controlling noise outside of the range. If the range is part of a larger building, the rangemaster must consider the noise exposure for workers and others occupying the building outside the range. Proper acoustic treatment of the range can mitigate these concerns. Additionally, reducing noise on an indoor or outdoor range may serve to avoid complaints from encroaching neighbors whether residential or commercial.

Administrative controls may mean reducing the number of shooters on a range at one time or shortening the duration in which shooters and instructors are on the range. This obviously impacts training time and scheduling. Therefore, it is up to each agency and rangemaster individually to determine if administrative controls can be utilized effectively to reduce employee risk of noise exposure. No rangemaster wants to give up training time, but it may be necessary to do more frequent, shorter duration training to minimize exposure to noise while other solutions for a range are being considered and implemented.

Lastly, personal protective equipment in the form of hearing protection is absolutely necessary for range operations. When considering hearing protection for shooters or instructors, several options are available that offer varying levels of attenuation. Below are brief descriptions and information about several types of hearing protection.

- Soft foam hearing protection: foam ear plugs are inexpensive but effective if used correctly. Some foam plugs are rolled up then inserted in the ear using the two-hand insertion method, while others such as 3M's No Touch earplug, may be inserted without rolling. The foam expands in the ear filling the space regardless of the individual shape. Many foam plugs can achieve 30+ dB Noise Reduction Rating (NRR) if inserted correctly using the instructions on the package. Foam plugs are often disposable as well and provide a cheap alternative for ranges to have on hand if a shooter is lacking hearing protection. While most foam plugs fit most shooters, some shooters may require a larger or smaller foam plug to fit their ear canal well. Stocking a wide range of sizes, shapes and NRR ratings can be highly beneficial to the rangemaster. As a general rule, foam earplugs should be disposed of after one use (e.g., one day at the range).

- Multi-use in-ear protection: another option is in-ear hearing protection that is reusable. These typically have a triple flange design of soft, flexible, polymer that is inserted into the ear. They are available in several sizes to fit a wide variety of shooters. Again, some shooters may require larger or smaller sizes to provide adequate protection. These plugs are inexpensive ($10 to $20) and can provide 24 to 30+ NRR ratings making them a good addition to the range bag for shooters in case they forget or have problems with their regular hearing protection. If considering these as agency supplied hearing protection, individual shooters should be tested with them inserted to ensure they provide the adequate protection.

- Custom molded ear plugs: a number of brands are available for custom molded ear plugs. If considered for use or issue by agencies, it is highly recommended that the molds be completed by personnel professionally trained to make them. Quantitative testing is available to verify the effectiveness of the ear plugs and is highly recommended to ensure a proper fit to the user. If made correctly, custom molded ear plugs can provide a NRR of 33 or higher and are reusable for several years of life. Changes in the user's weight, age, and so on can affect the efficacy of these plugs over time. It is recommended that these be tested regularly to ensure continued adequate performance and evaluate the lifecycle. The cost is higher than the ear plugs mentioned above ($65 +/-) however, these are typically long lasting for those on the range frequently. They also provide a good alternative for long gun shooting over ear muffs.

- Passive ear muffs: one of the most common forms of hearing protection, passive ear muffs are preferred by many shooters and agencies for use and issue to officers. The NRR rating can vary greatly from 18 or 19 NRR up to 33 dB or higher. Unlike in-ear hearing protection, the effectiveness of over the ear muffs can be compromised by the safety glasses worn or if they are worn in combination with a hat. In short, anything that breaks the seal can reduce the NRR of the muffs significantly. If thinner profile muffs are desired for long gun shooting, they will typically be a lower NRR due to reduced space for noise reducing insulation. Passive ear muffs provide effective hearing protection for rangemasters to have on hand for students or visitors, they are often adjustable to fit a wide range of people, and can be quickly disinfected with wipes between uses so they can be used by multiple individuals. Quality passive ear muffs can be purchased for less than $30 per pair making them a long-lasting, inexpensive and versatile option for ranges and rangemasters.

- Electronic earplugs and over the ear muffs: generic and custom earplugs and earmuffs also come in electronic versions. These are made to receive and transmit sound through a microphone and speaker in the plug or muff, allowing the wearer to hear normally or even amplify sounds around them. Older and less expensive electronic hearing protection is made with "stop gate" technology. This means that at a particular threshold, the electronics cut off the sound so it does not damage the wearer's hearing. Newer and more advanced models use "sound compression" technology which means that the sound coming in through the microphones to the speakers is continually compressed into a stream which will not exceed a threshold considered dangerous for human ears.[18] These allow wearers to hear constantly in their environment but always at a safe level while the stop gate versions have a discernible cut-off during loud noise. If using stop gate technology, it is important for the user to be aware of the attack time before buying or using them. Depending on the quality of the electronics, the time it takes for the electronics to recognize a sound that is past the allowable threshold and cut off the transmission to the user can vary (attack time). Some lesser quality, cheaper models do not cut off the impulse sound quickly enough thus reducing their effectiveness at preventing hearing damage. Most of the electronic systems are more expensive than the passive versions and range from fifty to hundreds of dollars depending on the brand, quality, and features. Electronic plugs and muffs often have a lower NRR rating than the passive versions. Regardless of whether the electronics are turned on or off, the NRR rating is what determines how effective they are at protecting the wearer's hearing.

- Another feature available in either passive or electronic over the ear muffs that may be useful to rangemasters and instructors are muffs that are made for two-way communication. These connect via Bluetooth or wire to two-way radios or other systems to allow for two-way communication between instructors or potentially one-way communication to student shooters who can be equipped with a receive only set. This can greatly improve range communication but, as with any technology, these units are subject to more frequent inoperability due to damage, dead batteries, or other technological issues. They are, as may be expected, also more expensive than other options.

Some ranges will recommend or require "double hearing protection". NIOSH has recommended this for use in most indoor range environments.[19] This means the shooter wears both in-ear hearing protection, such as foam plugs, AND over the ear hearing protection. It is important for rangemasters to understand that doubling up on hearing protection does not *double* the NRR of the protection. Nor can you simply add the two ratings together to come up with a new NRR. A simplified method of determining the increased NRR, according to OSHA, is to add 5 dB to the maximum NRR of the higher rated protection being worn.[20] So, if a shooter is wearing an ear plug with a rating of 30 dB and over the ear muffs with a rating of 27 dB, they would add 5 dB to the ear plug rating. The two systems together would provide a 35 dB NRR for the wearer.

Further, OSHA strongly recommends applying a 50% correction factor when estimating field workplace attenuation effectiveness of hearing protection. In their *Methods for Estimating HPD attenuation* they state, "OSHA's experience and the published scientific literature have shown that laboratory-obtained real ear attenuation for HPDs can seldom be achieved in the workplace."[21] Using the example above, if the wearer was using two forms of hearing protection which together had a 35 NRR (calculated with C-weighted measurements), OSHA recommends using a 50% correction to 17.5 dB field noise reduction rating. To be clear, this is not a regulation but rather a strong recommendation of how to calculate "real world" NRR by OSHA. Once again, a certified safety professional or industrial hygienist should be consulted to ensure that the hearing protection selected or provided is adequate to protect those individuals being exposed to gunfire on the range.

Hearing Conservation Programs

An ongoing hearing conservation program is an important part of a good workplace safety program. OSHA requires that employees exposed to levels of noise exceeding 85 dB be enrolled in a hearing conservation program.[22] If you are a rangemaster in a state under OSHA regulations or with an OSHA-approved state plan that applies to government workers this regulation applies to your agency. Even if you are not, this makes good sense to work with safety and risk management personnel to protect employees and ensure long-term hearing health.

Photo by author

Only trained personnel should conduct noise sampling

As part of the conservation program, hearing tests should be conducted according to OSHA standards by certified audiologists or a qualified vendor certified to conduct such tests. They should be completed as part of a recruit's pre-employment physical or onboarding and then annually for all officers. If an agency is not regulated by OSHA and resistant to having all officers tested, the rangemaster should, at least, advocate for having all firearms instructors tested annually. Enlisting the support of the organization's industrial hygienist in this effort is invaluable.

The first test establishes a baseline. For OSHA regulated agencies, this test has to be completed within 6-months of hire. Subsequent annual tests will show if there is a change in hearing over time. If there is hearing loss outside the normal rate attributed to aging, the employee and employer can make informed decisions about changes to exposure or hearing protection devices used.

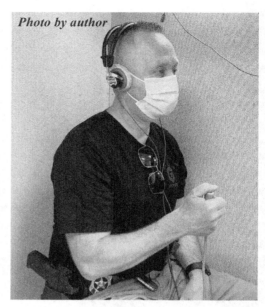

If an officer or instructor is exposed to gunfire or other loud noise, such as a noise flash diversionary device (flashbang), without proper hearing protection, they should consider completing an exposure report with worker's compensation. As we have discussed, even a single incident exposure to high levels of impulse noise can cause permanent hearing loss. It is important to document any such incidents.

A hearing conservation program is an important part of overall wellness for officers and range staff.

If your instructors are routinely exposed to sounds above the 120 dB range, and/or your tactical team members are exposed to flashbang devices that go as high as 140 dB, hearing protection alone may not be adequate. Pressure curves in the 120 to 140 dB range have been shown to penetrate the soft tissue and sinus cavities around the face and pass quickly through the relatively dense tissue of the brain in milliseconds.

Another way of thinking about exposure to percussive sounds that exceed 120 dB is taking a full powered punch in the face from a prize fighter - in 3 milliseconds! Continuous exposure to such percussive sound waves may have long-term impacts on the brain and nervous system.[23]

If a full-time firearms instructor has a continued increase in hearing loss, the agency may need to consider re-assignment of the officer to protect them against further hearing degradation. Any such discoveries likely linked to workplace exposures should be properly documented through worker's compensation.

Lead Exposure

Officers and range staff who routinely conduct training on live-fire ranges, where standard lead ammunition is used, have some exposure to lead. Exposure to lead, an ototoxin, can have serious health impacts including hearing related problems. Rangemasters should take appropriate steps to ensure the safety of range personnel and shooters so that they are not exposed to dangerous levels of lead.

Lead Exposure Details

Generally, lead enters the human body in two ways. One is the inhalation of airborne lead dust and the second is ingestion of lead particles, typically on the hands of the shooter transferred while eating or drinking, after firing or cleaning a firearm. While absorption through skin is possible, it is far less efficient and the lead has to be in contact with the skin for an extended period of time before it finds its way into the bloodstream.

Ammunition cartridge primers contain lead. If the base of a jacketed projectile is not covered by copper or other jacket metal, it can also be a source of airborne lead as the gun is fired. Additionally, the friction created by the bullet traveling through the rifled barrel of a firearm may produce particulate lead from some types of ammunition, that is released from the barrel when the projectile exits. Every time you fire a firearm with modern ammunition, there is an invisible cloud containing airborne lead surrounding you. Handguns, particularly revolvers, are more likely to create airborne lead at the firing point. In shoulder mounted weapons, the airborne lead is more likely to exit the muzzle, but that just puts the airborne lead at muzzle distance. Keep in mind that rifle and shotgun primers are larger and more powerful than pistol primers. Some airborne lead can be generated if the backstop is an outdated design (angled smash plate), but even most modern steel bullet traps generate some lead particulate (larger sized pieces).

Outdoor ranges don't have ventilation systems to keep the air moving away from the shooter. Depending on the air movement, or lack thereof, during a particular training session, shooters may be exposed to more or less lead particles in the air. Using non-reactionary steel targets at close range can also produce particulate lead that shooters can inhale if the air is moving toward them. On very dry ranges, shooting dirt berms can create significant dust that may contain lead particles from previously fired projectiles.

Inside a range, lead dust can collect on a variety of surfaces including firing booths, benches, desktops, control consoles, or almost any other surface. Shooters can also come in contact with lead when picking up spent brass casings. If the students shoot from alternate positions, such as kneeling or prone, they will come into contact with lead on the floor of the range. Officers or instructors may also be exposed to lead while cleaning firearms after they are done shooting. This can obviously occur at the range, station, or at home.

All of these examples serve as methods by which agency employees can be exposed to hazardous levels of lead. With forethought and proper mitigation actions, the rangemaster can greatly reduce the risk of lead exposure to range staff and shooters.

Determining Lead Exposure

OSHA has established standards for airborne lead monitoring and guidelines for housekeeping under 29 CFR 1910.1025. This includes full-shift personal air samples in which the employee wears an air sampling device

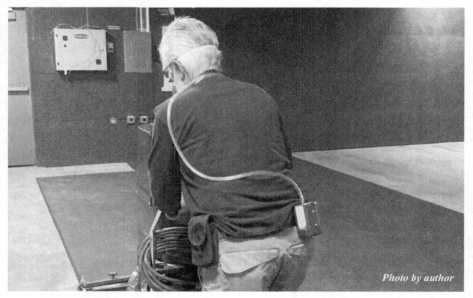

Photo by author

The pump worn by the employee samples particulate exposure

throughout a normal shift at the range facility. If the employee is exposed to more than the action limit (AL) of 30 micrograms per cubic meter of air (30 $\mu g/m^3$) averaged over an 8-hour period, the employer must offer medical surveillance. This should be done regardless of your agencies OSHA regulation status as an appropriate worker safety practice. Medical surveillance most often involves blood lead level testing but may also be done through urine testing (see below). If exposure to lead exceeds the permissible exposure level (PEL) for more than 30 days per year, employers must implement engineering and work practice controls to reduce exposure below the PEL.

While OSHA has no standard for contact surfaces, 1910.1025(h)(1) states that, "All surfaces shall be maintained as free as practicable of accumulations of lead." Testing of surfaces is typically through wipe sample detection. Colorimetric wipes are readily available for real-time detection of lead.[24] These change color (yellow/orange to pink/red) when exposed to acidic compounds such as lead.

Blood lead level tests should be completed for the NIOSH / OSHA Occupational Exposure Scale (more sensitive and more information than just a general blood lead level test). Blood tests should be done regardless if you have an outdoor range or indoor range as exposures above the PEL can occur at both. The best safety practice would be to include blood lead level testing as part of an officer's initial physical exam during the hiring process to establish a baseline for an employee who will be exposed to some degree of lead during their employment. After that, it may be cost prohibitive for an agency to provide ongoing testing for all officers, but active firearms instructors should get tested annually. Just as with hearing conservation, the first test establishes a baseline. Subsequent tests will show if there is an increase in lead levels over time.

The table below shows blood lead levels in micrograms per deciliter ($\mu g/dl$) with action needed according to the Centers for Disease Control. OSHA requires removal from exposure if the blood lead level is 50 $\mu g/dl$ or above. They are currently considering lowering this limit.

In addition to removal from the exposure, worker's compensation regulations or other governing guidelines may require that the employee be removed from the work environment, at least temporarily. A number of rangemasters and firearms instructors have been reassigned to alternative duties (including one of the authors) due to excessive blood lead levels. In addition to the negative, long-term impact on the employee's health of the exposure, mandated changes can be disruptive and potentially detrimental to the firearms program. All of this is completely avoidable through proper mitigation, safe workplace practices, and routine medical surveillance of employees.

Blood lead levels and corresponding actions according to the CDC	
Blood Lead Level	Action Needed
0-4 µg/dl	no action necessary
5-9 µg/dl	discuss health risk, minimize exposure, consider removal for pregnancy or other specific illnesses
10-19 µg/dl	decrease exposure, removal for pregnancy or other specific illnesses
20-29 µg/dl	remove from exposure
30-49 µg-dl	prompt medical evaluation

Lead levels can also be checked through a urine test. If a urine test is utilized, ensure it is not a "chelator-provoked" urine heavy metals test, meaning a chelating agent is ingested prior to the urine test. Prophylactic chelation is prohibited by OSHA for any employee.[25] The chelating agent is positively charged and attracts minerals and metals within the body. The subsequent urine test reading will be significantly higher. The problem with chelator-provoked urine tests is no reliable baseline chart could be established from previous studies since both exposed and unexposed participants showed similar increase in heavy metals exposure. Many medical practitioners consider chelator-provoked urine tests unreliable for determining actual levels of lead, mercury, etc.[26]

A final consideration is that the above blood lead levels were established by NIOSH and OSHA in 1974, when all cars ran on leaded gasoline. People with no occupational exposure to lead had relatively high "background" lead levels. Today, people with no occupational exposure should have a blood lead level of 0 to 1 µg dl, and a level of 5 µg dl is considered detrimental to human health by some research. OSHA is currently in the process of reviewing their lead exposure regulations; however, it may be some time before this is finalized.

Mitigating Lead Exposure

As with noise exposure, completely eliminating an officer's exposure to lead is challenging. One possibility for elimination is to conduct all training using lead-free ammunition on a range designated only for such use. As discussed in *Chapter 10: Indoor Ranges,* this can impact budgeting due to the expense for lead-free ammunition. Additionally, officers and instructors would be unable to shoot the issued duty ammunition. Nevertheless, conducting most training on a standard range, using lead-free ammunition, would be one way to reduce exposure for employees, if it is within the agency's ability to do so. It should be noted that mixing spent lead bullets with metals from non-lead alternative may render the material unfit for recycling and require more costly disposal.

Several other substitution options have been recommended by NIOSH. For example, the use of non-lead primers designed specifically for firing ranges would eliminate the airborne lead from this source. However, lead-free primers are more expensive than leaded primers, are less sensitive (more misfires), and can attract moisture and degrade quickly if not kept in cool, low humidity storage. Another substitution recommended by NIOSH is the use of total metal jacket ammunition in which the entire projectile is jacketed including the base. In jacketed ammunition where the base is left open to the exposed lead core, the bullet emits lead fume due to contact with hot propellant gases.

Proper range ventilation is one of the most important engineering controls an agency can put in place. Ensuring the ventilation system is working as designed, moving air as described previously, and filtering exhaust are important maintenance items for the rangemaster. Additionally, educating range staff on proper placement of equipment on the range so as not to block or disrupt ventilation is key to ensuring that personnel on the range are not unknowingly exposed to toxic lead particles. Finally, ensuring that supply and exhaust systems are balanced properly to maintain a negative air pressure inside the range (in comparison to the rest of the building) is critical. This keeps lead particles inside the range, avoiding contamination of the rest of the connected building. Once again, rely on an experienced range ventilation company for such work.

Some ranges commonly use compressed air in cleaning areas. Using compressed air for cleaning firearms can increase the risk of lead inhalation. OSHA 1910.1025 prohibits compressed air use for "housekeeping activities" for this reason.

Regular cleaning of contact surface areas is another important exposure mitigation measure. Any contact surface that may be contaminated with lead, both inside and outside the range, should be regularly wiped down using wipes made specifically for cleaning lead. These are widely available at industrial supply stores or online. Floors should be vacuumed using an explosion resistant HEPA vacuum, and sweeping (or other cleaning that generates dust in the air) should be avoided if possible. See *Chapter 10: Indoor Ranges – Maintenance* for further information.

Reinforcing good hygiene practices is another way to prevent or mitigate lead exposure. Encouraging thorough hand washing and use of NIOSH recommended hand wipes to remove lead before eating or leaving the range are positive practices. Rangemasters and instructors should not allow students to use their hats for collecting brass. Lead particulates can be deposited in them and later inhaled or ingested by the officers. Not allowing eating or drinking inside the range is another standard practice as well as an OSHA regulation to avoid lead ingestion. Employees who are pregnant or nursing should be strongly discouraged from entering range spaces in which lead exposure to any degree is possible. This means having positive, worker-wellness focused policies in place to exempt these employees from training, qualification, or other duties that would require them to be exposed to these hazards.

For full-time rangemasters and instructors, transferring lead particulate to your vehicle and into your home is a real consideration. Those exposed to higher levels of lead should consider having a set of their daily range wear (including footwear) tested for lead levels by an industrial hygienist; if the lead transfer levels are high, employees should consider showering and changing into street clothes before leaving for the day, if facilities allow. If this is not possible, range staff may consider changing clothes and bagging range clothing for immediate wash when arriving at home. Footwear may be left at the range or bagged separately and left in your vehicle. Wearing range clothing home, and interacting with significant others, pets or children without changing clothes is strongly discouraged, particularly if testing shows the possibility of lead transfer from your range clothing.

Personal protective equipment (PPE) should be worn by any personnel cleaning or performing maintenance on the range which may expose them to lead particulates. This PPE should include a properly fitted respirator, disposable (Tyvek or similar) coveralls, shoe coverings, and latex or other disposable gloves. These items should be disposed of properly after use according to any applicable regulations.

Other Considerations for Lead Exposure

If an assigned firearms instructor has a blood lead level of 20+ µg/dl, the agency should consider re-assigning the officer for a period of time (minimum 1 year) to allow blood lead levels to return to acceptable concentrations. As a heavy metal, it takes a long time for lead to leave a person's system. One of the authors once tested at 32 µg/dl, and was banned from working inside indoor ranges until his blood lead level had dropped to 16 µg/dl, which took several years.

Live-fire shoot houses can pose additional hazards of exposure if not mitigated properly. If your agency operates a live-fire shoot house, lead particulates can collect on the floor. If part of tactical team training involves deploying training flashbangs prior to entry, your officers could very well be entering rooms full of lead particulates suspended in the air. Again, surface wipe tests performed by a trained industrial hygienist will tell you if this is a concern or not. Live-fire shoot houses in particular would benefit from the use of non-toxic, lead-free ammunition at a minimum for the following reasons: mitigation of the lead exposure concern just discussed, far less ammunition is used during shoot house operations than range drills reducing the budget impact, and frangible ammunition is safer for close quarters shooting of targets and would avoid metal fragmentation off target frames or other objects. The ammunition would still allow for live-fire and real weapons manipulation.

Setting up a small shoot house or simulated rooms inside an indoor range induces two problems: (1) It disrupts the air flow for that part of the indoor range, creating an inhalation hazard for officers, and (2) It ensures that airborne lead that would otherwise be carried downrange is deposited inside the shoot house. As previously discussed, any objects used in training to simulate walls, cover, etc. should be placed between the shooter and the backstop. There should be no impediments to air flow from the supply to the shooter.

Lead exposure is serious and can be a career ending issue as well as a life-shortening health risk. Mitigation of exposure must be taken seriously by rangemasters who have a responsibility to properly educate range personnel and all officers on good hygiene practices. Range staff have an obligation to ensure engineering controls are in place and functioning. Training should be suspended if they are not. By implementing the suggestions outlined in this chapter, rangemasters can ensure that training can be conducted safely without exposing officers or staff to undue health risks.

Other Hazard & Exposure Considerations

Particulate exposure is not limited to just lead as described above. Outdoor dirt ranges as well as indoor ranges without proper positive air flow, and enclosed shoot houses can contain air particulates carrying lead, copper dust, valley fever spores, cedar fever allergens, and many other contaminates. These may be aggravated by the muzzle blast of firearms (e.g., fired from prone positions, etc.) or the impact of projectiles into softer surfaces such as dirt. N95 particulate facepiece respirators should be made available for voluntary use to shooters who are concerned about exposure in these situations. For further information on employer requirements, the rangemaster can consult OSHA 1910.134 concerning respirator protection.

Excessive sun exposure can lead to skin cancer. Pants, long sleeve shirts, and hats can minimize this exposure. Light colored long sleeve shirts are actually cooler in the heat than short sleeved shirts. Consider allowing the use of shemaghs - a large square piece of woven cloth derived from a traditional Arabian headdress called a keffiyeh - which provide warmth in the winter, and when moistened, provide cooling in the summer.

Sunscreen (SPF15 minimum) should be available for shooters who are concerned about possible excessive exposure to the sun during training. The SPF (sun protection factor) refers to the amount of time a person would be protected from a burn. SPF15 will allow a person to stay out in the sun 15 times longer than without sunscreen. Example: 10 minutes without sun screen is equivalent to 150 minutes (2.5 hours) with SPF15 sun screen.

The SPF rating only applies to UV-B rays (burns skin). To protect against UV-A rays (radiation) the sunscreen must contain Mexoryl, Parsol 1789, titanium dioxide, zinc oxide, or avobenzone. SPF 30 blocks 97% of UV-B rays, SPF 50 Blocks about 98% of UV- B rays. Higher SPF ratings don't offer much more protection. No SPF rating blocks 100%. Sunscreen loses its effectiveness after one to two years and should be discarded.[27]

Sunscreen should be applied 20 minutes before sun exposure and re-applied every two hours. Make it a part of the 2-hour break routine and make sure that shooters wash their hands before re-applying sunscreen to avoid unnecessary the lead exposure we just discussed.

Exposure to UV-A and UV-B light isn't limited to the skin. If you issue protective eyewear, not only should it meet ANSI Z-87+(2020) standards for shatter resistance, it should also block UV-A and UV-B rays. Cheap "convenience store" sunglasses can actually open up the pupil of the eye and allow damaging sun radiation further into the eye. Permanent eye sight damage can occur by using substandard eye protection. If you purchase eye protection from an industrial safety supplier, Safety Data Sheets should be available describing the level of protection from UV-A and UV-B. Many optometrists have instrumentation that can test the effectiveness of eyewear against damaging UV light.

Shooters can be exposed to insects such as mosquitoes, ticks, and chiggers, that can carry various diseases, such as Zika and West Nile Virus. Insect repellant should be available for shooters who are concerned about exposure to biting insects. If the agency is furnishing insect repellant, the rangemaster should be aware of what active ingredients it contains and share that with anyone using it. Some ingredients in repellents may cause irritation to skin, allergic reactions, or other medical risks. Application to clothing may be a better option than applying directly to the skin. EPA-approved insect repellant means it has been tested and approved for human safety and is effective when used according to the directions on the label.

Safety Data Sheets (SDS)

Safety Data Sheets are a topic that is not even on the radar for many rangemasters. They are often unaware of their responsibility to have Safety Data Sheets on file. While it is important to obtain SDS for various items, this is not a topic rangemasters need to put at the top of their priority list. Mitigating the exposure to hazards should be a higher priority.

Safety Data Sheets are documents that contain information related to occupational safety and health for various substances and products used by agency employees. For rangemasters those items would primarily be firearm cleaners, lubricants, and ammunition. However, there may be other general cleaning agents or other materials that warrant a copy of a SDS on file. A brief walk around the range facility will likely identify several items to add to the SDS binder such as the insect repellants discussed in the last section.

Agency employees have the right to review SDS documents. For this reason, the rangemaster should make the SDS available to employees in either hard copy format stored in an easy access binder or in digital format stored in a shared computer folder.

SDS were formally called Material Safety Data Sheets (MSDS). The problem with the former MSDS system was that the product manufacturer could put whatever information they felt was needed or necessary. The system did not require any uniformity of information. In 2012, OSHA created a new hazardous communication system called "HazCom 2012" to conform with the international standard called Globally Harmonized System (GHS). It was during this process that MSDS was changed to SDS.

The new SDS document contains 16 different categories of information that the product manufacturer must provide in order for the SDS to be valid. Most manufacturers that require a SDS for their products will provide them on their website for download. If it's not on their website, then the rangemaster can contact the manufacturer and request the needed SDS.

Rangemasters should have an SDS for every chemical used as part of their firearms program or range operations. Although OSHA only requires a SDS for hazardous materials, it's a good idea to have an SDS for every chemical in use.

Ammunition is considered a hazardous item and manufacturers have SDS for their ammunition products. Rangemasters should obtain a copy of the SDS for each type of ammunition they use and include it in their records.

Rangemasters can contact their agency's industrial hygienist, or contact their local OSHA / NIOSH representative for more information on the collection of SDS and the requirements for making them available for employees. A document regarding hazard communication standards and Safety Data Sheets can be found at https://www.osha.gov/hazcom.

[1] EPA. (2021). *The origins of the EPA.* United States Environmental Protection Agency: Washington, D.C. https://www.epa.gov/history/

[2] OSHA. (2022). *About OSHA.* United States Department of Labor: Occupational Safety and Health Administration: Washington, D.C. https://www.osha.gov

[3] ATF. (2022). *About the Bureau of Alcohol, Tobacco, Firearms and Explosives.* ATF: Washington, D.C. https://www.atf.gov/

[4] SAMMI. (2022). *UN 0012 1.4S ammunition by domestic road, rail, air & vessel.* Sporting Arms and Ammunition Manufacturers Institute, Inc. https://saami.org/

[5] ATF. (2022). *Explosive storage requirements.* ATF: Washington, D.C. https://www.atf.gov/

[6] NIOSH. (2018). *About NIOSH.* National Institute for Occupational Safety and Health: Washington, D.C. https://www.cdc.gov/niosh

[7] ANSI. (2022). *Introduction – a strong voice for the standards community.* American National Standards Institute: Washington, D.C. https://www.ansi.org

[8] ACGIH. (2022). *History.* American Conference of Industrial Hygienists. www.acgih.org

[9] Gregersen, E. (2018). *Decibel: unit of measurement.* Britannica. https://www.britannica.com

[10] OSHA. (2011). *Protecting yourself from noise in construction.* United States Department of Labor: Occupational Safety and Health Administration: Washington, D.C. https://www.osha.gov

[11] Brueck, Kardous, Oza, Murphy. (2014). *Measurement of exposure to impulsive noise at indoor and outdoor firing range during tactical training exercises.* National Institute for Occupational Safety and Health: Washington, D.C. https://www.cdc.gov/niosh/hhe/reports

[12] Hear-it. (2022). *Noise and hearing loss.* Hear-it. https://www.hear-it.org/

[13] Mayo Clinic. (2022). *Tinnitus.* Mayo Foundation for Education and Research. https://www.mayoclinic.org/

[14] OSHA. (2008). *Occupational noise exposure, 1910.95.* Occupational Safety and Health Administration: Washington, D.C. https://www.osha.gov

[15] Ibid.

[16] Katz, S. (2012). *A primer on indoor shooting range acoustics.* Troy Acoustics: Brunswick, GA.

[17] Bergiadis, B. (2019). *Shooting range acoustics.* Troy Acoustics. Presented at 2019 NSSF Shot Show.

[18] Tarr, J. (2016). *The benefits of electronic hearing protection.* Rifleshooter: Outdoor Sportsman's Group. https://www.rifleshootermag.com

[19] Brueck, Kardous, Oza, Murphy. (2014). *Measurement of exposure to impulsive noise at indoor and outdoor firing range during tactical training exercises.*

National Institute for Occupational Safety and Health: Washington, D.C. https://www.cdc.gov/niosh/hhe/reports

[20] OSHA. (2013). *Noise reduction rating.* OSHA Technical Manual (OTM) Section III: Chapter 5, Appendix E. Occupational Safety and Health Administration: Washington, D.C. https://www.osha.gov/otm

[21] OSHA. (2022). *Methods for estimating HPD attenuation.* Occupational Noise Exposure. Occupational Safety and Health Administration: Washington, D.C. https://www.osha.gov

[22] OSHA. (2004). *Minimum exposure for inclusion in the hearing conservation program (HCP).* Occupational Safety and Health Administration: Washington, D.C. https://www.osha.gov

[23] Bergiadis, B. (2019). *Shooting range acoustics.* Troy Acoustics. Presented at 2019 NSSF Shot Show.

[24] Esswein, E. & Ashley, K. (2003). *Lead in dust wipes – colorimetric screening method.* National Institute for Occupational Safety and Health: Washington, D.C. https://www.cdc.gov/niosh/docs

[25] OSHA. (2020). *1910.1025 – lead.* Occupational Safety and Health Administration: Washington, D.C. https://www.osha.gov

[26] Weiss, Campleman, Wax, McGill, & Brent. (2021). *Failure of chelator-provoked urine testing results to predict heavy metal toxicity in a prospective cohort of patients referred for medical toxicology evaluation.* Clinical Toxicology. https://doi.org

[27] NIOSH. (2018). *Sun exposure – recommendations.* National Institute for Occupational Safety and Health: Washington, D.C. https://www.cdc.gov/niosh

Chapter 12: TESTING & EVALUATION

Another obligation for many rangemasters is the testing and evaluation of equipment, ammunition, and a variety of other products used within firearms programs and range facilities. The importance of this responsibility should not be minimized. Decisions the rangemaster or firearms staff make about weapons, mounted lights, sighting systems, ammunition, holsters and so on can have serious impacts on training and field performance for many years. In this chapter we will suggest a few considerations for the rangemaster making these decisions to help avoid some common oversights.

Equipment Selection: Getting Started

Before you embark on selecting equipment for your agency, it will be well worth your while to spend a few minutes discussing with other department trainers what the agency's mission is and what officers will likely be faced with during their enforcement activities. You may be in a municipal agency whose primary function is patrol and criminal investigation in an urban setting or you may work for a sheriff's department where deputies patrol in rural areas and are also responsible for search and rescue. You may work in a jail and train officers or deputies for prisoner transport or you may work for a federal agency that handles physical security for government buildings. Whatever your agencies mission, the duties performed by officers will impact your equipment selection and must be considered.

Photo by author

Once you have determined what the mission is or, in other words, what your officers should be equipped to encounter based on their duties, it is time to begin deciding on the items you will purchase. Before beginning selection of equipment, it is important to understand that some items are necessary, while others are nice but not critical. For instance, a weapon mounted light on a rifle could be considered a necessity. Target identification for law enforcement is paramount. Officers must identify threats and distinguish them from victims, innocent bystanders, or other officers. Additionally, for proper handling and maintaining a solid shooting platform, having a light that is mounted to the weapon and able to be operated while maintaining a good shooting grip on the rifle is essential. Conversely, a thermal imaging or night vision scope with a laser range finder might be *nice;* however, it is clearly not *necessary* for the typical patrol officer threat identification whereas a good weapon mounted flashlight is invaluable.

Unfortunately, too many instructors get caught up in what would be nice to have rather than concentrating on what is necessary for the mission. Below are some suggestions on what you might consider to be necessary versus luxuries that you can live without.

1. Reliability: firearms and other equipment purchased must be thoroughly vetted for reliability. This means that they will operate under a variety of adverse conditions such as extreme temperature changes, various weather conditions, being dropped or hit against hard surfaces, and exposure to dirt, dust and other debris. Having a $2500 custom built pistol would be great; having a basic model pistol that fires every time the trigger is pulled is critical for a law enforcement officer.

2. Simplicity: As many of us know, the more complex a device is, the more there is to go wrong with it at an inopportune time. As mentioned above, attaching a good quality flashlight with a simple on/off switch can be a great advantage for the officer who works in reduced light conditions. Selecting equipment that is rugged, reliable, and simple to operate will be a great benefit to a firearms program from the standpoint of training and field performance.

3. Ambidextrous: When selecting equipment, another important consideration is whether it is equally functional both right and left-handed. In addition to being important for smooth, unencumbered

operation by officers who are either dominantly right or left-handed, many agencies train officers to fire and manipulate weapons with both hands (one-handed and two-handed). Therefore, considering the features for various equipment that allows for use by either hand is important.

Every piece of equipment you will evaluate as an instructor will have advantages and disadvantages. It is up to you to identify them, be aware of them, and decide if the advantages outweigh the disadvantages for the shooter in relation to the mission to be performed. For example, many agencies are currently considering some type of optical sighting system for pistols. Some obvious advantages to these sights are the ability to sight the weapon with both eyes open and focused on the target or threat. The fact that there is no need to align multiple planes (rear sight, front sight, and target) is another distinct advantage.

However, these systems are not without disadvantages. They are both electronic and battery operated making them vulnerable to failure to some degree, depending on the quality of manufacture. They must be zeroed on some interval, whereas most fixed sight handguns do not. If not adjusted correctly, the sighting dot can fade out in certain circumstances such as intense sunlight or in a dark environment when a weapon mounted light is used.

Most agencies and trainers, however, are finding that the advantages vastly outweigh the disadvantages, many of which can be addressed with proper operator training. These systems allow most shooters to shoot with both eyes open which increases peripheral vision. The shooter can focus on the target rather than the sights for better threat identification and many shooters are able to shoot faster and more accurately at distances beyond 10 yards. All of these factors lend themselves to moving forward with optical sight pistol programs.

Other pieces of equipment evaluated by rangemasters and instructors may not have the necessary advantages to move forward. This critical step of testing and evaluation cannot be overemphasized. Not every new invention is suited for use in the field of law enforcement. Regardless of how well an instructor "likes" something, the job is to determine if it will be useful for all officers in the field and if any disadvantages prohibit its use due to safety, reliability, or required tactics or techniques that conflict with those currently taught throughout the agency (not just in firearms). Critical thinking skills and examination, usually by more than one person, are necessary to identify and decide the potential usefulness of an item.

Budget

As mentioned in *Chapter 8: Budgeting,* the rangemaster often has responsibility for a budget for equipment and training. Therefore, they also have a responsibility to make sure that the money the agency has allotted for equipment and training is spent wisely. Accordingly, budget must also be a consideration when evaluating firearms, accessories, and other equipment. Part of budgeting is earning the trust of your administrators. As you present items for a supervisor or command staff to consider for purchase, make sure they meet the above criteria: necessary, reliable and appropriate for your agency's mission and officers. Presenting reasonable arguments as a subject matter expert that can be backed up with data and examples from other agencies will lend credibility to you as the rangemaster and to the training program you and your staff have built. Consider how requested equipment connects with training needs mentioned in *Chapter 4*.

When selecting any equipment, consideration should be given to the appropriate maintenance program to ensure that your equipment investments have a reasonable life expectancy. How will the equipment be replaced or updated when the time comes? Is there a budget allotted for that? These questions and others regarding budget must be part of the testing and evaluation process for firearms and equipment to ensure a long-lasting, sustainable program.

Firearms Selection

Rangemasters and their staff members are routinely charged with selection of firearms for issue to agency officers. As some might expect, choosing a firearm that will be issued to officers can be somewhat contentious for some instructor cadres and agencies. It is important to keep in mind the concepts discussed above and, at least attempt, to use some objective reasoning for the selection.

Many have probably either experienced or heard of an agency in which the rangemaster simply picked the gun (usually pistol) that they personally liked or thought was better than sliced bread, as the issued gun for the agency. That is obviously a poor way for any agency, regardless of size, to select a handgun.

An example, is an agency known to one of the authors that picked a very large frame handgun in a very difficult caliber to shoot. This was the issued handgun for all officers. If it didn't fit an officer, they were told they would likely not pass the firearms program. As rangemasters, we can do better.

Some agencies may (through choice or requirement) open a request for proposal (RFP) or bidding process to all pistol manufacturers. Other agencies may narrow their weapon choice down to a specific type, caliber, or even manufacturer they wish to carry. Regardless of the type of purchasing process you will use, listing out some of the features you are looking for in a pistol is a good place to start. Again, this should be a group activity if possible, involving several firearms staff members.

If you are using an RFP process, creating a list of features you are looking for will provide the specifications you are looking for in a new duty gun. If you are going to choose the specific gun, and obtain bids on that firearm, it will help to begin narrowing down manufacturer and model of what you want.

Photo by author

Some level of officer input is important in the selection process for firearms

As the instructors identifying the specifications, ample consideration should be given to the needs of *all* agency members and not just the top 10% shooters. With that in mind, once several competitors are identified, having time where officers from throughout the agency can come to the range and shoot the pistols being considered could be advantageous. In addition to receiving officer input, it offers an opportunity for instructors to see how each firearm fits individual shooters of different sizes and physical capabilities.

Below is a list of features, specifications, and options the range staff may consider during this selection. This list is by no means exhaustive but may provide a starting place for the rangemaster on weapon selection. For the purposes of clarity, we will discuss selection of handguns in this list but most of these items could be used for other weapon systems as well.

- Will the handgun be issued to every officer? Or, will officers be able to carry a personally owned (approved) handgun if they choose?
- What caliber(s) is the agency considering?
- What specific features should the pistol have? For example: ammunition capacity, same trigger pull weight each time, safety mechanisms, ambidextrous controls, etc.
- What accessories will be added or available to add to the pistol, such as weapon mounted lights or optical sights?
- Can the grip be adjusted to fit different shooter hand sizes and shapes?
- What is the availability of holsters and retention systems for the pistols being considered that also fit the desired accessories?
- What is the cost of the pistol, accessories, and holster gear?
- How many magazines will be issued to each officer?
- Is there any previous personal experience with the manufacturer(s) being considered and their history of customer service?
- What manufacturer warranties are available?

Certainly, other points can be considered and likely will be. Nonetheless, the intention for the above list is to get those involved in the decision started on a process of listing those issues that are most important for the agency and the shooters who will be using the weapon system. As mentioned in the introduction, this is a choice that will have an impact on the agency and its personnel for years to come and should not be taken lightly.

If feasible for your agency, one of the best ways to compare the "finalists" is to conduct and document in-house testing. There should be standardized evaluation of features and performance applied to all of the firearms that meet the basic specifications. This should be used up front to narrow the selection to several options and again over the implementation of a trial period (generally six months to a year.)

Below is a sample format for conducting test firing during firearms selection. This protocol is based on one used by a large agency in Arizona for many years. This protocol replicates firearms usage in agency training over a 10-year period to identify longevity and reliability issues. The protocol can be modified as the rangemaster sees fit for their agency.

1. Clean and lubricate the firearm upon arrival from the manufacturer. The cleaning and lubrication process should be the same for all firearms being considered and at every cleaning and lubrication interval.
2. No modifications are made to the firearms, except an approved weapon mounted light if carried by the agency.
3. A usage log must be kept with each firearm and completed faithfully. The log should document rounds fired, cleaning and lubrication intervals, and any malfunctions or problems along with the potential causes (e.g., ammunition, firearm, magazine, etc.)
4. Fire 1000 rounds of ball practice ammunition, conducting cleaning and lubrication every 250 rounds.
5. After the 1000 rounds of ball ammunition fired in step 4, fire 50 rounds of duty ammunition. Clean the firearm after firing the duty ammunition.
6. Repeat steps 4 and 5, four additional times for a total of 5000 rounds of ball ammunition and 250 rounds of duty ammunition per firearm.

At the conclusion of the test firing process, review the firearm log for any notable problems. Any malfunctions that occurred should be evaluated on the spot to determine the cause, or potential cause. The cause should be documented. Any recurring problems directly related to the firearm or magazines should be discussed with the manufacturer and may be a reason to remove the firearm from the selection process. This process, or a similar process, should be conducted before considering a particular firearm for field evaluations. See *Conducting Field Evaluations* below for more information.

When evaluating firearms, it is recommended to send one or two members of the range staff to an armorer course for the final makes being considered. If the manufacturer's sales department believes there is a substantial purchase pending, they may waive the tuition to the armorer course for a few individuals from a large agency. Smaller agencies can join with others in their region to host armorer courses. Agencies frequently get free seats in the course for hosting. Armorer courses can provide insight into how, and why a specific weapons system works mechanically, and any particular strengths or weaknesses of that system. It may also provide important information about ongoing maintenance and costs. This information can be invaluable when determining what system to choose for the agency.

Ammunition Selection

Along with selecting firearms, the rangemaster and their staff are often involved in the selection of duty and practice ammunition for any and all lethal weapon systems being used by the agency. Some may also be involved in the selection of less-lethal munitions; however, for this discussion we will stick to traditional firearms ammunition.

If required to use open bidding for ammunition contracts, consider specifying that duty ammo must meet all of the Federal Bureau of Investigation's (FBI) penetration expansion standards. The rangemaster may further specify the performance you desire through the FBIs testing to ensure you obtain ammunition that will be suitable for your purposes. Many quality options for duty ammunition from reputable manufacturers are available on state contracts. If buying from a state level contract which only offers one manufacturer or distributor, by choice or requirement, it may be wise to seek prior authorization to buy "off contract" from alternative sources if ammo starts becoming scarce.

If the rangemaster intends to test potential duty ammunition at their own facility, here are some guidelines to take into account. The FBI has set out a series of protocols by which it tests ammunition. These protocols should be utilized by any company you are considering purchasing duty ammunition from. The purpose of these protocols is to ensure the testing is done scientifically; that is, all tests are completed under the same conditions so that one round can be accurately compared to another, using the same conditions. This is more complicated than it may sound.

Examples of these protocols include mixing the ballistic gelatin to a standard density and temperature. The density must be tested by firing a .177 caliber shot at a particular velocity and ensuring penetration matches established standards. Then each test must be performed at particular angles, distances, and using specifically constructed barrier materials. Multiple tests under the exact same conditions must be performed to obtain truly comparable results between two or more duty rounds. This can be time consuming, resource intensive, and often, messy. It is typically not feasible, necessary or judicious for a rangemaster to take on this task unless they have a full-time staff they can dedicate to testing and who have been trained to conduct the tests to the FBI standard.

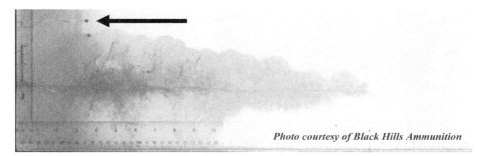

Photo courtesy of Black Hills Ammunition

Black Hills .308 GMX. Gelatin test projectile can be seen top left.

A larger department or a group of smaller agencies, may request that a duty ammunition manufacturer provide a ballistic gelatin demonstration and final results. If the manufacturer agrees, it is a good idea to record video for your own records. One advantage of these testing demonstrations is the ability to see the results of the testing using actual weapons the agency issues. Often testing is done with a test barrel or a particular firearm that they agency does not issue. An in person, manufacturer demo can be compared to FBI testing of the same ammunition to determine if there are significantly different results with the agency firearms.

If ammunition performance comes into question, it may be better for the rangemaster to be able to pass them on to the manufacturer representative instead of having them fall to range personnel, untrained in conducting FBI protocol tests. All of the data provided during the manufacturer's live-fire testing should be collected and retained. This is especially true if you select their product(s) for use.

An easier way to approach this entire affair is to request the FBIs ammunition testing results. They have done the vast majority of the hard work so the rangemaster doesn't have to. They also share this information with law enforcement by request. The rangemaster can contact the FBI Firearms Training Unit at the Quantico training facility in Virginia and request their latest ballistics testing data. Usually, this requires a formal request on organization letterhead and should not be shared outside the rangemaster's department, even with other LE agencies.

The electronic documents provided will include the results of testing of many different types of ammunition that can be considered for duty carry. The newer tests often include photos of the gelatin tests, and projectiles after being removed from the gelatin. It will also include the protocols used for testing so you have those on record. Finally, they included other resources such as staff presentations for the ammunition they select. To obtain an email address for requesting these documents, contact the nearest FBI office and ask to speak to one of their firearms instructors. They will be able to provide the information you need to request the ballistic information from Quantico.

Another thing the rangemaster may want to establish regarding selecting duty ammunition is the velocity from agency firearms. This is testing the rangemaster or instructors can do provided they have the correct equipment. The reason for conducting this testing is to establish muzzle velocity and any variations in muzzle velocity between individual rounds or lots. Why is it important to know the velocity of duty rounds? Every conventional jacketed hollow point (JHP) projectile needs to travel at a minimum velocity or it will perform like a FMJ round or "ball ammo" and not open up. Bullet design, bullet weight, and barrel length will all determine velocity. Variations between lot numbers of ammunition and different pistols of the same make, model and barrel length, should be in the + or - single digits. If the variations are in the double digits in feet per second (FPS), then accuracy between individual rounds, duty weapons, and terminal ballistics for both may be unacceptable.

Firearm velocity is measured by instruments called chronographs. There are two types of chronographs that can be purchased: (1) The sun shade or screen chronograph (older design) and (2) the doppler radar chronograph (newer design).

Using the sun shade chronograph, you fire a round through the opening in the sun shades. A photosensitive electric sensor is embedded in each end of the base, and measures the amount of time between the shadow of the bullet passing over the first sensor, then the second sensor, and automatically calculates the difference in feet per second (FPS) or meters per second, if you prefer. With this type of chronograph, the operator must allow for the mechanical offset between the sights and the centerline of the barrel to avoid damaging the equipment.

This chronograph only measures velocity near the muzzle, or realistic muzzle velocity. It cannot tell the user the velocity of the projectile as it travels downrange or how quickly it loses velocity. Therefore, depending on the distance of use, the testing may not have the desired information to evaluate terminal ballistics.

The second type of chronograph is the doppler chronograph. As the name implies, this instrument uses doppler radar to measure projectile velocity at various distances. It is capable of measuring projectile velocity from the

muzzle until the radar cannot sense the projectile, providing readings in 10-yard increments. The ability to do so is very important, as the trend toward Short Barreled Rifles (SBR's) and pistols have become more popular. Changes in barrel length have significant impact on projectile performance. There is a base line velocity that any projectile (pistol or rifle) designed to expand at termination must maintain or it will simply not expand; it will perform like a slow moving FMJ. Knowing this FPS threshold is important in understanding and choosing the correct duty ammunition for the relative weapon system.

The major disadvantage of the doppler chronograph is that it is much more expensive than the sunscreen chronograph. The choice for the type of chronograph needed will come down to the measurements needed at muzzle vs. distance and the budget available to the rangemaster to purchase the equipment.

Photo by author

Measuring duty round velocity will help rangemasters determine the performance and limitations of issued ammunition.

Due to the unpredictable nature of law enforcement deadly force encounters, rangemasters should attempt to identify duty ammunition that performs consistently during standardized testing through the various test protocols developed by the FBI.[1] While these tests do not predict "real world" performance of a round due to the nearly infinite number of variables involved, they do provide some comparative data on which the rangemaster can base their decision. If a round consistently obtains desirable penetration (without overpenetration) through a variety of materials or in bare ballistic gelatin, the round is likely sufficient for carry by officers. Individual agency environments and tasks should be considered as well. For example, a rural sheriff's office may have different considerations than an urban police department. What types of deadly force encounters have happened or are likely to happen? What ammunition would be best suited to those encounters?

The real proof of a duty cartridge's performance is still real-world officer-involved shootings. If your department has an OIS, review the incident to ensure bullets are performing accordingly. Have investigators request x-rays and photos of projectiles from the coroner or medical examiner. Keep copies in accordance with your agencies record keeping policy. If you are a smaller department where OISs are infrequent, reach out to rangemasters in your area that use the same duty ammunition and request anonymous or redacted data on projectile performance.

The illustration below is from a shooting in which the officer fired a patrol rifle at an armed, fleeing, homicide suspect who was firing rounds at officers. It is the longest known patrol rifle shooting on record at 326 yards. One round was fired (using open sights) and hit the suspect in the torso. Due to the distance, the velocity of the projectile dropped below 2200 fps at the time of impact which affected the projectile performance. X-ray shows .223 55 grain JHP projectile mostly intact after passing through the suspect's torso from the right side to left side. The small fragmentation near the projectile was likely the tip of the projectile that broke apart. While the round made the subject fall to the ground, it did not render him completely incapacitated. The arrest team

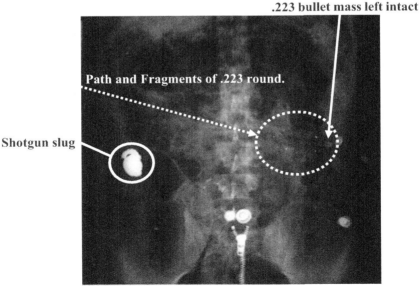

had to engage the suspect with a 12-gauge shotgun slug during their approach as the suspect reached for his handgun again. This is an example of data that can be used to verify field performance of ammunition used for duty.

For most agencies with patrol rifles that expect engagements at 250 yards or less, .223 jacketed hollow-point ammunition is an excellent choice. However, as this example illustrates, for law enforcement agencies with a designated marksmanship program, expecting engagements from 300-500 yards, .223 JHP ammunition may not the best choice.

Keep in mind that one or two officer involved shootings, do not meet the threshold for making sweeping changes in selection of equipment such as ammunition or weapons. Such a small sampling can be influenced by anomalies that are not the norm for performance. Shooting results, such as those pictured above, should be compared with other results using the same ammunition, whether from the rangemaster's agency or another agency. These results should then be compared with the test data. If you are seeing a concerning trend with field performance, reach out to other instructors or rangemasters as mentioned above and determine if they are seeing similar information. Networking, it's a thing.

Practice ammunition should be full metal jacket (FMJ) or total metal jacket (TMJ) (see *Chapter 11: Hazards & Exposures* for more information) with the same bullet weight, approximate muzzle velocity, and group sizing within practical distances (25 yards for pistol, 100 yards for rifle). If using frangible ammunition for steel targets or other uses, it may have significantly less bullet weight than duty or lead practice ammunition. As a result, it may perform differently. Range staff should test this out with agency firearms and know the variations so the ammunition can be used appropriately for training.

Practice ammunition should have high reliability standards to make the best use of the ammunition budget. More importantly, any damage caused by ammunition to agency or personal firearms should be covered by the ammunition manufacturer. It is inadvisable to allow use of handloaded ammunition in agency owned firearms. In most cases, this voids the firearm warranty and serious injury can result from improperly reloaded ammunition. Any problems with practice ammunition or performance that could cause damage to a firearm or injury to a shooter should be immediately reported to the manufacturer for remedy.

Agency Purchase vs. Private Purchase

Depending on agency policy regarding use of personally owned equipment, the rangemaster or instructors may have input into what personally owned equipment is authorized and the specifications of that equipment. If authorizing personally owned firearms for duty use, it is important to have an approved list of firearms along with what, if any, modifications are allowed. As new firearms come out, agencies will undoubtedly get requests from officers to carry them. It is important that the instructor cadre have an opportunity to weigh in on authorization of these firearms.

Some new models may be able to be authorized with minimal testing. For example, a new model of pistol from a known manufacturer with minor changes in size, appearance, or capacity can likely be approved with minimal evaluation. A firearm from a manufacturer the agency has not used before may require additional testing and evaluation to determine its suitability for duty use. In *Chapter 14: Firearms Policies* we will further discuss considerations for authorizing weapons, modifications, and other equipment.

Similarly, as new sights, lights or other equipment comes on the market, officers will likely want to make use of it. Some of it will be good and others not so much. Part of the responsibility of the rangemaster and instructor staff is to make recommendations for the authorization of these items based on how well the item will perform in the field along with its safety.

An example is a recently introduced pistol red dot sight from a well-known and highly regarded optics manufacturer. The company has a reputation of creating high quality gear that is very reliable. The problem is it's so large that no existing duty holster's rotating hood will fit over it. It would be unfortunate for an agency to invest hundreds or thousands of dollars into equipment that can't be used. Thoughtful testing and evaluation can help avoid such calamitous errors.

Conducting Field Evaluations

Evaluations in field conditions typically includes selecting a small group of individuals to test the item during duty conditions. Before doing so, such personnel should have the opportunity to try the equipment on the range or in a "practice" setting. They should be provided with an orientation to the item and its features and functions. No equipment should be fielded without some type of training and practice – even if the practice required is minimal.

Ideally, the officers selected for this will have the ability to objectively evaluate the pros and cons of such items and provide meaningful feedback for consideration. Sometimes having the input of those outside the instructor group can be good to get different perspectives that instructors may not have considered from their point of view as trainers. One group that can be good for such evaluations are those that serve as field training officers. This group should be very knowledgeable and active officers and should have some idea of what might be beneficial to a new recruit or be a distraction with little benefit.

Evaluators should keep track of specific performance, any failures, and unanticipated problems as well as unanticipated advantages discovered during testing. These observations should be provided to the rangemaster or person in charge of the project in writing. Additionally, maintenance should be documented, in the case of firearms or similar equipment, along with the number of rounds fired and any anomalies (e.g., failure to lock back, etc.)

Other Considerations

When evaluating a new item, it is a good idea to research other credible sources for testing and reviews. This may include other agencies, other instructors, or professional organizations. If you are a NLEFIA member, utilize the resource(s) of the Member's Forum and the rangemasters that are NLEFIA members. As an example, one of the authors was recently contacted by an agency in the Montreal, Quebec region regarding evaluating replacements for their aging duty pistols. The Montreal area rangemaster had heard that Los Angeles Police Department had recently gone through the same process and wanted to know if the author knew anyone involved in the selection of their new sidearm. With one phone call, a connection was made between the Montreal area rangemaster and a member of LAPD's testing and evaluation team. This is just one example of the benefits of a robust network of peers to call upon for needed information that will help guide your decisions and recommendations to command staff.

Conversely, be wary of social media hype by "influencers"; most of whom have never been a sworn law enforcement officer much less a rangemaster. Many of these influencers are compensated either through the social media platform or the manufacturer.

Evaluation of new and replacement equipment or ammunition is a key role for the rangemaster. Decisions made about weapons, manufacturers, sources of purchase and so forth can tie an agency to a product for years and involve thousands of dollars of agency funds. It is important for the rangemaster and their staff to take the time necessary to critically evaluate each option and provide the best recommendation possible to their staff. Even with thorough evaluation, a problem may be encountered with a product that was unforeseen. In these cases, it is important to know the warranty behind the product and ensure that any contracts for large purchase include a trial or warranty period in which the manufacturer must bring the product up to promised performance.

---

[1] Federal Bureau of Investigation. (2011). *FBI ammunition testing.* FBI Academy, Defensive Systems Unit, Ballistic Research Facility. Quantico, VA.

Chapter 13: CASE LAW

Disclaimer: The following chapter is intended to provide the reader with some of the case law relevant to firearms instructors and rangemasters. Nothing in this chapter should be construed to be legal advice. The summary of each case is written to provide the reader with a cursory overview of the case and what the authors believe are the salient points of the court's decision. Competent legal counsel should be obtained before relying on any of the cases below for critical agency decisions or as a legal defense.

A fundamental understanding of up-to-date case law is an important part of any use of force training program. Rangemasters and instructors must be familiar with a variety of key decisions to ensure that their instruction is in keeping with the law as it has been interpreted by the court system. Additionally, case law provides guidelines for what skills should be trained, how the legality of force applied will be determined by the court, when force may be applied, when officers or agencies are at risk of civil or criminal penalties, and what actions constitute discriminatory behavior. The information from an examination of the cases below and others can help a rangemaster shape their program and protect themselves, the officers they train, and their agency from legal liability.

It is important for trainers to understand the context in which court decisions are made and that the court is relying on the specific circumstances of one particular case to make the decision. While some decisions may have far-reaching impacts on how officers perform their duties, trainers should familiarize themselves with all of the facts of the case to understand the decision in the proper context. It is equally important to understand the issue that the court is considering. For example, in Popow v. Margate the court considered the training, or lack thereof, of the officers involved as part of a decision in a claim of failing to train. Conversely, in Tennessee v. Garner, the court focused on the constitutionality of a state statute authorizing the officer's actions. These two cases illustrate the vast differences in issues considered by the court and ultimately, the impact of those decisions.

The below cases are broken into several main topics. The first is cases relating to the use of force, what constitutes excessive force, and what force is constitutionally legal or not. The second topic includes cases related to an agency's responsibility to provide training and what constitutes a failure to train in the court's view. The third category includes several cases that involve qualifications and examine discriminatory practices to be avoided in a training program and in general. Lastly, several cases provide examples in which the court reviewed tactics and other training, the court's view on creating jeopardy and other related concepts.

The cases below are NOT an exhaustive list of all cases regarding a given topic. Rather they are key, relevant cases, in the authors' view, that provide current guidance for rangemasters and firearms instructors. Trainers should work cooperatively and proactively with their organization's legal counsel to ensure that training programs are consistent with the most current laws and legal decisions. Regular legal updates are an important part of continuing training for rangemasters, trainers, and officers, deputies or agents.

Sources: the below case analyses rely heavily on information and summaries of the specific cases found on the following websites:

- https://casetext.com/
- https://supreme.justia.com/
- https://caselaw.findlaw.com
- https://www.supremecourt.gov/opinions/

The authors claim no creative rights to the below case summaries and quotations. The majority of the text in each summary is taken from the original court rulings or summaries provided on these websites.

Cases Related to Use of Force and Excessive Force

<u>Tennessee v. Garner, 471 U.S. 1 (1985):</u>

A Memphis police officer shot and killed Garner as he was fleeing the scene of a burglary to a home. Despite a reasonable belief that Garner was unarmed, the officer believed he was justified in shooting Garner to prevent his escape from the scene of a felony crime based on a Tennessee statute that allowed officers to "use all the necessary means to affect the arrest" of a suspect that was resisting or fleeing apprehension.

The Supreme Court held that the Tennessee statute authorizing the use of "all necessary means" was unconstitutional and that deadly force may not be used against a fleeing suspect unless necessary to prevent the escape of someone whom the officer has probable cause to believe poses a threat of death or serious physical injury to the officer or others. In discussing the use of deadly force for apprehension, the court said that it is constitutionally unreasonable to use deadly force to prevent the escape of all felony suspects, regardless of the circumstances.[1]

Related cases: Monell v. New York City Dept. of Social Services, 436 U.S. 658, 98 S. Ct. 2018 (1978); United States v. Watson, 423 U.S. 411, 96 S. Ct. 820 (1976); United States v. Place, 462 U.S. 696, 103 S. Ct. 2637 (1983).

Bottom Line: force used by law enforcement must be reasonable. Shooting an unarmed, fleeing felon who poses no articulable risk to the officers or others is unreasonable and a violation of the Fourth Amendment.

Graham v. Connor, 490 U.S. 386 (1989):

The plaintiff, a diabetic, went into a store to purchase orange juice but left quickly because of the long line at the counter. Officer Connor conducted an investigatory stop and detained Graham on suspicion of a robbery. Graham sustained multiple injuries during the contact but was released after Connor learned no robbery had occurred. This case established a standard of objective reasonableness in uses of physical force by police rather than a substantive due process standard. The court applied the objective reasonableness standard from the perspective of a reasonable officer on scene and with the understanding that officers are often forced to make split-second decisions about the amount of force to be used in a particular situation. Information the court deemed relevant in determining the reasonableness of the officer's actions include:

1. Were the officer's actions objectively reasonable in light of the facts and circumstances at the time of the incident?
2. Did the officer rely on good and reasonable police practices? AND,
3. Did the officer in the situation act as another "reasonable and prudent" officer would have acted faced with a like or similar situation? (objective)

Further the court identified a three-pronged test of the legitimacy of force used against a suspect: "...proper application [of the Fourth Amendment] requires careful attention to the facts and circumstances of each particular case, including the severity of the crime at issue, whether the suspect poses an immediate threat to the safety of the officers or others, and whether he is actively resisting arrest or attempting to evade arrest by flight[2].

Related cases: Johnson v. Glick, 481 F.2d 1028 (2d Cir. 1973); Baker v. McCollan, 443 U.S. 137, 99 S. Ct. 2689 (1979); Tennessee v. Garner, 471 U.S. 1 (1985); Terry v. Ohio, 392 U.S. 1, 88 S. Ct. 1868 (1968).

Bottom Line: officers must use force that is objectively reasonable given the circumstances they are presented with at the time of the incident.

Photo by author

The court set a standard of objective reasonableness for use of force by police.

Thompson v. Hubbard, 131 U.S. 123 (1989):

Officer Hubbard responded to a robbery call in which shots were reported to be fired. Upon arrival he contacted Thompson who matched the description of a suspect in the call. Thompson initially complied but then turned and ran. Hubbard tried to grab him but only pulled his coat off. After a short foot pursuit, Thompson jumped over a fence between two buildings. Hubbard yelled at Thompson to stop. According to Hubbard, he reached for his waistband as if to draw a weapon while looking back at Hubbard. When

Thompson did not raise his hands, Hubbard shot once, hitting Thompson in the back and killing him. No weapon was found at the scene and no witnesses were present.

The attorney for the deceased argued that Hubbard's use of deadly force was objectively unreasonable because he should have considered that the waistband of Thompson's sweatpants was not strong enough to hold a firearm. The court did not agree. They stated in their ruling that an officer is not constitutionally required to wait until he sees the weapon before employing deadly force to protect himself against a fleeing suspect who turns and moves as if to draw a gun.[3]

Related cases: Ryder v. City of Topeka, 814 F.2d 1412 (1987); Graham v. Connor, 490 U.S. 386 (1989).

Bottom line: an officer does not have to wait to see a deadly weapon if there is probable cause that the suspect is armed and making a furtive movement toward such a weapon.

Plakus v. Drinski, 19 F.3d 1143 (7th Cir. 1994):

Plakus was involved in a single vehicle accident. He was located walking along the road by a Newton County, Indiana corporal. The corporal gave him a ride back to the scene where he was attended to by medical personnel. He was later arrested for driving under the influence. During transport, Plakus was able to open the back door of Corporal Koby's car and flee. Plakus fled to a nearby home whose occupants he knew. Officers and paramedics found him there where a confrontation ensued. Plakus armed himself with a fireplace poker and swung it at officers striking Koby on the wrist.

Plakus fled into the woods near the house where he was cornered in a clearing by officers. The officers spent 15 minutes or more trying to get Plakus to drop the poker and give up during which time he threatened Officer Drinski who was in the clearing with him. Finally, he raised the poker to swing at Drinski. Drinski retreated but ran into something. Plakus continued to advance and Drinski shot him once in the chest. Plakus ultimately died of his wound.

The plaintiff for the Plakus estate argued several claims that Drinski could not apply self-defense justification for this shooting. All of the plaintiff's arguments were denied by the court. More interestingly, the plaintiff argued that Plakus was wronged because Drinski had a duty to use alternative methods to resolve the situation. The court noted that this argument fails because in the synopsis it is clear that Drinski and other officers tried to get Plakus to drop the poker for between 15 and 30 minutes. He argues that the officers should have maintained distance, should have used chemical spray, or should have used a dog.[4]

The court rejected this argument and pointed out there is no precedent that the Constitution requires all feasible alternatives to avoid a situation where deadly force can justifiably be used. There is precedent, however, that where deadly force is otherwise justified under the Constitution, there is no constitutional duty to use non-deadly alternatives first.

Related cases: Ford v. Childers, 855 F.2d 1271 (1988); Carter v. Buscher, 973 F.2d 1328 (1992).

Bottom line: when deadly force is justified under the Constitution, officers are not required to use a lesser means of force.

Photo by author

Agencies must ensure officers clearly understand when deadly force is justified and appropriate and when it is not.

Harris v. Roderick, 933 F. Supp. 977 (D. Idaho 1996):

Six United States Marshals entered the property of Randall Weaver with a warrant to arrest him. They encountered Harris, Weaver, Weaver's 14-year-old son, Sammy, and the family dog at the intersection of two primitive roads. The plaintiff claims one of the U.S. Marshals, Roderick, shot the dog and Sammy fired two rounds into the trees where the marshals were and fled. Marshal Degan shot Sammy and severely wounded his arm, making him drop the gun he was carrying. Marshal Cooper then shot Sammy in the back, killing him. Harris admits to firing rounds into the woods in self-defense, one of which likely hit Marshal Degan, killing him.

The plaintiff claims Roderick and Cooper conspired to lie about the shooting in official reports and later to a grand jury that Harris fired first, starting the shootout. As a result of the information Roderick and Cooper provided, a contingent of Hostage Rescue Team members from the FBI were issued "Special Rules of Engagement" by a group of FBI and U.S. Marshal officials. These special rules of engagement stated that any armed adult observed in the vicinity of the Weaver cabin could and should be killed. This deviated from the FBI's standard rules of engagement that stated that deadly force may be used against a suspect "only if the person presents an immediate risk of death or great bodily harm to the agent or another person." The special rules of engagement were later modified to indicate "any armed male adult could and should be killed" if observed in the vicinity of the cabin.

FBI agents approached the Weaver cabin and were staged on a hill. Weaver, his daughter Sarah, and Harris approached a shed where they had placed Sammy's body. An FBI sniper shot Weaver with a .308 rifle wounding him. The group ran back to the cabin where Randy Weaver's wife Vickie was holding the door open with one arm and holding an infant with the other. The sniper fired again in an effort to kill both Vickie and Harris according to the plaintiff. The round struck Vickie Weaver in the head, killing her instantly, and struck Harris in the upper arm and chest severely wounding him. Harris remained in the cabin for several days with Randy Weaver, Sarah and his infant child that Vickie had been holding. He ultimately surrendered and after being hospitalized for some time was indicted on numerous felony charges including the death of Marshal Degan. He was acquitted at trial of all charges.

The Supreme Court reviewed motions from defendant U.S. marshals and FBI agents. Defendants claimed qualified immunity for actions resulting in the shooting and deaths of several people at the Weaver cabin. All motions were denied and the case referred back to the trial court. Roderick and Cooper claimed absolute immunity regarding the allegation of providing false testimony to the grand jury. They claimed that once the grand jury found that there was probable cause for charges against Harris and the Weavers, they were immune from any action. The court disagreed.

The court affirmed that Harris had met the 'heightened pleading' standard to bring a claim against the defendants. The court also ruled that the marshals and agents were not entitled to qualified immunity because 1) the law concerning the officials conduct was clearly established, and 2) under that law, a reasonable officer would not have believed the conduct to be legal. They cited Tennessee v. Garner and two related cases in determining that the marshals and agents did not have reason to fire on the suspects because there was no clear threat to the agents or others and the suspect's flight did not pose a danger to any other people.

Lastly, regarding the special rules of engagement to kill any armed adult - later changed to adult male - in an area, regardless of whether they posed a risk to another person the court ruled that these rules clearly violated the Fourth Amendment and were so extreme as to be "patently unjustified." The further stated that the special rules violated clearly established law and any reasonable law enforcement officer should have been aware of that fact.[5]

Related cases: Curnow v. Ridgecrest Police, 952 F.2d 321 (1991); Ting v. United States, 927 F.2d 1504, 1511 (1991); Tennessee v. Garner, 471 U.S. 1 (1985).

Bottom line: officers initiating a lethal confrontation when not in jeopardy then lying to cover it up is behavior that any officer would know was wrong; arbitrarily changing the "rules" of justification to use deadly force is a violation of the Fourth Amendment and once again, any reasonable officer should know this is illegal.

Plumhoff v. Rickard, 134 S. Ct. 2012, 188 L. Ed. 2d 1056, 572 U.S. 765, 24 Fla. L. Weekly Supp. 790 (2014):

Rickard was stopped by police, refused to produce ID and then fled in his car with a passenger. The pursuit was stalled momentarily when he spun out in a parking lot. He drove recklessly during a pursuit including accelerating when in contact with a police car and almost hitting an officer. One officer fired into Rickard's car three times. As he sped away, officers fired into the car 12 more times. The two separate shooting events took place within a total 10-second time frame. Rickard and his passenger died as a result of gunshot wounds and injuries when the vehicle crashed.

Rickard's minor daughter filed a § 1983 action alleging excessive force. The District Court denied the officer's motions for summary judgement and ruled that they had violated the Fourth Amendment by using excessive force. The Sixth Circuit Court of Appeals upheld the District Court's ruling and affirmed that the officers had violated the Fourth Amendment by using deadly force in this situation. The United States Supreme Court ultimately heard the case.

The plaintiff claimed the Fourth Amendment did not allow officers to use deadly force to stop a vehicle pursuit and even if the officers were allowed to use their firearms, they exceeded their authority to use force by shooting as many times as they did. The Supreme Court disagreed.

The Court ruled that the officers acted reasonably in stopping the pursuit. A "police officer's attempt to terminate a dangerous high-speed car chase that threatens the lives of innocent bystanders does not violate the Fourth Amendment, even when it places the fleeing motorist at risk of serious injury or death." Scott v. Harris, 385, 127 S. Ct. 1769, 167 L. Ed. 2d 686. Further the Court stated, "Rickard's outrageously reckless driving--which lasted more than five minutes, exceeded 100 miles per hour, and included the passing of more than two dozen other motorists--posed a grave public safety risk, and the record conclusively disproves that the chase was over when Rickard's car came to a temporary standstill and officers began shooting. Under the circumstances when the shots were fired, all that a reasonable officer could have concluded from Rickard's conduct was that he was intent on resuming his flight, which would again pose a threat to others on the road."

Regarding the number of shots fired, the Supreme Court states that the officers did not fire more shots than were necessary to end the public safety risk. They reaffirmed the concept of shooting to stop the threat by stating that if officers are justified in shooting to stop a public safety threat, they do not need to stop shooting until that threat has ended. In this case, during the 10 seconds in which the shots were fired, Rickard never stopped his illegal flight and even drove away after the first three shots were fired. They also confirmed that a passenger's presence does not bear on whether officers violated Rickard's Fourth Amendment rights as they are personal rights and cannot be vicariously asserted.

When addressing the officers claim of qualified immunity, the Court stated that an official is entitled to qualified immunity when there is no evidence that they violated any established law or constitutional right clearly established at the time. They also concluded that there is no clearly established law precluding officers from shooting at a fleeing vehicle to prevent public harm and thereby, they are entitled to qualified immunity.

The Supreme Court reversed the lower court decisions and ruled the officer acted reasonably to stop the actions of a suspect attempting to flee and driving in a manner that endangered others.[6]

Related cases: Graham v. Connor, 490 U.S. 386, 109 S. Ct. 1865 (1989); Scott v. Harris, 550 U.S. 372, 127 S. Ct. 1769, 167 L. Ed. 2d 686 (2007); Alderman v. United States, 394 U.S. 165, 89 S. Ct. 961 (1968); Ashcroft v. Al-Kidd, 563 U.S. 731, 131 S. Ct. 2074, 179 L. Ed. 2d 1149 (2011); Brosseau v. Haugen, 543 U.S. 194, 125 S. Ct. 596 (2004).

Bottom line: officers may shoot at a fleeing suspect when there is objectively reasonable evidence to believe that public harm will result from their continued flight. When justified to use deadly force to prevent a threat, officers may shoot until the threat ceases.

Kingsley v. Hendrickson, 135 S. Ct. 2466, 575 U.S. 959, 192 L. Ed. 2d 416, 192 L. Ed. 2d 435 (2015):

Michael Kingsley was being held as a pre-trial detainee in the jail on a drug charge. He placed a piece of paper over a light in his cell and refused several orders from jail personnel to remove it. Jail officers ultimately removed him from his cell and did so forcefully as he refused to cooperate with commands. They placed him in another cell face down on a bunk while handcuffed behind his back. Kingsley claims the officer slammed his head into the concrete bunk which officers deny. Both parties agree that the officers used a TASER on Kingsley for approximately 5 seconds and left him in the cell on the bunk for 15 minutes.

Kingsley filed a suit for a § 1983 Civil Rights Act violation and claimed that excessive force had been used by the jailers to punish him. The trial court denied the plaintiff's claim by jury decision. At issue in the appeal was whether Kingsley needed to prove the jail officers intended malice to punish him (a subjective standard) or if the jury only needed to determine if their actions were objectively unreasonable.

The case was ultimately heard by the Supreme Court which recognized there was disagreement among the Circuit Courts on this issue. The Supreme Court ruled that an objective standard rather than a subjective standard must be used in judging whether an officer applied excessive force. They also made a distinction between purposeful or intentional acts and accidental or negligent acts. If the actions of the officers are determined to be intentional, that is to say they intentionally applied the force, which was undisputed in this case, then the plaintiff need not prove their intent to achieve a particular outcome (e.g., punishment). The court or jury need only determine if the force used was objectively unreasonable. If the force is believed to be accidental or negligent then it falls beneath the threshold of constitutional due process.

The Supreme Court reversed the decision of the 7th Circuit Court of Appeals and remanded the case.[7]

Related cases: County of Sacramento v. Lewis, 523 U.S. 833, 118 S. Ct. 1708 (1998); Daniels v. Williams, 474 U.S. 327, 106 S. Ct. 662 (1986); Graham v. Connor, 490 U.S. 386, 109 S. Ct. 1865 (1989); Bell v. Wolfish, 441 U.S. 520, 99 S. Ct. 1861 (1979); Saucier v. Katz, 533 U.S. 194, 121 S. Ct. 2151 (2001).

Bottom line: force used against a person (intentionally) must be objectively reasonable based on the totality of the circumstances.

Cases Related to Failure to Train

Monell v. Department of Social Services of the City of New York, 436 U.S. 658 (1978):

Several female petitioners brought suit against the Department of Social Services, and the supervisory management of the department up to the Mayor of New York City for enacting policies that forced pregnant women to take unpaid leave prior to the leave being medically necessary. The issue brought to the Supreme Court was whether municipalities enjoyed qualified or other immunity in suits brought under a § 1983 Civil Rights Act violation.

The court concluded that local governing bodies (and local officials sued in their official capacities) can be sued directly under § 1983 for relief in situations where the alleged unconstitutional action implements or executes a policy, statement, ordinance, regulation, or decision officially adopted or promoted by those whose authority may be said to represent official policy. In addition, local governing bodies, like every other § 1983 "person," may be sued for depriving an individual's constitutional rights pursuant to governmental "custom" even though such custom has not been formally approved through the organization's official decision-making channels.[8]

Related cases: Edelman v. Jordan, 415 U.S. 651, 664, 94 S.Ct. 1347, 39 L.Ed.2d 662 (1974); McMillan v. Board of Education of State of New York, 430 F.2d 1145, 1148-49 (2d Cir. 1970); Cleveland Board of Education v. Lafleur, 414 U.S. 632, 94 S. Ct. 791 (1974).

Bottom line: governing entities can be sued for policies and practices including unofficial ones if promoted by those in authority positions who represent the entity.

Popow vs. City of Margate, 476 F. Supp. 1237 (D.N.J. 1979):

City of Margate police officer, George Biagi, was in pursuit of a kidnapping suspect in a residential neighborhood at night. Darwin Popow, hearing a commotion outside his house, stepped out of the house and, being mistaken for the kidnapper by Officer Biagi, was shot and killed. The wife of the deceased brought a suit against the City of Margate for a § 1983 Civil Rights Act violation and claimed that the city had failed to train its officers adequately.

During deposition, Officer Biagi stated that he had received training on deadly force almost 10 years prior to the incident while he was trained at the state police academy. He said the City of Margate only conducted firearms training twice per year and the training did not address shooting in low light, at moving targets, or in residential areas. Additionally, no training was provided regarding how to apply state law or policy to actual shooting situations. The court found the City of Margate's training of officers regarding shooting to be grossly inadequate.

In its ruling the court stated that police firearms training must be "regular" and it must be realistic citing the following as required training topics:[9]

- moving targets
- low light or adverse lighting conditions
- use of deadly force (firearms) in residential areas

- instruction on state laws, city regulations and agency policies
- instruction on how the above laws and regulations apply to actual situations

Bottom line: law enforcement agencies must train officers for situations they will likely encounter including and perhaps, especially deadly force decision making.

Photo by author

The Popow court stated that police training must be regular and realistic.

McClelland, v. Facteau, 610 F.2d 693 (10th Cir. 1979):

McClelland was stopped for speeding and arrested when he refused to sign the citation. He was not allowed to use a mobile phone in his truck to call an employee to retrieve the truck. He was not allowed to confer with an attorney. He was booked into the jail and a bond was assessed at $50. McClelland was questioned by a jailer without being read his rights or without representation of an attorney which he had previously asked for. He posted the bond, but before being released he was made to lean against the wall while Officer Facteau beat him in the presence of jailors Jimmie and Conn Brown.

In his suit, McClelland asserted that the chiefs of the New Mexico State Police and the Farmington City Police were directly liable for violations of his constitutional rights due to their failure to properly train and supervise their personnel to ensure that such violations did not take place. The chiefs argued that they could not be held liable for actions that they did not personally participate in. They also provided documentation that the officers had been trained properly and if the policies they set forth had been followed the plaintiff's rights would have been protected. The court upheld the summary judgement as to the failure to train claim; however, not for the failure to supervise claim. McClelland produced a number of newspaper articles alleging abusive and illegal behavior on the part of the agencies as well as Officer Facteau specifically. Representation for McClelland also cited two pending lawsuits regarding deaths within the jail prior to McClelland's contact. The court recognized that the chiefs are, in fact, responsible for the conduct of personnel they supervise when they know or should have known that conduct by a subordinate violated the law or policy. This part of the appeal was reversed and remanded to the trial court for consideration.[10]

Related cases: Rizzo v. Goode, 423 U.S. 362, 96 S.Ct. 598, 46 L.Ed.2d 561 (1976); Dewell v. Lawson, 489 F.2d 877 (10th Cir. 1974); Burton v. Waller, 502 F.2d 1261, 1285 (5th Cir. 1974), cert. denied, 420 U.S. 964, 95 S.Ct. 1356, 43 L.Ed.2d 442 (1975); Sims v. Adams, 537 F.2d 829 (5th Cir. 1976); Wright v. McMann, 460 F.2d 126 (2d Cir.), cert. denied, 409 U.S. 885, 93 S.Ct. 115, 34 L.Ed.2d 141 (1972).

Bottom line: Chief executives are responsible for conduct of subordinates and may be held liable if they know or should have known the subordinates violated law or policy.

Oklahoma City v. Tuttle, 471 U.S. 808, 105 S. Ct. 2427 (1985):

In this case an officer shot a man named Tuttle outside a bar while investigating the report of a robbery. Upon arrival, the officer had been told that no robbery occurred but while continuing to investigate the officer contacted Tuttle. Tuttle reached into his boot and was shot by the officer. A toy gun was later discovered in Tuttle's boot but the officer had not seen it. Tuttle's widow sued the police for excessive force and negligent training in a § 1983 Civil Rights Act violation. The officer was cleared but the case was argued to the U.S. Supreme Court, which found in favor of the city. Specifically, the lower courts (U.S. District Court and U.S. Court of Appeals) found that a single act of misconduct by an officer (or official) could equate to gross negligence or deliberate indifference on the part of the municipality to properly train or supervise its officers. The Supreme Court disagreed, indicating in their ruling that evidence of a single act of misconduct alone did not necessarily equate to proof of gross negligence or deliberate indifference on the part of the municipality. They intimated that additional evidence would have to be presented by the plaintiff to show sufficient cause for liability on the part of the municipality. It is important to note that the ruling of the Supreme Court, didn't address whether the training was, in fact, inadequate but rather the appropriateness of the jury instruction given in the case.

Each of the courts in their rulings acknowledged the evidentiary basis of deficient training within the department and in holding officers accountable for poor performance. So, while the plaintiff's case failed due to how they attempted to attach liability to the city, the appellate court and Supreme Court identified within their rulings a number of areas that are required for a department's firearms training to be adequate:[11]

- Stress and attitude
- Knowledge of law, policy, use of force principles, etc.
- Skill (marksmanship accountability)
- Moving targets
- Officers required to move during exercises
- Low light or adverse light conditions
- "Regular" in-service training
- Shotgun training (training on all weapons used by officer)
- Decision making – shoot or no-shoot decisions

Photo by author

Bottom line: agencies should train their officers regularly in skills they are reasonably expected to employ in their duties; however, a single act of misconduct does not necessarily equate to liability on the part of the agency for failure to train.

Kibbe v. City of Springfield, 777 F.2d 801 (1st Cir. 1985):

A relative of Clinton Thurston sued the City of Springfield as a result of him being shot in the head during a vehicle pursuit in which he fled from police officers. The pursuit involved at least ten officers, some of whom were supervisory personnel. At least three officers fired shots at his vehicle. A motorcycle officer, Theodore Perry, was the last to shoot at Thurston and fired the fatal shot to his head. As the car came to a stop, the officer who initiated the pursuit, Erich Risch, ran up to the car and ordered Thurston out. When he didn't comply, Risch hit him in the head with his flashlight. Ultimately, Thurston was taken to the hospital but neither EMS or attending medical staff had been told that Thurston had been shot. Perry also did not report this to the street supervisor on the scene. Sometime later when officers received a call from the hospital, police supervisory personnel alerted medical staff that Thurston may have been shot. The medical staff X-rayed his head and found a bullet in his brain but he expired a short time later.

The city argued that under Tuttle v. Oklahoma they could not be held liable for a single act of misconduct. The court disagreed. The fact that at least ten officers participated in the pursuit, that supervisor personnel were involved, and that at least three separate shooting events occurred during the pursuit, negated the city's argument of a single act of misconduct.

Further, in their decision against the city, the court cited the following: testimony by witnesses that Thurston did not pose a threat to the officers; testimony of little or no guidance for vehicle pursuits; a department policy of use of firearms that indicated other lesser means should be considered first which was arguably ignored by officers; another part of the policy which discouraged firing where there was a substantial risk to innocent bystanders arguably violated by two of the officers; overzealous announcements on the police radio by the dispatcher; and, considerable deficiencies in investigating officer involved shootings. These actions and deficiencies led the court to rule that the city was grossly inadequate in training its officers.[12]

The court cited a host of cases (listed below) that accept "inadequate training" as an actionable municipal custom or policy as described in the landmark Monell case.

Related cases: Monell v. New York City Department of Social Services, 436 U.S. 658 (1978); Owens v. Haas, 601 F.2d 1242, 1246-47 (2nd Cir.), cert. denied, 444 U.S. 980, 100 S.Ct. 483, 62 L.Ed.2d 407 (1979); Herrera v. Valentine, 653 F.2d 1220, 1224 (8th Cir. 1981); Wellington v. Daniels, 717 F.2d 932, 936 (4th Cir. 1983); Oklahoma v. Tuttle, 471 U.S. 808 (1985); Marchese v. Lucas, 758 F.2d 181, 188-89 (6th Cir. 1985); Voutour v. Vitale, 761 F.2d 812, 819-20 (1st Cir. 1985).

Bottom line: agencies are responsible for providing training and policies to guide officers in situations that could reasonably be encountered and for holding employees accountable to said training and policies. Not doing so may result in the agency being liable for failure to train.

Voutour v. Vitale, 761 F.2d 812 (1st Cir. 1985):

This is an appellate court case that was ruled on shortly after Oklahoma v. Tuttle as it refers to the pending decision of that case as it remands several items back to the District Court for consideration.

Voutour was driving a vehicle in Saugus, Massachusetts with two companions. The vehicle had numerous equipment problems. Voutour encountered Officer Vitale and Reserve Officer Wheeler in a patrol car near a Ford dealership. Not wanting to be contacted by police, Voutour left the area driving the wrong way on an exit ramp to Route 1. Voutour stopped some distance away to let one of his passengers out when Vitale and Wheeler drove by in the police car. They backed up and parked behind Voutour but did not activate any emergency equipment.

Reserve officer Wheeler approached the passenger side of the car with a flashlight in one hand and his gun in the other (disputed). When Wheeler grabbed the door handle, Voutour began driving away with Wheeler still holding on or being dragged (disputed). Vitale, claiming he was in fear for his partner's safety, fired upon Voutour. He claimed to be trying to shoot him in the shoulder. He struck Voutour in the neck rendering him a paraplegic.

Voutour filed a claim for a § 1983 Civil Rights Act violation and a claim under Massachusetts law for assault and battery against Voutour, Wheeler, the

Saugus Police Chief, Fred Forni, and the Town of Saugus. In the 1983 action, Voutour claimed Vitale's actions constituted excessive force depriving him of constitutional rights and failure to adequately train on the part of the Town and the Police Chief. The District Court summarily dismissed the claims against Wheeler, the Town of Saugus, and the Chief of Police citing a lack of clear connection to any violation of Voutour's civil rights. The jury in the case ruled for Officer Vitale on the 1983 excessive force claim and for Voutour on the assault and battery claim, awarding Voutour $1.5 million. Both plaintiff and defendant appealed and the case was considered by the U.S. Court of Appeals.

There was a dispute over the jury instructions that the Court of Appeals ruled on and remanded to the District Court. However, the Court ruled on two other issues regarding the summary judgment in the cases of Wheeler, the Town, and the Chief of Police. Voutour tried to link Wheeler to the excessive force claim against Vitale. Both the District and Appellate court agreed that there was no evidence that even if Wheeler had acted against training or practice by approaching the car without properly identifying himself, there was no way that he could have known with practical certainty that his actions would lead to Vitale shooting Voutour and causing injury. The Appellate Court disagreed with the District Court's summary judgement regarding the claim of failure to train and the liability attached to the Chief of Police and the Town.

In their judgement the Appellate Court stated that the evidence presented in the light most favorable to the plaintiff, clearly showed that training in the use of firearms was grossly inadequate for Vitale and as a whole for the Saugus police officers. Vitale had worked as a police officer for Saugus for 5 years but had not attended a police academy, as required at the time by Massachusetts state law, within 6-months of employment. Chief Forni testified that Vitale had firearms training from the Army and police training as a reserve from another department. Neither of these qualified as an exception from the law (no exceptions were listed in the law.)

Further, the only "in-service" training officers had undergone was 30-minute roll call training. Chief Forni stated in a reorganization proposal that this training was not "adequate or effective." He also testified that neither Wheeler nor Vitale had received firearms training. A letter written by one of the Chief's subordinates identifies three improper uses of service revolvers by officers (not Vitale). The Appellate Court felt this more than enough evidence for the case of failure to train to be heard by a jury and pointed to specific connections between the alleged constitutional deprivations and the actions of the Chief and the Town of Saugus. The District Court's decision of summary judgment was reversed.[13]

Related cases: Languirand v. Hayden, 717 F.2d at 227-28; Bennett v. City of Slidell, 728 F.2d 762 (5th Cir. 1984); Oklahoma v. Tuttle, 471 U.S. 808 (1985).

Bottom line: previous undocumented training in unrelated employment (military vs. civilian law enforcement) does not absolve an agency of their responsibility to train an officer to an adequate standard.

City of Canton Ohio v. Harris, 489 U.S. 378 (1989):

An arrestee fell down several times and was incoherent following her arrest; however, the officers summoned no medical assistance for her. She was left in a cell for about an hour and then released. She was transported by ambulance (provided by her family) and hospitalized for a week for several severe emotional ailments. She required another year of subsequent outpatient treatment. She sued to hold the city liable under 42 U.S.C. 1983 for violation of her right under the Due Process Clause of the 14th Amendment to receive necessary medical attention while in police custody.

Evidence was presented by the plaintiff to show that pursuant to a municipal regulation, shift commanders were authorized to determine, at their sole discretion, whether an arrestee required medical care. Evidence also showed that shift commanders received no training in determining the need for medical assistance beyond basic first aid. The municipality was held liable for failure to train the officers involved to provide medical assistance for detainees.[14]

Related cases: Oklahoma City v. Tuttle, 471 U.S. 808, 105 S. Ct. 2427 (1985); Monell v. New York City Dept. of Social Services, 436 U.S. 658, 98 S. Ct. 2018 (1978); Hays v. Jefferson County, 668 F.2d 869 (6th Cir. 1982); Pembaur v. Cincinnati, 475 U.S. 469, 106 S. Ct. 1292 (1986).

Bottom line: agencies who fail to train officers to handle situations that they will reasonably encounter may be held liable including if the failure results from a policy whether official or unofficial.

Walker v. City of New York, 974 F.2d 293 (2d Cir. 1992):

Plaintiff Walker was incarcerated for 19 years for a crime, which it was later revealed, he did not commit. Walker was accused of being an accomplice to an armed robbery. During the investigation he was identified as the primary suspect's accomplice by a known drug addict named Snider. In a line-up another man (a police officer) was identified by the victim rather than Walker. Snider also implicated another man named Givens who was discovered to have been in prison at the time of the robbery. Neither the ADA or the detective turned the documents from the line-up or statements from Snider over to the defense. The ADA, J. Paul Zsuffa, told the court during a pre-trial hearing that the line-up had never taken place. The detective, Robert Powell, said he didn't remember the line-up. Snider testified against Walker at trial and Walker was convicted.

After Walker's release 19 years later, he filed suit against the city for failure to train police officers and assistant district attorneys not to perjure themselves or suppress exculpatory evidence. The district court dismissed the suit, ruling that the city had no duty to train subjects that were so obvious as not to require training (i.e., not lying or hiding evidence).

The United States Court of Appeals, 2nd Circuit reversed the ruling identifying the following requirements that must be met to demonstrate a municipalities deliberate indifference in failing to train or supervise employees:

First, the plaintiff must show that a policymaker knows "to a moral certainty" that her employees will confront a given situation. Id. Thus, a policymaker does not exhibit deliberate indifference by failing to train employees for rare or unforeseen events.

The plaintiff must show that the situation either presents the employee with a difficult choice of the sort that training or supervision will make less difficult or that there is a history of employees mishandling the situation. Whether to use deadly force in apprehending a fleeing suspect qualifies as a "difficult choice" because more than the application of common sense is required. Instead, police officers must adhere to the rule of Tennessee v. Garner, 471 U.S. 1, 105 S.Ct. 1694, 85 L.Ed.2d 1 (1985), that deadly force may constitutionally be applied to a fleeing suspect only when "the suspect threatens the officer with a weapon or there is probable cause to believe that he has committed a crime involving the infliction or threatened infliction of serious physical harm" and when, "where possible, some warning has been given." Id. at 11-12, 105 S.Ct. at 1701. A choice might also be difficult where, although the proper course is clear, the employee has powerful incentives to make the wrong choice.

The plaintiff must show that the wrong choice by the city employee will frequently cause the deprivation of a citizen's constitutional rights. City of Canton, 489 U.S. at 390, 109 S.Ct. at 1205. Thus, municipal policymakers may appropriately concentrate training and supervision resources on those situations where employee misconduct is likely to deprive citizens of constitutional rights.

Where the plaintiff establishes all three elements, the court indicated that it can be said that the policymaker should have known that inadequate training or supervision was "so likely to result in the violation of constitutional rights, that the policymakers of the city can reasonably be said to have been deliberately indifferent to the need."

The appellate court ruled that, while Walker's claim that the police department's misconduct constituted deliberate indifference toward a failure to train was not adequate without further discovery of a pattern of police misconduct of perjury. The court stated that Walker should have the opportunity to demonstrate such a pattern and reversed the district court's decision to allow such an opportunity. Secondly, the appellate court ruled that the failure to train claims against the district attorney's office should be allowed to move forward. Walker demonstrated a complete lack of training on the part of the DA regarding the requirements of Brady v. Maryland, a decision that had occurred just seven years prior to the initial case in 1971. Therefore, the appellate court reasoned that there was a need to train on recent rulings such as obligations under Brady and those requirements were not as "obvious" at the time of the misconduct as they are when the suit was filed in 1990. The case was reversed and remanded to the district court.[15]

Related cases: City of Canton v. Harris, 489 U.S. 378 (1989); Oklahoma v. Tuttle, 471 U.S. 808 (1985) (single act of misconduct); Pembaur v. Cincinnati, 475 U.S. 469 (1986) (clarification of Tuttle); Monell v. New York City Department of Social Services, 436 U.S. 658 (1978) (municipal policy or custom and policymaker).

Bottom line: agencies may be held liable for failure to train when the topic of the necessary training is not obviously well known at the time of the incident. Plaintiffs may have to show a pattern of wrongful behavior to demonstrate the necessity for the training and support a failure to train claim.

Zuchel v. City and County of Denver, Colo., 997 F.2d 730 (10th Cir. 1993):

Zuchel is a 10th Circuit Court of Appeals decision. Two officers, Spinharney and Hays, responded to the report of a disturbance inside a fast-food restaurant. Upon arrival, the officers were told that Mr. Zuchel, the person causing the disturbance, had gone outside. Officers found Zuchel embroiled in an argument with several teenagers nearby. As they approached, Officer Hays said, "Hey," to get Zuchel's attention. She later testified that they were approximately 15 feet from him. Hays and two witnesses testified that Zuchel turned toward the officers with his hands in view. As he did, one of the teenagers said something to the effect of, "watch out, he has a knife,"; however, Hays said she saw nothing in his right hand but could not see his left. She began approaching Zuchel to take him under physical control when her partner, Spinharny said, "drop it," and shot Zuchel four times while he had his hands in the air. Two witnesses, one a security guard, testified that Zuchel had his hands in the air and they could not see a weapon. Zuchel died on the scene.

The parents of the deceased sued the City and County of Denver under a claim of a § 1983 Civil Rights Act violation alleging Officer Spinharny used excessive force and that the City and County of Denver failed to train officers properly in the use of deadly force.

The evidence presented by the plaintiff to demonstrate deliberate indifference on the part of the City and County of Denver and the Denver Police Department included a letter from the serving District Attorney (DA) that referenced six violent encounters involving shots fired by officers within six weeks. The DA recommended to the Police Chief that Denver Police implement additional training efforts to better prepare officers for response to violent encounters so they may minimize the number of these where possible. He specifically suggested live-fire, street relevant shoot / no-shoot decision making training. The Denver Police failed to implement any of the changes suggested by the DA prior to the Zuchel shooting.

Further testimony from members of the police department revealed that the only decision-making training completed was during the academy and was done by lecture and watching a video or movie. No live-fire decisional training was completed.

The court found in favor of the plaintiff that the city was deliberately indifferent in their failure to train officers in the use of firearms because they did not have live shoot/no-shoot training. The Appellate Court affirmed the District Court's decision and the jury's award to the plaintiff in the case.[16]

Related cases: Zuchel v. Spinharney, 890 F.2d 273 (10th Cir. 1989) (officer involved in this case); Canton v. Harris, 489 U.S. 378, 109 S. Ct. 1197 (1989); Ryder v. City of Topeka, 814 F.2d 1412 (10th Cir. 1987); U.S. v. Drake, 932 F.2d 861 (10th Cir. 1991)

Bottom line: agencies must provide officers with practical force decision making training (more than a video / discussion).

Brown v. Gray, 227 F.3d 1278 (10th Cir. 2000):

While running errands in his neighborhood, Clifton Brown became embroiled in a traffic dispute with Edmond Gray, an off-duty Denver police officer. Gray was not in uniform and was driving his personal car. The two drivers exchanged insulting hand gestures. At a stop light, Gray got out of his car and approached Brown's car with his gun drawn but not displaying any identification. He yelled at Brown that he was a police officer. The light turned green and Brown pulled away making a U-turn and then pulling to the side of the road to get Gray's license plate number. Gray pulled up behind him and again approached Brown's car on foot with his gun out, pointed at Brown. Gray claimed that Brown had menaced him with a handgun and he was attempting to arrest Brown. Conversely, Brown claimed Gray never displayed any identification. Brown put his car in gear and began to pull away when Gray fired several rounds into the car hitting Brown three times. Brown was badly injured, but drove for several blocks, summoned help and was taken to the hospital.

During the trial pursuant to a § 1983 Civil Rights Act violation claim, the policy of Denver police was introduced that said officers should "always (be) armed" and were "always on duty". Officers were intentionally not trained specifically about the differences in taking action off-duty versus on-duty.

Officers were told to respond "as though they were on-shift in all situations." It was acknowledged by Denver Police personnel during the trial that an off-duty officer is without a uniform, radio, police car, and other substantial equipment that they have available when on shift. An expert witness in police training, Patrick Murphy, referred to the lack of training for off-duty action on Denver's part as "a pervasive problem…creating a dangerous situation in which a shooting was a foreseeable result." The decision also states that,

The plaintiff was awarded $400,000 in damages and the appellate court affirmed that "The jury was thus presented with sufficient information to conclude that Denver policymakers were aware of and deliberately indifferent to the risks presented by the training program's deficiencies."[17]

Related cases: Oklahoma City v. Tuttle, 471 U.S. 808, 105 S. Ct. 2427 (1985); City of Canton Ohio v. Harris, 489 U.S. 378 (1989); Zuchel v. City and County of Denver, Colo., 997 F.2d 730 (10th Cir. 1993); Allen v. Muskogee, Oklahoma, 119 F.3d 837 (10th Cir. 1997).

Bottom line: if officers carry weapons off duty, they must be trained in appropriate off-duty response, use of force, and enforcement actions.

Cases Related to Qualification and/or Discrimination

Griffin v. City of Omaha, 785 F.2d 620 (8th Cir. 1986):

Marjorie Griffin and Sandra McWhorter were terminated from the Omaha Police Department (OPD) for failing their firearms qualification for the City of Omaha Police Academy. At the time the Omaha Police Department was under a consent decree which required an increase of black employment throughout the department. The district court found that the hiring requirements caused an increase in racial tensions throughout the department.

Griffin and McWhorter were part of the 1981 cadet academy class consisting of 34 cadets: fourteen white males, twelve black males, three Hispanic males, two white females and three black females. The 1981 recruit class had the greatest number of black officers in the OPD's history. Twenty-five members of the 1981 recruit class graduated; all nine recruits terminated were black, and included all three black females.

Griffin and McWhorter alleged that they had been wrongfully terminated and that they were treated differently than a similarly situated white male cadet because of their race and sex. They were terminated from the academy for failure to meet minimum firearms qualification standards while a white male cadet in the same situation was retained. They contended that they received both quantitatively and qualitatively inadequate firearms training compared to other cadets.

No written policy existed for scoring of "pre-qualification" shoots or for the final qualification shoot for cadets. It was a general practice that cadets who scored below 65 on any pre-qualification shoot were recommended for termination. None of the three black female cadets had used a firearm before. Based on their scores, four cadets were recommended for termination; all three black females and one white male. The three female recruits complained to the administration through the Midwest Guardians organization that the firearms training provided was inadequate. After considering these complaints, the training officers were ordered to provide additional firearms training for all four cadets.

Different training officers were assigned to provide remedial training to the cadets. The training was reviewed later by Louis Dirks, a training officer at the Law Enforcement Training Center at Grand Island, NE. He complimented the additional training provided to the white officer, Dussetschleger, who ultimately passed the final qualification; however, he severely criticized the additional training provided to the three females indicating that it was poorly documented, lacked sufficient diagnosis of the problems and did not provide useful techniques to the cadets for improvement. All three cadets scored a 65 or below on their final shoot. Only Griffin's average was above 70 for all shoots. Public Safety Director Friend testified that he adopted a new subjective standard for the cadets after the additional training was decided upon. This was the standard used to terminate the three black females.

Dirks testified that Griffin and McWhorter came to the Grand Island Training Center and he was able to diagnose their problems and qualify them within a weekend.

While the District Court denied Griffin and McWhorter's claim, the Appellate Court disagreed. The majority of evidence at trial focused on two issues: what were the OPD proficiency standards and did the appellants meet those standards; and, whether the training provided was adequate to qualify with firearms. The Appellate Court found that under the new subjective standards of the OPD, Griffin did pass. They also found that although the other two had not passed there was sufficient evidence that they had not received adequate training when others had. The Court criticized the changing of standards and the use of a subjective "deteriorating" standard. Thus, they found the District Court's ruling that the plaintiff's had failed to show evidence of discriminatory practices erroneous. The trial court's decision was reversed and remanded for further proceedings.

Of particular note in this case, a variety of firearms trainers testified during trial. All noted that losing 10 percent of a class and all the black females for failing to qualify was suspect. One trainer testified that of over 1100 cadets he had trained, only 1 had been dismissed for failure to qualify; another testified that of 230 cadets prior to this class in the OPD academy, only 4 had failed to qualify.[18]

Related cases: McDonnell Douglas Corp. v. Green, 411 U.S. 792, 93 S. Ct. 1817 (1973); Patterson v. Masem, 774 F.2d 251 (8th Cir. 1985); U.S. Postal Service Bd. of Govs. v. Aikens, 460 U.S. 711, 103 S. Ct. 1478 (1983); Craft v. Metromedia, Inc., 766 F.2d 1205 (8th Cir. 1985).

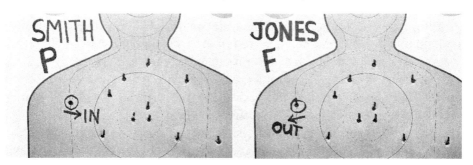

Agencies must have a standard and it must be applied to all employees equally. Disparate treatment (as illustrated) may result in exposure to liability.

Bottom line: agencies should establish official, written standards of performance; standards must be applied equally to all employees; adequate training, including remedial training, must be properly documented.

Ethridge v. State of Ala., 860 F. Supp. 808 (M.D. Ala. 1994):

Baxter Ethridge was hired as a provisional police officer for the town of Slocomb, Alabama. He had restricted use of his right arm and hand. At the time, municipalities were allowed to employ a provisional officer and have him or her perform the duties of the job pending satisfactory completion of at least 240 hours of training in a recognized police training school within 9 months of appointment.

In March 1992, Slocomb sent Ethridge to the Southwest Alabama Police Academy. Prior to sending Ethridge to the academy, the town police chief accompanied Ethridge to the police range and noted that he had difficulty controlling his sidearm while firing it. Nevertheless, Ethridge was sent to the academy to determine if he could meet the necessary qualifications.

When Ethridge began firearms training he was required to shoot with only his right hand as well as in a two-hand grip referred to as the Weaver stance. The Weaver stance required Ethridge to use his weaker right hand to support the pistol. Both of these requirements were written standards set forth by the Alabama Peace Officers Standards Commission. The minimum passing score for the pistol qualification was 70. Ethridge's three practice scores were 48, 58, and 58. His two official, for-record scores were 50 and 62. Ethridge was subjected to the same testing requirements as all of the other cadets.

Ethridge was dismissed from the academy due to his inability to qualify under the state standards. When he returned to Slocomb, he was provided one week's pay and terminated from employment. Ethridge filed a lawsuit in federal court claiming he was denied employment as a police officer in violation of federal and state law, specifically the Americans with Disabilities Act (ADA) and corresponding Alabama state law.

Ethridge's complaint alleged three separate theories for violation of the ADA: (1) He asserts that he could have passed the required handgun course if reasonable accommodation had been made and if he had not been subject to harsher, disparate treatment at the academy; (2) Ethridge asserts that it was unlawful for the Town of Slocomb to deny him employment on the grounds that he did not complete the requisite police training; and (3) he asserts that the requirement of a firearms course is itself discriminatory and that he could safety perform the function of a police officer without passing the course.

Prior to the hearing of this case, the parties reached a mutual agreement for Ethridge to re-test. After agreeing to the parameters of the test, Ethridge was allowed to retake the Alabama police qualification without using any particular stance and he was allowed to shoot with only one hand during any part of the qualification which normally would require the use of the Weaver stance. Ethridge failed to satisfactorily complete the course, scoring 52 and 56.

Further, testimony from instructors and witness cadets agreed that Ethridge was not treated more harshly or disparately but rather he received special attention and additional assistance during the firearms course. Multiple witnesses testified that Ethridge had difficulty loading, charging, unloading and clearing malfunctions from his pistol. They stated he frequently handled the gun in such a way that it was pointed at other cadets and instructors. At one point two instructors were working with Ethridge to attempt to find a way for him to hold and manipulate the gun in a safer manner. Ethridge was excluded from the night firing portion of training specifically because of safety concerns on the part of the instructors and the academy director.

The court found that Ethridge's claim that he could have passed the qualification but for the requirement of the Weaver stance and that he had received disparate and harsher treatment without merit. They also stated that the instructors were justified in excluding him from the night shoot for legitimate reasons of safety supported by articulable evidence. The court also found that the defendants need not have accommodated Ethridge's request to shoot one handed because the Weaver stance met the criteria of an essential job function as defined by ADA. Regarding this the court stated,

"Essential functions are those that an employee must be able to perform. Thus, although a disabled employee must be reasonably accommodated in order to perform the essential function, an employer need not hire an employee who cannot perform the essential function even with reasonable accommodation." See School Bd. of Nassau County, Fla. v. Arline, 480 U.S. 273, 287 n. 17, 107 S.Ct. 1123, 1131 n. 17, 94 L.Ed.2d 307 (1987); 29 C.F.R. §§ 1630.2(n) 1630.9, App.A.

Written descriptions of essential job functions are considered evidence of the necessity of those job functions.

Ethridge's claim against the Town of Slocomb that he should not have been dismissed on the grounds that he did not complete the police academy was denied. The court accepted that the law in Alabama was clear that a provisional police officer had to successfully complete the police academy training as a condition of his employment. Ethridge did not complete that training successfully and therefore, the Town could not employ him as a police officer by law.

Finally, the court addressed Ethridge's claim that the firearms course was discriminatory and he did not need to complete the course to function as a police officer. The defendants had the burden to show evidence that the firearms course and standard was relevant to the job. First, the course is required by Alabama Peace Officers Standards Commission which is created by state law. The South Alabama Police Academy conducted the course in accordance with state standards. The defendants also argued that safe handling and use of a firearm is necessary for "business" reasons of being a police officer and to ensure the safety of the police officer and the citizens they serve. The court found this to be a satisfactory argument and Ethridge was unable to provide evidence to the contrary.

Ethridge's claims were denied by the court and summary judgment was awarded to all defendants.[19]

Related cases: Chiari v. City of League City, 920 F.2d 311, 316-17 (5th Cir. 1991); School Bd. of Nassau County, Fla. v. Arline, 480 U.S. 273, 287 n. 17, 107 S.Ct. 1123, 1131 n. 17, 94 L.Ed.2d 307 (1987); Fitzpatrick v. City of Atlanta, 2 F.3d 1112, 1125-27 (11th Cir. 1993).

Bottom line: ADA mandated reasonable accommodation does not force an agency to hire a person who cannot perform an essential job function; courts rely significantly on written job duties to determine essential job functions; excluding someone from an activity or training for legitimate, articulable safety considerations does not equate to discrimination.

Hefley v. Village of Calumet Park, 239 F. App'x 276 (7th Cir. 2007):

Travis Hefley was a part time police officer for Calumet Park. In January of 2004, Susan Rockett, Assistant Chief, sent a memo to all police officers advising them that annual firearms qualifications would begin January 21 and that they must qualify by March 17. By March 5, Hefley had not qualified nor had he attended any of the sessions held by Sgt. Jones, the rangemaster.

Hefley received a written reminder from AC Rockett that part-time officers that did not complete the qualification by the deadline would be removed from the schedule. Hefley missed the next session but attended the last session on March 17 with another officer named Curtis Smith. At each of these sessions, Jones provided officers with training on their firearms and administered the annual test. At the end of the training, Jones administered the test and neither

Hefley, who is white, nor Curtis, who is black, achieved the passing score which was 76.

Jones notified Rockett that both officers had failed to qualify and asked her permission to give them an additional opportunity to take the test. Rockett agreed and notified both men that they could test for the final time on March 24. She reminded them if they did not pass, they could not resume patrol duties. When they met again, neither Hefley or Smith achieved a passing score. Hefley's top score was 60 while Smith's was 74. Both men were fired later that day.

Hefley contacted Chief of Police, Mark Davis and asked for another chance to qualify. He was directed to Assistant Chief Rockett who denied the request. In May, Smith reapplied for employment and passed his firearms test. He was rehired as a part-time officer. Hefley never reapplied.

Hefley sued the Village of Calumet and Chief Davis claiming discrimination under Title VII of the Civil Rights Act of 1964. The Court dismissed the case against Chief Davis and summarily dismissed the case against the Village stating that Hefley did not show prima facia evidence of discrimination. Specifically, he was not able to show that he was meeting his employers' expectations. Rockett notified him that he must pass qualification to continue employment and it is undisputed that he did not pass.

Hefley claims that his employer did not do enough to help him pass his firearms test. Both the District and Appellate courts agreed that an employer does not have to "bend over backwards to assist its employees with their job-related difficulties," Brummett v. Lee Enterprises, Inc., 284 F.3d 742 (7th Cir. 2002). Hefley also asserted that he had received positive performance evaluations previously which demonstrated that he could do the job effectively. The court rejected this argument because the plaintiff is required to show that he was meeting expectations at the time of the dismissal.

Lastly, Hefley was unable to support any claim of being treated differently than Smith. They were fired on the same day for failing to pass qualifications, demonstrating that both were treated the same. Hefley claims that Smith was given additional opportunities to qualify which is only true after Smith reapplied for employment. Hefley never reapplied so he is unable to compare himself to Smith in this respect. The standard of "similarly situated" means that two employees were directly comparable. Once Smith reapplied and Hefley chose not to, the two were no longer similarly situated.[20]

The Appellate Court affirmed the decision of the District Court and Hefley's case was dismissed.

Related cases: Mills v. Health Care Serv. Corp., 171 F.3d 450 (7th Cir. 1999); Phelan v. City of Chicago, 347 F.3d 679 (7th Cir. 2003); Ballance v. City of Springfield, 424 F.3d 614 (7th Cir. 2005); Brummett v. Lee Enterprises, Inc., 284 F.3d 742 (7th Cir. 2002); Johal v. Little Lady Foods, Inc., 434 F.3d 943 (7th Cir. 2006).

Bottom line: officers may be dismissed for failing to qualify when the expectations of performance are clearly made known and when expectations and testing are documented.

Chambers v. State, 523 S.W.3d 681 (Tex. App. 2017):

John Chambers was the chief of a small police department in Indian Lake, TX. He and one other officer were the only full time sworn employees; however, they regularly employed 20 to 30 reserve officers. The Texas Commission on Law Enforcement conducted an audit on the Indian Lake Police Department and found a number of deficiencies in paperwork required to be kept or submitted by law. The auditor notified Chambers of these deficiencies which included missing firearm qualifications for a number of the reserve officers.

Chief Chambers instructed his subordinate officer to complete qualification forms for fourteen reserve officers showing that they had passed a "firearms qualification practical pistol course" all on September 20, 2014. All of the forms indicated the reserve officers used the same Smith & Wesson .40 caliber handgun, whose serial number registered to Chambers. The fourteen reserve officers in question testified at trial that they had not completed the qualification course.

Chambers was indicted on fourteen counts of knowingly making false entries in governmental records, a jailable felony in Texas. Chambers appealed to the Texas State Court of Appeals and the court affirmed the trial court's judgment.[21]

Bottom line: agencies must keep proper documentation; documents generated by government officials (instructors) are "official documents" and if falsified, may subject the individual to penalties.

Cases Involving Tactics and Other Training

<u>Sager v. City of Woodland Park, 543 F. Supp. 282 (D. Colo. 1982)</u>:

Prior to the U.S. Court of Appeals decision on this case, a significant amount of litigation had taken place which is far afield from the issue we are concerned with from a training stand point. A very brief summary of the case is as follows:

While affecting the arrest of a teenager named Bryan Sager, a Woodland Park police officer, James Parr, pointed a shotgun at him. The facts of the case indicate Sager was in a prone position on the ground and offering no resistance. He was also unarmed. Officer Parr stood over him and pointed a shotgun at the back of his head while attempting to handcuff him. Parr shot Sager and killed him.

During the voluminous litigation, the City of Woodland Park moved to include the City of Colorado Springs Police Training Academy, who provided all initial training for Woodland Park police officers, as a defendant in the suit. They alleged that a police academy trainer showed a film in which a police officer holds a shotgun to the head of an arrestee while handcuffing him in the exact manner in which Bryan Sager was shot and killed. Plaintiff claims that this exact technique was used by a Woodland Park police officer and resulted in the officer shooting and killing the suspect.

The academy trainer confirmed that, in fact, a film was shown to cadets which depicted that technique; however, stated that the film was shown to illustrate an improper technique and "generate class discussion" however the students were not specifically told this was an improper technique.

The City of Colorado Springs as a third-party defendant in this case moved for summary judgment. Their motion was denied by the trial court and upheld by the appellate court. The court, ruling in favor of the plaintiff, stated that instructors and agencies are responsible for all of the training material they use, including videos. The Court further stated that the Colorado Springs Police Training Academy had a duty to train officers who attended properly, and that duty foreseeably extends to those wrongfully injured as a proximate result of such improper training.[22]

<u>Bottom line</u>: trainers and their employers are ultimately responsible for the content presented to police trainees. Examples of improper conduct used

during training must be clearly labeled and/or stated as improper by the trainer.

Quezada v. County of Bernalillo, 944 F.2d 710 (10th Cir. 1991):

Three deputies contacted Griego in a parking lot where she was sitting in her car with her head on the steering wheel. Upon contact the deputy initiating the contact found her to be despondent and she would only roll her window down slightly for the deputy. Two other deputies arrived a short time later.

During the contact, Griego picked up a pistol and loaded it. This was seen by the deputies. The initial deputy, Martin and another deputy, Murphy took cover. Deputy Sauser remained close to the vehicle and initially had his firearm pointed at Griego. While telling her to put the gun down, Griego put the gun to her temple and then in her mouth. She also waved the pistol around in a way the deputies later described as "aimless". She also took a drink of beer during the contact and the deputies recognized from the contact that she was intoxicated to some extent.

Although there was time, Deputy Sauser never sought cover. He instead placed himself on the driver's side of the car about 5 feet from it. At some point, Griego turned toward Deputy Sauser and made a movement he believed to be pointing her gun at him. He fired three rounds and struck Griego twice. She later died from the injuries. The other deputies testified they saw Griego make this movement as well.

Griego's mother filed a § 1983 Civil Rights Act violation claim of excessive force. During the trial, the District Court found that Deputy Sauser's actions were not objectively unreasonable (prior to the Graham v. Connor decision). The Appellate Court found that the District Court erred in this finding by not considering all of the evidence such as where Deputy Sauser chose to stand, training on dealing with suicidal subjects, cover available to Deputy Sauser, and so on. They reversed the lower court's decision in part and remanded the case for further proceedings.

The Court of Appeals stated, "...the district court found Deputy Sauser placed himself in a position of great jeopardy by standing in the open and close to Ms. Griego's car. Deputy Sauser disregarded his own safety by standing where he did. His actions left absolutely no room for error and forced the deadly confrontation because - given his vulnerable location - Deputy Sauser's only available option was deadly force. But for this negligence, deadly force would not have been required." They found that Deputy Sauser's actions were not objectively reasonable by the standard established by Graham v. Connor by creating the jeopardy he later relied upon for his justification of the use of deadly force.[23]

Related cases: Graham v. Connor, 490 U.S. 386 (1989); Tennessee v. Garner, 471 U.S. 1, 105 S. Ct. 1694 (1985); Street v. Parham, 929 F.2d 537 (10th Cir. 1991); Rozek v. Topolnicki, 865 F.2d 1154 (10th Cir. 1989).

Bottom line: an officer knowingly creating jeopardy he or she relies on later for justification of the use of deadly force is not objectively reasonable.

Photo by author

Recent court decisions have indicated that police must use reasonable tactics such as use of cover or barriers to avoid creating jeopardy.

Allen v. Muskogee, Oklahoma, 119 F.3d 837 (10th Cir. 1997):

Terry Allen had a dispute with his wife and left his house armed with several firearms and ammunition. This information was relayed to the Muskogee Police Department (MPD) from the Wagoner County Sheriff's Office. The MPD then received a 911 call from Allen's sister that he was in front of her house and was threatening suicide. Lt. Smith of MPD arrived on scene to find several bystanders near Allen's car. He told them to stand back and then approached the driver's door where Allen was seated. Allen had his right hand on a pistol resting on the arm rest between the seats.

Lt. Smith was joined by Officer McDonald on the driver's side of the car. Lt. Smith reached into the car to try to grab Allen's gun while McDonald was holding Allen's left arm. Another officer, Farmer, had arrived and opened the passenger door to help disarm Allen. Allen lifted the gun to point it at Farmer. McDonald and Smith fired 12 rounds striking Allen four times, killing him.

The trial court granted summary judgment for the defendant officers and the City of Muskogee. The plaintiff appealed. The Court of Appeals found that an examination of the objective reasonableness of the defendant's actions must include more than just their actions at the instant of the use of force. The court must consider the defendant's own reckless or deliberate conduct during the seizure that may have unreasonably created the need for such force.

The Court of Appeals found that not only was there evidence that the defendant officer's actions were unreasonable based on testimony from an expert witness who called their actions "reckless and totally contrary to proper police practices for dealing with armed, mentally ill people," but there was also evidence of inadequate and improper training of the officers on the part of the City. A lieutenant in charge of training testified that the officers had acted in accordance with their training in approaching the car and attempting to disarm the suspect. Lt. Smith and Glen McIntyre, the state firearms training coordinator, both testified that the officers had acted in accordance with their training indicating that they were trained to leave cover, approach an armed suspect and attempt to disarm them.

The expert witness, Dr. George Kirkham, was highly critical of this training calling it "out of sync" with training presented throughout the United States. The Court of Appeals found that the officers were trained to act recklessly and in a manner that created a high risk of death. They further stated that there was evidence to support that the officers had been trained to do precisely the wrong thing.[24]

The case was reversed and remanded to the lower court.

Related cases: Sevier v. City of Lawrence, 60 F.3d 695 (10th Cir. 1995); Graham v. Connor, 490 U.S. 386, 109 S. Ct. 1865 (1989); Romero v. Board of County Com'rs, 60 F.3d 702 (10th Cir. 1995); Tennessee v. Garner, 471 U.S. 1, 105 S. Ct. 1694 (1985); Canton v. Harris, 489 U.S. 378, 109 S. Ct.

1197 (1989); Zuchel v. City and County of Denver, Colo., 997 F.2d 730 (10th Cir. 1993).

Bottom line: officers and agencies may be liable when officers are trained to act recklessly and in a manner that creates a high risk of death. As in Quezada, officers may not create the jeopardy they later rely on for justifying the use of deadly force.

[1] *Tennessee v. Garner*, 471 U.S. 1 (1985). https://supreme.justia.com

[2] *Graham v. Connor*, 490 U.S. 386 (1989). https://supreme.justia.com

[3] *Thompson v. Hubbard*, 131 U.S. 123 (1989). https://caselaw.findlaw.com

[4] *Plakus v. Drinski*, 19 F.3d 1143 (7th Cir. 1994). https://casetext.com

[5] *Harris v. Roderick*, 933 F. Supp. 977 (D. Idaho 1996). https://casetext.com

[6] *Plumhoff v. Rickard*, 134 S. Ct. 2012, 188 L. Ed. 2d 1056, 572 U.S. 765, 24 Fla. L. Weekly Supp. 790 (2014). https://www.supremecourt.gov/opinions/

[7] *Kingsley v. Hendrickson*, 135 S. Ct. 2466, 575 U.S. 959, 192 L. Ed. 2d 416, 192 L. Ed. 2d 435 (2015). https://caselaw.findlaw.com

[8] *Monell v. Department of Social Services of the City of New York*, 436 U.S. 658 (1978). https://supreme.justia.com

[9] *Popow vs. City of Margate*, 476 F. Supp. 1237 (D.N.J. 1979). https://casetext.com

[10] *McClelland, v. Facteau*, 610 F.2d 693 (10th Cir. 1979). https://casetext.com

[11] *Oklahoma City v. Tuttle*, 471 U.S. 808, 105 S. Ct. 2427 (1985). https://supreme.justia.com

[12] *Kibbe v. City of Springfield*, 777 F.2d 801 (1st Cir. 1985). https://casetext.com

[13] *Voutour v. Vitale*, 761 F.2d 812 (1st Cir. 1985). https://casetext.com

[14] *City of Canton Ohio v. Harris*, 489 U.S. 378 (1989). https://supreme.justia.com

[15] *Walker v. City of New York*, 974 F.2d 293 (2d Cir. 1992). https://casetext.com

[16] *Zuchel v. City and County of Denver, Colo.*, 997 F.2d 730 (10th Cir. 1993). https://casetext.com

[17] *Brown v. Gray*, 227 F.3d 1278 (10th Cir. 2000). https://caselaw.findlaw.com

[18] *Griffin v. City of Omaha*, 785 F.2d 620 (8th Cir. 1986). https://casetext.com

[19] *Ethridge v. State of Ala.*, 860 F. Supp. 808 (M.D. Ala. 1994). https://casetext.com

[20] *Hefley v. Village of Calumet Park*, 239 F. App'x 276 (7th Cir. 2007). https://casetext.com

[21] *Chambers v. State*, 523 S.W.3d 681 (Tex. App. 2017). https://casetext.com

[22] *Sager v. City of Woodland Park*, 543 F. Supp. 282 (D. Colo. 1982). https://supreme.justia.com

[23] *Quezada v. County of Bernalillo*, 944 F.2d 710 (10th Cir. 1991). https://casetext.com

[24] *Allen v. Muskogee, Oklahoma*, 119 F.3d 837 (10th Cir. 1997). https://casetext.com

Chapter 14: FIREARMS POLICIES

When it comes to agency policies, there are two areas where the rangemaster should be heavily involved: firearms and use of force (deadly force section). It is vital that both of these topics involve input from the rangemaster or instructor staff as subject matter experts. While that doesn't always happen like it should, in cases where range staff does have input, they should approach the task earnestly and give their recommendations considerable thought. At a minimum, rangemasters should attend any meetings or committees that involve firearms or use of force for the following reasons:

- To advise and remind leaders of current policy and training standards covered in the firearms and use of force policy.
- To ensure proposed changes to the firearms or use of force policies are not in conflict with proper firearms training and use of force law.
- To ensure valid policy changes are clearly understood and can be correctly implemented by the firearms unit/staff.
- To ensure that other policies which overlap with firearms, such as building searches, high risk stops, arrest control, etc. are consistent with the current firearms training program where those policies intersect.

If an agency does not have a current firearms or use of force policy, or if the policy is significantly out of date, the rangemaster should draft and propose a new or significantly updated policy which is in line with current law and relevant industry practices. As we have mentioned several times throughout the book, rangemasters need not "re-invent the wheel" by trying to fashion a policy from scratch with no assistance. Networking with other rangemasters can be a powerful tool that can save someone facing a major policy rewrite, time, energy, and frustration. Requesting current firearms policies from other agencies or rangemasters will provide a good starting place for writing a new policy or revising an outdated one.

Definitions and General Guidelines

The firearms policy should address several key topics regardless of agency size or configuration. The policy should start with definitions for any special words or terms that are unique to firearms that employees may not readily understand. These definitions will give clear meaning of the guidelines provided throughout the policy. Words such as *duty handgun, issued handgun,* or *plain-clothes handgun* could have different meanings for different agencies. Are these owned by the agency, owned by the officer or a combination of the two? Are some guns allowed to be carried in uniform and others not? Similarly, words like *on-duty* and *off-duty* may need to be defined within the firearms or use of force policy. If an officer is working in uniform at an off-duty job, paid by a private organization, are they *on-duty* or *off-duty* for the purposes of this policy? Any term that could be easily misunderstood or defined in more than one way deserves consideration of inclusion in this section.

Photo by author

Also included at the beginning of the policy should be any "general guidelines" that apply to all firearms. Examples of these general guidelines may include:

- All firearms used in an official capacity must be registered with the agency using form X.
- Prior to carrying any firearm in an official capacity, the firearm must be inspected and approved by an agency certified armorer.

For simplicity, the policy can then be sectioned out to address each type of weapon system (pistol / revolver, shotgun, rifle) with each section addressing the same topic, but specific to the firearm system. The following sections are not all inclusive, but they represent the minimum topics that should be covered within an agency's firearms policy.

Firearms Safety and Security

The Firearms Safety Rules discussed in *Chapter 2* are often dictated by a higher authority such as a POST organization and will likely not change frequently. Further, it should be an expectation of all officers to comply with those rules all the time. As such, they should be considered an essential part of the firearms policy.

Additionally, guidelines for weapon security and storage should be outlined within the policy. In some states, safe storage laws have been enacted. If that is the case, the rangemaster should ensure policy matches law where required. At the very least, a statement regarding the officer's responsibility to take reasonable precautions to ensure that weapons used for their job are not accessed by unauthorized persons is a prudent addition to the policy.

Authorized Firearms – Duty and Off-duty

A section of the policy should be dedicated to outlining weapons that are authorized for duty carry as well as off-duty. If the agency issues firearms, the policy should outline under what conditions those weapons may or are required to be carried by officers. It may also include what weapons by make, model, and caliber are issued to officers. Similarly, if any personally owned firearms may be carried on-duty, whether in uniform or plain-clothes, the policy should outline that as well. This may also include identification of authorized firearms by make, model, and caliber.

Another section of the policy should be set apart to address firearms that can be used for purposes other than those included with "duty firearms." These may include off-duty handguns, back-up handguns, weapons carried in undercover assignments, and so on. These may be contained in one section or split into multiple sections as the needs of the agency dictate. Once again, the agency may specify these by make, model, and/or caliber as necessary.

A separate section(s) should be dedicated to other weapon systems such as rifle or shotgun. It should outline whether these weapons are mandatory or voluntary and for whom that applies. The policy should include the requirements to carry those firearms and any specifications of those systems. If the program is voluntary, how does an officer qualify for carry? It should state whether the firearms are issued or personally owned. This part of the policy may also include the specifications for such weapons so it is clear what will be allowed for carry or not.

If policy within the organization is cumbersome to change, the rangemaster may suggest wording in the policy that allows handguns, rifles, or shotguns "from an approved list" to be carried. For issued firearms it may state, "officers will be issued an agency authorized handgun for duty carry," or something to that effect. Within the policy, it can state that, "the rangemaster will maintain a list of all approved [handguns, rifles, shotguns] authorized for carry." This may be an addendum to the policy manual, part of a standard operating procedure (SOP) manual or stand-alone document (Approval List). The idea being to have a document that is more easily updated than policy if the policy requires multiple levels of review or another complicated process.

Authorized Accessories or Modifications

Whether the agency allows personally owned firearms or not, there should be a statement or section within policy regarding authorized or prohibited accessories or modifications to firearms. Accessories may include different sights or optics, weapon mounded lights (WML), different grips or grip wraps, slings, stocks for shoulder-fired guns, pressure switches for WMLs, or just about anything else you can think of. Modifications might be gunsmithing, milling of slides for optical sights, custom trigger work, aftermarket parts (triggers, springs, etc.), ambidextrous controls, and on and on.

The firearms policy should state not only firearms permitted for private purchase and use but what, if any modifications are allowed. If none are allowed, the policy should state that as well, indicating that the firearm must be "factory specification" or something similar. Along with authorized modifications (or not) there should be an approval process outlined for new weapons (particularly personally owned firearms) to be approved before they are carried. Included in this area of policy, having a requirement for any firearm used for official purposes to be inspected by a factory certified armorer as part of the approval process is recommended.

Photo by S. Wood

Policy should clearly state what firearms and accessories are authorized.

The rangemaster should consider very carefully whether to allow any aftermarket parts to be added to issued or personally owned firearms which change the internal workings of the firearm. Such items often void the firearm warranty. Most duty-worthy, law enforcement handguns have a five-to-six-pound trigger weight. Allowing aftermarket springs or kits that reduce that to three pounds or less with parts not designed by the manufacturer of the firearm is a risky proposition and generally *not* recommended.

Rangemasters should be careful about how much "stuff" they include in the policy. As with firearms above, not every specification detail has to be in policy. Once it becomes part of policy, it becomes difficult to revise. For example, when it comes to accessories and modifications, rangemasters should not list every accessory/modification in policy. Instead of listing all of the brands and models of weapon mounted lights that are authorized, the policy should simply state, "Weapon mounted lights are authorized for use. The rangemaster will maintain a list of authorized brands and models (Approval List). Only the items on the rangemaster's approval list are authorized for use." This allows the rangemaster to easily modify the list as technology changes or as problems arise. The rangemaster may still need approval from their chain-of-command to make the revision to the Approval List, but a policy revision will not be needed for the change. Policy should include who can install the accessories. For example, "only an agency certified armorer may install accessories," or "accessories must be installed by trained range personnel."

Authorized magazines should not be overlooked in the policy as part of the accessory section. It should outline what magazines and how many are required to be carried on-duty or off-duty. It should also address whether the officer is allowed to carry any supplemental magazines in a "rapid deployment bag" or on their person. These should be identified by make, style and capacity as with other equipment. Magazines are often a cause for weapon malfunctions so the rangemaster should consider whether aftermarket magazines are allowed for duty, or only factory magazines.

As this book is being written, one of the authors is advising a part-time rangemaster from a rural department that has a "problem child". The part-time officer in question is heavily influenced by social media channels with competitive shooters, and routinely modifies his personally purchased duty weapons to have the latest competition accessories, etc. The officer has been advised twice to remove unauthorized modifications from his pistol (light spring kit, "enhanced" trigger) and patrol rifle (drop - in aftermarket trigger group) and is coming up on his third violation. At what point do such violations reach disciplinary action? If an officer is intentionally violating one policy, how well are they complying with other policies such as search and seizure, arrest, and others?

Authorized Ammunition

The next section that should be included in a firearms policy outlines authorized ammunition. The policy should clearly state the number of rounds to be carried while in different roles and for different weapon systems. As indicated above with magazines, the policy should indicate whether the officer can supplement his normal issued or duty load with additional magazines and ammunition.

The policy (or an addendum) should include the specifics of ammunition carried for each system. This should be listed by manufacturer, product model, bullet weight, and so on. If additional ammunition is authorized, requiring the officer to carry the exact same type that the agency issues is highly recommended. It may be appropriate to include a frequency in which that ammunition needs to be changed out as well. Officers should carry specific amounts of ammunition, as indicated in policy. This will aid investigators of officer-involved shootings and other situations where an officer discharged their firearm, to account for ammunition fired or not fired.

Photo by author

The rangemaster may consider adding a statement about what practice ammunition is authorized for use in agency-owned firearms. Since some remanufactured or reloaded ammunition can void the firearm warranty, it may be wise to restrict its use. Only allowing use of practice ammunition from specified manufacturers may be a prudent step in protecting the agency's investment in issued firearms.

Required Training

Outlining the initial training and recurring training time in policy is recommended. This section should include frequency, required attendance, minimum hours, etc. Initial training may be set by a state standard but if not, consider the minimum time needed to establish a baseline of training for an officer in agency policies, procedures, tactics, and expectations of performance. If a new officer is coming from another agency, it is difficult to tell how they were previously trained or if they have received any ongoing training at all since leaving an academy. Having several days to a week to work with new officers will likely make their transition into the agency much smoother. Whatever this requirement, it should be clearly spelled out in the agency policy.

Including required firearms training in policy helps it be seen by administrators as something that is important and necessary to accomplish. Setting minimum hours helps ensure that those hours are less likely to be reduced. Even administrators who are not "pro-training" may think twice about lowering the standards for the agency if the required minimum training hours are listed in policy.

The policy should include a number of hours per year that are required by officers, the number of sessions they must attend, and/or frequency. This may correspond to required continuing education requirements from a higher authority like a POST organization or it may be solely driven by the agency. For many agencies, it is inevitable that an officer will miss some training due to illness, major case investigations, military leave, modified duty from injury, or any number of other reasons. Allowing for some flexibility and make-up of training within the policy is reasonable and wise.

Qualifications

Firearm qualifications should also have its own section of policy. This section should be carefully crafted to ensure practice matches policy and covers all of the necessary components of testing officer's ability. If an officer fails to qualify, they can be disciplined, suspended, or terminated. Therefore, it is important for the rangemaster to get this section of policy right.

The qualification section should clearly spell out how frequently officers are required to qualify on a given weapon system. It should include how many attempts they have to pass and what time frame those attempts must be completed within. This should include any specifics about the qualification course and who administers the qualification.

The qualification course may be referred to by name or number designation such as "POST qualification", "Qualification #1", or it may be referred to as, "the agency-approved qualification" which may allow more flexibility for modifying the course of fire over time without having to change policy.

Any rules for the qualification may be listed in policy or can be referred to in policy by a statement such as, "rules for the qualification will be included on the qualification form and reviewed with officers before their first attempt."

The policy should clearly spell out the protocol for a failure to qualify and should include the following:

- Notification of supervisory chain of command
- Any written advisement
- Change in duty assignment while remedial training takes place
- Potential consequences if the officer is unable to qualify successfully
- Time period, if any, before officer is allowed to attempt to qualify again
- Restrictions from working off-duty or overtime

The remedial training protocol should be included in this section and outline the minimum amount of time that an officer must complete, if any, and who conducts the remedial training. If an officer completes remedial training, how many more attempts do they get to qualify? What period of time do those attempts occur within? What happens if they fail those attempts? All of these questions should be answered within the policy.

It is a good practice not to conduct qualifications one-on-one with an instructor and student; however, that practice is not feasible for many agencies. At a minimum, if a shooter is on their last attempt to qualify before discipline or dismissal, having another person present (instructor, supervisor, etc.) to verify the qualification was conducted appropriately and scored correctly is a prudent custom. It is only recommended to include this in policy if it is able to be adhered to in practice.

Other Firearms Policy Considerations

The rangemaster may consider a few other items to add to their firearms policy if not included in another part of the policy manual. Firearm carry options, holster gear allowed, and retention required relevant to on-duty or off-duty carry, may be subjects the rangemaster should consider addressing. Some types of carry may require additional training to ensure it is done safely. An example would be inside the waistband holsters or shoulder holsters which require the wearer to draw or holster differently than most training from a weapon side hip holster.

Another consideration is any expectations, requirements, or standards for range staff. An example might be if range instructors have to qualify at a higher standard or maintain a specific certification. Another consideration is formalizing a range instructors' authority while conducting live-fire training or qualifications on the range. Their ability to enforce safety rules and standards up to and including removing someone from the range should be spelled out in the event the problem person is someone of higher rank. Lastly, policy may include any authorization to offer medical surveillance to range personnel. This may include offering regular blood lead level testing or hearing testing in addition to an agency hearing conservation program. See *Chapter 11: Hazards & Exposures* for more information.

Use of Force Policy

The use of force (UOF) policy should address several topics for each of the force options the agency allows. Obviously, the rangemaster should be mostly concerned with the deadly force section of the policy. While there are many ways officers can apply deadly force, the policy will primarily cover the use of firearms. That should be where the rangemaster focuses their attention.

Like the firearms policy, the use of force policy should have a "general guidelines / information" section at the beginning that covers items such as the elements of force, escalation and de-escalation, when to provide medical treatment, etc. There should also be a section for definitions of key words or terms used in the policy. Rangemasters should ensure the policy addresses the following issues regarding use of deadly force and provide input as the subject matter expert to ensure these policies follow law and current standard practices.

Use of Deadly Force by an Officer

The policy should obviously cover when an officer is authorized to use deadly force within their duties. This section should, at a minimum, mirror the state or federal law applicable to the agency. Further, the rangemaster should ensure it is consisted with established case law such as *Tennessee v. Garner* and *Graham v. Connor*. See *Chapter 13: Case Law* for additional examples.

The rangemaster should ensure that any additional restrictions placed on officers are consistent with the training provided and are practical for the dynamic encounters that officers face. Overly restrictive policies, that attempt to address every possible scenario, often fall short when applied to actual incidents with fluidly changing circumstances. Constructing policies that provide clear guidelines for officers while allowing the flexibility to adapt to a wide variety of suspect actions and individual circumstances will often serve the officers and the agency better.

Other Expected Actions by Officers

The use of force policy should outline other actions to be taken by officers in the case of an officer involved critical incident such as a shooting. These include actions such as rendering medical attention to anyone injured, including the suspect, when it is safe and practical to do so. This should be worded carefully so as not to require the officer to put themselves at undue risk to provide medical attention to a suspect who has caused or attempted to cause others harm.

Another action that may be required in policy is the notification of the chain of command by supervisory personnel on scene. If there is a specific investigative protocol for such incidents (there likely should be), notification for that response should be outlined as well. There may be additional items outlined but any actions should obviously prioritize safety of persons and control of the scene over notifications or other administrative or investigative actions.

Shooting At or From Moving Vehicles

The policy should address the issue of shooting at moving vehicles, when that action is authorized and when it is not. It may include a general statement about an officer's duty to avoid creating jeopardy (see *Quezada v. County of Bernalillo* in *Chapter 13: Case Law)*. It should provide any other guidance the agency sees fit on this issue.

In the same section, the policy should address officers shooting *from* moving vehicles. Is this action strictly prohibited? Several recent incidents have involved officers returning fire while pursuing a suspect(s) in a vehicle. Is that appropriate? If so, under what circumstances? What about the use of an armored rescue vehicle or officer/citizen down tactics? If the agency has an air unit, what about using firearms from a helicopter in the air? Is there additional training that is needed? All of these questions, which are relevant to the agency's composition and expected response actions, should be addressed.

Photo by R. Reed

Warning Shots

The policy should address whether warning shots are authorized or prohibited. Most agencies have prohibited warning shots for good reasons such as the liability of using a firearm when deadly force may not be authorized. Additionally, the control, or lack thereof, over where those projectiles ultimately come to rest and the damage or injury they may cause. Regardless of the agency's views, the issue should be clearly addressed for the benefit of officers knowing what actions are permitted or not.

Use of Firearms Against Animals

The use of force policy and/or the firearms policy should include guidance relative to the use of firearms against animals. This section should differentiate between the use of firearms against aggressive animals and euthanasia of injured animals.

In addressing use of firearms against aggressive animals, the policy should outline when use of a firearm is authorized as well as other considerations for the officer such as distance, barriers, and other force options such as pepper spray. Once again, providing clear guidance that is flexible for dynamic situations is key to addressing such issues.

Regarding the euthanasia of injured animals, the policy should further differentiate between wildlife and domesticated animals. Wildlife will likely fall under the jurisdiction of a state wildlife management agency and may require authorization, specific actions, or notifications that an animal has been put down. This policy should conform to those regulations. Additionally, it should outline proper notifications to dispatch and/or supervision that such action is taking place in case of reported shots fired. Finally, it should outline safety considerations such as use of hearing protection, proper background and ensuring other persons in the area will not be injured.

Euthanasia of domestic animals may require additional direction for the officer in policy. Consider that domestic animals are personal property and as such have monetary value. Destroying these animals without authorization of the owner may open the agency to civil liability. Generally, in the case of domesticated animals that are injured, notifying the owner and/or requesting veterinary assistance is preferred before destroying the animal. The agency may consider some sort of written or recorded request from an owner before destroying a domestic animal.

Rangemaster Participation in UOF Policy Changes

Again, it is important that rangemasters attend meetings and committees that discuss use of force. There is a case where the chief of a large agency called a meeting to discuss use of force. The agency rangemaster was invited to the meeting and the rangemaster brought one of his firearms instructors along. During the meeting the agency's lawyer suggested a policy revision to allow officers to use warning shots to gain compliance from non-compliant suspects. The rangemaster and firearms instructor made counter-arguments to the chief that allowing warning shots was a bad idea because officers are responsible for every round fired regardless of the direction and purpose. They pointed out that the agency would be opening itself up to increased liability if warning shots were allowed. The chief agreed and the lawyer conceded. If the rangemaster and instructor had not been at the meeting, the outcome may have been much different and detrimental to the entire agency.

Participation of subject matter experts in critical policy decisions is extremely important. While the chief and executive management are the decision makers, depending on their career movement they may lack the expertise to formulate prudent policy in specific knowledge areas. Even if they have served in instruction positions, if it has been years since they last instructed a topic, the current trainers and experts should be called in for advice as in the above example. This practice will often lead to better overall policies for the agency.

Proposing Policy Changes

The rangemaster may need to propose policy changes from time to time. Oftentimes, they will have their best chance of success by addressing one or more of these topics during their proposal:

- How the change will reduce liability for the agency
- How the change will save the agency money (or at least will not cost additional money)
- How the change will reduce the chance of a claim involving ADA, EEO, OSHA, EPA, etc.*

Rangemasters should compare their policy proposal to the policies of surrounding agencies before presenting the change. However, if the rangemaster is trying to be progressive and proposing something no other agency is doing yet, then the proposal will definitely need to address two or more of the bullet points above. It will be important to demonstrate the benefits, such as those listed, and show that they outweigh any drawbacks.

One of the most important elements of a successful proposal is *timing*. Good timing could mean having the right chain of command in place, or it could be the result of recent events in which change is now being considered. Either way, if the timing isn't right then the likelihood of being successful with a policy change is minimal. In these cases, rangemasters should keep their proposal in a drawer, ready to go in an instant, for when the timing becomes right. Learning how to "read the tea leaves" of when the environment for change is right can be challenging. Part of becoming a good rangemaster will be learning how the executives make decisions, what motivates their decision-making, and when they are likely to be open to new ideas or not.

It can be frustrating for rangemasters when their recommendations are ignored; however, it is important for them to maintain a seat at the table. When they come prepared with data, current best practices supported by national training organizations, and a thorough knowledge of statutory and case law, they can often sway administrators toward needed changes or away from unsound practices.

A recent example is a rangemaster who proposed their agency complete a test and evaluation (T&E) of pistol optical sights. When the chief was asked for approval for the T&E, he instantly and adamantly denied the request. Understanding the chief was a somewhat impulsive decision maker, the rangemaster put the request away and moved on with their daily business. Just over two weeks later, the chief was standing in the doorway of the rangemaster's office asking about the proposal and requesting a presentation to the executive staff. The presentation was provided and testing was approved. Ultimately, the optical sight program was approved and is being implemented. In this case the rangemaster knew he needed to let the chief have time to digest the initial request and that prodding, pushing, or nagging, would have only encouraged the chief to dig into his position. The value of understanding the chain of command and the process they use to come to decisions cannot be overstated.

* Americans with Disabilities Act (ADA), Equal Employment Opportunity (EEO), Occupational Safety and Health Administration (OSHA), and Environmental Protection Agency (EPA).

Chapter 15: INVESTIGATIONS

Rangemasters may have to conduct administrative investigations from time to time. An investigation is initiated if the situation is a possible policy violation or criminal act. Situations that may require an investigation include, but are not limited to, the following:

- Unintentional discharges (injury vs. no injury)
- Seriously injured person during training
- Missing firearms, ammunition, spare parts, etc. (possible theft)
- Unauthorized firearm modifications / parts
- Failure to qualify

First, if the agency's rangemaster is a non-supervisory employee (officer, deputy, or civilian) then they probably have not been trained on conducting administrative investigations. In these situations, the investigation should be conducted by the agency's internal affairs unit or by a supervisory employee.

If the rangemaster is of supervisory rank and has been trained to conduct administrative investigations, then the rangemaster may conduct the investigation. However, it is always good practice to advise the internal affairs unit of the situation to see if they want to conduct the investigation. The process for who and how the investigation is carried out is likely outlined in policy and, in that case, the established process should be followed.

If the allegation is a criminal act or a policy violation that could lead to major discipline or termination, then the internal affairs unit may want the investigation or may be assigned by policy or command decision. If the allegation is a policy violation that will only result in minor discipline, then the internal affairs unit may leave the incident for the rangemaster to investigate.

The rangemaster must understand their role in the investigatory process. Ideally, this is defined in policy. The rangemaster may or may not be the supervisor of the subject of the investigation. That may alter their role depending on the agency protocols for internal investigations. For example, if the rangemaster is not the supervisor of the subject, they may only be the "finder of fact" and not recommend discipline; however, if the rangemaster is the subject officer's supervisor, they may be charged with recommending discipline as part of the process. This will vary from agency to agency.

If the rangemaster is tasked with conducting the investigation, then they follow normal investigative procedures and complete the investigation as soon as practical or by any timeline set forth by the agency. Once the investigation is completed, it is forwarded through the chain-of-command (usually the officer's chain-of-command) to the appropriate review person or committee to determine the outcome.

Investigation of an Unintentional Discharge

One of the most common investigations rangemasters will conduct are unintentional discharges (UD) that occur within the range facility. If an injury resulted from the UD, then the agency's internal affairs unit may conduct the investigation. There may be a parallel criminal investigation conducted by investigators from within the agency or from an outside agency.

As indicated above, conducting an investigation may involve different tasks and roles depending on agency protocol. Below are some typical things the rangemaster will need to determine if they are assigned to conduct an investigation of a UD:

- What are the basic facts surrounding the incident? Where did it occur? Who was present or involved? What happened?
- Was someone injured and, if so, what are the extent of those injuries?
- Which policies, if any, may have been violated?
- What was the cause of the incident?
- Were any training or equipment issues contributing factors to the incident?

If the firearms policy includes adherence to the Firearms Safety Rules, short of a mechanical failure which is rare, there will almost always be a violation of policy where an unintentional discharge occurs. That being said, the rangemaster should be diligent in eliminating any other contributing factors before assigning responsibility to the subject officer. If injuries occur, there are likely other policies and laws that may come into play as described above.

If a UD results in injury and the investigation is completed by the internal affairs unit, the rangemaster should be available for questions the investigators may have regarding training practices, equipment, protocols and so on. After the investigation is complete, it is a good idea for agencies to allow the rangemaster to review the investigation and outcome to determine if changes need to occur in training or equipment to avoid a similar occurrence in the future. This review should be included in policy where possible.

A rangemaster may have to investigate or provide input regarding unintentional discharges or other firearms related incidents.

Even if the cause of the UD seems obviously to be operator error, the investigator should have the involved firearm inspected by an armorer to verify it is functioning correctly. This simply eliminates that as a possible cause and, in the case where there is a problem, may reduce the responsibility of, or exonerate the subject officer.

What if one of the range staff (instructor, armorer, RSO, etc.) is the subject of the investigation? What if a firearms instructor has a UD and the investigation determines the instructor is "at fault"? That has happened on numerous occasions across the nation. Has the instructor lost credibility? Should they be removed from the firearms training staff for a period of time and have to re-establish their credibility?

It is common practice to remove the instructor from the firearms staff, and all training responsibilities, for a period of time (1-3 years) if they are found "at fault" for a policy violation related to firearms, especially if the act was conducted during training in the presence of students.

However, with that being said, each situation should be judged on its own facts and circumstances. There is a case in which an experienced, and highly respected, agency firearm instructor had a UD (no injury) with a student's rifle while conducting an inspection of the rifle at the beginning of a training session. During the investigation, the rangemaster discovered a unique set of circumstances in which it was very probable that the same result would have happened with other experienced firearms instructors. That information was disclosed in the investigation and the rangemaster was able to discuss the circumstances with the reviewing committee. The end result was the firearms instructor received minor discipline for the incident but was able to keep his position as a full-time firearm instructor for the training unit. He had to rebuild his reputation, but that didn't take long due to his long-standing history of being an excellent instructor prior to the event in question.

Investigations should remain confidential to the extent possible. Those with a need to know should be included during the investigation but these reviews should not be the source of gossip within the firearms program.

Theft of Agency Property

Theft may not be a common investigation for rangemasters, but the potential is there, and it has happened. Again, in these cases, the rangemaster should check with the internal affairs unit to see if they want the investigation. However, they may run a parallel criminal investigation as the rangemaster conducts an administrative investigation.

The importance of having a sign out log and doing inventory of sensitive items, such as firearms, spare parts, ammunition, etc., on a regular basis cannot be overstated, as this is how a rangemaster will identify a potential theft situation has occurred. Many times, it can be a case of misplaced items or an instructor forgetting to log out the equipment. In any case, only certain personnel should have access to inventoried sensitive items. This will help minimize the possibility of theft, and if a theft does occur it will narrow down the possible culprits.

There is a case in which a retired sergeant, who served as a rangemaster for a large agency, was hired as a full-time civilian firearms instructor by a smaller agency (150+ officers). The current full-time rangemaster for the agency was an officer. The retired sergeant started advising the officer on some changes they needed to make because there was a lack of control over access to the armory and sensitive items contained within. The armory was controlled by a key card digital access door. The problem was, every officer in the agency had the ability to open the armory door at all hours of the day. In addition, there were sensitive items that were missing and the rangemaster did not know if someone borrowed the items and didn't notify him or if the items were stolen.

The retired sergeant proposed restricting access to the armory to ten select people (several adjunct firearms instructors, several specific supervisors and command staff) so the armory could still be accessed when armory staff was not at work if needed. In addition, once the restricted access was in place, they conducted an initial inventory of all sensitive items, established sign out logs, and advised the ten individuals about the sign out logs. From there they started doing monthly inventories and auditing which of the ten people were accessing the armory and at what times of the day. Now if any sensitive items go missing, it is much easier for them to identify the timeframe in which it went missing and who accessed the armory during that timeframe.

Photo by author

The fact that an item(s) is missing from the armory doesn't mean a theft has occurred. However, with good systems in place, if it does occur it will be easier to identify and resolve.

Unauthorized Modification Violation

An investigation may be initiated if an instructor or armorer determines that an officer made unauthorized modifications to their firearm (agency or personally owned). In addition to the rangemaster or assigned investigator determining that, in fact, there was an unauthorized modification, they will need to determine the intent or knowledge of the subject officer. Is it clear the officer knew this was an unauthorized modification? Was it clearly reviewed in training with new officers? Is this a change in policy that hasn't been discussed in training? Or, is it clearly intentional by the officer's actions?

In the example provided in *Chapter 14: Firearms Policies,* in which the subject officer had received two prior reprimands for such modifications, it may be very clear that they knew this was against policy. In which case, the rangemaster is now investigating an intentional violation of policy.

In a similar incident, an officer had an unauthorized vertical grip attached to a rifle. It was discovered that when the officer arrived at training, he would remove the grip and then reinstall it after training before returning to his patrol duties. These actions indicate an intent to avoid detection of the unauthorized modification by range staff. As such, it should be treated differently than the officer who may have been ignorant of policy…at least on the *first* violation.

Failure to Qualify Investigation

A rangemaster may be called upon to review or investigate several issues surrounding a failure to qualify. They may need to review the process that has been conducted for remedial training prior to disciplinary action or termination, they may need to investigate an integrity violation related to a failure to qualify, or they may be required to investigate an allegation of discriminatory practices regarding qualifications. Each of these will require the rangemaster to complete a thoroughly documented investigation, likely for review by others.

As described in *Chapter 6: Documentation,* failures to qualify and any remediation should be documented. If an officer is facing discipline or termination due to a failure to qualify, the rangemaster should confirm that the qualification process and any remedial efforts were conducted and documented as outlined in policy. It may be warranted for the rangemaster to confirm the diagnosis and solution efforts as part of the review and investigation into the failure to qualify.

If the rangemaster has been notified that an officer has intentionally violated rules during a qualification, they may need to initiate an investigation for an integrity violation. For example, a common qualification rule is that shooters are not allowed to make up rounds in one stage that they were unable to fire during another stage due to time constraints. If an officer is found to be doing so by a range instructor and the rules were clearly made known prior to the qualification, the range instructor should mark the attempt as a failure to qualify and, potentially notify a supervisor or rangemaster of an integrity violation. The rangemaster will then need to investigate to ensure the rules were reviewed or known to the shooter as agency protocol dictates and determine whether the violation was intentional or not. Integrity violations should be taken very seriously. They often can result in significant discipline or termination.

Another area that may require an investigation is if an officer claims that they failed to qualify due to some disparate treatment by range personnel. Several case law examples exist for such claims. See *Chapter 13: Case Law* for additional information. In these cases, it will be important for the rangemaster to interview the instructors, other officers/students that were present, and the officer making the claim to form a clear picture of what has occurred. Once again, the rangemaster must confirm that agency protocol for a failure to qualify and any required remediation was followed as outlined. The investigation should assure that all steps were documented appropriately. It may also be necessary to compare the case being investigated to similar previous failures to qualify and remediation efforts to ensure the one in question was conducted in a similar fashion. Any discrepancies should be thoroughly looked into before further recommendations are made. In the end, it is important to establish that the agency had a standard, that the standard was applied equally (if that is the case), and that the person did or did not meet the standard.

Rangemasters may be assigned to investigate the above issues or others that arise within the firearms or range facility domain. It is important to maintain the integrity of the program and position by conducting fair and objective reviews of these incidents and maintaining as much impartiality as possible. The rangemaster should always be able to seek assistance on specific protocols for internal investigations from those who may conduct them more frequently within the organization to ensure they are done correctly.

Chapter 16: RANGE STAFF SELECTION & DEVELOPMENT

One of the many duties of a rangemaster is to select and develop their firearms training staff. There is an obvious difference between large agencies that can have officers serving as full-time firearms instructors, and medium to small agencies where their firearms instructors serve full-time in other positions and firearms training is a collateral duty.

However, in both cases the rangemaster needs to select the best people possible to serve as firearms instructors, armorers, range safety officers (RSO), etc. For the purposes of this chapter, we will concentrate exclusively on selecting and developing firearms instructors. However, many of the selection and development concepts we outline here can apply to selecting and developing armorers and RSOs as well.

Firearms Instructor Selection Process

When selecting firearms instructors, the rangemaster first has to ask themselves what kind of firearms instructor they want. Do they want non-certified candidates that will be selected and then sent to a firearms instructor (FI) certification course, or do they want a candidate that is already a certified firearms instructor? Maybe the rangemaster allows both types of candidates to apply and those that already have a FI certification receive extra points during the selection process.

One thing is for sure, rangemasters should be looking for candidates that have a passion for teaching and mentoring. If the candidate is primarily looking for a collateral duty that will get them some overtime, an opportunity to escape their current job, or unlimited access to the ammunition locker, then they may not turn out to be a very good instructor due to their ulterior motives.

Rangemasters should also be looking for candidates that have above-average firearms skills. They don't need to be the best shooters in the agency. Being the best shooter does not always translate into being a good instructor. As long as the candidate can perform the skills that they will be asking students to perform, then that is good enough for consideration. If selected, the instructor must be able to step up in front of a group of students (recruits or tenured officers) and perform a live-fire demonstration correctly with better than average marksmanship.

Another requirement consideration is candidate experience. As a FI, they will be instructing other officers and recruits on the proper application of deadly force and tactics, from a position of authority. Having a minimal level of experience to speak from, will help to ensure credibility on the part of the instructor. An individual does not necessarily need to have extensive law enforcement experience to become a new instructor but a couple of years (at the current agency or a previous one) is not unreasonable as a minimum requirement for the position.

Once a rangemaster has identified the qualities and characteristics they are looking for in a firearms instructor, they must design the selection process in a way that will expose the appropriate candidates. However, that is harder than it sounds to accomplish, especially if the agency already has a selection process protocol that the rangemaster must follow.

Ideally, the rangemaster will have some degree of freedom to create the selection process. If so, here are some tasks to consider for selection:

- Candidates should submit a resume and letter of interest. The resume should be a set format or template to ensure each candidate is submitting the specific information the rangemaster is looking for.

- Check the candidate's history - Candidate's personnel file is reviewed for any awards and discipline. The rangemaster should consider removal of candidates from the selection process if they have discipline relating to firearms, poor decision making, negative use of force issues, or integrity within the previous 3 years. Their credibility may come into question if appointed and reflect negatively on the program.

- Test the candidate's knowledge - Eligible candidates should take a written test. The written test should have questions related to firearms policy, use of force policy, firearms instructor manual, and range operations manual (if you have one). The answers should come directly from the documents to avoid any controversy. Test questions should not be open-ended or subjective in manner.

- <u>Test the candidate's skills</u> - Eligible candidates should take a shooting test. The shooting test should not be any standard firearms qualification for reasons discussed in *Chapter 5: Firearms Qualifications*. The rangemaster should design a separate shooting test specific to the selection process.

- <u>Test the candidate's ability to process information and make decisions</u> - Eligible candidates should participate in an oral board with a minimum of three board members. The board members should consist of the rangemaster, and two experienced firearms instructors. A board member can also be someone of higher rank as long as the person has experience as a firearms instructor. The board should not have anyone who does not have the technical knowledge and expertise of being a firearms instructor. The oral board should include scenario-based questions related to firearms training or range operations that forces the candidates to make a decision and justify their actions.

- <u>Test the candidate's ability to teach</u> - Eligible candidates should be asked to teach a portion of an outline in front of observers (usually in front of the oral board panel before or after the oral board portion is completed for simplicity). The candidate is given a firearm, a few magazines, and some inert (dummy) rounds and asked to teach

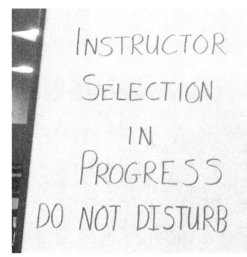

Photo by author

something simple as loading & unloading, reloads, or malfunction clearances. During the presentation the board is watching how the candidate handles the firearm, how well they convey the information, and if the candidate covered everything in the outline, or if they added information not in the lesson.

Each one of these selection tasks should be graded on a point scale. The number of points possible for each task is based on their level of importance to the rangemaster. The total possible points for the selection process should be 100 points for simplicity. If the rangemaster is going to create an eligibility list that will last one to two years, they must ensure only reasonably qualified candidates are added to the list. Accordingly, there should be a cut-off score. For example, the candidates must score 70 or above to make the list.

Some performance during the skills test or teaching portion, such as a safety violation, may be justification for removal from the process. This should be considered ahead of time and added to the process documentation.

If an officer's seniority (time in service) is to be considered for points, then it should only be considered if there is a tie between candidates. Seniority does not always translate into being a good instructor, so it should not be considered during the regular selection process. It should only be an advantage if there is a tie between equally qualified candidates. That is where seniority has its privilege.

Examples of written test questions, shooting test, oral board questions, and teach-back evaluation form may be found in *Appendix F – I*.

Instructor Development

A Rangemaster has to ensure their range staff stays current with their technical knowledge and continues to improve as presenters of information. The initial (basic) firearms instructor course is just the "academy" for firearms instructors. If recruits don't know everything there is to know about policing when they graduate the academy, then we should not expect officers to know everything there is to know about firearms training when they graduate the basic firearms instructor course. Unfortunately, many rangemasters and agency leaders immediately look at new firearms instructors as being "experts". They are not.

Consequently, rangemasters need to ensure their firearms instructors continue to attend training. This should include both operator level firearms training to keep their personal skills up, and advanced instructor development training to continue to grow as instructors. Beware of advertised "instructor training" courses, as many of them are merely advanced shooting courses that include a simple teach back at some point during the course to check the "instructor training" box. That does not constitute true instructor training.

Instructor level classes should be vetted by experienced instructors first. If the course purports to be "instructor level training," the primary focus should be on learning how to teach the particular topic(s) of the course rather than on shooting. There will likely be some shooting during most advanced firearms instructor training; however, the shooters should merely be training aids for other students to learn how to properly coach, run a drill, or conduct the particular training the course focuses on.

Photo by author

NLEFIA Tactical Firearms Instructor Class - Colorado

There are several resources rangemasters can consider to get their staff additional training. The first one is easy and will probably cost nothing in most cases. Training with instructors from surrounding agencies can be highly beneficial for the new FI. New instructors will begin to get to know other instructors in the area and start their networking which we have referred to throughout the book. If a nearby agency is conducting their own firearms training or instructor development training then the rangemaster should contact them and see if they have any open spots available.

The next option is to host training from a reputable organization or training company. By hosting the training, the rangemaster will likely receive a few free slots and there are no travel expenses. If a surrounding agency is hosting the training, that would be the next best option. The rangemaster may not receive free spots but the travel expense will be minimal.

Another option is to check with federal agencies. FLETC, FBI, and DEA will often allow state and local agencies to attend their firearms programs.

Rangemasters should check with state and national firearms instructor associations for additional training opportunities. Washington state (WSLEFIA), Colorado (CLEFIA), Georgia (GALEFI), Massachusetts (MLEFIAA), and Minnesota (MALEFI) have state-level firearms instructor associations. The National Law Enforcement Firearms Instructor Association (NLEFIA), the International Association of Law Enforcement Firearms Instructors (IALEFI), and the International Law Enforcement Educators and Trainers Association (ILEETA) all provide training courses or annual conferences to attend.

The rangemaster should also check out the National Tactical Officers Association (NTOA) and state level tactical officers' associations for training courses or conferences. Sometimes, they offer courses that are beneficial to firearms instructors whether shooting courses or not.

Rangemaster Development

We would be remiss if we did not include the responsibility for the rangemaster to train their replacement(s). As instructors develop within the program, the rangemaster should be identifying those that have an interest in and the skills to take over their position at some point. Developing these individuals into the next generation of rangemasters ensures that the experience gained will not be wasted and that the program will continue to grow and improve. Ideally, the rangemaster should strive to have several instructors trained to be able to run the program or facility. In addition to eventual job succession, there will be people available to run the facility or program when the rangemaster is occupied with other tasks or on vacation. It is also good to have these individuals trained up so the rangemaster can counsel with them about significant decisions or take them to policy revision meetings like the one mentioned in *Chapter 14: Firearms Policies.*

The bottom line is this: firearms programs are only as good as the firearms instructors who develop and conduct them. So, if a rangemaster wants a top-notch firearms program, then their staff has to be top notch also.

Do not be the rangemaster with an over-sized ego, that stagnates their program with rigid dogma, or that builds a self-serving kingdom and refuses to share information with anyone. Instead, be the rangemaster that leads by example, is the consummate student of the craft, who shares ideas and is constantly looking for ways to improve the program. Be the rangemaster that shares what they have learned and the mistakes they have made with the next generation so the program that you have built with your team can carry on.

Chapter 17: FINAL THOUGHTS

In considering how we wanted to wrap up this book, we decided to each write out the personal and professional comments and advice that we want to pass on to the next generation of law enforcement rangemasters. It was an opportunity for us to reflect back on our firearms instructor and rangemaster careers, and tell you the things we wished someone had told us when we started our journey down the rangemaster road.

Each of us has a passion for teaching and a desire to leave the profession better that we received it. We hope this has shown through in the pages of this text. We encourage you to strive to leave the profession and the job of rangemaster better than you received it.

Author: Paul Wood

Wear hearing protection. Of all of the things I have to say, that is probably the most valuable. So many instructors I've met have hearing damage from spending years around ranges with inadequate protection or training in poorly designed facilities. But I'm guessing you already picked up on that from some of the previous chapters, so...I will dispense some additional free advice...which is usually worth what you pay for it.

Just like many others in this business, I was brought up, as a firearms instructor, in a very structured program. There was most definitely a "right way" and "wrong way" to do things. The mentor I had was a good one and taught me lots of things about being an instructor that I still use today. However, it took me a long time, and many mistakes to realize that I didn't want to be an "always - never" instructor. That is, I decided I wanted to be more open minded and flexible in my thinking rather than the instructor that says, "always do this," or "never do that."

Now, there are a few "absolutes" in firearms training. The Firearms Safety Rules are four good examples. But those absolutes should be few and far between. Too often, when we (firearms instructors) see a new technique, training concept, or philosophy, we are very quick to dismiss it, usually with some derogatory name calling thrown in for good measure. We justify our position with statements like, "we've always done it this way," or "the way we do it has always worked." While that may be true, there is no guarantee that the "way we've always done it" has been right, good, or will always work for every shooter in the future.

We need to be more objectively critical in our evaluation and more creative in our application of new ideas. As subject matter experts in our field, we should challenge ourselves when shown a new technique or idea to find a way or a time in which we could use that technique or idea to our advantage. As instructors, it is our job to help new and tenured officers think critically about the options and approaches available to them. Each one will have advantages and disadvantages. Part of our job is to help students see the pros and cons and evaluate the appropriate time and place to employ such techniques.

The same can be said for equipment. We should be able to critically evaluate various types of equipment, and identify strengths and weaknesses. Through that evaluation, we can determine if one outweighs the other and thereby determine if we would recommend using the item or advise against it. These recommendations should always come with the reasons why we have reached that conclusion.

With all that preamble, some ideas are just stupid. Take for example, warning shots. I read an article not long ago advocating of the use of warning shots in law enforcement. This is a terrible idea and doing so would very likely result in significant liability for an agency, injuries to officers or citizens or both. It seems if you are firing a warning shot, you are either (1) using a deadly weapon when you are not authorized to apply deadly force or, (2) *not* applying deadly force when there is, in fact, a deadly threat to the officer or someone else. Both of which are disturbing circumstances and also, quite possibly, illegal and/or unconstitutional. My point here is that having an open mind does not mean you have to let your brain fall out of your head and adopt *every* idea, technique, or piece of equipment that comes along. On the contrary, rangemasters should be very picky about what they approve or don't.

The balance is to consider and endorse ONLY those things that will give your officers, in your community, and working environment, a distinct advantage during a lethal force encounter. What will make them better, avoid having to use deadly force, or allow them to use that force in a far superior way to their attacker? Does the technique, *in fact,* make shooters safer, faster, more accurate, etc.? Do you have the training time available for officers to become proficient? Does it connect to or improve ideas or techniques already taught? All instructors should know *why* any technique, tactic, or equipment

has been integrated and the reason should make sense to the instructors and at least most of the officers…you won't be able to please everyone.

Be a thinker. Be someone who considers new ideas. Don't jump on every bandwagon that comes down the trail but DO avoid being the "always - never" instructor. And whatever you do…trust me on the hearing protection.

Paul Wood

"It's a _drill_ not a scenario…"

Paul began his career in law enforcement in 1990 with the Larimer County Sheriff's Office in northern Colorado, becoming a sworn deputy in 1993. He was selected to be a firearms instructor in 1994 and is certified to teach pistol, revolver, shotgun, and carbine rifle. Paul provided firearms instruction for new deputies, reserve deputies and in-service training while working as a patrol deputy in various assignments.

In 1997, Paul became an officer with Fort Collins Police, an agency of more 230 sworn officers in the same area of Colorado. He became a collateral duty firearms instructor for the agency the same year he was hired. With Fort Collins Police, Paul served as a patrol officer, field training officer, and academy trainer for a variety of topics such as high-risk contacts, building searches, leadership, and procedural law in addition to serving on the firearms team. In 2002 Paul was promoted to sergeant. Since then, he has supervised various patrol squads, a detective squad responsible for gang investigations, fugitive apprehension, and high-risk warrant service, and a property crimes detective unit.

While serving in these assignments, Paul continued teaching firearms. He developed an agency patrol rifle program in 2000 along with two other instructors and implemented rifles agency wide several years later. He became the assistant coordinator of the firearms program in 2000 and the rangemaster in 2006. Paul led the firearms team through the selection of agency issued pistols in 2010 moving away from a history of individually purchased handguns. In 2007, Paul began teaching pistol and rifle instructor development courses. Paul is a certified live-fire shoot house instructor and has provided advanced firearms training for several local SWAT teams and firearms instructor cadres. In 2017, Paul developed a police academy firearms program which was certified by Colorado POST and implemented in 2018. During the implementation of this program, Paul mentored five other instructors to become POST lead academy instructors. He continues to mentor and develop lead instructors today.

As a firearms training sergeant and the rangemaster, Paul has served on 16 use of force review boards to date as a subject matter expert in the use of deadly force. He has also testified as an expert witness concerning firearms operation and use. He has reviewed and written multiple policies on use of force, tactics, investigations, firearms, technology and training. He is also the principal author of many firearms/use-of-force training manuals, curriculum materials, and industry magazine articles. Paul has presented training at conferences for the International Association of Chiefs of Police and the National Sheriffs' Association. In 2019, his agency created the first full-time rangemaster position in its history and Paul was the first to fill the assignment. As the rangemaster he oversees the agencies indoor range, firearms program, and serves on a technical advisory committee for a regional training center shared between Fort Collins and Loveland police departments.

Paul is a Charter Member and Staff Instructor for the National Law Enforcement Firearms Instructor's Association (NLEFIA) and became an NLEFIA instructor in 2015. Since then, he has worked with the NLEFIA staff to develop and teach several instructor certification and development courses. Paul has implemented the philosophies and training practices learned from NLEFIA into his agency's firearms program and enjoys passing on what he has learned to the next generation of firearms instructors.

Author: Benjamin Kurata

I want to give my deepest thanks to my co-authors, Paul Wood and Jason Wuestenberg. Together, they embody the core values of NLEFIA in action – continually striving for better, continually learning from others, and executing with the highest of expectations and standards. It is truly a privilege and a pleasure to train and work with them on projects like this book.

There is a funny saying in law enforcement... "There are two things cops hate...change and the way things are." The truth is law enforcement is an ever-changing career field. And, that holds true for an agency's firearms program.

Show me a department that does NOT make a continuous investment in its firearms instructor staff and I will show you a department that just needs to keep adding zeros to its legal defense budget. It's part of the annual fight that every Rangemaster has to be prepared for - the annual budget. It's ironic how departments that can't find funding to keep their F.I. staff trained up somehow find millions of dollars to settle an excessive use of deadly force civil suit. Your job is to fight and win those tough internal battles that will keep every officer in your agency safer, and better able to make the right decisions when projectiles start flying. Don't expect any certificates of commendation or service medals. An enlightened command staff will know when what you trained just saved officer(s) lives and the department's reputation.

There's an old saying, "Develop your staff, or someone else will." What this pandemic has shown us is how thin the front line of first responders is really stretched. Be a reason why suitable candidates want to work for your agency rather than the one next door. Develop your peer networks because they can literally save your bacon with the battles they have fought and won. And never be so vain to (1) think there's nothing to be improved upon with your firearms training program, and (2) never ask for help!

I am Charter Member 002 at NLEFIA and serve on the Board of Advisors. In this capacity, <u>I am here to support you</u>, the agency Rangemaster, Firearms Instructor, Range Safety Officer, and Armorer. If I can help in any way, you can email me at office@nlefia.org.

Benjamin Kurata

"If it's not written down... it didn't happen!"

Ben began his law enforcement career in 1975 in Michigan. With his background in competitive bullseye and PPC shooting (Google it), Ben started working with his department's problem shooters years before he received his first firearms instructor certification from the National Rifle Association in 1990.

Ben first inherited rangemaster responsibilities when he joined the SigArms Academy as one of four full time firearms instructors in 2000. As collateral duty to designing, delivering, and evaluating Academy courses, Ben was responsible for the Academy's 500+ firearms, including three Armorer's kits that were in constant motion between classes. Along with accountability for the firearms came everything related, including two separate ammunition inventories: conventional ball and hollow point ammo for the outdoor ranges, and non-toxic frangible from the indoor range, the first lead-free range in the United States. All materials related to ensuring successful classes at the Academy or "on the road" fell under Ben's responsibilities. This included firearms, support gear, ammunition, targets, safety gear, cleaning supplies, spare parts, and Sig swag all had to be ordered, inventoried, and accounted for after each course was held.

During his tenure at SigArms, the first rangemaster class was developed and delivered at the Academy between 2001 and 2002. Ben was the lead instructor for two blocks of instruction: low light and force-on-force training. He also assisted and taught any other course module as necessary.

Ben transitioned from SIG in 2004 to co-found the Action Target Academy. The rangemaster course kept it's 5-day format, but was presented by a single instructor, as the Action Target Academy was a mobile training team (MTT).

From 2008 – 2010 Ben was the rangemaster for International Training, Incorporated (ITI) at the Dilley, TX site. ITI's primary clients were U.S. Department of Defense and the U.S. State Department. Ben was responsible for the armory which housed full complement of Sig Sauer P229s, Beretta M9s, Glock 17s, Colt M4s and Kalashnikov automatic rifles or AKs. The only thing that Ben was NOT responsible for at ITI was the separate bunker that contained C4 det cord and kilo blocks.

In 2015, when Jason Wuestenberg started NLEFIA, Ben was Charter Member 002 and recruited several other Charter Members. He was asked, along with several other current and former rangemasters among the NLEFIA staff instructors, to condense the rangemaster class from its previous 5-day format, which included range training, into its current 3-day format, which is all interactive classroom instruction. Ben has taught a variety of classes for

NLEFIA to include being the lead instructor on numerous Rangemaster Instructor Development courses.

It has been Ben's privilege to be a part of Rangemaster from its inception in 2001 through today, and to contribute to this book.

Author: Jason Wuestenberg

The best advice I can give to new and current rangemasters is "network". Make friends with an attorney from the legal unit. Make friends with a supervisor in the finance department. Make friends with an industrial hygienist. Bring these folks out and let them shoot some firearms. Let them see what you do. Take them out for lunch. These people are going to help you when you need help in their respective areas.

Network with rangemasters and lead firearms instructors from surrounding agencies and across your state or region. These networks are great for passing on information or inquiring if they have any information about a particular topic. Invite them to your training. Ask to attend their training to learn. Don't just work in your agency bubble.

Continue to better yourself as a leader and continue to seek out training opportunities for your firearms instructors. The better your instructors are, the better your firearms training programs are. The better your training programs are, the better the agency officers will perform. The better officers perform, the better your reputation will be. I received numerous calls from Sergeants and Lieutenants working the streets thanking me for the great job I was doing with the patrol rifle program because the rifle operators on their scene performed flawlessly. And, I always asked them to tell my Lieutenant what they told me so my Lieutenant would be in the loop on our performance.

A good reputation will get you invited to a seat at the table. What table? The Chief/Sheriff's table...the Policy Review Committee table...the Use of Force Committee table...the Training Needs Committee table...the Uniform/Equipment Committee table...etc., etc., etc. I had a seat at four different tables at my agency for the last six years of my career as a Firearms Sergeant / Rangemaster. The rangemaster position can be one of the most influential positions in the agency, if the rangemaster themself has a good reputation.

The hardest part about being a rangemaster is establishing a standard…a standard on how the firearms instructors will perform…a standard on how training will be conducted…and a standard on how officers attending the training will conduct themselves. And there will likely be people who do not meet your standards. And, as a rangemaster you will have to deal with them accordingly. This often results with some people within your agency resenting you to some degree. That is the cost for establishing and upholding standards. While there were a small number of officers in my agency who didn't like me because of the standards I set, there were far more officers who appreciated the standards I set because it meant their accomplishments had meaning and value. As a rangemaster, you're never going to make everyone happy. You have to find a balance between making decisions that protect the agency and making decisions that benefit the officers. It can be a hard job…but I found it very rewarding and I was proud to retire from that position.

I wish every rangemaster and lead firearms instructor the best of luck. As long as I am the Executive Director for NLEFIA, readers can contact me at director@nlefia.org for any rangemaster-related questions. Go forward and do good things!

"No-go … Bro!"

Jason Wuestenberg

Jason Wuestenberg retired from the Phoenix Police Department (AZ) in 2017 after 22+ years of service. Jason served more than half of his career at the Training Bureau as a full-time firearms and tactics instructor. Jason served at the Firearms Unit for five years and was a certified instructor in every firearms discipline (pistol, revolver, shotgun, carbine, and precision rifle). He became certified as a shoot house instructor and conducted live-fire training in the agency's shoot house for various units and patrol squads. Jason was also certified to conduct video simulation training and testing for judgmental use of force and decision-making skills.

Following that assignment, Jason served nearly 3 years at the Tactical Training Unit and was certified as a reality-based training (RBT) instructor, defensive tactics instructor, OC instructor, impact weapons instructor, less-lethal instructor, Taser instructor, ballistic shield instructor, and driving/PIT instructor. Jason conducted force-on-force training for various patrol tactics such as building searches, active shooter intervention, crisis entry for patrol, counter-ambushes, high risk vehicle stops, and etc.

After promoting to Sergeant, Jason served as a precinct rangemaster at a precinct indoor range while working as a patrol sergeant. After 3 years in patrol, Jason returned to the Training Bureau to serve as one of two Firearms Sergeants / Rangemasters and supervise the agency's patrol rifle program which consisted of 300+ rifle operators. He supervised four full-time instructors and nearly 20 adjunct instructors. Jason established (10-year lease) and managed the agency's two north side ranges located at the Ben Avery Shooting Facility (BASF) in north Phoenix. BASF sits on 1650 acres and is the largest public operated shooting facility in the United States. BASF is operated by the Arizona Game & Fish Department.

During his time as a rangemaster, Jason became a firearms Subject Matter Expert (SME) for Arizona Peace Officer Standards and Training (AZ POST) which allowed Jason to train and certify other officers as AZ POST firearms instructors. Jason also sat on the expert panel for the agency's Use of Force Board and was a member of the Firearms Committee, Tactical Review Committee, and Training Needs Committee. Jason held the rangemaster position for six years before retiring.

Jason has trained police recruits, in-service-personnel, SWAT personnel, military personnel, armed security guards, and civilians in firearms and tactics. He has been a presenter at several national conferences and has conducted firearms instructor development training in Canada and England (UK). In addition to writing numerous training curricula during his career, Jason has also authored several articles for various publications.

Jason started the National Law Enforcement Firearms Instructors Association (NLEFIA) in 2015 to provide advanced training and certification courses to law enforcement firearms instructors across the nation. As of the publication of this book, Jason currently holds the Executive Director position where he oversees 15+ development / certification courses and supervises nearly 20 staff instructors and two office personnel.

GLOSSARY OF FIREARMS TERMS

A

Aberrations: Imperfections in the image of an object as seen through a lens or a system of lenses. They are the result of light rays failing to pass through a single point after refraction. There are six aberrations in general: spherical, chromatic, astigmatic, coma, curvature of field, and distortion.

Abrasion: In the bore of a firearm, abrasion (cutting away of metal) may be caused by improper cleaning methods or by firing ammunition to which abrasive particles have adhered. Not to be confused with erosion, which is a "washing away" of metal in the bore by the action of superheated powder gases.

Accelerator: A device found in some semiautomatic and automatic firearms that, through mechanical advantage or spring energy, transfers kinetic energy from one part of the mechanism to another with the resultant speeding up of the action (e.g., Browning M2 machine gun). Also, a name used for the Remington-Peters "accelerator" cartridge in .30-30 and .30-06 calibers where a sub-caliber bullet (e.g..224) is encased in a sabot which is loaded into either a standard .30-30 or .30-06 caliber case.

Accidental Discharge: The unexpected and/or unintentional discharging of a firearm due to the rare circumstance of a mechanical or other equipment failure outside the user's intent or control which causes a firearm to discharge. *Accidental Discharge* is sometimes used to denote the unintended discharge of a firearm due to user error; however, that circumstance is more properly referred to as a *negligent* or *unintentional* discharge. Also see, "Negligent Discharge" and "Unintentional Discharge".

Accuracy: The term describing a firearm's ability to shoot consistently where aimed. Also used to describe the measure of the dispersion of the group fired with firearms using single projectiles. The optimum would be one hole no larger in diameter than a single projectile hitting at the point-of-aim.

Accurize: To improve the accuracy of a rifle or handgun, normally by mechanical improvements or adjustments.

Achromatic Lens: A lens made up of a combination of glasses having different focal powers so that the image formed is free of unwanted colors.

ACOG: An abbreviation for Advanced Combat Optical Gunsight. The ACOGs are internally adjustable compact telescopic sights with tritium illuminated reticule patterns for use in low light or at night. Many models feature bright daytime reticules using fiber optics which collect ambient light. The ACOGs combine traditional, precise distance marksmanship with close-in aiming speed. Although the ACOGs have many features which are advantageous for military use, they were developed by Trijicon without government funding. Many ACOG's feature the Bindon Aiming Concept or BAC. Also see, "Bindon Aiming Concept".

ACP "Automatic Colt Pistol": A proprietary descriptive abbreviation added after the caliber notation of certain cartridges originally developed for use in Colt designed pistols. E.g., .25 ACP, .32 ACP, .380 ACP, .45 ACP.

Action: The working mechanism of a firearm that is necessary to complete the cycle of operation. Various types exist, including single-shots, multi-barrels, hinge, box lock, revolvers, slide or pump-actions, lever-actions, bolt-actions, semi-automatics and full automatics. Also see "Cycle of Operation".

Action Release: The part of a firearm that unlatches or opens the action to give access to the chamber.

Action Shooting: A generic term for a variety of shooting games usually characterized by extreme speed of fire, relatively powerful handguns, medium to large targets and short to medium ranges. Often called "Combat Shooting." IPSC-style competitions, bowling pin and falling plate matches are all typical of this type of shooting.

Active Safety Device: An active safety device is one which requires the user to actively engage or respond to the device for it to be effective. There are various gradations to these types of devices, from those which are totally dependent on the user, such as trigger locks, to those which act automatically but require a user to respond to the device, such as loaded chamber indicators.

Adjustable Choke: The ability to vary the size of a choke on a shotgun, either by the use of screw in chokes or through the use of an outer ring that when turned opened up or closed down the choke. Also see "Choke".

Adjustable Barrel Band: A band put around a rifle barrel near the fore-end of the stock to hold the barrel in the channel. By turning a screw that goes through the stock fore-end and into a bolt attached to the band, the tension between the barrel and the fore-end can be varied.

AK: Abbreviation for Avtomat Kalashnikov. From the Russian for Automatic Kalashnikov also called the Kalashnikov Avtomat. Most well-known example is the AK47.

Aluminum Case: A cartridge casing made of aluminum. The case that holds the bullet, powder and primer can be made from various metals. Brass is the most common material used in ammunition cases, but aluminum is also popular. Unlike brass cases, aluminum cases cannot be reloaded.

Ammunition: This generally refers to the assembled components of complete cartridges or rounds i.e., a case or shell holding a primer, a charge of propellant (gunpowder) and a projectile (bullets in the case of handguns and rifles, multiple pellets or single slugs in shotguns). The commonly used term "bullet" actually refers to the projectile itself, and not the complete cartridge that is loaded into a firearm. Sometimes called "fixed ammunition" to differentiate from components inserted separately in muzzleloaders. Also see "Cartridge".

Ammunition Lot: A quantity of cartridges made by one manufacturer under uniform conditions from the same materials. Ammunition within a lot is expected to perform in a uniform manner, and is identified by a code number printed on the case and the individual boxes.

Annealing: The process of making brass more malleable by controlled heating followed by rapid cooling. Usually applied to the neck and shoulder area of cases which are to be reformed to a caliber or design different from the original (makes them less prone to cracking during the reforming process). This should not be done to the head of the case, since reducing the strength of this part may result in failures.

Antique Firearm: By federal definition, a firearm manufactured prior to January 1, 1899 or a firearm for which ammunition is not generally available or a firearm incapable of firing fixed ammunition.

Anvil: The internal metallic part of a Boxer primer. The anvil is raised in the center to form a cone, and has three legs which rest against the bottom of the primer pocket, spanning the flash hole. It offers concentrated resistance to the firing pin as it dents the primer, crushing the priming compound between them, which is ignited by the resulting sharp friction. The blow from the firing pin crushes the priming mixture against the anvil causing ignition of the primer and the gun powder in the case.

Aperture Sight: A sight consisting of a post front sight, and a small aperture rear sight (often easily adjustable). When looking through the sights the front sight is lined up in the aperture of the rear peep hole with the top of the front sight either centered in the hole or at the bottom center of the hole (adjustable user preference) and the target appearing just above the front sight post. This type of sight is the most common type of fixed sight used on military and law enforcement rifles. Also see "Peep Sight".

Armorloy: A hard plated firearm finish resembling stainless steel that is more durable and protective than bluing or parkerizing.

Armor Piercing Ammunition: see "Bullet".

Armorer: One that repairs, inspects, assembles, and test firearms usually to ensure conformity to factory specifications. An armorer differs from a gunsmith in that an armorer does not have the knowledge, skill, or authority to make alterations to a firearm beyond keeping it within factory specifications usually by parts replacement.

Armory: A place where arms, ammunition, and equipment are stored. Also, a place where arms are repaired or inspected.

Arsenal: A manufacturing or storage facility for arms and ammunition. Government facility where firearms and ammunition are stored, repaired, or manufactured.

Assault Rifle: A military/law enforcement type firearm designed to provide both semi-automatic or fully-automatic fire. This term is an English translation from the German sturmgewehr, which means "storm rifle". It is distinct from a high-powered rifle because it is chambered for a less powerful cartridge. After the development of smokeless powders in the late 1800s, the high-powered rifle was chambered for a cartridge that could accurately strike a target at 1,000 yards. The problem was, of course, that gun battles generally did not take place at more than 350 yards and that humans cannot see a person at 1,000 yards accurately enough differentiate between enemy soldier and a friendly soldier. It was also learned that most wounds from small arms did not occur from pinpoint, aimed fire. Instead, wounds occurred from throwing as many projectiles (bullets) as possible. Thus, a weapon with a high rate of fire and high ammunition capacity was called for. In 1942, the sturmgewehr was born. The cartridge was far less powerful but smaller and lighter than the one then used in the German Army up to that point. The new cartridge also made it much easier to incorporate an automatic firing system in the gun. In 1947, after the war, the Soviets copied the theory into what is known today as the AK-47 (Avtomat Kalishnikov, 1947). By U.S. Army definition, the term "Assault Rifle" means a selective-fire rifle, chambered for a cartridge of intermediate power. If applied to any semi-automatic only firearm, regardless of its cosmetic similarity to a true assault rifle, the term is incorrect.

ATF: Alcohol, Tobacco, Firearms, and Explosives (Bureau of). Also see "BATFE".

Auto: Slang for an automatic, or more likely a semi-automatic firearm.

Auto Loading: see "Semi-Automatic".

Auto Rim (or Rimless): Used to indicate that the rim of a case is the same diameter (or smaller) as the rest of the case. With this type of case the headspace is kept by the mouth or neck of the case rather than the rim, with the rim existing for extraction purposes only. Designed so that cartridges would stack well in a box or drum magazine.

Automatic: A firearm designed to feed cartridges, fire them, eject their empty cases and repeat this cycle as long as the trigger is depressed and cartridges remain in the feed system. Examples: machine guns, submachine guns, selective-fire rifles, including true assault rifles. This term is also commonly used for semi-automatic pistols [see below] and rifles instead of the term fully automatic. A fully automatic firearm is capable of firing multiple rounds of ammunition with a single pull of the trigger. The speed at which it can fire is known as its cyclic rate. As an example, the Colt M16 rifle used by the armed forces has a cyclic rate of 600 rounds per minute. The possession, use, and transportation of full-automatic firearms has been tightly controlled under federal law since 1934. Also see "NFA 34" and "Cyclic Rate".

Automatic Pistol or Rifle: Generally, refers to self-loading firearms as a class, both fully automatic and semi-automatic. This term is often used to describe what is actually a semi-automatic pistol or rifle, and can lead those who hear it to believe a firearm is a fully automatic weapon when in truth it is not. It is best to refrain from using nonspecific terms such as this to avoid confusion.

Azimuth: As applied to sight corrections, it is the angle to the right or left in the horizontal plane through which the sights are moved to align the bore with the line of sights. Windage corrections are made in azimuth while range corrections are made in elevation.

B

Back Bore: Modification to a shotgun barrel to decrease shot pattern spread. Typically used on "tactical" shotguns or "scatter guns" so the shot stays together in a tight group retaining more mass for longer range.

Backstop: Material that stops projectiles that have passed through a target; it may be of natural material, such as a hillside, or man made for the purpose of stopping projectiles from leaving the designated range area. Also see "Bullet Trap".

Backstrap: That part of the revolver or pistol frame that is exposed at the rear of the grip.

Baffle: (1) A sound barrier used to contain or to reduce, redirect or suppress sound waves created by firearms. (2) A physical barrier used to contain or deflect projectiles into a bullet trap. Baffles may serve both of these purposes and be placed overhead, along the side or at ground level on a range. They may be constructed of a variety of materials

Ballistic Coefficient: A measure of the aerodynamic efficiency of the projectile. In reloading the bullet shape class. Also, the ratio of the sectional density of a bullet to its coefficient of form. The ballistic co-efficient represents the projectile's ability to overcome air resistance in flight. The ballistic co-efficient of a projectile determines its ability to resist air drag, maintain velocity and energy as it flies, and shoot flat. The higher the co-efficient more aerodynamic the projectile, reducing its air resistance and making it less susceptible to wind deflection, velocity degradation or energy loss. The ballistic co-efficient of a projectile must be known in order to calculate accurate trajectories.

Ball And Dummy: A training exercise wherein the shooter makes an effort to employ all the control factors for firing a good shot. The ammunition inserted into the firearm by the coach is a random selection of live or inert, also known as "dummy", ammunition. This training aids the shooter in overcoming reaction to the recoil and loud noise of firing, preventing uncontrolled reflexes from disturbing the hold, and perfecting sight alignment.

Ball Powder: This is a trade name for a double-base smokeless powder developed by Olin Industries. The grains have a spherical, or flattened spherical, shape.

Ballistics: (1) The science which studies the behavior of projectiles in motion. Interior ballistics deals with the propulsion and motion of a projectile within a gun or firing device. Exterior ballistics is concerned with the motion of the projectile while in flight, and includes the study of the trajectory, or curved flight path, of the projectile. Terminal ballistics is concerned with the phenomena occurring at the termination of the projectile's flight; such termination may result from impact on a solid target or explosion of the projectile. (2) In criminology, the term ballistics is applied to the identification of the weapon from which a projectile was fired. Microscopic imperfections in a gun barrel make characteristic scratches and grooves on projectiles fired through it.

- Sight Height and Factory Ballistic Data: Because everyone may have a different far-zero setting and their sights may be mounted at various heights above the barrel, the most consistent way to tabulate the trajectory of a projectile is to measure the amount of drop from the line of departure (also see "Line of Departure") at various ranges (true drop). In practice, the true drop is of little use to the shooter since he or she is concerned with the drop from the line of sight. As a result, ballistics tables generally assume a certain far-zero setting and sight height and then tabulate the apparent drop from the line of sight. You can determine the assumed far-zero setting because the bullet drop will be zero at that range.

- Wound Ballistics: The medical and technical study of wounds created by ballistic projectiles, typically bullets and shot as fired from firearms. Wound Ballistics includes the evaluation of literature in the field of forensic & wound ballistics, as well as encouraging and promoting new work in wound ballistics. The leading agency for scientific study of Wound Ballistics is the International Wound Ballistics Association or IWBA

Barrel: A cylindrical tube of varying length, attached to a loading and firing mechanism, that contains and directs the pressure from a propellant (burning gunpowder) to the rear of a bullet, which is then forced down the barrel's interior length (bore), which accelerates, stabilizes, and directs the projectile to an intended target. Because of the seal created between the projectile and the surface of the barrel, gas produced by the burning gunpowder remains trapped behind the bullet once it leaves the cartridge case. As a result, the bullet continues to accelerate until it exits the firearm at the muzzle. Thus, the longer the barrel (generally speaking), the higher the velocity achieved by the projectile.

Barrel Band: A metal band, either fixed or adjustable, around the fore-end of a gun that holds the barrel to the stock.

Barrel Bushing: A firearm component designed to support the muzzle end of the barrel on some semi-automatic pistols. The bushing can also be subjected to customization intended to increase the accuracy of the weapon.

Barrel Erosion / Barrel Wear: The gradual wearing away of the rifling lands immediately ahead of the chamber throat, resulting in accuracy loss. Metal surface is burned away by the intensely concentrated powder flame at this point.

Barrel Fitting: A term usually applied to the fitting of a rifled and chambered barrel to an action so that the relation between the chamber and bolt face leaves the proper amount of headspace.

Barrel Length: The distance from the front of the chamber to the muzzle. Rifle and shotgun barrel length is strictly regulated by law in the US. This measurement does not include accessories or barrel extensions like flash suppressors or muzzle brakes. The barrel length of a revolver is the distance from the muzzle to the breech end immediately in front of the cylinder.

Barrel Liner: A thin steel tube usually permanently inserted into the barrel to either change the caliber, restore the firearm, or to make the firearm more functional when the barrel is formed from softer material. Also called a sleeve.

Barrel Lock: (also "Bore Lock" and "Barrel Insert") A rod or cable that is inserted through muzzle, through the barrel, and out the breech of a firearm where the end of the rod is locked or ends of the cable are locked together, rendering the firearm incapable of being loaded or fired. Also see "Chamber Insert" and "Trigger Lock".

Barrel Lug: A general term for any projection extending at right angles to the barrel.

Barrel Pitting: A term for corrosive damage to the bore of a barrel usually caused by the use of ammunition assembled with a primer that contains corrosive compounds (all early primers). If a firearm was discharged using this type of cartridge the corrosive compound would coat the bore and slowly disintegrate the metal of the bore causing a series of "pits".

Barrel Rib: Additional structure along the top of the barrel that allows for quicker alignment of the muzzle with the target, stiffens the barrel, and adds weight to improve the balance of the firearm (also see "Ventilated Barrel Rib").

Barrel Throat: (see "Throat").

Barrel Time: The interval between the time the bullet starts to leave its seat until it reaches the muzzle. This is significant because is it linked to recoil time, which affects the point-of-impact.

Barrel Whip: The movement of the barrel as the projectile travels through it.

Barricade: A structure on the range that is used as part of a course of fire. Barricades are usually wooden in construction and are used to simulate cover.

Baseline: An imaginary line from the muzzle to the target from which other measurements are taken (usually applied to long gun shooting for zeroing, and trajectory calculations.)

BATFE: Bureau of Alcohol, Tobacco, Firearms, and Explosives (aka ATF): A division of the Treasury Department that has the authority to regulate many aspects of the firearm market. BATFE is responsible for licensing firearms dealers, controlling the importation of firearms, and tracking firearm production. BATFE also works with law enforcement agencies to track firearms used in crimes. However, the jurisdiction of BATFE does not allow it to set safety standards or regulate in any way the production of domestic firearms.

Battery: The term battery refers to the position of readiness of a firearm for firing where all the components are in the proper position. A semi-automatic is said to be "out of battery" when the slide or bolt is retracted enough to prevent the firing pin from striking the primer (thus preventing the gun from firing). Failure to return to battery is a fairly common mode of failure for semi-automatics. Common causes for semi-automatics failing to return to battery during normal operation include a loose, insufficient grip on a semi-automatic pistol, under lubrication and weak springs. This problem is usually easily fixed by a competent armorer.

Battery Cup: A type of primer used in shotshells which makes use of an outside cup to support it in the case.

Bayonet Lug: A fitting on a firearm to which a bayonet is attached. Under the so called "Assault Weapons Ban", a bayonet lug can no longer be manufactured or mounted onto a civilian or sporting firearm.

BB: A spherical pellet of plated steel of .175-inch diameter for use in air guns. Also, a spherical pellet of lead or steel of .180-inch diameter for use in shotguns. Similar pellets are used to test the density of ballistic gelatin prior to firing a projectile into it.

Bead Sights: A round sight normally used at the muzzle end of a shotgun. Also, the front sight on some older rifles, in which the sight is viewed as a round ball or bead on a narrow post. Bead sights usually consist of a post or bead front sight mounted on a barrel length rib running along the top of the barrel. There is no rear sight to speak of. Used primarily on shotguns, bead sights offer very quick target acquisition by lining the rib up with the bead and the target and are favored by many shotgunners. However, they lack the preciseness of small peep or blade sights and so are used almost exclusively for close range shotgun applications.

Beavertail: A fore-end design with generous proportions (wider than normal) that allows a shooter to grasp the wood without touching the barrel. Also used to describe the upper extension of the backstrap on various pistol designs, intended to protect the shooter from hammer pinch or the slide cutting the web of the shooter's hand.

Bedding: (Also "Bedding Block") In rifles that have one-piece stocks, the point of attachment of the receiver and the stock. Also refers to the fit or fitting of the metal parts of the barrel and receiver with the stock. The barrel lays in and is attached to the bedding.

Bell: To open or flair the mouth of a case slightly in order to seat a bullet more easily. Also used in reference to a rifle barrel which is worn at the muzzle (as in "a belled muzzle").

Belt: The narrow band around the rear section of some cartridge cases, forward of the extractor groove that is intended to strengthen the case. Usually associated with magnum caliber cartridges.

Belt Feed: A reference to an ammunition feeding mechanism used by machine guns. Cartridges are linked together in a flexible belt that may be made of canvas or metal. The machine gun draws the ammunition through the receiver in a continuous cycle (sometimes destroying the belt as it goes) and will continue to fire as long as the trigger is held down and ammunition remains on the belt (some belts can be added to as the weapon is firing).

Belted Cartridge: A band which is formed into the head of some cases (magnum type) to strengthen the case and headspace the cartridge. The .300 Weatherby Magnum a belted cartridge

Benchrest: A term used to indicate a rest of some type that a firearm is placed on to steady the arm for precision shooting. A benchrest is typically used to steady scoped rifle when performing a "Sight-In" so as to not introduce variables cause by the movement of the shooter. Less commonly the term can refer to a type of competitive shooting that emphasizes extreme accuracy.

Berdan Primer: Invented by Colonel Hiram Berdan of the U.S. Army in the 19th c., this is the most common type of center-fire primer manufactured outside the U.S. It makes use of an anvil formed in the case itself. Cases that are Berdan Primed typically can NOT be easily reloaded, unlike American style Boxer Primed cartridges (also see "Boxer Primer").

Berm: An embankment used for restricting projectiles to a given area or as a dividing wall between ranges. Also backstop, baffle.

Bindon Aiming Concept: An advanced, automatic zooming, two eye aiming method used in modern ACOG or Advanced Combat Optical Gunsights. Using the two-eye aiming method, when the rifle is being moved, the perceived image is unmagnified, permitting extremely rapid target acquisition. As soon as the rifle movement is stopped and the shooter is close to the proper aim on target, the targeted image "zooms" into magnification, permitting greater accuracy with higher hit ratios (also see "ACOG"). A brief explanation of Bindon Aiming Concept follows: Human vision is based upon a binocular (two eyes) presentation of visual evidence to the brain. The word binocular literally means using both eyes at the same time. We most often associate this word with binocular instruments such as field glasses or a binocular microscope. These instruments specifically strive to present the object to be viewed the same way to both eyes.

Vision research material was examined for its assistance to understand the optically aided firearm aiming process. Three major types of optical enhancement were compared. There are strong customer preferences in reticule designs, some simple reticules enhance the speed of target acquisition, others allow for greater precision in a given time limit. The simple substitution of a bright red dot for the usual cross-hairs makes it very easy to keep both eyes open. Just as in the Single point or Armson O.E.G. sighting, the brain merges the two images. During dynamic movement, the scene through the telescope blurs because the image moves more rapidly due to magnification. The one eye sees the bright dot against the blurred target scene, so the brain picks the scene from the unaided eye. The shooter swings the firearm towards the target while perceiving the dot indicating where the weapon is pointed. As soon as the firearm begins to become steady in the target area, the brain switches to the magnified view.

Bipod: A stabilizing device used on rifles. A bipod consists of two legs set in an "A" frame configuration, attached to the fore-end stock or front end of the barrel. The legs are set on a solid surface to help keep the rifle steady for a more accurate shot. Most firearms experts consider the fore-end stock as the best mounting location for a bipod.

Birdshot: Many small pellets contained in a shotshell intended for hunting small game, birds or shooting clay targets. Birdshot comes in a variety of sizes (smaller and lighter than buckshot). The large number of shot in the shotshell spread out when fired, making it easier to hit a small or moving target. The size of birdshot is given as a number or letter, with the larger number the smaller the shot size. The size designation was originally based upon the size of a mesh through which the shot would pass. The finest size generally used is #9 which is approximately .08" in diameter and the largest common size is #2 which is approximately .15" in diameter. Also see "Shot".

Blackout: Condition where the exit pupil of a scope is smaller than the pupil of the shooter, which results in the target image forming on only part of the eye, with a surrounding black ring. This makes it more difficult to focus on the target.

Blade Sights: Blade sights (also called rifle sights) consist of a post or blade front sight and a notched rear sight. When looking through the sights, the front sight is lined up in the notch of the rear sight, with the tops even and the target appearing just above the composite sight picture. As with all fixed sights the focus should be on the front sight, causing the rear sight and the target to be out of focus. This type of sight is the most common type of fixed sight used on handguns and civilian rifles.

Blank Cartridge (or "Blank"): A round designed to produce noise that is loaded with black powder or a special smokeless powder but lacking a projectile. Used mainly in starting races, theatrical productions, troop exercises and in training dogs. Blank rounds can produce considerable energy and propel expanding gases and particles out of the barrel with considerable force causing injury or damage. Blank cartridges can also produce sound pressure levels nearing those of live ammunition requiring the use of appropriate hearing protection.

Blind Box Magazine: An integral magazine with a permanently closed bottom.

Blow-Back (or Blow-Forward): A system of a self-loading firearm where the bolt, slide or barrel is not locked into battery, but allowed to move by direct gas pressure on the cartridge case head as soon as the cartridge is fired so as to shorten the time (or lessen the force) needed to cycle the action. The major disadvantage of this system is case deformation, a premature loss of pressure, and corresponding loss of velocity of the projectile.

Blown Primer: Malfunction condition where the primer has fallen completely out of its pocket when the cartridge is extracted after firing.

Bluing: One of the most, if not the most, common firearms finishes used. Bluing is essentially a oxidation (rust) process that is controlled by applying oil which mixes with the nitrates used in the process. The process leaves a dark blue or black finish on the steel and iron parts of a firearm. Bluing is a comparatively low-cost process done to give additional protection to the metal and make it harder for traditional rust to form, however there are more durable and protective (and expensive) finishes available.

Bolt: Used in many types of firearms, the bolt is a metal cylinder or block that drives the cartridge into the chamber of a firearm, closes and locks the breech (by rotation, engaging in lugs, tilting, etc.), and usually contains the firing pin (or striker) and extractor. The bolt can be operated manually, by excess gas and pressure from the barrel, by recoil or electrically by some type of drive mechanism.

Bolt Action: Chamber loading and breech closure of a firearm by means of a manually operated bolt that moves in front to back motion. May also include a up and down motion to rotate and lock the bolt in the forward position or the bolt may lock with just a forward motion by means of cam to provide bolt rotation for lock up at the forward end of the stroke.

Bolt-a-ron: A synthetic polymer (hard plastic) that is used to construct holsters and other firearms accessories.

Bolt Carrier: A component that supports the bolt in its movement and may contain the means of rotating or otherwise locking the bolt.

Bolt Face: The forward end of the bolt which supports the base of the cartridge.

Bolt Handle: Used on bolt action firearms to provide a place to grasp and manually operate the bolt of the firearm.

Bolt Release: A lever or catch on a bolt action firearm that, when depressed, allows the bolt to be removed from the firearm for cleaning and inspection. The trigger mechanism is also used as the bolt release on some bolt action firearms instead of a separate lever.

Bore: The interior of a firearm's barrel, said by some to include the chamber, but by others, excluding the chamber. Also, the diameter of the barrel as measured across the lands of a rifled barrel.

Bore Diameter: Diameter of the bore. In rifled firearms the bore diameter is the original dimension of the barrel before the rifling grooves are cut or swayed. Bore diameter is expressed in caliber (inches and/or millimeters) or gauge.

Bore Sight (or Bore Sighting): Technique for aligning sights or an optical scope with the axis of the bore. Done by looking through or shining a light or laser down the bore of a firearm and manually aligning the sights or the scope cross hairs to the same place the bore is pointing. May be part of the sight alignment procedure. When sighting in, a scope tool such as a collimator can be used.

Box Magazine: (see "Magazine").

Boxer Primer: Type of ammunition ignition or priming device invented by the British Colonel Boxer in the 19th century, this is the most common type of center-fire primer used in the U.S. today. Boxer Primers have a 3-legged internal anvil, permitting the use of a single, central flash hole in the case head. Such cases can be conveniently deprimed by means of the decapping pin in standard reloading dies. This type of primer is used in most American made rifle and pistol ammunition. Boxer Primed cartridges are easy to reload (also see "Berdan Primer").

Brass: When talking about firearms it is a synonym for the expended or unloaded metallic cartridge case, stemming from the fact that most cartridge cases are made of brass (alloy of copper and zinc). Also see "Cartridge".

Break (or Break Open) Action: (see "Hinge Action").

Break In: A barrel wear-in process for the initial use of a new rifle barrel, by alternately firing and cleaning, a progressively larger number of shots, until a certain number has been reached. This process must be completed before load development for the rifle is started, and/or before the rifle is sighted in for a specific load.

Breech: The rear part of a gun barrel; the entrance to the chamber through which the cartridge is inserted (also may be called the throat). Also used by some to indicate all essential working parts of a gun.

Breech Block (Breechblock): The part of the action that fits securely against the cartridge keeping it snug in the breech and locks the action to allow maximum efficiency and safety during firing.

Breech Bolt: The locking and cartridge head support mechanism of firearms that operate in line with the axis of the bore.

Breech Face: That part of the breechblock or breech bolt against which the head of the cartridge case or shotshell rests during firing.

Breech Loader: A gun which loads through the breech end of the barrel. The advantages to being a breechloader include being able to load more quickly and with less effort, a greater rate of fire, and being able to easily load the gun from awkward positions, or while mounted. Until the invention of the metallic cartridge, most breechloaders were impractical. A major problem they had was severe gas leakage.

Bridge Mount: A bridge-type scope mount is one that spans the loading port in the receiver of a bolt-action rifle.

Buckshot: A varying number of medium sized pellets contained in a shotshell intended for hunting medium size game. Buckshot comes in a variety of sizes (larger and heavier than birdshot). The smallest buckshot (number 4) is about .25 caliber; the largest (000) is about .36 caliber.

Buffer: A resilient component in a self-loading firearm that is designed to be struck at the end of a bolt or slide's rearward movement and to adsorb part of the force that would otherwise be transmitted directly to the frame or stock of the firearm. Designed to reduce wear and smooth and control the reload cycle. May also refer to the compound loaded into a shotshell along with the shot to cushion and protect the shot from deforming during discharge.

Bull Barrel: A heavier, thicker than normal barrel with little or no taper that is intended to increase stability and reduce muzzle rise and felt recoil in precision-shooting firearms.

Bullet: The projectile expelled from the cartridge of a firearm. It is not a synonymous term with cartridge (also see "Cartridge"). Traditionally bullets are made of solid lead, or lead with a jacket of harder metal, although they can be made of other materials, in many different shapes (round-nosed, flat-nosed, hollow-pointed, etc.), weights and constructions, each designed to have specific characteristics in flight, on impact with the target, and after penetrating the target. The following is a listing of common terms used to describe bullets:

- Armor Piercing: By federal definition, "a projectile or projectile core which may be used in a small arm and which is constructed entirely (excluding the presence of traces of other substances) from one or a combination of tungsten alloys, steel, iron, brass, bronze, beryllium copper, or depleted uranium". A projectile specifically designed to penetrate hardened, or armor-plated targets such as tanks, trucks, and other vehicles.
- Boattail: A bullet design having a tapered base or truncated conical base design, which raises the ballistic coefficient factor by reducing the aerodynamic drag, providing greater stability at subsonic velocities. Drag partly comes from the effects of cavitation (turbulence) and the progressive reduction of the diameter toward the rear of the bullet allows the air to fill in the void.
- Bonded Hollow Point (BHP): Same as the JHP, but the metal jacket has been chemically bonded to the lead core to ensure that the jacket cannot separate from it on impact. This is desirable for when a bullet may need to penetrate glass or thin metal and still remain intact.

- Cannelure: A groove around the circumference of a jacketed bullet into which the mouth of the cartridge case is crimped.
- Frangible: Bullets or other projectiles designed to easily break apart upon impact, in order to minimize ricochet and splatter, thus reducing the chance of a secondary target impact.
- Full Metal Jacket (FMJ): Sometimes known as "hardball", a bullet completely enclosed (except for the base) in a hard metal jacket (usually an alloy of copper, sometimes mild-steel). Fully jacketed bullets have round or pointed noses, and tend to expand less and penetrate better than bullets with an exposed nose.
- Head Height: The height of a bullet from its shoulder to the tip of its point.
- Hollow Point (HP): A type of bullet with a hollow cavity formed into its nose, designed to expand on impact with the target.
- Jacket: An envelope (usually of a harder material than the core, like copper) wrapping and enclosing the lead core of a bullet. The jacket prevents the lead core from melting and leaving large deposits of lead fouling in the bore. Fully jacketed and semi-jacketed bullets have different performance characteristics from simple lead bullets.
- Jacketed Flat Point (JFP): Same as the FMJ, however instead of the nose of the bullet being rounded or pointed, it ends in a flat plate.
- Jacketed Hollow Point (JHP): A bullet constructed of a soft lead core enclosed in a hard metal jacket (usually an alloy of copper), except that a portion of the bullet nose is left exposed and hollowed out. On the force of impact, the hollow cavity forces the bullet nose to open up and expand more than a soft nose bullet does, resulting in less penetration but greater damage to the target due to the larger diameter of the now expanded bullet.
- Jacketed Pre-Fragmented (JPF): A bullet that consists of a metal jacket as in the JHP, but instead of the core being solid lead, it consists of a number of separate projectiles, such as lead shot (the most common), metal disks, or polymer, (or any combination) compressed into the jacket. The tip of the bullet usually has a polymer "cap" with a round-nose profile to ensure reliable feeding. JPF bullets are usually much lighter than normal bullets, and travel at extreme velocities.

- Jacketed Soft Point (JSP): A bullet constructed of a soft lead core enclosed in a hard metal jacket (usually an alloy of copper), but with the bullet tip left exposed. On the force of impact, this exposed, soft lead tip of the bullet is forced to open up and expand, resulting in less penetration but greater damage due to the larger diameter of the now expanded bullet. Jacketed Soft Points are commonly used for hunting large game.
- Jacketed Truncated Cone (JTC): Very similar to the JFP, but the sides of the bullet are straight and end in a flat plate, as opposed to the JFP where the sides are more rounded. The JTC bullet has the profile of a cone with a flat plate at the tip instead of a point.
- Lead Hollow Point (LHP): Same as the JHP, but the bullet is constructed completely of lead and has no jacket.
- Lead Round Nose (LRN): A bullet that is constructed completely of lead, with no metal jacket and a rounded nose.
- Lead Truncated Cone (LTC): Same as JTC, however the bullet is constructed completely of lead and has no metal jacket.
- Meplat: The flat nose of a flat nosed bullet.
- Partition Bullet: A jacketed bullet with its core divided into two chambers. The first chamber is designed to expand. The rear chamber is held together to provide better penetration.
- Plated Hollow Point (PHP): Same as the JHP, however, instead of the lead core being enclosed by a metal jacket, it is instead coated with a thin layer of chemically deposited metal.
- Plated Round Nose (PRN): Same as LRN, however, instead of the lead core being enclosed by a metal jacket, it is instead coated with a thin layer of chemically deposited metal.
- Round Nose, Flat Tip (RNFT): Same as LRN, except that the very end of the tip is cut to present a small flat cross section.
- Rubber Bullet: A specialty bullet generally fired from a shotgun or a firearm specially designed to shoot rubber bullets. Intended to inflict less-lethal damage to a target. Used for crowd control purposes in a riot or for other volatile situations where deadly force is inappropriate.
- Sabot: A lightweight carrier surrounding a heavier projectile of reduced caliber, allowing a firearm to shoot ammunition for which it is not chambered. For example, a hunter could use his .30-30 deer rifle to shoot small game with high velocity .22 center-fire bullets.

- Semi Jacketed Hollow Point (SJHP): Same as the JHP, except the jacket does not completely cover the lead core. Usually a small section (about 2mm or 1/8") at the top of the bullet is left exposed. This is an older design, but is still common in the .38 special, .357 Magnum and .44 Magnum calibers.
- Semi Wad Cutter (SWC): Very similar to the LTC, however the base of the bullet has a slight ridge or shoulder. Thus, the diameter of the base of the cone is slightly smaller than the base of the bullet itself. This causes the bullet to cut neater holes in paper targets, instead of ripping the paper.
- Slug: A slang term synonymous with "bullet". May also be descriptive of a slug used in a shotgun.
- Soft point: A type of jacketed bullet in which the soft lead core is exposed at the tip, so that upon impact with the target the bullet deforms to cause more damage. Most bullets designed for hunting are soft points.
- Spire Point: A bullet with a cone-shaped nose.
- Spitzer: A type of bullet having a sharply pointed nose.
- Teflon: Trade name for a synthetic sometimes used to coat hard bullets to protect the rifling. Other synthetics, nylon for instance, have also been used as bullet coatings. None of these soft coatings has any effect on lethality.
- Total Metal Jacket (TMJ): Same as the FMJ, however, unlike the FMJ where the metal jacket encloses the whole bullet except the base, the TMJ bullet's base is also enclosed by the jacket.
- Tracer: A bullet used in military applications that contains a compound in the tip of the bullet that burns as the bullet passes through the air. Typically, tracer ammunition is used with machine guns and is set to fire every fifth round to indicate the point-of-impact.
- Wad Cutter (WC): A bullet with no extension past the mouth of the case and a completely flat face. Only usable in some types of firearms and not as aerodynamically stable as other bullets. Used for target shooting only, the flat face cuts very neat round holes in paper targets. Especially favored in light, target loads.

Bullet Trap: Any barrier, natural or man-made, intended to deflect or capture fired bullets and contain them within a specific area (range). Bullet impact areas at firing ranges can be constructed of dirt, sand, compressed or granulated rubber, steel, or virtually any other material that will capture bullets and prevent them from exiting the training area.

Bullpup: A bullpup configured firearm is one where the receiver is behind the trigger group as far back in the stock as possible. This design allows for a fairly long barrel to be fit into a firearm with a fairly short overall length. The major advantage of this configuration is maneuverability and concealment. The major disadvantage is that spent brass is usually ejected quite close to the face of the shooter.

Burn Rate (also Burning Rate): A term which is used to describe the rapidity with which a given powder will burn. The term itself is a relative one based on a comparison with other powders.

Burr Hammer: An exposed hammer having a somewhat circular, serrated projection at the top to provide a gripping surface for cocking. The large Mauser military pistol, the Browning Model 1935, and the Colt Commander have burr hammers. The circular burr or projection usually has a hole drilled through it.

Butt: On long guns the butt is the shaped end of the buttstock that is placed against the shoulder. On handguns the butt is the rear lower portion of the frame onto which the grip is attached.

Butt Pad: (see "Recoil Pad").

Butt Plate: A protective plate attached to the rear of the buttstock of long guns. May be used for cosmetic reasons, for protection of the stock, for cushioning, or for aiding in the duplication of rifle position. Can be made of metal, rubber, plastic or other materials that protects and reinforces the butt of the firearm stock.

Buttstock: That portion of the stock on a long gun located behind the receiver and usually including a shaped area (called the "butt") for placing the stock against the shoulder for support while shooting or to rest the firearm on when placing it in a rack.

C

Caliber: The nominal diameter of a projectile of a rifled firearm (not a shotgun) or the diameter between lands in a rifled barrel. In the United States, usually expressed in hundreds of an inch; in Great Britain in thousandths of an inch; in Europe and elsewhere in millimeters. Not all calibers indicate true bore diameter. For example, the .44 Magnum is not .44 inches in diameter; it is .429 inches in diameter. A .38 Special is not .38 inches; it is .357 inches. The .357 Magnum, though, is truly .357 inches in diameter. A 9mm is .355 inches. Some calibers are also confusing. A .45 Long Colt is a revolver cartridge. A .45 ACP (Automatic Colt Pistol) is an automatic cartridge. They are not interchangeable.

Caliper: An instrument for measuring diameters. It is made in the form of a scaled rule with sliding jaws, or in the form of a compass.

Cam: A rotating or sliding piece in a mechanical linkage used especially in transforming rotary motion into linear motion or vice versa. An example is the cam pin in an AR-15 bolt assembly.

Capacity: Number of cartridges a firearm will hold.

Carbine: In common usage, a rifle with a relatively short barrel (generally one with a barrel 22 inches in length or shorter) originally designed for use from horseback. An alternative origin for the term is a rifle designed to fire straight cased, lower velocity cartridges. The primary role of the carbine is to provide a lighter, defensive long gun with easy maneuverability and reduced weight. Many so called "assault rifles" might be more properly classed as a "carbine". Any rifle or carbine with a barrel less than 16 inches long is a "short barreled rifle" (SBR) must be registered with the Bureau of Alcohol, Tobacco, Firearms, and Explosives. Also, this term is used to refer specifically to the U.S. Carbine, Caliber .30 M1, which was adopted by the U.S. military in 1941, and which saw extensive use in World War 2, the Korean War, and Vietnam.

Carbon Fiber: Exceptionally strong and lightweight synthetic fiber made especially by carbonizing acrylic fiber at high temperatures.

Carrying Handle: A handle integral to the receiver, or attached to the center, of a long gun designed to allow for a firm balanced grip on the firearm for extended carry (used mostly on military rifles).

Cartridge: A single, complete round of ammunition. Commonly misnamed "bullet", it consists of four parts. The cartridge components are:

(1) The Case: Also called "brass", the case is a tube shaped, closed bottom, container usually made of brass (plain or nickel plated to reduce corrosion), but cases have also been made of aluminum, steel, tin, or plastic (aluminum and plastic cases cannot be reloaded). The case can be shaped with either straight sides or in a "necked" configuration so as to hold a smaller diameter bullet with a large quantity of powder behind it. The case also has a formed bottom referred to as the "rim" to aid in extraction of the spent case. As the gunpowder burns, the case expands to seal against the side of the chamber, forcing the expansion of gas down the barrel. The case is the foundation of the cartridge which contains the remaining basic components, the powder, primer and bullet.

(2) The Powder: A chemical compound which either explodes (black powder) or burns rapidly (smokeless powder), producing a mass of gas which expands, propelling the bullet down the barrel. Most modern firearms use smokeless powder because it burns slower and cleaner, and it is capable of driving bullets to much higher velocities than black powder.

(3) The Primer: A small amount of explosive, located at the rear end of the case. Most modern primers consists of a cup, a charge of explosive and an anvil that is pressed into the center of the rear of the case (center-fire). Upon being struck by the firing pin, the anvil is crushed into cup, igniting the explosive. This creates a burst of extremely hot embers that are propelled through a flash hole in the bottom of the case. The embers ignite the powder within the case and combustion occurs. The only notable exception to the center (rear) location of the primer is modern .22 ammunition that contains the primer compound in the rim of the case (rim-fire) and is ignited by striking the rim. Rim-fire primers were more common at the end of the nineteenth and the beginning of the twentieth centuries than they are today.

(4) The Bullet: Too often in news stories, writers confuse a bullet with the entire cartridge. Bullets are generally not explosive. A bullet is usually a piece of lead, commonly jacketed with copper or a copper compound to reduce lead fouling in the barrel. The bullet is seated in the mouth of the case on top of the powder charge. Upon powder combustion, the bullet is propelled out of the case, down the barrel of the firearm (spinning rapidly if the barrel is rifled), and out the muzzle. Rifling makes the firearm far more accurate than a smooth bore (such as in a musket).

Cartridge Shoulder: A modern cartridge case shaped like an ordinary round bottle having an abrupt reduction in diameter near the forward end. This abrupt step is called the shoulder. For rimless cases, this shoulder is the means of preventing the cartridge from going too far into the rifle chamber.

Case (or Casing): The envelope (container) of a cartridge. For rifles and handguns, it is usually of brass or other metal; for shotguns it is usually of paper or plastic with a metal head and is more often called a "hull." Also see "Cartridge".

Case Hardened: A treatment to the surface of steel parts (receivers, frames, etc.) where carbon (and/or nitrogen) is diffused into the outer layer of steel at high temperature. The carbon combines with the outer layer of steel to make it nearly glass-like in its hardness while the core of the steel remains softer. The result is a very durable surface with an attractive mottled appearance. A possible liability of improper case hardening is that the steel may become too brittle and crack or break during firing and injure the shooter.

Case Trimmer: A device used to remove excess material from a case mouth. Metallic cases stretch after extensive reloading and firing because the brass flows forward. These cases must be trimmed back.

Caseless Cartridge (Caseless Ammunition): A cartridge that does not use a case to contain the bullet, powder, and primer. Instead, the powder is formed into a solid mass and the bullet is directly attached to that mass. There may or may not be a primer also affixed to that mass. This design is intended to reduce the weight of the ammunition, save on materials, and eliminate components needed for extraction of the spent case. Two of the major disadvantages of this design is that the chamber must be sealed tightly to prevent the escape of excess gas and that caseless cartridges are more prone to ignite by residual heat within the chamber (cook off).

Cease-Fire: As a verb - the command to stop shooting and await further instructions from the lead range instructor. As a noun - time or period of range inactivity while targets are changed or other activities are conducted.

Center Fire: A type of cartridge in which the primer is located in the center of the casing's base. To fire this type of cartridge, the firing pin must impact in the center of the casing's base. Also see "Cartridge", and "Rim Fire".

Chamber: With the exception of the revolver, the rear part of the barrel that is formed to accept the cartridge to be fired. A revolver employs a multi-chambered rotating cylinder that is separated from, and directly to the rear of, a stationary barrel. It is common to say a firearm is chambered in a certain caliber and most firearms are chambered for only one type of cartridge. It is cumbersome, expensive and uncommon to change most firearms to chamber a different cartridge than that it was originally built for. However, a few firearms, by design, allow certain components to be changed which will allow different types of cartridges to be chambered and fired. Also used to refer to the action of placing a cartridge in the chamber (e.g., "chambering a round").

Chamber Insert: Also known as a "Chamber Flag", chamber inserts are designed to hold the action in an open position and prevent a cartridge from being inserted into the chamber (see also "Barrel Lock" and "Trigger Lock"). Chamber inserts differ from barrel locks in that they are placed directly into the chamber rather than inserted through the barrel.

Chamber Throat: (see "Throat").

Chamfer: To ream a taper on the inside of a case mouth or primer pocket.

Charge: The amount of powder used in the case at each loading.

Charge: The amount, by weight, of the powder in a cartridge. Also refers to the amount of shot used in a shotshell. May also refer to the action of loading a cartridge into the chamber of a firearm.

Charging Handle: The handle of a semi-automatic or fully automatic firearm used to cycle the firearm manually without firing. Also known as cocking handle, cocking knob or operating handle.

Checkering: A functional decoration to reduce handling slippage that is applied to pistol grips, stocks, and other areas. Checkering consists of a series pointed pyramids cut into the wood or metal in various spacings and sizes. Checkering is measured in LPI or lines per inch. Typical checkering is either 20 or 30 LPI.

Cheek Piece: A lateral projection from the comb of the stock. Provides additional support and contact to the cheek when the rifle is shouldered in the firing position. Assists with quickly aligning the shooting eye with an attached optic. Also see "Monte Carlo Stock".

Choke: A constriction at or near the muzzle of a shotgun barrel that affects shot dispersion to keep it from spreading out too quickly (also see "Adjustable Choke"). Degree of choke is measured by the approximate percentage of pellets in a shot charge which hit within a 30-inch circle at 40 yards. For example, with a "Full Choke" 65 to 75% of the pellets will hit in a 30-inch circle at 40 yards. The following list gives the accepted percentages obtained with various chokes: Full Choke 65-75%, Improved Modified 55-65%, Modified 45-55%, Improved Cylinder 35-45%, and Cylinder Bore 25-35%. Some rifled arms are also slightly choked as an aid to increased accuracy. This is especially true of precision air guns. The noted barrel maker Harry Pope made choked rifle barrels.

Chronograph: An instrument used to measure the velocity of a projectile. As velocity is one of the variables in determining bullet performance a chronograph is used to determine the speed or velocity of the projectile.

Class Three: Refers to a group of firearms originally controlled by the 1934-gun control act and then further restricted in 1986 by a rider to gun legislation that actually eased some facets of the 1968-gun control act. The firearms in this class are fully automatic firearms and long firearms with short barrels. It is still possible for any law-abiding citizen to own any weapons in this group by paying a "Stamp Tax", along with submitting the required forms, two set of pictures and two sets fingerprints to the FBI and successfully passing a background check.

Clicks: Term used for adjustment increment on an optical sight. The amount of change is measured by "clicks" turned. Typical optical rifle scopes move 1/4 MOA (Minute of Angle) per click, but some adjust to 1/8 MOA and others like ACOG's as specified in the user's manual. Common, non-magnification, red-dot systems move 1/2 MOA per click. Some, often lesser quality, optical sights will not have tactile clicks but, rather, free moving screws which make it more difficult to gauge adjustments.

Clip: A device for holding a group of cartridges together with no spring or automatic follower to feed cartridges to the receiver. In this usage there are two kinds of clips: Stripper clips and en bloc clips: Stripper clips hold 5 to 10 rounds of ammunition by their bases and are used to load magazines quickly. To load the magazine, the clip is placed in a guide which is either a part of the gun, or a separate guide which slips onto the magazine. En bloc clips hold the cartridges together by their bases and their bodies; the clip and the rounds are inserted into the magazine as a unit. When the last round is loaded, the clip is automatically ejected from the magazine. A typical example of this type of clip is those used in the M1 Garand rifle. This type of clip is often incorrectly referred to as "detachable magazine".

Cock: To ready the mechanism of a gun for firing by moving the hammer or striker of a firearm into a position where it is latched back under spring tension, as in "to cock the hammer."

Cocked And Locked: A slang term for the practice of carrying a single-action, semi-automatic pistol with a round in the chamber, the hammer cocked and the manual safety engaged. This is the typical defensive carry condition for these types of pistols.

Cocking Handle: The handle of a semi-automatic or fully automatic firearm used to cycle the firearm without firing. Also known as charging handle, cocking knob, or operating handle.

Cocking Indicator: Any device which the act of cocking a gun moves into a position where it may be seen or felt in order to notify the shooter that the gun is cocked. Typical examples are the pins found on some high-grade hammerless shotguns which protrude slightly when they are cocked, and also the exposed cocking knobs on bolt-action rifles. Exposed hammers found on some rifles and pistols are also considered cocking indicators.

Cold Range: A range that does not allow shooters to carry loaded weapons away from the firing line. For safety and liability reasons, this is the usual practice. The vast majority of ranges in the US are cold ranges.

Also, when no one is touching their firearms (and/or no firearms are loaded) and people may be downrange, there is a cold range. At events, declaring the range "cold" or "hot" is at the discretion of the range officer (RO). Once the RO has called the range hot, no one should pass the firing line. The range is declared "cold" after all firearms are cleared to allow target pasting and administration of the range and targets. Also see "Hot Range".

Collapsible Stock: A stock for a long gun that telescopes toward or away from the receiver to shorten or lengthen the overall length of the firearm. This may be for adjusting to different shooters, more convenient transportation, or covert carry. Also see "Folding Stock".

Comb: The upper edge of a rifle or shotgun buttstock where the shooter's cheek rests.

Combat Shooting: A generic reference to a shooting sport (generally using handguns) that seeks to simulate the use of small arms as an instrument of personal protection in a tactical or combat scenario. The term is often used for any type of practical firearms skills training.

Compensator: A device attached to, or forming a part of, the muzzle of a firearm which is designed to divert some of the escaping gas upward to counter the tendency of the muzzle to rise.

Compressed Charge: A charge of powder which so nearly fills the case that it is compressed when the bullet is seated.

Concealed Hammer: A firearm that uses a hammer but surrounds it with housings it in such a way that it is not possible for the shooter to manually cock the hammer by using an external device such as a hammer spur. A firearm with a concealed hammer can only be fired by first cocking the hammer with the trigger, slide, hinge, or bolt depending on the type of firearm. Some revolvers use a concealed hammer so as to allow the shooter to fire the weapon inside a pocket or other clothing without causing a malfunction (also see "Exposed Hammer" and "Hammer").

Cook Off: Premature ignition of the propelling charge by the heat absorbed from a chamber made hot by prolonged firing.

Copper Fouling: The partial obstruction and loss of accuracy caused by accumulated metal residue in the barrel of a firearm. Copper fouling is the same as leading or lead fouling, but is caused from the copper covering on copper jacketed bullets. The fouling occurs when the metal particles fill in the grooves of a rifled barrel, which make the firearm shoot more like a smooth bore. Accuracy is lost because the fouled rifling is not imparting adequate spin and stability on the projectile. Several chemicals are available to remove both lead and copper from the barrel of a firearm.

Cordite: A chemical used as propellant. Smokeless powder composed of nitroglycerin, guncotton, and a petroleum substance usually gelatinized by addition of acetone and pressed into cords resembling brown twine. Cordite is most commonly found in British military ammunition, circa WWI and WWII.

Course of Fire: The particular conditions of each shooting event, specifying the number of shots, movement, and distance and time limits. A course of fire may involve some set of standard exercises or may involve a scenario designed to simulate a real-world situation. The description of the course of fire would describe all the targets relative position on the course and the shooters actions at each target. It also specifies and safety precautions or restrictions applicable to that course.

Co-witness(ed) Sights: Most frequently used when mechanical or open sights can be viewed (co-witnessed) through an optical sight mounted on the same firearm. Common on many carbine rifles with low or one-power optics or on optical pistol sights. Co-witnessing allows the shooter to use the mechanical sights if the optical sight fails.

Crane: The crane is the pivoting arm that allows the cylinder of a modern revolver to swing to the side, after a release catch is pressed, to allow loading and unloading the revolver.

Creep: The movement of the trigger before it releases the striker or hammer.

Crimp: The process wherein the bullet of a cartridge is fixed firmly in the mouth of the case. With shotshells the term applies to the closure at the hull mouth. Common crimps are: roll, flat, star, fold, stab, semi-circular, split ring, and rose.

Crimped Primer: A forcing inward of the brass around the top of the primer pocket over the top of the primer. This is frequently found on military cartridges and is done to prevent set-back of primers. The crimp must be removed before repriming the case. Most commercial consumer cartridges do not have crimped primers.

Cross Dominant: In reference to the shooters eye dominance, to be cross-dominant means that you are right-handed, and yet rely on your left eye to aim, or vice versa. While it is more common to be left-handed and left-eye dominant, or right-handed and right-eye dominant, many shooters are cross dominant as well. Also see "Eye Dominance".

Cross-Bolt Safety: A device that blocks the firing mechanism of a firearm.

Crossfire: (1) A shot accidentally fired on a target assigned to another shooter. (2) Two or more shooters/officers placing themselves in such a positional relationship to the intended threat that a shot from one shooter may miss the intended target and strike another shooter. Also referred to in law enforcement as a "blue-on-blue" shooting.

Crosshairs: A cruciform reticule in an optical sight, also commonly referred to as crosswires (also see Graticule" and "Reticle").

Crowning (or Crown): The rounding or chamfering normally done to a barrel muzzle to ensure that the mouth of the bore is square with the bore axis and that the edge is countersunk below the surface to protect it from impact damage. Traditionally, crowning was accomplished by spinning an abrasive coated brass ball against the muzzle while moving it in a figure eight pattern until the abrasive had cut away any irregularities and produced a uniform and square mouth.

Cycle of Operation: The series of operations necessary to cause a firearm to discharge one round and return to a state of readiness. May be performed by hand or by an automatic mechanism. The cycle consists of: 1) chambering the round; 2) closing and possibly locking the breech; 3) firing; 4) unlocking and opening the breech; 5) extracting spent case; 6) ejecting the spent case; 7) cocking the firing mechanism; and 8) feeding the next cartridge into place. Not all of these functions may be present. For example, a blowback weapon does not perform locking and unlocking, a caseless weapon does not perform extraction and ejection, and the cycle may not be in the order given (e.g., cocking can take place before extraction) but the entire cycle must be followed by any firearm to function.

Cyclic Rate: A term used with fully automatic weapons to describe the rate at which the weapon fires. Expressed as number of rounds per minute (also see "Automatic").

Cylinder: That portion of a revolver that is immediately behind the barrel, that revolves and that contains a number of chambers into which cartridges are placed. Most commonly, a cylinder will contain six chambers, but some revolver cylinders are made with as few as four chambers and as many as ten.

Cylinder Bore: A shotgun barrel having the same diameter throughout, i.e., without choke. Necessary if it is used to fire solid slugs.

Cylinder Bore Choke: see "Choke".

Cylinder Gap: The maximum allowable space between the front of the cylinder and the rear of the barrel in a revolver.

Cylinder Release: A catch operated by either a thumb or finger that releases the cylinder so that it can be swung out from a revolver on the crane to allow for ejecting spent cases and for loading new cartridges. This is true of most modern revolvers, although some older designs used a loading gate or a break open action instead.

Cylinder Stop: A small "hand" or lever that protrudes from the trigger mechanism of a revolver that stops the cylinder's rotation during the cocking stroke so that a chambered cartridge lines up with the firing pin at the rear and the barrel at the front.

D

Deburring Tool: The deburring tool removes burrs from the inside and outside of newly-trimmed case mouths.

Decock: The process of un-cocking or returning the hammer or striker to the down or forward and unsprung position on a firearm.

Decocker (Decock Lever): Used on a double-action semi-automatic pistol, a decocker is a lever designed to lower a cocked hammer to a safe position without pulling the trigger or discharging the weapon.

Delayed Blowback: A variant of the blowback principle in which the blowback operation is by some means retarded (e.g., by a fluted or grooved chamber).

Derringer: Currently used as a generic term applied to a variety of small pistols, often lacking a trigger guard, with single or multi-barreled versions (rarely more than two), that are designed to be kept in a pocket. Derringers generally fire single-action with no magazine and no cylinder. A derringer contains one chamber for each barrel, and each chamber must be manually reloaded after discharge. This term has also been used inaccurately to describe small revolvers. Originally associated with small handguns designed by Henry Derringer.

Detachable Magazine: see "Magazine".

Die: A tool, in hand loading, that reforms cartridge cases and seats bullets; or, in bullet manufacturing a tool that swages bullets or cores, extrudes lead wire or draws jackets.

Disconnector: A component of a self-loading firearm which disconnects the trigger from the sear after each shot. It can only be reconnected by the shooter releasing the trigger. The disconnector prevents a semi-automatic weapon from firing in the fully automatic mode. A select fire weapon disables the disconnector when placed on fully automatic.

Dominant Eye: The stronger eye; the eye through which a person usually views an object as when sighting a firearm.

Double Action (abbreviated "DA"): A handgun that can both cock and release the hammer or striker by a pull on the trigger, thus the trigger is said to be performing two actions or "Double Action" (also see "Single Action"). In double-action revolvers, pulling the trigger or pulling back the hammer also revolves the cylinder.

Double Action Only (abbreviated "DAO"): A double-action only handgun can only be fired by pulling the trigger to both cock and release the hammer, striker, or firing pin to initiate the discharge of the handgun. There is no provision or ability for the shooter or the firearm to set or keep the hammer, striker, or firing pin in the cocked position for release in a single-action method of operation.

Double Barrel: A firearm with two barrels either side by side or one on top of another. Commonly used with shotgun design although both rifles and handguns have been designed with more than one barrel.

Double Base Powder: Smokeless powder made with nitroglycerine and nitrocellulose base.

Double Set Trigger: A device which consists of two triggers, one to cock the mechanism that spring-assists the other trigger, substantially lightening the other trigger pull.

Double Tap: A quick succession to two-shots fired rapidly from a semiautomatic pistol, rifle or shotgun, or a revolver. Also, as a verb, to describe the act of firing a double-tap. When doing a double tap the shooter does not line up (sight alignment or sight picture) the second shot. The shot is lined up once, and then the trigger is pulled rapidly twice. For most shooters (with some training) double taps can be practical and accurate at short distances.

Double Trigger: Double triggers are used in various applications. Many older double-barreled firearms used a separate trigger for each barrel. Some select fire automatic weapons use two triggers, one for semi-automatic mode and the other for fully automatic mode. Also see "Double Set Trigger" and "Single Trigger".

Double-Barrel: A firearm with two barrels, either side-by-side or one over the other.

Dovetail: A flaring machined or hand cut slot that is also slightly tapered toward one end. Cut into the upper surface of barrels and sometimes actions, the dovetail accepts a corresponding part on which a sight is mounted.

Down Range: A term used when describing any field of fire to indicate the direction of the targets and bullet impact area. On a formal range, there would be clear firing lines and a definitive direction. Also see "Up Range".

Drift: Deviation of a projectile from the line of departure due to its rotational spin or the force of wind. Also, the sideways movement of the bullet in flight, caused by the rifling. Note: The sights are usually designed to provide an average compensation for drift at the usual range over the firearms employment, but additional adjustment may be required for longer ranges.

Drop Safety: A device designed to passively or actively prevent the accidental discharge of a firearm if it is dropped. On revolvers and pistols without drop safeties or with actively engaged safeties, the hammer in the uncocked position can rest directly on the firing pin. If such a firearm is dropped, a blow to the hammer or muzzle can transfer enough energy to the firing pin to cause an accidental discharge. Drop safeties are typically hammer or firing pin blocks, or transfer bars. Also see "Grip Safety", "Magazine Safety", and "Thumb / Finger Safety".

Drum Magazine: A large-capacity magazine in which cartridges are arranged in a spiral around a central wind-axis.

Dry Fire (Dry Firing): A term used to describe the act of practicing gun handling (including pointing to a target and pulling the trigger) without live ammunition in the firearm. Instructors often encourage dry firing as a training technique. By firing the gun unloaded a shooter becomes accustomed to pulling the trigger without flinching or jerking in an attempt to control recoil. This is also a method used to develop hand/eye coordination and sight alignment techniques. Dry-firing normally does not hurt or damage most modern handguns. If unsure, check with the specific manufacturer or a certified armor or gunsmith for your firearm. Be very sure that the gun is unloaded before any dry-fire practice.

Dual or "Staggered" Column Magazine: A magazine that has an interior side to side dimension approximately 1½ times wider than the cartridge it was designed to hold. Thus, when cartridges are inserted in the magazine they stagger first to one side and then the other, giving the magazine the ability to hold more rounds for a given height. The detractor is that the magazine is wider, and if designed to insert into the grip of a pistol, the grip must be wider as well. Many pistols and rifles use this type of magazine and it is also known as a "double stack magazine". Also see "Magazine" and "Single Column Magazine".

Dud: Slang for a cartridge that fails to fire after its primer is struck by the firearm's firing pin.

Dummy cartridge: An inert training cartridge that is the same dimension as a live cartridge and can be inserted into the firearm, but which will not fire. Most dummy cartridges have a fluorescent-colored insert for the bullet or are entirely fluorescent colored to differentiate them from live ammunition. Sometimes referred to as "snap caps" or "dummy ammo". Also see "Snap Caps".

Duplex Load: The use of two different powders in loading the same cartridge.

E

Effective Range: The maximum distance for a shooter at which he or she can confidently hit the target. Also refers to the useful range of the projectile(s). Also see "Range".

Ejection port: A port that spent cartridge casings are ejected through on the side of the receiver of a firearm.

Ejector: Fixed component inside the receiver of a firearm that pushes a spent cartridge out the ejection port as the extractor pulls the spent cartridge to the rear.

Ejector Rod: A push rod designed to eject spent cartridges from the chambers in the cylinder of a revolver.

Ejector Rod Shroud: A shroud of metal machined as a part of the barrel of a revolver that surrounds and protects the ejector rod from damage.

Emergency Reload: The process of reloading a firearm in as rapid a motion as possible so as to return the weapon to use as quickly as possible. Speed reloads generally do not take into consideration that some cartridges may still remain in the cylinder or the cast-off magazine of the firearm because of the desire to bring the firearm to a "fully loaded" state as quickly as possible. Unlike the "Partial Magazine Reload", the live rounds that were in the firearm are discarded in favor of a fully loaded cylinder or magazine.

Empty Gun Reload: Reloading a firearm that has run out of ammunition. Sometimes referred to as a "combat" reload.

Elevation: A term used to indicate adjusting the sighting mechanism of a firearm so as to raise or lower the impact point of the weapon.

Elevation Scale: Graduations on an adjustable rear sight or scope sight that indicate elevation readings for various distances.

English Stock: A very straight, slender-gripped stock.

Enhanced Model: A firearm that has features not found on earlier models. Such features may enhance function, accuracy, convenience, use, or appearance.

Erosion: The wearing away of the bore due to friction and/or gas cutting.

Explosive: Any substance (TNT, etc.) that, through chemical reaction, detonates or violently changes to gas with accompanying heat and pressure. Smokeless powder, by comparison, deflagrates (burns relatively slowly) and depends on its confinement in a gun's cartridge case and chamber for its potential as a propellant to be realized.

Exposed hammer: A firearm where the hammer is exposed on the outside of the weapon and where it can be cocked by direct manual pressure on the hammer spur. Many firearms with an exposed hammer can be fired one of two ways, by first cocking the hammer with the trigger, slide, hinge, or bolt depending on the type of firearm and then releasing the hammer with the trigger or by cocking the hammer with the thumb and then releasing it with the trigger. Many older style revolvers can be fired by using only the second method (e.g., a "single-action" revolver). Also see "Concealed Hammer" and "Hammer".

Extended Magazine Release: A magazine release that is larger or longer than normal. Typically found on competition guns, extended magazine releases allow a shooter to more easily release the magazine with their weapon hand while retrieving a fresh magazine with the support hand during empty gun reloading. Extended controls are not always compatible with retention holsters used for law enforcement.

Extended Slide Release: A slide release that is larger than normal (usually protruding from the side of the gun) to allow for easier single hand operation. Extended slide releases are often added to duty and competition pistols so the shooter can "thumb" the slide release without changing the shooting grip after a reload. Extended controls are not always compatible with retention holsters used for law enforcement.

Extraction: The removal of a cartridge or case from the chamber of a firearm.

Extractor: A small "hook" or grapple on one side of the bolt face which hooks over the rim of a cartridge as it is pushed into the chamber. The extractor is designed to pull the spent case from the chamber after the weapon is fired. The extractor pulls the case back with the rearward movement of the bolt until the spent case strikes the ejector which then pushes it out of the ejection port.

Extractor Groove: The groove around the head of a cartridge case that provides a grip surface for the extractor of the firearm.

Eye Dominance: In reference to the shooters dominant or aiming eye. It is most common to be right-handed and right-eye dominant, or left-handed and left-eye dominant, but it is not unheard of to be cross-dominant as well. Proper determination of eye dominance is important to beginning firearms instruction.

Eye Protection: For shooting firearms, some form of glasses or goggles designed to protect shooters from minute particles sprayed in the air as a part of shooting a firearm. Glasses for shooting should be impact rated, as defined by the American National Standards Institute (ANSI), as Z87.1 or Z87+ and should have "wrap-around" or side protection to prevent particles or fragments from impacting the wearer's eye from the side.

Eye Relief: The distance between the eye and the ocular lens at which the entire field of view of a scope is visible simultaneously.

F

Factory Ammunition: Also, Factory Round. Ammunition that has been produced by a major manufacturer using new brass cartridges or other new cartridge and shell casing materials. Because of the high-quality assurance achieved by most major ammunition makers there is little chance that firearm damage or shooter injury will occur due to faulty cartridges. Additionally, firearms makers design their arms in concert with major ammunition makers to ensure safe, consistent operation and function within design parameters. For this reason, most firearms makers will void their warranties if "factory ammunition" is not used. Also see "Reloading" for additional discussion of factory and reloaded ammunition.

Failure To Feed: A malfunction condition where although the magazine contains cartridges, no cartridge is fed into the chamber as the slide, bolt or action moves forward into the locked in battery position. This malfunction is often caused by an improperly seated or fitted magazine, under lubrication of the firearm, weak recoil springs, or improper alignment of the slide or action.

Falling Block: A single-shot action where the breech block drops straight down when a lever is actuated. On some rifles the lever also cocks the hammer.

Feed: The act of moving a live cartridge from the magazine of a self-loading firearm to the chamber.

Feed Lips: The curved-in portion at the open end of a box magazine that retains the cartridges in the magazine and that positions the top cartridge for pickup (stripping) by the bolt or slide for feeding into the chamber of a firearm. Damaged feed lips (mostly in detachable magazines) are a common cause for feeding malfunction. The feed lips of all magazines should be regularly inspected for proper condition (also see "Follower" and "Magazine").

Feed Ramp: The part at the lower rear of the barrel or as a part of the receiver that slopes upward into the chamber to facilitate feeding the cartridge from the magazine of a self-loading firearm. Note: The feed ramp can be polished to facilitate better feeding and function of all types of ammunition. Some older types of semi-automatic pistols, such as the Walther PPK must have the feed ramp polished in order to properly feed hollow point cartridges.

Feeding Path: The path a cartridge follows within the action.

Feet Per Second: Standard measurement for the velocity of a bullet as it leaves the barrel. Abbreviated FPS or (fps).

FFL (Federal Firearms License): An FFL holder is needed in the transfer of ownership of many types of firearms across state lines, and within most states as well. Agencies must purchase firearms from an FFL dealer or distributor and complete specific paperwork to be exempted from firearms excise tax. Most gun stores (of which all have an FFL) will manage the transfer of personal firearms for a small fee.

Field Load: A shotshell loaded for hunting small game animals and birds.

Field Of Fire: The area which a weapon or a group of weapons may cover effectively with fire from a given position.

Field of View: Regarding scopes or binoculars, the term refers to the diameter of the field of vision at any one range or the field of vision in degrees of angle. It is the usual practice to give the field of view in feet at 1,000 yards for binoculars and 100 yards for scopes.

Field Strip (of Field Stripping): Disassembling a firearm to the point where it can undergo routine cleaning and lubrication. This usually refers to the limit of disassembly allowed by the operator without specialized training (see "Armorer").

Finish: The outward appearance of the firearm that varies depending on the type of material, level of polishing, and chemical finish. Also see "Bluing", "Parkerizing", "Nickel Plating", "Stainless Steel".

Fire: Act of discharging a firearm. Also, a range command to initiate a sequence wherein a firearm is deployed and discharged down range.

Firearm: A device which launches a projectile using the energy generated by the burning of gunpowder. Under the National Firearms Act, the word designates machine guns, rifles, shotguns, handguns, etc., but not air guns. The term firearm and small arms are synonymous; however, the term weapon and firearm are not synonymous. Also, by federal definition, under the 1968 Gun Control Act, antiques are excepted from the definition.

Firearms Instructor (FI): A trained and certified instructor able to provide training and correction, through diagnosis, to shooters in a given topic such as handgun shooting, carbine rifle shooting, covert carry, etc.

Firing Line: The line at which shooters position themselves to shoot down range to the targets. Usually designated for line drills. May also designate different firing points for a solo or team drill.

Firing Pin: The device that strikes the primer of a cartridge, initiating the sequence of events that causes a firearm to discharge. The firing pin can be a standalone component or it can be part of other components such as a hammer or striker.

Firing Pin Safety: A small lever or post that engages in a notch on the firing pin that is only withdrawn by the intentional movement of the trigger mechanism during firing. A firing pin safety is designed to prevent movement of the firing pin (and accidental discharge) if the firearm is dropped or otherwise mishandled.

Firing Pin Spring: A spring which controls or dampens the movement of the firing pin. A firing pin spring may hinder the forward movement of the firing pin until struck by the hammer or it may force the striker or firing pin forward when released by the trigger mechanism depending on the design of the firearm. Some firearms do not contain a firing pin spring and the firing pin is "floating". One such firearm is the AR-15.

Fit And Finish: Term used to describe the quality of over-all firearm workmanship.

Flash Blindness: Impairment of vision resulting from an intense flash of light such as the flash from a firearm muzzle (especially at night). This can be prevalent in rifles with barrels less than 10 inches which do not have an effective method of eliminating the excessive flash, such as a flash suppressor or an acoustic suppressor.

Flash Gap: The distance between the face of a revolver's cylinder and the breech end of the barrel. U.S. industry standards call for a gap of .006-inch, with a .003-inch tolerance in either direction.

Flash Hider / Flash Suppressor: A muzzle attachment intended to reduce visible muzzle flash and audible noise caused by the burning propellant. Although they can reduce the visibility of the firearm's location when fired they are primarily designed to prevent the shooter's vision from being blinded by the flash at night. Many flash hiders also act as a Muzzle Brake.

Flash Hole: The hole between the primer pocket in a metallic cartridge and the portion of the cartridge holding the powder charge.

Flash Suppressor: Muzzle attachment designed to cool emergent gases and prevent or reduce muzzle flash.

Flechette: A thin, fin-stabilized projectile resembling an arrow and much smaller than the bore of the weapon in which it is fired and which therefore needs to be supported in the bore by some form of sabot.

Floating Barrel (or Free Floating): A barrel bedded so as to avoid contact with any point on the stock. Floated barrels increase accuracy by avoiding the stress of physical contact between the barrel and the stock.

Floating Firing Pin: On a revolver, a firing pin that is mounted inside the frame, as opposed to being pinned to the hammer. In other use a firing pin that is unrestrained by a spring or other mechanical means.

Floor Plate (floorplate): The metal plate at the bottom of fixed box cartridge magazine permanently attached to the rifle. In this usage the floor plate is usually hinged at the front and held by a release spring located just ahead of the trigger guard. Also, can mean the bottom plate of a detachable box magazine.

Folding stock: A buttstock on a long gun that is designed to fold to the side, top or bottom to reduce the overall length of the arm for transport or covert carry.

Follow Through: The part of aiming and firing in which the aim is maintained after the shot is fired.

Follower: A metal or plastic platform against which the last cartridge or cartridges in a tubular, box, or drum magazine rest, and the means by which the magazine spring forces (pushes) an entire column of cartridges successively into position for feeding into the chamber as each cycle of operation is completed until the magazine is empty. In a tubular magazine, the follower is simply a round plunger riding over the end of the magazine spring. In a box or drum magazine, it is a more carefully shaped platform sometimes provided with ribs or grooves to assist in aligning the cartridges with the feed lips or the magazine for feeding into the chamber. Also see "Feed Lips" and "Magazine".

Forcing Cone: A short tapered section of the bore of a revolver at the breech, just forward of the cylinder face, designed to force a bullet into the rifling of the barrel upon discharge. Also, the forward part of the chamber in a shotgun where the chamber diameter is reduced to bore diameter. The forcing cone aids the passage of shot into the barrel.

Fore-Stock (or Fore-arm): The front portion of a one-piece or two-piece shoulder arm stock. Located under the barrel, the fore-stock serves as a hand-hold. It can also be called a forend or handguard.

Forward Assist: A manually operated lever or handle on a self-loading firearm designed to force a bolt (malfunctioning due to dirt, or powder buildup) forward and into lock-up so that the weapon may be fired.

Fouling: A residue left in the barrel of a firearm by burning powder (powder fouling) or metallic residue left in the barrel of a firearm by the passage of a bullet (lead or copper fouling).

Fouling Shots: Shots fired for the purpose of clearing the bore of cleaning solution and to "settle the barrel" preparatory to sighting and record shots.

Frame: Also known as the receiver, the frame is the basic structure or housing to which all other firearms components are attached including the breech, chamber(s), firing mechanism, and grips (generally only used as a term on handguns). Also see "Receiver". Generally, this is the serialized part of the firearm that is controlled for sale by law.

Free Floating Barrel (Free Float): A firearm action bedded in the stock so that the barrel does not contact the stock at any point. Also known as Floating Barrel. Free Floated Barrels increase accuracy by avoiding stress, flex or warp caused by physical contact with the stock or shooter.

Freebore: The transition area between a firearm's chamber and the beginning of the rifling that is designed to force the bullet into the rifling (also called "Leade").

Front Sight Ramp: A piece of metal on the top of the barrel near the muzzle on which the front sight is mounted.

Front Strap: That part of the revolver or pistol grip frame that faces forward and often joins with the trigger guard. The front strap is often checkered or stippled to give shooter's hand a reduced slippage surface.

Fully Automatic: A firearm designed to fire continuously as long as the trigger is depressed and ammunition remains in the feeding mechanism (as opposed to semi-automatic).

Full Choke: see "Choke".

Furniture: A slang term used when describing the stocks or grips of a firearm. Usually indicates that the stocks or grips are made from wood.

G

Gas Block: A device that replaces the front sight post and gas vent on an AR-15 rifle. Typically found on flat top and long-range variants, some include provisions for detachable sight posts.

Gas Operated: A firearm designed to bleed off and redirect a portion of the gas pressure generated in the barrel during discharge to assist in unlocking the breechblock or slide of a firearm to begin the cycle of operation. The gas is directed through a small port drilled in the side of the barrel and into a small cylinder containing a piston that acts on the unlocking mechanism. On some firearms the gas is directed to the gas cylinder by means of a long tube. The piston may act directly on the unlocking mechanism or through the use of intermediate linkages. Some firearms also allow the pressure directed to the cylinder to be varied by means of a gas regulator.

Gas Port: A small hole in the barrel of a gas-operated firearm through which expanding gases escape to power the auto loading system or reduce recoil.

Gas Retarded: A type of delayed blowback operation in which a portion of the powder gasses is bled off from the barrel to retard the rearward travel of the slide (e.g., Heckler & Koch "squeeze cocker" pistol).

Gas Tube: Component of a gas operated rifle that conveys the propellant gasses from the barrel to the bolt carrier group. Some sophisticated systems include adjustable gas systems for match accuracy, single fire and for different load variations.

Gauge: The bore size of a shotgun determined by the number of spherical lead balls of bore diameter that equals one pound. While most ammunition is described in terms of caliber, shotgun ammunition (called a shell or shotgun shells) is described in terms of gauge, and the direction of the scale is reversed: the lower the gauge, the bigger and more powerful the shell.

Ghost Ring Sights: Ghost ring sights consist of a post front sight, and a large aperture rear sight. When looking through the sights, and focusing on the front sight, the ghost ring rear sight, instead of a small peephole, will appear as a large thin fuzzy ring, hence the word "ghost ring". Used primarily on shotguns and short-range rifles/carbines, ghost ring sights offer very quick target acquisition. However, they lack the preciseness of small rear peep or blade sights and so are used mostly for close range competition rifle and shotgun applications. Ghost ring sights also present a higher profile and may not be as durable as other sights.

Gilding Metal: An alloy of 90 or 95 percent copper and the rest zinc used for bullet jackets.

Grain: The smallest unit of the British and U.S. system of weights. A unit of weight (7,000 grains equal one pound) commonly used to measure the weight of ammunition components (bullets and powder charges). Black powder and its substitutes are measured in grains by volume. Modern powders are measured by weight. Note that a grain is not the same a granule of powder.

Graticule: The cross-wires or other aiming mark in the field of view of a telescopic sight. In the United States this has been called a reticule or reticle, however technically a reticule must have a method for determining range where the graticule is a standard cross hair.

Grip: In handguns, the grip is the handle, that part of a handgun that is used to hold it securely during use. In rifles and shotguns, the portion of the stock to the rear of the trigger is considered the grip or wrist. Grips are often made of wood, rubber, or synthetic materials and can be custom designed to fit the user's hand.

Grip Bushing: A small additional piece used to hold the grips in place on certain types of handguns. The grip bushing screws into a hole on the side of the frame, the grip is placed over it and held in position by it. The grip screw is threaded into the hole in the center of the bushing to hold the grip on the firearm.

Grip Safety: Originally designed in the 1880s, to prevent accidental discharge. To discharge a handgun equipped with a grip safety, the safety lever, located on the front or back of the grip, must be compressed. When holding the handgun in a normal shooting position, the fingers or palm (depending on the design) of the shooter's hand compresses the safety lever, thus unlocking the trigger. If the shooter releases the lever, the locking mechanism automatically re-engages. Also see "Drop Safety", "Magazine Safety", and "Thumb / Finger Safety".

Grooves: The recessed portion of rifling. Swaged impressions or cuts spiraled through a bore to rotate projectiles. Also see "Rifling".

Group / Group Size: The distribution of bullets on a target fired with a single aiming point and sight setting. Group size is expressed as the distance between centers of the farthest holes and is most easily determined by measuring the extreme spread from outside to outside and subtracting one bullet diameter.

Guard Position: A ready position with handgun or rifle in which the firearm is lowered below the line of sight. The position is variable depending on the target, threat, or lack thereof present. Also see "Low Ready".

Gunpowder: A mixture of chemical compounds of various compositions, particle sizes, shapes and colors which, when ignited by the primer, burns rapidly to generate a gas that serves as a propellant. This production of gas dramatically increases the pressure inside the cartridge or chamber. Once the pressure reaches a threshold (determined by the way the cartridge is manufactured or the chamber is loaded), the bullet is discharged from the case or chamber, through the barrel, and out the muzzle down range. Ignited smokeless powder emits minimal quantities of smoke from a firearm's muzzle; the older black powder emits relatively large quantities of whitish smoke.

H

Half Cock: A number of firearms allow the hammer to be manually cocked. On some of these guns the hammer has two latching positions, half cock and full cock. When the hammer is latched to full cock the firearm is ready to fire, but when latched at the half cock position, the sear is captured and the hammer cannot be released by simply pulling the trigger. Originally designed as a safety position for the hammer on single action firearms, half cock is considered unreliable as a safety by modern standards.

Hammer: The hammer serves to generate the energy needed to ignite the primer and fire the bullet. The hammer is that component of a firearm that either has the firing pin attached to it, or that strikes the firing pin. When the hammer is pulled back into the cocked position (either directly or by another mechanism), it compresses the mainspring, thus generating potential energy. When the trigger is pulled, the potential energy stored in the mainspring is released, forcing the hammer forward to strike the primer of the cartridge in the chamber directly, or to strike the firing pin, which then strikes the primer, causing the firearm to discharge. Also see "Concealed Hammer", "Exposed Hammer" and "Striker".

Hammer Block: A safety device designed to keep the hammer from moving far enough forward to strike the primer without the trigger being deliberately depressed. A hammer block safety is designed to prevent an accidental discharge if the firearm is dropped or otherwise mishandled.

Hammer Spur: A small extension affixed to the back of an exposed hammer designed to aid in manually cocking the hammer prior to release.

Hammer Strut: A bar or lever that connects the hammer to the mainspring.

Hammerless: Some "hammerless" firearms do in fact have concealed hammers, which are located completely within the action housing. Truly hammerless guns, such as the Savage M99, have a firing mechanism that is based on a spring-activated firing pin called a striker.

Hand: The part of a revolver which turns the cylinder as the gun is cocked, thus aligning a chamber containing a cartridge with the barrel and hammer or firing pin.

Hand Loading: The process of assembling cartridges from all new components as well as the process of taking previously fired cartridge cases and then reassembling them using a new primer, powder and projectile. Also see "Reloading".

Handgun: A firearm designed to be held and fired with one hand, capable of being concealed on the person and with a barrel less than 16 inches long. Said by some to be a synonym for pistol, but in correct usage "handgun" is a general term used to indicate both a pistol or a revolver. In other words, a "pistol" and a "revolver" are both handguns, but "pistol" and/or "revolver" are also specific terms that are not interchangeable with one another. Also see "Pistol" and "Revolver".

Hangfire: An ignition failure in a cartridge which results in delay before the main charge burns. Invariably due to faulty materials in the cartridge. Hangfires are quite dangerous as it may be mistaken for a misfire, the firearm turned or moved for inspection, and a unintentional target struck when the firearm discharges.

Headspace: The fit of a cartridge in a chamber measured as the distance from breech face to the rear of that part of the chamber which stops the cases forward movement. Insufficient headspace hinders complete chambering; excessive headspace permits case stretching or separation.

Hearing Protection: Any of a wide variety of devices specially designed to fit inside or over the ear and worn to attenuate the report of a firearm discharge to prevent hearing damage. All reputable hearing protection manufacturers provide a noise reduction rating (NRR) to buyers indicating the effectiveness of the attenuation of the hearing protection if properly worn.

Heavy Barrel: A rifle barrel of greater than standard outside diameter that is designed to reduce barrel deflection from heat or sling wrap-up. Also, a heavy handgun barrel. Also see "Bull Barrel".

Heel: Back end of the upper edge of the buttstock at the upper edge of the buttplate or recoil pad.

High Brass/High Cup: Shotshells having a high metal head construction.

High Capacity Magazine: An inexact, non-technical term indicating a magazine holding more rounds than might be considered "average". Some laws have defined a "high-capacity magazine" as a magazine that holds more than ten rounds.

High Power: A term applied to the first smokeless powder cartridges with velocities of approximately 609.6 meters per second (2,000 feet per second).

High Power Rifle: Generally, a rifle that uses center-fire ammunition.

High Ready: A position of readiness where the shooter is holding a firearm in such a manner that the muzzle is pointed upward often to avoid pointing the muzzle at something low or on the ground such as a person. See also "Muzzle Up" and "Temple Index".

Hinged Frame Action: A design where a level located on the top, side or under the frame is used to open the action. The barrel or barrels then pivot either up, down or to the side for loading or unloading. When the action is closed, the barrel(s) breech swings against the standing breech. Also, an older method of opening a handgun for reload that involved releasing a catch and swinging the barrel down to expose the chamber(s) for spent case extraction and insertion of the new round(s).

Holding: The action of keeping the sights on the target while pressing the trigger.

Holster: A firearms accessory designed to hold a firearm on your person in such a way as to make it available for use as needed. Holsters are made to fulfill a variety of purposes such as, concealment, comfort, speed in drawing, security from snatching, protection from adverse field conditions, style, etc. Holster selection is usually a trade off in features depending on intended use. Sometimes used as a range command to return a firearm to the holster. Below are some common types of holsters.

- Ankle holster: holster which straps around the lower leg, calf, or ankle. Usually concealed by a pant leg.
- Belly-band holster: several types of holsters which wrap around the chest or waist with a wide belt or band and have a holster attached or integrated into the band. Usually worn under the clothing for concealment.
- Cross-draw holster: any holster which requires the shooter to reach across their body to retrieve the firearm. Cross draw holsters can be worn as shoulder or belt holster or under clothing on bands around the chest.
- Inside the waistband holster (IWB): holster or concealment method used for concealed carry of a firearm where the firearm is inside the waistband of the pants or trousers. Note: so-called "appendix holsters"

are IWB holsters carried in the front of the waist in the "appendix" position.

- Outside the waistband holster (OWB): holster worn on the belt outside the waistband. Traditional belt holsters are examples of OWB.

- Small of the back holster (SOB): a holster specifically designed to be worn at the center of the back on the beltline (usually OWB). The shooter reaches behind their back with their weapon hand to draw the handgun which is typically carried horizontally with the bottom of the grip oriented upward.

- Shoulder holster: type of holster in which a harness is slung over one or both arms and the holster is (typically) under the support side arm requiring the shooter to reach across their body (cross draw). Shoulder holsters may orient the firearm vertically (muzzle up or down) or horizontally.

Hoplophobe: An individual with an unreasonable fear of weapons in and of themselves, or of the practice of weapon craft and gunnery. From the Greek hoplon meaning tool or weapon and phobes meaning fear.

Hot Range: A range that allows shooters to carry loaded weapons away from and on the firing line. This practice is most commonly found on law enforcement ranges where every officer carries a loaded firearm most of the time. Operating a hot range requires that all personnel have demonstrated a high degree of safe handling of firearms and are aware of and follow all applicable safety rules.

Hot Round: A nonspecific term describing a round that is more "powerful" than usual rounds of its caliber. In this context "powerful" might mean greater muzzle velocity, greater felt recoil, or greater power factor.

Hull: "Hull" is to shotguns what "casing" is to handguns and rifles. Refers to the spent or unloaded shotshell (shotgun shell).

I

IDPA (International Defensive Pistol Association): The governing body of a shooting sport that simulates self-defense situations and real-life encounters. Cardboard or paper targets with scoring areas specifically designed for IDPA are routinely used in law enforcement training.

Ignition: The action of setting the powder charge on fire. Historically, this source of ignition could be a spark from a flint, a felt lit on fire, a match or even a torch. In modern firearms the primer ignites the powder charge.

Improved Cylinder Choke: see "Choke".

Inertial Firing Pin: A firing pin that is too short to contact the cartridge's primer when the hammer is resting on it and can only hit the primer when driven forward under the momentum of the hammer blow. The system used in the Browning 1911 pistol is an example of an inertial firing pin.

Internal Scope Adjustment: A mechanism sealed inside telescopic rifle sights by which the reticule or crosshairs can be adjusted vertically for elevation and horizontally for windage without moving the scope tube in its mounting.

Intrinsic Safety Device: These are safety devices which are permanently attached to the handgun, either during manufacture or by the user. These include such devices as loaded chamber indicators, magazine disconnectors, manual thumb safeties, transfer bars (a type of drop safety), grip safeties, built-in locks and personalized guns.

IPSC "International Practical Shooting Confederation": The governing body for much of the action/combat shooting competition conducted worldwide. Often used as a term for this type of competition. Cardboard or paper targets with scoring areas specifically designed by IPSC are regularly used in practical law enforcement training.

Iron Sights: Fixed sights on a gun (not necessarily made of iron). The term is used to differentiate them from optical sights (scopes). Also called metallic or mechanical sights.

Isosceles Stance: Common handgun shooting stance in which both hands grip the handgun and the extended arms form an isosceles triangle, giving the stance its geometric name.

J

J Frame: A term used by the Smith & Wesson firearms company for many years to designate a frame size in their popular line of double action revolvers. The frame designations in this series are "J" small, "K" medium, "L" large, and "N" very large.

Jacket: A thin coating of metal, usually copper or a copper alloy, covering the core (often lead) of a projectile. See also "Full Metal Jacket" and "Total Metal Jacket".

Jam: An inaccurate slang term used by many when referring to a *malfunction.* In correct usage a "jam" is an interruption in the cycle of operation caused by malfunctioning components or ammunition that results in the firearm ceasing to function. A "jam" is a more serious condition than a malfunction in that the firearm must be taken out of service and repaired by a qualified armorer or gunsmith to restore function. Examples of jams would include damaged or broken firing pins, extractors, springs, or other components, or improperly loaded ammunition that causes a projectile to only travel partway down the barrel (squib load). Also see "Malfunction" and "Stoppage".

K

K Frame: A term used by the Smith & Wesson firearms company for many years to designate a frame size in their popular line of double action revolvers. The frame designations in this series are "J" small, "K" medium, "L" large, and "N" very large.

Keyhole: The elongated hole formed by an unstable bullet hitting the target sideways, rather than point first, due to the failure to remain balanced in flight.

Kick: see "Recoil".

Knurling: A series of regular ridges or rectangles cut or rolled onto a metal surface to prevent slipping. Often used on hammer spurs, bolt handles, and sight adjustment knobs. Knurling on a firearm often indicates parts that are intended to be moved by the user, thus providing a grip-able surface.

Kurz: German word meaning "short." Used in cartridge designations, such as 9mm Kurz, which in the U.S. is known as the .380 ACP.

Kydex: A synthetic polymer (hard plastic) that is used to construct holsters and other firearms accessories.

L

L Frame: A term used by the Smith & Wesson firearms company for many years to designate a frame size in their popular line of double action revolvers. The frame designations in this series are "J" small, "K" medium, "L" large, and "N" very large.

Laminated Stock: A gunstock made of many layers of wood glued together under pressure. They are very resistant to warping.

Land & Groove Impression: The impression left on the bearing surface of a bullet caused by the rifling in the barrel through which it was fired.

Lands (or Land): The raised portion of rifling. The lands are portions of the bore left between the grooves of the rifling in the bore of a firearm. In rifling, the grooves are usually twice the width of the land. Land diameter is measured across the bore, from land to land. Also see "Rifling".

Lanyard loop: A small metal or plastic loop affixed to the firearm to hold a strap that is also affixed to the person carrying the firearm. Intended to keep the firearm from being accidentally dropped and lost.

Laser Sights: A sighting device mounted on a firearm, usually in the same manner as scope, that projects a low intensity laser beam on to a target to indicate the point-of-aim.

Lead Fouling: A thin deposit of lead left in the rifling grooves of a firearm after the firing of lead bullets. If allowed to build up, it will have a detritus effect upon the accuracy of the firearm. Lead fouling is one of the primary reasons for the adoption of jacketed or plated bullets.

Lead Free (Ammunition): Designation for ammunition that is free of lead components. This ammunition is often used in "lead free" indoor ranges to reduce the exposure of lead to users of the range. Components of the primer containing lead are replaced with other chemical components and the projectile is often made of compressed copper and other non-lead alloy metals.

Leade: The transition area between a firearm's chamber and the beginning of the rifling that is designed to force the bullet into the rifling (also called "Freebore").

Leading: Particles from shot or bullets that stick to the metal surface of the bore. This is due to heat or friction.

Leather: When used in firearms circles the term "leather" refers to holsters, belts, and other firearms accessories.

Lever Action: A firearm action where the cycle of operation is completed by the manual operation of a lever below the receiver that also acts as the trigger guard. The lever is a handle located under and a bit behind the trigger that hinges at a point forward of the trigger. When the lever is pushed down and forward, a spent cartridge is ejected from the firing chamber. Bringing the lever back and up into firing position loads a cartridge into the chamber (if the magazine is loaded) and cocks the hammer so that the weapon is ready to fire again. A secondary purpose of the lever is to serve as a trigger guard

Lightweight (L.W.): A firearm that is constructed of lightweight material such as aluminum alloy in the receiver or frame.

Line of Departure: An imaginary line extending from the muzzle of a firearm along the path of the projectile if it were to leave the barrel traveling in a straight line without being influenced by any other forces such as gravity.

Line of Sight: An imaginary straight line from the eye, through the sights, to the point-of-aim. Often used as a reference in zeroing various sights on firearms.

Live Ammunition: Ammunition containing primers and propellants capable of firing bullets or other projectiles.

Load: The combination of components used to assemble a cartridge or shotshell. Also refers to the act of preparing a firearm for firing by inserting ammunition into the chamber(s), and/or magazine or other feeding mechanism.

Loaded: A firearm is loaded when a cartridge is in its firing chamber. Generally used to refer to a gun that contains ammunition. However, there are some legal subtleties. For a semi-automatic, most people assume that when a gun is described as loaded there is a round in the chamber. This may or may not be the case in technical legal terms as for any type of handgun, the firearm may be considered "legally loaded" if ammunition is attached to it in any way.

Loaded Chamber Indicator: A small device found on some pistols which displays a warning when the chamber contains a cartridge. These were first developed for use in the early 1900s by European handgun manufacturers. Often the chamber indicator is a small pin that is built into the mechanism of the pistol. When a cartridge is in the chamber, and the action is closed, the pin protrudes from the top, back, or side of the gun.

Loading Density: Ratio of the volume of the powder charge to the volume of the case. The higher the better in terms of accuracy.

Loading Gate: A small port covered by some type of door (the "Gate") either hinged or spring-loaded, that when opened, allows for feeding cartridges into the magazine or chambers of a firearm. Loading gates can be found on revolvers and a variety of long guns.

Loading Port: The opening in the receiver where a cartridge may be placed either directly into the chamber or into the magazine.

Lock Time: The amount of time between when the trigger is pulled and the gun fires. Generally, the faster the lock time the better, because this makes it easier to shoot accurately. In order to obtain the fastest lock time, some modern firearms have been built which set off the primer via an electric impulse, rather than through mechanical means.

Lock Up (Lockup): The process of locking the action closed and placing the firearm in a condition of full readiness to fire. Also used to describe a proper two-hand grip on a pistol to control recoil.

Locked Breech: A firearms action in which the barrel and breech face remain locked together during the initial part of the firearm's discharge. Most powerful auto pistols use the locked-breech principle; most low-powered ones are blowback designs.

Locking Lugs: A number of projections machined as part of the breech bolt that are designed to fit into corresponding slots (recesses) in the receiver to lock the breech of a firearm in a closed position for firing.

Long Action: A rifle designed for longer, higher power, cartridges.

Long Gun: Generic term used to describe rifles and shotguns.

Long Rifle: Designation for .22 caliber rim fire ammunition that is the longest length and highest velocity of the .22 family (excluding the .22 magnum). Abbreviated LR.

Low Brass/Low Cup: Shotshells with a low metal head construction.

Low Ready: A shooting position where the shooter holds the gun pointed downrange and angled downward at approximately 45 degrees. Starting at the "Low Ready" is sometimes used as a substitute for drawing from a holster for certain range exercises. Also see "Guard Position".

Luger: American name for the German "Parabellum" semi-automatic pistol introduced in 1900. The Parabellum was designed by Georg Luger, and based on the earlier Borchardt pistol. The official German military nomenclature was "Pistole '08" or "Po8." At first, it was chambered for the 7.65mm Parabellum round. Soon, it was modified to use the 9mm Parabellum cartridge, which is what most people refer to today when talking about a "9mm." "Luger" is now a trademark owned by the Stoeger Arms Co.

M

M1911: The official US military designation for the Colt .45 semiautomatic pistol adopted by the US in 1911. This gun was designed by John Moses Browning, and originally produced by Colt. During military trials, the Browning-Colt design beat out several competing designs, including one from Savage and a .45 caliber version of the German Parabellum (Luger). Early use showed that it could be improved and in 1921 the M1911A1 was introduced, which featured a few changes like a recontoured frame, shorter trigger, and a rounded backstrap. The M1911A1 remained the standard "official" US military handgun until it was replaced as the official handgun in the 1980s by the Beretta M9. The 1911 design has been manufactured by, and modified by, more gun manufacturers and gunsmiths that any other firearm ever made.

Machine Gun: A firearm of military significance, often crew-served (operated by more than one person), that on trigger depression automatically and continuously feeds and fires cartridges of rifle size or greater until the ammunition supply is exhausted or the trigger is released.

Machine Pistol: A pistol that has select fire capabilities, and is magazine fed. Some have shoulder stocks or braces.

Magazine: A device for holding and feeding a group of cartridges. Types of magazines include box (fixed and detachable), tube, and drum. Detachable magazines for the same firearm may be offered by the firearm's manufacturer or other manufacturers with various capacities. A firearm with a five-shot detachable magazine, for instance, may be fitted with a magazine holding 10, 20, or 50 or more rounds. Box magazines are most commonly located under the receiver with the cartridges stacked vertically. Tube or tubular magazines run through the stock or under the barrel with the cartridges lying horizontally. Drum magazines hold their cartridges in a circular mode. All magazines hold a group of cartridges together and incorporate some type of follower to positioning the cartridge is such a way as to be picked up by the slide or bolt of a firearm when loading the chamber. As a cartridge is taken from the magazine the follower pushes another cartridge into place. This cycle continues until the magazine is empty. Also see "Feed Lips", "Clip", "Dual or Staggered Column Magazine", "Follower", and "Single Column Magazine". Many people incorrectly refer to box magazines as "clips" even though a clip is more strictly defined as device for holding a group of cartridges only with no ability to feed cartridges to the receiver.

A magazine may also refer to a storage area for explosives designated by the Bureau of Alcohol, Tobacco, Firearms and Explosives. Magazines are not typically required for storage of small arms ammunition but are often required for storage of explosive materials and have a variety of specifications for construction and proximity to other structures.

Magazine Cut Off: Disengages magazine feed from firearm.

Magazine Disconnector (or Magazine Safety): A magazine disconnector is a passive mechanical safety device which is designed to prevent the discharge of a round in the chamber of a pistol when the magazine is removed from the pistol. Like the loaded chamber indicator, the magazine disconnector was originally developed in the early 1900s by European gun manufacturers and was intended to prevent accidental discharges. Because the pistol will not fire with the magazine removed the handler may come to believe that the pistol is unloaded even when there is a live round in the chamber.

Magazine Floorplate: see "Floor Plate".

Magazine Follower: A spring-actuated platform that pushes cartridges or shells to the feeding position. When checking that a firearm is completely unloaded, the magazine must be removed (detachable magazines) or the follower must be clearly in view (non-removable magazines). This is especially important with tubular magazines.

Magazine Holder (or Pouch): A holder or pouch fabricated from cloth, plastic, or metal designed to hold spare magazines.

Magazine Plug: A part inserted into a magazine to reduce its capacity. It is also the part in the end of a tubular magazine that closes the end and retains the spring.

Magazine Release: A lever or button on the side of a firearm that when depressed releases a detachable magazine from the firearm for unloading or so that a new magazine may be inserted.

Magazine Safety: A safety device found on some semi-automatic handguns that prevents firing unless the magazine is inserted into the firearm. See also "Magazine Disconnector".

Magazine Throat: A metallic insert found in some plastic magazines that aligns the next cartridge to be fed into the chamber.

Magazine Well: The opening in the bottom of the receiver or grip of a firearm intended to receive a detachable magazine. The magazine well may be modified in a manner intended to make it easier and faster to insert new magazines.

Magnum: From the Latin for "more." A term usually indicating a relatively heavily loaded metallic cartridge or shotshell which generates higher velocity and energy as compared to other cartridges or shotshells firing projectiles of the same diameter and, by extension, a firearm safely constructed to fire the heavier loads.

Magnum Cartridge: Centerfire, rimfire and shotshell ammunition that is larger, more powerful or produces higher velocities than standard calibers.

Mainspring (or Hammer Spring): The spring that drives a hammer or striker forward to ignite the primer upon release by pressing the trigger.

Mainspring Guide: Usually a rod-like device that keeps the mainspring from kinking when compressed.

Mainspring Housing: Used on some firearms to surround and contain the mainspring. The mainspring housing additionally may be a modifiable item for firearms customization.

Malfunction: A firearm or ammunition's failure to perform; not firing when the trigger is pressed. By definition, malfunctions are able to be diagnosed and cleared by the shooter in very little time, with no tools, and no gunsmithing knowledge, returning the firearm to full function in the field. Failures to feed ammunition, fire when the trigger is pressed, extract spent casings, or eject spent casings are examples of malfunctions. Also see "Jam" or "Stoppage".

Mannlicher Stock: A full length slender fore-end extending to the muzzle.

Marking Cartridge: A simulated ammunition cartridge used for force-on-force training. Marking cartridges are generally fired through specialty firearms which are incapable of firing standard ammunition (for safety) and contain a colored marking pellet to show "hits" on opposing role players during a training exercise.

Martini Action: A hammerless single shot rifle action operated by a lever where the breechblock's movement is contained within the receiver and pivots at the rear.

Master Eye: see "Dominant Eye".

Match Action: A firearms action that is specially prepared for shooting in competition or for match use. Typically Match Actions have a squared and true bolt face, action and locking lugs. The mechanical tolerances are closer or measured to a higher standard to facilitate improved accuracy and reliability. A Speed Lock Spring and light weight firing pin are often used to decrease lock time and facilitate near immediate ignition when the trigger is pulled. The trigger on most match guns is of a two (2) stage design or machined and adjusted to a very light trigger pull weight.

Match Barrel: A rifle or handgun barrel specifically designed or prepared for shooting in competition or shooting matches. A typical rifle match barrel is of a heavier contour and is designed for extreme accuracy and for less barrel sag when fired from a hot barrel. Often match barrels are made of higher-grade steel or stainless steel with lands and groves broach cut to increase accuracy and to lessen the chance of fouling. Many Match Rifles have specific rifling twists for the specific bullet weight and for the distance to the target. Most Match Guns are not well suited for defensive or hunting use.

Match Grade Ammunition: Ammunition manufactured to much closer tolerances than regular ammunition to produce rounds that consistently perform to the highest of standards.

Maximum Ordinate: The highest point above the baseline (line from the muzzle to the target) that the bullet reaches in its flight.

Mean Point-of-impact: The mathematical center of a group of shots (usually 3 to 5) fired at the same point-of-aim. Abbreviated MPI.

Mechanical Off-set: See "Sight Over Bore Height".

Mechanical Sights: Sighting systems on firearms usually consisting of a front post and rear notch or aperture of various types in contrast with optical sights which include some type of glass lens, projected hologram, dot or reticule.

Mercuric Primer: A primer in which the priming mixture contains fulminate of mercury as one of the ingredients. Fulminate primers sometimes deteriorate in storage and also have a destructive effect on the brass of the cartridge cases. When fired, their residue can accelerate bore corrosion and pose a health risk as airborne mercury is released.

Metallic Cartridge: A cartridge with a metallic case. In contrast, early cartridge cases were made of linen, paper, etc.

Metallic Sights: In competitive rifle or pistol shooting, the term generally indicates a sight combination not containing glass elements, except that a single corrected lens may be used in the rear sight as a substitute for that in the shooter's eyeglasses. Also see "Iron Sights".

Micrometer: A very precise measuring device that is typically hand held. Used in hand and ammunition reloading to measure bullets and cases.

Micrometer Sight: A finely adjustable target sight.

Mid-Range Trajectory: Refers to the distance the bullet rises above the line of sight. Mid-range trajectory is calculated halfway between the muzzle and the target.

Mil: An angular measurement used in fire control. Originally it was the angle subtended by one/one thousand of the range; that is one yard at one thousand yards. For ease of division, it is now taken as much as 1/6400th of a circle or 3.375 minutes. Thus, one mil at 1,000 yards subtends .982 yards. Used in zeroing and trajectory calculation as an alternative to minute of angle (MOA).

Minute Of Angle (MOA): The arc subtended by an angle of one minute (1/60th of a degree) at any range, usually 100 yards. A minute of angle or (MOA) at 100 yards is 1.0471680" - so close to one inch that for all practical purposes it is considered an inch. Therefore, 1 MOA = 1 inch at 100 yards. This measurement is used on scopes and optics. In practical use, one would adjust the scope or optics so the bullet strike or point-of-impact (POI) and the aiming point or point-of-aim (POA) coincide at a desired distance. For an adjustment to zero at 100 yards, follow this example: If the POI was 3 inches to the left of and 4 inches below the POA, one would move the adjusting knobs on the scope or optics 3 MOA (3 inches) to the right and 4 MOA (4 inches) up. Some scope adjusting knobs are in 1/4 MOA or 1/4 inch at 100-yard increments, so you cannot always say 4 clicks as 4 clicks on a 1/4 MOA scope is only 1 MOA. Abbreviated MOA.

Misfire: The failure of a cartridge to fire after the primer is struck. The condition of a cartridge not firing when an attempt to fire it is made. It can be caused by either a defective cartridge or a defective firearm. Do not confuse with hangfire, which is a delay in firing.

Modern Firearms: Firearms manufactured after January 1, 1949 (also includes Curio Relics).

Modified Choke: see "Choke".

Modular Weapons System: Generic term and military noun nomenclature for a series of quick attachment systems used to accommodate the use of various devices and accessories on a firearm. The Modular Weapons System or MWS adds flexibility and adaptability to a proven rifle design. The MWS has recently been adopted by the U.S. Army and type classified.

Monte Carlo Stock: A type of rifle stock with a very high comb that provides elevated eye alignment when using a telescopic sight.

Mouth: Refers to the opening at the forward end of the cartridge casing where the bullet is inserted and then crimped in place.

MRBF: Mean Rounds Between Failure. A term used when expressing the reliability of a certain firearm.

Multi-Barreled: A firearm with more than one barrel, the most common being the double-barreled shotgun.

Mushroomed Bullet: Refers to a projectile which has hit an object and expanded (usually as designed) opening up and flattening at the nose in a shape that resembles a mushroom, thus the name.

Muzzle: The open end of the barrel from which the projectile exits. The front end of a barrel.

Muzzle Blast: The release of gas from the muzzle following the bullet's departure from the barrel. It always produces noise (called "report") and is often accompanied by light called muzzle flash.

Muzzle Brake: An attachment to or an integral part of the muzzle end of the barrel (often slotted) that functions by diverting a portion of the powder gas from a fired round to the side or even partially to the rear to reduce perceived recoil. Also known as a compensator.

Muzzle Crown: A treatment of the mouth of the muzzle that creates an even, circular opening by shaving away metal that may be worn into a more oval pattern. Accuracy is often improved by crowning the muzzle.

Muzzle Energy: A bullet's energy, measured in foot pounds, as it emerges from the muzzle.

Muzzle Flash: The incandescent flash in the air at the muzzle of a gun following the departure of a bullet; caused by the sudden release, expansion and expulsion of powder gasses and burning powder grains, and contact with the oxygen in the air. Also see "Flash Hider / Flash Suppressor" and "Muzzle Blast".

Muzzle Up: A rifle or pistol ready position in which the muzzle of the firearm is pointed upward to avoid covering anything the operator does not wish to shoot. Often used when a muzzle down position would be unsafe. Sometimes in this position, the operator will place the front sight in view so if a threat is presented, the operator will raise the buttstock of a long gun or extend their arms for pistol, bringing the weapon on target by pivoting on the front sight axis.

Muzzle Velocity: The speed of a projectile as it leaves the muzzle of a firearm measured in feet per second or meters per second (industry standard is measured 15 inches from the muzzle).

N

N Frame: A term used by the Smith & Wesson firearms company for many years to designate a frame size in their popular line of double action revolvers. The frame designations in this series are "J" small, "K" medium, "L" large, and "N" very large.

Neck: The upper section of a cartridge case that grips the bullet.

Neck Size: To bring the neck of a case back to its original dimensions to hold a new bullet. Cases fired in the same chamber need neck sizing (resizing) only.

Necking Down: The use of forming dies to reduce both the outside and inside diameter of a cartridge case neck.

Negligent Discharge: The unexpected and/or unintentional firing of a firearm that causes unintentional or unexpected damage or injury due to a violation of safety rules on the part of the person handling the firearm. This term usually indicates a more serious burden of responsibility on the part of the firearm handler than the term "Accidental Discharge". Negligent is often used as a legal term and may be used as a determination after the investigation of a firearm discharge. Also see "Accidental Discharge" and "Unintentional Discharge".

NFA 34 (National Firearms Act of 1934): A set of federal regulations passed into law in 1934 that govern the sale and possession of certain classes of firearms.

NIB: Abbreviation for New In Box. A firearm that is new and in its original box.

Nickel Plated: A hard plated firearm finish resembling chrome that is more durable and protective than bluing or parkerizing.

Noise Reduction Rating (NRR): A standardized measurement of the effectiveness of hearing protection to attenuate noise exposure for the wearer. NRR is measured in decibels, and determined under laboratory conditions. Achieving the advertised NRR requires that the user wears the hearing protection as instructed, that it fits appropriately, and that nothing is interfering with the protective abilities (e.g., glasses or hats breaking the seal of ear muffs, etc.).

Non-Corrosive: Usually refers to primers having a priming mixture which is free of corrosive compounds. Most modern primers are non-corrosive.

O

O Frame: A term used by the Colt firearms company to designate the frame of pistol built on the Browning 1911 patent for a semi-automatic handgun, the "Colt .45 Auto".

Octagon Barrel: A barrel on a firearm that has eight flat sides instead of a round barrel.

Offhand: Another term for the standard standing (unsupported) shooting position.

On Target: Holding a firearm in a position of full readiness with a complete sight picture, requiring only the press of the trigger to strike the target.

Open (Mechanical or Metallic) Sights: Non-magnifying devices on the front and rear ends of a firearm used to assist aim. There are several different types of open (mechanical or metallic) sights.

Open Bolt System: A firing system for automatic and semi-automatic firearms where the bolt remains in the rearward position after each cartridge is fired or when firing is stopped. The firing pin is generally in a fixed position in the bolt. This system allows for faster cooling of the action. This system works in a manner exactly opposite to that of the closed bolt system familiar to most shooters. Therefore, care must be taken with an open bolt firearm as natural, but, in this case, wrong tendency of "closing the bolt" fires the cartridge. The Israeli-made, Uzi sub-machine gun and the U.S. M3 sub-machine gun ("grease gun") are examples of open bolt designs.

Operating Handle: The handle of a semi-automatic or fully automatic firearm used to cycle the firearm without firing. Also known as charging handle, cocking handle or cocking knob.

Operating Rod: A long rod extending from the gas piston that may be attached to a cocking knob or handle.

Optical Center: Optical access or line joining the centers of curvature of two lens surfaces. The optical access does not always coincide with the mechanical access. When a system of lenses is used it is important that the optical access of the individual components be aligned.

Optical Sight: Sight involving the use of lenses. Optical sights may involve fixed or variable magnification or no magnification. Some optical sights involve an etched or crosswire "reticle" while others involve the use of a projected LED dot or holographic aiming reticle. A wide variety of optical sights exist but generally the term refers to any sighting system in which the shooter looks through a lens to aim.

Out Of Battery: The condition where the breeching mechanism is not in proper position for firing.

Over and Under: A term used with double barreled weapons to indicate one barrel mounted on top of the other. Generally, a shotgun design but can be a rifle or rifle/shotgun combination.

Overall Length (OAL): The total length of a cartridge, measured from bullet tip to base of case or the total length of a firearm measured from butt to muzzle

P

Palm Rest: A projection on the fore-end of a free rifle, with a shaped knob on the end to fit the half-closed hand, that a shooter grasps to support the rifle in offhand shooting. The palm rest can be adjusted for height and moved along the fore-end or pivoted toward the butt or toward the muzzle. It allows the shooter to support the rifle more steadily than he can with a conventional stock.

Parabellum: Means "prepare for war". From a Latin maxim "si vis pacem, para bellum," which means, "if you want peace, prepare for war". It is a descriptive term used for weapons and ammunition developed by the Deutsche Waffen-Und Munitions-fabrik, Berlin (the Luger pistol) and (today more commonly) the 9mm cartridge it chambered.

Parallax: A phenomenon occurring with telescopic sights where the primary image of the objective lens does not coincide with the reticule. In simple terms it is a noticeable shift in reticle placement while looking through an optical sight from different angles. Many "reflex" or "red dot" sights are advertised as *parallax free* which is technically not possible; however, for practical purposes, it means that regardless of where the reticle (red dot) is viewed in the optic, if it is on the intended point-of-aim the round will strike there (provided no error occurs on the part of the shooter and the weapon and sight are zeroed properly). This may be tested with such sights by adjusting the weapon and firing it when the aiming reticle is at the 12 o'clock, 3 o'clock, 6 o'clock, and 9 o'clock positions viewed through the lens or, alternatively, firing when the aiming reticle is in each corner of a square optical sight lens.

Parkerizing: One of the most common firearms finishes used on military weapons. Parkerizing is essentially a controlled rusting process that leaves a rough, rust-resistant, grey/green, oxide finish on the steel and iron parts of a firearm. Parkerizing is a comparatively low-cost process done to give additional protection to the metal and make it harder for traditional rust to form, however there are more durable and protective (and expensive) finishes available.

Partial Magazine Reload: A reload in which a partially expended detachable magazine in a firearm is exchanged for a fully loaded one AND the partially expended magazine is retained by the shooter for future use if necessary. Sometimes referred to as a "Tactical" reload.

Passive Safety Device: A passive safety device is one which automatically engages when the firearm is not in use, without any input from the user, and then automatically disengages to allow the gun to be discharged. Examples include magazine disconnectors, transfer bars, firing pin blocks, grip safeties and personalized guns.

Patridge Sights: A common handgun sight system consisting of a wide, flat-topped post front sight and a corresponding square-notch rear sight. Named after the late E. E. Patridge, who popularized it around the turn of the century (1900).

Pattern: The distribution of a charge of shot fired from a shotgun. This should be measured at a standard distance of 40 yards and within a 30-inch circle.

Peep Sight: Peep sights consist of a post front sight, and a small aperture rear sight (commonly easily adjustable). When looking through the sights the front sight is lined up in the aperture of the rear peep hole with the top of the front sight either centered in the hole or at the bottom center of the hole (adjustable user preference) and the target appearing just above the front sight post. As with all fixed sights the focus should be on the front sight, causing the rear aperture to appear as a small fuzzy ring and the target to be out of focus. This type of sight is the most common type of fixed sight used on military and law enforcement rifles. Also see "Aperture Sight".

Pellet (or Pellets): Small spherical projectiles loaded in shotshells and more often called "shot". Also, the skirted projectiles used in pellet guns.

Penetration: The depth that a projectile travels into a target before it stops.

Personalized Firearms: This term has both an old and a new meaning. The old meaning refers to the process of adding or making custom features to a firearm, thus making it uniquely one person's gun. The new meaning of the term refers to a relatively new type of firearm that prevents anyone, other than an authorized user, from firing the gun. This personalization is achieved by the use of a magnetic or electronic lock has been built into the grip of the gun that can only be unlocked when an authorized user wears an identifying magnetic ring or radio transmitter bracelet. When placed next to the grip of the handgun in the proper orientation, the ring or bracelet unlocks the trigger and allow the weapon to be fired.

Pistol: In contemporary American usage, the term "pistol" is limited to handguns in which the barrel and chamber form a single unit (i.e., self-loaders and single shots.) It is considered by many to be erroneous to apply the term "pistol" to a revolver. The origin of this word is particularly obscure. Some trace it to the Italian town of Pistoia, an early gun making center. Another explanation derives from a Bohemian handgun called a "pist'ala" from a Czech word for "pipe". Several other more fanciful etymologies exist. Also see "Handgun" and "Revolver".

Pistol Grip: The handle of a handgun or protrusion on the buttstock or fore-end of a shoulder-operated firearm that resembles the grip or handle of a handgun. A "semi-pistol grip" is one less pronounced than normal; a "vertical pistol grip" is more pronounced than normal.

Point Blank Range: Any distance at which a given firearm can hit the target with reasonable accuracy without the need to compensate for bullet drop. The "point blank diameter" refers to the area on the target where those hits are considered reasonably accurate, thus helping establish point blank range.

Point-of-aim (POA): The place or point on a target that intersects the straight line generated by the alignment of the shooters eye with the sighting system of a firearm.

Point-of-impact (POI): The point at which a projectile hits the target.

Polymer: A chemical compound or mixture of compounds formed by polymerization and consisting essentially of repeating structural units. Also, a chemical compound with high molecular weight consisting of a number of structural units linked together by covalent bonds. Polymers are used in the manufacture of many modern firearm parts such as pistol frames and rifle stocks, grips, etc.

Polymer Frame: A modern handgun frame or receiver made of polymer or plastic. The polymers used in modern handgun frames and receivers typically consist of high strength synthetic fibers that are mixed with hard but forgiving plastics. The combination of the materials is a little different for each manufacturer and the exact recipe is a trade secret. The key is to get a material that is of low weight and high strength, without becoming brittle. Also reduced machining time and therefore a reduced manufacturing cost.

Polymer frames actually give a little under recoil and this helps to dissipate and absorb some of the perceived recoil. Many of the polymer framed handguns also have some steel components in them.

Pope Rib: A rib integral with the barrel. Designed by Harry M. Pope, famed barrel maker and shooter, the rib made it possible to mount a target scope low over the barrel.

Port: The word port as it relates to Firearms has many uses and definitions. In most cases the term port refers to an opening or vent manufactured into the firearm. Additional uses are:

- Barrel Port: The openings or vents cut or machined into the muzzle end of a barrel to allow gas to escape and to reduce perceived recoil. Also called Barrel Porting and Ported Barrel.
- Cylinder Port: Openings in the cylinder face or frame of a revolver for the passage of loaded ammunition and removal of expended cartridges.
- Ejection Port: Opening where expended cartridges and shells are removed from the action or magazine.
- Firing Port: A hole in an armored vehicle or a fortified structure for observation or for firing weapons.
- Loading Port: An opening in a firearm for the insertion of ammunition into the magazine, chamber, breech or cylinder.
- Magna Port: A commercial porting process where ports are burned into the muzzle of a firearm. The Porting is designed to reduce felt recoil and muzzle lift on all types of firearms.
- Muzzle Port: The openings or vents cut or machined into the muzzle end of a barrel to allow gas to escape and to reduce perceived recoil.

Porting: May mean either lowering the ejection port of a self-loading pistol to ensure greater reliability and less damage to cases upon ejection or the practice of drilling gas vents in a barrel to reduce muzzle jump. The proprietary Magna port system is a well-known example of this.

Powder: The propellant used in most firearms. It produces a large volume of gas when ignited. There are two basic types, black powder (an explosive) and smokeless powder (a propellant). Also see "Smokeless Powder".

Powder Burn: Charring caused by gunshot residue.

Powder Charge: The amount of powder by weight in the case of smokeless powder.

Powder Scale: A device used to weigh charges of powder.

PPC "Practical Pistol Course": A course of fire developed by the FBI that involves shooting at human-shaped silhouettes from a variety of ranges and shooting positions. Shot competitively, usually by police. The custom heavy-barreled revolvers favored in these competitions are known as "PPC revolvers".

Pressure: Force per unit area, measured in interior ballistics terms of pounds per square inch. The force exerted against the cartridge case, base of the bullet, chamber and bolt face by a burning charge of powder in the chamber of a firearm.

Pressure Barrel: A heavy-walled barrel fitted with instrumentation to measure pressure.

Pressure Peak: The maximum chamber pressure reached by gases that result from the ignition and burning of powder in a cartridge case or shotgun shell. In a rifle or shotgun, maximum pressure normally occurs when the bullet or shot charge has moved less than one-quarter of the distance through the barrel.

Primer: That part of a cartridge which is struck by the gun's firing pin, detonates, and thus ignites the powder charge. There are two main types of priming systems currently in use, rimfire and centerfire. In a rimfire cartridge, e.g. .22s, the priming compound is spun into and contained in a hollow space in the case rim. In a centerfire primer, the compound is in a small metal cup inserted into the base of the cartridge case. There are two types of centerfire primers "Boxer" or "Berdan". The Boxer primer is made up of a cup and an anvil, with the priming compound sandwiched between the two. The Berdan primer does not have a self-contained anvil, using instead an anvil that is a part of the casing. Also see "Percussion Cap".

Primer Pocket: The cavity in the base of a cartridge which receives and supports the primer.

Projectile: A term used with firearms to describe ball, shot or bullet fired from a firearm.

Prong Buttplate: A buttplate for use on a free rifle that has a prong projecting from the toe, or from the toe and the heel. The prongs aid in maintaining the butt of the rifle in fixed position against the shoulder, the prong that fits under the armpit serving to balance the rifle on the fulcrum afforded by the palm rest.

Proof Mark: A mark or stamp placed on firearms to indicate meeting rigid standards. In European guns, they are quite specific, indicating proof house and all proofs performed, sometimes also the date of proof. Proof marks are applied to all parts actually tested, usually on the barrel, and often before blueing, and without sights. In the U.S., there is no federalized or government proof house, only the manufacturer's in-house proof mark indicating that a firearm has passed their internal quality control standards per government specifications.

Proof Test: The firing of a deliberate overload to test the strength of a firearm barrel and/or action.

Propellant: In a firearm the chemical composition (gunpowder) that is ignited by the primer to generate gas. In air or pellet guns it means compressed air or $CO2$.

Pull-Through: The cord used to pull a bore brush or cleaning patch through the bore of a firearm.

Pump Action: see "Slide Action".

Q

Quick Detach (QD): Usually referring to an easily removable attachment for a scope mount or sling swivel.

R

Ramp: A fixed component of a firearm directly in front of the top round in a magazine designed to direct cartridges up and into the chamber of a firearm as they are stripped from the magazine by the slide or bolt.

Range: A term generally used to indicate a place to shoot firearms that has been developed and maintained for that purpose. This term can also be used when describing the distance that a certain firearm can throw a bullet, the distance that a firearm is most effective within, or the distance from the firearm to the target.

Rangemaster: A person of authority or seniority that manages an agency's firearms program and oversees the daily operations of a shooting range. Typically, a supervisory position or position of leadership. Ideally a certified firearms instructor with notable experience. Also, a person responsible for maintaining the range and ensuring the safety of all present. The rangemaster has the authority to direct shooter conduct while at the range, up to and including expulsion.

Range Safety Officer (RSO): A staff member trained and/or certified to run an exercise on a range and monitor safety but not to provide instruction. Range safety officers may be tasked with monitoring shooters during exercises, running a qualification (not training), or other tasks assigned by the rangemaster or lead firearms instructor depending on the agency use of these positions.

Rate Of Twist: see "Rifling Twist".

Rebated Rimless: The type of cartridge case in which the extraction rim is much smaller than the rest of the casing. Used in firearms where it is necessary to completely enclose the case in the chamber but still have it held by the bolt, and also in order to allow a large case to be manipulated by a standard size bolt face.

Receiver: This term is generally only used as a term on long guns. Means the housing for a firearm's breech (portion of the barrel with chamber into which a cartridge or projectile is loaded) and firing mechanism, including the bolt, firing pin, mainspring, trigger group, and magazine or ammunition feed system. The barrel is threaded into the somewhat enlarged forward part of the receiver, called the receiver ring. At the rear of the receiver, the butt or stock is fastened. In semi-automatic pistols, the frame or housing is sometimes referred to as the receiver.

Receiver Bridge: That section of a bolt-action rifle receiver above and behind the ejection port.

Receiver Ring: The portion of a receiver into which the barrel is threaded.

Recoil: The rearward movement of a firearm in the opposite direction to that of the bullet at the moment of discharge. The motion or "kick" of a firearm on firing. Recoil in shooting is the practical effect of Newton's Third Law of Motion: for every action there is an opposite and equal reaction.

Recoil Operated: A form of locked-breech semi-automatic operation in which the barrel and breech remain locked together during the peak pressure, then move rearward under recoil (opposed to gas returning from the barrel or a piston) to effect unlocking and completion of the cycle of operation. Many high-power pistols use this system.

Recoil Pad: A pad attached to the butt of a buttstock to absorb part of the firearm's recoil.

Recoil Shield: On a revolver, the recoil shield is the metal extensions on the firearm's frame that cover the exposed back of the cylinder on either side of the gun. It is designed to prevent fired or unfired cartridges from sliding out of the cylinder and to protect the exposed primers of cartridges in the chambers on either side.

Recoil Spring (or Return Spring): The spring on a self-loading firearm's action which returns it into battery after firing.

Release Trigger: A trap (shotgun sport) shooting trigger that fires the gun when the trigger is released, not pressed.

Reload: The process of putting more cartridges into a firearm that has run out of ammunition. Also, could be a reference to a cartridge that has been reassembled with a new primer, powder, and projectile. Also see "Reloading".

Reloader: Term used to describe the press used to load or reload ammunition cartridges. There are several types of reloading presses, they include the turret press, the progressive type and the single stage reloader. Also may refer to someone who loads or reloads ammunition cartridges.

Reloading: A process of taking empty, previously fired cartridge cases, inspecting them, cleaning them, resizing them, and then reassembling them using a new primer, new powder and new projectile to make a new cartridge. This term is distinct from "Hand Loading" which can encompass reloading but is also inclusive of the processes of assembling cartridges from all new components. Reloading is done for various reasons, some of which are; to save money, to build custom cartridges otherwise unobtainable, and/or as a hobby.

Remaining Energy: A projectile's energy in foot pounds at a given range.

Report: The sound made by firing a gun. Also see "Muzzle Blast".

Resolving Power: The ability of a lens or system of lenses to show two closely spaced objects as distinct, one from the other. The measure of resolving power is customarily taken as the angle subtended by two objects that are just far enough apart to make it possible to see them as two distinct points.

Reticle (also Reticule): The lines (crosshairs) that are visible when looking through a scope and that are used to determine the point-of-aim. Also said by some to be a form of graticule (also see "graticule") which incorporates markers which are a specified distance apart and can thus be used in range finding and that the word "reticle" is wrongly used interchangeably with "graticule".

Revolver (Revolver Action): A firearm, usually a handgun, with a multi-chambered revolving cylinder that rotates to successively align each chamber with a single barrel and firing pin each time the hammer is cocked (single action), or the trigger is pulled (double action). The number of chambers in the cylinder can vary between models, ranging from 4 to 10. The direction of cylinder rotation is also variable, either being clockwise or counter-clockwise, depending on the design. Also see "Handgun" and "Pistol".

Rib: see "Barrel Rib".

Ricochet: A term descriptive of the unintentional deflection of a bullet when striking a hard object. Ricochets are commonly misunderstood in the belief that a bullet can bounce from surface to surface in the manner of a pool ball against the cushions of a pool table. Bullets rarely deflect from a surface greater than 10 degrees of angle from their path of flight and when so deflected, bullets tend to travel parallel to the surface that deflected them. A more common effect, often mistaken as a ricochet, is "splash" where a bullet will strike a solid object, fragment, and pieces may actually travel back along the flight path to strike the shooter.

Rifle: A shoulder held firearm with a rifled barrel. Rifles can be of almost any caliber, from .22 to .50 BMG (Browning Machine Gun). As with handguns, though, the power is in the cartridge, not the firearm. The term rifle derives from the rifling of the barrel. Also, the act of forming the rifling in a gun barrel.

Rifle Sights: same as "blade sights".

Rifled Barrel: A barrel with a spiral pattern of grooves cut into its bore for the purpose of imparting a spin on the projectile as it is forced through it.

Rifled Slug: A large diameter single projectile, designed to be fired through the smooth bore of a shotgun. The rifling is actually cast as part of the slug and imparts some spin to the slug by friction with the bore.

Rifling: A set of parallel spiraling grooves that run the length of the interior of the barrel which cause the bullet to spin upon firing to improve its stability in flight, thus imparting greater accuracy. Rifling is present in all true rifles, in most handguns and in some shotgun barrels that are designed for increased accuracy when using slugs (a slug is a single projectile from a shotgun rather than the more common "shot"). Rifling may rotate to the left or the right, the higher parts of the bore being called lands, the cuts or lower parts being called the grooves, and with the grooves usually cut twice the width of the land. Many types exist, such as oval, polygonal, button, Newton, Newton-Pope, parabolic, Haddan, Enfield, segmental rifling, etc. Most U.S. made barrels have a right-hand twist, while British gunmakers prefer a left-hand twist. In practice, there seems to be little difference in accuracy or barrel longevity. Also see "Rifling Twist".

Rifling Twist: The rate of spiral of the grooves of a rifle barrel expressed as a ratio of length to rotation. Typically, the number of inches a bullet moves down the barrel for one revolution. For example, 1:9, would mean a bullet would make one full rotation after moving 9 inches down the barrel. Also see "Rifling".

Rim: The edge on the base of a cartridge case. The rim is the part of the case that the extractor grips to remove the cartridge from the chamber. The rim may be the same diameter as the casing, smaller or larger depending on the type and design of the ammunition.

Rim Fire (Rimfire Cartridge): A rimmed or flanged cartridge where the priming mixture is spun into the outer rim of the casing base. Once a very common cartridge in all calibers, the most notable modern example that remains is the .22 rim-fire. To fire this type of cartridge, the firing pin must impact on the outer rim.

Rimless Cartridge Case: A centerfire cartridge case with the case head of the same diameter as the body.

Rimmed Cartridge Case: A cartridge case with a base or head larger in diameter than the body of the case.

Rod: A rod used for cleaning a firearm. It is used to check for obstructions prior to loading the firearm. It may also be referred to as a ramrod, proving stick or dummy rod.

Rolling Block Action: A single shot action, designed in the U.S. and widely used in early Remington arms. Also known as the Remington-Rider action, the breechblock, actuated by a lever, rotates down and back from the chamber. The firing pin is contained in the block and is activated by hammer fall.

Rotary Magazine: The cartridges are arranged about a central rotating spindle or carrier.

Round: Synonym for a cartridge. A military term meaning one single cartridge, as in a "round of ammunition". Also, one shot fired by a firearm.

Round Butt: A revolver that has a forward curve in the lower rear grip area.

S

S&W: Abbreviation for Smith & Wesson, prominent American maker of revolvers and firearms since the 1850s. S&W's introduced the first commercially-produced breech loading revolver.

Safety: A device designed to prevent discharge of a firearm until discharge is intended. Also see "Grip Safety", "Firing Pin Safety", "Hammer Block", "Magazine Safety", "Thumb / Finger Safety", "Transfer Bar" and

"Trigger Safety". Also, a state of mind and actions intended to reduce the risk of personal harm.

Safety Slug (or Glaser Safety Slug): Frangible ammunition designed to prevent over penetration and for enhanced safety in training and close quarters shooting environments. Glaser Safety Slug, Inc. developed the first frangible bullet in 1974 to provide reduced ricochet and over-penetration danger with improved stopping power over conventional bullets. In 1987, Glaser developed the round-nose frangible bullet offering guaranteed feeding reliability. In 1988 Glaser introduced the compressed-core bullet to maximize bullet weight and the number of bullet fragments. This precision formed bullet also produces target grade accuracy, seldom found in a personal defense bullet. In 1994 Glaser improved fragmentation reliability to below 1000 feet per second through the use of soft, rather than hard plastic in the bullet tip.

Scope: An abbreviated term for "telescopic sight" or "telescopic scope". A magnifying optical aiming device usually mounted to the receiver or slide of a firearm to assist in aiming the weapon. A scope may be designed with either a fixed or variable magnification and with various fields of view and reticules.

Scope Mount: A set of metallic rings on a base that secures a scope to a firearm.

Scout Rifle: A concept popularized by the late Col. Jeff Cooper. A scout rifle, generally, is a bolt action carbine firing a medium power round suitable for taking large game (e.g., .308), fitted with a long eye-relief telescopic sight mounted on the barrel, and a backup set of iron sights.

Sear: A small lever that engages in a notch on the lower portion of a firearm with a hammer to hold the hammer in a cocked or halfcocked position or on the lip of a striker. The sear is directly acted on as a part of the trigger mechanism. When the trigger is depressed, the sear is retracted which then releases the hammer or striker, discharging the firearm.

Seating Depth: The depth to which a bullet is seated below the case mouth.

Seating Die: The reloading die that presses the bullet into the neck of the cartridge case, crimping the case if so desired.

Sectional Density: A bullet's weight, in pounds, divided by the square of its diameter in inches.

Select Fire (or Selective Fire): A firearm's ability to be fired full automatic, semi-automatic, or in some cases, in burst-fire mode at the option of the shooter.

Selector: In a double-barreled firearm, the selector is a device to allow the shooter to choose the barrel used by the first pull of the trigger. In select-fire firearms, it is the lever that chooses between semi-automatic, burst, and/or automatic firing and between a high and low rate of automatic firing.

Self-Feed: An overall descriptive term of a firearm that uses gas pressure or recoil, rather than manual operation, to complete the cycle of operation. Both semi-automatic and fully automatic firearms are self-feeding.

Semi-Automatic: Term used to describe firearms which use part of the energy produced when the gun is fired to automatically eject the empty case and reload the chamber with a new cartridge. On semi-automatics the trigger must then be released and then pulled again to fire the next cartridge (as opposed to fully-automatic).

Serial Number: A unique number applied to a firearm in order to identify the individual firearm.

Set Trigger: A special trigger that allows for most of the pressure necessary to release the hammer to be overcome by use of another lever or button, leaving the trigger in a state where only very light pressure is needed to fire the weapon.

Shock (or Hydrostatic Shock): The transference of the kinetic energy of a bullet to animal tissue or other liquid or semi-liquid mediums.

Shoot House: A specially designed range, usually for training military or law enforcement personnel, which is structured like a building with various walls, corners and doors to simulate movement and engagement inside a building. Shoot houses may be specifically built for live-fire or restricted to force-on-force training with marking cartridges.

Shooting Platform: A combination of a shooter's stance and grip to support the firearm and control recoil during shooting. Used as an instructional term to help shooters understand proper techniques for efficient and effective shooting methods.

Short Action: A rifle designed for shorter, lower power, cartridges.

Shot: Round lead (or other metal alloys) balls loaded into shotgun shells. The two main divisions of shot: "Birdshot" small shot (less than .24 inches); and "Buckshot" heavy shot (.24 inches or larger) shotshells. Also see "Birdshot" and "Buckshot".

Shotgun: A shoulder held firearm generally with smooth-bored barrel(s) primarily intended for firing multiple small, round projectiles, (shot, birdshot, pellets), larger shot (buck shot), single round balls (pumpkin balls) and cylindrical slugs. Some shotgun barrels have rifling to give better accuracy with slugs or greater pattern spread to birdshot. Shotguns are used in hunting, target shooting, police, military and self-defense applications. Shot is effective to about 40 meters or less; slugs to about 100 meters or less.

Shotshell: The cartridge for a shotgun (also called a shell). A shotshell case (or "Hull") may be made entirely of metal or plastic or partly of plastic or paper with a metal head. Most shotshells also carry a load of many small pellets rather than a single projectile, although many different types of loads exist, including single projectiles (slug) and other specialty loads. Small shotshells are also made for rifles and handguns and are often used for vermin control.

Shoulder: The projection of a bottle necked cartridge case from the neck to the case body; or, the point at which the head of a projectile joins the cylindrical rear portion.

Side by Side: A term used with double barreled firearms (usually a shotgun) to indicate one barrel mounted to the side of the other.

Sight Alignment: The relationship of the front sight to the notch of the rear sight as seen by the shooter's eye.

Sight Ears: The projections on both sides of the front or rear sights of a rifle that serve to protect the sights.

Sight Height: Can be used to reference to the height of the front sight post or rear sight notch or aperture. May also be used to indicate the height of the line of sight through the sights over the centerline of the bore of the firearm. Also see "Sight Over Bore Height".

Sight In (or Sighting In): A term used to describe the action of adjusting the sighting elements of a firearm. Adjustments are made after firing the weapon a number of times and determining a consistent placement of the bullets. Adjusting the sights will compensate for any degree of placement of the shot other than the intended location. Also see "Zeroing".

Sight Over Bore Height: The distance from the centerline of the bore to the centerline of the sighting system in which the shooter looks through.

Sight Picture: A term indicating that the front sight and rear sight are properly aligned with the focus on the front sight and that the target is positioned correctly as a part of this entire "picture". Having acquired a proper sight picture, all that is necessary to strike the target is to correctly pull the trigger.

Sight Radius: The distance between the sighting point on the rear sight and the sighting point on the front sight. Generally, the longer the sight radius, the easier it is to hit a specific point-of-aim.

Sight(s): Aiming device attached to the top of the barrel, receiver or slide. They are used to align the firearm with a target. Any of a variety of devices, mechanical and optical, designed to assist in the aiming of a firearm.

Single Action: A handgun that can only be fired by first manually cocking the hammer or striker, accomplished by direct manual action (pulled back by the thumb) or by the action of the bolt or slide. The hammer or striker is then released by pulling the trigger; thus, the trigger is said to be performing only one action or "single action". Also see "Double Action". This term has been misused to denote handguns that allow the hammer to be cocked only one way, either by direct manual action (pulled back by the thumb), or by a long pull on the trigger.

Single Column Magazine: A magazine that has an interior side to side dimension the same width as the cartridge it was designed to hold. Thus when cartridges are inserted in the magazine they stack on top of one another.

The detractor to this type of magazine is reduced capacity when compared to a dual or "staggered" column magazine, although if designed to insert into the grip of a pistol, the narrower magazine means that the grip will be narrower as well (beneficial to those with smaller hands). Many pistols and a few rifles use this type of magazine. Also see "Magazine" and "Dual or Staggered Column Magazine". Also referred to as a "single stack magazine".

Single Shot: A firearm mechanism lacking a magazine, where separately carried ammunition must be manually placed in the firearm's chamber for each firing.

Single-Stage Trigger: A single-stage trigger is designed to operate in one smooth range of motion with no take-up or slack in the trigger. Single-stage triggers will often have a lighter pull weight when compared to two-stage triggers. Also see "Two-Stage Trigger".

Single Trigger: Most often used to describe a single trigger on a double-barrel gun. It fires both barrels one after the other by successive pulls. Obviously, this term can also describe any firearm with only one trigger. Also see "Double Trigger" and "Double Set Trigger".

Sleeve: An insert of special material placed in a barrel to reduce bore erosion, renew an eroded bore. They are also used to strengthen a barrel or alter the diameter to accept a different caliber of ammunition. Also called a barrel liner.

Slide: A major part of a semi-automatic pistol that surrounds the barrel and that contains the ejection port. As its name implies, the slide moves backwards (either manually or upon discharge), opening the breech area of the handgun, ejecting a spent case, possibly cocking the hammer or striker, and then striping a new cartridge from the magazine and placing it into the chamber.

Slide Action: A firearm action mechanism used on rifles and shotguns that is activated by manual operation of a horizontally sliding handle (that almost always doubles as the fore-end stock) and that is almost always located under the barrel. There, it serves as a device to hold the gun and steady it the same as a fixed fore-end stock. To eject a case/hull and load the next cartridge/shotshell, the handle is pulled back as far as it will go toward the buttstock, and then pushed back out as far as it will go toward the muzzle. "Pump-action" and "trombone" are synonyms for "slide-action."

Slide Safety: A device that blocks the firing mechanism of a firearm.

Slide/Bolt Release (Catch): A lever or catch designed to hold the slide or bolt of a self-loading firearm open in preparation for inspection or reloading. Many self-loading firearms are designed so that the follower of the magazine will push up on the slide/bolt release when the last cartridge from that magazine is stripped and fired causing the slide or bolt to stop in its rearward position. This allows a new magazine to be quickly inserted and the release pressed stripping a new round and readying the firearm for the next shot very rapidly.

Sling: A fabric or leather strap attached to a firearm so that the weapon can be hung from the neck, shoulder or arm without the need of holding it in the hands at all times. A sling may also be used as a shooting aide, when wrapped around the arms properly, to obtain a secure grip on the firearm preparatory to discharge.

Sling Swivels: Metal loops affixed to the gun, so as to be able to rotate, to which the sling is attached.

Slug: The most common use of this term is to describe the hollow based lead bullet used primarily in shotguns. Also, to "slug" a barrel, is to force a soft lead projectile through the bore of a gun to determine bore and groove diameter. Also, a slang term synonymous with "bullet". Also see "Bullet".

Small Bore (Smallbore): Generally, refers to a .22 caliber firearm or rim-fire ammunition.

Smokeless Powder: The propellant powder used in modern ammunition, invented during the 1880s by the Frenchman M. Vielle. Smokeless powder has either a nitrocellulose or nitroglycerin base, or both (in which case it is referred to as "double based"). Like black powder, it is black in color, but this is generally due to a graphite coating which improves metering. It is not an explosive, but rather a flammable solid that burns extremely rapidly releasing a large volume of gas. Its burning rate can be controlled by the shape and size of the granules. Faster burning powders (e.g., Bullseye™) are generally used in pistols, while slower powders (IMR 4064™) are used in rifles. Commonly called "gunpowder", it is classified as a "Flammable Solid" by the Department of Transportation. Note that small arms ammunition, unless it has explosive filled projectiles, does not explode in a fire but rather burns vigorously.

Smooth Bore (Smoothbore): A gun barrel which is not rifled. The original gun and muskets were smoothbore. Most shotguns are smoothbore.

Snap Cap: A non-firing mechanical device that resembles a cartridge and is constructed (usually out of plastic) with a spring-loaded plunger in place of a primer, bullet, and powder charge. It is intended to be chambered in a firearm during dry-fire practice to cushion the firing pin so as to avoid damaging or breaking the firing pin.

Sniper Rifle: An inflammatory phrase having no legal or technical meaning or definition. Generally, this term is applied to a scoped rifle, firing a high-powered cartridge, that is intended to engage a target at long ranges. Although this term can be used to describe the weapon used by trained snipers (military and police), this description also be used to describe many hunting rifles (essentially the same rifle used for a different purpose). As such, using the phrase "sniper rifle" is a misnomer and should be avoided.

Snub Nosed: Descriptive of a small revolver (usually) with an unusually short barrel.

Speed Loader: A device intended to hold a number of cartridges in such a manner as to aid in reloading a revolver.

Speed Reload: Sometime used as another term for an empty gun reload. This term is also used synonymously with "emergency reload" in which a partial magazine is dropped and not retained. Also see "Empty Gun Reload" and "Emergency Reload".

Spent Bullet: A bullet near the end of its flight which has lost nearly all its energy. Despite a loss in energy, spent bullets can still penetrate targets.

Spot Anneal: The annealing of a small spot on a piece of steel while leaving the rest of the steel hard. This technique is frequently applied to rifle receivers which are too hard to drill and tap for scope blocks.

Spotting Scope: A single-lens scope, usually of 20 power or greater and used with a tripod for long-range target observation, adjusting fire, and estimating effects of wind speed and direction.

Square Butt: A revolver that is not curved in the lower rear grip area.

Squeeze Cocker: A specially designed mechanism that places a firearm in a cocked condition by squeezing the grip of the weapon (used in the Heckler & Koch "squeeze cocker" pistols).

Squib (or Squib Load): A round that is under loaded. When a squib is fired there is insufficient force to push the bullet clear of the barrel. The gun must be field stripped so that the bullet can be removed (usually with a cleaning rod). Firing another shot before clearing a squib is not safe and may cause injury to the shooter or to onlookers as well as damage to the firearm. Most squibs occur because of careless reloading practices. They are extremely rare in factory ammunition.

Staballoy: Designates metal alloys made from high-density depleted uranium with other metals for use in kinetic energy penetrators for armor-piercing munitions. Several different metals such as titanium or molybdenum can be used for the purpose. The various staballoy metals have low radioactivity that is not considered to be a significant health hazard.

Stage: In a qualification, fired at more than one range or in more than one position, each range or position is referred to as a stage of the qualification.

Staging Area: The designated zone behind the firing line, usually farthest from the bullet impact area on a range, where the next relay of shooters can complete their preparations for the stage or training exercise and receive instruction and advice from their coach or instructor.

Staggered Column Magazine: A box magazine that has two staggered columns of cartridges that increase capacity but not length of the magazine.

Stainless Steel: Although often referred to as a firearm finish, stainless steel is actually the replacement of standard steels with a steel containing a high percentage of chromium, making it more rust resistant. The biggest advantage of a stainless-steel firearm is that it is very difficult for rust to form. The disadvantage to stainless steel weapons is that parts do not tend to slide on one another as smoothly as milder steels do.

Stamp Tax: see "Class Three".

Stance: The posture assumed by a shooter or marksman while firing a shot. Proper stance is important in competition and in tactical or defensive uses of firearms as the shooter is more stable and has the ability to move and engage targets properly from a steady and efficient shooting position.

Stock: The wooden, metal, plastic or fiberglass portion of a rifle or shotgun, to which the barrel, action, trigger action, etc., are attached and which is used to hold it securely. Stocks are used on long guns, grips on handguns.

Stop Plate: A small round steel target that falls back and down when shot. Used to indicate a shooter has reached the end of a course of fire.

Stoppage: An interruption in the cycle of operation of a firearm which may occur for a variety of reasons. Also see "Malfunction".

Stopping Power: A popular but non-specific and non-scientific term used to describe the defensive or offensive effectiveness of a particular type of ammunition. Usually stopping power is quantified as a number expressing the percentage of times a first hit stops a threat (not necessarily kills). Most published writings on this including the popular pulp fiction by Marshal and Sannow have been completely discredited by medical professionals, scientists and ballistics engineers. There are many factors in determining a rounds effectiveness, such as velocity, bullet weight, penetration depth, weight retention and bullet expansion. Penetration and expansion are determined by muzzle velocity, bullet design, and shot placement. Because of this stopping power or the terminal effect varies greatly, even within a single caliber. The end result and terminal effect of any particular bullet varies greatly based on the target itself, to include the targets clothing, body position relative to the shooter, their mindset and whether drugs are involved. Anecdotal evidence exists on both extremes of bullet performance, but generally "center of mass" hits with defensive type hollow point ammunition is the most effective combination for stopping an aggressor.

Stove Pipe: Term used to describe a pistol feeding malfunction. Occasionally, semi-automatics firearms fail to fully eject a spend cartridge. When this happens, the empty shell can be trapped as the slide closes. Sometimes the shell will protrude from the slide open end up, giving the appearance of a stove pipe, hence the use of the term. A good firearms instructor can provide training on how to quickly clear a stove pipe. The correct procedure allows shooter to return the gun to operational status very quickly.

Striker: In many modern arms the traditional hammer is replaced an axially mounted, spring-propelled firing pin that is acted on directly by the trigger mechanism. In operation a striker can function in a "double-action" or "single-action" manner. In double-action firearms the trigger mechanism draws the striker back against spring pressure and then releases it to spring forward to strike the primer on the cartridge. In single-action firearms the striker is "cocked" (drawn back against spring pressure and latched back) by some other mechanism and then released to strike the primer on the cartridge by the trigger mechanism. Also see "Hammer".

Stripper Clip: see "Clip".

Strong Hand: In shooting, the primary usage or dominant hand. For a right-handed person, the right hand. For a left-handed person, the left hand. Also see "Weapon Hand".

Sturmgewehr: German for "storm rifle" or assault rifle. Also see "Assault Rifle".

Submachine Gun: A fully automatic, magazine-fed firearm that fires pistol ammunition, such as 9mm or .45 ACP, that is intended for close-range combat. In military environments they are traditionally deployed in special operations commando units where mobility is key, or tank crews where space inside the vehicle is tight. In police environments they are deployed in counter-terrorist or special weapons units. The weapon is designed to be fired with two hands and generally has a shoulder stock or brace.

Subsonic: Below the speed of sound. Sound travels at 1118 feet per second (340 meters per second) at sea level. An object such as a bullet moving at a greater speed generates a sound-wave (the sonic bang). Thus, a firearm that is silenced or suppressed must fire sub-sonic ammunition, otherwise the noise of the bullet's sonic bang will be heard.

Supersonic: Above the speed of sound. Greater than 1118 feet per second at sea level. In metric 340 meters per second.

Support Hand: In shooting, the off-hand or non-dominant hand. For a right-handed person, the left hand. For a left-handed person, the right hand.

Support Side: The side of the shooters body of the non-dominant hand. For a right-handed person, the left side. For a left-handed person, the right side.

Suppressor: A device for attachment to a firearm's muzzle for reducing the report. Often inaccurately referred to as a "silencer". May also be referred to as a "sound suppressor". The device can also be integral to the firearms barrel.

Swage: To pressure-form by forcing through or into a die.

Swaged: A part that has been tapered or shaped in such a way as to be one directional; e.g., a swaged pin must be removed in one direction (right to left) and replaced in the opposite direction (left to right).

T

Tactical Reload: see "Partial Magazine Reload".

Take Down: A firearm designed to be disassembled readily into two or more sections for ease of carrying, storage, or shipping.

Take Down Pins: Removable or sliding pins that are slid or removed from a gun so it can be taken apart.

Take Down Release: A lever or button that when depressed allows a firearm to be taken apart into various components for inspection and cleaning.

Tang: Metal prongs or rods that extend from the rear of a receiver (upper, middle, and/or lower) of a long gun to connect the receiver to the buttstock.

Tang Safety: A device that blocks the firing mechanism of a firearm that is located in the tang. Also see "Tang".

Target: A mark or item to shoot at, something fired at with a gun. Many types of targets exist for shooting competition and recreation. Target types include paper with a traditional bulls eye or concentric rings and circles, human form type silhouette targets, typically used by law enforcement, metal plates of varying sizes and shapes to include game animal forms, and clay or frangible items used for skeet or trap shooting. Targets can be made of just about anything, the most common being paper and cardboard.

Target Ammunition: Ammunition which is designed to be used for shooting (paper or steel) targets. Since the design priority is accuracy rather than terminal effect in soft tissue or stopping power, target ammunition is not loaded "hot". Target ammo does not include "defensive features" such frangibility or a hollow point. It is usually less expensive than ammunition designed to be carried for defense.

Target Grips: Oversize wood grips designed to give the shooter firm control on a competition handgun.

Target Hammer: A hammer with an unusually large spur to facilitate manual cocking with the thumb.

Target Trigger: A wider trigger, many times found with a grooved surface, that is designed to give the target shooter firm, full control.

Telescopic Sight: see "Scope".

Temple Index: A muzzle up ready position for pistol in which the hand holding the pistol is indexed on the side of the head, near the temple, with the muzzle up and trigger finger straight. Often used for operating around vehicles or in confined spaces or when a muzzle down position would be unsafe.

Ten Ring: The innermost ring of the black section of the target.

Throat: Sometimes used as a definition of the leade or freebore; The transition area between a firearm's chamber and the beginning of the rifling that is designed to force the bullet into the rifling. Also used as a definition of the open end of a firearm's chamber that receives and guides the cartridge into the chamber.

Throating: The practice of polishing, enlarging and re-contouring the feed ramp and chamber mouth opening of an auto pistol's barrel to ensure more reliable functioning, especially with semi-wadcutter and other non-standard bullets.

Thumb / Finger Safety: A safety device in the shape of a lever or button operated by the thumb or forefinger designed to render the trigger mechanism inoperable in the safe position. This type of safety may also lock the side or bolt, move the firing pin out of reach of the hammer, insert a block between the hammer and firing pin, or lock the hammer. Also see "Grip Safety", "Drop Safety", and "Magazine Safety".

Timing: The alignment of the chambers of a revolver with the bore. In a revolver which has seen a lot of use, the timing can be "off," so that the chambers do not perfectly align with the bore, causing the gun to spit lead from the barrel-cylinder gap.

Toe: The bottom part of the butt of a rifle or shotgun.

Toggle (or Knee) Action: A unique action developed for the "Luger" pistol. Instead of a traditional slide as most semi-automatic pistols use, the Luger has a breach block that is actuated by a hinged, spring loaded, lever with knurled, round, griping lugs on each side. To open the action the knurled lugs are pulled to the rear and up. It is these knurled lugs that give the Luger its most distinctive feature.

Top Strap: That section of a revolver's frame that spans the top of the opening for the cylinder. It may also be slightly grooved, the groove serving as rear sight, or it may carry at its rearward end an adjustable sight.

Trajectory: The vertically curved path taken by a projectile after it leaves the barrel of a gun. If you draw an imaginary straight line exactly parallel to the center of the bore, the bullet will fall away from that line.

Transfer Bar: A safety device used with handguns to prevent accidental discharge of the firearm. The transfer bar is actuated as a part of the act of pulling the trigger. When the hammer is released, the transfer bar is imposed between the hammer and a floating firing pin, transferring the impact to the cartridge primer. The transfer bar is designed to prevent an accidental discharge if the firearm is dropped or otherwise mishandled.

Trigger: A small lever protruding from the action intended to be pulled on by the fore-finger. Pressing the trigger causes hammer or striker to release, or an electric circuit to close, which then causes the cartridge to be fired.

Trigger Control: The ability of the pistol shooter to apply pressure on the trigger to fire the weapon without disturbing the sight alignment or sight picture.

Trigger Guard: A metal or plastic ring surrounding and protecting the trigger from being pulled or depressed accidentally. It is designed to prevent the trigger from snagging as the firearm is handled or as handgun is removed from or placed into a holster. Some vintage handguns do not have trigger guards.

Trigger Job: Polishing or machining work done to improve the trigger pull by making it lighter, smoother and/or more precise. Can be dangerous unless performed by a qualified gunsmith.

Trigger Lock: A device intended to render the trigger of a firearm inaccessible and inoperable. Trigger locks come in a variety of styles, and can be purchased with key or combination locks. The most common trigger lock design covers the trigger mechanism on either side with two steel or plastic blocks which clamp over the trigger guard and lock together making the trigger inaccessible. If the trigger lock does not fit the gun properly or is improperly installed, the trigger may still be operated and if installed incorrectly on a loaded gun may result in an accidental discharge. Also see "Barrel Lock" and "Chamber Insert".

Trigger Pull: Length of the travel of the trigger. Force or weight in pounds applied pressing the trigger needed to cock the firearm and/or release the hammer/striker.

Trigger Safety: A small lever on the face of a trigger intended to prevent an accidental discharge. The lever locks the trigger in the forward position and only allows the trigger to be depressed by a direct, deliberate pressure on the trigger face.

Trigger Shoe: An additional part that is attached to a handgun trigger to make the trigger wider than the original factory trigger. It is also used to effectively move the placement of the trigger further out from the handgun's frame, making it more comfortable for people with longer fingers. Caution should be used whenever a trigger shoe is employed as the trigger shoe may actually extend past the side of the trigger guard and catch on the holster causing an accidental discharge.

Trim To Length: The length a cartridge case should be trimmed to after it has stretched past its "maximum case length".

Tritium Sights: Sights that have been manufactured (or modified) to include small vials of tritium, a mildly radioactive and luminescent substance with an approximate half-life of 12 years. The addition of tritium sights to a firearm makes the sights easier to see in low light situations, but require periodic replacement to remain effective.

Tubular Magazine: A tube-shaped magazine in which cartridges or shotshells are arranged end-to-end. It may be located under the barrel or in the butt stock. Also see "Magazine".

Turret Press: A reloading press with a rotating multi-station turret top for positioning dies and powder measure in their appropriate sequence.

Twist: see "Rifling Twist".

Two-Stage Trigger: These trigger mechanisms have two phases of operation. There is typically a lighter take-up or slack stage so when pressing the trigger, it moves easily to a point and then encounters additional resistance. During the second stage, the hammer or striker is released and the gun is fired. This type of trigger is commonly found in pistols of various types. Rifles such as the AR-15, can be equipped with either two-stage triggers or single-stage triggers, depending on preference. Also see, "Single-Stage Trigger".

U

Unintentional Discharge: The discharge of a firearm which was unintended by the operator or handler. An unintentional discharge can be further broken down into two categories:

(1) A voluntary unintentional discharge meaning the operator intentionally pressed the trigger believing the firearm to be unloaded. For example, during disassembly, function testing, or dry-fire practice, or;

(2) An involuntary unintentional discharge meaning the operator placed their finger on the trigger (knowingly or unknowingly) but did not consciously intend to press the trigger. The pressing of the trigger may occur through a startle response or other stress response, or through careless handling of the firearm (e.g., picking a firearm up incorrectly, grabbing a firearm that is falling, etc.)

Unintentional discharge can be used to describe "what happened" prior to the ruling or official finding of an investigation where the terms "accidental discharge" or "negligent discharge" may be applied through the result of the investigative facts.

Unload: The complete removal of all unfired ammunition from a firearm.

Up Range: Area of a shooting range opposite the bullet impact area. Also see "Down Range".

V

Velocity: The speed of a projectile expressed as distance per unit time. Usually measured in feet per second (fps) at a given range.

Ventilated Barrel Rib: A specialized barrel rib with cutouts along its length that help to dissipate heat from the barrel and cut down heat shimmer along the sighting plane. Also see "Barrel Rib".

Vernier Caliper: A slide-type graduated instrument used to measure overall cartridge and case lengths precisely.

Vernier Sights: An additional component to a "peep sight" system that allows for greater elevation adjustment than normal.

Vertex: The highest point of a bullet's trajectory. See also "Maximum Ordinate".

W

Wad: A cardboard disk or cardboard or plastic cup commonly used in shot shells to separate the powder charge from the shot or slug. When fired the wad seals propellant gases behind the shot load or slug, and holds the shot together as it travels down the barrel. Upon exiting the muzzle, the wad decelerates rapidly and drops to the ground leaving the shot or slug to travel on to the target.

Weapon Side: The side of the shooters body of the dominant or primary hand. For a right-handed person, the right side. For a left-handed person, the left side.

Weaver Stance: A two-handed pistol shooting that involves the shooter standing slightly bladed to the target; the weapon side arm is extended and pushes the pistol toward the target whilst the support side arm is bent and pulls the pistol back toward the weapon side shoulder. The isometric tension created by this grip is intended to control recoil. Also see "Stance" and "Isosceles Stance".

Web: That portion of a cartridge case between the bottom of the primer pocket and the interior of the case. Also used to describe the part of the hand between the thumb and forefinger where the backstrap of the pistol grip is placed.

Weapon Mounted Light (WML): A high intensity flashlight mounted directly to a firearm so as to be in line with the barrel/bore and illuminate whatever the firearm is pointed at. Used in law enforcement for threat identification and engagement. WMLs can be mounted in a wide variety of ways and activated by various types of switches. These lights can be used on both handguns and long guns.

Wheel Gun: A slang term for revolver.

Wildcat Cartridge (Wildcat): A cartridge made by altering or modifying an existing cartridge case of standard design. Such ammunition is in distinction to that produced by ammunition companies for use in firearms of commercial manufacture. Most wildcats are made by altering one or more of the dimensions of an existing cartridge case in order to change the caliber, the length or the powder capacity. Such alterations are made in the hope of obtaining higher velocity, flatter trajectory or greater accuracy. Once adopted by an ammunition company, and placed on the market through normal commercial channels, such a cartridge ceases to be a wildcat.

Wind Velocity: The horizontal direction and speed of air motion. For most ballistic calculations in the U.S., wind speed is measured in miles per hour.

Windage: A term used to indicate adjusting the sighting mechanism of a firearm so as to move the point-of-impact from side to side. Also used to describe the lateral drift of the bullet in flight caused by wind.

Wing Safety: A device that blocks the firing mechanism of a firearm.

X

X-Ring: Center of a target. Bulls-eye.

Y

Yaw: The angle between the longitudinal axis of a projectile and the line of the projectile's trajectory (usually caused by the projectile spinning erratically around its own axis). Yaw is usually considered to exist before a bullet achieves full gyroscopic stability.

Youth Dimensions: Usually refers to shorter stock dimensions and/or lighter weight enabling youth/women to shoot and carry a lighter, shorter firearm.

Z

Zero (Also True Zero): Adjustment of the sighting system so that the point-of-impact and point-of-aim coincide at a specific distance.

- Battle Zero: A zero (true zero) distance that establishes an effective "point blank range" for military or combat applications.
- Event Zero: Changing the sight elevation and/or windage to establish point-of-aim / point-of-impact for a specific distance and to adapt to specific environmental conditions. After the event, the sights are returned to the zero (true zero) setting.
- Mechanical Zero: Adjusting the sighting system to the centermost setting of mechanical adjustment for windage and elevation. This can be a starting place for establishing a zero (true zero).
- Point Blank Range: Any distance in which a given firearm can hit a target without the need to adjust sights or change the point-of-aim to compensate for bullet drop. *Example:* a typical AR-15 rifle with a 50-yard zero (true zero) has a point blank range from 0 yards to 250 yards to hit the torso of a human silhouette. Beyond 250 yards, the sights must be adjusted or the operator must hold a different point-of-aim to hit the same area of the target.

Zeroing: The act of setting the sights so that a projectile will hit the center of the intended target at a specific, desired distance.

Appendix A: SITE SAFETY PLAN

Training Date:		Training Time:	
Lead Instructor:			
Safety Officer:			
[Other Position]:			Radio: ☐

Training Location: **Police Training Facility – 123 1st Ave. – Anytown, STATE
Land Line – (303) 555-1212
Lat: Xº Y' Z" N / Long: Xº Y' Z" W**

Facilities:

Firing Range		Classroom		Other

First-aid:

* Individuals with advanced medical training:

* A **trauma first aid kit** is located:
* A separate first aid kit is available for minor injuries. See an instructor for treatment.
* A fire extinguisher will be readily available [LOCATION] as well as [LOCATION] in the classroom.

Communications:

* Instructors will have a cellular phone on their person.
* A portable radio will be in the range prior to initiating any training.
* In the event of an emergency the instructor in charge at the range will be:

	OR	

Procedure to summons Emergency Medical Services (EMS):

* At all times, there will be a minimum two ways to contact EMS. (1) a handheld radio capable of contacting [Police Communications Center] and (2) a cellular phone with confirmed coverage. For non-emergency contact [Police Dispatch] at 303-555-1111.

* The Lead Instructor or their designee will be responsible for initiating the emergency medical response to the range. In the event the Lead Instructor is incapacitated another instructor will initiate the response. Students will also be briefed on this process in the event a student is responsible for initiating the response.

Transport:

- Emergency transport will be by ambulance by contacting [Police Dispatch].

- The Lead Instructor has discretionary authority to make other transportation arrangements if deemed in the best interest of the injured person.

Injury Procedures:

- In the event of ANY INJURY, Call CEASE FIRE if necessary and notify an Instructor IMMEDIATELY. An instructor will use the radio OR phone to contact dispatch for an injury that requires advanced emergency care. Instructors will render first aid as needed.

- The Lead Instructor, Safety Officer or their designee will provide direction to students to safely secure any loaded firearms and maintain the integrity of the scene for potential investigation.

- In the event emergency transportation is needed for an injury, an ambulance will be dispatched by [Police Dispatch].

- The nearest hospital is [HOSPITAL NAME] at [ADDRESS] – Emergency entrance is off [STREET].

- The nearest TRAUMA center is **[NAME] at [ADDRESS]**.

- The nearest Fire Station is [NAME] at [ADDRESS].

- In the case of a minor injury the student will report the injury to an instructor who will ensure that the injury is treated. The instructor or Safety Officer will also inform the student the requirement to complete a Workman's Compensation Form for their employer if applicable.

- The Lead Instructor will also evaluate the cause of the injury to see if it was caused by training and adjust the training accordingly.

- In the case of serious injury **all training** will cease. The Lead Instructor will notify the Rangemaster and their chain of command of the injury. Training may resume after the agency's investigation is complete. In the event the death or gunshot wound occurred during a reserve or full academy, then training can only resume after [investigative or POST rule procedure].

Prior to conducting any firearms related training review the following:

NLEFIA Firearms Safety Rules
1. Know the status of your firearm at all times.
2. Never point your firearm at anything you are not willing to shoot.
3. Keep your trigger finger straight along the frame / receiver until you are on target and have decided to fire.
4. Identify the threat and environment before firing

Appendix B: RANGEMASTER JOB DESCRIPTION

Job Title:	Rangemaster	Reports to:	Training Lieutenant
Grade:		Classification:	
Reviewed and approved by:		Date:	
HR review and approval:		Date:	

Job Summary:

The Rangemaster has overall responsibility for the firearms training program for XYZ Police Department and operation of the XYZ Police range facility. This includes ensuring that the firearms training program meets or exceeds all applicable state, federal, and local standards and that the police range and operations conducted thereon are compliant with applicable regulations.

Essential duties and responsibilities:

- Remain current on local, state and federal use of lethal force issues, court decisions, and pending legislation / court cases to ensure that all firearms training meets or exceeds requirements described by applicable local, state and federal case law, department use of force policy, and current best practices in the public policing profession.
- Coordinate on a routine basis with Agency management, XYZ legal counsel, other department instructors (examples: defensive tactics, EVOC) to ensure consistency and continuity of training across disciplines.
- Select and supervise personnel from other sworn, armed operating divisions of XYZ Police Department who report directly to the Rangemaster while firearms training and qualification are being conducted at the range facility.
- Immediately stop training on the range if any unsafe weapons handling is detected.
- Authorized to make physical contact with any employee if necessary to prevent a potential injury.
- With assistance from Firearms Instructors and Range Safety Officers, document any serious safety infractions on the range during training as well as any training related injuries.
- Recording the following: all firearms owned by the Department, all issued firearms and related equipment (magazines, ammunition, holsters, duty belts, etc.), all training and duty ammunition purchasing and issuance.
- Ensure officers are trained in all aspects of the use of Agency authorized firearms.
- Ensure officers are trained in the tactics used for deployment of firearms and the safe resolution of situations with varying levels of conflict and risk to the officers or others.
- Ensure proper evaluation of officers' skills in the use of various firearms including but not limited to: safe handling, marksmanship, presentation from a sling or holster, weapon manipulation, tactics, threat identification, decision making, communication, tactical skills, de-escalation, weapon transitions and transitional thought process.
- Acts as a resource for the agency in matters concerning firearms, range operations, and use of deadly physical force.
- Ensures that training material provided to officers is consistent with state and Federal law as well as Agency policy and procedure.
- Ensures remedial training is provided in accordance with Agency policy when deficiencies are identified in officer performance related to firearms training.

- Ensures following items are documented: attendance of officers at training, individual officer qualification with various firearms, deficiencies in training or qualification, injury to anyone during training, damage to equipment or property during training, issuance of equipment, or other items as assigned.
- Responsible for staffing, upkeep, and scheduling of the XYZ Police Department Range Facility located at 123 Range Road.
- Responsible for the safety of all firearms training conducted at the facility, including, but not limited to:
  o Federal and State OSHA compliance for exposure to airborne lead, hearing conservation, vision protection;
  o Medical Emergency procedure and regular review and coordination with EMS;
  o Managing a part time staff of Firearms Instructors and Range Safety Officers;

Non-essential duties and responsibilities:
- Attend quarterly state POST instructor meetings.

Required education and experience:
- Minimum 3-years as a certified firearms instructor is preferred.

Required Certifications in <u>addition</u> to all certifications required for XYZ [police officer] [supervisor]:

- Current certification in CPR and First Aid.
- POST approved basic firearms instructor certification.
- POST approved rifle instructor certification.
- Must complete the NLEFIA Rangemaster Development course within 2 years of appointment to position.

Physical Requirements of the Job (% of time standing, % of time sitting, lifting, walking, etc.):
- Sitting: 50 %
- Standing, walking 50%
- Giving instructions and range commands with or without a loudspeaker system 50%
- Lifting to shoulder height weights up to 50 pounds 10%
- Assuming conventional and unconventional shooting positions (prone, sitting, kneeling, standing) as part of routine instructional demonstrations 10%
- Use of a computer workstation while sitting 50%

Environmental Condition:
- Wet or humid conditions 33%
- Work near moving mechanical parts 20%
- Fumes or airborne particles 50%
- Toxic or caustic chemicals 10%
- Outdoor weather conditions 50%
- Work in near total darkness 10%
- Exposure to moderate noise environment 33%
- Exposure to loud noise environment 33%
- Exposure to extremely loud noise environment 33%
- Exposure to defensive/offensive weapons 100%

Appendix C: FIREARMS INSTRUCTOR JOB DESCRIPTION

Job Title:	Firearms Instructor	Reports to:	Rangemaster
Grade:		Classification:	
Reviewed and approved by:		Date:	
HR review and approval:		Date:	

Job Summary:

The Firearms Instructor is a part-time adjunct, shared reporting officer position related to the training of sworn officers in the use of firearms and the application of deadly force. This job is conducted in addition to the duties of a sworn officer. The Firearms Instructor assists the Rangemaster in ensuring the firearms program is conducted safely and consistent with applicable laws and Agency policy.

Essential duties and responsibilities:

- Maintain current proficiency with all Department issued firearms systems including appropriate support equipment such as magazines, ammunition, and routine preventative maintenances of said systems.
- Instruct officers in all aspects of the use of handguns, rifles, and other firearms.
- Train officers in the tactics used for the deployment of firearms and the safe resolution of situations with varying levels of conflict and risk to the officer or others.
- Evaluate officers' skills in the use of various firearms including but not limited to: safe handling, marksmanship, presentation from a sling or holster, weapon manipulation, tactics, threat identification, decision making, communication, tactical skills, de-escalation, weapon transitions and transitional thought process.
- Act as a resource for peers regarding both investigative and training questions regarding firearms.
- Ensure that training material provided to officers is consistent with state and Federal law as well as Agency policy and procedure.
- Ensure that safety protocols for firearms training are adhered to by all officers' present and that the training environment is reasonably safe for employees within the constraints of training personnel for deadly force encounters under live-fire conditions including but not limited to:
  o Federal and state OSHA compliance for exposure to airborne lead, hearing conservation, and vision protection.
  o Medical emergency procedure and regular review and coordination with EMS.
- Provide First Aid as necessary for any injuries on the range and aids injured persons in receiving appropriate medical treatment of any injuries sustained during training.
- Document attendance of officers at training, individual officer qualification with various firearms, deficiencies in training or qualification, injury to anyone during training, damage to equipment or property during training, issuance of equipment, or other items as assigned.
- Provide remedial training when deficiencies are identified in officer performance related to firearms training.
- Assist the Rangemaster in planning training, developing lesson plans, designing live-fire drills, preparing training materials, creating props or other training aids, and recommending changes in policy or procedure.

- Assist the Rangemaster in evaluating equipment and recommending changes in technology.
- Assist the Rangemaster with department inventory of firearms, ammunition, and equipment related to the firearms program.
- Immediately stop training on the range if any unsafe weapons handling is detected.
- Authorized to make physical contact with any employee if necessary to prevent a potential injury.
- With assistance from Range Safety Officers, document any serious safety infractions on the range during training as well as any training related injuries.
- Assists Rangemaster with maintenance and scheduling of XYZ Police Department's range facility located at 123 Range Road.

Non-essential duties and responsibilities:
-

Required education and experience:
- Firearms Instructors are selected from sworn, armed personnel of the XYZ Police Department.
- Candidates for position must be off probationary employee status and have a minimum of 2 years of field law enforcement experience.

Required Certifications in <u>addition</u> to all certifications required for XYZ [police officer] [supervisor]:

- Current certification in CPR and First Aid.
- POST approved basic firearms instructor certification within one year of appointment to position.
- POST approved rifle instructor certification within one year of appointment to position.

Physical Requirements of the Job (% of time standing, % of time sitting, lifting, walking, etc.):
- Sitting: 25 %
- Standing, walking 75%
- Giving instructions and range commands with or without a loudspeaker system 50%
- Lifting to shoulder height weights up to 50 pounds 10%
- Assuming conventional and unconventional shooting positions (prone, sitting, kneeling, standing) as part of routine instructional demonstrations 25%
- Use of a computer workstation while sitting 25%

Environmental Condition:
- Wet or humid conditions 33%
- Work near moving mechanical parts 30%
- Fumes or airborne particles 60%
- Toxic or caustic chemicals 10%
- Outdoor weather conditions 60%
- Work in near total darkness 30%
- Exposure to moderate noise environment 30%
- Exposure to loud noise environment 40%
- Exposure to extremely loud noise environment 30%
- Exposure to defensive/offensive weapons 100%

Appendix D: RANGE SAFETY OFFICER JOB DESCRIPTION

Job Title:	Range Safety Officer	Reports to:	Rangemaster
Grade:		Classification:	
Reviewed and approved by:		Date:	
HR review and approval:		Date:	

Job Summary:

The Range Safety Officer (RSO) is a part-time adjunct, shared reporting officer position related to the training of sworn officers in the use of firearms. This job is conducted in addition to the duties of a sworn officer. The RSO assists the Rangemaster in ensuring the firearms program is conducted safely and consistent with Agency policy.

Essential duties and responsibilities:

- Ensure all weapons handling, manipulations, and firing is done in a safe manner consistent with the firearms training program.
- Ensure that safety protocols for firearms training are adhered to by all officers' present and that the training environment is reasonably safe for employees within the constraints of training personnel for deadly force encounters under live-fire conditions including but not limited to:
  o Federal and state OSHA compliance for exposure to airborne lead, hearing conservation, and vision protection.
  o Medical emergency procedure and regular review and coordination with EMS.
- Immediately stop training on the range if any unsafe weapons handling is detected.
- Authorized to make physical contact with any employee if necessary to prevent a potential injury.
- Provide First Aid as necessary for any injuries on the range and aids injured persons in receiving appropriate medical treatment of any injuries sustained during training.
- With assistance from Firearms Instructors, document any serious safety infractions on the range during training as well as any training related injuries.
- Document attendance of officers at training, individual officer qualification with various firearms, deficiencies in training or qualification, injury to anyone during training, damage to equipment or property during training, issuance of equipment, or other items as assigned.
- Maintain current proficiency with all Department issued firearms systems including appropriate support equipment such as magazines, ammunition, and routine preventative maintenances of said systems.

Limitations of duties and responsibilities
- The RSO is specifically not authorized to instruct or give constructive feedback to shooters. The RSOs function is maintaining safety within the training environment.

Non-essential duties and responsibilities:
- May assist the Rangemaster with administrative tasks as appropriate and assigned.

Required education and experience:
- RSOs are selected from sworn, armed personnel of the XYZ Police Department.

- Candidates for position must be off probationary employee status and have a minimum of 1 year of field law enforcement experience.

Required Certifications in <u>addition</u> to all certifications required for XYZ [police officer] [supervisor]:

- Current certification in CPR and First Aid.
- Must complete Range Safety Officer orientation course before assuming range duties.

Physical Requirements of the Job (% of time standing, % of time sitting, lifting, walking, etc.):
- Sitting: 25 %
- Standing, walking 75%
- Giving instructions and range commands with or without a loudspeaker system 50%
- Lifting to shoulder height weights up to 50 pounds 10%
- Use of a computer workstation while sitting 25%

Environmental Condition:
- Wet or humid conditions 33%
- Work near moving mechanical parts 30%
- Fumes or airborne particles 60%
- Toxic or caustic chemicals 10%
- Outdoor weather conditions 60%
- Work in near total darkness 30%
- Exposure to moderate noise environment 30%
- Exposure to loud noise environment 40%
- Exposure to extremely loud noise environment 30%
- Exposure to defensive/offensive weapons 100%

Appendix E: ARMORER JOB DESCRIPTION

Job Title:	Armorer	Reports to:	Rangemaster
Grade:		Classification:	
Reviewed and approved by:		Date:	
HR review and approval:		Date:	

Job Summary:

The Armorer is a part-time adjunct, shared reporting officer position related to the training of sworn officers in the use of firearms. This job is conducted in addition to the duties of a sworn officer. The Armorer assists the Rangemaster in ensuring that all Agency issued firearms are maintained within factory specifications and are duty ready.

Essential duties and responsibilities:

- Maintain a twelve (12) month rolling inventory of parts expected to be replaced in maintaining Agency issued firearms and coordinate with the Rangemaster for budgeting purposes.
- Maintain an inventory (to the box of 20 or 50) of duty and practice ammunition and provide a monthly report to the Rangemaster on the current status of the ammunition inventory.
- Report any issues with quality, consistency, or sourcing of replacement parts to the Rangemaster promptly.
- Report any issues with quality, consistency, or sourcing of practice or duty ammunition to the Rangemaster promptly.
- Ensure that all Agency issued firearms are maintained within factory specifications.
- Coordinate with the Rangemaster on any firearms taken out of service for repair, when the firearm is returned to active service, and firearms that have been returned to the factory.
- Report any non-authorized modifications to issued duty weapons to the Rangemaster immediately, including but not limited to:
  o Light trigger mechanisms
  o Light spring kits
  o Unauthorized grips, sights, magazines, ammunition, etc.
- Assist in maintaining the safety of all Firearms Training conducted at the facility including, but not limited to:
  o Federal and state OSHA compliance for exposure to airborne lead, hearing conservation, and vision protection.
  o Medical emergency procedures and regular review and coordination with EMS.
- Responsible for notifying the Rangemaster 6-months or more prior to the expiration of any armorer or other required certifications.

Limitations of duties and responsibilities
- The Armorer is specifically not authorized to perform work on non-Agency owned firearms (personally owned firearms), test and evaluation firearms, or firearms that have been transferred from evidence without specific authorization from the Rangemaster.

Non-essential duties and responsibilities:
- May assist the Rangemaster with administrative tasks as appropriate and assigned.

Required education and experience:

- Armorers are selected from sworn or non-sworn personnel of the XYZ Police Department.
- Candidates for position must be off probationary employee status and have a minimum of 1 year of field law enforcement experience.

Required Certifications in <u>addition</u> to all certifications required for XYZ [police officer] [supervisor]:

- Current certification in CPR and First Aid.
- Must obtain a factory armorer certification for the specific firearm system prior to assuming maintenance duties.
- Must maintain a factory armorer certification for all firearms serviced.

Physical Requirements of the Job (% of time standing, % of time sitting, lifting, walking, etc.):
- Sitting: 75 %
- Standing, walking 25%
- Lifting to shoulder height weights up to 50 pounds 10%
- Working at a work table or bench with common hand tools 75%
- Use of a computer workstation while sitting 25%

Environmental Condition:
- Wet or humid conditions 33%
- Work near moving mechanical parts 30%
- Fumes or airborne particles 60%
- Toxic or caustic chemicals 10%
- Outdoor weather conditions 10%
- Work in near total darkness 0%
- Exposure to moderate noise environment 70%
- Exposure to loud noise environment 20%
- Exposure to extremely loud noise environment 10%
- Exposure to defensive/offensive weapons 100%

Appendix F: INSTRUCTOR SELECTION WRITTEN TEST

Police Department
Rifle Instructor Selection Process / Written Test

Applicant Name & Serial #: _____   Date: _____

Final Score: _____ / 20   Graded by: _____

NOTE: One point per question / 20 points possible. You must get the entire question correct to get full credit for the question. There is no "partial credit" available.

1. List the POST four firearm safety rules.

     a. _____

     b. _____

     c. _____

     d. _____

2. According to the department rifle policy (Ops 4.25.6), if a rifle operator has not qualified on a rifle in over two years, they must attend which training to become certified again?

     a. 40-hour Rifle Operator certification course

     b. 10-hour Rifle Operator Re-Certification course

     c. 4-hour Rifle Operator Refresher Course

     d. No training, they just complete a rifle qualification

3. According to the POST Rifle Instructor manual, what are the three methods of discharging a firearm?

     a. _____

     b. _____

     c. _____

4. According to the department rifle policy (Ops 4.25.6), when a rifle operator fails the second qualification attempt:

     a. The rifle operator is not authorized to deploy with the rifle.

     b. The rifle operator will relinquish their duty rifle ammunition.

     c. The rifle operator has 7 days to complete the third rifle qualification attempt.

     d. All of the above.

     e. A and B only.

5. According to the POST Rifle Instructor manual, the use of the mechanical safety on an AR-15 is left to the discretion of each agency. On the XYZ Police Department, the mechanical safety will be used (placed in the SAFE position):

   a. Only during tactical reloads and while moving

   b. Whenever the rifle is not being fired

   c. Only when the rifle operator deems it necessary

   d. All of the above

6. According to the department rifle policy (Ops 4.25.6), which of the following is NOT considered a *pattern of failure* to remove a rifle operator from the rifle program?

   a. Single fails the rifle qualification four consecutive quarterlies

   b. Double fails the rifle qualification two consecutive quarterlies

   c. Double fails the rifle qualification on any two quarterlies within a year time frame

   d. When a rifle operator has failed 50% or more of rifle qualification over an established period of time

7. According to the department rifle policy (Ops 4.25.6), rifle operators will notify a supervisor of a rifle deployment as soon as possible.

   True / False

8. According to the department rifle policy (Ops 4.25.6), employees who have deployed with a rifle will not initiate any physical hand-to-hand confrontation. However, they may make hands-on arrest when exigent circumstances exist.

   True / False

9. According to the POST Rifle Instructor manual, Minute of Angle (MOA) means 1/60th of one degree, and is equivalent to _____ inch at _____ yards.

10. According to the POST Rifle Instructor manual, what are the three types of ballistics?

    a. _____

    b. _____

    c. _____

11. According to the department rifle policy (Ops 4.25.6), rifle inspections, modifications, and repairs can be completed by any certified rifle instructor.

    True / False

12. According to the Authorized Rifle Equipment list dated December 2015, any mil-spec 30-round metal magazine can be used for duty purposes.

    True / False

13. According to the POST Rifle Instructor manual, list the six fundamentals of marksmanship.

    1. _____
    2. _____
    3. _____
    4. _____
    5. _____
    6. _____

14. According to the department rifle policy (Ops 4.25.6), personally owned rifles will be inspected, modified, and repaired by the Rifle Training Squad.

    True / False

15. According to the AZ POST Rifle Instructor manual, the number of inches for the barrel rifling to make one full revolution is called...

    a. Barrel twist
    b. Twist rate
    c. Rifle twist
    d. Ballistic rate

16. According to the POST Rifle Instructor manual, what two external forces are always acting on a bullet in flight?

    a. Wind and humidity
    b. Bullet weight and gravity
    c. Gravity and air resistance
    d. Air density and temperature

17. According to the department rifle policy (Ops 4.25.6), rifles will only be deployed when an _____ situation exists.

18. According to the department rifle policy (Ops 4.25.6), which of the following is NOT a part of condition 2 carry...

    a. Magazine inserted
    b. Bolt locked to the rear
    c. Chamber empty
    d. Weapon on safe

19. You are zeroing a rifle operator at 50 yards. The group impact is 6 inches low and 5 inches right. What is the correction in MOA?

    _____ MOA up / _____ MOA right

20. Using the answers in Question 19, what is the clicks for an optic with ½ MOA adjustments.

    _____ clicks up / _____ clicks right

Appendix G: INSTRUCTOR SELECTION SAMPLE SKILLS TEST

Shooting Practical Course of Fire – Rifle*

Distance	Description	Time	Reps
100 yds	2 rounds standing, 1 round prone	12 sec	1
50 yds	Start with 1 round mag in rifle. 2 rounds standing, empty gun reload, 2 rounds intermediate position, tactical reload, 2 rounds prone	20 sec	1
25 yds	3 rounds primary side, 3 rounds support side	10 sec	1
25 yds	1 round to the head	3 sec	2
15 yds	Side-step left or right, then shoot 2 rounds to the body, 1 round to the head	4 sec	1
15 yds	5 rounds while moving from 15 yards to 10 yards	4 sec	1
10 yds	Independently tested - 5 rounds to the body	2 sec	1

*Using TQ-21 Target

Other Modifications for Shooting Tests:

- Shoot the standard pistol qualification using two targets and double the ammunition count. Time frames, distances and course of fire remains the same; however, every course of fire must be shot on both targets within standard time frames.

- Shoot pistol qualification using double distances. Time frames and course of fire remain the same. Example: 25-yard line drill is shot at 50 yards, 15-yard line drill is shot at 30 yards, 5-yard line drill is shot at 10 yards, etc.

Appendix H: INSTRUCTOR RESUME SCORE SHEET

Total Resume Score (40 points possible): _____   Applicant: _____

Evaluator: _____

Firearms Instructor Selection Process Resume Score Sheet

Below are sections outlined in the resume section of policy and is a guideline for evaluating the resume. The Firearms Training Unit has several roles, so consideration should be given to individuals who have backgrounds that would be beneficial to the unit in these areas.

Assignment History / Previous Work History
5 points possible .... Score: _____

Assignment history (including prior jobs) or responsibilities, which may assist them in performing the duties of a firearms instructor.
__ Police-related prior teaching experience   Notes:
__ Non-police prior teaching experience
__ Other Rifle-related Specialty Positions

Qualifications
10 points possible .... Score: _____

This includes certifications that will assist them in being a firearms instructor, such as firearms / rifle instructor and other certifications necessary for this position.
__ POST GI / Firearms / Rifle Instructor   Notes:
__ Pistol Armorer
__ Rifle Armorer
__ Other Instructor Certs: _____
__ Other Armorer Certs: _____

Education / Professional Development
10 points possible ....Score: _____

This may include college education, non-firearms instructor certifications applicable in/outside of the Department, outside firearms training, specific inside Department firearms training, etc. that will assist them with their duties while assigned to the Firearms Training Unit.
__ AA Degree __ BA Degree __ Master's Degree   Notes:

__ Other Instructor Certs: _____

__ Shooting Schools: _____

__ Other Non-Shooting Related Training: _____

Miscellaneous information
10 points possible ....**Score:** _____
Information they have included that will assist them in performing the duties of a
Department firearms instructor.
  __ Worked as adjunct instructor   Notes:
  __ Worked indoor range / recruit training
  __ Expert Shooter
  __ Expert Rifle
  __ Misc. Skills: _____

Professional Memberships
5 points possible ....**Score:** _____
This could include professional memberships in the field of firearms and/or training
related to the duties of the Rifle Training Detail, may include subscriptions.
    __ NRA   __ NLEFIA   __ IALEFI   __ ILEETA   __ NTOA

     Notes:

Appendix I: ORAL BOARD INTERVIEW QUESTIONS

Police Department

Firearms Instructor Selection Process

<u>Oral Board Interview</u>

Applicant Name & Serial #: _____   Date: _____

Evaluator: _____   Score: _____

Final Score (average score of the three evaluators): _____

This is the oral board interview for the Firearms Instructor selection process. You will be given 30 minutes to answer seven questions. Please indicate when you are finished answering a question so we can ask the next question. If at any time you want to have a question repeated, please ask. If at any time you want to go back to a previous question, please ask. There is a notepad and pen for you to take notes during this process. The notepad and pen will remain with us at the end of the process.

Following the seven questions, there will be a short teach-back demonstration which will be explained later. Do you have any questions?

Questions #1: (10 points)
Tell the Board why you are the best candidate for the Firearms Instructor position.

_____ Expert Shooter Award
_____ Adjunct instructor
_____ Assists with teaching recruits & in-service personnel
_____ Teaches other topics
_____ Good computer skills
_____ Good general craftsman skills
_____ Problem solver
_____ Minimum supervision
_____ Team player

Other Notes:

Question #2: (10 points)

While conducting a live-fire drill during annual training at the range, you observe an officer clutch his chest and fall to the ground. Tell the Board what you would do?

_____ Call cease fire
_____ Determine injury
      _____ Gunshot wound
      _____ Possible heart attack
      _____ Other
_____ Obtain trauma kit / AED
_____ Call for fire dept
_____ Send someone out to range entrance to escort fire
_____ Treat in place vs. self-transport
_____ Make range safe / unload other shooters
_____ Protect scene for investigation
_____ Notify supervisor
_____ Delegate duties

Other Notes:

Question #3: (10 points)

While teaching empty gun reloads and the use of the safety during a 40-hr rifle operator certification course, an officer who you know has combat experience states "You shouldn't be putting the safety on during empty gun reloads...you're going to get someone killed teaching that." Tell the Board how would you handle this situation?

_____ Mention legal and civil ramifications of failing to use the safety
_____ The use of the safety does not slow a shooter down
_____ Emphasize dept philosophy and training
_____ Adopted from military special operations community
_____ Applicant successfully defended the use of safeties
_____ Applicant was respectful & professional to the officer

Other Notes:

Question #4: (10 points)

You are conducting quarterly pistol training and a participating officer is exhibiting a negative attitude to the point where it is affecting the others officers and the training. Your supervisor is away at a meeting. Tell the Board how you would handle this situation?

_____ Separate / Speak to the officer away from the group
_____ Communicate / Try to determine the problem, and remedy it
_____ Educate / Remind the officer of the importance of training and a good attitude
_____ Re-Acclimate / Get the officer back into the training
_____ Monitor the officer
_____ Advise the supervisor
_____ If problem continues, remove the officer from training with supervisor approval

Other Notes:

Question #5: (10 points)

A rifle operator comes to you frustrated and states his zeroing groups look like "buckshot pattern". Tell the Board what you would do to identify and fix the problem?

_____ If using iron sights, check if small aperture is being used
_____ If using iron sights, check carry handle screws
_____ If using optic, check optic mount
_____ Check barrel for tightness
_____ Check chamber & barrel for cleanliness
_____ Check officer's shooting platform
_____ Instructor shoots rifle to verify

Other Notes:

Question #6: (5points)

You come to work on Monday and see there is no scheduled training on the training calendar for the week. Tell the Board what you would do to be a productive member of the unit.

_____ Range / trailer maintenance
_____ Check & maintain ammo / supply inventory
_____ Clean / repair weapons
_____ Review / revise outlines
_____ Develop drills
_____ Research outside training
_____ Test & Eval new equipment
_____ Assist other trainers
_____ Patrol shift

Other Notes:

Question #7: (5 points)

Inside the rifle case there is a rifle. Please tell the Board what parts, if any, are unauthorized for use.

_____ Checks to ensure the rifle is unloaded and shows it is clear
_____ Pistol grip
_____ Ambidextrous safety selector
_____ Dust cover
_____ Optic

Other Notes:

Teach-back portion: (40 points)

You will have 10 minutes to teach empty gun reloads to the Board. There is no outline for you to follow. This is a demonstration of your current knowledge, instructional habits, and public speaking skills. Do you have any questions?

_____ Introduction
_____ Safe weapon handling
_____ Demo multiple techniques
_____ Discussed pros & cons of various techniques
_____ Demo both right- and left-handed techniques
_____ Used mechanical safety appropriately
_____ Speaks well in front of group

Other Notes

Notes:

RANGEMASTER

Printed in Great Britain
by Amazon

הגדה של פסח

haggadah

THE KOL MENACHEM HAGGADAH

THE SLAGER EDITION

הגדה של פסח haggadah

THE KOL MENACHEM HAGGADAH

*With commentary and insights
anthologized from
Classic Rabbinic Texts and
the works of the Lubavitcher Rebbe*

Compiled and Adapted by
Rabbi Chaim Miller

THE GUTNICK LIBRARY OF JEWISH CLASSICS

קול מנחם

לכשיפוצו מעיינותיך חוצה

THE KOL MENACHEM HAGGADAH

with commentary from classic Rabbinic texts,
and the Lubavitcher Rebbe,
Rabbi Menachem Mendel Schneersohn.

ISBN-13: 978-1-934152-13-3   ISBN-10: 1-934152-13-7
(Nusach Ashkenaz)

Published and Distributed by:
Kol Menachem
827 Montgomery Street,
Brooklyn, NY 11213
1-888-580-1900
1-718-951-6328
1-718-953-3346 (Fax)
www.kolmenachem.com
info@kolmenachem.com

First Edition — March 2008
Two impressions . . . March — April 2008
Third impression . . . January 2009

Kol Menachem is a not-for-profit organization. Proceeds
from the sales of books are allocated to future projects.

בהזמנות לפנות:
"חיש" — הפצת המעיינות, כפר חב"ד
טל': 03-9600770   פאקס: 03-9606761
chish770@gmail.com   www.chish.co.il

היכל מנחם, ירושלים, רחוב ישעיהו 22
טל': 02-5384928, פאקס 02-5385015, ת.ד. 5955
hmj@neto.bezeqint.net

ENGLAND & EUROPE: MENDEL GORMAN info@jerusalemthegolden.com
AUSTRALIA: GOLD'S: 95278775 OR SHAUL ENGEL: 0438260055
SOUTH AFRICA: chabadbooks@mweb.co.za • 0117861561

Dedication of the
KOL MENACHEM HAGGADAH

**The Kol Menachem Haggadah
is dedicated to
our dear friends**

DAVID & LARA SLAGER

and their children
Hannah and Sara Malka

NEW YORK / LONDON

*May the merit of
spreading words of Torah
illuminated by the teachings of Chasidus
to thousands across the globe
be a source of blessing
for them and their family
for generations to come.*

❧ *Contents*

Key: [TH]=Textual–Historical; [JL]=Jewish Law; [PG]=Personal Growth; [MI]=Mystical–Inspirational (see p. xxx).

Key: [TH]=Textual–Historical; [JL]=Jewish Law; [PG]=Personal Growth; [MI]=Mystical–Inspirational (see p. xxx).

Key: [TH]=Textual–Historical; [JL]=Jewish Law; [PG]=Personal Growth; [MI]=Mystical–Inspirational (see p. xxx).

Key: [TH]=Textual–Historical; [JL]=Jewish Law; [PG]=Personal Growth; [MI]=Mystical–Inspirational (see p. xxx).

Key: [TH]=Textual–Historical; [JL]=Jewish Law; [PG]=Personal Growth; [MI]=Mystical–Inspirational (see p. xxx).

Key: [TH]=Textual–Historical; [JL]=Jewish Law; [PG]=Personal Growth; [MI]=Mystical–Inspirational (see p. xxx).

⊗⊗ *Foreword*

T HE PASSOVER SEDER IS PROBABLY THE MOST universally observed
of all Jewish practices, which has rendered its "script," the
Haggadah, a place in virtually every Jewish home. Often, the Seder
is a deeply moving experience, even—or perhaps, especially—for
Jews who seem to demonstrate little other affiliation to their faith. The
informal home setting, the presence of family members spanning
a number of generations, the sense of tradition and historical
continuity that the Haggadah evokes, the striking qualities of the
Passover customs and rituals, and the lively spirit (enhanced, no
doubt, by four cups of wine), make the Seder an especially positive
and vibrant experience. To this day I recall nervously reciting the
Four Questions as a tiny child of two or three at our family Seder,
the words of my late grandfather reciting the Haggadah still ringing
in my ears: "*In each and every generation a person must see himself
as if he had personally left Egypt....*"[1]

Like much of Jewish tradition, the Haggadah text dates back to
antiquity. While minor differences in liturgy have emerged over
time, our Haggadah is virtually identical to the text used, for example, by Maimonides in the 12th century, and the core of the
Haggadah is to be found in the *Mishnah*, compiled in the 2nd
century CE.[2]

But the principle of recounting the chronicle of the Egyptian
Exodus on the first night of Passover is as old as scripture itself.
"*You shall tell it to your son on that day,*" states the Torah, "*saying,
'It is because of this that God did for me when I left Egypt.'*"[3] The
Haggadah is simply a Rabbinical formula (the compiler of which is
unknown), designed to ensure that we carry out that Biblical obli-
gation correctly, by stressing the appropriate themes and relevant
points. And, as anybody who has attended a Seder will testify, the

---

1.   Below, p. 127.
2.   For the historical development of the Haggadah see Rabbi M. M. Kasher,
     Haggadah Sheleima (Jerusalem 1967), pp. 17–9.
3.   *Shemos* 13:8.

discussion is never limited to the printed text—*"Whoever discusses the Exodus from Egypt at length is praiseworthy."*[4]

Leading a Seder can, at times, be quite a humbling experience. Besides the tension generated by the sheer length of the evening's proceedings, and the presence of guests who might be hungry or somewhat disgruntled, the greatest challenge of the evening is the need to communicate. Not everybody is a naturally gifted storyteller, master of ceremonies, or teacher of children, but on this night, the head of every Jewish family is forced to take on all of these roles. The tools are at our hands: a rich and inspiring Haggadah text, the "hands-on" message of the Seder plate, and a host of Pesach rituals which arouse curiosity and invite commentary.

But what am I going to say? is the question on the lips of every Seder-leader. How will I capture the attention and the imagination of the guests, especially the children?[5] What insights hold the key to bringing this experience alive, to making it personally relevant?

Faced with the challenge of "performing" for the evening and infusing meaning into this ancient story, many people amass a considerable collection of Haggados over the years. It is no surprise, then, that the Haggadah is the most published work in Jewish history.[6]

Therefore, no excuse is required to add one further contribution to this rich body of literature. I hope that this effort will make a meaningful impression on a variety of readers from different backgrounds, especially as it contains the thoughts of an especially

---

4.   P. 39 below.

5.   In 1987, the Rebbe suggested that every single child should have his or her own illustrated Haggadah, to capture his or her interest as much as possible at the Seder (see *Hisvaduyos* 5747, vol. 2, p. 766).

6.   Shmuel Wiener's *Bibliographie der Oster Haggadah* 1500–1900 already lists some 909 editions. Avraham Yari's *Bibliography of the Passover Haggadah* (Jerusalem, 1960) refers to 2,717 different versions. T. Wiener cites a further 330 editions in his appendix to Yari's work (*Studies in Bibliography and Book-lore*, vol. 7, Cincinnati, 1965).

   The Chabad–Lubavitch Library in New York houses a significant collection of some 2,000 editions of the Haggadah published over the last 450 years, including Shmuel Wiener's own collection of some 400 Haggados, acquired by the Previous Rebbe in 1894.

   The first known print of the Haggadah was in Guadalajara (c. 1482). The only extant copy is in the National Library in Jerusalem.

great luminary whose impact on Jewish thought and communal life has been colossal.

The Kol Menachem Series

In 2001, I founded, together with Rabbi Meyer Gutnick, the Kol Menachem Foundation, dedicated to organizing the teachings of the Lubavitcher Rebbe, Rabbi Menachem Mendel Schneersohn,[7] and making them universally accessible and useful.

Our first project was a new edition of the Chumash (Pentateuch), with a running commentary anthologized from some eighty classic, Rabbinic sources, alongside a digest of the Rebbe's thoughts, entitled *Toras Menachem*.

The Chumash was warmly received by a broad cross-section of the Jewish community worldwide, including some of the leading scholars of our day. This was soon followed by a commentary on the Haftarah cycle (readings from the Prophets). A number of foreign language translations of the Chumash have since been initiated, of which the Hebrew and Spanish editions have now been published, in part.

Last year we published the first volume in a new series on the teachings of Maimonides (Rambam), aimed at introducing the reader to the Thirteen Principles of Faith in an intellectually stimulating and engaging fashion (an area which had received surprisingly little attention, even with the exponential growth of Jewish publishing in recent years). Again, this was very well received, encouraging us to expand our activities to further projects.

The Lubavitcher Rebbe's Literary Corpus

In the foreword to the Kol Menachem Chumash, I presented a brief review of the vast body of printed teachings of the Rebbe and how they came into being.

For whatever the reason may be, the Rebbe's immense religious and social contribution to Jewish communities worldwide has, in the public eye at least, eclipsed his intellectual and scholarly achieve-

---

7.   For biographical notes on the Rebbe's life see Aryeh Solomon, *The Educational Teachings of Rabbi Menachem M. Schneersohn* (New Jersey: Jason Aronson 2000), pp. 307-40.

ments.[8] People know the Rebbe as a great leader who inspired a generation of young men and women to selflessly dedicate their lives to Jewish communal work. His embracing, non-judgmental approach has been emulated by virtually every segment of Jewry, and he has thus been rightly proclaimed as "the man who turned Judaism outwards."[9] But, sadly, the same recognition could not be yet said for his scholarly achievements.

This is staggering when one considers that the Rebbe is, to my knowledge at least, one of the most published Rabbinic thinkers in history, with over two-hundred volumes of his writings, discourses, and correspondence in print.[10] The Rebbe's close aides relate that even while leading the Chabad movement, he spent the majority of his time isolated, in private study. He took virtually no phone calls, and private meetings with his followers, communal activists,

8.   Thus while a fair amount has been written about the Rebbe himself and the Chabad movement, little attention has been given to evaluating his contribution to Torah thought. The only full-length studies are Solomon, *Educational Teachings*, and Rabbi Faitel Levin, *Heaven on Earth: Reflections on the Theology of Rabbi Menachem M. Schneersohn* (Kehos Publication Society, 2002), and both works are confined to one aspect of the Rebbe's thought. Brief but valuable insights can be gleaned from Rabbi Jonathan Sacks, *Torah Studies* (Kehos, revised edition 1996), pp. viii-ix; Rabbi Alter B. Metzger, *Chasidic Perspectives, A Festival Anthology* (Kehos, 2002), p. vii; and Rabbi Yanki Tauber, *The Inside Story* (Va'ad Hanachos ha-Temimim, 1997), pp. xiv-xix.

      In Hebrew: For a general overview see Rabbi Ch. Y. Eisenbach, *Raban Shel Yisrael* (*Merkaz Chabad-Lubavitch*, Tel-Aviv, 1988). A number of studies focus on specific contributions of the Rebbe's scholarship: Rabbi Tuvia Bloy, *Klalei Rashi* (Kehos, 2nd ed. 1991); Rabbi Mordechai Menasheh Laufer, *Klalei Rambam* (Kehos, 1991); Rabbi Yehoshua Newhouser, *Ha-Tzafnas Pane'ach be-Mishnas ha-Rebbi* (Va'ad le-Hafatzas Sichos, 2002). A number of articles on specific contributions are found in *Sefer ha-Yovel Karnos Tzadik* (Kehos 1992), p. 641ff; and see also Rabbi Yehoshua Gross, *Ha-Rambam le-ohr Toras Kevod Kedushas Admur Shlita*, in *Kovetz Hadras Melech*, vol. 3 (Kolel Avreichim Chabad, 1985). Some articles in the biographical anthology *Raban Shel Yisrael* (Sifriyas Kfar Chabad, 2005) also touch on the Rebbe's scholarship.

      The first significant attention to the Rebbe's thought from the academic community was a convention in New York University in 2005, entitled *Reaching for the Infinite, the Lubavitcher Rebbe—life, teachings and impact*.

9.   A phrase coined by Rabbi Jonathan Sacks, Chief Rabbi of the United Hebrew Congregations of the Commonwealth.

10. No complete Bibliography has yet been compiled. For a partial list see Solomon, *Educational Teachings* p. 451ff.

or those seeking his counsel were scheduled for the late hours of the night.

The Rebbe's towering scholarly achievement was a weekly essay, which appeared regularly from 1969-1992,[11] each complete with as many as a hundred annotations and cross-references to the complete gamut of Rabbinic writings (now published in the thirty-nine volumes of *Likutei Sichos*[12]). His style is an unusual combination of penetrating analysis, lateral thinking, an acute attention to detail, alongside a tendency to gravitate towards theological and mystical themes. On studying these discourses in the original Yiddish or Hebrew, one is immediately taken aback by their sheer intellectual brilliance.

The Jewish people have, of course, been blessed with many great minds and incisive thinkers over the centuries, but it always struck me that there is something very unique about the Rebbe's intellectual path. At the risk of oversimplification I would say that it represents a convergence of two very different talents which, due to their conflicting nature, rarely coincide in one individual.

On the one hand, the Rebbe excelled in what we would call, in contemporary parlance, "left-brain" wisdom.[13] He possessed a careful, sober mind and his arguments were always well-honed and eminently reasonable, making it his declared goal to reach an absolutely objective perspective. When analyzing a classic commentary on the Chumash or Talmud his first question was always: Is this what the text actually says, or is the author "reading in" his own ideas, however subtly, into the text? In the spirit of a search

---

11. With the exception of 1972 and 1975. Essays also appeared, in a less developed form, during the years 1958 and 1963. See Solomon, *Educational teachings,* pp. 24-25. I refer to them here as "essays," even though their published title is *"Sichos"* (talks), since in the vast majority of cases they represented an earlier talk that had been totally rewritten, often with much new material added by the Rebbe during the editorial process. In some instances, only a tiny fraction of the essay had been included in the earlier talk on which it was based.

12. Published by Va'ad le-Hafatsas Sichos (Kehos) from 1962 to 2001 (viewable online at http://www.otzar770.com/library/).

13. There is remarkable correlation between the contemporary classification of right- and left-brain wisdom, to the Kabbalistic concepts of *chochmah* and *binah,* the intellectual components to be found on the right and left side of the *sefirotic* tree. See below pp 22–3; p. 108.

for objective truth, the Rebbe's own suggestions were often subject to self-scrutiny, and he was quick to point out their limitations and flaws, sometimes revising them at a later date if he found them, on reflection, to be problematic.[14] Even more remarkable was his attention to detail. He would scrutinize a comment of *Rashi*, or a passage from the Talmud, down to the finest nuances of language and style. This would then be compared with a host of other textual variants, or similar source materials. Typically, at the outset of one of his essays, as many as fifteen or twenty textual problems may have been raised that require closure. While attention to detail is common in Rabbinic writings, the extreme to which it was taken in *Likutei Sichos* is extraordinary.[15]

The flip side of the Rebbe's intellectual approach is what you might call a "right-brained," holistic or mystical perception. In stark contrast to the detailed and careful logic of a left-brained analysis, the mystical talent enables a teacher to penetrate through the limitations of logic and worldly phenomena, uncovering deeper themes that unify many disparate conceptual or textual elements. This is typically an inspirational experience for the student, leading him to feel liberated from the confines of conventionality, as he is lifted to a more meaningful and true-to-home vantage point. Mystical ideas are also self-validating due to the very depth of their insight. Unlike conventional reasoning, which must constantly re-assert its authenticity in the face of never ending criticism and re-evaluation, mystical insight automatically dispels doubt, as light banishes darkness, leaving the student with a clarity of insight which has sometimes been compared to intellectual "vision," where ideas are simply "seen" to be correct and true. Much has been written about the Jewish mystical tradition, so I will not dwell upon it further here.

The Rebbe excelled in both of these areas, demonstrating the extreme thoroughness that one would normally associate with an academic, and the elevated intuition of a mystic. What seems to be unprecedented is not merely the presence of these two talents

---

14. See, for example, *Sichas Shabbos Parshas Chukas Balak* 5746, par. 13.
15. See *Likutei Sichos* vol. 16, p. 533, where the Rebbe makes some brief notes about his attention to textual detail, comparing it with other schools of rabbinic analysis.

simultaneously, but the success in *integrating* them into a single outlook and approach.[16]

For example, a typical essay will begin with a strictly analytical discussion, isolating various problems with a text and highlighting the limitations of different solutions which have been proposed. At this point the reader's "left-brain" has already been well exercised, and very often strained, by the display of intellectual agility and textual mastery.

When the solutions come, however, they invariably arise from the "right-brain." In the majority of cases, the Rebbe will not jump straight into a mystical explanation. The first solution typically draws on *lomdus,* the conceptual approach to Jewish learning.[17] A discussion of the rudimentary underlying principles of the text ensues, leading to a clarification of its conceptual underpinning, which is then skillfully applied to resolve all the earlier problems. I call this "rightbrain" because it is not a single, direct solution *per se*, but a deeper, holistic appreciation of the character of the text, an elevated viewpoint from which the earlier disparate points of confusion are now reframed into a unified scheme where each detail supports the general thesis.

This now provides the author with an ideal platform to launch into a mystical commentary. The conceptual approach, while not actually a form of mysticism, nevertheless shares the same qualities of a profound, far-reaching insight, and the ability to perceive things holistically. So after the *lomdus* has liberated the seemingly contradictory elements of the text from their prior atomistic state, harmonizing them into a single, cohesive system, mystical insight then takes this same process a stage further, raising the perception to a more spiritual, intuitive or even suprarational, viewpoint.

But, most remarkably—and this is the point I have been trying to bring out from the very start—our final, elevated point of reference does not eclipse the mosaic of details with which we grappled at the outset. On the contrary, now we see how a deeper, conceptual or mystical truth is accurately reflected in every detail. The text thus comes "alive," as all its disparate elements, which earlier were

---

16. See conversation between the Rebbe and Rabbi Moshe Grossberg in *Ha-Melech bi-Mesibo,* vol. 2, p. 259.

17. See Yosef Blau ed., *The Conceptual Approach to Jewish Learning,* (New Jersey: Yeshiva University Press, 2006)

sources of confusion, now "shine" as expressions of our freshly discovered thematic focus.

So, as an "academic-mystic," for want of a better term, the Rebbe managed to bring some of the electricity, inspiration and inner unity of a Torah text to be felt palpably in the dryest and most technical of details. The result is twofold. On the one hand, it enhances the reader's appreciation of the text itself, whose sanctity and precision have now been underscored through highlighting a number of previously imperceptible "soul" qualities. And, on the other hand, Jewish mystical teachings, which often suffer from being elusive and vague, have been rendered much more accessible, as our detailed observations of the text now act as tangible "handles" through which rational beings such as ourselves can "grasp" the mystical truths that lurk beneath them.

With all this in mind, one can imagine the difficult task which we face when attempting to communicate the Rebbe's Torah in its full, original glory. The convergence of technical, scholarly and mystical discourse in just a few pages, with the complicated symbiosis that exists between these different schools of thought, makes an accurate rendition or simplification of this material virtually impossible. Even when reading the original, a legally attuned reader might be confused by the mystical passages, and another reader might lack the ability to plow through the complex analysis. Add to that the sheer volume of the material, and we are left with a corpus which for many, both quantitatively and qualitatively, verges on the impenetrable.

It has therefore been most welcoming that the Rabbinic, scholarly community has acclaimed the Kol Menachem series as capturing at least a tiny glimpse of the profundity of the Rebbe's Torah. But, in light of the above, I cannot stress enough that the reader is highly encouraged to tackle this material in its original form.

The Sources Available to Us

I will not repeat here what was stated in the foreword to the Kol Menachem Chumash concerning the delivery and publication of the Rebbe's Torah, but a few words are in order concerning some sources which are particularly relevant to the Haggadah.

a.) *Likutei Ta'amim u'Minhagim*

In 1946, a number of years before he ascended to the leadership of the Chabad-Lubavitch movement, the Rebbe published a commentary on the Haggadah entitled *Likutei Ta'amim u'Minhagim* ("an anthology of explanations and customs").[18] Rabbi Immanuel Schochet has discerned four general categories of comments that were included by the author: i.) Source references for the passages and practices mentioned in the Haggadah. ii.) Textual variants of the Haggadah with their various implications. iii.) A clarification of customs specific to Chabad tradition. iv.) Reasons and explanations for the passages in the Haggadah and for the laws and procedures of the Seder.[19]

Essentially, *Likutei Ta'amim u'Minhagim* is an anthology of classical writings, ranging from the Talmud to the primary (Medieval) and later authorities.[20] A number of points, however, are noteworthy.

First, in quite a number of instances the author does offer his own highly original solutions and explanations. Second, despite the apparent straightforward nature of the work, there is much taking place "behind the scenes." In other words, the omissions here are just as significant as the comments that are included. Often, there will be a number of standard interpretations for a passage, but the Rebbe will select just one, presumably because he maintained that

18. Published by Kehos. (In its early printings the commentary bore a slightly di - ferent title, *Likutei Minhagim ve-Ta'amim.*) This was the first totally original work that the Rebbe authored. (*Ha-Yom Yom*, which appeared in 1942, was an anthology of the Previous Rebbe's teachings.)

Chasidim have noted an interesting parallel with the first Rebbe of Chabad, the *Alter Rebbe*, whose *Laws of Pesach*, composed while under the tutelage of his master Rabbi Dovber ("the Maggid") of Mezritch, was the first part of his *Shulchan Aruch* to be published, (a point noted by the Rebbe at the beginning of *Likutei Ta'amim u'Minhagim*). Likewise, the first work of the Rebbe concerned laws and customs of Pesach, and was composed while under the tutelage of his Rebbe and teacher, Rabbi Yosef Yitzchak of Lubavitch.

19. Forward to second edition of the English translation of *Likutei Ta'amim u'Minhagim* (Kehos, 1985). See also S. Vitzhandler, *Haggadas Raban Shel Yisra'el* in *Ha-Tamim*, issues 7-8 (2001).

20. In later editions, additions and emendations were made. In the fourth edition (1963), which coincided with the 150th anniversary of the *Alter Rebbe's* passing, the Rebbe added a number of comments and anecdotes, the majority of which related to the *Alter Rebbe*.

this is the most relevant or satisfying. So what superficially appears to be a mere anthology can be seen, on closer examination, to be a critical evaluation of all of the Rabbinic literature pertaining to the Haggadah. In fact, this "esoteric" dimension of the Haggadah was brought to light in subsequent correspondence with Rabbi Shlomo Yosef Zevin (1890–1978), editor of the *Encylopedia Talmudis,* in which the Rebbe revealed some of the tremendously complex decision making that went into writing some of the passages.[21]

Many outstanding Torah luminaries were highly impressed with *Likutei Ta'amim u'Minhagim,* such as Rabbi Zevin,[22] Rabbi Yitzchak Zev Soloveitchik (1886–1959)[23] and Rabbi Reuvein Margolies (1889–1971).[24] Each year, many Chabad scholarly journals offer an array of articles by senior scholars and their students, which

21.   See *Igros Kodesh* vol. 2, p. 241; ibid. p. 260; and also below p. 145. For a review of the Rebbe's general correspondence with Rabbi Zevin see Rabbi Shalom Wolpo, *Shemen Sason me-Chaveirecha* vol. 2 (1998), pp. 68–110.

22.   In his *Sofrim u'Sefarim* (Tel Aviv: Avraham Zioni, 1959), Rabbi Zevin praises *Likutei Ta'amim u'Minhagim* as "a remarkable work, which is quite unique. It is suited for Jews of all backgrounds, Chasid and non-Chasid alike. If I was not concerned for the aversion of Chasidim to define a Torah text in secular terms, I would say that it is a scientific work of the finest caliber." For the Rebbe's response see *Igros Kodesh* vol. 18, pp. 487–8.

     Rabbi Zevin, who possessed a large personal collection of Haggados, once told Rabbi Mordechai Shmuel Ashkenazi, the current Chief Rabbi of Kfar Chabad, that "on Seder night I use the Rebbe's Haggadah" (*Sichas ha-Shavuah* (*Tze'iray Agudas Chabad,* Israel), issue 1005).

23.   Rabbi Solveitchik spoke of the Haggadah highly and used it at his own Seder (Wolpo, *Shemen Sason,* vol. 3 (2003), p. 169).

24.   Rabbi Ashkenazi relates that, in his youth, on a visit to the Rambam Library in Tel-Aviv, he noticed that *Likutei Ta'amim u'Minhagim* had been mistakenly recorded in the library catalog as a work authored by the third Lubavitcher Rebbe, the *Tzemach Tzedek* (1789–1866, who had the same name as the Rebbe). When Rabbi Margolies, the library's director, was informed of the mistake, he remarked, "I was aware that the Rebbe is a great Torah scholar, but not to this extent. I was convinced that this was the work of an author from previous generations" (*Sichas ha-Shavuah ibid.*). (Incidentally, the Rebbe once remarked: "I am named after the *Tzemach Tzedek,* and so I try to emulate him"—*Ha-Melech bi-Mesibo,* vol. 2, p. 259). For the Rebbe's relationship with Rabbi Margolies, see Wolpo, *Shemen Sason,* vol. 3, pp. 74-80.

     For more on the Rebbe's Haggadah see review of Meir Madan in *Machanayim* (1957, issue 32, cited (in part) in *Sichas ha-Shavuah,* issue 537).

attempt to decipher the underlying thought processes behind many of the Rebbe's comments.[25]

Another important point is that *Likutei Ta'amim u'Minhagim* pioneered a new genre of Haggadah which focused on the objective, scholarly analysis of Jewish law and custom, in contrast to the more subjective, personal insights which dominated most Haggados prior to this date. This precedent appears to have inspired later scholarly Haggados, such as *Iyunei ha-Hagadah*[26] and the encyclopedic *Seder ha-Aruch*.[27] In fact, even the original Artscroll Haggadah[28] was significantly influenced by *Likutei Ta'amim u'Minhagim.*

With the above in mind, I hardly need to emphasize that the current work is in no way intended to replace *Likutei Ta'amim u'Minhagim,* which stands as the standard, authoritative Chabad Haggadah.

b.) *Biurim*

As years passed by, passages from *Likutei Sichos* which discuss the Haggadah were appended to *Likutei Ta'amim u'Minhagim,* which was renamed *Likutei Ta'amim u'Minhagim u'Biurim* ("an anthology of reasons, customs *and explanations*"). Reprinted a number of times, with an increasing number of pages, the complete version was printed by Kehos in 1995 in two volumes (1076 pages). In addition to commentaries on the Haggadah, the work also contains a considerable section addressed to an analysis of various Passover laws.

c.) *Communal Letters*

Throughout the entire period of his leadership, the Rebbe composed communal letters in connection with special dates during the year, including the festival of Pesach, addressed to the global Jewish community ("to the sons and daughters of Israel, wherever they may be found"). Written in a pastoral tone, and drawing richly on Jewish sources, these letters offer a frank and upbeat message,

25. See, for example, *Kovetz Ha'aros u'Biurim Oholei Torah* (archives to be found at http://www.haoros.com).
26. Rabbi Chaim Banish, Jerusalem 1988.
27. Rabbi Moshe Weingarten, 3 vols, Jerusalem 1991–3.
28. Rabbi Joseph Elias, 1977.

charged with Chasidic optimism, but never shying away from real issues and problems. All the letters have been published (in Hebrew translation from the Yiddish original, with an introduction) in *Igros Melech* (*Kehos* 1992), in two volumes.[29] The letters pertaining to Pesach are also to be found in *Likutei Ta'amim u'Minhagim u'Biurim.*

d.) *Oral Commentaries on the Haggadah*

During the Rebbe's own Seder, he did not interrupt the proceedings to add any of his own commentary. Instead, for many years (1951–1970), he called a public *farbrengen* (gathering) on the second night of Pesach at around 1:30 AM, after most of the community had completed their own Sedarim, at which time he delivered his commentaries to the Haggadah.[30] This arrangement had the advantage of enabling an entire community of his disciples to be present, which clearly would not have been possible if the commentaries had been offered privately. From 1957 onwards, the crowd was also privileged to hear a *ma'amar* (Chasidic discourse) relating to Pesach.

Generally speaking, the Rebbe would finish speaking at around 4:00 AM, and the Chasidim would escort him home, singing a festive Chasidic melody such as *Mimitzrayim Ge'altanu*,[31] or *Al Achas Kama ve-Chama*.[32]

While a number of insights from these *farbrengens* were included in *Likutei Sichos* (and later in *Likutei Ta'amim u'Minhagim u'Biurim)*, the majority were not. They were later published in *Sichos Kodesh* and (in part) in *Toras Menachem, Hisvaduyos*,[33] from

---

29. A partial collection of the letters pertaining to the first half of the Jewish year (*Tishrei–Adar*) from 1949-1978, in English translation, is found in *Letters by the Lubavitcher Rebbe* (Va'ad le-Hafatsas Sichos 1979).

30. For more details about these *farbrengens,* see overview of Rabbi Michoel Seligson in *Hiskashrus* issue 506.

31. Below, p. 198.

32. P. 116.

33. An ongoing project of Va'ad Hanachos Lahak to render all of the Rebbe's talks which do not appear in *Likutei Sichos* into Hebrew, with extensive annotations and cross-references. To date, thirty-four volumes have been published (1992–2006), covering the Rebbe's talks from 1950-1962 (viewable online at http://www.livingwiththerebbe.com).

During the years 1981–1992 Va'ad Hanachos Lahak published a Hebrew

students' notes. (See our foreword to *Chumash Kol Menachem* for the important distinction between publications edited by the Rebbe and those that were not.)

e.) *The Rebbe's hanhagos*

While his mother-in-law, Rebbetzin Nechamah Dina Schneersohn, was still alive (until 1970), the Rebbe conducted all the festival meals (including the Seder) in her apartment, in the presence of a number of guests. On Pesach night, Chasidim were able to enter after they had completed their own Seder at home.

On these occasions, it was possible to observe the precise detail with which the Rebbe himself observed the laws and customs of the Seder. These "*hanhagos*" were later collected and published in *Otzar Minhagei Chabad*,[34] along with all other extant source materials relating to Chabad festival custom. Below we will discuss the significance of the *hanhagos*.

f.) *Informal Discussions at the Festival meals.*

During the above-mentioned Festival meals, informal conversations took place between the Rebbe, his brother-in-law, Rabbi Shemaryahu Gurary,[35] and the other guests. Many of these discussions, which contained original Torah insights, were later published in *Ha-Melech bi-Mesibo*.[36] Naturally, the discussions at the Pesach meals often related to both the festival in general and to the Haggadah.

g.) *Other Chabad Haggados and Pesach anthologies.*

See Bibliography on p. 236.

rendition of each of the Rebbe's talks, shortly after they were delivered, later collected in 43 volumes of *Hisvaduyos* 5742–5752 (viewable online at http:/ www.otzar770.com/library/).

34.   Rabbi Yehoshua Mondshine, Kehos 1996.

35.   Rabbi Shemaryahu Gurary, also known as the *Rashag* (1897–1989) was the eldest son-in-law of Rabbi Yosef Yitzchak Schneersohn, the sixth Rebbe of Chabad. He possessed an extensive knowledge of Chabad Chasidic thought and was a devoted follower of the Rebbe until his passing.

36.   2 vols., Kehos 1993.

The Structure of the Current Work

The Kol Menachem Haggadah is comprised of the following elements.

1.) *Hebrew text of the Haggadah*

We are publishing the Haggadah in two editions, one following *Nusach ha-Arizal,* the liturgical variant of the Haggadah used in Chabad communities[37]; and another edition following the Ashkenazic text which is the most commonly used variant among English-speaking Jews.

2.) *English Translation*

A new translation has been prepared, which aims to render the meaning of the text with clarity, avoiding the use of archaic or over-ly formal English, so as to offer an easy read which remains loyal to the original text.

---

37.   For a general introduction to *Nusach ha-Arizal* see Rabbi Nissen Mangel, introduction to *Siddur Tehillas Hashem* with English translation (Kehos).

  The authoritative texts of the *Alter Rebbe's Nusach ha-Arizal* are *Siddur Torah Ohr* (Rabbi Avraham David Lavut, 1887; corrected version published by the Rebbe in 1941) and *Siddur Tehillas Hashem* (corrected version pub-lished by the Rebbe in 1956). See introduction of Rabbi Shalom Dovber Levin to *Hagahot le-Siddur Rabeinu ha-Zaken* (Kehos, 2006), and, at length, Rabbis Gedalia Oberlander and Nachum Greenwald (eds.), *Ha-Siddur* (Heichal Menachem, Monsey, 2003).

  In 1987, the Rebbe instructed *Tze'iray Agudas Chabad* (*Tzach*) of Israel, who were in the process of preparing a new edition of the Haggadah (for children), to reproduce the liturgical text from the above sources, without dividing paragraphs, highlighting words, or adding additional punctuation marks (*Hiskashrus* (1998), issue 194). However, in Rabbi Yekusiel Green's *Haggadah for Pesach in the Light of Chasidus* (see Bibliography), which the Rebbe had seen before publication (see letter printed before the preface), changes were made to the text in all of these areas. This was also the case with *Haggadah for Pesach Annotated Edition* (Kehos, 2005).

  Thus, while these minor enhancements to the text appear to have become accepted, and it is possible that the Rebbe's instruction to *Tzach* was specific to the occasion, we can glean at the very least from the Rebbe's instructions that the *Siddur Torah Ohr* and *Siddur Tehilas Hashem* remain the authorita-tive sources of the *Alter Rebbe's Nusach ha-Arizal.* Consequently, while we have followed the precedent of Green and Kehos, the reader should bear in mind that what is presented here is in no way intended to be an improved or corrected version of the *Nusach.*

3.) *Directions*

The directions in the Ashkenazic edition follow the prevailing customs in most communities, though the reader should note that a total uniformity of practice does not exist, and what is written here is intended as a general guideline.

4.) *Classic Questions*

As in our previous works, a prominent section entitled "Classic Questions," contains the thoughts of over one hundred important Jewish thinkers, from Talmudic times up to the twentieth century, that address issues of importance pertaining to the Haggadah and its observances. In preparing this commentary, we relied heavily, though not exclusively, on the sources cited by *Likutei Ta'amim u'Minhagim*. As in previous works, many passages are paraphrased, rather than translated, though there are numerous exceptions to this rule.[38]

In the Kol Menachem Chumash, virtually every part of the Classic Questions was cross-referenced to a discussion in the Toras Menachem commentary (see below). In the Haggadah, however, the focus is slightly different. Here the intention of the Classic Questions is to present the reader with *core knowledge* of the Seder ritual and the Haggadah text, so that he or she will be well informed about the details of the evening's proceedings. Consequently, there is less common ground here between the two commentaries (Classic Questions and Toras Menachem), though in many instances there are cross-references (indicated by bold highlights in Toras Menachem).

5.) *Toras Menachem*

As the name suggests, this is a digest of the Rebbe's commentaries on the Haggadah, adapted for the English reader.[39] The com-

---

38. The reader should also bear in mind the following.

    i.) If the citation in Classic Questions has no given source, it is taken from the stated author's commentary on the Haggadah.

    ii.) Sometimes, this may be from a Haggadah that was not composed by the author himself, but compiled from his writings.

    iii.) In an instance where the author offers a number of interpretations, we may cite only one.

39. In reference to publishing his own teachings in English translation, the Rebbe wrote: "As I have mentioned many a time, what matters is the content and not

mentaries have been compiled in a similar fashion to those found in the previous volumes in this series, but the reader is asked to bear the following points in mind.

i.) *Choice of Sources*

Any attempt at adapting the works of a great Torah luminary must obviously be painstakingly loyal to the original teacher. Thus, to a very great extent, the sources which I choose to draw on in all my works are a reflection of the Rebbe's own emphasis in his talks. For example, in the Chumash I gave a lot of attention to the *Toras Menachem* commentaries on *Rashi*, since this had clearly been a priority for the Rebbe himself. In fact, our projects in general are selected with this point very much in mind. The *Principles of Faith* was chosen because it is a recurring theme in the Rebbe's talks, and the current work was undertaken largely because the Rebbe spoke so much about the Haggadah and the themes of exile and redemption.[40]

ii.) *Types of Commentary*

I would divide the commentaries presented here in Toras Menachem into four categories:

a.) *Textual–Historical.* Insights into the basic meaning of the Haggadah text, or the events surrounding the Egyptian exodus.

b.) *Jewish Law.* An in-depth analysis of the finer points of the festival laws and customs.

c.) *Personal Growth.* Lessons in life, drawn from traditional and Chasidic wisdom as it relates to the contemporary Jew.

d.) *Mystical–Inspirational.* Insights which unravel the spiritual dynamics of the Haggadah, drawing especially from the wisdom of the Kabbalah.

In previous works, different threads in the *Toras Menachem* commentary were delineated visually by the use of highlighted frames set off from the main body-text. With the Haggadah, however, this has not been possible for typographical reasons.

---

the literal translation. Therefore, you should ensure that the language is clear and the style appropriate, for the main objective is that the readers should appreciate what is written" (*Igros Kodesh* vol. 28, p. 267).

40. For the connection between Jewish leadership and the themes of exile and redemption, see below p. 43.

(It would have resulted in too many "boxes" on a relatively small page.) Therefore, somewhat regrettably, this attractive feature has now been lost. To partially compensate, at least, I have included in the Table of Contents a brief abstract of each insight to be found in *Toras Menachem*, along with a note as to which of the four above categories it seems to belong.

iii.) *Method of adaptation*

Generally speaking, the Rebbe's commentaries on the Haggadah are esoteric and complex. On the other hand, an English rendition such as this is likely to have a broad audience, due to the sheer popularity of the Pesach Haggadah. I also had to bear in mind that, while it could be used as a text for study, the main use for this book will be at the informal setting of the Seder table. This created a considerable challenge of presenting some very hard material in a universally accessible form.

The result is that I have tried very hard to *communicate* the ideas here as much as possible, resulting in what one of our reviewers referred to as a "folksy" style. It really is a soul-wrenching experience to focus constantly on loyalty to the original text, on the one hand, and the need to relate to the reader, on the other, and I pray that there has been at least some degree of success. But if you do find some passages challenging at times, please bear in mind everything that I have said above. There is only so much one can distill the Rebbe's wisdom without totally losing its richness.

Finally, to the credit of our excellent research department, even those readers who are familiar with many of the Rebbe's insights into the Haggadah are likely to find a lot of new material here. And while we have only been able to present a tiny fraction of the Rebbe's thoughts on each subject, there is definitely much food for thought in the following pages.

Acknowledgments

I would like to gratefully acknowledge the following people for their assistance in preparing this work. Most especially, Rabbi Itzick Yarmush, who stood at my side throughout every stage, from the initial research, through discussing and planning the commentaries, and then, after they were written, checking them carefully against the original sources. I am also grateful to the following for their assistance: Rabbis Shmuel Rabin, Zvi Homnick, Mendy Lent, Mendy Angyalfi, Asher Lowenstein and Eli Shear; and to our proofreaders: Chaya Sarah Cantor, Yehudis Homnick and Laurence Saffer.

It is once again my pleasure and honor to dedicate this volume in the Kol Menachem series to **David and Lara Slager**. The Slager family have set a fine example to the Jewish community, both in their personal lives and with their outstanding philanthropic efforts towards an impressive array of causes across the globe. We are proud to have them as members of the Kol Menachem family, and wish David, Lara, and their precious children Hannah and Sara Malka, all the abundant blessings that they deserve.

Finally, I extend my heartfelt wishes to the backbone of our organization, **Rabbi Meyer Gutnick,** who, seven years ago, had the courage to invest in an unknown author, and since then has been an unfailing source of material support and moral encouragement. Motivated by a great love for the Rebbe, and recognizing the urgency of spreading his Torah teachings, Rabbi Gutnick has chosen to invest his own natural talent at "getting things done" into a very worthy cause. In the merit of this, and all his many other impressive philanthropic efforts, may God bless him, together with his dear wife Shaindy, and all their wonderful children and grandchildren, with *chasidishe nachas* and only revealed and open goodness.

May we soon merit the true and complete redemption, when all the Jewish people will be totally free to observe God's commands and study His Torah, and, *"Just as in the days when you left the land of Egypt I will show you wonders."*[41]

Rabbi Chaim Miller
Rosh Chodesh Adar II 5767

41. Michah 7:15.

הגדה של פסח **Haggadah**

THE KOL MENACHEM HAGGADAH

סֵדֶר בְּדִיקַת וּבִיעוּר חָמֵץ

➤ ON THE EVE OF 14TH NISSAN (THE NIGHT BEFORE THE SEDER), INSPECT THE HOUSE FOR CHAMETZ. (IF THE EVE OF THE 14TH OCCURS ON SHABBOS, THE SEARCH IS CARRIED OUT ON THURSDAY NIGHT, AND THE BURNING ON FRIDAY MORNING.)

➤ MANY HAVE A CUSTOM TO PLACE TINY (WRAPPED) PIECES OF BREAD IN VARIOUS PLACES AROUND THE HOUSE (ACCORDING TO THE KABBALAH—TEN PIECES).

➤ SEARCH WITH THE LIGHT OF A WAX CANDLE. IT IS CUSTOMARY TO COLLECT THE CHAMETZ WITH A FEATHER AND WOODEN SPOON.

➤ BEFORE THE SEARCH, RECITE THE FOLLOWING BLESSING AND START TO SEARCH WITHOUT SPEAKING. AFTERWARDS, YOU MAY SPEAK ONLY ABOUT MATTERS RELEVANT TO THE SEARCH UNTIL THE SEARCH IS COMPLETED.

➤ ONE SHOULD NOT SUFFICE WITH A SUPERFICIAL SEARCH. BE CAREFUL TO CHECK ALL THE CORNERS, NOOKS AND CRANNIES OF THE ROOMS WHICH REQUIRE SEARCHING, AS WELL AS POCKETS OF CLOTHING.

בָּרוּךְ אַתָּה יְהֹוָה אֱלֹהֵינוּ מֶלֶךְ הָעוֹלָם, אֲשֶׁר קִדְּשָׁנוּ בְּמִצְוֹתָיו וְצִוָּנוּ עַל בִּעוּר חָמֵץ:

CLASSIC QUESTIONS

● **If a person did not find any Chametz during his search, has he still fulfilled the *mitzvah*?**

SHIBOLEI HA-LEKET: Yes. The *mitzvah* is to search for Chametz, not to find it.

● **Why, then, do we put down pieces of Chametz?**

CHOK YA'AKOV: Holding onto the Chametz that we find will remind us to recite the declaration the next day (overleaf).

Alternatively, if a person searched for some time and found no Chametz he might become disheartened and give up his search too quickly. Therefore, we put down pieces of Chametz to encourage him along the way (*Orach Chaim* 432:14).

LIKUTEI TA'AMIM U'MINHAGIM: This enables us to say the words, "All leaven...which I did or did not *see*" (the following morning), since we actually saw Chametz during the search.

● **Why do we make the blessing on "disposal of Chametz" now, if we only destroy it tomorrow?**

ROSH: Because immediately after the search we nullify the Chametz verbally, which, according to Torah law, is a means of removing it.

And even though we will only complete the disposal of Chametz tomorrow, when we burn it, we nevertheless begin the *mitzvah* of removing it now. Therefore, the blessing is made at this point (*Pesachim* 1:10).

The Search and Disposal of Chametz

➤ On the eve of 14th Nissan (the night before the Seder), inspect the house for Chametz. (If the eve of the 14th occurs on Shabbos, the search is carried out on Thursday night, and the burning on Friday morning.)

➤ Many have a custom to place tiny (wrapped) pieces of bread in various places around the house (according to the Kabbalah—ten pieces).

➤ Search with the light of a wax candle. It is customary to Collect the Chametz with a feather and wooden spoon.

➤ Before the search, recite the following blessing and start to search without speaking. Afterwards, you may speak only about matters relevant to the search until the search is completed.

➤ One should not suffice with a superficial search. Be careful to check all the corners, nooks and crannies of the rooms which require searching, as well as pockets of clothing.

Blessed are You, God, our God, King of the universe, who has sanctified us with His commandments and commanded us about the disposal of Chametz.

CLASSIC QUESTIONS

● **Should the search be performed before or after *ma'ariv* (the evening prayer)?**

Alter Rebbe's Shulchan Aruch: If one prays with a congregation, *ma'ariv* is recited before the search.

If one prays alone, the search must be performed immediately upon nightfall, before reciting *ma'ariv*.

However, if a person normally recites *ma'ariv* with a congregation, but tonight he prays at home, then he must pray before the search, as we are concerned he might forget to pray at all (*Orach Chaim* 431:7-8).

Hayom Yom: The search for Chametz takes place after the evening prayers (14th Nissan).

(This, among other reasons, is because the Chasidic custom is to spend a very long time on the search, and so if *ma'ariv* was not recited first it would be delayed excessively—see *Igros Kodesh* vol. 2, p. 343.)

● **What is the symbolism behind the search for Chametz?**

Tur Barekes: Our Sages taught that Chametz (leaven) is symbolic of evil in general and the evil inclination in particular: *"We want to do Your will, but the yeast in the dough is holding us back"* (*Brachos* 17a).

The search for Chametz thus represents seeking out evil that has been misplaced and "scattered." On a personal level this corresponds to a soul reckoning for hidden sins that are to be found in the "crevices" of our conscious minds, such as inappropriate thoughts etc.

On a cosmological level, we are taught that the Sin of Adam, and later the Sin of the Golden Calf, caused evil to be "scattered" in all the spiritual worlds. Our search for Chametz thus represents an

➤ AFTER THE SEARCH, WRAP THE CHAMETZ CAREFULLY AND SAFEGUARD UNTIL TOMORROW. ANY CHAMETZ FOODS WHICH ARE TO BE EATEN TOMORROW SHOULD BE KEPT IN A SAFE PLACE.

➤ NOW RECITE THE FOLLOWING DECLARATION, RELINQUISHING ANY REMAINING CHAMETZ FROM YOUR POSSESSION THAT WAS NOT FOUND (OR SOLD). IF YOU DO NOT UNDERSTAND ARAMAIC, YOU MUST SAY IT IN ENGLISH.

כָּל חֲמִירָא וַחֲמִיעָא דְּאִכָּא בִרְשׁוּתִי, דְּלָא חֲמִיתֵהּ וּדְלָא בְעַרְתֵּהּ וּדְלָא יָדַעְנָא לֵיהּ, לִבְטֵל וְלֶהֱוֵי הֶפְקֵר כְּעַפְרָא דְּאַרְעָא.

➤ ON THE FOLLOWING MORNING (SEE A LOCAL JEWISH CALENDAR FOR THE SPECIFIC TIME, WHICH VARIES FROM YEAR TO YEAR), BURN ALL THE REMAINING (UNSOLD) CHAMETZ.

➤ AFTER THE CHAMETZ HAS BEEN BURNED IN THE FIRE, RECITE THE FOLLOWING DECLARATION, RELINQUISHING ANY REMAINING CHAMETZ FROM YOUR POSSESSION. IF YOU DO NOT UNDERSTAND ARAMAIC, YOU MUST SAY IT IN ENGLISH.

כָּל חֲמִירָא וַחֲמִיעָא דְּאִכָּא בִרְשׁוּתִי דַּחֲזִתֵּהּ וּדְלָא חֲזִתֵּהּ דַּחֲמִתֵּהּ וּדְלָא חֲמִתֵּהּ דְּבַעֲרְתֵּהּ וּדְלָא בְעַרְתֵּהּ לִבְטֵל וְלֶהֱוֵי הֶפְקֵר כְּעַפְרָא דְּאַרְעָא.

═══ CLASSIC QUESTIONS ═══

attempt to track down this scattered evil and eliminate it (431:1).

● **What special stringency applies to the Biblical command to remove Chametz?**

MINCHAS CHINUCH: In the case of other positive commands, such as the requirement to eat Matzah, or to take the Four Species on Succos, a person would not be liable for failing to observe the mitzvah until the very end of the day. But here, a person fails to fulfil the mitzvah of removing Chametz every moment that Chametz remains in his possession (Mitzvah 9, par. 3; see Sichas Shabbos Parshas Vayikra 5743, par. 34).

ARIZAL: If a person is careful to avoid even the tiniest amount of Chametz on Pesach he will be spared from [unintentional] sin throughout the entire year (cited in Ba'er Heitev 447:1; see Likutei Ta'amim u'Minhagim).

➤ After the search, wrap the Chametz carefully and safeguard until tomorrow. Any Chametz foods which are to be eaten tomorrow should be kept in a safe place.

➤ Now recite the following declaration, relinquishing any remaining chametz from your possession that was not found (or sold). If you do not understand Aramaic, you must say it in English.

ALL LEAVEN and leavened products that are in my possession, which I did not observe, did not dispose of, or do not know about, are hereby nullified and ownerless, like the dust of the earth.

➤ On the following morning (see a Local Jewish Calendar for the specific time, which varies from year to year), burn all the remaining (unsold) Chametz.

➤ After the Chametz has been burned in the fire, recite the following declaration, relinquishing any remaining chametz from your possession. If you do not understand Aramaic, you must say it in English.

ALL LEAVEN and leavened products that are in my possession, which I did or did not see, which I did or did not observe, which I did or did not dispose of, are hereby nullified and ownerless, like the dust of the earth.

=== CLASSIC QUESTIONS ===

● **In principle, must Chametz be disposed of by burning it?**

Mishnah: Rabbi Yehudah says: The only way Chametz may be eliminated is through burning it.

The other Sages say: One may also crumble it and scatter it to the wind or cast it into the sea (*Pesachim* beg. ch. 2).

Tur Barekes: In the future, God will destroy the forces of evil with fire (see *Malachi* 3:19). In the current era, when evil has not yet been eliminated, Jewish law allows for different ways through which Chametz (evil) can be removed. But our practice is to burn the Chametz as an expression of our fervent hope for the coming of Mashiach when all evil will be burned (445:1).

סֵדֶר הַגָּדָה
The Order of the Haggadah

➤ **MATZAH**: TAKE THREE WHOLE SHMURAH MATZOS AND PLACE THEM, ONE ON TOP OF THE OTHER, SEPARATED BY NAPKINS. (MANY HAVE THE CUSTOM TO INSERT THE MATZOS INTO COMPARTMENTS UNDER THE SEDER PLATE.)

➤ THE SEDER PLATE IS THEN ARRANGED ACCORDING TO YOUR FAMILY CUSTOM. (THE PREDOMINANT CUSTOM IS TO FOLLOW THE ARRANGEMENT OF THE ARIZAL, DISPLAYED OPPOSITE).

➤ SOME HAVE THE CUSTOM TO BRING THE SEDER PLATE TO THE TABLE BEFORE KIDDUSH, WHILE OTHERS BRING IT AFTER KIDDUSH.

=== **CLASSIC QUESTIONS** ===

● **Why does the Kabbalah teach that the items must be placed on top of the Matzos, and not on a separate plate?**

REBBE RASHAB: According to the Kabbalah, spiritual illumination reaches this world by intense "lights" being channeled down into "vessels" which help to restrain the "lights" so that they will not be too overwhelming for the creations. In our case, the Matzos allude to the "vessels" and the various items allude to the "lights." The items are therefore placed upon the Matzos, alluding to the notion of the "lights" being channeled down into the "vessels."

Therefore concave Matzos are preferred, since they physically depict the significance of Matzos as "vessels" or "containers" of light (*Sefer ha-Sichos* 5698, p. 260).

=== **TORAS MENACHEM** ===

הַקְּעָרָה — *The Seder Plate*

Why do the wicked prosper? Why has history been dominated by a phenomenon that we refer to as "exile," where Jews have been denied religious freedom by oppressive regimes? And what can be done to put an end to all of the above?

The Kabbalistic symbolism of the Seder plate provides the key (see *Classic Questions*). Jewish mysticism teaches that the source of everything, all physical and spiritual existence, is light. Not the stuff made of photons, but a Divine "light," in the metaphorical sense, which is emanated by God.

But just as looking at the sun would render a person blind, too much Divine light would also be more than we could cope with. So the light's intensity must be counterbalanced by a series of "vessels" which filter the light, dampening its overwhelming qualities.

So, thanks to the vessels we are able to exist. And since the vessels do not filter out *all* of the light, we are left with at least some spiritual illumination.

This whole scheme is what you might call a cosmic system of "law-and-order," where each created entity gets just as much light as it needs. Angels, for example, get more than us, because their role in life is to sing to God in a constant state of ecstasy. Our mission, on the other hand, is to worship our Creator in a context of relative concealment from Him, so we are granted less light.

There is, however, a way of "cheating the system," a means of obtaining more light than one needs or deserves, through functioning "above the law," and drawing from a more ethereal realm where the rules do not apply.

To understand why this is the case, consider the following observation. When you are asleep, two things

➤ **(1) SHANKBONE**: THE SHOULDER BONE OF A LAMB WITH SOME MEAT ON IT, ROASTED.

➤ **(2) EGG**: A ROASTED OR BOILED EGG.

➤ **(3) BITTER HERBS**: GRATED HORSERADISH.

➤ **(4) CHAROSES**: A THICK PASTE OF GROUND APPLES, NUTS, OTHER FRUITS, WINE, AND CINNAMON.

➤ **(5) KARPAS**: CELERY, PARSLEY, RADISHES, OR BOILED POTATO.

➤ **(6) CHAZERES**: ROMAINE LETTUCE.

ביצה EGG — זרוע BONE — מרור BITTER HERBS — כרפס KARPAS — חרוסת CHAROSES — חזרת CHAZERES — כהן COHEN — לוי LEVI — ישראל YISRAEL

CLASSIC QUESTIONS

● **How does the Seder plate depict the *Sefiros*?**

ARIZAL: The three Matzos represent the three intellectual faculties of *Chochmah*, *Binah* and *Da'as*. The six items (Bone, Egg etc.) correspond to the six emotional faculties of *Chesed*, *Gevurah*, etc.

KOCHO D'R' ELIEZER B'RASHBI: If the Matzos represent the higher, intellectual faculties, then why are they placed *below* the other six items, which represent the lower, emotional faculties? (Addendum.)

LIKUTEI TA'AMIM U'MINHAGIM: The Rebbe Rashab's explanation (opposite) resolves the question posed by *Kocho d'R' Eliezer b'Rashbi*. For the Matzos represent the *vessels* of the intellectual faculties, whereas the items represent the *lights* of the emotional faculties. And lights always *go down* into vessels.*

TORAS MENACHEM

happen: i.) Your brain functions in a more *disorderly* fashion, which is why you can dream the most bizarre things; ii.) in a dream, emotions and ideas are often felt in a much more *intense* fashion than when you are awake. These two phenomena are actually connected. Normally, when you are awake, the light of your soul is projected down into your cerebral apparatus (your "vessels"), which harnesses that light in a useful, orderly fashion. But when you fall asleep, the soul withdraws into itself, thereby losing the stability which the vessels provided, but gaining a certain intensity that had inevitably been dampened by the vessels.

The same is true for the world in general. When God (the "soul" of the world) projects Himself down into His "vessels," law and order prevails and the righteous prosper. But when He withdraws back "into himself away from the vessels," light is bestowed indiscriminately, the wicked prosper, and we have exile on our hands. *Ending the exile is thus a process of drawing God's light back into His "vessels."*

So on Pesach, the festival of our redemption, we are granted the power to achieve this remarkable feat, to neutralize the negative forces which have controlled history by starving them of the unjustly earned light. And that is why the Seder plate vividly depicts the channeling of light into vessels, because, from the perspective of the Kabbalah, all of tonight's activities will be aimed at restoring that cosmological law and order.

(Based on *Likutei Sichos* vol. 32, p. 196; *Toras Chaim, Shemos* p. 23*ff* and 241b ibid.)

---

*ראה אגרות קודש כרך כ"א ע' רצג (ובהנסמן שם בהערה) שהתירוץ המובא בס' כחו דר' אליעזר ברשב"י שם מאת מהרה"א שפירא ממונקאטש "במחכת"ר, אינו מתקבל". וראה באריכות בספר "שמן ששון מחביריך" ח"ג (הרב שלום דובער הלוי וולפא, תשס"ג) ע' 61 ואילך.

סִימָן סֵדֶר שֶׁל פֶּסַח

קַדֵּשׁ · וּרְחַץ · כַּרְפַּס · יַחַץ ·

מַגִּיד · רָחְצָה · מוֹצִיא · מַצָּה ·

מָרוֹר · כּוֹרֵךְ · שֻׁלְחָן עוֹרֵךְ ·

צָפוּן · בָּרֵךְ · הַלֵּל · נִרְצָה ·

סִימָן סֵדֶר שֶׁל פֶּסַח — *The Steps of the Pesach Seder.*

At the most basic level, the "Steps of the Pesach Seder" were included here as a memory aide, to assist a person in recalling the precise sequence of events that are to be carried out tonight.

But the Seder, of course, is not merely a sequence of rituals; each feature of the evening's proceedings speaks a certain message to us, which we will discuss in some depth at each junction later on. Now, at the outset, the Haggadah presents us with the Seder "at a glance," identifying for us fifteen important "signposts" that will help us to chart the precarious path from personal exile to redemption.

PART ONE — Coping with exile (steps 1–9).

1–2.) KADEISH-URCHATZ: *We make Kiddush and then wash our hands.*

According to the Kabbalistic Haggadah of the *Arizal*, these first two steps are joined by the Hebrew letter *vav.* This is somewhat confusing since the

Kabbalah also teaches that the spiritual forces which *Kadeish* and *Urchatz* manifest are *oppositely* charged: Kadeish is rooted in the right side of the mystical Godhead, whereas *Urchatz* emanates from the left. Later we will discuss exactly what this means practically (pp. 22–3), but for now just bear in mind that we are speaking here about *joining* and harmonizing the *opposite,* contradictory elements of our personalities, our souls, and ultimately, the entire universe.

3.) KARPAS: *We dip a vegetable in salt water and eat it.*

The only way we can transcend the limitations of our own existence is by surrendering to something greater than ourselves. This is the inner message of dipping, where one food *surrenders* its flavor into the liquid in which it is dipped (see p. 25).

4.) YACHATZ: *We break the middle Matzah. The smaller half becomes "poor man's bread." The bigger half, is put away for the Afikoman.*

Every small half-Matzah must have a corresponding large half, which means that if you can only see

The Steps of the Pesach Seder

Kadeish · Urchatz · Karpas · Yachatz · Maggid · Rachtzah · Motzi · Matzah · Maror · Koreich · Shulchan Oreich · Tzafun · Bareich · Hallel · Nirtzah ·

the "small piece of Matzah" in your life, God surely has the "large piece" hidden away somewhere for you (see p. 26).

5.) MAGGID: *We tell the Exodus story.*

For most people, this needs little commentary. It's all about *empathizing* with the plight of our ancestors, *reliving* the exodus in a way that makes the spiritual message of Judaism immediate and relevant, and *communicating* that message to others, especially the children (see p. 128*ff*).

6–8.) RACHTZAH–MOTZI–MATZAH: *We wash our hands, acknowledge God as the source of all sustenance, and eat Matzah.*

According to the *Zohar*, Matzah is "Bread of Faith." Consuming it refines and hones our "sixth sense" of spiritual intuition. On the second night, the Matzah is our "Bread of Healing" (p. 146).

9.) MAROR: *We eat Bitter Herbs.*

Basically, this is all about coping with life's bitter moments by perceiving them as growing pains. We'll talk about this at length later on (p. 125, 149).

PART TWO — Anticipating redemption (10-14)

10.) KOREICH: *We eat a sandwich of Matzah and Bitter Herbs, as Hillel did in Temple times.*

This inevitably focuses our attention on the rebuilding of the Temple (see p. 153).

11-13.) SHULCHAN OREICH–TZAFUN–BAREICH: *festive meal, eat Afikoman, and Grace after Meals.*

This alludes the festive meal which God will make for the righteous in the future. The climax of the meal is the Afikoman, reminding us of the Paschal lamb, which we will eat once again in the Messianic Era (p. 175, 188).

14.) HALLEL: *Songs of praise.*

This corresponds to a later phase in the Messianic Era, where the spiritual (represented here by song) will predominate entirely over the physical (p. 187).

PART THREE — God's response (step 15).

15.) NIRTZAH: *Acceptance.*

We hope that our efforts will be found pleasing and "accepted" above on high (p. 180, 204).

קַדֵּשׁ

ON FRIDAY NIGHT, RECITE KIDDUSH ON PAGE 14.

ON SATURDAY NIGHT, RECITE KIDDUSH ON PAGE 16.

KIDDUSH FOR WEEKDAY NIGHT

➤ IT IS CUSTOMARY FOR THE HEAD OF THE HOUSEHOLD TO WEAR A WHITE KITTEL DURING THE SEDER.

➤ KIDDUSH MAY NOT BE STARTED UNTIL NIGHTFALL.

➤ AS A DISPLAY OF FREEDOM, EACH PERSON SHOULD HAVE HIS CUP FILLED BY SOMEONE ELSE.

═══════════════ CLASSIC QUESTIONS ═══════════════

● **How is tonight's Kiddush different from the Festival Kiddush throughout the year?**

LIKUTEI TA'AMIM U'MINHAGIM: Because, in addition to being Kiddush, sanctifying the festival day, this is also one of the Four Cups of wine which our Sages enacted that every person should drink on this night.

Consequently, there are a number of special laws that apply to this Kiddush that do not apply during the year.

a.) During the year, there is an option to make Kiddush over bread. Tonight, we must make Kiddush over wine.

b.) During the year somebody else may make Kiddush on our behalf. Tonight, every person must drink the cup of wine himself (*Alter Rebbe's Shulchan Aruch, Orach Chaim* 472:22).

c.) Tonight a person should push himself to drink the Four Cups even if it causes him severe discomfort, and even if he cannot afford the wine (*Nedarim* 49b; *Pesachim* 92b).

d.) During the year we are permitted to bring in the Festival (or Shabbos) early and make Kiddush while it is still light. But tonight, we may only make Kiddush after nightfall (*Terumas ha-Deshen* ch. 137).

This is because all Four Cups of wine must be consumed after nightfall, since the timing of this *mitzvah* must coincide with the timing of the *mitzvah* of Matzah, which may only be carried out after nightfall (*Alter Rebbe's Shulchan Aruch* ibid. 2).

e.) Tonight, we try to drink the whole cup of wine, or at least the majority of it (ibid. 19), [making sure that this is at least the prescribed quantity of 2.9 U.S. fl. oz/ 86ml].

● **Must women drink Four Cups of wine?**

TALMUD: Yes, because they, too, benefited from the miracle of the Exodus from Egypt (*Pesachim* 108b).

● **Why is no blessing recited on this *mitzvah* of drinking Four Cups?**

KOLBO: Because the *mitzvah* is performed in four separate parts with interruptions in between.

● **Why *Four* Cups?**

SHEMOS RABAH: Because the Torah uses four expressions of redemption, which promised liberation from four decrees of Pharaoh against the Jewish people.

Kiddush: Sanctify the Day

ON FRIDAY NIGHT, RECITE KIDDUSH ON PAGE 15.

ON SATURDAY NIGHT, RECITE KIDDUSH ON PAGE 17.

KIDDUSH FOR WEEKDAY NIGHT

➤ IT IS CUSTOMARY FOR THE HEAD OF THE HOUSEHOLD TO WEAR A WHITE KITTEL DURING THE SEDER.

➤ KIDDUSH MAY NOT BE STARTED UNTIL NIGHTFALL.

➤ AS A DISPLAY OF FREEDOM, EACH PERSON SHOULD HAVE HIS CUP FILLED BY SOMEONE ELSE.

CLASSIC QUESTIONS

The four expressions of redemption are: *"I will bring you out...I will save you...I will redeem you...I will take you"* (*Shemos* 6:6-7).

The four decrees were: 1.) *"They embittered their lives with hard labor."* 2.) *"If it is a boy you must kill him."* 3.) *"Every boy who is born, you shall cast into the Nile."* 4.) *"You shall not continue to give straw to the people to make bricks"* (*Shemos* 1:14, 16, 22; 5:7; *Shemos Rabah* 6:4; *Eitz Yosef* ibid. 112).

TOLA'AS YA'AKOV: According to the Kabbalah, the Exodus shattered all four forces of *kelipah* (evil).

BEREISHIS RABAH: In the butler's dream (*Bereishis* 40:11-21), Pharaoh's cup is mentioned four times (88:5).

JERUSALEM TALMUD: The Four Cups correspond to the Four Exiles (Babylonian, Persian, Greek and Roman).

Alternatively, they represent the Four Cups of Catastrophe with which God will coerce the nations of the world to drink, while at the same time He will give Four Cups of Consolation to the Jewish people (*Pesachim* 10:1).

SHALOH: The Four Cups correspond to the four letters of the Tetragrammaton (*Siddur Shaloh*).

TORAS MENACHEM

קִידוּשׁ — *Kiddush.*

The Talmud teaches that in a leap year, when an extra month of Adar is added, Purim is always celebrated in the second month of Adar, and not the first. The reason, says the Talmud, is because, we wish to *"juxtapose redemption to redemption"* (*Megilah* 6b), i.e., to celebrate the redemption of Purim in close proximity to the redemption of Pesach.

Where do we find the "proximity" between these two festivals expressed in the respective *mitzvos* of each day?

Perhaps we could point to a certain symmetry in the way Jewish law requires us to *drink* on these two festivals. The Kiddush of Pesach is unusual in that: a.) wine must be used, and not bread; and b.) each person is required to drink the cup of wine *himself* (see **Likutei Ta'amim u'Minhagim**).

And we find these very same conditions stipulated in the laws of Purim. *"A person is required to become intoxicated on Purim"* (ibid. 7b)—he may not delegate the task to another. And he must drink *wine* (*Rashi* ibid.), just as the Pesach Kiddush must be on wine.

(Based on *Sichah* of 2nd night of Pesach 5725)

סַבְרִי מָרָנָן וְרַבָּנָן וְרַבּוֹתַי:

בָּרוּךְ אַתָּה יְהֹוָה אֱלֹהֵינוּ מֶלֶךְ הָעוֹלָם, בּוֹרֵא פְּרִי הַגָּפֶן:

בָּרוּךְ אַתָּה יְהֹוָה אֱלֹהֵינוּ מֶלֶךְ הָעוֹלָם, אֲשֶׁר בָּחַר בָּנוּ מִכָּל־עָם וְרוֹמְמָנוּ מִכָּל־לָשׁוֹן וְקִדְּשָׁנוּ בְּמִצְוֹתָיו, וַתִּתֶּן־לָנוּ יְהֹוָה אֱלֹהֵינוּ בְּאַהֲבָה מוֹעֲדִים לְשִׂמְחָה, חַגִּים וּזְמַנִּים לְשָׂשׂוֹן, אֶת־יוֹם חַג הַמַּצּוֹת הַזֶּה, זְמַן חֵרוּתֵנוּ, מִקְרָא קֹדֶשׁ, זֵכֶר לִיצִיאַת מִצְרָיִם. כִּי בָנוּ בָחַרְתָּ וְאוֹתָנוּ קִדַּשְׁתָּ מִכָּל־הָעַמִּים, וּמוֹעֲדֵי קָדְשֶׁךָ בְּשִׂמְחָה וּבְשָׂשׂוֹן הִנְחַלְתָּנוּ: בָּרוּךְ אַתָּה יְהֹוָה, מְקַדֵּשׁ יִשְׂרָאֵל וְהַזְּמַנִּים:

➤ Do not repeat this blessing if you said it at candle lighting.

בָּרוּךְ אַתָּה יְהֹוָה אֱלֹהֵינוּ מֶלֶךְ הָעוֹלָם, שֶׁהֶחֱיָנוּ וְקִיְּמָנוּ וְהִגִּיעָנוּ לַזְּמַן הַזֶּה:

➤ Recline to the Left and Drink the Entire Cup (or at least the majority of it), preferably without Pausing. (Continue p. 22.)

Attention, my masters and teachers!

Blessed are You, God, our God, King of the universe, who creates the fruit of the vine.

Blessed are You, God, our God, King of the universe, who has chosen us from among all nations, and raised us above all tongues, and sanctified us through His commandments. And You, God, our God, have lovingly given us festivals for rejoicing, holidays and seasons to be cheerful—the day of this Festival of Matzos, the time of our freedom, pronounced holy, as a memorial of the Exodus from Egypt. For You have chosen us and sanctified us above all the nations, and Your holy festivals, in rejoicing and cheerfulness, You have given us as an inheritance. Blessed are You, God, who sanctifies Israel and the seasons.

➤ Do not repeat this blessing if you said it at candle lighting.

Blessed are You, God, our God, King of the universe, who has kept us alive, sustained us, and brought us to this season.

➤ Recline to the Left and Drink the Entire Cup (or at least the majority of it), preferably without pausing. (Continue p. 23.)

KIDDUSH FOR FRIDAY NIGHT

➤ IT IS CUSTOMARY FOR THE HEAD OF THE HOUSEHOLD TO WEAR A WHITE KITTEL DURING THE SEDER.

➤ KIDDUSH MAY NOT BE STARTED UNTIL NIGHTFALL.

➤ AS A DISPLAY OF FREEDOM, EACH PERSON SHOULD HAVE HIS CUP FILLED BY SOMEONE ELSE.

(SAY QUIETLY—וַיְהִי־עֶרֶב וַיְהִי־בֹקֶר)

יוֹם הַשִּׁשִּׁי: וַיְכֻלּוּ הַשָּׁמַיִם וְהָאָרֶץ וְכָל־צְבָאָם: וַיְכַל אֱלֹהִים בַּיּוֹם הַשְּׁבִיעִי מְלַאכְתּוֹ אֲשֶׁר עָשָׂה, וַיִּשְׁבֹּת בַּיּוֹם הַשְּׁבִיעִי מִכָּל־מְלַאכְתּוֹ אֲשֶׁר עָשָׂה: וַיְבָרֶךְ אֱלֹהִים אֶת־יוֹם הַשְּׁבִיעִי וַיְקַדֵּשׁ אֹתוֹ, כִּי בוֹ שָׁבַת מִכָּל־מְלַאכְתּוֹ אֲשֶׁר־בָּרָא אֱלֹהִים לַעֲשׂוֹת:

סַבְרִי מָרָנָן וְרַבָּנָן וְרַבּוֹתַי:

בָּרוּךְ אַתָּה יְהֹוָה אֱלֹהֵינוּ מֶלֶךְ הָעוֹלָם, בּוֹרֵא פְּרִי הַגָּפֶן:

בָּרוּךְ אַתָּה יְהֹוָה אֱלֹהֵינוּ מֶלֶךְ הָעוֹלָם, אֲשֶׁר בָּחַר בָּנוּ מִכָּל־עָם וְרוֹמְמָנוּ מִכָּל־לָשׁוֹן וְקִדְּשָׁנוּ בְּמִצְוֹתָיו, וַתִּתֶּן־לָנוּ יְהֹוָה אֱלֹהֵינוּ

KIDDUSH FOR FRIDAY NIGHT

➤ It is customary for the head of the household to wear a white Kittel during the seder.

➤ Kiddush may not be started until nightfall.

➤ As a display of freedom, each person should have his cup filled by someone else.

(SAY QUIETLY–And it was evening and it was morning,)

THE SIXTH DAY. The skies, the earth and all their numerous components were completed. On the seventh day, God completed His work that He had made. On the seventh day, He rested from all His work that He had done. God blessed the seventh day and He sanctified it, because on it God rested from all His work that He had created, to make.

Attention, my masters and teachers!

BLESSED ARE YOU, God, our God, King of the universe, who creates the fruit of the vine.

BLESSED ARE YOU, God, our God, King of the universe, who has chosen us from among all nations, and raised us above all tongues, and sanctified us through His commandments. And You, God, our

בְּאַהֲבָה שַׁבָּתוֹת לִמְנוּחָה וּמוֹעֲדִים לְשִׂמְחָה,
חַגִּים וּזְמַנִּים לְשָׂשׂוֹן, אֶת־יוֹם הַשַּׁבָּת הַזֶּה וְאֶת־
יוֹם חַג הַמַּצּוֹת הַזֶּה, זְמַן חֵרוּתֵנוּ, בְּאַהֲבָה מִקְרָא
קֹדֶשׁ, זֵכֶר לִיצִיאַת מִצְרָיִם. כִּי בָנוּ בָחַרְתָּ וְאוֹתָנוּ
קִדַּשְׁתָּ מִכָּל־הָעַמִּים, וְשַׁבָּת וּמוֹעֲדֵי קָדְשֶׁךָ
בְּאַהֲבָה וּבְרָצוֹן בְּשִׂמְחָה וּבְשָׂשׂוֹן הִנְחַלְתָּנוּ: בָּרוּךְ
אַתָּה יְהֹוָה, מְקַדֵּשׁ הַשַּׁבָּת וְיִשְׂרָאֵל וְהַזְּמַנִּים:

➤ DO NOT REPEAT THIS BLESSING IF YOU SAID IT AT CANDLE LIGHTING.

בָּרוּךְ אַתָּה יְהֹוָה אֱלֹהֵינוּ מֶלֶךְ הָעוֹלָם,
שֶׁהֶחֱיָנוּ וְקִיְּמָנוּ וְהִגִּיעָנוּ לַזְּמַן הַזֶּה:

➤ RECLINE TO THE LEFT AND DRINK THE ENTIRE CUP (OR AT LEAST THE
MAJORITY OF IT), PREFERABLY WITHOUT PAUSING. (CONTINUE P. 22.)

KIDDUSH FOR SATURDAY NIGHT

➤ IT IS CUSTOMARY FOR THE HEAD OF THE HOUSEHOLD TO WEAR A WHITE KITTEL
DURING THE SEDER.

➤ KIDDUSH MAY NOT BE STARTED UNTIL NIGHTFALL.

➤ AS A DISPLAY OF FREEDOM, EACH PERSON SHOULD HAVE HIS CUP FILLED BY
SOMEONE ELSE.

סַבְרִי מָרָנָן וְרַבָּנָן וְרַבּוֹתַי:

בָּרוּךְ אַתָּה יְהֹוָה אֱלֹהֵינוּ מֶלֶךְ
הָעוֹלָם, בּוֹרֵא פְּרִי הַגָּפֶן:

God, have lovingly given us Sabbaths for rest, festivals for rejoicing, holidays and seasons to be cheerful—this Sabbath day and the day of this Festival of Matzos the time of our freedom, pronounced holy in love, as a memorial of the Exodus from Egypt. For You have chosen us and sanctified us above all the nations, and Your holy Sabbath and Festivals which, lovingly and willingly, with rejoicing and cheerfulness, You have given us as an inheritance. Blessed are You, God, who sanctifies the Sabbath and Israel and the seasons.

➤ DO NOT REPEAT THIS BLESSING IF YOU SAID IT AT CANDLE LIGHTING.

BLESSED ARE YOU, God, our God, King of the universe, who has kept us alive, sustained us, brought us to this season.

➤ RECLINE TO THE LEFT AND DRINK THE ENTIRE CUP (OR AT LEAST THE MAJORITY OF IT), PREFERABLY WITHOUT PAUSING. (CONTINUE P. 23.)

KIDDUSH FOR SATURDAY NIGHT

➤ IT IS CUSTOMARY FOR THE HEAD OF THE HOUSEHOLD TO WEAR A WHITE KITTEL DURING THE SEDER.

➤ KIDDUSH MAY NOT BE STARTED UNTIL NIGHTFALL.

➤ AS A DISPLAY OF FREEDOM, EACH PERSON SHOULD HAVE HIS CUP FILLED BY SOMEONE ELSE.

Attention, my masters and teachers!

BLESSED ARE YOU, God, our God, King of the universe, who creates the fruit of the vine.

בָּרוּךְ אַתָּה יְהֹוָה אֱלֹהֵינוּ מֶלֶךְ הָעוֹלָם, אֲשֶׁר בָּחַר בָּנוּ מִכָּל־עָם וְרוֹמְמָנוּ מִכָּל־לָשׁוֹן וְקִדְּשָׁנוּ בְּמִצְוֹתָיו, וַתִּתֶּן־לָנוּ יְהֹוָה אֱלֹהֵינוּ בְּאַהֲבָה מוֹעֲדִים לְשִׂמְחָה, חַגִּים וּזְמַנִּים לְשָׂשׂוֹן, אֶת־יוֹם חַג הַמַּצּוֹת הַזֶּה, זְמַן חֵרוּתֵנוּ, מִקְרָא קֹדֶשׁ, זֵכֶר לִיצִיאַת מִצְרָיִם. כִּי בָנוּ בָחַרְתָּ וְאוֹתָנוּ קִדַּשְׁתָּ מִכָּל־הָעַמִּים, וּמוֹעֲדֵי קָדְשֶׁךָ בְּשִׂמְחָה וּבְשָׂשׂוֹן הִנְחַלְתָּנוּ: בָּרוּךְ אַתָּה יְהֹוָה, מְקַדֵּשׁ יִשְׂרָאֵל וְהַזְּמַנִּים:

➤ HOLD YOUR FINGERS TO THE LIGHT OF THE CANDLES.

בָּרוּךְ אַתָּה יְהֹוָה אֱלֹהֵינוּ מֶלֶךְ הָעוֹלָם, בּוֹרֵא מְאוֹרֵי הָאֵשׁ:

בָּרוּךְ אַתָּה יְהֹוָה אֱלֹהֵינוּ מֶלֶךְ הָעוֹלָם, הַמַּבְדִּיל בֵּין קֹדֶשׁ לְחוֹל, בֵּין אוֹר לְחֹשֶׁךְ, בֵּין יִשְׂרָאֵל לָעַמִּים, בֵּין יוֹם הַשְּׁבִיעִי לְשֵׁשֶׁת יְמֵי הַמַּעֲשֶׂה. בֵּין קְדֻשַּׁת שַׁבָּת לִקְדֻשַּׁת יוֹם טוֹב הִבְדַּלְתָּ, וְאֶת־יוֹם הַשְּׁבִיעִי

Blessed are You, God, our God, King of the universe, who has chosen us from among all nations, and raised us above all tongues, and sanctified us through His commandments. And You, God, our God, have lovingly given us festivals for rejoicing, holidays and seasons to be cheerful— the day of this Festival of Matzos the time of our freedom, pronounced holy, as a memorial of the Exodus from Egypt. For You have chosen us and sanctified us above all the nations, and Your holy festivals which, in rejoicing and cheerfulness, You have given us as an inheritance. Blessed are You, God, who sanctifies Israel and the seasons.

➤ Hold your fingers to the light of the candles.

Blessed are You, God, our God, King of the universe, who creates the lights of fire.

Blessed are You, God, our God, King of the universe, who distinguishes between sacred and mundane, between light and darkness, between Israel and the nations, between the seventh day and the six workdays. You have distinguished between the holiness of the Sabbath and the holiness of the Festival, and You have sanctified

מִשֵּׁשֶׁת יְמֵי הַמַּעֲשֶׂה קִדַּשְׁתָּ, הִבְדַּלְתָּ וְקִדַּשְׁתָּ

אֶת־עַמְּךָ יִשְׂרָאֵל בִּקְדֻשָּׁתֶךָ: בָּרוּךְ אַתָּה

יְהֹוָה, הַמַּבְדִּיל בֵּין קֹדֶשׁ לְקֹדֶשׁ:

➤ DO NOT REPEAT THIS BLESSING IF YOU SAID IT AT CANDLE LIGHTING.

בָּרוּךְ אַתָּה יְהֹוָה אֱלֹהֵינוּ מֶלֶךְ הָעוֹלָם,

שֶׁהֶחֱיָנוּ וְקִיְּמָנוּ וְהִגִּיעָנוּ לַזְּמַן הַזֶּה:

➤ RECLINE TO THE LEFT AND DRINK THE ENTIRE CUP (OR AT LEAST THE
MAJORITY OF IT), PREFERABLY WITHOUT PAUSING. (CONTINUE P. 22.)

═══════════════ CLASSIC QUESTIONS ═══════════════

● **Why must we lean when drinking the Four Cups of wine?**

ALTER REBBE'S SHULCHAN ARUCH: Because this *mitzvah* is to commemorate redemption and freedom. For the Four Cups were instituted by the Sages, corresponding to the four expressions of redemption in the Torah portion of *Va'eira*: "*I will bring you out... I will redeem you...I will take you...I will save you.*" (*Shemos* 6:6-7)...

Therefore they require leaning, as an expression of freedom (*Orach Chaim* 472:14).

● **When may we drink the Four Cups?**

ALTER REBBE'S SHULCHAN ARUCH: One must drink the Four Cups in the prescribed order. Namely, one pauses to recite the Haggadah between the First and Second Cups, and between the Third and Fourth Cups. Between the Second and Third cups one pauses to eat Matzah and to recite Grace after Meals.

If a person fails to pause for these activities and drinks the cups sequentially, he does not fulfil the *mitzvah* of the Four Cups, and it is considered as if he had drunk just one cup (ibid. 16).

═══════════════ TORAS MENACHEM ═══════════════

ד' כוסות — *The Four Cups.*

As they are written in the Torah, the four expressions of redemption appear in the following order:

1. *I will bring you out;* 2. *I will save you;* 3. *I will redeem you;* 4. *I will take you...*(*Shemos* 6:6-7).

However, when they appear in the *Alter Rebbe's Shulchan Aruch*, the sequence has changed:

1. *I will bring you out;* 2. *I will redeem you;* 3. *I will take you;* 4. *I will save you.*

Why did the *Alter Rebbe* deem it necessary to change the sequence here?

Perhaps the following could be suggested. The *Alter Rebbe* recorded the four expressions in this sequence to reflect the law that "*one must drink the Four Cups in the prescribed order*" (see *Classic Questions*), and

the seventh day above the six workdays. You
have distinguished and sanctified Your people
Israel with Your holiness. Blessed are You, God,
who distinguishes between holy and holy.

➤ DO NOT REPEAT THIS BLESSING IF YOU SAID IT AT CANDLE LIGHTING.

BLESSED ARE YOU, God, our God,
King of the universe, who has kept us alive,
sustained us, brought us to this season.

➤ RECLINE TO THE LEFT AND DRINK THE ENTIRE CUP (OR AT LEAST THE
MAJORITY OF IT), PREFERABLY WITHOUT PAUSING. (CONTINUE P. 23.)

TORAS MENACHEM

finding that the sequence of the "expressions" in the
Torah did not reflect the order of the Cups, he found
it necessary to switch them around.

His logic would appear to be as follows.

1. Kiddush (First Cup) is connected to "*I will bring
you out...*" (וְהוֹצֵאתִי) since it mentions the words "as
a memorial of bringing you out (יְצִיאַת) of Egypt."

2. We recite the Second Cup over *Magid*, recounting the story of the Exodus at length. This corresponds to the verse "*I will redeem you with an
outstretched arm and with great acts of judgment*,"
which emphasizes the miracles of the Exodus. There
is also a connection between "*I will redeem you*" and
the concluding blessing of *Maggid* which stresses that
God "has *redeemed* us and *redeemed* our fathers...
Blessed are You, God, who *redeemed* Israel."

3. "*I will take you as a people for myself and I will
be a God to you*," refers to the day when the Torah
was given (see *Midrash ha-Gadol* and *Bachaye* ibid.). This
alludes to the Grace after Meals (Third Cup), since
in Grace we are obligated to praise God for giving us
the Torah (such that if a person omits the phrase, "*the
Torah which you have taught us*," he does not fulfil
his obligation—*Brachos* 48b).

4. The expression "*I will save you from their labor*"
is given no further clarification by scripture, alluding
to the future era of which we are told: "*A person does
not know what will transpire until it occurs, for these
matters were concealed from the prophets*" (*Rambam,
Laws of Kings* 12:2). This expression therefore corresponds to the Fourth Cup over which Hallel is recited,
since the focus of Hallel is very much on the future
redemption (see below, p. 180).

An interesting point that arises from the *Alter
Rebbe's* analysis is the extent to which the theme
of redemption has penetrated every aspect of this
mitzvah of the Four Cups. Without the above insight,
we would have imagined that the Four Cups are *as
a whole* reflective of "redemption and freedom" (see
Shulchan Aruch cited in *Classic Questions*), but that each
cup nevertheless has its own independent significance (Kiddush, Grace etc.). But with the above in
mind we see that even the *specific* cups are directly
associated with redemption and freedom, since they
each commemorate one of God's four redemptive
promises to the Jewish people in Egypt.

(Based on *Likutei Sichos* vol. 11, pp. 20-1)

וּרְחַץ

Wash the Hands

➤ THE HEAD OF THE HOUSEHOLD WASHES HIS HANDS WITHOUT MAKING A BLESSING
(SEE OPPOSITE). (IN MANY HOUSEHOLDS, THE SEDER PARTICIPANTS ALSO WASH
THEIR HANDS).

➤ IT IS CUSTOMARY FOR THE HEAD OF THE HOUSEHOLD TO HAVE THE WATER
BROUGHT TO HIS SEAT.

CLASSIC QUESTIONS

● **Why do we wash our hands at this point?**

TALMUD: Because the law requires us to do so
before eating a food dipped in liquid (the next step
of the Seder). This is in order not to impart the liquid
(and thereby the food) with ritual impurity from our
hands, for ritual impurity is transmitted more easily
to a wet substance (see *Pesachim* 115a and *Rashi* ibid.).

● **Why do we not make a blessing?**

ALTER REBBE'S SHULCHAN ARUCH: In a case of halachic
doubt we do not make a blessing, for fear that
we would be uttering God's name in vain. In this
instance, there is a view (*Tosfos* ibid.) that washing the
hands before touching dipped food was a *mitzvah*
only practiced in Temple times (*Orach Chaim* 158:3).

● **If during the year I follow the opinion of
Tosfos and do not wash before dipping food,
should I still wash now?**

CHOK YA'AKOV: Yes, because this is part of the Seder,
designed to arouse the interest of the children (*Orach
Chaim* 473:28).

● **Why does this step's title, *Urchatz*, begin
with the letter *vav* (meaning "and"), which is not
the case with the other steps?**

LIKUTEI TA'AMIM U'MINHAGIM: This renders *"Urchatz"*
as a two-syllabled word. It thus enables the steps
of the Seder, arranged in stanzas of two words, to
rhyme: *Kadesh, Urchatz; Karpas, Yachatz, etc.* (see
also addendum).

TORAS MENACHEM

❧ **וּרְחַץ** — *Urchatz.*

What is the *inner* reason why *Urchatz* is the only
step of the Seder which begins with the letter *vav*
("and"), suggesting a special connection with the
preceding step, *Kadesh*? (See *Classic Questions.*)

The Kabbalists taught that the various steps of the
Seder allude to different aspects of the *sefiros*, the

scheme of Divine attributes which are mirrored in the
soul of man. In particular, the first two steps, *Kadesh*
and *Urchatz*, correspond to the first two *sefiros*,
Chochmah (conception) and *Binah* (cognition).

Unlike the other *sefiros* which operate relatively
independently of one another, *Chochmah* and *Binah*
are a single functional unit, "*two friends that never
separate*" (*Zohar* III 4a). And this is the mystical expla-

How to Wash

☞ BEFORE WASHING THE HANDS CHECK THAT THEY ARE CLEAN AND DRY.

☞ POUR PLENTY OF WATER (AT LEAST THREE OUNCES) TWICE OVER YOUR RIGHT HAND SO THAT THE WATER COVERS THE ENTIRE HAND UP TO THE WRIST.

☞ PASS THE CONTAINER INTO YOUR RIGHT HAND AND POUR WATER TWICE OVER YOUR LEFT HAND, EXACTLY AS BEFORE.

☞ LET GO OF THE CONTAINER AND DRY YOUR HANDS THOROUGHLY.

☞ DO NOT MAKE A BLESSING.

TORAS MENACHEM

nation why the steps of the Seder embodied by these two *sefiros* are linked by a *vav:* to reflect their intimate working relationship.

Why are *Chochmah* and *Binah* so utterly dependent on each other?

Chochmah is the seat of the soul's creativity. Its perception is holistic: it has an extremely broad view of concepts and ideas, and it acquires knowledge intuitively rather than rationally. *Chochmah*'s "eye" can read different themes simultaneously, perceiving how they converge into a simple core idea, or "point."

Binah, on the other hand, is quite the opposite. It focuses very much on details and data, analyzing them carefully and sequentially. Its logic is well reasoned and precise; and it excels at taking the raw ideas which it is fed by *Chochmah* and fleshing them out with ornate detail, appropriate descriptions and helpful analogies.

Chochmah and *Binah* are "*two friends that never separate*" because each excels in what the other lacks. Besides initially generating the ideas, which *Binah* could not do on its own, *Chochmah*'s constant influence is required to prevent *Binah* from losing the bigger picture as it focuses on the detail. *Chochmah* must always be at hand to help its "friend" synthesize its findings and to place in context the rather dizzying amount of information that *Binah* tends to produce.

But as much as *Binah* is helpless without *Chochmah*, *Chochmah* alone is a mere "side-dish" to the "main course" of true intelligence which *Binah* offers. Intuition, creativity and holistic perception are, of course, wonderful, but of what use are they unless we have the apparatus to translate those whims of abstraction into solid, well-honed ideas? *Chochmah* has all of the inspiration, but none of the communication skills necessary to bring its message across. *Chochmah* may be a master of *context*, but without *Binah* there is no *text* at all.

So that inconspicuous *vav* at the beginning of *Urchatz* represents our ability to harmonize an inner tension that exists within us all: the rational versus the intuitive, the practical versus the idealistic, the tangible versus the transcendent.

There is no easy solution. Our souls are powered by highly contrasting faculties which need to work together so that we can lead fulfilling lives and carry out our God-given mission in this world. In short: We must listen to *both* of our minds, and give each of them the respect that they deserve.

(Based on *Sichah* of *Erev Pesach* 5750)

כַּרְפַּס

➤ DO NOT TAKE A VEGETABLE THAT MAY BE USED FOR BITTER HERBS.

➤ DIP A SMALL PIECE OF VEGETABLE (LESS THAN 0.9 OZ) INTO SALT WATER, MAKE THE FOLLOWING BLESSING, AND THEN EAT IT. HAVE IN MIND THAT THIS BLESSING ALSO APPLIES TO ALL THE BITTER HERBS EATEN LATER. (MOST PEOPLE DO NOT LEAN.)

בָּרוּךְ אַתָּה יְהֹוָה אֱלֹהֵינוּ מֶלֶךְ הָעוֹלָם, בּוֹרֵא פְּרִי הָאֲדָמָה:

=== CLASSIC QUESTIONS ===

● **Why do we dip the vegetable in salt water and eat it?**

TALMUD: To arouse the interest of the children, since it is not something we do during the rest of the year (*Pesachim* 114a-b).

=== TORAS MENACHEM ===

כַּרְפַּס — *Dip and Eat the Vegetable (Halachah).*

The stated reason for *Karpas*, eating a vegetable that has been dipped in salt-water, is to arouse the interest of the children. The commentators explain that this rather odd practice is likely to capture the children's attention, since dipping is not something we do the rest of the year (see *Classic Questions*). In fact, we find this is one of the Four Questions posed by the child later on: *"On all nights we need not dip even once, but on this night we do so twice!"*

There seems, however, to be a glaring inconsistency here. Even a small child will be familiar with the fact that we *do* carry out a "dipping" ceremony at other times. On *Rosh ha-Shanah*, for example, we dip an apple in honey. Furthermore, every time we eat bread during the year there is a requirement to dip it in salt. (In fact, many follow the *Arizal's* custom to dip the bread in salt three times). So how could one say, *"On all other nights we need not dip even once"*?

A simple solution to this problem, which even a child could appreciate, is that tonight's ritual is unique in that *it revolves around the dipping itself.*

On *Rosh ha-Shanah*, our main intention is to recite a prayer for a sweet new year, to which the apple dipped in honey is secondary. Likewise, during the year when we dip the bread in salt, the emphasis is not the dipping *per se*, but the presence of the salt on the table (since the table resembles the Altar on which salt was always placed), or the general mixing of the salt with the bread, *in whatever fashion* (to resemble the mixing of salt with the sacrifices). The notion of dipping is thus an outgrowth of the general need for salt. This is not a "dipping ceremony" at all, but a "salt ceremony" that has evolved in such a way that it involves some dipping.

In fact, in one of his discourses, the *Alter Rebbe* states this point unequivocally: *"The essential principle is not that we bring salt and dip the bread in it. Rather, our main intention is that the bread should somehow acquire the flavor of salt....The dipping is not a crucial point here"* (*Short Discourses*, p. 500).

So, in the final analysis, we see that tonight is the only occasion when normative Jewish practice requires dipping for dipping's sake.

Dip & Eat the Vegetable

➤ DO NOT TAKE A VEGETABLE THAT MAY BE USED FOR BITTER HERBS.

➤ DIP A SMALL PIECE OF VEGETABLE (LESS THAN 0.9 OZ) INTO SALT WATER, MAKE THE FOLLOWING BLESSING, AND THEN EAT IT. HAVE IN MIND THAT THIS BLESSING ALSO APPLIES TO ALL THE BITTER HERBS EATEN LATER. (MOST PEOPLE DO NOT LEAN.)

Blessed are You, God, our God, King of the universe, who creates the fruit of the earth.

TORAS MENACHEM

(While the above definition of salt dipping is satisfying, for a person initiated in the finer points of Jewish law, it is ultimately unnecessary. From a strictly halachic viewpoint "dipping" here refers to dipping *in a liquid* (which is why we are required to wash our hands first—see above, p. 22), and the salt in which we dip our bread throughout the year is, as a general rule, dry. Tonight, by contrast, both of our dippings are wet: the vegetable in salt-water, and the Bitter Herbs in Charoses, a paste made with wine. So there is really no question in the first place: from the perspective of Jewish law we *never* dip bread in salt.)

(Based on *Sichas Shabbos Parshas Kedoshim* 5741)

כַּרְפַּס **‏** — *Dip and Eat the Vegetable* (*Kabbalah*).

According to the Kabbalah, *tibul*, dipping, is symbolic of *bitul*, surrender (or negation) of the self, which is why in Hebrew we find that one word is an anagram of the other: טִיבּוּל = בִּיטוּל (*Siddur im Dach, Sha'ar Kavanos ha-Mikvah*). And one doesn't need to be a mystic to appreciate why. The purpose of dipping a food into a flavoring agent is so that the food should *surrender* some of its own taste and "give way" to a more desirable quality found in the flavoring agent.

But, ironically, while dipping food suggests an experience of surrender and self-negation *for the food substance*, it bears the very opposite connotation for *the dipper himself*.

What drives a person to dip? Because, as something of a connoisseur, he knows that the food is lacking its full gourmet potential and that it would be enhanced greatly by the right sauce—hardly a moment of self-surrender and ego nullification!

But on Pesach, all this changes. Pesach is a festival of *bitul*: We eat unleavened bread which has no chance to rise, symbolic of humility; and we celebrate the birth of our nation, a point in history when Israel's spiritual standing was very low, and we had little of which to be proud.

So our dipping tonight is inevitably different from any dipping throughout the year. Normally, dipping food is an expression of culinary expertise, an exercise aimed at enriching those pleasures of life that our egos so desperately pursue. But tonight, when our souls are awakened, we realize that there is something more important, more noble—and, ironically, more rewarding—than the pursuit of happiness for its own sake. A voice within is telling us that only through genuine *bitul* can we make a transition from the distorted, egocentric, human view of reality, to a more true, theocentric standpoint. After all, a genuine mystical union with our Creator must be on His terms, and not on ours.

God took us out of Egypt so that we would be free to serve Him: free from the Egyptians and, more significantly, free from the obsessive desire for self-enrichment which draws us away from our true calling in life. So tonight, let us emulate the *Karpas* and "dip ourselves" too, endeavoring to surrender to God, and not make our observance of His law contingent on our own, mortal understanding.

(Based on *Sichos of Nights of Chag ha-Pesach* 5748)

Break the Middle Matzah

➤ BREAK THE MIDDLE MATZAH INTO TWO, ONE PIECE BIGGER THAN THE OTHER.

➤ REMOVE THE LARGER PIECE (NOW DESIGNATED AS THE AFIKOMAN), WRAP IT IN A CLOTH AND SET IT ASIDE.

➤ THE SMALLER PIECE OF MATZAH IS LEFT BETWEEN THE TWO WHOLE MATZOS.

➤ SOME PLACE THE AFIKOMAN BRIEFLY ON THEIR SHOULDERS (TO REMEMBER HOW THE JEWISH PEOPLE LEFT EGYPT WITH MATZOS ON THEIR SHOULDERS).

CLASSIC QUESTIONS

● **Why do we break Matzah now and leave the broken piece on the Seder plate?**

ALTER REBBE'S SHULCHAN ARUCH: Because we are required to recite the Haggadah in the presence of Matzah which is suitable to fulfil the *mitzvah* [of eating Matzah on this night, and this must be a broken piece specifically].

This law is implicit in the verse, *"You shall eat it with Matzos, bread of oni"* (*Devarim* 16:3)...on which our Sages expounded (*Pesachim* 115b):

a.) It is a bread upon which we "recite" (*onin*) many things, [i.e. recite the Haggadah].

b.) Scribally, the word *oni* is written *ani* (without a *vav*), which means "poor man." Thus our Sages expounded: *"Just as it is the way of a poor man to*

TORAS MENACHEM

৪৩ יַחַץ — *Break the Middle Matzah.*

When *Yachatz* is performed, two radically different Matzah "identities" emerge.

➤ One half of the Matzah, the smaller piece, becomes *"poor man's* bread." The larger piece (Afikoman), on the other hand, is symbolic of the Paschal lamb which was eaten in a manner of *majesty* and *royalty*.

➤ The smaller piece remains on the table; but the larger piece must be hidden away.

➤ The smaller piece is an "exile" Matzah, over which we bemoan the slavery of our ancestors in Egypt; the larger piece is a "redemption" Matzah with which we look forward expectantly to the day when we will eat the Paschal lamb once again.

➤ The smaller piece reminds us of the Egyptian Exodus whose effects were eventually reversed, with further exiles following; the larger piece alludes to the future redemption whose effects will be permanent and everlasting.

So the question is: How could one *single* piece of Matzah harbor such a split personality? After it is broken into two, we see that the middle Matzah combined two utterly divergent themes. How could they have co-existed in one single cracker?

Yisrael Ba'al Shem Tov, founder of the Chasidic movement which revived mysticism, joy and sincere worship of God as the focal point of Judaism, would sometimes sign his name "Yisrael from Okop." Okop is not the name of a town—the Ba'al Shem Tov actually originated from the Galician town of Tlost. Rather, Okop means "trench" in Polish.

מַגִּיד

Tell the Exodus Story

➤ THE SEDER PLATE IS LIFTED UP WITH THE MATZOS UNCOVERED.

➤ THE HAGGADAH SHOULD BE RECITED LOUDLY, JOYOUSLY AND WITH INTENSE CONCENTRATION. IT IS CUSTOMARY THAT EVERY PERSON READS ALONG OUT LOUD.

═══════════════ CLASSIC QUESTIONS ═══════════════

use a broken loaf of bread, here too we are to use a broken matzah." I.e., the Matzah which we use for this *mitzvah* must not be whole, but broken. And it is in the presence of this Matzah that the Haggadah is recited (*Orach Chaim* 473:36).

● **Why do we break the *middle* Matzah?**

TUR: Because we will fulfil a *mitzvah* with the upper Matzah before we will fulfil a *mitzvah* with the middle Matzah (see below p. 142*ff*), and we want the Matzos to be in the correct order so that we do not "pass over a *mitzvah*" (*Orach Chaim* ch. 473).

● **Why is the bigger piece chosen for the Afikoman?**

ALTER REBBE'S SHULCHAN ARUCH: Because the Afikoman is considered to be a very "important" *mitzvah* since it takes the place of the Paschal lamb [which was eaten roasted, "in a manner of importance"] (ibid. 35).

● **Why is the Afikoman broken into five pieces?**

LIKUTEI TA'AMIM U'MINHAGIM: Breaking the Afikoman off the middle Matzah is, according to the Kabbalah, symbolic of a "sweetening" of the Divine attribute of *Gevurah* (severity).

The middle Matzah represents severity, a trait characterized by our Patriarch Yitzchak (note that "Yachatz" and "Yitzchak" share the same letters); whereas the Afikoman represents kindness (*"afiko man"* means "bring out food," suggestive of charity and kindness). So creating the Afikoman (kindness) from the middle Matzah (severity) suggests a softening of severity into kindness. And since, according to the Kabbalah, there are five forces of severity, we break the Afikoman into five pieces, to ensure that each harsh force is softened.

● **Why is the Afikoman put aside?**

YA'AVETZ: So that we do not eat it inadvertently during the meal (*Siddur Ya'avetz*).

═══════════════ TORAS MENACHEM ═══════════════

Tlost was originally a walled town, but at some point in history the walls were destroyed, leaving numerous trenches. The Ba'al Shem Tov's parents were so desperately poor that they could not afford even a modest home in which to live, so they sought refuge in one of these trenches. And that is where the Ba'al Shem Tov was born—hence the signature: "Yisrael from the trench."

While the Ba'al Shem Tov himself was not the actual Mashiach, we are nevertheless promised that the mystical revival which he initiated will ultimately be responsible for ushering in the Messianic Era (*Kesser*

Shem Tov, par. 1). Thus, when telling the above story, Rabbi Shalom Dov Ber of Lubavitch, concluded: "*From the Ba'al Shem Tov's trenches we have been granted the strength to get out of all other trenches, for the Ba'al Shem Tov's influence is unfaltering.*"

One cannot help but marvel at the irony here. The enormous influence of the Ba'al Shem Tov, which will eventually be responsible for the global utopia of the future era, had such pitiful and humble beginnings. All men will one day enjoy wealth and physical abundance thanks to a person who lived in a trench!

But this, precisely, is the point. As the Psalmist said,

הָא לַחְמָא עַנְיָא
דִּי אֲכָלוּ אַבְהָתָנָא
בְּאַרְעָא דְמִצְרָיִם.

CLASSIC QUESTIONS

● **Why do we not recite a blessing before fulfilling the *mitzvah* of recounting the Exodus?**

Rif: Because in Kiddush we already discharged this obligation when saying, *"A memorial of the Exodus from Egypt"* (cited in *Avudraham, Seder ha-Haggadah*).

Rashba: We do not recite a blessing on a *mitzvah* that has no minimum *shiur* (prescribed amount). In this case, any amount of discussion would be sufficient to fulfil one's obligation (ibid.).

Alter Rebbe: The solutions of *Rif* and *Rashba* are difficult to accept, because, in contrast to the rest of the

year when we can fulfil our obligation to remember the Exodus with a few brief words, tonight on the anniversary of the Exodus itself we are required to discuss it at length.

Rather, we do not make a blessing on reciting the Haggadah for the same reason we do not make a blessing on the *mitzvah* to recite *Bircas ha-Mazon* (Grace after Meals). Namely, because we do not make a blessing on a blessing. Thus, since the Haggadah is itself words of blessing, we do not make a blessing on it (*Sefer ha-Sichos* 5697, p. 219; see *Likutei Sichos* vol. 3, p. 1016).

TORAS MENACHEM

"Out of the straits I called upon God; God answered me with expansiveness" (Psalms 118:5). The very wide can only come after we have been constrained through the very narrow.

And it is this dynamic which the middle Matzah embodies. Poverty and redemption emerge from the same, single piece of Matzah to teach us that the tragic and the tremendous follow one after the other.

So even if you look around and see a fractured world with no remedy in sight, do not despair. In truth, Mashiach is just around the corner, and we will soon emerge from our trenches, with the help of "Yisrael from Okop."

(Based on *Sichah* of 2nd night of Pesach 5720)

֎ **הָא לַחְמָא עַנְיָא** ֎ — *This is the Bread of Affliction.*

The precise significance of this passage seems, at first glance, to be rather confusing. The fact that it follows right after the heading "*Maggid*" ("*Tell the Exodus story*"), appears to suggest that with these few lines we start to recall the chronicle of our ancestors' departure from Egypt.

But from both the *context* and the *content* of the passage, this is evidently not the case. According to Jewish law, the *mitzvah* of telling the Exodus story is carried out in response to the question of a child—the "*Mah Nishtanah*"—something which only occurs in the *following* section. So the context of these few

THIS IS THE BREAD OF AFFLICTION
that our ancestors ate in the land of Egypt.

CLASSIC QUESTIONS

● **Did our ancestors really eat Matzah *"in the land of Egypt"*? The Torah states that they ate Matzah after *leaving* Egypt** (*Shemos* 12:39)**?**

AVUDRAHAM: From a personal experience of being imprisoned in India, Ibn Ezra testified that prisoners are fed Matzah, which is satisfying in small amounts because it is slow to digest. Thus, as slaves, the Jewish people were fed Matzah in Egypt.

SFORNO: The Egyptian slavedrivers did not allow the Jewish people time to bake leavened bread in Egypt, so they baked Matzah (*Devarim* 16:3).

MAHARAL: The assertion that the Jewish people ate Matzah in Egypt is not substantiated by Scripture, the Mishnah, or the Talmud (*Gevuras Hashem* ch. 51).

● **Why is this passage written in Aramaic, unlike the remainder of the Haggadah, which is in Hebrew?**

KOLBO: This passage was composed at a time when the spoken language of the Jewish people was Aramaic, and was thus phrased in a way that everybody would be able to understand. The last sentence, however, (*"next year we will be free men"*) was written in Hebrew so that the Babylonians would not understand it, since they may interpret it as a rebellion against the government (ch. 51).

LIKUTEI TA'AMIM U'MINHAGIM: The remainder of the Haggadah was composed in Temple times, as is clear from the Mishnah (*Pesachim* 116a). Therefore it was composed in Hebrew.

TORAS MENACHEM

lines, placed *before* the *Mah Nishtanah*, suggests that we have yet to begin telling the story. This notion is confirmed by the *content* of the text. Here we speak, not of redemption and freedom, but of our current, gloomy exile. People are hungry and need feeding. *"Now we are here...Now we are slaves,"* and it is only next year that we hope that the redemption will have arrived. Unlike the Exodus story which *"begins with shame and ends with glory"* (*Pesachim* 116a), the current passage ends, for the time being, in shame: *"now* we are slaves."

So if this is not the Exodus story, then what is it? And why do we read it straight after announcing *"Magid,"* that we are about to begin the story?

A simple solution would be to propose that this passage is nothing more than a traditional invitation to guests: *"All who are hungry, let them come and eat! All who are needy, let them come and conduct the Pesach Seder!"*

But this cannot be the entire purpose of these lines, as, once again, the context proves otherwise. For why

כָּל־דִּכְפִין יֵיתֵי וְיֵיכוֹל,
כָּל־דִּצְרִיךְ יֵיתֵי וְיִפְסַח.
הַשַּׁתָּא הָכָא, לְשָׁנָה הַבָּאָה
בְּאַרְעָא דְיִשְׂרָאֵל. הַשַּׁתָּא עַבְדֵי,
לְשָׁנָה הַבָּאָה בְּנֵי חוֹרִין:

===== CLASSIC QUESTIONS =====

● **If we were redeemed then how could it be that "Now we are slaves"?**

MAHARAL: People ask: What was the benefit of the Exodus to us, since we are now subjugated by other regimes? What difference does it make if the Egyptians or somebody else is persecuting us?

This is a foolish question. For when the Jewish people came out of Egypt a tangible, positive change

occurred to them, rendering them intrinsically free. The Jew now possesses an essential quality which means that he deserves to be free by virtue of who he is, and an essential quality is never lost due to something circumstantial, such as a subsequent exile (*Gevuras Hashem* ch. 61).

REBBE RAYATZ: The Egyptian Exodus opened up the spiritual "conduit" through which all future redemptions would flow (*Sefer ha-Ma'amarim* 5708, p. 164).

===== TORAS MENACHEM =====

would we only issue an invitation to guests now, after beginning the Seder and drinking the First Cup?

Rather, we declare, *"This is the bread of affliction etc.,"* in order to pose—and answer—an important question that will be troubling the reader when embarking upon the Exodus story; a question so troubling that if it were to remain unanswered our ability to carry out the evening's celebrations would be severely compromised. In fact, without a solution, we will be wondering whether there is any contemporary relevance to the Seder at all.

The question is: How can we celebrate *redemption* if we are now in *exile?* Or, to put it bluntly, the political freedom accomplished through the Exodus may be a fascinating and marvelous piece of ancient history, but its effects do not appear to have lasted. Jews are currently scattered around the globe, subjugated to regimes that are, in so many instances, hostile to the observance of Judaism, and, *"in each and every*

generation they rise against us to destroy us" (below p. 64). So why relive a past glory when right now we seem to be doomed once again?

In order to make this point, the Haggadah begins: "This is the bread of *affliction* which our ancestors ate *in Egypt.*" This declaration was not intended to be literal (for as **Maharal** has shown, our ancestors did *not* eat Matzah as slaves in Egypt), but rather, satirical. The Haggadah is essentially bemoaning the apparent failure of the Exodus: "Do you really think that our ancestors ate Matzah of *redemption*? No! We see in retrospect that their freedom was short-lived; their 'Matzah of redemption' was really Bread of Affliction, because the effects of the redemption have now been reversed and it is as if they never left Egypt at all. In hindsight we see that when they ate that Matzah on their departure from geographical Egypt, they were really still "in Egypt," metaphorically speaking.

All who are hungry, let them come and eat! All who are needy, let them come and conduct the Pesach Seder!

Now we are here; next year we will be in the Land of Israel. Now we are slaves; next year we will be free men.

TORAS MENACHEM

"You say this is Bread of *Redemption*? Can't you see that the redemption failed, and it is for us Bread of Affliction!

"And what is the proof? That there are so many poverty-stricken Jews who cannot afford to eat, or to carry out a Seder: *'All who are hungry, let them come and eat! All who are needy, let them come and conduct the Pesach Seder!'* If we have truly enjoyed redemption then why are our brothers starving?

"In short, how can we possibly celebrate the Seder when, *'Now we are here...Now we are slaves'?"*

A formidable question, indeed.

To fathom the answer, let us briefly address a theological problem which arises from the above discussion. If God is absolutely perfect, and He personally came to redeem us, then how could it have turned out to have been an imperfect redemption which was later annulled?

Apparently, we need to draw a distinction between *God's* redemptive power and *our* ability to receive and internalize those energies.

When we came out of Egypt, God illuminated our souls, imbuing us with faith and a desire to be religious, but these emotions soon dissipated. However, this is not to be perceived as a failure on God's part. Obviously, He could have transformed us into angels if He had so desired, but, in God's eyes, the truly great person is one who struggles with his darker side, overcoming and ultimately mending his own weaknesses and flaws. So He granted us the spiritual

illumination required to liberate ourselves, but He left "the ball in our court."

The redemptive energy that began to shine at the Exodus never ceased, which is why we find a requirement to take the Exodus to heart every single day: *"In each and every generation—and likewise each and every day—a person must see himself as if he personally left Egypt"* (*Pesachim* 116b; *Tanya* ch. 47).

But we have *to want* to be good people; to take that inspiration and make a concerted effort to refine our far-from-perfect personalities. We cannot blame God for our troubled history, only ourselves, since *"we were exiled from our land because of our sins."*

So the answer to our troubling question, how we could celebrate redemption while still in Exile, is that *"Next year we will be in the Land of Israel....Next year we will be free men."* The Exodus from Egypt was the time when God first began to grant us the redemptive powers to heal ourselves and the world around us, and He has never stopped doing so. We merely have to take advantage of this gift, and then "next year we will be free men."

Tonight's activities are therefore extremely pertinent and relevant to our present condition. For if every day God helps us to emerge from our internal—and external—battles, then certainly on this auspicious day, when He redeemed us for the first time, we ought to refocus on redirecting ourselves to a life of sincerity, dedicated only to what is right and holy.

(Based on *Likutei Sichos* vol. 17, p. 80*ff*; *Sichah* of 2nd night of Pesach 5726).

> THE MATZOS ARE COVERED AND THE TRAY IS REMOVED (OR PUSHED TO THE SIDE). THE CUP OF WINE IS FILLED FOR THE SECOND TIME.

> THE FOLLOWING IS ASKED BY THE YOUNGEST SON.

מַה-נִּשְׁתַּנָּה הַלַּיְלָה הַזֶּה מִכָּל-הַלֵּילוֹת.

שֶׁבְּכָל-הַלֵּילוֹת אָנוּ אוֹכְלִין חָמֵץ וּמַצָּה, הַלַּיְלָה הַזֶּה כֻּלּוֹ מַצָּה:

שֶׁבְּכָל-הַלֵּילוֹת אָנוּ אוֹכְלִין שְׁאָר יְרָקוֹת, הַלַּיְלָה הַזֶּה מָרוֹר:

═══ CLASSIC QUESTIONS ═══

● **Why do we fill the Second Cup now?**

RASHI: This will encourage the children to ask the question: "Why are we pouring a second cup of wine before the meal? We don't normally do that" (*Pesachim* 116a).

ALTER REBBE'S SHULCHAN ARUCH: The children's interest will thus be aroused, leading them to ask the *Mah Nishtanah* (*Orach Chaim* 473:40).

● **Why is a *young* child chosen to ask the *Mah Nishtanah*?**

LIKUTEI TA'AMIM U'MINHAGIM: A parent loves a small child unconditionally, not because of the child's talents or qualities. We thus encourage a small child to say the *Mah Nishtanah* to bring to light God's unconditional love for the Jewish people, as in the verse, *"Israel was a youth and I loved him"* (*Hoshea* 11:1).

For this reason, our custom is that even the adults say the *Mah Nishtanah*—and they preface it with the words "Father, I wish to ask you Four Questions," even if their father is no longer alive—since God's

unconditional love as a Father extends to all Jews (see *Sichah* of 2nd night of Pesach 5712).

● ***"Tonight we dip twice"*—Don't we dip the Sandwich also, which makes *three* times?**

TUREI ZAHAV: The Maror and the Chazeres (bitter herbs in the Sandwich) are counted as one "dip," since in both cases we are dipping the same thing: bitter herbs (*Orach Chaim* 475:6).

● **Why does the *Mah Nishtanah* not include a question about the Four Cups of wine?**

MAHARAL: The Four Cups of wine are a Rabbinic *mitzvah*, and in the *Mah Nishtanah* we only ask questions about Biblical commandments, (or Rabbinic enactments that are appended to Biblical commandments). Thus: 1. Matzah is a Biblical requirement; 2. Maror is essentially a Biblical requirement (though it only has this status in Temple times); 3. Dipping is carried out with Maror; 4. Leaning is carried out when eating Matzah (*Gevuras Hashem* ch. 52).

> ➤ THE MATZOS ARE COVERED AND THE TRAY IS REMOVED (OR PUSHED TO THE SIDE). THE CUP OF WINE IS FILLED FOR THE SECOND TIME.

> ➤ THE FOLLOWING IS ASKED BY THE YOUNGEST SON.

WHY IS THIS NIGHT
different from all other nights?

ON ALL OTHER NIGHTS we eat Chametz or Matzah, but on this night only Matzah!

ON ALL OTHER NIGHTS we eat any kind of vegetables, but on this night bitter herbs!

═══════════════ CLASSIC QUESTIONS ═══════════════

● **Why do we say the *Mah Nishtanah*?**

ALTER REBBE'S SHULCHAN ARUCH: The *mitzvah* of reciting the Haggadah should be carried out in response to questions that are posed, as the verse states: *"When your son will ask you...You shall say to him, 'We were slaves, etc.'"* (*Devarim* 6:20-21; 473:14).

● **How do the Four Questions allude to the future redemption?**

REBBE RASHAB: *Dipping*: The spiritual purification (like "dipping" in a ritual bath) was not completed in the earlier exiles; but with this final exile we will "dip twice": the purification of the body and the revelation of the soul.

Matzah: During the earlier exiles our worship of God involved our Godly soul (Matzah) and our animal soul (Chametz), but following this final exile we will use only the Godly soul, for the spirit of impurity will depart.

Maror: During the earlier exiles there were various forms of envy (symbolized by green) between Torah-scholars. After the final exile only "bitter greens," a sharp envy: *"Each pious man will be scorched by the 'canopy' of his fellow"* (*Bava Basra* 75a).

Reclining: Eating without leaning alludes to a diluted form of spiritual pleasure. In the future, everyone will lean, reaching the highest levels of pleasure (*ha-Yom Yom* 19th Nissan).

═══════════════ TORAS MENACHEM ═══════════════

📖 מַה נִּשְׁתַּנָּה — *Why is this night different?*

Why are the child's questions such a focus of the Pesach observance in particular? (See *Classic Questions*.)

Because the Exodus from Egypt was the birth of the Jewish nation (see Ezekiel ch. 16), and therefore it is an appropriate time to stress Jewish education. In fact we find that the Haggadah itself takes its name from the principle of education, from the verse,

"You shall tell (*ve-higadeta*), your son" (*Shemos* 13:8; *Pesachim* 116b).

Interestingly, according to the *Arizal's* Haggadah, the first of the Four Questions concerns the custom of dipping. When we consider that the remaining questions focus on requirements of Jewish law, it is striking that the *first* question should concern a matter of mere custom. This points to the importance of making Jewish custom a priority in Jewish education.

שֶׁבְּכָל־הַלֵּילוֹת אֵין אָנוּ מַטְבִּילִין אֲפִילוּ פַּעַם אֶחָת, הַלַּיְלָה הַזֶּה שְׁתֵּי פְעָמִים:

שֶׁבְּכָל־הַלֵּילוֹת אָנוּ אוֹכְלִין בֵּין יוֹשְׁבִין וּבֵין מְסֻבִּין, הַלַּיְלָה הַזֶּה כֻּלָנוּ מְסֻבִּין:

➤ THE SEDER PLATE IS RETURNED TO ITS PLACE AND THE THREE MATZOS ARE PARTIALLY UNCOVERED.

═══ CLASSIC QUESTIONS ═══

● **According to the Kabbalah, why are there *four* questions?**

ARIZAL: Because there are four spiritual worlds between us and God—*Atzilus* (Emanation), *Beriah* (Creation), *Yetzirah* (Formation), and *Asiyah* (Action)—and each question corresponds to one of the spiritual worlds.

═══ TORAS MENACHEM ═══

Living, as we do, in a secular world, educating our children in the path of Torah and *mitzvos* is no easy matter. Since there is a limit to how many do's and dont's a child might be willing to listen to, a parent might be tempted to choose his or her battles wisely and make the mandatory parts of Judaism the focus of the child's education. Certainly the Biblical precepts are important, and Rabbinic law too is endorsed by a Biblical mandate; "but perhaps," a person may think, "it would be counterproductive to subject my child to even more discipline, just to enforce the observance of the customs?"

This would be a grave error indeed, as the *Mah Nishtanah* shows. The child's *first* question concerns, not Biblical or Rabbinic law, but Jewish custom, because it is the customs which arouse the children's interest the most. And, practically speaking, customs greatly enrich the "flavor" of Judaism, helping the child to foster a strong Jewish identity which is so crucial in protecting ourselves from the "inferiority complex" of wanting to imitate others.

The customs are just as much a part of Judaism as all the other laws, and there is immense pedagogic value in preserving them, down to the tiniest detail.

(*Ma'amar* of 11th of Nissan 5740, s.v. *ki yishalcha*; *Likutei Sichos* vol. 32, p. 189, note 32; vol. 1, p. 244*ff*)

ד' קוּשְׁיוֹת — *The Four Questions.*

While one question would, in theory, have been sufficient to enable us to respond to a child's inquiry (see *Classic Questions* on previous page), nevertheless, the universal Jewish practice is to ask *Four* Questions.

Nothing in Torah is haphazard or incidental. In this case, **Arizal** taught that there is immense significance to the notion of Four Questions: they are a reflection of the fundamental infrastructure of the spiritual cosmos which, according to the Kabbalah, is divided into four spiritual worlds (see *Classic Questions*). Unlike many Jewish practices which typically focus on manipulating one particular spiritual force or emanation, the *Mah Nishtanah* encompasses the entire Chain of Emanation stretching from God down to man.

It seems rather peculiar, however, that we relate to even the highest of the spiritual worlds here by a ritual of question-asking. True spirituality is all about revelation and illumination, whereas questions represent concealment and a lack of clarity, so how could we draw down illumination from above with *questions*?

A number of different solutions could be offered.

a.) Technically speaking they are not *questions*, but *inquiries*. A *question* represents concealment, a tendency to be critical and hostile to the truth. An *inquiry* is merely a request for further illumination.

WHAT ARE WE
DOING NOW?
*The matzos are
uncovered since
the Exodus story
is to be recited
over "Lechem
Oni," bread
over which
many things
are declared
(Pesachim 115b).*

ON ALL OTHER NIGHTS we do not dip even once, but on this night we do so twice!

ON ALL OTHER NIGHTS we eat sitting upright or reclining, but on this night we all recline!

➤ THE SEDER PLATE IS RETURNED TO ITS PLACE AND THE THREE MATZOS ARE PARTIALLY UNCOVERED.

TORAS MENACHEM

---

b.) The Four Questions do not emanate from the Four Worlds themselves, but from forces of evil (*kelipos*) which correspond to the Four Worlds. For example, the highest world, *Atzilus,* is in a state of absolute surrender to God. An example of the corresponding *kelipah* would be a person who is totally surrendered to God *but he is proud of the fact* (see *Ohr ha-Torah, Vayikra* vol. 2, p. 566).

c.) Questions are a symptom of the relative concealment of one spiritual realm compared to the realm above it.

"The Ba'al Shem Tov once said that he could refute even the most brilliant Torah insight. This is because the Torah journeys down from spiritual world to spiritual world, and in each location it takes different expression....Each world yearns to be influenced by its superior, for it lacks some quality which is filled by the higher world....Likewise, the Torah takes on a different expression in each world corresponding to the qualities of that world, and so the idea as it exists in any particular world must possess some inherent weakness or flaw, whereas in the higher world that problem does not exist. But there is nevertheless another problem to be found in that higher world, which is solved in an even higher world, and so on.

"Since the Tzadik of the generation is connected to all worlds, he is able to tell us what is lacking in one world, and how that void is filled by the world above it (*Ginzei Nistaros, Ohr Yisra'el* p. 41).

d.) The Festival of Pesach is characterized by great Divine revelation *"With great awe...the revelation of the Shechinah"* (p. 91). Since this holiness is showered on us from above, we must make some effort, at least, down below, in order to internalize it. So the four inquiries represent the human contribution: an interest and a willingness to absorb something higher.

(Based on a discussion at the Rebbe's 2nd Seder 5730)

ברכה **ד' קוּשְׁיוֹת בְּלֵיל שֵׁנִי** — *The Four Questions on the Second Night.*

After the Four Questions have been fully answered on the first night of Pesach, why is the child required to ask them again on the second night?

Because questions and incorrect presumptions, which enhance the clarity of the final conclusion are themselves considered to be an integral part of the Torah. Thus we find that the requirement to make a blessing before studying Torah applies even if one studies only an incorrect presumption or opinion, never reaching the final conclusion, because even this has the status of "Torah." Furthermore, even after studying the final answer, we can still go back and learn the questions and incorrect presumptions, since they, too, form part of the sacred Torah text.

In Judaism, questions are as much a part of the text as the answers themselves, such that they must be repeatedly studied and emphasized.

(Based on *Sichah* of night of *Simchas Torah* 5736, par. 25)

ברכה **הַלַּיְלָה הַזֶּה כֻּלָּנוּ מְסֻבִּין** — *On this night we all recline.*

At the time of the Exodus we can appreciate how Jews might have asked the first three of the Four Questions. Matzah and Maror were Biblical commands at that time, and, according to the *Ba'alei Tosfos,* even the "dipping" was fulfilled by dipping blood on their doorposts (*Da'as Zekeinim* to *Shemos* 12:8). But where do we find they fulfilled the precept of leaning, which was a later, rabbinic enactment?

However, this too is hinted at by the *Midrash Rabah*: The *Midrash* bases an account of Moshe eating his Paschal lamb on the verse, "While the King was *reclining* at his table" (*Shir ha-Shirim* 1:12).

(*Sichah* of 2nd night of Pesach 5730).

עֲבָדִים

הָיִינוּ לְפַרְעֹה בְּמִצְרָיִם

וַיּוֹצִיאֵנוּ יְהֹוָה אֱלֹהֵינוּ מִשָּׁם

בְּיָד חֲזָקָה וּבִזְרֹעַ נְטוּיָה.

וְאִלּוּ לֹא הוֹצִיא הַקָּדוֹשׁ בָּרוּךְ הוּא

CLASSIC QUESTIONS

● **Why were the Jewish people punished with Egyptian exile?**

MIDRASH: *"Moshe returned to God and said, 'O God! Why have you mistreated this people?'"* (Shemos 5:22). Moshe said to God: I took the Book of *Bereishis* (Genesis) and I read it. I observed the deeds of the generation of the Flood and how they were judged fairly; and the deeds of the generation of the Dispersion, and of the Sodomites, how they were judged fairly. But what did *this* people do that they deserved, more than the generations that preceded them, to be enslaved? (*Shemos Rabah* ibid.)

SHALOH: We find that all three of the Patriarchs gravitated at some point away from their home towards settling in Egypt. This was in order to rectify the sin of Adam, for which he was sent away from his home in the Garden of Eden. (The parallel between

Egypt and the Garden of Eden is indicated by the verse *"like the garden of God, and like the land of Egypt"* —*Bereishis* 13:10). And this, too, is the inner reason why the Jewish people were exiled in Egypt: to become spiritually refined, purified and cleansed from the soul-contamination which persisted from the days of Adam (*Maseches Pesachim*, discourse 6).

● *"God took us out from there."* **How urgent was this?**

TZROR HAMOR: The Jewish people were living in Egypt for an extended period, during which time they were strongly influenced by the surrounding culture....If God, in His kindness, had not shattered the forces of impurity and taken the Jewish people out at that moment...they would have been trapped there forever (commentary to *Shemos* 12:40).

TORAS MENACHEM

∞ וַיּוֹצִיאֵנוּ יְהֹוָה אֱלֹהֵינוּ מִשָּׁם בְּיָד חֲזָקָה וּבִזְרֹעַ נְטוּיָה — *God, our God, took us out from there with a strong hand and with an outstretched arm.*

Why does the Haggadah stress that "God took us out from there with *a strong hand*"? What is the message behind this strikingly anthropomorphic metaphor?

To understand exactly how God took our ancestors out of Egypt we first need to explain why they were exiled there in the first place. According to **Shaloh**, we are to view the events in Egypt as a form of spiritual repair for Adam's sin: *"The Jewish people were exiled in Egypt to become spiritually refined, purified and cleansed from the soul-contamination which persisted from the days of Adam."*

We were slaves

to Pharaoh in Egypt,

but God, our God, took us out from there with a strong hand and with an outstretched arm (after *Devarim* 6:21).

If the Holy One, blessed be He, had not taken our ancestors out of Egypt, then we,

---

TORAS MENACHEM

Suffering can indeed bring about a purification of the soul, but *too much* suffering has the opposite effect of numbing the soul. So when the Egyptians persecuted us excessively (see below p. 76), the Jewish people became cold and indifferent to their God and, instead of gaining from the experience of exile, they became corrupted by it. If history had been left to run its course, the purpose of the exile would never have been fulfilled; instead of the intended spiritual refinement and purification, permanent and irreparable corruption would have occurred (see *Tzror Hamor*).

But despite the necessity of the Exodus, it was, in a sense, a perversion of celestial justice. The Heavenly Court had "sentenced" the Jewish people to a term of spiritual "rehabilitation" in Egypt, and there was no reason to sanction their freedom until the exercise had borne its fruit. Even when it became clear that this "sentence" had proven ineffective and the Jewish people were never going to be rehabilitated in Egypt, the Heavenly Court insisted that justice must prevail: The Jewish people will only come out when they deserve to come out, when their spiritual refinement and purification is complete.

So this was one of those cases where harsh justice had proven to be counterproductive to the overall good. God therefore chose to override the court's decision, and set the Jewish people free. A complete spiritual refinement would just have to wait for another day.

And this is the meaning of the Haggadah's statement, "God took us out from there *with a strong hand.*" An extra stamp of Divine authority was needed to overturn what, in hindsight, had become a catastrophic verdict from the Heavenly Court.

(Based on *Likutei Sichos* vol. 17, pp. 87-8)

וְאִלּוּ לֹא הוֹצִיא הַקָּדוֹשׁ בָּרוּךְ הוּא אֶת־אֲבוֹתֵינוּ מִמִּצְרַיִם — *If the Holy One, blessed be He had not taken our ancestors out of Egypt....*

How could the Haggadah assert that if God *"had not taken our ancestors out of Egypt, then we... would still be enslaved to Pharaoh in Egypt,"* when God had promised Avraham unconditionally that his descendants would be freed after a fixed time: *"They will enslave and oppress them for 400 years"* (*Bereishis* 15:13)?

The Torah teaches us that even when a slave is freed from bondage he may nevertheless choose not to leave, saying: *"I love my master...I will not go free"* (*Shemos* 21:5). Having become accustomed to the "conveniences" of enslavement—freedom from any financial responsibility; all basic needs catered to, *etc.,*—the slave is sadly reluctant to regain once again the dignity of personal autonomy.

With this in mind we can appreciate that scripture's promise to let the Jewish people free after four hundred years poses no contradiction to the notion that

אֶת־אֲבוֹתֵינוּ מִמִּצְרָיִם, הֲרֵי אָנוּ וּבָנֵינוּ וּבְנֵי
בָנֵינוּ מְשֻׁעְבָּדִים הָיִינוּ לְפַרְעֹה בְּמִצְרָיִם.
וַאֲפִילוּ כֻּלָּנוּ חֲכָמִים כֻּלָּנוּ נְבוֹנִים כֻּלָּנוּ
זְקֵנִים כֻּלָּנוּ יוֹדְעִים אֶת־הַתּוֹרָה, מִצְוָה
עָלֵינוּ לְסַפֵּר בִּיצִיאַת מִצְרָיִם. וְכָל־הַמַּרְבֶּה
לְסַפֵּר בִּיצִיאַת מִצְרָיִם הֲרֵי זֶה מְשֻׁבָּח:

TORAS MENACHEM

"we...would still be enslaved to Pharaoh in Egypt," because, in all likelihood, *the Jewish people would have themselves returned to Egypt*, especially upon encountering difficulties in the desert.

It is only because "the Holy One, blessed be He" *actively* took us out of Egypt, illuminating our souls with a desire to serve Him, that we managed to stay out of Egypt. The scriptural promise of a four-hundred year exile would have been sufficient to end our physical servitude, but we needed God's personal help to rid us of the slave mentality so as to ensure that we would choose to remain free.

In fact, even with this Divine assistance, we still find that the Jewish people longed to return to Egypt (see *Bamidbar* 11:4-5; 14:4), so we can imagine that without the miracle of the Exodus, they would have had no qualms in actually returning.

It is only because "God took us out from there" that we stand here as free men today.

(Based on *Likutei Sichos* vol. 17, p. 88)

מְשֻׁעְבָּדִים הָיִינוּ לְפַרְעֹה בְּמִצְרָיִם — *We would still be enslaved to Pharaoh in Egypt.*

The Haggadah seems to be stating the obvious here. If God *"had not taken our ancestors out of Egypt, then we...would still be enslaved to Pharaoh in Egypt."* Clearly, if we had not left, we would still be there. What insight is the Haggadah trying to teach us?

One of the most sophisticated concepts to be found in any study of *halachah* is that of *peulah nimsheches* (a legally ongoing event). This is where an event which has ceased from the onlooker's perspective, is nevertheless from a legal perspective considered to be repeating itself every moment.

While there are many examples of this phenomenon, the most pertinent to our case relates to the principle of *hekdesh,* consecrating property for use in the Temple. Jewish law permits a pledge of consecration to later be annulled, which—explains the *Rogatchover Ga'on*—indicates that the initial act of consecration must have been a legally ongoing event: *"Every moment it is consecrated anew, for the fact that the vow of consecration could be annulled at any moment shows that it is constantly being renewed by his initial declaration"* (*Tzafnas Pane'ach*, *Arachin* 4:28). In other words the law perceives it as if the person's verbal declaration of consecration is being uttered every second, thereby maintaining the object's consecrated status. Annulling the vow is thus merely a case of decreeing that the ongoing "speech" should cease.

In the current passage, the Haggadah teaches us that the Exodus, too, is a *legally ongoing event.* "If the Holy One, blessed be He, had not taken our ancestors out of Egypt," *i.e. in an ongoing fashion that continues to this day,* "then we...would still be enslaved to Pharaoh in Egypt."

Why was it necessary for God to make the Exodus an ongoing activity? This can be gleaned from the case of *hekdesh.* The reason why a verbal stream is required to continuously render an object consecrated is because the very notion goes against the grain. Mundane, physical objects do not, as a rule, become "holy," any less than a rock stays in the air when it is thrown upwards. So to maintain holiness in a physical object requires ongoing input.

our children, and our children's children
would still be enslaved to Pharaoh in Egypt.

Even if we were all men of wisdom,
people of understanding, experienced and
knowledgeable in the Torah, we would still
be obligated to tell the story of the Exodus
from Egypt. And whoever discusses the
Exodus from Egypt at length is praiseworthy.

═══ CLASSIC QUESTIONS ═══

● *"We would be enslaved to Pharaoh in Egypt."*
How is this feasible?

LIKUTEI TA'AMIM U'MINHAGIM: It does not mean that
we would still be slaves to the same Pharaoh,
because he would be long dead. Rather, we would
be slaves to another king of Egypt who, in accordance with the ancient Egyptian custom, would also
be called Pharaoh (see *Rashi* to *Tehillim* 34:1).

Although today's leaders of Egypt are not called
Pharaoh, perhaps if the Jews had not left the country,
Egypt would still be the same superpower and con-
tinue to call their kings by the name Pharaoh.

═══ TORAS MENACHEM ═══

Likewise, the notion that we have been redeemed
from Egypt, never to return, goes against the grain
of the natural course of history—for who is to say
that a similar scenario might not repeat itself again?
It thus requires an ongoing Exodus. So, ultimately,
the Exodus was not merely a past event which had a
profound effect on the future, but a phenomenon that
shapes history on a day-to-day basis.

(Based on *Likutei Sichos* vol. 5, p. 174*ff*;
Sichah of 2nd Night of Pesach 5724)

⮰ וַאֲפִילוּ כֻּלָּנוּ חֲכָמִים ⮰ — *Even if we were all men
of wisdom, etc.*

At first glance, this statement is hard to compre-
hend. The requirement to discuss the Exodus on the
night of the 15th of Nissan is a Biblical commandment,
so why would one imagine that scholars would be
exempt? Even if they *know* the story already, Biblical
law requires them to *relate* it verbally on that night.

Most of us are willing, at some point or another, to
engage in behavior that violates our beliefs and con-
victions. This weakness, of course, is the cause of all
sinful behavior. We *know* what the upright and moral

thing is, but *doing it* is another story. The Sages
referred to this general phenomenon of cognitive dis-
sonance as "Egypt," *Mitzrayim*, since it represents a
constriction (*maytzar*) or blockage between the mind
(what we ought to do) and the heart (what we are
excited and motivated to do).

How do we "leave Egypt" and ensure a consistency
between mind and heart? Perhaps the answer is to
have a crystal-clear understanding of our principles.
Maybe our hearts sway from what is right because we
do not fully appreciate *why* it is right?

In response, the Haggadah says: "*Even if we
were all men of wisdom, people of understanding,
and knowledgeable in the Torah, we would still be
obligated to tell the story of the Exodus from Egypt.*"
Even if our minds appreciated the ethics of the Torah
perfectly, a certain blockage (*maytzar*) between the
mind and heart would remain. Even if we were so
wise that we were careful never to sin, our *Mitzvos*
would still be somewhat half-hearted, because *understanding* does not necessarily engender *excitement*.

The only way to truly "leave Egypt," to bridge
the chasm between mind and heart, is through a
suprarational commitment to the Torah. So long as

מַ**עֲשֶׂה** בְּרַבִּי אֱלִיעֶזֶר וְרַבִּי יְהוֹשֻׁעַ וְרַבִּי אֶלְעָזָר בֶּן־עֲזַרְיָה וְרַבִּי עֲקִיבָא וְרַבִּי טַרְפוֹן שֶׁהָיוּ מְסֻבִּין בִּבְנֵי בְרַק, וְהָיוּ מְסַפְּרִים בִּיצִיאַת מִצְרַיִם כָּל־אוֹתוֹ הַלַּיְלָה עַד שֶׁבָּאוּ תַלְמִידֵיהֶם וְאָמְרוּ לָהֶם: "רַבּוֹתֵינוּ, הִגִּיעַ זְמַן קְרִיאַת שְׁמַע שֶׁל שַׁחֲרִית":

═══ CLASSIC QUESTIONS ═══

● **Why does this incident appear here?**

ABARBANEL: Because it proves what the Haggadah has just stated: 1. Even if we were *all men of wisdom* etc. we would still be obligated to tell the story of the Exodus from Egypt. 2. And whoever discusses the Exodus from Egypt *at length* is praiseworthy.

CHIDA: This incident demonstrates that two types of Jews whose ancestors were not enslaved are nevertheless required to recount the Exodus story. They are: a.) members of the Tribe of Levi (*kohanim* and levites); and, b.) converts.

In this case, Rabbi Elazar ben Azaryah and Rabbi Tarfon were *kohanim*, Rabbi Eliezer and Rabbi Yehoshua were levites, and Rabbi Akiva was from a family of converts (*Simchas ha-Regel*).

● **Is it surprising that Rabbi Elazar ben Azaryah and Rabbi Akiva discussed the Exodus all night?**

IMREI SHEFER: Yes. These two Sages maintain that the Paschal lamb may only be eaten until midnight, and Rabbi Eliezer states further that there is no obligation to discuss the Exodus after midnight. Nevertheless,

═══ TORAS MENACHEM ═══

observance is contingent on our own intellectual appreciation of Judaism, only so much enthusiasm will percolate through into the heart. But when we act out of dedication to a Higher Authority, then our passion to do the right thing will be insatiable.

(Based on *Sichah* of 2nd night of Pesach 5721; *Ma'amar* s.v. *Kimay Tzayscha* 5719)

רַבּוֹתֵינוּ הִגִּיעַ זְמַן קְרִיאַת שְׁמַע שֶׁל שַׁחֲרִית ◆◆
— *Teachers! The time has come for reciting the morning Shema.*

Taken at face value, it seems that if it were not for the students' announcement here, the rabbis would

not have stopped to recite the morning *Shema* at all. How is such a notion conceivable?

According to the Jerusalem Talmud a person whose life is dedicated to Torah study (*toraso umnaso*) is exempt from reading the *Shema* (*Brachos* 1:2).* Since relating the story of the Exodus is a form of Torah study, these full-time scholars were exempt from reciting the *Shema*, and did not plan to stop studying. The students, however, had not reached this level of *toraso umnaso* and were thus required to exempt themselves from the Seder and recite the *Shema*.

On an ordinary night, that is what would have happened: the Sages would have continued to study and the students would have said the *Shema*. But on

─────────

*The Babylonian Talmud appears to contest this ruling, stating that a person who is dedicated to Torah study *is* obligated to interrupt his studies in order to recite the *Shema* (*Shabbos* 11a. This view is echoed by the Code of Jewish Law, *Orach Chaim*, end of ch. 106.) However, it could be argued that there is no difference of opinion here: the Jerusalem Talmud simply refers to a person whose level of dedication to Torah study is of a higher caliber (see *Likutei Sichos* vol. 17, p. 357*ff*). [Thus, in the Haggadah's discussion here, the Sages were on this higher level, whereas the students were not.]

Upon reaching this passage the Rebbe Rashab exclaimed, "A fine gathering!" With these words he actually drew these tzadikim back into this world to the extent that he actually could see them with his eyes (Sichah of 2nd Night of Pesach 5712).

I**T ONCE HAPPENED** that Rabbi Eliezer, Rabbi Yehoshua, Rabbi Elazar ben Azaryah, Rabbi Akiva and Rabbi Tarfon were reclining at a Seder in Bnei Brak. They were discussing the Exodus from Egypt that entire night, until their students came and said to them: "Teachers! The time has come for reciting the morning *Shema!*"

===== CLASSIC QUESTIONS =====

in practice, we see that these two Sages continued to discuss the Exodus all night.

●**Why are the Sages cited in this order? And why are we informed that the Seder took place in Bnei Brak?**

LIKUTEI TA'AMIM U'MINHAGIM: Rabbi Akiva was the Rabbi of Bnei Brak, where this incident occurred. Nevertheless, Rabbi Eliezer and Rabbi Yehoshua are mentioned before him, since they were his teachers.

Rabbi Elazar ben Azaryah is also mentioned before Rabbi Akiva, due to his esteemed lineage and his status as Nasi (leader of the Supreme Court).

While Rabbi Tarfon was also one of Rabbi Akiva's teachers, he later became his colleague of equal standing. So being that the Seder occurred in Rabbi Akiva's town, Rabbi Akiva is mentioned first.

●**Why did the students interrupt their teachers at the *earliest* time to recite the morning *Shema*, when many hours of the morning still remained?**

REBBE RAYATZ: The *Shema* is intended to bring a person to appreciate God's unity: "Hear O Israel, God is our God, God is one." According to the Kabbalah, this is achieved progressively: the evening Shema brings a person to perceive a lower level of unity (*yichudah tata'ah*), whereas the Shema recited the following morning lifts a person to a more profound appreciation of unity (*yichudah ila'ah*).

After listening to their teachers, the students exclaimed that they had already, *while it was still night,* been uplifted to the level of the morning *Shema*. They were effectively saying: If your goal is to inspire us then you have completed your task! (*Sefer Hasichos* 5704 p. 88).

===== TORAS MENACHEM =====

Pesach night, a person is not merely required to study about the Exodus, he must *discuss* it, i.e., share it with his students. So, in this case, the teachers could not remain aloof on their own, higher level of Torah study; they were forced to focus downwards, towards the level of the students. And now, finding themselves closer to the students' level, *the teachers became obligated to recite the Shema, just like the students.*

With the above in mind, we can appreciate how this incident offers support for the previous passage of the Haggadah, *"Whoever discusses the Exodus from Egypt at length is praiseworthy"* [see **Abarbanel**]. At first glance, the Haggadah's choice of proof seems peculiar: Here we have a case where a Seder was halt-

ed to do something else *more important*. If anything, this highlights more the greatness of saying Shema as a *mitzvah* which takes priority over the need to "discuss the Exodus at length," something that hardly belongs here in the Haggadah, a text aimed at bringing to light the greatness of the Exodus.

However, based on the above we can appreciate the Haggadah's intention in citing this incident, since here we learn an important clarification of what it means to "*discuss* the Exodus at length." Tonight the story must not merely be recounted in a way that we find personally engaging; it must be focused directly at the level of our students and children.

(Based on *Sichah* of 2nd night of Pesach 5725)

אָמַר רַבִּי אֶלְעָזָר בֶּן־עֲזַרְיָה:

הֲרֵי אֲנִי כְּבֶן־שִׁבְעִים שָׁנָה, וְלֹא זָכִיתִי שֶׁתֵּאָמֵר יְצִיאַת מִצְרַיִם **בַּלֵּילוֹת** עַד שֶׁדְּרָשָׁהּ בֶּן זוֹמָא, שֶׁנֶּאֱמַר: "לְמַעַן תִּזְכֹּר אֶת־יוֹם צֵאתְךָ מֵאֶרֶץ מִצְרַיִם כֹּל יְמֵי חַיֶּיךָ".

"יְמֵי חַיֶּיךָ" — הַיָּמִים.

"כֹּל יְמֵי חַיֶּיךָ" — **הַלֵּילוֹת.**

CLASSIC QUESTIONS

● **Why did Rabbi Elazar ben Azaryah say, "I am like a seventy year old man"?**

Talmud: When Rabbi Elazar ben Azaryah was asked to become head of the Academy, he went and consulted his wife.

She said to him, "But you have no white hair!" (He was eighteen years old that day).

A miracle occurred for him and eighteen rows of hair on his beard turned white. That is why Rabbi

Elazar ben Azaryah said, "I am *like* a seventy-year-old man (*Brachos* 27b).

Rashi: He meant, "I already look elderly," but he was not really old. He began to look aged on the day that Rabban Gamliel vacated the leadership and he took office, and on that day Ben Zoma expounded this verse (*Brachos* 12b).

Arizal: If one adds the age that Rabbi Elazar ben Azaryah reached in his former incarnation to his present eighteen years, it makes a total of seventy.

TORAS MENACHEM

הֲרֵי אֲנִי כְּבֶן שִׁבְעִים שָׁנָה 🙠 — *I am like a seventy year old man.*

Why did Rabbi Elazar ben Azaryah bemoan that despite having reached old age he "did not merit" to fully fathom the law, when in fact he was not old at all (see *Talmud*)?

The answer is that spiritually speaking he *was* old, as *Arizal* writes that he carried fifty-two years from a previous incarnation. And that is why he miraculously sprouted white hair (as the *Talmud* states), to demonstrate that this spiritual seniority had permeated his conscious, bodily existence to the extent that even his hair was old.

The Kabbalah teaches that, like Rabbi Elazar ben Azaryah, most of us are incarnations of souls that lived in previous generations (see *Sha'ar ha-Gilgulim* ch. 20). So the lesson from this passage of the Haggadah is that, as latter generation Jews, we have an elevated spiritual potential by virtue of the good deeds performed by our "former selves," in previous incarnations. And since only good persists, but not evil, we have only to benefit from our souls' past history.

No wonder, then, that we will be the generation to finally bring Mashiach, since we are charged with the spiritual potential from all our illustrious forefathers.

(Based on *Likutei Sichos* vol. 1, p. 246*ff*)

RABBI ELAZAR BEN AZARYAH SAID:

QUICK INSIGHT
Presumably, this is what Rabbi Elazar ben Azaryah actually said at the previously mentioned Seder in Bnei Brak (Likutei Ta'amim u'Minhagim).

I AM LIKE a seventy-year-old man and I did not yet merit [to find a Scriptural proof, that in addition to the daytime obligation] to mention the Exodus from Egypt [there is also an obligation to mention it] every night—until [today, when] Ben Zoma demonstrated a proof from the following verse:

"That you should remember the day you left Egypt all the days of your life" (Devarim 16:3).

[Ben Zoma explained that if the verse would merely have stated,] "the days of your life," there would already be a sufficient proof for a daytime obligation [to mention the Exodus]. The fact that the verse stresses *"all* the days of your life," indicates a further obligation [to mention the Exodus] in the evenings.

TORAS MENACHEM

כֹּל יְמֵי חַיֶּיךָ — *All the days of your life.*

Here, the Haggadah points to the greatness of the Exodus from Egypt, that even after leaving Egypt, there is a legal obligation to remember the Exodus from Egypt, "all the days of your life," both by day and at night.

The reason for this is because the Exodus from Egypt is *"a major foundation and strong pillar within our Torah and our faith"* (Sefer ha-Chinnuch, mitzvah 21), which introduced the entire concept of "redemption"—that Jews left the state of slavery and became intrinsically free (see p. 152). Furthermore, as noted above (p. 38), the Exodus is an ongoing event.

In practical terms, Exodus means a freedom of the soul from the confines and "imprisonment" of the body (and the world in general), so as to achieve a total unity with God through observance of Torah and its commandments. Since this theme is so central to

Torah and Judaism, there is a directive to "remember the day you left Egypt *all the days of your life,"* to the extent that *"In each and every generation, and likewise each and every day, a person must see himself as if he personally left Egypt"* (Tanya, ch. 47).

In this daily obligation, there are two levels:

a.) "A *daytime* obligation"—when the light of God shines we must attempt to break out of our internal constraints.

b.) "In the evenings"—even in a time of darkness, when the light of God does not shine, during the darkness of Exile, there can *and must* be the "Exodus from Egypt."

By Divine providence, Rabbi Elazar ben Azaryah was appointed leader of the Jewish people on the same day as he discovered the above insight (as *Rashi* states). This points to the fact that the goal of a true Jewish leader is to connect "all the days of your

וַחֲכָמִים אוֹמְרִים:

"יְמֵי חַיֶּיךָ" — הָעוֹלָם הַזֶּה.
"כֹּל יְמֵי חַיֶּיךָ" — לְהָבִיא לִימוֹת הַמָּשִׁיחַ:

═══════════════ CLASSIC QUESTIONS ═══════════════

● **How are we to understand Ben Zoma's view, that the Exodus won't be mentioned in the future?**

RASHBA: The *mitzvah* of recalling the Exodus could more accurately be described as a verbal declaration of miracles which God has performed for us, so as to remind us of His providence and to strengthen our trust in Him. Thus, according to Ben Zoma, when we will recall the miracles of the future redemption, which will be of a greater magnitude than those of the Exodus, we will achieve the goal of this *mitzvah* to an even greater extent (*Chidushei Agados* ibid.).

═══════════════ TORAS MENACHEM ═══════════════

life" of every single Jew in this physical world with redemption from limitations in general, and with the theme of global redemption. And this form of leadership is especially pertinent "in the evenings," during the time of Exile.

Therefore, it is precisely on the day that Rabbi Elazar ben Azaryah ascended to lead the Jewish people that he was enlightened with this idea.

(*Sichas Shabbos Parshas Shemos* 5752)

◊◊ **כֹּל יְמֵי חַיֶּיךָ לְהָבִיא לִימוֹת הַמָּשִׁיחַ** — *"All the days of your life," includes also an obligation to mention the Exodus in the Messianic Era.*

Our view of the Exodus from Egypt tends to be colored by the historical events that followed. We know that soon afterwards, the Jews worshipped the Golden Calf, were forced to wander in the desert for forty years, and even after conquering the Land of Israel they were later exiled from it. So we tend to perceive the Exodus as a "high point" in Jewish history which was later followed by several "lows," such as the state in which we find ourselves now, after the destruction of the Temple. Recalling the Exodus thus instills us with hope that we will once again return to a "high point" with the final redemption through Mashiach.

At the time of the Exodus, however, this was not how the Jewish people perceived the matter. They certainly did not see themselves as enjoying a special moment of Divine kindness which would inspire them through the later difficulties that were to follow. Rather, they hoped that God would take them imme-

diately to their final destination, where the Temple would be built and they would live forever in a state of peace and spiritual bliss.

Indeed, this was God's very intention, as the Midrash teaches: *"If the Jewish people had waited for Moshe [to descend the mountain], and not performed that act [of worshipping the Calf], there would not have been any further exiles"* (*Shemos Rabah* 32:1).

In the Zohar we find the theme elaborated further: *"When the Jewish people left Egypt, God wanted to make for them a land...and build for them a Temple.... But they angered Him in the desert which led to their deaths, and God brought their children into the land. The Temple was then built by man, which is why it did not last"* (*Zohar* III 221a).

Our initial reaction to these sources, that God intended the Exodus from Egypt to be a final redemption, is that we are reading here of a plan which unfortunately did not materialize. Plan 'a' was an immediate and permanent entry into the Land of Israel; plan 'b' was what actually happened—three further tragic exiles before the final redemption will ultimately materialize. Upon the failure of plan 'a,' the ideal scenario, it became necessary to resort to plan 'b.'

By looking at the events from this perspective, we naturally perceive the Exodus and the final redemption as two distinct entities, one partially successful, and the other perfect and eternal. We are thus left with a problem that when the imperfect redemption is surpassed by a perfect one, what will be the point in continuing to recall the previous, imperfect redemption?

THE SAGES SAID:

"The days of your life," would be sufficient to include the current era.

[The fact that the verse states] "*all* the days of your life," includes [also an obligation to mention the Exodus] in the Messianic Era.

TORAS MENACHEM

However, there is another approach to understanding these texts which helps to reconcile the difficulties mentioned above. Namely, that the Exodus and the final redemption are two elements or phases *of one single process.*

It is not the case that the original plan to enter the land and build a permanently enduring Temple was aborted and replaced with an alternative course. Rather, the original plan is still in effect, only it has suffered various hiccups and delays along the way. The Exodus from Egypt and the future redemption are thus one and the same thing: the Exodus was that moment when God decided to start bringing us to our land and give us a Holy Temple forever, and it is a decision that He never revoked. (He may have changed His mind about how quickly the promise is to be fulfilled, but the promise itself was never retracted.) Thus, while the route may have been more tortuous than expected, the period between His first redemptive act and the complete fulfillment of that plan can only be described as the consummation of one single process.

Viewed from this perspective, our entire history is actually a process of "leaving Egypt" or "heading towards complete redemption," which are both essentially the same thing.

(From *Rambam: Principles of Faith 8 & 9,* [*Kol Menachem* 2007], p. 328*ff*)

≈8 **לְהָבִיא לִימוֹת הַמָּשִׁיחַ** — *An obligation to mention the Exodus in the Messianic Era.*

Why did the Sages maintain that we will mention the Exodus from Egypt—an incomplete redemption which was followed by many national catastrophes—after the final, permanent redemption has arrived? Does it make sense to mention an inferior "product" when one is in possession of a superior one?

The Egyptian Exodus symbolizes the Jew who is distant from God but makes a sincere, concerted effort to come closer. For, in Egypt, the Jews were steeped in idolatry, but they nevertheless fled from their homes into a barren desert, trusting that God would take care of them.

The final redemption, on the other hand, represents the Jew who is close to God and finds it easy to serve Him. For the striking change that we will find in the future era is that of global transformation, from a world dominated by corruption to one that is totally free of evil and sin. In the microcosm, this represents the Jew who has transformed his natural, animalistic urges, to become totally pious; a person who positively enjoys the worship of his Creator.

The age-old question is: Who is greater? Our spiritually compromised friend who tries hard to be better—the spiritual warrior? Or the pious saint who is enraptured and enthralled with the worship of God?

There is, of course, no straightforward answer. The saint is definitely more spiritually "beautiful" and must surely please His Creator greatly. But the warrior demonstrates more effort and dedication: he still retains strong ties to the unholy and the profane, and yet he repeatedly tears himself away from the pleasures of this world to do a *mitzvah.* So both types of Jew have their own irreplaceable contribution to make.

Therefore, in the future, when we will all be saints, there will remain a need to perpetuate the "warrior" type of service in our daily lives, so that its unique quality will not cease to be. Of course, we will not be able to actually fight the evil inclination, for evil will then be something we only read about in history books; but we will at least be able to mention the superiority of a warrior-type service. Therefore, the Sages maintained that, in the future, we will continue to mention the Exodus from Egypt, the symbol of the spiritual warrior, on a daily basis.

(ibid., pp. 326-7)

בָּרוּךְ הַמָּקוֹם

בָּרוּךְ הוּא, בָּרוּךְ שֶׁנָּתַן תּוֹרָה לְעַמּוֹ יִשְׂרָאֵל, בָּרוּךְ הוּא.

כְּנֶגֶד אַרְבָּעָה בָנִים דִּבְּרָה תוֹרָה: אֶחָד חָכָם, וְאֶחָד רָשָׁע, וְאֶחָד תָּם, וְאֶחָד שֶׁאֵינוֹ יוֹדֵעַ לִשְׁאוֹל:

CLASSIC QUESTIONS

● **Why do we bless God at this point?**

AVUDRAHAM: A *darshan* (one who expounds a text in public) usually begins: "In the name of God...." Since we are about to read a passage which expounds upon scripture, we too begin, "Blessed is God."

SHIBOLEI HA-LEKET: We are now about to recite four verses where the Torah instructs us to tell the Exodus story to our children. Since telling the story is a Biblical commandment, we should, in principle, make a full blessing (see p. 28). Since this is not done in practice, we say the word "Blessed" here to allude to the concept of a blessing. And we say it four times, corresponding to the four verses that follow.

MALBIM: In times gone by, the head of the household would say, "Blessed is the All-present One," and everybody would respond, "Blessed be He!" Then he would say, "Blessed is He who gave etc.," and everybody would respond again "Blessed be He!"

● **Why is God referred to as "All-present"?**

MIDRASH: Because He constitutes the place of the world, but He is not limited to its place (*Bereishis Rabah* 68:9).

● **Does the Torah actually mention Four Sons?**

RASHI: No. The Torah mentions in four different places that one must tell the story of the Exodus to your son. From the different context in each case, the Haggadah derives that we are speaking of four different types of sons.

● **Why do the Four Sons appear here in a different order than their verses in the Torah?**

AVUDRAHAM: They are listed here in order of intelligence. The Wicked Son, though rebellious, is highly intelligent, and the Simple Son has some wisdom, at least.

BLESSED IS THE ALL-PRESENT ONE!

BLESSED IS HE! BLESSED IS HE WHO GAVE THE TORAH TO HIS PEOPLE ISRAEL. BLESSED IS HE!

THE TORAH SPEAKS OF FOUR SONS: ONE WISE, ONE WICKED, ONE SIMPLE, AND ONE CLUELESS.

TORAS MENACHEM

ברוּךְ הַמָּקוֹם...בָּרוּךְ שֶׁנָּתַן תּוֹרָה לְעַמּוֹ יִשְׂרָאֵל 👁️
— *Blessed is the All-present One!...Blessed is He Who gave the Torah to His people Israel.*

Why is God referred to here in particular as the "All-present One"? And why does the Haggadah choose to give its fourfold blessing here when introducing the Four Sons, and not, for example, when speaking of the Four Questions, or the Four Cups?

The answer is because the core of the blessing, "Blessed is He *who gave the Torah to His people Israel*," belongs here, in reference to the Four Sons. For while the Four Cups and the other parts of the Seder are mere *details* within the Torah, the goal of teaching our children is a *general* theme of the Torah itself. By way of illustration: a.) In our most central prayer, the *Shema,* we emphasize *"and you shall teach it to your children."* b.) In the blessings on Torah study we stress, "May we *and our children and the children of Your entire people...be students of the Torah."* c.) And *"after three generations the Torah seeks its home"* (*Bava Metzia* 85a).

To underscore this point further, God is referred to here as "the All-present One," i.e. how He expresses himself in this physical world. For in the heavens above there are no children, since the angels cannot be fruitful and multiply. Only down here can the crucial imperative of *"you shall teach it to your children,"* be fulfilled.

(Based on *Sichah* of 2nd Night of Pesach 5730)

כְּנֶגֶד אַרְבָּעָה בָנִים דִּבְּרָה תּוֹרָה 👁️ — *The Torah speaks of Four Sons.*

In a Torah scroll, if one letter is missing, regardless of what letter it may be, it compromises the sanctity of all the other letters. Thus, the fact that *the Torah speaks of Four Sons,* means that: a.) All Four Sons are *crucial* to the Jewish people as a whole. b.) All Four Sons, regardless of their standing, are *equally* important, just as every letter is crucial to the Torah, regardless of what letter it may be.

Our job, then, is to positively influence all Four Sons, i.e. to bring "blessing" to all of their lives

חָכָם מַה הוּא אוֹמֵר?

"מָה הָעֵדֹת וְהַחֻקִּים וְהַמִּשְׁפָּטִים
אֲשֶׁר צִוָּה יְהֹוָה אֱלֹהֵינוּ אֶתְכֶם?"

וְאַף אַתָּה אֱמָר־לוֹ כְּהִלְכוֹת הַפֶּסַח:
"אֵין מַפְטִירִין אַחַר הַפֶּסַח אֲפִיקוֹמֶן":

CLASSIC QUESTIONS

● **How do we see that this is a question from the Wise Son? And what is our response to him?**

RITVA: This son is clearly wise since he demonstrates an understanding of the different types of precepts of the Seder: *Commemorative laws*—Matzah and Maror that commemorate the slavery of Egypt; *Suprarational laws*—e.g. many details of the Paschal lamb ritual, such as not breaking any bones; and the other *civil laws*. Being that he has demonstrated such advanced knowledge, our response is to take his education a step further, in the spirit of the verse, *"Give instruction to a wise man, and he will be yet wiser"* (Prov. 9:9). We therefore *"instruct him in the laws of the Paschal lamb,"* and teach him other laws, even the Rabbinic enactments that have no basis in Scripture, such as the rule that *"we do not serve any dessert after the Paschal lamb."*

● **"The Wise Son, what does he say?"** Why not just state, **"The Wise Son says"?**

REBBE RAYATZ: "What does he say," (מַה הוּא אוֹמֵר) could also be rendered, "What he is, he says." From just a few words that a person says, one can discern his true character (cited in *Likutei Ta'amim u'Minhagim*).

TORAS MENACHEM

(hence the repetition of the word "blessed" *four* times here).

What blessing ought we to bring? "*One* Wise, *one* Wicked, *one* Simple, and *one* Clueless"—an awareness of the One God who is the source of all blessing.

(Based on *Likutei Sichos* vol. 1, p. 249ff)

৪৯ **חָכָם** — *The Wise Son.*

Why does the Wicked Son follow straight after the Wise Son, rather than being banished to the end of the table for his rebellious spirit?

One of the answers is that the Haggadah wishes to suggest that the Wise and Wicked Sons have something very significant in common.

While Judaism does not encourage slavish intellectual conformity, it does not endorse critical rationality either. Instead, we are encouraged to pursue a carefully nuanced path of mental creativity tempered by a deep sense of intellectual humility. We seek knowledge with passion and constantly look for new approaches to old problems, but all of this is coupled with an awareness of the ultimate fallibility of human knowledge which will always defer to the absolute and comprehensive truth of the Torah.

Thus, the highest and purest form of Torah study is not to challenge accepted norms through questions, but to enhance our knowledge through diligent and *patient* study.

Of course, questions can be a very helpful pedagogic tool, but from an idealistic point of view at least, the critical tone of a question is a move away from the intellectual humility which is the hallmark of a Torah approach. The Wise Son's questions thus represent a very subtle tendency towards critical rationality, which, ultimately, could lead him astray. To hint to this point, the Wise and Wicked sons are placed side by side.

THE WISE SON

WHAT DOES HE SAY? "What are these commemorative laws, suprarational laws and civil laws which God, our God, has commanded you?" (*Devarim* 6:20).

You should instruct him in the laws of the Paschal lamb: "We do not serve any dessert after the Paschal lamb" (*Mishnah, Pesachim* 119b).

CLASSIC QUESTIONS

● **In stating "which God...has commanded *you*" doesn't the Wise Son "exclude himself from the community," just like the Wicked Son?**

MACHZOR VITRY: No, because he makes clear that he includes himself in the community by stressing, "God *our* God."

The reason why the Wise Son says, "What are the testimonies etc. which God has commanded *you*," is because the son (in the verse), who did not leave Egypt, is addressing the father, who did. The father was in Egypt at the time when the commandments of Pesach were given (*Laws of Pesach* par. 95).

TORAS MENACHEM

Where do we see this flaw in the question of the Wise Son? And what is our response to him?

In his question, the Wise Son makes a distinction between commandments that cannot be understood by human reason ("suprarational laws"), and those that can ("commemorative laws" and "civil laws"). Since the Wise Son's weak point is lack of intellectual humility, he overly "discriminates" between laws motivated by reason and those which require pure religious devotion. His mistake is that *all* commandments, even the intellectually palatable ones, must *primarily* be observed out of a sense of the fallibility of human knowledge and obedience to a Higher Authority. The fact that a certain law makes more sense should not color the religious perception of it.

Our response to the Wise Son is: "*We do not serve any dessert after the Paschal lamb*," because we do not wish to lose the flavor of the meat from our mouths. Now one might ask: If the Paschal lamb commemorates the salvation of Jewish life, ("*It is a Pesach offering to God because...He saved our houses*"—*Shemos* 12:27), then it is presumably a message that is not easily forgotten. So why should we be concerned that its significance will be sidelined by

eating dessert? Could we possibly forget so quickly that God saved our lives?

The answer, sadly, is yes. In fact our greatest religious flaw is an insensitivity to life and death, at least in a spiritual sense. For "life," according to Scripture, means to be attached to God ("*You who remain attached to God are alive today*"—*Devarim* 4:4), from which it follows that any sin is effectively spiritual "suicide."

Why, then, do we not flee from sin? The Sages explained that we are simply irrational: "*A person does not sin unless a nonsensical spirit enters him*" (*Sotah* 3a). And being that our greatest religious enemy is "*a nonsensical spirit*," attempting to fight it with logic would be futile. The only solution is a *suprarational* dedication; a sensitivity to the inviolability and sanctity of all the Torah's laws.

So the Wise Son is warned: "*We do not serve any dessert after the Paschal lamb*." Even the most powerful intellectual conviction—such as the saving of life represented by the Paschal lamb—can soon be eroded. We must always remember the fallibility of human wisdom which can be bribed with something so little as a mere helping of dessert.

(Based on *Sichos* of 2nd Night of Pesach 5718 & 5724)

רָשָׁע מַה הוּא אוֹמֵר?

"מָה הָעֲבוֹדָה הַזֹּאת לָכֶם?"

"לָכֶם" וְלֹא לוֹ. וּלְפִי שֶׁהוֹצִיא

אֶת־עַצְמוֹ מִן הַכְּלָל, כָּפַר בְּעִקָּר.

וְאַף אַתָּה הַקְהֵה אֶת־שִׁנָּיו וֶאֱמָר־לוֹ:

"בַּעֲבוּר זֶה עָשָׂה יְהוָה לִי בְּצֵאתִי מִמִּצְרָיִם".

"לִי" וְלֹא לוֹ, אִלּוּ הָיָה שָׁם לֹא הָיָה נִגְאָל:

CLASSIC QUESTIONS

● **Why does the Wicked Son follow after the Wise Son?**

ARIZAL: The Four Sons correspond to the four spiritual worlds. The Wise Son corresponds to the highest world Atzilus (Emanation) and the Wicked Son to the lowest world Asiyah (Action). Why should Atzilus be placed next to Asiyah? Because Asiyah is in need of much light, which must be drawn from the highest world, Atzilus.

Also, the Wicked Son, placed second in the list of four, corresponds to the Second of the Four Cups of wine. For on the Second Cup we say the words, "In the beginning our fathers were idol-worshippers" (Pri Etz Chaim, Sha'ar Chag ha-Matzos ch. 7) .

TORAS MENACHEM

&❧ רָשָׁע — The Wicked Son.

The Wicked Son is placed next to the Wise Son because only the Wise Son is capable of revealing the inherent good in his errant brother (see Arizal).

We might imagine that to pursue "outreach," to teach the uninitiated about the Torah way of life, there is nothing to be gained by being advanced in one's own Judaism. After all, why would it be necessary to be a Torah scholar merely in order to teach Alef-Beis to another Jew? Why would there be a need to observe the commandments meticulously in order to share one or two commandments with an absolute beginner? Wouldn't the scholars and pious ones better spend their time in study and prayer, leaving their junior colleagues to reach out to the unaffiliated?

The Haggadah teaches us here that nothing could be further from the truth. "The higher one is," goes the old Chasidic adage, "the lower down one can reach" (Torah Ohr 4b). In order to touch the hearts of those who, possibly through no fault of their own, have become estranged from Judaism, much illumination is required. It is the most profoundly pious and scholarly Jew who will be the most powerful magnet for the most secular of his brothers.

And this explains why we recite the main part of the Haggadah, reliving the Exodus story, over the Second Cup of wine, which corresponds to the Wicked Son (see Arizal). For by bringing all Jews, even the "wicked," back to the fountains of Torah we will once again enjoy exodus and redemption from this final exile.

(Based on Likutei Sichos vol. 1, p. 247ff)

THE WICKED SON

WHAT DOES HE SAY? "What is this bothersome ritual service to you?" (*Shemos* 12:26).

He says *"to you,"* but not *to himself*. In declaring immunity from the law, he has denied a basic principle of Judaism.

You should therefore also blunt his teeth and say to him: "It is because of this that God did for me when I left Egypt" (*Shemos* 13:8). *"For me,"* but not *for him!* If he had been there, he would not have been redeemed.

CLASSIC QUESTIONS

● **What mistakes does the Wicked Son make?**

SHIBOLEI HA-LEKET:

1.) He excludes himself by saying "What is this service *to you?*"

2.) He does not mention God.

3.) He refers to worshipping God as "bothersome."

● **What, exactly, is his question? And how is it answered?**

RITVA: Why are you imposing all this bother of the Seder on us which is delaying the meal? Therefore we are told to "blunt his teeth" which desire to chew and eat.

● **Will the "Wicked Son" be part of the true and final redemption?**

RASHI: *"You will return to God your God and He will listen to His voice...and God will return your captives (from Exile)"* (*Devarim* 30:2-3)— The day of the ingathering of exiles is as momentous and difficult as if He, Himself, would need to carry, literally in His grasp, *every individual* from his place, as it is said, "You shall be plucked, *one at a time,* Children of Israel" (Isaiah 27:12).

TANYA: Most definitely, every person will eventually repent, whether in this incarnation or another, because *"No one banished from Him by his sins will remain banished"* (Cf. II Sam. 14:14; ch. 39).

TORAS MENACHEM

☞ **אֵלּוּ הָיָה שָׁם לֹא הָיָה נִגְאָל** — *If he had been there, he would not have been redeemed.*

This response to the Wicked Son has classically been perceived as a form of harsh rebuke. We tell the one who has "declared immunity from the law," that he has no share in the entire Exodus story, and "if he had been there he would not have been redeemed" (see *Torah Temimah* to *Shemos* 12:26).

But *our* approach to the Wicked Son should not be a harsh one, which is likely to alienate him altogether. Rather, with affection and love we should explain, "If he had been *there*, he would not have been redeemed": from *the Egyptian exile* the Wicked Son would not have been redeemed, but from our final exile he will be saved along with the rest of the Jewish people. For when the Torah was given at Sinai, God forged an intrinsic, unbreakable connection with every Jew, regardless of his ethical and spiritual standing.

Apparently, though, the Israelites in Egypt also had an inextricable soul-connection with God, since we see that He refers to them as "my first-born child" (*Shemos* 4:22). Does this not suggest an

תָּם מַה הוּא אוֹמֵר?

"מַה־זֹּאת"? וְאָמַרְתָּ אֵלָיו: "בְּחֹזֶק יָד
הוֹצִיאָנוּ יְהֹוָה מִמִּצְרַיִם מִבֵּית עֲבָדִים":

וְשֶׁאֵינוֹ יוֹדֵעַ לִשְׁאוֹל:

אַתְּ פְּתַח לוֹ, שֶׁנֶּאֱמַר: "וְהִגַּדְתָּ לְבִנְךָ
בַּיּוֹם הַהוּא לֵאמֹר, בַּעֲבוּר זֶה עָשָׂה
יְהֹוָה לִי בְּצֵאתִי מִמִּצְרָיִם":

TORAS MENACHEM

unbreakable, parent-like bond? Why, then, was the "Wicked Son" in Egypt not redeemed?

The answer is that even our bond to God as His "children" is not unbreakable because ultimately *free choice* is more powerful. While there is a natural, powerful love between a parent and a child, the child may choose, if he wishes, to have nothing to do with his parent. The ties of blood represent a natural affinity, but with free choice—that unique quality that distinguishes us from the rest of the Animal Kingdom—we can choose to go against our nature.

But the power of choice works in both directions: God, too, is free to exercise His choice, *and at Sinai God chose the Jewish people*. So now, even if we temporarily "declare immunity from the law," He continues to choose us, in a way that is permanent and unconditional. And because He constantly beams the message that He wants us, every Jew—even the Wicked Son—will eventually listen to that inner voice and return to God (see *Rashi* and *Tanya* above).

(Based on *Likutei Sichos* vol. 11, p. 2*ff*)

דאם תָּם וְשֶׁאֵינוֹ יוֹדֵעַ לִשְׁאוֹל — *The Simple Son and the Clueless Son.*

Our responses to these two sons appear, at first glance, to be the wrong way around. The Simple Son, who is more advanced than the Clueless Son, shows at least some interest in the rituals of the evening,

asking *What is this?* So surely, we should have explained to him, *"It is because of this etc.,"* that we were redeemed from Egypt in the merit of the special *mitzvos* performed tonight. The Clueless Son, however, shows no interest at all, so would it not have been appropriate to try and grab his attention with the impressive miracles of the Exodus, saying *"With a strong hand God took us out of Egypt"*?

The key to answering this question lies in the fact that the Clueless Son is placed here last of all. Could he possibly be worse than the Wicked Son?

Of course, in terms of practical observance, the Clueless Son vastly surpasses the Wicked Son. He performs the necessary rituals and he certainly does not challenge any sacred practices or texts.

But the Clueless Son is sadly further from being redeemed than his wicked brother, for he suffers from two maladies that, when they strike together, defy any simple cure—ignorance and apathy. The Wicked Son may be a terror, challenging everything we do, but at least he takes an interest in the evening's activities. Judaism angers him, but at least that shows that there is "somebody home." When the Wicked Son finally comes around to our way of thinking, he will be a passionate Jew and an asset to his people.

But the Clueless Son has almost "immunized" himself against Judaism. It is not that his soul lacks passion, for when it comes to other endeavors, such

THE SIMPLE SON

WHAT DOES HE SAY? "What is this?" Say back to him: "With a strong hand God took us out of Egypt, from the house of slavery" (*Shemos* 13:14).

WITH THE CLUELESS SON

YOU MUST TAKE THE INITIATIVE, as the verse states: "You shall tell your son on that day, saying, 'It is because of this that God did for me when I left Egypt'" (ibid. 13:8).

TORAS MENACHEM

as making money, we see his great talents and drive. But Torah seems to just make him "switch off"; nothing in the Seder seems to engage his interest. "Just tell me what to do so I can get it over and done with," he says.

So, by placing the Clueless Son last, the Haggadah warns us that apathy is the greatest danger of all.

Our only hope is to say to him, *"It is because of this that God did for me when I left Egypt."* You are a fine, religious Jew, but your observance is lifeless and performed by rote. It is time for you to "leave Egypt." It is *"because of this,"* the *mitzvos* of the Paschal lamb and Matzah that our ancestors left Egypt, both of which represent a *passionate dedication* to Judaism, and not mere observance by rote.

The Simple Son however, is already engaged in the Seder and even asks questions, so we do not need to prove to him the *necessity* of leaving Egypt. All that is required is to show him the right approach, namely that we must always act *"with a strong hand."*

The lesson here is a powerful one. We should never be perturbed by those who are angry and antagonistic towards Judaism. For such individuals are blessed with passion, a gift that needs not, God forbid, to be extinguished, but rather, *redirected* for the good.

(Based on *Sichah* of 2nd Night of Pesach 5725)

☙ הַבֵּן הַחֲמִישִׁי — *The Fifth Son.*

While the "Four Sons" differ from one another in their reaction to the Seder Service, they have one

thing in common: they are all present at the Seder Service. Even the so-called "Wicked" son is there, taking an active, though rebellious, interest in what is going on in Jewish life around him. This, at least, justifies the hope that some day also the "Wicked" one will become wise, and all Jewish children attending the Seder will become conscientious, Torah-and-*mitzvos*-observing Jews.

Unfortunately, there is, in our time of confusion and obscurity, another kind of a Jewish child: the child who is conspicuous by his absence from the Seder Service; the one who has no interest whatsoever in Torah and *mitzvos*, laws and customs; who is not even aware of the *Seder-shel-Pesach*, of the Exodus from Egypt and the subsequent Revelation at Sinai.

This presents a grave challenge, which should command our attention long before Passover and the Seder-night. For no Jewish child should be forgotten and given up. We must make every effort to save also that "lost" child, and bring the absentee to the Seder table. Determined to do so, and driven by a deep sense of compassion and responsibility, we need have no fear of failure.

The regrettable truth is that the blame for the above-mentioned "lost generation" lies squarely on the shoulders of the parents. It is the result of an erroneous psychology and misguided policy on the part of some immigrants arriving in a new and strange environment. Finding themselves a small minority and encountering certain difficulties, which are largely unavoidable in all cases of resettlement,

יָכוֹל מֵרֹאשׁ חֹדֶשׁ — תַּלְמוּד לוֹמַר: "בַּיּוֹם הַהוּא". אִי בַּיּוֹם הַהוּא, יָכוֹל מִבְּעוֹד יוֹם — תַּלְמוּד לוֹמַר "בַּעֲבוּר זֶה": "בַּעֲבוּר זֶה" לֹא אָמַרְתִּי אֶלָּא בְּשָׁעָה שֶׁיֵּשׁ מַצָּה וּמָרוֹר מֻנָּחִים לְפָנֶיךָ:

TORAS MENACHEM

some parents had the mistaken notion, which they injected also into their children, that the way to overcome these difficulties is to become quickly assimilated with the new environment, by discarding the heritage of their forefathers and abandoning the Jewish way of life.

Finding the ensuing process somewhat distasteful, as such a course is bound to be full of spiritual conflict, some parents were resolved that their children would be spared the conflict altogether. In order to justify their desertion and appease their injured conscience, it was necessary for them to devise some rationale, and they deluded themselves, and deluded their children, by the claim that in their new surroundings the Jewish way of life, with the observance of the Torah and *mitzvos* did not fit. They looked for, and therefore also "found," faults with the true Jewish way of life, while in their non-Jewish environment everything seemed to them only good and attractive.

By this attitude the parents hoped to assure their children's existence and survival in the new environment. But what kind of existence is it, if everything spiritual and holy is traded for the material? What kind of survival is it, if it means the sacrifice of the soul for the amenities of the body?

In their retreat from Yiddishkeit, they turned what they thought was an "escape to freedom" into an escape to servitude, pathetically trying to imitate the non-Jewish environment, failing to see that such imitation, by its caricature and inferiority complex, can only call forth mockery and derision, and can only offend the sensibilities of those whose respect and acceptance they are so desperately trying to win.

The event of the Exodus from Egypt and the Festival of Passover are timely reminders, among other things, that not in an attempt to imitate

the environment lies the hope for survival, deliverance and freedom, but rather in the unswerving loyalty to our traditions and true Jewish way of life.

Our ancestors in Egypt were a small minority, and lived in the most difficult circumstances. Yet, as our Sages relate, they preserved their identity and, with pride and dignity, tenaciously clung to their way of life, traditions and distinct uniqueness; precisely in this way was their existence assured, as also their true deliverance from slavery, physical and spiritual.

There is no room for hopelessness in Jewish life, and no Jew should ever be given up as a lost cause. Through the proper compassionate approach even those of the "lost" generation can be brought back to the love of God and love of the Torah, and not only be included in the community of the "Four Sons," but in due course be elevated to the rank of the Wise Son.

(excerpted from communal letter, 11th Nissan 5717)

&8 **יָכוֹל מֵרֹאשׁ חֹדֶשׁ** 8&— *One might think [that the discussion of the Exodus story must be] from the beginning of the month.*

Much has been written about what actually happened when the Torah was given at Sinai. Besides the addition of new laws which had not been commanded to Adam, Noach or Avraham, more importantly, there was a *qualitative* change in the nature of the law. Namely, *that it was now possible to sanctify the mundane.*

The commandments performed by the Patriarchs, for example, did not affect the physical world. When Ya'akov put on (a precursor of) *tefillin*, nothing happened to the object itself. *Ya'akov* was spiritually uplifted by the experience, but the physical object had become no more sacred than it was at the outset.

ONE MIGHT THINK [that the discussion of the Exodus story] must be from the beginning of the month. The Torah therefore says, "[You shall tell your son] *on that day*" (ibid.).

However, "On that day," could mean while it is still daytime [when the Paschal lamb is offered]. The Torah therefore states [the additional words], "Because of *this*"—i.e. only when Matzah and Bitter Herbs are placed before you.

=== CLASSIC QUESTIONS ===

● Why might you think that the Haggadah is to be recited at the beginning of the month?

MA'ASEI NISIM: Because that is when Moshe first taught the laws of Pesach to the Jewish people.

● Couldn't a person place Matzah and Bitter Herbs before him at an earlier date?

TERUMAS HA-DESHEN: The Haggadah means at a time when there is an *obligation* to do so.

=== TORAS MENACHEM ===

This innovation of Sinai—the license to sanctify—is no small matter. Kabbalists actually perceived this phenomenon as the guiding force behind world history. The Messianic dream of a global utopia where all men would finally learn to conquer their character flaws and worship the One God in harmony, will not, according to Jewish mystical thought, be brought about by political means. Our selfishness and the world's corruption is a symptom of a more fundamental evil, that physical matter, by its very nature, conceals God. We do not see Him, or feel Him, so it is only natural that we perceive ourselves as independent beings. The inevitable consequence is that we aggressively pursue the goal of self-preservation.

So neither Communism, nor Capitalism, nor any other 'ism, will save the world, because all these systems are only capable of managing and curbing our inherent tendency to self-worship. None of these approaches are capable of *changing* man for the good. And being humanly contrived, they will always possess flaws and inefficiencies that will inevitably be exploited.

The Kabbalah, on the other hand, has a different approach—very much a long-term solution, but an effective one. *The goal is to gradually erode away the arrogant, untruthful nature of physical matter itself.* Our sense of total independence—and the hostile self-preservation that it engenders—is a lie. Really it is God who provides for us, along with our six billion brethren on this planet, and we should focus our energies on worshipping Him, rather than fighting with others for some daily bread. But the ego blinds us to the truth. And this, explained the Kabbalists, is not an inherently human problem, but a symptom of the arrogance of physical matter itself.

At Sinai, we were given 613 tools, each of which have the effect of gradually cajoling the world into being more translucent and sensitive to God's presence. Eventually, we are promised, the cumulative effect of all these *mitzvos* over the centuries will bring a real, and permanent change for the good, humbling the world and its inhabitants into a Messianic state of unity and spirituality (*Torah Ohr* 27c-d).

So, *"one might think that the discussion of the Exodus must be from the beginning of the month,"* when, as a prelude to Sinai, the commandments of Pesach were issued to the Jewish people for the first time. Even though the time to observe these com-

מִתְּחִלָּה עוֹבְדֵי עֲבוֹדָה זָרָה הָיוּ אֲבוֹתֵינוּ,
וְעַכְשָׁו קֵרְבָנוּ הַמָּקוֹם לַעֲבֹדָתוֹ.
שֶׁנֶּאֱמַר: "וַיֹּאמֶר יְהוֹשֻׁעַ אֶל־כָּל־הָעָם, כֹּה־אָמַר
יְהוָה אֱלֹהֵי יִשְׂרָאֵל: בְּעֵבֶר הַנָּהָר יָשְׁבוּ אֲבוֹתֵיכֶם

═══ CLASSIC QUESTIONS ═══

● **Why do we say this passage?**

TALMUD: *"We begin with shame (and end with glory)"* (Mishnah).

Rav said: This means we say, "In the beginning our ancestors were idol-worshippers."

Shmuel said: This means we say, "We were slaves to Pharaoh in Egypt" (*Pesachim* 116a).

RIF: In practice we say both passages.

AVUDRAHAM: Shmuel thought it would be inappropriate to stress any "shame" other than the difficulties that the Jewish people experienced in Egypt, since the Exodus is tonight's topic of discussion.

Rav maintained that a greater contrast between "shame" and "glory" is achieved by stressing the very low spiritual standing from which our ancestors originally came (commentary to עבדים היינו).

● **"In the beginning our ancestors were idol-worshippers." Who does this refer to?**

RAMBAM: Our ancestors during and prior to the days of Terach (*Laws of Chametz and Matzah* 7:4).

RASHBATZ: Avraham originally worshipped idols, like his father Terach, but later he came to recognize his Creator, and smashed the idols. As a result of this, God drew Avraham close to worship Him.

═══ TORAS MENACHEM ═══

mandments had not yet arrived, the very fact that man had now been granted a license to sanctify the mundane was such a momentous event that, apparently, it should be the focus of our celebrations.

But, the Haggadah teaches us, the answer is no. We celebrate redemption *"only when Matzah and Bitter Herbs are placed before you."* For *possessing* the license alone is not enough; the main thing is that it should be *used* to make a real, practical impact on the global community.

(Based on *Likutei Sichos* vol. 16, p. 215*ff*)

◈ **מִתְּחִלָּה** — *In the Beginning...*

This passage is recited to fulfil the *Mishnah's* directive to *"begin with shame and end with glory,"* that the Exodus can only be fully appreciated by contrasting it with the gloomy state of affairs that preceded.

While conventionally the "glory" referred to here is considered to be the Exodus from Egypt itself, perhaps we could suggest a novel interpretation. In the blessing recited after recounting the Exodus story, we conclude with prayers for the future redemption,

"...gladdened in the rebuilding of Your city...We shall eat of the sacrifices...We will then thank You with a new song for our redemption..." (below p. 141).

When compared to the miracles and spiritual bliss of the final redemption, the Egyptian Exodus was vastly inferior. In fact, the contrast is so stark that we might even refer to the imperfect Exodus, after which we suffered a further 3000-year exile, as "shameful" compared with the future redemption, which will endure forever. So, "we begin with shame," *the story of the Egyptian Exodus*, and "end with glory," a description of the final redemption.

(*Sichah of Acharon Shel Pesach* 5747, par. 19)

◈ **עוֹבְדֵי עֲבוֹדָה זָרָה הָיוּ אֲבוֹתֵינוּ** — *Our ancestors were idol-worshippers.*

On the verse, *"Avraham was old, well on in years"* (*Bereishis* 24:1), our Sages commented that Avraham served God his entire life to the extent that all of his days were "perfect" (*Zohar* I 129a). This seems to contradict the fact that in the earlier part of his life Avraham was taught to worship idols by his father,

I N THE BEGINNING our ancestors were idol-worshippers, but now the All-present One has brought us close to His worship, as the verse states: "Yehoshua said to all the people, this is what God, the God of Israel, said: 'Your ancestors used to live across the river—

====== CLASSIC QUESTIONS ======

● **Wasn't Yehoshua stating the obvious here?**

LIKUTEI TORAH: According to the Kabbalah, "the other side of the river" refers to an exalted level of spirituality which God granted to Avraham (and the other Patriarchs—see *Zohar* III 99a). The goal of this "soul infusion" is expressed by the next verse, "I led him

through the whole land of Cana'an." I.e. this intense spirituality should be drawn down into this world.

So Yehoshua was effectively teaching us how the Patriarchs were able to bring about a revolution against the idol-worshipping culture of their time: by virtue of a spiritual gift from above (*Vayikra* 47a).

====== TORAS MENACHEM ======

as *Rashbatz* stresses here. How, then, can the *Zohar* assert that all Avraham's days were perfect?

The simple explanation is that God's law is reasonable. If He asks you to do something, He gives you a reasonable amount of time to put it into practice. For example, it is impossible that on the day the *mitzvah* of *tefillin* was first given to the Jewish people that sufficient pairs of *tefillin* could have been made available for the million or so adult men in the desert. But it would be ludicrous to suggest that they would have *transgressed* the requirement to observe this *mitzvah* until a reasonable time to gather the materials and make the *tefillin* had passed.

Likewise, so long as Avraham could not have *reasonably* been expected to recognize God, he was not culpable for failing to do so. And since he was granted a fair "grace period" to establish a full philosophical appreciation of monotheism, during which time he was not guilty of rebelling against God through idol-worship, it turns out that all Avraham's days were "perfect" and free of sin.

(Based on *Likutei Sichos* vol. 35, p. 68*ff;* vol. 17, p. 82)

◈◈ **וְעַכְשָׁו קֵרְבָנוּ הַמָּקוֹם לַעֲבֹדָתוֹ** — *Now the All-Present One has brought us close to His worship.*

How can the Haggadah state, "*Now* the All-Present One has brought us close," when this is something that occurred in the times of Avraham?

Idol worship may seem a concept that is foreign to our modern lives, but in truth, a mistake not dissimilar from that of the idol-worshippers can easily be made in our own business activities. Men of old may have worshipped the sun and the moon, but don't we "worship" our jobs and our clients? Don't we make the mistake of imagining "market forces" as working independently from God?

Just as then there was a need to see the sun and the moon as mere tools of God, "an axe in the hand of the chopper," likewise, we should see the marketplace as nothing other than a Divine tool by which God—and God alone—provides our sustenance. Our business efforts in and of themselves do not bring us wealth; they merely make a "vessel" into which God may channel His blessings.

So the need to rid ourselves of "idolatry," in its subtle, contemporary form, so as to come "close to His worship," is also applicable now, as much as ever.

(Based on *Sichah* of 2nd Night of Pesach 5724)

◈◈ **בְּעֵבֶר הַנָּהָר יָשְׁבוּ אֲבוֹתֵיכֶם** — *Your ancestors used to live across the river.*

The Kabbalistic understanding of these words (see *Likutei Torah*) appears to be in stark contrast to the literal interpretation of the verse. The Kabbalah teaches that "*across the river*" points to an exalted spirituality granted by God to Avraham; whereas,

מֵעוֹלָם, תֶּרַח אֲבִי אַבְרָהָם וַאֲבִי נָחוֹר, וַיַּעַבְדוּ אֱלֹהִים אֲחֵרִים":

"וָאֶקַּח אֶת־אֲבִיכֶם אֶת־אַבְרָהָם מֵעֵבֶר הַנָּהָר, וָאוֹלֵךְ אוֹתוֹ בְּכָל־אֶרֶץ כְּנַעַן, וָאַרְבֶּ* אֶת־זַרְעוֹ וָאֶתֶּן־לוֹ אֶת־יִצְחָק: וָאֶתֵּן לְיִצְחָק אֶת־יַעֲקֹב וְאֶת־עֵשָׂו, וָאֶתֵּן לְעֵשָׂו אֶת־הַר שֵׂעִיר לָרֶשֶׁת אוֹתוֹ, וְיַעֲקֹב וּבָנָיו יָרְדוּ מִצְרָיִם":

*וָאַרְבֶּה קרי

TORAS MENACHEM

when taken at face value, "across the river" refers to the corrupt idol-worshipping locale in which Avraham was born. A far cry from exalted spirituality!

The two interpretations also paint Avraham's role in a very different light. The Kabbalah depicts Avraham as a pious saint, gifted with such an intense spirituality that he was effectively "immune" to the corruption that surrounded him. But a plain reading of the verse seems to imply that Avraham *was* influenced by his surroundings, but he managed to heroically tear himself away.

While Torah interpretation is, of course, multifaceted, the numerous insights into any one verse are ultimately different "facets" of the *same* gem. There must, therefore, be a certain exegetical "symbiosis" between them. How is this to be understood in our case?

The mission with which we have been charged, as champions of true monotheism, is to mend the rift between God's absolute unity and the world's apparent diversity. To effect this repair, two basic approaches are at our disposal, each possessing their own respective advantages and disadvantages.

The *Human Hero Model* sees a man-initiated attempt to draw closer to God by combatting the diversity and "me-ness" of this world.

But man alone possesses neither the strength nor the inspiration to carry out this task unaided; and there is a limit to how high we can reach without God's helping hand.

Thus there is a need for the *Divine Influence Model*, where man is showered with inspiration from Above to carry out his mission. But here, too, there is the obvious danger of being given *too much* help from Above, thus denying man the basic privilege of being responsible for his own achievements.

So to reach the goal of true monotheism, to engender a seamless compatibility between God and His world, a carefully nuanced approach is required that draws from *both* models.

And this is the underlying message implicit in our verse. The fact that a single verse embraces both the *Divine Influence Model* (the Kabbalistic interpretation) and the *Human Hero Model* (the literal interpretation), suggests the need for a unified approach. Somewhere in our souls is the sensitivity to discern a carefully charted "middle path."

(Based on *Likutei Sichos* vol. 20, p. 298*ff*)

תֶּרַח אֲבִי אַבְרָהָם 🙚🙘 — *Terach, Avraham's father.*

In the Torah, the first of the Patriarchs is mentioned by two names. Initially born as Avram, he challenges the idol worship of his father, and, eventually, upon reaching spiritual perfection he is renamed Avraham. So "Avraham" represents the complete rejection and triumph over the values imparted to "Avram" by his father.

Why, then, does the Haggadah refer here to "Terach, *Avraham's* father"? Surely, Terach was Avram's father, not Avraham's father?

Terach, Avraham's father and Nachor's father—
and they served foreign gods.

"**B**UT I TOOK your father Avraham from
across the river, and I led him through
the whole land of Cana'an. I multiplied his
offspring, and I gave him Yitzchak; and to
Yitzchak I gave Ya'akov and Eisav. To Eisav
I gave Mount Sei'ir to possess it, and Ya'akov
and his sons went down to Egypt'" (Joshua 24:2-4).

CLASSIC QUESTIONS

● Why is וָאַרְבֶּ ("I multiplied") written without a letter *hei* at the end, which could also be read as
וָאָרִיב, "I quarreled with him"?

RASHI: God is saying, "I put him through a number of quarrels and tests before I gave him offspring."

TORAS MENACHEM

The answer is that when two men enjoy an essential bond, they are bound together in every respect. Avraham may have parted from the ways of Terach, and rejected everything that Terach stood for, but, as father and son, they were still bound together inextricably.

(Based on *Sichah* of 2nd Night of Pesach 5713)

וָאַרְבֶּה אֶת זַרְעוֹ וָאֶתֶּן לוֹ אֶת יִצְחָק — *I multiplied his offspring, and I gave him Yitzchak.*

How could *one* son, Yitzchak, be considered as God having "*multiplied*" Avraham's offspring?

Various insights could be offered. a.) The verse refers to an increase in quality, not quantity. The satisfaction which Avraham was to have from Yitzchak was equivalent to having many children. b.) Or, simply, we might read the verse as saying that *through* Yitzchak a nation of Jewish people arose.

At the literal level, however, perhaps the following could be argued. *Rashi* was troubled by this very question, and therefore suggested that, in this case, we are forced to take on a masoretic reading of the verse: "*I put him through a number of quarrels and*

tests before I gave him offspring." Here, the "quarrels" clearly refers to Yishmael, who was only given the status of Avraham's "offspring" after Avraham's quarrel with Sarah about Yishmael's eviction (*Bereishis* 21:13); and "tests" refers to Yitzchak.

With this in mind, we could explain why the Haggadah chose to cite the whole of verse 24 here. For, if our goal is merely to prove "*that the All-present One has brought us close to His worship*" from amid idol worship, then we only need the first part of verse 24: "*I took your father Avraham from across the river;*" the details of Avraham's children are irrelevant. And if the Haggadah chose to digress slightly with the extended chronicles of Avraham's descendants, then why not cite the continuation of the story in verses 26-7, which discuss the Exodus itself?

However, the Haggadah's intention was not to digress here at all, but rather, to prove how God "*brought us close* to His worship," i.e. how the Patriarchs were selected by God. First we read that after Yitzchak and Yishmael were born (after "*I multiplied his offspring*"), Yitzchak was selected, "*I gave him Yitzchak.*" And later, after Ya'akov and Eisav were born, Eisav was rejected, "*I gave Mount Sei'ir*"

בָּרוּךְ שׁוֹמֵר הַבְטָחָתוֹ לְיִשְׂרָאֵל

בָּרוּךְ הוּא, שֶׁהַקָּדוֹשׁ בָּרוּךְ הוּא חִשַּׁב אֶת־הַקֵּץ לַעֲשׂוֹת כְּמָה שֶׁאָמַר לְאַבְרָהָם אָבִינוּ בִּבְרִית בֵּין הַבְּתָרִים. שֶׁנֶּאֱמַר:

CLASSIC QUESTIONS

● *"He calculated the End...."* When is "the End" of our current exile?

Talmud: Rav said: "All the Ends have passed. Now the matter depends solely on repentance" (*Sanhedrin* 97a).

TORAS MENACHEM

to possess it." Thus we have proven that it was only Ya'akov and his family who remained chosen and "brought close" by God.

(Based on *Sichah* of 2nd Night of Pesach 5727; *Likutei Sichos* vol. 1, p. 110; vol. 17, p. 328)

❧ שֶׁהַקָּדוֹשׁ בָּרוּךְ הוּא חִשַּׁב אֶת־הַקֵּץ — *For the Holy One, blessed be He, calculated the End.*

The *Talmud* states: "*All the Ends have passed. Now the matter depends solely on repentance.*" This appears to pose a number of problems.

a.) Even after the Talmudic era we find that many illustrious figures such as *Saadia Gaon, Rashi, Rambam, Ramban, Rabeinu Bachaye, Abarbanel, Arizal, Ohr ha-Chayim* and *Chasam Sofer,* to name but a few, each predicted a precise date for the End of Days. Chabad leaders such as the *Alter Rebbe, Rebbe Rashab* and Rabbi Yosef Yitzchak of Lubavitch also proclaimed the time of Mashiach's coming. How is this to be reconciled with the statement that "*all the Ends have passed*" already in the time of the *Talmud?*

b.) The *Talmud's* statement itself is confusing. Surely there is only *one* actual End of Days, all other predictions being incorrect. Why, then, does the *Talmud* lend them all legitimacy, stating that "*all Ends have passed*"?

As we will discuss in the following insight at length (p. 63), the transition from exile to redemption is a gradual, cumulative process, beginning at the very inception of the exile itself. "*The full perfection of the Messianic Era,*" writes the *Alter Rebbe,* "*and the period of Resurrection, namely, the revelation of God's infinite light within this physical world, is a product of our acts of worship throughout the period of exile*" (*Tanya,* chapter 37). Or, as our Sages so graphically put it: On the day the Holy Temple was destroyed, "*the savior and redeemer of the Jewish people was born*" (*Eichah Rabah* 1:51). The process of *actively* bringing the redemption had begun.

If our eyes were sufficiently attuned, we would already see "*the revelation of God's infinite light within this physical world*" which has been drawn down here by all the *mitzvah* acts performed throughout the generations. The moment of redemption will thus

Blessed is He Who keeps His Promise to the Jewish People!

Blessed is He! For the Holy One, blessed be He, calculated the End when He would carry out what He had told our father Avraham at the Covenant of the Parts, as the verse states: "And He said to Avram,

---

TORAS MENACHEM

---

represent a mere change in perspective—the ability to see something that is already present, and not a change in the world's actual condition.

Exceptional *tzadikim* (pious ones) and great Jewish leaders, whose eyes were attuned to things spiritual, were capable of perceiving this cumulative, redemptive potential in their own lifetimes. So when they "predicted" the End of Days, it was not some sort of mathematical guess-work. Rather, they *saw* how much spiritual progress had been achieved so far, and from this they figured how many acts of worship were still necessary to reach "the full perfection of the Messianic Era."

The only moot point here, which leaves room for confusion, is the exact proportion of this "full perfection." When it came to evaluating the spiritual growth achieved in the past, the *tzadik* made no mistake because he saw it with his own eyes. But what always remained somewhat uncertain was how great the future redemption will be.

Or, to put it in other words, since the "full perfection of the Messianic Era is a product of *our* acts of worship throughout the period of exile," the question is rather: What are *we* capable of? How great are the Jewish people, at the end of the day?

So in all those cases where a *tzadik* predicted an "End" but Mashiach did not come, it was ultimately *because he had in some way underestimated the full, potential achievements of the Jewish people.*

Of course, such great *tzadikim* were not mistaken, in the literal sense of the word. Even in primary Torah sources we find different views expressed as to the extent of the "full perfection" of the Messianic Era. For example, *"Shmuel said, 'The only difference between this world and the Messianic Era is an end to subjugation to foreign regimes'"* (Sanhedrin 99a). Yet other sages dissented, and depicted a fuller redemption, replete with Divine intervention and miracles.

Likewise, different *tzadikim* who predicted various dates for the "End" perceived what the spiritual limits of the Jewish people would be from their own point of view, and we only see in retrospect how they underestimated the fullest potential of Israel. Nevertheless, since the Torah leaves room for a number of different interpretations of this issue, the *Talmud* attributes to all of them a certain legitimacy, referring to more than one theoretical possible notion of the "End."

(Furthermore, as the Haggadah stated above (p. 45), even in the Messianic Era we will mention the Egyptian Exodus, from which we see that a later "End" can somehow incorporate an earlier one).

Similarly, Rav himself argued that "all the Ends have passed," because, in his own estimation, enough had already been achieved to realize "the full perfection of the Messianic Era." But clearly, subsequent sages, who suggested later dates for the End, understood that the Jewish people were capable of more.

"וַיֹּאמֶר לְאַבְרָם, יָדֹעַ תֵּדַע כִּי גֵר יִהְיֶה זַרְעֲךָ
בְּאֶרֶץ לֹא לָהֶם וַעֲבָדוּם וְעִנּוּ אֹתָם, אַרְבַּע
מֵאוֹת שָׁנָה: וְגַם אֶת־הַגּוֹי אֲשֶׁר יַעֲבֹדוּ דָּן
אָנֹכִי, וְאַחֲרֵי־כֵן יֵצְאוּ בִּרְכֻשׁ גָּדוֹל:"

➤ COVER THE MATZOS AND HOLD THE CUP IN YOUR HAND.

TORAS MENACHEM

Where does all this leave us now? The most recent "End" predicted (by the Previous Lubavitcher Rebbe, Rabbi Yosef Yitzchak Schneersohn), was in 5703 (1943). Since then, many decades have passed, and no leader has emerged who is able to predict another "End." The only explanation, therefore, is that while in the times of the *Talmud* it was not yet the case that, "all the Ends have passed," *this is true now, in the most literal sense.*

"The End" refers to a limitation imposed by God, that He refuses to bring the redemption until a certain time—or, to be precise, a certain amount of worship—has been completed. But now, He could not possibly demand anything more from us. In 5703 we were clearly very close indeed (as the Previous Rebbe said, "we are standing ready in our uniforms to greet Mashiach and it only remains for us to polish our buttons"), and since then we have suffered the remaining atrocities of the Holocaust, only to witness Judaism flourish in the subsequent decades. So the "End" has now, for sure, passed; in other words, sufficient worship must have been carried out to satisfy God's demands for *"the full perfection of the Messianic Era."*

The glaring proof of this point is that in our generation we have witnessed drastic changes in human civilization which were predicted long ago by the Sages as signs of imminent redemption. At the end of Tractate *Sotah* we have been warned that as a prelude to Mashiach's coming *chutzpah* (insolence) will be predominant; government policy will be agnostic; people will be so sinful that they cannot rebuke each other; people who fear sin will be despised; truth will be absent; the young will shame their seniors in public; children will rebel against their parents; and a man's enemies will be the members of his own household (*Sotah* 49b). Does this not bear an uncanny resemblance to contemporary society?

Furthermore, and this is perhaps more remarkable, we see global changes *for the good* that have strong messianic overtones. For example, Jewish law has always obligated us to spread monotheism and morality amongst non-Jews (*Rambam, Laws of Kings* 8:10), but throughout history it has never been possible to fulfil the *mitzvah*, since it would have endangered our very lives to be seen as proselytizing members of other faiths. Yet, nowadays, the gentile world welcomes our efforts in this area, and admires us for it. So, without doubt, *"All the Ends have passed,"* for why would God send signs of redemption such as these—and so many others—to this world if the time was not already ripe?

In fact, it could no longer even be said that *"the matter depends solely on repentance,"* since one thought would suffice for this purpose (see *Shulchan Aruch, Even ha-Ezer* 38:31; *Igeres ha-Teshuvah* ch. 1), and, by now, virtually all Jews must have contemplated *teshuvah* at some time or another.

So the question remains: If there is no limitation being imposed by God (no "End"), and man is ready for the redemption, then where is Mashiach?

Obviously, nobody can answer this question. But what we *can* do is seek an uncharted path which might bridge the remaining gap.

In the past, an acute messianic awareness is something we found almost exclusively among Jewish leaders. They were the ones who calculated the "End" and, to a great extent, the people relied on their leaders to bring them to the redemption.

Now, however, that "all Ends have passed," *the responsibility must pass from the leader to the people.* Every Jew, man, woman and child, should make it his or her business to develop an acute longing for Mashiach. We should take to heart *Rambam's*

'You should know that your descendants will be strangers in a land that is not theirs where they will be enslaved and oppressed for four hundred years. Then I will pronounce judgment on the nation whom they will serve, and afterwards they will leave with great wealth'" (*Bereishis* 15:13-14).

➤ COVER THE MATZOS AND HOLD THE CUP IN YOUR HAND.

=== CLASSIC QUESTIONS ===

● **How did God keep His promise in full?**

TALMUD: God said to Moshe: Please, go and tell Israel to please ask from the Egyptians vessels of silver and gold, so it cannot be said by that righteous man [Avraham]: God fulfilled for them, *"They will be enslaved and oppressed,"* but He did not fulfill for them, *"afterwards they will leave with great wealth."*

Upon hearing this, the Jews said to Moshe: "If only we could escape with our lives!"

A parable: A man was kept in prison and people were telling him, "Tomorrow, they will release you from the prison and give you plenty of money."

He answered them, "Please, let me go free today and I will ask for nothing more!" (*Brachos* 9a-b).

IYUN YA'AKOV: Surely God was obliged to keep His word in any case, so why does the *Talmud* imply that the Jews left with "great wealth" merely due to a potential complaint of Avraham?

To answer this question the *Talmud* explains that the Jewish people themselves were willing to forgo the great wealth so as to leave Egypt a moment sooner. Avraham, however, was insistent that the Jewish people be rewarded in full (ibid.).

● **Why was it decreed that the Jews must be exiled if they had not sinned?**

ARIZAL: To extract sparks of holiness which had fallen into the hands of the forces of evil (*Likutei Torah, Parshas Vayeitzei*).

=== TORAS MENACHEM ===

ruling that *"a person should always see...the world as equally balanced between good and evil and by doing one good deed, he can bring salvation to himself and to the entire world"* (*Laws of Teshuvah* 3:4). In other words, all the details of our observance, even those which have no open connection with the redemption, need to be infused with messianic fervor and hope. For if God is ready, and the world is ready, then the only thing that could possibly remain is for people's hearts to be ready for Mashiach.

Of course, this is no easy matter. To observe Jewish law properly requires an excruciating attention to detail and a strong will to obey fixed rules. Messianic fervor, on the other hand, demands quite the opposite emotion: the desire to break free from confinement and embrace the transcendent.

Nevertheless, these two simultaneous qualities are demanded from us—after all, the elusiveness of God's

redemption could not be captured by one simple emotion. It is a carefully nuanced path of passion and persistence, obsession and obedience; a harmony of the radical and the traditional that is now required.

(Based on *Sichas Shabbos Parshas Devarim* 5740; *Purim* 5747; *Motzaie Shabbos Parshas Bo* 5737; *Shabbos Parshas Vayigash & Vayechi* 5747)

וְאַחֲרֵי כֵן יֵצְאוּ בִּרְכוּשׁ גָּדוֹל ‏ 🙾 — *And afterwards they will leave with great wealth.*

The *Talmud* relates that after many years of slavery, Israel's spirit was sufficiently crushed that they were willing to forego "great wealth" so as to leave Egypt without delay. Avraham, however, was not willing to let this opportunity pass. His insistence was that the Jewish people must leave with their promised fortune and as a result, says the *Talmud*, God obliged.

וְהִיא שֶׁעָמְדָה לַאֲבוֹתֵינוּ וְלָנוּ, שֶׁלֹּא
אֶחָד בִּלְבָד עָמַד עָלֵינוּ לְכַלּוֹתֵנוּ,
אֶלָּא שֶׁבְּכָל־דּוֹר וָדוֹר עוֹמְדִים עָלֵינוּ לְכַלּוֹתֵנוּ,
וְהַקָּדוֹשׁ בָּרוּךְ הוּא מַצִּילֵנוּ מִיָּדָם:

➤ PLACE THE CUP BACK ON THE TABLE AND UNCOVER THE MATZOS.

TORAS MENACHEM

But if the Jewish people *themselves* were willing to forgo this opportunity to become rich, then what business did Avraham have in vetoing their decision? Surely they were entitled to relinquish their own rights to the silver and gold of Egypt?

Evidently, the "great wealth" was much more than the "icing on the cake" of redemption. If this opportunity had been missed, something fundamental would have been sorely lacking in the whole Divine plan of exile and redemption.

To fathom this point, we need to turn ourselves briefly to the most tormenting of all existential questions: Why are we here? How do we make sense of the pain, desire, pleasure and fear that are the stuff of the human experience?

Conventionally, Judaism teaches us to perceive life as a war between the good and evil within our souls, where we are given, in every instance, the free choice as to which direction to take. But since evil is an offense to God, only existing so as to give us free choice, it will not persist forever. Axiomatic to this drama is an end to life as we know it, when evil will be eliminated and man will be rewarded for his positive decisions throughout history.

While generally satisfying, a significant weakness of this theology is that we are left with a certain discord between the period of struggle (worship) and the period of relief (reward). As long as we are worshipping God, our actions take on a super-human significance in that we are carrying out *His* will, something far greater than any mortal achievement or experience. But then, in an apparent anticlimax, we are promised an eternal period of *our* reward, which will clearly be limited to the scope of human experience. It seems that having acted as loyal agents of God for so many years, we will be sent to "retire" for eternity with a

meager spiritual "pension" which could never compete with the *real,* meaningful action of our erstwhile "career." For us it might be more of a pleasurable experience than sweating away in exile, but in the broader picture it seems nothing less than being doomed to eternal mediocrity.

We need, therefore, to explain how the future period of reward and redemption will represent genuine *progress* from the period that precedes it.

Enter the *Arizal,* Rabbi Yitzchak Luria, the celebrated Kabbalist of 16th Century Tzefas, whose fresh insight into the mystical teachings of the Kabbalah gives the story of mankind a new twist.

Central to our discussion is the doctrine of *Tikun,* the global restitution of a primordial, spiritual defect which occurred at the outset of creation. Of course we all know that the world is flawed and that man is here to fix it, but *Tikun* depicts *how* and *why* this is the case, with a remarkably precise and vivid imagery.

Initially, we are told, there was light: God emanated and radiated His presence outwards. But since the Divine plan was heading towards the creation of finite beings, it was necessary that this light should be captured and crystallized in special "vessels" that would absorb some of the light's sting.

Then, quite strangely, a sort of cosmic "catastrophe" occurred, a pivotal event which explains the whole drama of history and determines man's place in it: *The light proved too much for the vessels and they shattered.*

As a result of this disaster, sparks of God's light trapped in the fragments of these vessels were scattered throughout all the worlds. To lift up the scattered sparks of light and to restore them to their home is the essential task of man in the process of *Tikun.*

**WHAT ARE WE
DOING NOW?**
*The custom of
raising the cup
here is Kabbalistic
(unlike below
p. 132, when we
raise the cup
as a Halachic
requirement)
(Likutei Ta'amim
u'Minhagim).*

AND IT IS THIS that has stood by our fathers and us! For not just one alone has risen against us to destroy us, but in each and every generation they rise against us to destroy us—and the Holy One, blessed be He, saves us from their hand!

➤ PLACE THE CUP BACK ON THE TABLE AND UNCOVER THE MATZOS.

CLASSIC QUESTIONS

● *"And it is this...."* What does "this" refer to?

LIKUTEI TA'AMIM U'MINHAGIM: To *God's* promise to the prophets to redeem us from this final exile, as we said above, *"Blessed is He Who keeps His Promise to the Jewish People."*

ARIZAL: "This" refers to *our* inner fountains of faith.

TORAS MENACHEM

This notion of the "breaking of the vessels" adds tremendous color and depth to the two most pressing of all theological issues: the existence of evil, and man's role in eliminating it. As long as the damage is not mended, an inner flaw persists in everything that exists. For when the vessels were broken, some of the light diffused back to its source, but some fell downwards, providing a source of sustenance to the forces of evil. The aim of creation, therefore, is to extract the remaining sparks that are trapped in this world so as to restore the earlier, ideal order.

The point which now emerges so powerfully is that we are the architects of our own redemption. Gone is the notion of a human struggle and test, followed by a totally disparate era of Divine grace and relief. Now salvation means nothing other than the cumulative effect of returning all the sparks to their source, through observing the *mitzvos,* which inevitably starves the forces of evil of their sustenance. The perfection of the future is no longer seen as an alternative or replacement for the struggle of history, rather, it is the *natural result* of that struggle.

Our "reward," therefore, will be nothing other than the sense of satisfaction that our very own hands have brought the Divine plan to its conclusion. God no longer "pays" us for our work with something that is spiritually inferior to the holy work itself; rather, *"the reward for the mitzvah is the mitzvah itself"* (*Avos* 4:2), i.e., we will be granted a thorough appreciation of the colossal significance of our own actions, which we performed as agents of God. *Tikun* thus sees every Jew as an active protagonist in the great messianic struggle.

Since an object's financial value is a measure of its general worth and importance, it therefore gives us an idea of how many sparks are invested in the object. So when the Torah tells us that the Jewish people left Egypt with "great wealth," it means that they succeeded in extracting all the sparks that were buried in Egypt, ever since the breaking of the vessels, ensuring that the trapped Divine light returned safely to its source.

In the final analysis, therefore, God's promise to "leave with great wealth" was not a footnote to the general notion of redemption, but rather, *it represented the very purpose of the exile itself.* No wonder, then, that even if the Jewish people were willing to forgo this bounty, God nevertheless *"kept His promise to the Jewish people"*—that they would be the central players in healing the cosmos and restoring it to its original harmony.

(Based on *Likutei Sichos* vol. 3, p. 827*ff;* vol. 29, pp. 14-15; *Sichas Shabbos Parshas Eikev* 5749)

וְהִיא שֶׁעָמְדָה לַאֲבוֹתֵינוּ וְלָנוּ — *And it is this that has stood by our fathers and us!.*

What is the connection between the literal interpretation of the word "this," that it refers to *God's* promise to redeem us (*Likutei Ta'amim u'Minhagim*), and the Kabbalistic interpretation (*Arizal*), that it refers to *our own* reserves of faith?

The answer is that when we have faith in God, it inspires Him, so to speak, to have faith in us, and consequently, He keeps His promise to redeem us.

(Based on *Sichah* of 2nd Night of Pesach 5721)

צֵא וּלְמַד מַה־בִּקֵּשׁ לָבָן הָאֲרַמִּי לַעֲשׂוֹת לְיַעֲקֹב אָבִינוּ, שֶׁפַּרְעֹה לֹא גָזַר אֶלָּא עַל הַזְּכָרִים וְלָבָן בִּקֵּשׁ לַעֲקוֹר אֶת־הַכֹּל, שֶׁנֶּאֱמַר:

"אֲרַמִּי אֹבֵד אָבִי, וַיֵּרֶד מִצְרַיְמָה וַיָּגָר שָׁם בִּמְתֵי מְעָט, וַיְהִי־שָׁם לְגוֹי גָּדוֹל עָצוּם וָרָב":

"וַיֵּרֶד מִצְרַיְמָה" — אָנוּס עַל־פִּי הַדִּבּוּר.

CLASSIC QUESTIONS

● **Why is the unusual term "Go out and learn" used? And how does this portion relate to the previous passage of the Haggadah?**

Ra'avan: The previous passage discussed how when *"they rise up against us to destroy us...God saves us from their hand."* The Haggadah now brings further proof for this statement: *"Go out and learn,"* that we know this is the case from the fact that when Lavan sought to eliminate Ya'akov and his family, God saved them.

● **Where do we see in the account of Ya'akov's life that Lavan *"sought to eliminate everyone"*?**

Shibolei ha-Leket: Upon reaching Ya'akov, who had fled from his home, Lavan said *"I am sufficiently strong to harm you,"* except that *"the God of your father spoke to me last night, saying 'beware'"* (*Bereishis* 31:29).

● **Why was Ya'akov *"compelled by Divine decree"* to go down to Egypt?**

Shibolei ha-Leket: Ya'akov would never have willingly gone to Egypt since he knew that it would eventually result in the slavery of his descendants.

Rashbatz: However, it had already been decreed at the "Covenant of the Parts" that Avraham's children would live in exile in another land, as the verse states, *"Your descendants will be strangers in a land that is not theirs"* (*Bereishis* 15:13). So Ya'akov was effectively compelled to go.

Likutei Ta'amim u'Minhagim: From a literal reading of the Torah it appears that Ya'akov went down to Egypt willingly, and was not "compelled." (Even here, the verse states that "he went down," not that he was "brought down"). Perhaps this is why *Rambam* omitted this passage from his text of the Haggadah.

TORAS MENACHEM

צֵא וּלְמַד מַה בִּקֵּשׁ לָבָן הָאֲרַמִּי לַעֲשׂוֹת לְיַעֲקֹב אָבִינוּ — *Go out and learn what Lavan the Aramean sought to do to Ya'akov our Patriarch.*

Like every Torah text, the precise choice of phrase here hints to powerful lessons in our daily lives. A problem that affects some people is an inability to absorb new ideas because their current outlook is too rigid. Having "lived life" and gone through a variety of experiences, it is only natural for a person to make certain presumptions about human nature and morality, about what is "normal" and acceptable.

Any new insight which challenges this firmly established outlook is intuitively rejected. The person finds it difficult to relate to ideas that do not sit well with his preconceived notions, which, as years pass by, are gradually carved in stone.

So the Haggadah teaches us: *"Go out and learn."* If you want to learn and be open to new ideas you first need to "go out" of your limited viewpoint of life. Cast away your preconceptions and you will find that your mind becomes greatly enriched.

(Based on *Sefer ha-Sichos* 5704, p. 91)

WHAT ARE WE
DOING NOW?
Following an
explicit directive
of the Mishnah
(Pesachim 116b),
we now expound
upon four verses
in Devarim
(26:5-8) in detail.

G O OUT and learn what Lavan the Aramean wanted to do to our father Ya'akov. Pharaoh only decreed against the males, but Lavan wanted to eliminate everyone, as the verse states:

"An Aramean sought to destroy my father. He went down to Egypt and sojourned there, few in number; and he became a nation there — great, mighty and numerous" (Devarim 26:5).

"He went down to Egypt" — compelled by Divine decree.

TORAS MENACHEM

פַּרְעֹה לֹא גָזַר אֶלָּא עַל הַזְּכָרִים וְלָבָן בִּקֵּשׁ לַעֲקוֹר אֶת הַכֹּל — *Pharaoh only decreed against the males, but Lavan sought to eliminate everyone.*

Lavan (Laban) was Ya'akov's father-in-law for whom he worked for many years while raising his family. During this time, Lavan was guilty of numerous acts of subterfuge and dishonesty, and the Haggadah informs us here that Lavan actually sought to eliminate Ya'akov and his descendants completely.

But why would Lavan wish to eliminate *his own family,* including his daughters and grandchildren? Was he simply insane?

What the Haggadah means to say is that Lavan's influence would have eventually *resulted* in the annihilation of his family, not that he actually intended to kill them. Here we are referring not to a physical demise, but to a form of moral and psychological deterioration.

Lavan was a cutthroat businessman who believed in the "survival of the fittest," and that honesty is not necessarily the best policy. So Lavan does not represent a Hitler, a Stalin or a Pharaoh, but a very common outlook which, unfortunately, is the *modus operandi* of the business world. Somehow we are led to believe that personal gain is of such paramount importance that it justifies the maltreatment of others, and even subterfuge or fraud. And all of this stems from the basic presumption that our own pleasure is of paramount importance, and that everything else must take second place.

Such an attitude is gravely misguided. Our Patriarch

Ya'akov understood that a life without meaning and purpose, a life without values and a sense of responsibility to a higher, spiritual calling, is no life at all. So if the children would be guided by Grandpa Lavan's influence, then Ya'akov's mission would be totally uprooted.

The lesson here is obvious. Our children need to be taught that there is a "Super-being" in this world, and that there is such a thing as "right" and "wrong." Life is not a game of seeking personal gain and outsmarting our colleagues and customers. Dishonesty is wrong, even if you never get caught, and true happiness will ultimately be found through acting as a God-fearing, upright citizen.

(Based on *Sefer ha-Sichos* 5704, p. 91; *Sefer ha-Ma'amarim* 5709, p. 221; *Sichas Yud Beis Tamuz* 5744)

וַיֵּרֶד מִצְרַיְמָה אָנוּס עַל פִּי הַדִּבּוּר — *"He went down to Egypt," compelled by Divine Decree.*

Why are we so religiously uninspired? Why is it so difficult for us to commit to higher standards of ethical behavior and *mitzvah* observance? Why is our appreciation of the spiritual caliber of Judaism so weak and tenuous?

Our Sages referred to this general mood of confusion and apathy as "exile," based on the conviction that Israel's subjugation to other nations has been responsible for compromising its fine qualities and intellectual heritage. We are but a scattered remnant, a glimmer of our former selves, so is it any wonder that the ways of the secular world rule supreme and Jewish values are degraded?

"וַיָּגָר שָׁם" — מְלַמֵּד שֶׁלֹּא יָרַד יַעֲקֹב
אָבִינוּ לְהִשְׁתַּקֵּעַ בְּמִצְרַיִם אֶלָּא
לָגוּר שָׁם, שֶׁנֶּאֱמַר: "וַיֹּאמְרוּ אֶל פַּרְעֹה לָגוּר
בָּאָרֶץ בָּאנוּ, כִּי־אֵין מִרְעֶה לַצֹּאן אֲשֶׁר לַעֲבָדֶיךָ
כִּי־כָבֵד הָרָעָב בְּאֶרֶץ כְּנָעַן, וְעַתָּה יֵשְׁבוּ־נָא עֲבָדֶיךָ
בְּאֶרֶץ גֹּשֶׁן":

TORAS MENACHEM

Of course, this might leave all but the greatest optimist in a state of despair. If the situation is so dire, how could it be repaired? Will it ever be possible to heal such a severely fractured world?

For a mystic, however, the question would be in the reverse: not *why* did the exile occur, but *how could* it have occurred? Consider for a moment that the soul which enlivens all of us is highly conscious of its Creator and that this intimate connection can never be compromised. We literally have a "piece of God" inside us and we take it wherever we go, no matter how far from our homeland we may be scattered and how severe our subjugation to other regimes may be. Therefore, the *Talmud* states that wherever the Jews were exiled, *"the Divine presence was with them"* (*Megilah* 29a), because the fact that their souls accompanied them meant that God was always there.

So the question is: *how could* this epidemic of spiritual apathy known as "exile" have occurred? If our souls are instinctively and intuitively aware of God, then surely we should have been immune to any sort of spiritual regression? Why did our souls fail to protect us?

There is no satisfactory answer to this question. It simply makes no sense at all. The only thing we can say is that God must have a grand plan which requires us to operate in a spiritually compromised state. That is what God has decreed, and no further insight can be gathered.

Thus the Haggadah declares: "He went down to Egypt, *compelled by Divine decree."* This uninspired state, this "journey down to Egypt" makes no sense at all; it is simply forced upon us "by Divine decree."

But, ultimately, the message is an encouraging one. For if we had truly regressed, if our exile had genuinely ruined our fine qualities, then the solution would be a very difficult one indeed. But in truth, our souls are immune to the exile, and the fact that we have fallen so low is because God has forced something upon us which essentially goes against the grain.

And that means that the solution is not too far away. As soon as this "Divine decree" will be annulled, we will naturally and effortlessly return to our true exalted state as "children of God, your God."

(Based on *Likutei Sichos* vol. 2, p. 540*ff*)

❧ וַיָּגָר שָׁם — *And he sojourned there.*

Ba'al ha-Turim writes that Ya'akov's last seventeen years in Egypt were the best of his life (commentary to *Bereishis* 47:28). As a small child, the *Tzemach Tzedek* (Rabbi Menachem Mendel of Lubavitch, 1789-1866) found this difficult to understand. "How could it be," he asked his grandfather, Rabbi Shneur Zalman of Liadi, "that Ya'akov's *best* years were spent in a corrupt and idolatrous land?"

His grandfather answered, based on the *Midrash*, that this was because there was a *yeshivah* (Torah academy) in Goshen, and therefore Ya'akov and his family were able to study Torah.

In this exchange, both the question and answer are hard to grasp. One would have imagined that Ya'akov's best years were spent in Egypt simply because he had now been reunited with his son Yosef, after so many years of estrangement. And if this is not the explanation, then why would the mere opportunity to study Torah in Egypt make this the greatest

"And he sojourned there" — this teaches that our father Ya'akov did not go down to settle in Egypt, but only to live there temporarily, as the verse states: "They said to Pharaoh, 'We have come to sojourn in the land, for your servants' flocks have no pasture, since the famine is severe in the Land of Cana'an. Now, please, let your servants settle in the Land of Goshen'" *(Bereishis 47:4).*

═══════════════ CLASSIC QUESTIONS ═══════════════

● **How do we know that Ya'akov only intended to be in Egypt temporarily?**

RA'AVAN: The verse uses the term "sojourn" (*lagur*), which indicates that he did not want to be there permanently, but only until the famine in the Land of Israel had ended.

● **Why did they settle in Goshen?**

RASHBATZ: Because it was near their homeland and thus easy to return from there.

═══════════════ TORAS MENACHEM ═══════════════

period of Ya'akov's life? Wouldn't his best years of Torah study have been spent in the Holy Land?

In the spiritually "safe" environment of the Land of Israel, Torah study was a form of *nourishment* for Ya'akov's soul; whereas in the religiously threatening atmosphere of Egypt, it was a form of *medicine,* to protect and heal him from the negative influences of his environment. And just as medicine is much more expensive than food, one has to spend much more energy and effort in Torah study for it to yield its medicinal properties. So Ya'akov's best years were spent in Egypt, while living in an environment which sought to compromise his connection to Torah, because this forced him to study the Torah with additional intensity.

(Based on *Sichas Shabbos Parshas Vayechi* 5732)

◈◈ וְעַתָּה יֵשְׁבוּ נָא עֲבָדֶיךָ בְּאֶרֶץ גֹּשֶׁן ◈◈ —*Now please let your servants settle in the Land of Goshen.*

The *Midrash* relates that when Pharaoh took our Matriarch Sarah into his house (see *Bereishis* 12:14*ff*), he showered her with gifts as an expression of his great love for her, including a document bequeathing her the land of Goshen as an inheritance. *"Therefore,"* says the *Midrash, "the Jewish people later settled in the Land of Goshen"* (*Pirkei d'Rabbi Eliezer,* ch. 26).

But if the Jews actually *owned* the land, how could their stay there be described as part of 210 years of Egyptian *exile?* How was it a fulfillment of God's

decree to Avraham that "Your descendants will be strangers in a land that is *not theirs*" (*Bereishis* 15:13)?

Two possible answers could be suggested:

a.) According to the *Midrash,* Ya'akov and his family established a *yeshivah* (academy) in Goshen where they dedicated themselves to Torah study, and, *"If any person takes upon himself the yoke of Torah, then the yoke of government and the yoke of worldly cares is removed from him"* (*Mishnah, Avos* 3:5). So even though they were in their own land at the time, the experience of exile was simulated by the self-imposed yoke of intense Torah study.

b.) More simply, one could argue that so long as a Jew is not found in his homeland, the Land of Israel, he remains in a foreign land *even if he owns it.* So even while dwelling in the Land of Goshen, which was their own private property, Ya'akov and his descendents were deeply pained to find themselves in "*a land that is not theirs,*" a land which did not possess the importance and holiness which was befitting them. And this itself was a subtle form of suffering or "exile."

(Based on *Likutei Sichos* vol. 15, pp. 408-9)

◈◈ בְּאֶרֶץ גֹּשֶׁן ◈◈ — *In the Land of Goshen.*

The Egyptian exile was more difficult to withstand than all the subsequent exiles—including the one in which we find ourselves now—for four reasons:

1. The Egyptian exile preceded the giving of the Torah. Therefore, Judaism was not yet a complete,

"בִּמְתֵי מְעָט" – כְּמָה שֶׁנֶּאֱמַר: "בְּשִׁבְעִים נֶפֶשׁ יָרְדוּ אֲבֹתֶיךָ מִצְרָיְמָה, וְעַתָּה שָׂמְךָ יְהֹוָה אֱלֹהֶיךָ כְּכוֹכְבֵי הַשָּׁמַיִם לָרֹב":

CLASSIC QUESTIONS

● **Scripture only makes explicit mention of sixty-nine members of Ya'akov's family at the time they entered Egypt. Who was the seventieth?**

PIRKEI D'RABBI ELIEZER: God joined them as the seventieth, as the verse states, *"I will go down with you to Egypt"* (Bereishis 46:4; Pirkei d'Rabbi Eliezer ch. 39).

IBN EZRA: Ya'akov himself was the seventieth soul (Bereishis 46:23; see also Rashbam, Hadar Zekeinim, Ralbag, Abarbanel and Ohr ha-Chayim).

TALMUD: Yocheved (Moshe's mother) was the seventieth soul. She is not listed, since she was born just as they entered Egypt (Bava Basra 123b; see Rashi to 46:15).

● **What is the significance of *seventy* souls?**

RASHI: The seventy members of Ya'akov's family correspond to the seventy nations of the world. The Sanhedrin (Jewish Supreme Court) also had seventy judges (commentary to Bereishis 35:11).

TORAS MENACHEM

God-given system, which meant that its ability to inspire the people with courage and resilience was limited.

2. If a person suffers a particular type of tragedy several times, God forbid, the first occasion is always the hardest, being a totally new experience. Thus, on a national level, the first exile in Egypt was the most difficult for the Jewish people.

3. In the subsequent exiles the Jewish people were scattered over the world, whereas here they were together. This meant that in Egypt our enemies were able to persecute us all together in one swoop, whereas in later exiles, even when one part of the nation suffered, another was able to have at least some peace.

4. Egypt was unparalleled in history as an oppressor, to the extent that, prior to the Exodus, not one person had ever slipped through their fingers and fled the country (Mechilta and Rashi to Shemos 18:9).

Despite these four elements of hardship which were unique to the Egyptian exile, we are taught that the Jewish people nevertheless established and maintained a *yeshivah* (Torah academy) in Goshen (Rashi to Bereishis 46:28).

From here we can learn the importance of both supporting *yeshivos* financially, and of giving our children a *yeshivah* education. Formal Torah study is simply the secret of the Jewish people's survival— *"ever since the days of our Patriarchs there was never a time without a yeshivah"* (Yomah 28b)—and if it was

possible to support full-time Torah students in Egypt, then it is certainly possible to do so in our times.

(Based on *Likutei Sichos* vol. 1, p. 95ff)

בְּשִׁבְעִים נֶפֶשׁ יָרְדוּ אֲבֹתֶיךָ מִצְרָיְמָה — *When your fathers went down to Egypt they were seventy souls.*

Scripture only names sixty-nine souls who went down to Egypt, and the commentators offer various suggestions as to who the elusive seventieth soul was: Yocheved, Ya'akov, or perhaps God Himself? (See *Classic Questions*.) Apparently, the identity of the seventieth soul reflects a certain perception of this crucial moment when Ya'akov's family "went down to Egypt," where they would subsequently be enslaved, redeemed and given the Torah. The addition of one more element was necessary to ensure that this mission would be successful, to charge the people with an extra "soul power." But, argue the commentators, what was the crucial extra ingredient needed?

The most straightforward approach was taken by **Pirkei d'Rabbi Eliezer**, that "God joined them as the seventieth soul," because, understandably, they needed Divine assistance to overcome the immense ordeals that lay ahead. Likewise, **Ibn Ezra's** view, that Ya'akov was the seventieth soul, is easy to appreciate, because Ya'akov was their Patriarch whose pristine soul would surely inspire them and charge them with resilience.

"Few in number" — as the verse states: "When your fathers went down to Egypt they were seventy souls, but now God your God has made you as numerous as the stars of the skies" *(Devarim 10:22).*

But how are we to understand that the Jewish people's historic mission received crucial assistance at this point from the soul of Yocheved, a baby girl?

(Of course, Yocheved's role was instrumental in that she would later give birth to Moshe, the redeemer of the Jewish people. But there must also be some quality about Yocheved *herself* that made her addition at this point so important).

Judaism is, essentially, a "feminine" religion. As a religious and ethical system, it seeks to change the world into a better place, but its approach to achieving this goal is a uniquely feminine one.

"A man's nature," says the *Talmud, "is to conquer, but it is not a woman's nature to conquer"* (*Yevamos* 65b). Conquering means to subdue, to overcome and to possess by force. A man wishes to acquire, to expand his empire, and he does so by utilizing whatever power he has at his disposal.

But a woman desires not to conquer, but to *nurture.* She takes a fertilized egg and, for nine months, patiently provides all the support required for it to develop. When the child is born, the same task continues: Her instinct and natural talent is to offer support and affection to her child, and to provide everything that the child may need, both physically and emotionally. As a homemaker, the woman excels in bringing beauty and serenity to her environment. Everything she touches is enhanced—the decorations, the furnishings, the food—and the overall mood in the home is largely to her credit.

In other words, a woman transforms her world from within, by nurturing it, bringing its latent qualities to the surface, and helping it to grow at its own pace.

Judaism's mission is monotheism, to demonstrate how the diverse aspects of this world are expressions of one God. This could be done in two ways. A masculine approach would be to "impose" God on the world, to show how everything is *insignificant* compared to its Creator, and to *coerce* people to be righteous.

But if God is truly One then we can do more than that: we can reveal how even the tiniest detail of this world is *significant* because it contains a spark of the Divine, and its inner identity is nothing other than an expression of God. We can embrace people *as they are,* encouraging them to come to an awareness of the truth *by themselves,* and *support* their efforts to become better people.

So true monotheism is feminine. It seeks to nurture the inner sanctity of every being on this planet, not by degrading it, conquering it or replacing it with something else, but by bringing its true, Godly identity to the surface.

And that is why, at this moment in history when the monotheistic mission began to unfold, the seventy souls of Ya'akov's family were "completed" by Yocheved, a woman. Because the ultimate goal of monotheism—to teach all seventy nations about God (cf. *Rashi*)—lies in the feminine approach.

(Based on *Likutei Sichos* vol. 20, p. 218*ff*)

וְעַתָּה שָׂמְךָ יְהוָה אֱלֹהֶיךָ כְּכוֹכְבֵי הַשָּׁמַיִם לָרֹב — ◌
Now God, your God, has made you as numerous as the stars of the skies.

Every Jew is a complete world in himself and has a God-given task from the Creator-of-man; a task that has to be carried out in the fullest measure, according to the capacities that have been given him. This task has to be carried out by each person himself, individually, without relying on someone else, or on the Jewish community, to carry out his task for him.

On the other hand, he must know that he is a part of the *one people*, composed of millions and millions of Jews (may their numbers increase), a nation blessed *"as numerous as the stars of the skies."*

In a deeper sense, it is *one people* that is composed of all generations of Jews, from the time of the giving of the Torah to the end of time.

It is clear, therefore, that everyone's task is an integral part of the whole community of Israel and that the good of the community outweighs personal considerations and personal interests.

It also follows that when a Jew acts for the benefit of the community, for the good of the *one people* that

"וַיְהִי- שָׁם לְגוֹי" — מְלַמֵּד שֶׁהָיוּ יִשְׂרָאֵל מְצֻיָּנִים שָׁם:

"גָּדוֹל עָצוּם" — כְּמָה שֶׁנֶּאֱמַר: "וּבְנֵי יִשְׂרָאֵל פָּרוּ וַיִּשְׁרְצוּ וַיִּרְבּוּ וַיַּעַצְמוּ בִּמְאֹד מְאֹד, וַתִּמָּלֵא הָאָרֶץ אֹתָם:"

CLASSIC QUESTIONS

● **How were the Jewish people "distinct"?**

ABARBANEL: They did not change their names, language, religion or style of clothing (from *Shemos Rabah* ch. 1 and *Midrash Lekach Tov, Parshas Va'eira*).

RI BEN YAKAR: A group of people which is dispersed and indistinguishable from their neighbors cannot properly be called a nation, since there is no reason to refer to them separately. The fact that the verse refers to them as a "nation" indicates that they were distinctive there, preserving their language and dress and observing the *mitzvos*.

MIDRASH: The Israelites were redeemed from Egypt on account of four things: They did not change their language or style of dress; they did not speak *lashon hara* (gossip); and not one person was involved in illicit behavior (*Vayikra Rabah* 32:5).

● **How did the people "swarm"?**

RASHI: The women had sextuplets.

TORAS MENACHEM

embraces *all* generations, he draws strength from the inexhaustible wellspring of the *eternal people*, and he is bound to succeed in this effort, and thereby also in all of his personal affairs, both material and spiritual.

May God grant that everyone, man and woman, should indeed be thoroughly permeated with the thought and remembrance, of both extremes: That he (or she) is a complete world, which he (or she) must make a true living Jewish world, and at the same time—a part of the *one people* comprising all generations, which gives each and every Jew, man, woman, and child, extraordinary capacities, coupled with an extraordinary privilege and responsibility toward the Jewish community; hence there is no room for being discouraged by any difficulties in carrying out one's God-given task; all the more so, considering that the difficulties are all his, whereas the benefit is (also and especially) for the Jewish community.

(Excerpt from communal letter, 25 Adar II 5742)

☙ **וַיְהִי שָׁם לְגוֹי** — *And he became a nation there.*

A nation is usually formed by a group of individuals who share a common characteristic, geographic location or belief system. The Jewish people, on the other hand, acquired their national identity by Divine selection, as *Rambam* writes, "*God chose Israel as His heritage and He crowned them with commandments*" (*Laws of Idol Worship,* end of ch. 1).

At first glance, one would imagine that God chose the Jewish people due to some superior quality that inspired Him to take this nation for Himself. But, explains Chasidic thought, opting for a superior product over an inferior one is not really a "choice" at all. Could you say, for example, that when offered a gift of either $100 or $1000, a person genuinely *chose* the latter? If something is objectively more valuable or impressive there simply is no decision to be made. A real choice, which is an expression of individuality, must be a subjective one, where all the options are effectively equal but the person nevertheless expresses a personal preference for one of them.

This makes it a little easier to understand how God could have chosen a group of Israelites who had sunk into idol worship and sin, not too different from their fellow Egyptians. God did not select us due to

"And he became a nation there" — this teaches that the Israelites were recognizably distinct there.

"Great, mighty" — as the verse states: "And the children of Israel were fruitful and swarmed and increased and became very, very strong; and the land became filled with them" (*Shemos* 1:7).

TORAS MENACHEM

any positive quality, but simply because He chose to do so arbitrarily. His choice tells us something about Him, more than something about us.

(In fact, this is the inner reason why He chose us *specifically* when we had sunken so low and were serving idols, because then it was obvious that the choice was not based on our merits, but rather, on God's personal preference, so to speak.)

However, while we were not in need of any merit to be selected by God, we did at least need to be identified so that the actual "choice" could take place. God chose a single nation, so there had to be a certain level of cohesiveness among us, some distinctive qualities which made clear what the definition of an "Israelite" was.

Therefore it was crucial that the Jewish people did not change their names or dress—not because this was a particular merit or an expression of loyalty to tradition, but simply because it enabled us to be *identified* as a single nation so that God could choose us. Likewise, it was crucial that we did not speak *lashon hara* (gossip), not because of the sinful nature of this activity—for the people were in any case very sinful—but because the Israelites needed to stay *distinct* from their neighbors, the Egyptians, and not gossip to them about other Jews.

For us, the message is an uplifting one. If being Jewish depended on having some sort of merit, then there would always remain the possibility that we would cease to exist as a nation if that merit was lacking. But since we know that God chose the Jewish people regardless of their merits, we are assured that the nation of Israel will endure forever.

(Based on *Likutei Sichos* vol. 31, p. 10*ff*)

שֶׁהָיוּ יִשְׂרָאֵל מְצֻיָּנִים שָׁם — *The Israelites were recognizably distinct there.*

Like in Egypt, it is just as important today that a Jew remains distinct from the world around him. When it comes to food, a Jew must keep kosher; his

clothing must be free of *shatnez* (forbidden wool and linen mixture), and he must wear *tzitzis*. His ethics and values are to come from Jewish law, and not from his surrounding culture.

All this could be perceived as sending the message that we should isolate ourselves from the rest of the world as much as possible so as to remain "distinct." Perhaps the Haggadah is telling us to disengage from reality, sever our connections with the people around us and retreat into the safe haven of an utterly Jewish enclave?

Nothing could be further from the truth. As much as we are to be *apart* from the world, we must also be *part* of it. The Divine plan, to sanctify every corner of this globe, requires us to be involved with society and to be in touch with reality; to be genuinely *in* the world so that we can influence it positively.

Nevertheless, the Jew must *also* remain "distinct" so that he is not swallowed up by secularity, and always remains conscious of his sacred mission.

(Based on *Sichah* of the 2nd night of Pesach 5717)

וּבְנֵי יִשְׂרָאֵל פָּרוּ וַיִּשְׁרְצוּ — *The children of Israel were fruitful and swarmed.*

The term "swarmed" (*vayishretzu*) is a derivative of the word *sheretz*, which means "vermin." This indicates that the Jewish people multiplied as quickly as mice, having sextuplets (see *Rashi*). Likewise, the *Midrash* teaches, *"The verse compares them to the greatest of the vermin, the mouse, which gives birth to six at a time"* (*Yalkut Shimoni*).

This begs the question: Why does the Torah use such an unflattering term in reference to the Jewish people, a word which speaks of vermin? Would it not be preferable for the verse to say explicitly that each woman had sextuplets, so as to avoid such a disparaging turn of phrase?

If the Torah would have stated that women were having six children at a time, we would presume that it was an outright miracle. But such a conclusion

"וָרָב"

— כְּמָה שֶׁנֶּאֱמַר: "רְבָבָה כְּצֶמַח הַשָּׂדֶה נְתַתִּיךְ, וַתִּרְבִּי וַתִּגְדְּלִי וַתָּבֹאִי בַּעֲדִי עֲדָיִים, שָׁדַיִם נָכֹנוּ וּשְׂעָרֵךְ צִמֵּחַ, וְאַתְּ עֵרֹם וְעֶרְיָה: וָאֶעֱבֹר עָלַיִךְ וָאֶרְאֵךְ מִתְבּוֹסֶסֶת בְּדָמָיִךְ, וָאֹמַר לָךְ בְּדָמַיִךְ חֲיִי וָאֹמַר לָךְ בְּדָמַיִךְ חֲיִי":

CLASSIC QUESTIONS

● **The Haggadah cites *two* verses to prove that the Jewish people were numerous (Ezekiel 15:5-6), but how does the *first* verse prove this point?**

LIKUTEI TA'AMIM U'MINHAGIM: The words *"By your blood you shall live"* indicate that the Jewish people increased even more when they were persecuted, as the verse states, *"As much as they would afflict them, so did they multiply"* (Shemos 1:12).

● **Why are the Jewish people compared to "plants of the field"?**

ABARBANEL: We would have assumed that due to the intense suffering of the Egyptian exile many children must have died. Therefore the verse tells us that they were like plants of the field, which need no care and grow without special attention.

● **How were the people "naked and bare"?**

MECHILTA: When the time had arrived for the Jewish people to be freed, they did not possess any *mitzvos* with which to busy themselves in order to be worthy of redemption, as the verse states, *"You were naked and bare."*

Therefore, God gave them two *mitzvos*: the blood of the Pesach lamb, and the blood of circumcision, for they circumcised themselves on that night, as the verse states, *"I saw you weltering in your bloods."* (The use of the plural, "bloods," suggests two types of blood.)

Because they were immersed in idolatry, God said to them, *"Draw and buy for yourselves"* lambs and sheep (Shemos 12:21), as if to say, "Withdraw from idolatry and buy for yourselves a lamb in order to fulfill a *mitzvah*!" (Mechilta to Shemos 12:6).

TORAS MENACHEM

would not fit in with a literal reading of the story here. A few verses later we read that the Egyptians made plans to curb the growth of the Jewish people: *"Come let us act cunningly with them, lest they increase"* (v. 10), and "acting cunningly" would obviously be insufficient to stop an open miracle from God.

Apparently, the Egyptians perceived the rapid growth of the Jewish people as being a natural phenomenon, albeit an admittedly unusual one. It was not, they imagined, the hand of God, but something which nature itself had made possible.

As a hint to this, when describing the way in which the Jewish people multiplied, the Torah employs a term which describes a rapid *natural* reproduction.

(Based on *Sichas Shabbos Parshas Shemos* 5748)

Just as the Jewish people left the Egyptian exile after "swarming and increasing," there is a parallel to be found with our generation, the culmination of the current exile:

a.) Our Sages teach that Mashiach (the Messiah) will come when all the souls stored in heaven have come down to earth (*Yevamos* 62a). Thus, by having another child, we hasten the redemption.

b.) *"Any person who teaches another Torah is considered to have given birth to him"* (Sanhedrin 19b). Thus, each of us should seek to have an abundance of spiritual "children." (Interestingly, the *Midrashic* view is that each woman gave birth to twelve or even sixty children—*Shemos Rabah* 1:8).

c.) The Alter Rebbe (Rabbi Shneur Zalman of Liadi) taught that the first commandment of the Torah,

"And numerous" — as the verse states: "I caused you to thrive like the plants of the field, and you increased, and grew, and became very adorned, your bosom fashioned and your hair grown long; yet you were naked and bare. When I passed over you and saw you weltering in your bloods, I said to you, 'By your blood you shall live,' and I said to you, 'By your blood shall you live!'" (Ezekiel 16:6-7).

TORAS MENACHEM

to "be fruitful and multiply," means also, to "give birth" to another Jew by bringing him or her close to observant Judaism. In our generation, the last of the current exile, we must simply endeavor to reach every Jew!

(Based on *Sichas Shabbos Parshas Shemos* 5722; *Vayikra* 5743; *Behar-Bechukosai* 5751, note 128)

☙ רְבָבָה כְּצֶמַח הַשָּׂדֶה נְתַתִּיךְ — *I caused you to thrive like the plants of the field.*

Ultimately, we can only thrive, physically or spiritually, if we are independent. So long as we rely on someone else to feed us, to teach us or to inspire us, there will always be a limit to growth. But when we can earn a living by ourselves, study Torah unaided and inspire ourselves on a daily basis, then there is no limit to what we can achieve; it is simply a matter of how much effort we are willing to invest.

Independence, and the immense benefits that it brings, cannot be acquired overnight. Any job must have a period of apprenticeship, and to acquire the skills necessary to study unaided, many years of tutelage are required. So in order to become a powerful, independent entity we first must undergo a period of total dependence, a time when we do nothing but absorb.

For an egocentric creature such as man, this is no easy task. Our nature is to lead and not to follow. We all want to be rich so that we can give to others and exercise power over them, and not poor so that we are forced to receive our bare livelihood from others. Thinking and acting independently are the instinctive norms for a human being, which makes any period of dependency very difficult.

But if we wish to acquire new skills there is no alternative. For a short while at least, we need to dismantle our defenses, open our minds and listen to somebody else.

Chasidic thought sums up this process with an esoteric rule of thumb: *Any "something" that wishes to be transformed into a greater "something," must first become a "nothing."*

A physical illustration of this process is the planting of a seed. Initially the seed is a self-sufficient entity: It is rich in nutrients, well protected by its shell and has a long shelf-life. But it is small—pitifully small—and needs desperately to grow.

The transition from seed to tree, from an independent "something" to a much greater and more sophisticated "something," must first pass through a phase of "nothing": *the seed must shed its outer shell and absorb from the earth.* Only in this way can it benefit from the vast repositories of nutrients in the ground which it will need in order to become a tree.

In Egypt, our ancestors' spiritual standing was pitifully low. Even the adults only had simple, undeveloped faith, like that of a small child. In order to grow to the extent that they were fit to receive the Torah, to be "very adorned" with the commandments, they had to shed their outer shell and "decompose" like a seed, through the Egyptian exile.

This is why the Haggadah employs the analogy of plants, *"I caused you to thrive like plants of the field,"* because it accurately depicts the way in which the Jewish people ascended to greatness, through the experience of exile—the phase of "nothing" in-between two "somethings".

(Based on *Sefer ha-Ma'amarim* 5722, p. 177; *Likutei Torah, Pekudei* 4d; *Sha'arei Ohrah*, 63a)

☙ וְאַתְּ עֵרֹם וְעֶרְיָה — *You were naked and bare.*

According to *Mechilta*, the two *mitzvos* of slaughtering the Pesach lamb and becoming circumcised were demanded of the Jewish people at this point to eliminate a spiritual handicap: the absence of merit through which to be redeemed.

"וַיָּרֵעוּ אֹתָנוּ הַמִּצְרִים וַיְעַנּוּנוּ, וַיִּתְּנוּ עָלֵינוּ עֲבֹדָה קָשָׁה":

"וַיָּרֵעוּ אֹתָנוּ הַמִּצְרִים" — כְּמָה שֶׁנֶּאֱמַר: "הָבָה נִתְחַכְּמָה לוֹ, פֶּן־יִרְבֶּה וְהָיָה כִּי־תִקְרֶאנָה מִלְחָמָה וְנוֹסַף גַּם־הוּא עַל־שֹׂנְאֵינוּ וְנִלְחַם־בָּנוּ וְעָלָה מִן־הָאָרֶץ":

CLASSIC QUESTIONS

● **How did the Egyptians "treat us badly"? And where do we see this in the verse, "Come, let us act cunningly"?**

ORCHOS CHAIM: The verse cited here does not mention any actual harm done by the Egyptians to the Jews. Therefore the term "treated us badly" must mean that the Egyptians *perceived us* as being an evil threat, which is why they plotted against us, "Come let us act cunningly." They treated us as bad.

LIKUTEI TA'AMIM U'MINHAGIM: "They treated us badly" means that their intention was not merely to enslave us (to "make us suffer"), but to find ways of being bad to us and mistreating us as much as possible. This is clearly proven by the verse that depicts plotting and scheming, "Come, let us act cunningly..."

SHALOH: The term *vayareiu osanu* could also be rendered "they made us bad," indicating that the Egyptians made us into evil people like themselves because we learned from their ways. And since the Jewish people are *"a wise and understanding people"* (*Devarim* 4:6), it was necessary to *"act cunningly"* in order to lead the Jews to act foolishly and sin (162a).

TORAS MENACHEM

At first glance, one single *mitzvah* would appear to be sufficient for this purpose, to ensure that the Jewish people were no longer "naked" of *mitzvos*, but the *Mechilta* taught that two *mitzvos* were in fact necessary. This is because the process of withdrawing from idolatry involved two distinct elements:

a.) The positive involvement with good deeds and *mitzvos*. This was achieved through circumcision, which allows the Jew to enter into a covenant with God.

However, the occupation with good alone would not have been sufficient, as the people may still have remained passively attached to their former idolatrous ways. Therefore, a further act was required to withdraw from and renounce the idolatrous practice of Egypt. And this was:

b.) The public renunciation of the god of Egypt. The Jewish people were commanded to kill a lamb, which was the deity of Egypt, and splash its blood on their doorposts. This achieved a total disassociation from their previous idolatrous ways.

In our days too we must endeavor to ensure that no Jewish person leaves this current exile "naked and bare" of *mitzvos*. The immense accomplishment of bringing a Jew to observe just one *mitzvah* cannot be overestimated.

(Based on *Likutei Sichos*, vol. 16, p. 114*ff*)

וַיָּרֵעוּ אֹתָנוּ הַמִּצְרִים ◈ — *The Egyptians treated us badly.*

The classic perception of our ancestors' predicament in Egypt is that they were in a situation of dire emergency. Of the "fifty gates of impurity" which the mystics describe, the Jews had sunk through forty-nine and were on the verge of reaching the point-of-no-return. God therefore took them out of Egypt prematurely, before their mission in exile had been completed, which is why we were ultimately forced to return to exile and finish a task which was left incomplete. If only the Egyptian exile had been allowed to run its full course, the Messianic Era would

"The Egyptians treated us badly, they made us suffer, and they imposed hard labor upon us!" *(Devarim 26:6)*

"The Egyptians treated us badly" — as the verse states: "Come, let us act cunningly with them lest they increase. For if a war will occur, they will join our enemies, fight against us and depart from the land" *(Shemos 1:10)*.

CLASSIC QUESTIONS

● **Who advised Pharaoh to "act cunningly"?**

TALMUD: There were three advisors in that plan (to "act cunningly" and kill the male Jewish babies): Bilam, Iyov (Job), and Yisro (Jethro). For consenting to the plan, Bilam was ultimately killed himself (see *Bamidbar* 31:8). For remaining silent, Iyov was later afflicted with suffering (*Iyov* ch. 1-2). For fleeing, Yisro merited that his descendants would sit as judges in the Temple's Chamber of Hewn Stone (*Sotah* 11a).

IYUN YA'AKOV: Yisro acted correctly and opposed Pharaoh's plan, and he was thus forced to flee in order to save his life (ibid).

TORAS MENACHEM

have been with us long ago....

Why, indeed, did the Jews fall so low? If God's original intention was that from Egypt we would move permanently to the Land of Israel, what caused this plan to be forfeited?

To solve this problem we need to turn to a famous question posed by many of the commentators, that if the exile in Egypt was a Divine decree (*"Your descendants will be strangers in a land that is not theirs. They will be enslaved and oppressed for four hundred years"*—Bereishis 15:13), why were the Egyptians punished for carrying out something which was ostensibly God's will?

One solution, suggested by *Ramban*, is that God had only decreed that the Jews should be exiled, not that they should be persecuted and tormented. The Egyptians were therefore punished because they *added* to God's decree and maltreated the Jews. *Ramban* offers three examples: "They threw their children into the Nile, they embittered their lives with harsh labor, and they plotted to eliminate the Jews entirely."

Here, the Haggadah informs us of a fourth example: "They treated us badly," which, according to **Shaloh** means, "they made us bad"—they imparted Egyptian impurity into our souls. This "additional evil" had even greater repercussions than the three acts mentioned by *Ramban*: it spiritually corrupted the Jews through

forty-nine gates of impurity, causing the entire mission of the Egyptian exile to be prematurely aborted, as we have explained. And, precisely because of that, we sit here tonight, still in exile, still picking up the pieces from the events in Egypt.

Nevertheless, the first redemption was not a complete failure, because it gives us the inspiration, strength and spiritual fortitude necessary to leave our present exile—speedily in our days.

(Based on *Likutei Sichos* vol. 17, pp. 87-8)

◆◆ **הָבָה נִתְחַכְּמָה לוֹ** — *Come, let us act cunningly with them.*

At first glance, all three of the **Talmud's** judgments appear to be unjust (see *Classic Questions*). Bilam was an advisor to Pharaoh, which meant that he was under a moral obligation to act in the best interests of his own country. Pharaoh's objection seemed reasonable: the Jews were multiplying at a rapid pace and it was therefore conceivable that "*if a war will occur, they will join our enemies, fight against us and depart from the land.*" It simply seems unfair that he should be punished so harshly for acting in the interests of what was essentially his own nation's security.

Iyov, too, seems to have been penalized far too heavily. After all, he said absolutely nothing, so why should he have been condemned to such terrible suffering?

"וַיְעַנּוּנוּ" — כְּמָה שֶׁנֶּאֱמַר: "וַיָּשִׂימוּ עָלָיו שָׂרֵי מִסִּים לְמַעַן עַנֹּתוֹ בְּסִבְלֹתָם, וַיִּבֶן עָרֵי מִסְכְּנוֹת לְפַרְעֹה אֶת־פִּתֹם וְאֶת־רַעַמְסֵס":

"וַיִּתְּנוּ עָלֵינוּ עֲבֹדָה קָשָׁה" — כְּמָה שֶׁנֶּאֱמַר: "וַיַּעֲבִדוּ מִצְרַיִם אֶת־בְּנֵי יִשְׂרָאֵל בְּפָרֶךְ":

TORAS MENACHEM

And even Yisro's reward seems unjustified, because it appears that he failed to act in the best interests of the Jewish people. When Yisro stated his position, the case was already lost, since his single vote could not form the majority necessary to overturn Pharaoh's plan. So would it not have been more prudent of Yisro to negotiate some "damage control," rather than just to anger Pharaoh and run? Yisro could have argued that at least the surviving Jewish girls should be given kosher food and a Jewish education. What was gained by self-righteously declaring Pharaoh to be wrong, a move for which Yisro would inevitably forfeit any further negotiating power that might have benefitted the Jews?

In truth, however, it was Bilam and Iyov who acted purely out of self-interest, betraying the Egyptian people whom they had been appointed to advise. Unlike Pharaoh, Bilam was highly attuned to spiritual matters (he was a prophet) and he knew that the Jewish people would always enjoy Divine protection. He was fully aware that if Egypt persecuted the Jews, then Egypt would ultimately be destroyed. But rather than "lose face" with Pharaoh and inform him of the "ugly" truth, Bilam told Pharaoh exactly what he wanted to hear, thereby betraying the nation he was appointed to advise for an immediate personal gain.

Iyov too acted purely out of self-interest. If the *Talmud* had said that he was in favor of Pharaoh's plan, we might think that he had made an honest mistake in perceiving the Jewish people as a national threat. But by saying *nothing* he clearly wished to remain a "friend" of both sides, while in truth assisting

none of them. He valued his own image more than the safety of the Egyptian people, or the Jews.

But Yisro was a man of integrity, a person who was willing to say openly and unashamedly that Pharaoh's plan was bad for Egypt (and bad for the Jews). Of course he was fully aware that this was not what Pharaoh wanted to hear, but his duty was to the Egyptian people whom he was appointed to lead and protect, and not to Pharaoh personally. When faced with a dilemma, he chose a path which was morally and ethically correct, rather than being "politically correct," and therefore he was greatly rewarded.

The lesson is a simple yet powerful one. Those of us who have positions of responsibility in the community would do well to learn from Yisro: Your responsibility lies not with defending your own honor or seeking grace from the authorities, but in acting with the best interests of those whom you represent in mind.

(Based on *Sichah* of Purim 5731, par. 8)

וַיִּבֶן עָרֵי מִסְכְּנוֹת לְפַרְעֹה אֶת פִּתֹם וְאֶת רַעַמְסֵס
— *And they built storage cities for Pharaoh—Pisom and Ra'amses.*

A position maintained by a number of secular historians for many years is that the pyramids in Egypt were built by the Jewish slaves—a notion which appears to be alluded to by this verse.

At first glance, this theory appears to be inconsistent with a teaching of *Rashi* in his commentary to the Torah. "They brought the tabernacle to Moshe," writes *Rashi*, "because they were unable to erect it....

"They made us suffer" — as the verse states: "They appointed taskmasters over them to afflict them with their burdens, and they built storage cities for Pharaoh—Pisom and Ra'amses" *(Shemos 1:11).*

"And they imposed hard labor upon us" — as the verse states: "The Egyptians enslaved the children of Israel with crushing labor" *(ibid. 13).*

CLASSIC QUESTIONS

● **What, exactly, is "crushing labor"?**

RAMBAM: What is "crushing labor"? A task that has no end, or a pointless task, intended solely to work a person so that he may not rest *(Laws of Slaves 1:6; see Hagahos Maimonios ibid).*

TORAS MENACHEM

No person could erect it because of the weight of the beams" *(Rashi to Shemos 39:33).*

Now, if the Jewish people had successfully erected the pyramids, which necessitated transporting huge stones over large distances, it is rather difficult to conceive why they were unable to lift up the wooden beams of the Tabernacle which must have been incomparably lighter.

The answer, quite simply, is that while Pharaoh desired to place unfair demands on the Jewish people which were detrimental to their health, God would not do the same. So when they found that lifting the beams was too physically demanding, they came to Moshe and exclaimed, "A reasonable God could not possibly require us to lift such a heavy weight. Serving Him cannot require something which makes us suffer!"

Consequently, writes *Rashi*, God informed Moshe, *"You work with your hands and it will appear as if you are erecting it, but it will actually go up by itself."*

Our efforts to come closer to God through observing the Torah and sharing it with others are not intended to be an unbearable load. Of course, there have been occasions in history when Jews were forced to die for their religion, but this is very much the exception rather than the rule. In the vast majority of cases, God does not want our observance to be overburdensome,

and it is His intention that we come closer to Him in reasonable, manageable steps.

(Based on *Sichas Shabbos Parshas Naso 5745, par. 34ff*)

וַיַּעֲבִדוּ מִצְרַיִם אֶת בְּנֵי יִשְׂרָאֵל בְּפָרֶךְ ❧ — *The Egyptians enslaved the children of Israel with crushing labor.*

A modern-day equivalent of "crushing labor," if we follow **Rambam's** definition (see *Classic Questions*), is the obsession that some people have with making money. It goes without saying that the quest for personal wealth can easily become a "task that has no end," that consumes a person's every waking moment and leaves no room for any other pursuits. But why would it be considered "a pointless task"? Surely there are very real gains to be made by investing more time and energy into making money?

In truth, however, as Jews we believe that our income for the current year has already been decreed by God on *Rosh ha-Shanah* (the first day of the year). Of course, it is only *"with the sweat of your brow you will eat bread"* (*Bereishis 3:19*), and much effort is required to cash our heavenly "check." But the fact remains that all the entrepreneurial endeavors in the world will not help a person earn one cent more than has been decreed for him for that year.

So overworking is, in essence, a "pointless" task. It will not make you any more wealthy than if you

"וַנִּצְעַק אֶל־יְהֹוָה אֱלֹהֵי אֲבֹתֵינוּ, וַיִּשְׁמַע יְהֹוָה אֶת־קֹלֵנוּ וַיַּרְא אֶת־עָנְיֵנוּ וְאֶת־עֲמָלֵנוּ וְאֶת־לַחֲצֵנוּ":

"וַנִּצְעַק אֶל־יְהֹוָה אֱלֹהֵי אֲבֹתֵינוּ" — כְּמָה שֶׁנֶּאֱמַר: "וַיְהִי בַיָּמִים הָרַבִּים הָהֵם וַיָּמָת מֶלֶךְ מִצְרַיִם,

---

CLASSIC QUESTIONS

Talmud: R. Elazar said: *perech* ("crushing labor") alludes to *peh rach* ("with a gentle mouth"), meaning that the Israelites were enticed to work through smooth talk and pay, until they became accustomed to hard labor.

R' Shmuel bar Nahmani said in the name of R' Yochanan: They exchanged men's work for the women's work and the women's work for the men's, and this was especially difficult, as they were not accustomed to it (*Sotah* 11b, according to *Rashi*).

TORAS MENACHEM

work a reasonable amount, more than our guidebook in life, the Torah, deems appropriate.

How much work is *reasonable*?

The answer is really quite simple. First, one has to discharge one's basic obligations. Obviously, a person has to look after his health, which means eating and sleeping sufficiently, and following medical advice. Then there are the obligations to his family: to spend time rearing his children and ensuring that his wife has the support she needs. And, then, of course, there are religious obligations: daily prayer, regular Torah study, Shabbos and festival observance, etc.

From the time that remains, a person may choose to dedicate as much as he wishes to earning a living—but never more. Stealing time from your essential obligations in order to earn more money is quite simply a "pointless task," because you will never earn more than God has allotted to you, and God would never expect you to shun your obligations to your family and to religious worship for the sake of financial gain.

So close your store at a normal hour! Don't spend nights in the office denying your family precious

time. Take time out of your busy schedule to pray and study Torah. And make sure to look after your health.

We've left Egypt now. The "crushing labor" has ended. Do all of the above, and your wallet will not suffer because this, after all, is the true freedom we are celebrating tonight.

(Based on *Likutei Sichos* vol. 3, p. 848*ff*)

בְּפָרֶךְ 🙠 — *With crushing labor.*

The "crushing labor" of our current exile is the arduous task of refining our much-to-be-desired character traits. It is sad but true that unlike in earlier generations when people were predisposed to be refined, decent and wholesome, today, virtually everyone is naturally drawn to deceit, arrogance and stubbornness. Our fuses are so terribly short, such that we erupt with the slightest provocation; and we are such jealous, proud people.

"What is hateful to you, do not do to your neighbor—that is the whole Torah, and the rest is commentary" (*Shabbos* 31a). Since the "entire Torah" is

"And we cried out to God, the God of our fathers. God heard our voice and He saw our affliction, our toil and our oppression" (*Devarim* 26:7).

"And we cried out to God, the God of our fathers"
— as the verse states: "After many days had passed, the

---

addressed to our interpersonal relations, we are left with a very arduous task indeed, the "crushing labor" of refining our coarse character traits, which are highly resistant to change.

The *Talmud* presents us with two insights as to how to carry out this crushing labor (*perech*).

1.) *Go against your nature.* Even a small act which goes against a person's nature helps to transform his or her personality tremendously. The Egyptians understood this when they "changed the men's work for the women's, and the women's for the men's," since it is especially difficult for a person to do something which he is unaccustomed to, even if it is easier than his usual work. So by doing something that goes against your nature you help to "crack" the unrefined qualities in your personality.

2.) *Try your best to be soft and nice to others.* The *Talmud* teaches that when dealing with other people, "A man should always be gentle (*rach*) as the reed and never unyielding like the cedar" (*Ta'anis* 20a). *Peh-rach* means "gentle mouth," indicating that our crushing labor, the primary challenge which we face every day, is to subdue our natural obstinacy before our fellow man. We should always endeavor to be soft and easygoing and not angry or hot-headed with others who defy or insult us. It is truly a "crushing labor" never to become jealous of our friend or to hate him, nor to feel superior to others, but that is the task which faces us.

"A soft answer turns away anger" (*Proverbs* 15:1). Being easygoing has a calming effect on others and a therapeutic effect on yourself, calming your inner fire

of anger and negative energy. It also has a calming effect Above, so to speak, so that God will deal kindly with you too.

(Based on *Torah Ohr* 51c; *Ma'amarei Admor ha-Emtzoie, Vayikra* vol. 1, Discourses for Pesach, p. 118*ff*)

℺ וַנִּצְעַק אֶל יְהוָה — *And we cried out to God.*

Rabbi Shmuel of Lubavitch taught: *"Even a Jewish groan which, God forbid, is prompted by physical misfortune, is a great act of teshuvah (penitence). Most certainly then, a groan prompted by an undesirable spiritual status is a lofty and effective teshuvah. The groan pulls a person out of the depths of evil and places him on a firm footing in the realm of good"* (*ha-Yom Yom*, 3rd of *Tammuz*).

Why is a "groan" in and of itself considered to be a great religious act, that of returning to God?

When a person sins, there is a tendency for him to write off his rebellious act as insignificant, or even non-existent. Several arguments are available at his disposal. One option is to justify the act with all sorts of rationalizations, claiming that it was in fact appropriate.

Another approach is to admit that the act was wrong but to be lenient with oneself. "Look, I did something wrong," he says, "but considering the circumstances it was not so bad. I have such a big *yetzer hara* (evil inclination)! My job forces me to mix with all sorts of people and to contend with many powerful temptations. In fact, considering the tests I face, I think I've done pretty well. Somebody else would probably have fallen much lower."

וַיֵּאָנְחוּ בְנֵי־יִשְׂרָאֵל מִן־הָעֲבֹדָה וַיִּזְעָקוּ, וַתַּעַל שַׁוְעָתָם אֶל־הָאֱלֹהִים מִן־הָעֲבֹדָה":

"וַיִּשְׁמַע יְהֹוָה אֶת־קֹלֵנוּ" – כְּמָה שֶׁנֶּאֱמַר: "וַיִּשְׁמַע אֱלֹהִים אֶת־נַאֲקָתָם, וַיִּזְכֹּר אֱלֹהִים אֶת־בְּרִיתוֹ אֶת־אַבְרָהָם אֶת־יִצְחָק וְאֶת־יַעֲקֹב":

CLASSIC QUESTIONS

● **Why were the prayers to God so crucial? How does this relate to the end of our exile?**

BACHAYE: Even though the appointed time had come for the redemption, the people did not yet deserve it. But when so many of them cried out to God because of the hard work, He accepted their prayers. This is a hint to our future redemption which also depends on *teshuvah* (repentance) and prayer (*Shemos* 2:23).

MIDRASH: All the thousands that perished in battle in the days of David, perished only because they did not demand [from God] that the Holy Temple be built (*Midrash Tehilim* 17:4).

BEIS YOSEF: The Jewish people will not be redeemed until they will confess [their sins] and *demand* the Kingdom of Heaven, the Kingdom of the House of David and the Holy Temple (*Orach Chaim* 188).

TORAS MENACHEM

(Of course, we are supposed to use such arguments to look upon *others* in a favorable light, but not to defend our *own* wrongdoings.)

A third reaction to sinning is to admit having done wrong and not try and justify or excuse ourselves, but to simply smile and say, "Sometimes I like to spoil myself a little bit." We don't feel guilty because, *"love covers all sins"* (Proverbs 10:12). Our prejudice towards ourselves enables us to overlook the "occasional" transgression.

When a person is courageous and honest, choosing not to employ any of the above tactics, and he is willing to face the ugly truth that he has sinned and rebelled inexcusably against his Creator, his *"groan prompted by an undesirable spiritual status is a lofty and effective act of teshuvah."* Because the essence of *teshuvah* is a willingness to come to terms with the painful fact that the present situation is undesirable, and that empty excuses must be replaced with genuine self-evaluation. The moment that realization

comes, the transformation is instant. In one moment, our Rabbis taught, a person can change from being wicked to righteous (see *Kidushin* 49b). It's just a question of being honest with oneself.

(Based on *Likutei Sichos* vol. 1, p. 129*ff*; *Sichas Shabbos Parshas Shemos* 5725, end of par. 3)

֍֎ **וַיִּזְעָקוּ וַתַּעַל שַׁוְעָתָם אֶל הָאֱלֹהִים** — *They cried out, and their prayer rose up to God.*

This verse is a focal point in the chronicle of the redemption from Egypt. The sincere cries and pleas of the Jewish people were instrumental in "inspiring" God, so to speak, to enact the awesome miracles of the Exodus which began to unfold from this point.

Being that the Egyptian Exodus was the "prototype" of all future redemptions, many sources indicate that the final act of our current exile will also be the fervent prayers and cries of the Jewish people: *"O God, how long shall the adversary taunt? Shall the enemy*

king of Egypt died. The children of Israel groaned from the hard work, and they cried out. And their prayers, prompted by the hard work, rose up to God" (*Shemos* 2:23).

"God heard our voice" — as the verse states: "God heard their cry, and God remembered His covenant with Avraham, Yitzchak, and Ya'akov" (ibid. 24).

═══════════════ CLASSIC QUESTIONS ═══════════════

● **Why did God remember the Patriarchs?**

MIDRASH: *"The voice of my beloved! Behold, he comes leaping upon the mountains, skipping upon the hills"* (Song 2:8). Rabbi Yehudah said: What does "leaping upon the mountains" mean? God is saying: "If I look at the deeds of the Jewish people they will never be redeemed. Rather, what do I look at? At their holy ancestors—as the verse states, *'I also heard the groans of the Jewish people...[and I remembered*

═══════════════ TORAS MENACHEM ═══════════════

blaspheme your name forever?"* (*Psalms* 74:10).

In fact, some texts, such as the **Midrash** and **Beis Yosef**, indicate that we should not only *pray* for the true and final redemption, we should actually *demand* it from God. As the Psalmist declared, *"Do not keep silent, O God! Do not hold your peace and be still, O God!"* (83:2).

(Of course, this does not imply for a moment that we are impudently telling God what to do, or attempting to change His mind. God *already* wants to bring the redemption and it is only that He is waiting for the "cue" from us, because *"God longs for the prayers of the righteous"* (*Yevamos* 64a; *Chulin* 60b). Our impatient pleas will merely have the effect of "drawing" God's *existing* desire for redemption down into this world.)

In a sense, the imperative for redemption is even more pressing now than it was then. In Egypt the Jews cried out because they could no longer bear the *physical* labor which God had decreed upon them; but we have suffered not only physical atrocities throughout history, culminating with the Holocaust, but in our days even the *spiritual* goal of the exile has long been completed (see p. 62).

It is simply unfathomable why, when Jews gather together, they do not make an uproar and demand the redemption from God. The unfortunate fact is that even when they do pray for Mashiach, it is nothing more than lip-service, for if their words were sincere there is absolutely no doubt that the redemption would already be here.

We can only hope that ultimately a small group of stubborn Jews will be found who are so adamant in their pleas for redemption that they elicit a response from Above.

When the prophet Michah pleaded for Israel's redemption, God replied: *"Just as in the days when you came out of the land of Egypt, I will show you marvelous things"* (Michah 7:15). This, explains *Radak*, means to say: *"You will be redeemed for the same reason your ancestors were redeemed in Egypt"*—simply because "they cried out and their prayers rose up to God."

(Based on *Sichos* of *Shemos* and *Tzav* 5743; *Yisro* 5745; 28th of *Nissan* 5751; *Likutei Sichos* vol. 30, p. 182)

וַיִּזְכֹּר אֱלֹהִים אֶת בְּרִיתוֹ אֶת אַבְרָהָם אֶת יִצְחָק וְאֶת יַעֲקֹב — *And God remembered His covenant with Avraham, Yitzchak and Ya'akov.*

The extraordinary spiritual transformation brought about by the Exodus is depicted metaphorically by King Solomon in his *Song of Songs* as God "leaping upon the mountains" and "skipping upon the hills." This rich imagery is decoded by the **Midrash** (and **Talmud**) which interprets "mountains" as referring

"וַיַּרְא אֶת־עָנְיֵנוּ" — זוֹ פְּרִישׁוּת דֶּרֶךְ אֶרֶץ — כְּמָה שֶׁנֶּאֱמַר: "וַיַּרְא אֱלֹהִים אֶת־בְּנֵי יִשְׂרָאֵל וַיֵּדַע אֱלֹהִים":

"וְאֶת־עֲמָלֵנוּ" — אֵלּוּ הַבָּנִים, כְּמָה שֶׁנֶּאֱמַר: "כָּל־הַבֵּן הַיִּלּוֹד הַיְאֹרָה תַּשְׁלִיכֻהוּ

CLASSIC QUESTIONS

My covenant]' (Shemos 6:2). I will redeem them in the merit of their ancestors." Therefore the verse states, "leaping upon the mountains," for "mountains" refers specifically to the "Patriarchs" (Shemos Rabah 15:4).

TALMUD: And "skipping upon the hills" refers to the merit of the Matriarchs (Rosh ha-Shanah 11a).

● **How were husband and wife separated?**

MIDRASH: One interpretation is that the Egyptian taskmasters did not allow the Israelites to return home at night (Shemos Rabah 1:12).

ARIZAL: The women were prevented by the police from attending mikvah (Sefer ha-Likutim, Shemos 1:12).

TORAS MENACHEM

to the Patriarchs, and "hills" to mean the Matriarchs. The message, therefore, is that the quantum spiritual "leap" of the Exodus was elicited by God, not as a consequence of Israel's activities—for they were steeped in sin and idol worship—but in the merit of the Patriarchs and Matriarchs, as the Haggadah indicates here.

On closer examination, however, this interpretation appears to have generated a certain tension between the Midrashic understanding of the verse and its literal meaning. According to the Midrash, the merit of the Patriarchs and Matriarchs was sufficient to bring about the redemption, which suggests that, spiritually speaking, they were higher than it, and were therefore able to "give birth" to it. But, at the literal level, the redemptive "leap" was "upon the mountains" and "upon the hills," i.e., it was a revelation above and beyond anything which had been experienced by our ancestors, despite their immense spiritual stature (as "mountains" and "hills").

So what are we to conclude? Was the saintliness of our Patriarchs the cause and spiritual "father" of the Exodus? Or are we now celebrating a leap far beyond anything that they enjoyed?

In essence, both statements are true, but they need to be placed in the correct context. Later in the

Haggadah we read: "'God brought us out of Egypt,' not through an angel, not through a saraf and not through a messenger, but the Holy One blessed be He, in His glory, He alone" (page 89). This, explains the commentators, is because the Jews had fallen so low, into such a depraved state of idolatry and impurity, that they were approaching a point-of-no-return. Therefore, only God Himself could redeem them, because no spiritual messenger would be able to penetrate the overwhelming impurity of Egypt. Even an angel would be swallowed up alive.

This personal "visit" from God is described as a spiritual leap, because, compared to any prior revelation that had been witnessed throughout history—even by the Patriarchs and Matriarchs—it was totally unprecedented.

One might imagine that before God would carry out this remarkable act, He would first wait for man to do something exceptional in order to elicit a response from Above. After all, any meaningful relationship must be give-and-take, and not all-give or all-take. But in this case, the revelation was so high that there was simply nothing the Jewish people could possibly have done to deserve it or to directly elicit it. When God Himself comes to visit, there is really nothing we can do to properly and appropriately invite Him.

"Referring to the separation of husband and wife" is a parenthetical statement, and not a point which the Haggadah is attempting to prove Scripturally (Likutei Ta'amim u'Minhagim).

"And He saw our affliction" — ["our affliction"] referring to the separation of husband and wife — as the verse states: "God *saw* the children of Israel, and God took note" (ibid. 25).

"Our toil" — this means [the decree against] the children, as the verse states: "Every boy who is born you

---

CLASSIC QUESTIONS

● **Why are children referred to as "labor"?**

MACHZOR VITRY: Because they are a person's vigor, as the verse states, *"You are my firstborn, my strength, my first (drop of) vigor"* (Bereishis 49:3).

SHIBOLEI HA-LEKET: Because a person devotes toil and strenuous effort to raising and educating his children. The *Talmud* likewise states, *"What is 'a man's handi-work?'* (after Ecc. 5:5) *It is a man's sons and daughters"* (Shabbos 32:2).

TORAS MENACHEM

But God did not want to come *totally* uninvited. He created us to be partners in the immense task of bring-ing spiritual illumination to this world, so if we could not directly initiate the fantastic revelations of the Exodus, at least we could offer God some sort of "invi-tation," albeit an insufficient one, so as to have some measure of involvement. And since we were inviting God to make a "leap," to shower us with a totally unprecedented revelation, our "invitation," too, had to consist of some sort of personal spiritual "leap."

It was in this vein that the Sages taught that *"our ancestors were redeemed from Egypt in the merit of their faith"* (Mechilta, Beshalach 14:31), the faith that they still retained as a legacy from the Patriarchs and Matriarchs. When the Jews demonstrated a "leap of faith"—most notably, when they slaughtered the Egyptian deity and displayed its blood on their doorposts—God, too, responded with a "leap" of revelation: *"God brought us out of Egypt... in His glory, He alone."* Their faith was not so great that it *directly* merited redemption; it simply provided a sort of "cue" for the utterly disproportional revelation which was to follow.

So, ultimately, both interpretations of our verse are consistent. The Egyptian Exodus vastly sur-passed anything which the Patriarchs bequeathed us (it was *"upon* the mountains"). But if the Exodus is to be associated with any human "prompt" or "cue," we can only point to the kernel of faith which had been passed down to every Jew from Avraham, Yitzchak and Ya'akov; Sarah, Rivkah, Rachel and Leah.

(Based on *Ma'amar* s.v. *Kol Dodi* 5736)

וְאֶת עֲמָלֵנוּ אֵלּוּ הַבָּנִים — *"Our toil" means the children.*

The verse which the Haggadah cites here does not even mention the word "toil," so how does it prove the point that *"'our toil' means the children"*?

The answer is, simply, that there is no proof to be found here. The Haggadah only wishes to dem-onstrate how children are connected to the story of Egyptian exile; we are not given an explanation why *"'our toil' means the children."*

But no information is lacking: *The Haggadah sim-ply deemed it self-evident that children are associated with toil.*

The Haggadah's intuitive connection between "chil-dren" and "toil" teaches us that rearing children is inevitably and inextricably associated with tireless dedication, for which no shortcuts can be found. This rule is far-reaching and applies to many different sorts of "children":

a.) *Students.* The Torah states, *"You should teach them diligently to your children"* (Devarim 6:7), on which our Sages explained, *"'Your children'—this means your students"* (Sifri ibid.). The Haggadah's rule that children are synonymous with toil means that a proper teacher must show the utmost dedica-

וְכָל־הַבַּת תְּחַיּוּן": "וְאֶת־לַחֲצֵנוּ" — זוֹ הַדְּחַק כְּמָה שֶׁנֶּאֱמַר: "וְגַם־רָאִיתִי אֶת־הַלַּחַץ אֲשֶׁר מִצְרַיִם לוֹחֲצִים אֹתָם":

"וַיּוֹצִאֵנוּ יְהוָה מִמִּצְרַיִם בְּיָד חֲזָקָה וּבִזְרֹעַ נְטוּיָה וּבְמֹרָא גָּדֹל וּבְאֹתֹת וּבְמֹפְתִים":

CLASSIC QUESTIONS

● **Why were the boys killed and not the girls?**

Midrash: Pharaoh's astrologers told him, "The redeemer of the Jews has been conceived!".… Why did he decree that the boys should be cast into the Nile rather than killing them directly, which would leave no room for any child to escape their attention? Because the astrologers told him that this redeemer would meet his end through water. They thought that this meant drowning (but in truth, Moshe met his end due to the "waters of strife"—*Bamidbar* 20:12-13).

Of what use were the girls to Pharaoh, such that he *actively* encouraged, "Every girl *you shall* keep alive?" What he meant was, "Let's kill the boys and take the girls as wives for ourselves," for the Egyptians were steeped in depravity (*Shemos Rabah* 1:18, according to *Aitz Yosef*).

● **What new element of "oppression" are we informed of here?**

Abarbanel: Here we refer to the *method* by which the Jews were required to carry out their jobs. We already know that the Jews were forced to carry out back-breaking labor; now we are told that the Egyptians did not let the Jews calmly perform their responsibilities, but constantly put pressure on them to work more.

TORAS MENACHEM

tion and concern for his or her students, both inside *and* outside the classroom. We must toil even with the good students, and with those who seem to be progressing well, because "'our toil' means the children"—*all* the children.

b.) *Spiritual "offspring."* The Chasidic interpretation of the command to "be fruitful and multiply," is that *"a Jew must make another Jew"* (*Sefer ha-Sichos* 5691, p. 262), that is to say, we have a sacred duty to alert others to the importance and beauty of observant Judaism. But this task of producing spiritual "children" requires so much time and effort! We need to toil—literally—to show people that we care, and to hold their hand while they grow in knowledge and observance, one step at a time.

c.) *Physical Children.* To have children, to "be fruitful and multiply," is the first of the 613 com-

mandments recorded in the Torah. It was written first—explained Rabbi Yosef Yitzchak, the previous Lubavitcher Rebbe—to teach us that having children is the most important thing of all, the Torah's first priority (ibid.).

If you are a couple who unfortunately experience difficulty having children, do not be deterred by what the doctors say, because there is a God in this world. Turn to Him and say, "I need desperately to fulfill the first and most important commandment in Your holy Torah!" And do not rest until He listens to you, because sometimes children are associated with toil *even before they are conceived*: the toil of our heartfelt prayers to God.

And tonight is an auspicious time for your prayer, because on Pesach we celebrate how God broke all the laws of nature, bringing ten miraculous

shall cast into the Nile, and every girl you shall keep alive" (ibid. 1:22). *"And our oppression"* — this means the pressure, as the verse states: "And I have also seen the oppression with which the Egyptians are oppressing them" (ibid. 3:9).

"God brought us out of Egypt with a strong hand, with an outstretched arm, with great awe, with signs and with wonders" (Devarim 26:8).

TORAS MENACHEM

plagues on Egypt, and He even split the sea in half. Regardless of what the doctors might say, you must place your absolute trust in God in Whose hand all nature rests. Toil in sincere prayer and you will be blessed with children.

(Based on *Sichos* of 2nd Night of Pesach 5714-6)

כָּל הַבֵּן הַיִּלּוֹד הַיְאֹרָה תַּשְׁלִיכֻהוּ — *Every son who is born you shall cast into the Nile.*

Thank God, we do not face the threat of physical extermination by an anti-Semitic political regime in our days, but the danger of "casting our children into the Nile" still persists in the metaphorical sense.

In Egypt, it does not rain. All agricultural life—which in those days was the main source of income and sustenance—was nourished by irrigation from the Nile.

So the contemporary equivalent of *"every son who is born you shall cast into the Nile"* is the misplaced concern about how a child is going to earn a living as soon as he is born. Unfortunately, some people are so concerned about their child's career and future prospects in life, the need to succeed in society and to earn a handsome living, that they deny the child a reasonable Jewish education. "How could he succeed in life," they wonder, "if he spends part of the day, or all of the day, studying Bible and Talmud, while others are spending all their time devoted to secular and academic studies?"

The only solution, they conclude, is to "cast the child into the Nile" as soon as he is born: to arrange the child's education from the moment of birth in such a way that it maximizes his career prospects.

This is the advice of Pharaoh! Remember that God runs this world, which means that it *is* possible to have a proper Torah education and still succeed in life. The skills necessary for an impressive career certainly do not need to be acquired in early childhood. Don't be perturbed by your neighbors and peers who are rearing doctors and lawyers from the womb. Give your child the right to a Jewish education, and he, his children and his children's children, will be eternally grateful to you.

(Based on *Likutei Sichos* vol. 1, pp. 112-3)

וְכָל הַבַּת תְּחַיּוּן — *And every girl you shall keep alive.*

According to the **Midrash**'s interpretation—that Pharaoh *actively* sought to corrupt the Jewish girls— we see a certain symmetry between the first and second half of our verse. *"Every son who is born you shall cast into the Nile,"* refers to a physical destruction; and, *"every girl you shall keep alive"* refers to a spiritual "annihilation," through assimilation into Egyptian culture and corruption by its depraved citizens.

To people such as ourselves, it might seem that complete isolation from Torah values and observance is ultimately preferable to being physically obliterated. But we do find instances where our Sages espoused a contrary viewpoint. *"Where is the proof,"*

"וַיּוֹצִאֵנוּ יְהוָה מִמִּצְרַיִם" — לֹא עַל יְדֵי מַלְאָךְ, וְלֹא עַל יְדֵי שָׂרָף, וְלֹא עַל יְדֵי שָׁלִיחַ, אֶלָּא הַקָּדוֹשׁ בָּרוּךְ הוּא בִּכְבוֹדוֹ וּבְעַצְמוֹ, שֶׁנֶּאֱמַר: "וְעָבַרְתִּי בְאֶרֶץ־מִצְרַיִם בַּלַּיְלָה הַזֶּה, וְהִכֵּיתִי כָל־בְּכוֹר בְּאֶרֶץ מִצְרַיִם מֵאָדָם וְעַד־בְּהֵמָה, וּבְכָל־אֱלֹהֵי מִצְרַיִם אֶעֱשֶׂה שְׁפָטִים, אֲנִי יְהוָה":

"וְעָבַרְתִּי בְאֶרֶץ־מִצְרַיִם בַּלַּיְלָה הַזֶּה" — אֲנִי וְלֹא מַלְאָךְ. "וְהִכֵּיתִי כָל־בְּכוֹר בְּאֶרֶץ מִצְרַיִם" — אֲנִי וְלֹא שָׂרָף. "וּבְכָל־אֱלֹהֵי מִצְרַיִם אֶעֱשֶׂה שְׁפָטִים" — אֲנִי וְלֹא הַשָּׁלִיחַ. "אֲנִי יְהוָה" — אֲנִי הוּא וְלֹא אַחֵר:

═══════ CLASSIC QUESTIONS ═══════

● **Why did God *Himself* bring us out of Egypt?**

ZOHAR: Here we see the power of God, and His greatness that surpasses everything. God said, "This Egyptian nation is impure and filthy and it does not deserve that a holy angel or *saraf* should be sent there, among those wicked, cursed and filthy people!" (*Zohar* I 117a, *Midrash ha-Ne'elam*)

ARIZAL: The spiritual impurity of Egypt was so strong that if an angel had descended there it would have drowned, God forbid, in the forces of evil (commentary to the *Siddur*).

MAHARAL: Each angel has its own jurisdiction, and the Angel of Egypt would not have allowed another angel to enter (*Haggadah* of the *Maharal*).

BACHAYE: If the slaying of the firstborn would have been carried out by God's ministering angels, they would have expressed only his attribute of severity and punished the Jewish people too, for the Jews did not deserve to be saved. Therefore, the judgment was enacted by God Himself, who has both attributes of severity and compassion, so that the Jews could be saved while the Egyptians were punished (commentary to *Shemos* 12:12).

═══════ TORAS MENACHEM ═══════

they asked, *"that causing a person to sin is worse than actually killing him? Because by murdering him one kills him only in this world; but through causing him to sin, one kills him both in this world and the next"* (*Bamidbar Rabah* 21:4; *Rashi* to *Devarim* 23:9).

Following this logic it would seem that Pharaoh's planned corruption of the girls was, in fact, harsher than his intended annihilation of the boys!

In our days, there are, tragically, so many Jews who lack even the most rudimentary Torah knowledge

"God brought us out of Egypt" — not through an angel, not through a *saraf* and not through a messenger, but it was the Holy One blessed be He, He himself in His glory, as the verse states: "I will pass through the land of Egypt on this night, and I will slay all the firstborn in the land of Egypt, from man to beast, and upon all the gods of Egypt I will perform acts of judgment, I, God" (*Shemos* 12:12):

᳐ "I will pass through the land of Egypt on this night"—I and not an angel.

᳐ "I will slay all the firstborn in the land of Egypt"—I and not a *saraf*.

᳐ "Upon all the gods of Egypt I will perform acts of judgment" —I and not a messenger.

᳐ "I, God"—it is I, and none other!

═══ CLASSIC QUESTIONS ═══

● **What is the difference between an "angel," a "saraf" and a "messenger"?**

ABARBANEL: "An angel" refers to the chief angel of mercy, Michael. "A *saraf*" (fiery angel) refers to a punishing angel, from the camp led by the angel Gavriel. "A messenger" refers to the master angel of nature, Metatron, who is appointed over the lower worlds.

VILNA GA'ON: The "messenger" refers to Moshe, who was not told to *do* anything specific by God at the moment of redemption. Rather, it was the collec-tive *mitzvos* of circumcision and the Paschal lamb, performed by all the Jewish people, which directly caused the redemption.

● **What is added by *"It is I and none other"*?**

ALSHICH: A person might think that God only destroyed the Egyptian deities and not those of the other nations because the other deities actually have some power. To counteract this notion, God says, "It is I and none other," as if to say, "no other deity has any power at all, even those which I did not destroy" (*Toras Moshe, Shemos* 12:12).

═══ TORAS MENACHEM ═══

and basic *mitzvah* observance. If spiritual "death" is worse than physical extinction, as our Sages assert, then it follows that *saving a person spiritually is even more urgent than saving his physical life.*

How imperative it is then, that we make every effort possible to seek out our Jewish brothers and sisters and share with them the beauty of Judaism, especial-ly the inspirational wisdom to be found in the mystical tradition. For when it comes to saving lives—spiritual or physical—nothing else can take priority.

(Based on *Likutei Sichos* vol. 1, pp. 111-2; *Vayeira* 5749)

᳐ **לֹא עַל יְדֵי מַלְאָךְ... אֶלָּא הַקָּדוֹשׁ בָּרוּךְ הוּא בִּכְבוֹדוֹ וּבְעַצְמוֹ** — *Not through an angel... but it was the Holy One, blessed be He, He Himself.*

The Kabbalists elaborate at length on the distinction between the *manifestations* of God, and His *essence*. *A manifestation* is a kind of Divine "mood," where God openly demonstrates a distinct form of behavior. For example, countless scriptural verses, as well as our own lives, attest to moments of Divine kind-ness, Divine harshness, Divine compassion, Divine forgiveness, etc.

"בְּיָד חֲזָקָה" — זוֹ הַדֶּבֶר, כְּמָה שֶׁנֶּאֱמַר:
"הִנֵּה יַד־יְהֹוָה הוֹיָה בְּמִקְנְךָ אֲשֶׁר
בַּשָּׂדֶה בַּסּוּסִים בַּחֲמֹרִים בַּגְּמַלִּים בַּבָּקָר וּבַצֹּאן,
דֶּבֶר כָּבֵד מְאֹד":

"וּבִזְרֹעַ נְטוּיָה" — זוֹ הַחֶרֶב, כְּמָה שֶׁנֶּאֱמַר:
"וְחַרְבּוֹ שְׁלוּפָה בְּיָדוֹ נְטוּיָה עַל
יְרוּשָׁלָיִם":

"וּבְמֹרָא גָּדֹל" — זוֹ גִּלּוּי שְׁכִינָה — כְּמָה
שֶׁנֶּאֱמַר: "אוֹ הֲנִסָּה אֱלֹהִים

TORAS MENACHEM

God's *essence*, by contrast, is totally abstract. It never changes. It can neither be excited nor subdued. And it defies any description whatsoever.*

God's *essence* is His true, inner self, as opposed to His *manifestations* which only give us a limited, veiled glimpse into the workings of the Creator.

As humans, we cannot see or experience God's *essence*, because we can only relate to something tangible, and the *essence* is totally abstract. If we do see Him, hear Him or feel Him, we are sensing a manifestation, for otherwise there would be no "handles" for us to grasp on to, nothing concrete for our limited senses and minds to fathom.

But there is one telltale sign to know when God's essence is at work in this world—namely, *when two paradoxical entities coexist in harmony.*

Divine kindness *must* be kind, and Divine punishment *must* punish, because they are both specific, "honed" manifestations; but God's essence can reward and punish *simultaneously.* When the essence is at work it is as if He is in a "good mood" and a "bad mood" at the same time.

When the Haggadah states that *"God brought us out of Egypt, not through an angel etc., but it was the Holy One blessed be He, He Himself,"* it is telling us that the slaying of the firstborn, the start of the actual Exodus, was carried out by God's essence. Therefore we find, *"He smote and healed"* simultaneously (Isaiah 19:22): at the same time God was punishing the Egyptians He healed the Jewish people from the pain of their recent circumcisions (*Zohar* II, 36a).

Why was it so crucial for God's essence to redeem us? Why would a lesser revelation or manifestation not have sufficed?

Since we are created in the image of God, we too possess *essence* and *manifestations.* Sometimes we

---

*In fact, we cannot even say that His *essence* is infinite, because that, too, is a formal definition, and consequently, a subtle limitation. If He is infinite, then He cannot *also* be finite, so we have compartmentalized Him as an *exclusively* infinite being. His "manifestations" are certainly infinite—He is infinitely kind, infinitely powerful, infinitely knowledgeable, *etc.*—but His *essence* is totally abstract, neither infinite nor finite.

"With a strong hand" — this refers to the pestilence, as the verse states: "Behold, the *hand* of God will place a very severe pestilence upon your livestock in the field — upon the horses, the donkeys, the camels, the cattle, and the sheep" (*Shemos 9:3*).

"With an outstretched arm" — this refers to the sword, as the verse states: "His sword drawn in His hand, *stretched out* over Jerusalem" (*Divrei ha-Yamim* I 21:16).

"With great awe" — ["great awe"] referring to the revelation of the *Shechinah* (Divine Presence) — as the verse states: "Or has any deity performed miracles, coming

"Referring to the revelation of the Shechinah" is a parenthetical statement, and not something which the Haggadah is attempting to prove scripturally (Likutei Ta'amim u'Minhagim).

CLASSIC QUESTIONS

● **Why are the three plagues of Pestilence, Slaying of the firstborn ("sword") and Blood** (see overleaf) **singled out here? And why are they in this particular order?**

LIKUTEI TA'AMIM U'MINHAGIM: These plagues express the greatness of God's acts in three progressively more impressive levels:

1.) He destroyed their property (cattle).

2.) He killed their firstborn.

3.) He struck the Nile and thereby "performed acts of judgment" even upon their gods, for the Egyptians were known to worship the Nile.

TORAS MENACHEM

are good and devout, holy and pure, righteous and kind; but at other times we can be nasty, irreverent, cruel and unforgiving. All this, however, is relevant only to the *manifestations* of our personalities. In essence, man is good. Nothing can change or contaminate our inner core of faith in God and loyalty to Him. Our spiritual blemishes are only skin deep.

In Egypt, the Jews had sunk to unprecedented levels of impurity and sin. In other words, their *manifestations* were totally corrupted and contaminated. So the only way in which they could be redeemed was "*not through an angel, not through a saraf and not through a messenger*," but through "*the Holy One blessed be He Himself in His glory*"— God's essence. Only this was able to bring to light that our essence remains good and holy, regardless of our spiritual circumstances and standing.

What can we learn from all of this in our day-to-day lives? That in order to redeem another Jew—to save our brothers and sisters from the tides of assimilation—we must dedicate ourselves to the task with nothing less than our very essence. "Of course," a person may argue, "outreach is important, but do I have to invest my very life into it? Does it really have to be engraved on my heart?"

The Haggadah teaches us that it does. *"It is enough for the servant that he should be like his master"* (*Brachos* 58b). If God our Master, "He Himself in His glory," immersed His very essence into redeeming Jewish people lost in a secular culture, then surely we, His servants, can do the same.

(Based on *Sichos* of *Shabbos Parshas Beshalach* 5714; 2nd night of *Pesach* 5717; *Likutei Sichos* vol. 3, p. 866)

לָבֹא לָקַחַת לוֹ גוֹי מִקֶּרֶב גּוֹי, בְּמַסֹּת בְּאֹתֹת וּבְמוֹפְתִים וּבְמִלְחָמָה וּבְיָד חֲזָקָה וּבִזְרוֹעַ נְטוּיָה וּבְמוֹרָאִים גְּדֹלִים, כְּכֹל אֲשֶׁר־עָשָׂה לָכֶם יְהוָה אֱלֹהֵיכֶם בְּמִצְרַיִם לְעֵינֶיךָ:

"וּבְאֹתֹת" — זֶה הַמַּטֶּה, כְּמָה שֶׁנֶּאֱמַר: "וְאֶת־ הַמַּטֶּה הַזֶּה תִּקַּח בְּיָדֶךָ אֲשֶׁר תַּעֲשֶׂה־בּוֹ אֶת־הָאֹתֹת":

"וּבְמוֹפְתִים" — זֶה הַדָּם, כְּמָה שֶׁנֶּאֱמַר: "וְנָתַתִּי מוֹפְתִים בַּשָּׁמַיִם וּבָאָרֶץ,

➤ WHEN SAYING EACH OF THE WORDS דָּם וָאֵשׁ וְתִימְרוֹת עָשָׁן REMOVE WINE FROM THE CUP (EITHER WITH YOUR FINGER OR BY SPILLING).

דָּם וָאֵשׁ וְתִימְרוֹת עָשָׁן":

CLASSIC QUESTIONS

● **How and why do we spill out wine?**

DARKEI MOSHE: One sprinkles a little wine with the finger to remember how the Egyptians recognized that the plagues were *"the finger of God"* (Shemos 5:15; Tur Orach Chaim 473, par. 18).

PRI ETZ CHAIM: I heard in the name of Rabbi Chaim Vital [the Arizal's disciple], that rather than dipping his finger into the cup, he would spill a little bit from the cup itself. Perhaps this was a hint to the Kabbalistic teaching that the plagues were enacted by God's attribute of *malchus* [the final attribute in the sefirotic chain, which receives and collects all the emanations from the Divine attributes above it], alluded to by the cup [which is a *receptacle*.

Therefore the spilling must be from the cup—*malchus*—itself.] (Sha'ar Chag ha-Matzos ch. 7).

KESER SHEM TOV (GAGUINE): This custom of spilling out wine was originally an exclusively Ashkenazic custom. However, when it was adopted by the Arizal, Sefardim began to practice it too (vol. 3, p. 130).

PESACH ME'UBIN: All the wine should be spilled out of the cup and replaced, after the cup has been cleaned, since: a.) We do not wish to keep wine upon which God's punishments, the plagues, have been recited. b.) The wine has been dirtied by inserting the finger into it (sec. 261).

ALTER REBBE'S SIDDUR: One should not remove wine by dipping with the finger. Rather, one should spill

to a nation and taking it for Himself out from another nation, with signs and wonders, with a war, a strong hand, an outstretched arm, and with awesome acts — like everything that God, your God, did for you in Egypt, before your eyes?" (*Devarim* 4:34).

"*With signs*" — this refers to the staff, as the verse states: "You shall take this staff in your hand, with which you will perform the *signs*" (*Shemos* 4:17).

"*With wonders*" — this refers to the blood, as the verse states: "I will show *wonders* in heaven and on earth,

➤ WHEN SAYING EACH OF THE WORDS "BLOOD, FIRE AND PILLARS OF SMOKE" REMOVE WINE FROM THE CUP (EITHER WITH YOUR FINGER OR BY SPILLING).

blood, fire and pillars of smoke." (Joel 3:3)

CLASSIC QUESTIONS

from the cup itself. One spills into a broken dish. One should have in mind:

- The cup represents *malchus* (see *Pri Etz Chaim*).
- The wine spilled from it represents God's attribute of anger and fury, which *malchus* has [received and collected from above].
- We direct the anger and fury to the forces of evil (*klipah*), symbolized by the broken dish, (because the *klipah* is irreversibly and irreparably cursed).

- This process is powered by the attribute of *Binah* ("comprehension") [which causes the Divine attributes to be revealed from a state of latency, just as detailed comprehension brings the profundity in an abstract idea to light].

LIKUTEI TA'AMIM U'MINHAGIM: In his *Siddur*, the Alter Rebbe instructs the reader with a mystical *kavanah* (intention; concentration) to be followed when spilling out the wine, based on the Kabbalistic text *Mishnas Chasidim*. This is striking when one

TORAS MENACHEM

שְׁפִיכַת הַיַּיִן — *Spilling of the wine.*

Even adherents of the **Alter Rebbe** should respect the opposing view, that the wine is to be sprinkled using the finger, because this is a practice followed by many Jewish people. Furthermore, in a *halachic*

work an author would not even give consideration to something which was not a valid legal opinion. The fact that the *Alter Rebbe* deemed it necessary to issue a ruling against placing one's finger in the cup indicates that he nevertheless considered it to have a firm basis (*ha-Melech bi-Mesibo* vol. 2, pp. 108-9).

דָּבָר אַחֵר:

"בְּיָד חֲזָקָה" — שְׁתַּיִם.

"וּבִזְרוֹעַ נְטוּיָה" — שְׁתַּיִם.

"וּבְמוֹרָא גָדוֹל" — שְׁתַּיִם.

"וּבְאֹתוֹת" — שְׁתַּיִם.

"וּבְמוֹפְתִים" — שְׁתַּיִם:

עֶשֶׂר מַכּוֹת שֶׁהֵבִיא הַקָּדוֹשׁ בָּרוּךְ הוּא עַל
הַמִּצְרִים בְּמִצְרַיִם. וְאֵלּוּ הֵן:

CLASSIC QUESTIONS

considers that the Alter Rebbe rarely includes any Kabbalistic *kavanos* such as these.

Here, however, he was forced to do so due to *halachic* considerations. The *Talmud* teaches that *"we do not say a blessing over a cup that symbolizes punishment"* (*Brachos* 51a), which in this case seems to leave us with a problem, being that the spilling of the wine represents God's punishments through the plagues.

In fact, due to this concern *Pesach Me'ubin* suggests that one should empty the entire cup after the spilling has been carried out and replace it with fresh wine.

To resolve the problem, the Alter Rebbe included this mystical *kavanah* which clarifies that the theme of punishment only applies to the wine *spilled out of the cup*. Consequently, by having this *kavanah* in mind one ensures that the remaining wine is positive and "joyful," thereby precluding the need to dispose of it.

● *"Another explanation."* **What's the logic here?**

LIKUTEI TA'AMIM U'MINHAGIM: Each noun in the verse refers to one plague and its adjective strengthens it to indicate two. The words *"signs"* and *"wonders"* are in the plural, and therefore they each indicate two plagues.

Another explanation:

"With a strong hand" — suggests two plagues;

"With an outstretched arm" — another two;

"With great awe" — another two;

"With signs" — another two;

"With wonders" — another two.

These

are the Ten Plagues which the Holy One, blessed be
He, brought upon the Egyptians in Egypt. They are:

TORAS MENACHEM

אֵלּוּ עֶשֶׂר מַכּוֹת — *These are the Ten Plagues.*

Conventionally, we tend to perceive the Ten Plagues as a series of harsh punishments for the Egyptian nation—which, of course, they were. But there is another element which, while often overlooked, is no less significant. In fact it is arguably the most important theme here, since it frames the plagues in a broader historical (and philosophical) context.

The Torah stresses repeatedly that the Ten Plagues were enacted so that *"Egypt shall know that I am God"* (*Shemos* 7:5. See also ibid. 17; 8:6,18; 9:14,29; 11:7; 14:4,18). In other words, the goal of the plagues was to bring the Egyptian nation, which believed in the many gods of nature and chance, to an appreciation that there is in fact one God who rules this world. Repeated miraculous intervention was intended to teach the people a lesson, that the disparate physical and astrological forces of which they were aware are nothing but an *"axe in the hand of a lumberjack"*

(after Isaiah 10:15), a mere set of tools with which God Himself controls the world. If He so desires, then these tools follow a predictable path; but if He chooses otherwise, then nature breaks down and yields to a miracle.

Viewed from this angle, the plagues are not so much a form of Divine oppression *against* Egypt but rather, something that was intended *for their benefit*, to teach them a valuable religious truth. The harshness of the plagues was only necessary because the Egyptians were highly resistant to the message. They were such devout polytheists—a belief in which their ego was heavily invested—that it would take a series of national catastrophes to prove the truth of monotheism to them. But in theory, at least, they could have learned the same lesson much more easily.

How can we be certain that teaching the Egyptians about God was the *primary* purpose of these great miracles? Where is the proof that they were

➤ WHEN SAYING THE TEN PLAGUES REMOVE THE WINE AS BEFORE, TEN TIMES.

דָּם. צְפַרְדֵּעַ. כִּנִּים. עָרוֹב. דֶּבֶר. שְׁחִין. בָּרָד. אַרְבֶּה. חֹשֶׁךְ. מַכַּת בְּכוֹרוֹת:

TORAS MENACHEM
---

not inherently plagues of punishment, but plagues of pedagogy? Furthermore, of what importance is it to Jews and Judaism that a *gentile* nation *"should know that I am God?"* Aren't we celebrating our *own* national redemption here?

In retrospect, we know that the Egyptian Exodus was an incomplete redemption by the simple fact that many of its effects were reversed by further exiles. It was certainly our first national redemption, and it was a "prototype" which all further redemptions were to follow; but to understand properly what the Exodus *should* have been, we need to turn to a description of the future Messianic redemption, which, we are promised, will be a perfect and final one.

"He will repair the whole world," writes *Rambam* in reference to Mashiach (the Messiah), *"to serve God with one accord"* (*Laws of Kings* 11:4); and then, *"the single preoccupation of the entire world will be nothing other than to further their knowledge of God"* (*ibid.* 12:5). In a similar vein, *Rashi* states, in his commentary to the verse, *"Hear O Israel, God is our God, God is One"* (*Devarim* 6:4): *"God, who is right now our God and not the God of the idol-worshippers, will in the future be one [universally accepted] God."*

The stress here, that non-Jews will play a central role in the future redemption, such that Mashiach will busy himself with teaching the "whole world," is, at first glance, difficult to fathom. If the entire creation is *"for the sake of the Torah and for the sake of the Jewish people"* (*Rashi* to *Bereishis* 1:1), why is it so important that *non-Jews* should *"further their knowledge of God?"* Is this the dream for which we have yearned

for thousands of years? Isn't the Jewish concept of a Messianic utopia one where Jews are free to worship God and gentiles simply don't get in the way?

Apparently not, according to *Rambam*. While he does frame the *initial* phase of the future redemption as *"mere freedom from political oppression"* (ibid. 2), it is clear from the above citation that in order for the Messianic Era to reach full fruition it is crucial that all nations (*"the whole world"*) occupy themselves with worshipping God and probing the subtleties of true monotheism. For this is the dream which the prophets predicted long ago: *"God will be King over the entire earth"* (*Zechariah* 14:9), that *all* the inhabitants of the earth will view God as their "King," and develop a *personal* relationship with Him.

Judaism is not a mere path to personal salvation which brings its worshippers eternal bliss, leaving a corrupt and profane world behind them, but a global plan to bring awareness of God to every corner of the Earth. The very definition of a *mitzvah* is a command *to positively influence an element of the world*, by imparting it with some sanctity and spirituality, and ultimately, we believe, the cumulative effect of all the *mitzvos* will reach a crescendo, leading the world and all its inhabitants to recognize God (see p. 55).

So if non-Jews would never have their own relationship with God it would mean that our *mitzvos* didn't really do their job. They were just a means for us to get to heaven, but they didn't sanctify the world and make it a place that is receptive to its Creator. And if a non-Jew's religious worship had to be directly connected with a Jew, it would mean that we failed to

➤ WHEN SAYING THE TEN PLAGUES REMOVE THE WINE AS BEFORE, TEN TIMES.

Blood · Frogs · Lice · Wild Creatures · Pestilence · Boils · Hail · Locusts · Darkness · Slaying of the Firstborn.

TORAS MENACHEM

introduce monotheism as a universal "currency" that everybody could benefit from and appreciate.

While it is definitely true that God created the world, *"for the sake of the Torah and for the sake of the Jewish people,"* the Torah's own self-stated goal was always a globalization of monotheism in a way that it would be accepted by all nations and all peoples. But only the 613 commandments, which were given exclusively to the Jewish people, are endowed with sufficient spiritual potency to achieve this goal.

If the Egyptian exodus had been a perfect one, the nations would have come to *"know that I am God,"* without the havoc and destruction of the plagues. In fact, God saw it as tragic that the Egyptians had to be destroyed, rather than learn their lesson: "'*My handiwork is drowning in the sea,' said God to the angels, when they requested permission to sing, 'and you want to sing praise!'"* (*Megilah* 10b). But, sadly, the Egyptians had proven to be too obstinate and, as human beings with free choice, they refused to accept the truth of one God. The time had clearly not yet come for complete redemption, and at this point in history, God's plan could only be furthered, unfortunately, through destruction.

But regardless of the approach—destruction through plagues, as it was in the past, or "repair" through Mashiach, as it will be in our days—the theme remains the same. Our task as Jews is to act as a source of genuine ethics and spirituality for the entire world, so that all nations "*shall know that I am God.*" And then, "*God will be King over the entire earth. On that day, God will be one and His Name will be one*" (*Zechariah* 14:9).

(Based on *Likutei Sichos* vol. 25, pp. 189-191; vol. 23, p. 177-8; vol. 27, p. 255)

With the above in mind, we will now examine the Ten Plagues briefly to see how each furthered the goal that *"Egypt shall know that I am God."* Clearly, God could just have slayed the firstborn right away, for maximum impact. But, instead, He devised an incremental sequence of plagues, each conveying their own unique lesson. So, in each case we need to explain: What message did this plague teach that the Egyptains did not know before?

BLOOD: EGYPT'S DEITY IS POWERLESS

Why was Blood the first plague? Because *"rain does not fall in Egypt, and since the Nile irrigates the earth the Egyptians worshipped it. Therefore, God first struck their deity"* (*Rashi* to *Shemos* 7:17).

This plague was, in effect, a two-pronged attack on the Egyptian faith in their idol: a.) The *entire* Nile was afflicted, rendering their deity *totally* helpless. b.) No water outside the Nile was affected, such that "the Egyptians dug *around* the Nile for water to drink" (*Shemos* ibid. 24). This magnified the embarrassment: Their deity was "out of commission," yet, at the same time, every other source of water was functioning perfectly, even wells right next to the Nile!

FROGS: EGYPT'S DEITY CAUSES NATIONAL DISASTER

This was the second of two plagues which "struck their deity," since the frogs came out of the Nile which they worshipped. This further reinforced the ineffectiveness of the Egyptian deity, since:

a.) The plague of *Blood* was, to some extent, passive. It posed no harm or danger to the people, since they had other sources of water and the blood was not poisonous. With the plague of *Frogs*, however, the Egyptians' own deity became an *active* source of havoc and national disaster.

➤ WHEN SAYING THE WORDS דְּצַ"ךְ עַד"שׁ בְּאַחַ"ב REMOVE WINE AGAIN THREE TIMES.

רַבִּי יְהוּדָה הָיָה נוֹתֵן בָּהֶם סִמָּנִים:

דְּצַ"ךְ. עַד"שׁ. בְּאַחַ"ב:

➤ NOW REFILL THE CUP WITH FRESH WINE (AND DISPOSE OF THE SPILLED WINE).

═══════════════════ CLASSIC QUESTIONS ═══════════════════

● **Why did Rabbi Yehudah refer to the plagues with a mnemonic?**

TALMUD: [Permanent knowledge of] the Torah can only be acquired with the help of mnemonics (*Eruvin* 54b).

SHIBOLEI HA-LEKET: What is the wisdom behind Rabbi Yehudah's mnemonic? Couldn't anybody just join together the first letter of each word?

In Psalms (ch. 78 and 105), the plagues are presented in a different order to the sequence that they appear in the Torah. Rabbi Yehudah therefore informed us that our primary reference should be the Torah's sequence.

Also the *gematria* (numerical equivalent) of the words *Detzach Adash Be'achav* is 501, alluding to the total of 500 plagues at the sea described in the following passage of the Haggadah, plus the "finger" of God = 501.

SIDDUR KOL YA'AKOV: 501 is also the *Gematria* of the Hebrew word *asher* ("that"). Thus when Pharaoh said, "Who is God that (*asher*) I should listen to his voice," he was sent the Ten Plagues in response.

ABARBANEL: The plagues fall into three groups aimed at teaching three different lessons. The three plagues *Detzach* proved the existence of God; *Adash,* His providence; and *Be'achav* His power over nature.

═══════════════════ TORAS MENACHEM ═══════════════════

b.) The frogs remained in the Nile (ibid. 8:5,7) as a permanent reminder to the Egyptians that their own deity had terrorized them.

c.) This was the first plague that contained an element which the Egyptian sorcerers could not duplicate. For while generally *"the sorcerers did the same thing with their spells and brought up frogs"* (ibid. 3), they were unable to duplicate God's miracle that *"there was one frog initially, but when they hit it swarms of frogs streamed out"* (*Rashi,* ibid. 2).

LICE: SORCERY IS LIMITED; GOD IS UNLIMITED

This was the first plague which the Egyptian sorcerers were unable to duplicate at all (ibid. 8:14), leading them to exclaim, *"It is the finger of God!"* (ibid. 15). The message that *"Egypt shall know that I am God"* had now been brought home clearly and effectively.

An interesting question here is whether the lice affected the Egyptians only, or whether the Jews suffered too? Some commentators maintain that

the Jews were not affected, but scripture itself only indicates a distinction between Jews and non-Jews from the fourth plague and onwards. And *Rashi,* who adhered strictly to a literal interpretation of the Torah, makes no indication that the Jews were unaffected by the blood, frogs or lice.

But if the Jews were affected too, then how would the message be communicated clearly to Pharaoh that the God of Israel was at work?

In the case of the first two plagues, *Blood* and *Frogs,* the answer is not too hard to fathom. As mentioned above, the purpose of the plagues (according to *Rashi*) was to strike the Nile because it was the deity of Egypt. So if *any* part of the Nile had remained unaffected Pharaoh would remain convinced that his god was not completely helpless. It would seem that the God of Israel was not able to totally overturn the god of Egypt! Therefore, it was crucial that the entire Nile be afflicted.

➤ WHEN SAYING THE WORDS *DETZACH ADASH BE'ACHAV* REMOVE WINE AGAIN
THREE TIMES.

Rabbi Yehudah would refer to them with a mnemonic:

Detzach · Adash · Be'achav

➤ NOW REFILL THE CUP WITH FRESH WINE (AND DISPOSE OF THE SPILLED
WINE).

TORAS MENACHEM

But why was it necessary for the lice to affect the Jewish people too? This plague had nothing to do with the Nile, being an attack on the Egyptians themselves.

The answer is that even the Egyptians were aware that sorcery, which is carried out by man, is limited. To be convinced that God is at work, they would have to witness something unlimited.

If the lice had only affected a portion of the population, the plague would have a limited feel to it, and it would not have provided irrefutable proof that this was a miracle of *God*. The fact that the Egyptian sorcerers could not duplicate the miracle was indeed impressive, but perhaps Moshe and Aharon were simply more skilled sorcerers than they? In their eyes, the only real evidence of "the finger of God"—that they were witnessing something beyond the power of sorcery—would be an *unlimited* phenomenon. Therefore, it was necessary that the lice infest everyone, even the Jews.

WILD CREATURES: GOD ACTS DIRECTLY

This was the most devastating plague yet. All those that had preceded it consisted of just one attacking species, whereas now the Egyptians were terrorized by a *mixture* of wild creatures ("*wild animals, snakes and scorpions*"—*Rashi* to 8:17), which would have obviously wrought a greater degree of havoc. In fact, it is precisely to stress this point that the Torah refers to this plague simply as an *arov* ("mixture") without clarifying what the mixture was, since the key development here was the havoc caused by a number of different species unleashed together.

Another important feature here (and with *Pestilence*), is that neither Moshe nor Aharon did anything dramatic to initiate the plague, unlike in the previous instances where Aharon's staff had been instrumental in bringing about each plague. However impressive

a plague might be, the fact that it was prompted by a ritual performed by a human being must have made it harder for the Egyptians to believe that the miracle was coming directly from God, and not via sorcery. So the fact that the mixture of wild creatures came automatically, without intervention by Moshe or Aharon, must have conveyed the message more powerfully to the Egyptians that God's hand was at work. In fact, this is precisely why we find no indication in Scripture that they attempted to duplicate this plague (or the next), for the lack of human intervention proved clearly that it was from God and was beyond the capabilities of sorcery.

PESTILENCE: OUR LIVELIHOOD COMES FROM GOD

This is the first plague in which the Egyptians suffered the crippling loss of their main source of long-term income, their livestock. With the previous plague, the mixture of wild creatures was merely "incited" against Egypt (8:17), and vegetation ("*the land*") was destroyed (ibid. 20), but we find no indication that the Egyptian cattle were killed. Here however, "the livestock of the Egyptians died" (9:6), which, considering that a person values his livestock with his very life (*Mechilta* to *Shemos* 17:3), must have been a tremendously severe blow.

The great value of a person's livestock is highlighted further by one extreme case in Jewish Law, where Shabbos may be transgressed to save livestock on the basis that it is equated to *pikuach nefesh* (danger to life) for the owner! (*Magen Avraham, Orach Chaim* ch. 248, par. 16). Clearly, then, this plague which destroyed the economic foundation of Egypt must have driven home the power of God in an unprecedented fashion.

BOILS: SORCERY COMPLETELY DISCREDITED

Here, for the first time, we read that "the sorcerers *could not stand before Moshe* due to their

רַבִּי יוֹסֵי הַגְּלִילִי אוֹמֵר:

מִנַּיִן אַתָּה אוֹמֵר שֶׁלָּקוּ הַמִּצְרִים **בְּמִצְרַיִם עֶשֶׂר** מַכּוֹת וְעַל **הַיָּם** לָקוּ **חֲמִשִּׁים** מַכּוֹת?

בְּמִצְרַיִם מַה הוּא אוֹמֵר: "וַיֹּאמְרוּ הַחַרְטֻמִּים אֶל־פַּרְעֹה **אֶצְבַּע** אֱלֹהִים הִיא".

וְעַל **הַיָּם** מַה הוּא אוֹמֵר: "וַיַּרְא יִשְׂרָאֵל אֶת־**הַיָּד** הַגְּדוֹלָה אֲשֶׁר עָשָׂה יְהֹוָה בְּמִצְרַיִם וַיִּירְאוּ הָעָם אֶת־יְהֹוָה וַיַּאֲמִינוּ בַּיהֹוָה וּבְמֹשֶׁה עַבְדּוֹ":

TORAS MENACHEM

boils" (9:11). This is somewhat difficult to understand because, presumably, the sorcerers had also been affected by the plague of lice, so why do we not find that they "could not stand before Moshe" as a result of being covered in lice?

Apparently, the "inability to stand" here refers not merely to the embarrassment of their physical appearance, but to a much deeper emotional humiliation. "The sorcerers could not stand before Moshe," because their egos had now been completely deflated.

Why did this happen only now for the first time with the plague of boils? Hadn't the sorcerers already admitted defeat with the plague of lice when they confessed that *"it is the finger of God"*?

Human nature is such that your ego becomes somewhat threatened when another person does something that you can't do. But to admit that your capabilities are limited doesn't mean that you lose all self-esteem, because at least within your own realm of expertise you are competent.

A much greater form of humiliation is if somebody else does a thing which you *can* do, but he does it much better than you. By beating you "on your own turf," he renders your contribution insignificant, and

you cannot help but feel totally worthless. This is what happened with the plague of *Boils*. In the case of *Lice*, the sorcerers admitted that the miracle was simply beyond their capabilities, because *"sorcery cannot control creatures smaller than a barleycorn"* (*Rashi* to 8:14). The next two plagues, *Wild Creatures* and *Pestilence,* were clearly supernatural, since they had begun without any initiation ritual by man, and no sorcerer can produce results without some sort of action or incantation first. So they did not even attempt to duplicate these two plagues.

But this was not yet the ultimate insult to the Egyptian's faith in their own powers. For while they had been forced to admit that God was greater than them, at least they could still do some impressive sorcery within the limits of nature.

However, with the *Boils*, Moshe brought about a plague that was essentially *within* the capabilities of sorcery, and it was initiated by a dramatic ritual where soot was cast into the air, just as a sorcerer might do. But while this was a feat which the Egyptians could have duplicated to some extent, it was nevertheless accompanied by "numerous miracles" (*Rashi* to 9:8) which were well beyond the capabilities of the sorcerers.

RABBI YOSE HAGLILI SAYS:

FROM WHERE DO YOU DERIVE that the Egyptians were struck by *ten* plagues in Egypt, and were struck by *fifty* plagues at the sea?

Concerning the plagues in Egypt the verse states: "The sorcerers said to Pharaoh, 'It's the *finger* of God'" (*Shemos* 8:15).

And concerning the plagues at the sea the verse states, "Israel saw the great *hand* which God had enacted on the Egyptians, and the people feared God. They believed in God and in Moshe, His servant" (*Shemos* 14:31).

TORAS MENACHEM

So now they *"could not stand before Moshe"* because they saw how God was all-powerful, both in the supernatural and the natural arena.

HAIL: PRECISION AND OMNIPOTENCE OF GOD

This plague was significantly harsher than all those that had preceded it, as its warning clearly indicated: *"This time I am sending (a plague like) all my plagues upon your heart... in order that you should know that there is none like Me in the entire earth"* (9:14, according to *Rashi* as interpreted by *Mizrachi*). Consequently, this plague inspired Pharaoh to confess, *"This time, I have sinned"* (ibid. 27). It also terrorized the Egyptian people to the extent that when Moshe warned them about the next plague they begged Pharaoh to let the Jews go (10:7).

Hail also taught the Egyptians two graphic lessons about God's omnipotence:

a.) *"Moshe scratched a line on the wall for Pharaoh and said, 'Tomorrow, when the sun reaches this point, the hail will come down!'"* (*Rashi* to 9:18). For the first time, the Egyptians were shown the extreme precision of God.

b.) The highest revelations of God allow opposites to co-exist. It is one thing for God to be extremely punishing or extremely kind, but it is more impressive for Him to exhibit both qualities at the same time. Thus, in contrast to the previous plagues which were *only* punishing, here, for the first time, the Egyptians

were informed of an element of mercy: *"Gather in your livestock and all that you have in the field. The hail will fall on any man and beast that is found in the field and not brought into the house"* (9:19). (Some commentators maintain that with the plague of *Pestilence,* animals could also be saved by bringing them into the house. But even according to that opinion, God's mercy stands out here where He *actively* told the Egyptians to save their animals: *"Gather in your livestock."*)

This unique power of God to "fuse opposites" was also demonstrated by the hail itself: *"There was a miracle within a miracle, fire and hail mixed—for the hail is [frozen] water—but to carry out the will of their Creator they made peace"* (*Rashi* to 9:24).

LOCUSTS: MAN'S FREE CHOICE IS IN GOD'S HAND

Locusts was an unprecedented scenario in the sequence of plagues. It was the first plague where a.) Pharaoh's heart had actually been hardened (9:12), and nevertheless, b.) Moshe was commanded to warn Pharaoh of the consequences of his actions.

What was the point in warning Pharaoh if his heart had been hardened? *Rashi* explains that the simultaneous hardening of Pharaoh's heart, together with a warning, achieved the effect of "ridiculing" or "mocking" Egypt (*Rashi* to 10:2). Pharaoh and his servants would have to face the terror of an upcoming attack, and yet they would be powerless to protect

כַּמָּה לָקוּ **בָּאֶצְבַּע?** עֶשֶׂר מַכּוֹת.

אֱמוֹר מֵעַתָּה: בְּמִצְרַיִם לָקוּ **עֶשֶׂר** מַכּוֹת, וְעַל הַיָּם לָקוּ **חֲמִשִּׁים** מַכּוֹת:

רַבִּי אֱלִיעֶזֶר אוֹמֵר:

מִנַּיִן שֶׁכָּל־מַכָּה וּמַכָּה שֶׁהֵבִיא הַקָּדוֹשׁ בָּרוּךְ הוּא עַל הַמִּצְרִים בְּמִצְרַיִם הָיְתָה שֶׁל **אַרְבַּע** מַכּוֹת?

TORAS MENACHEM

themselves from it, since Pharaoh's free choice was diminished. This must have sent the people of Egypt into a state of utter turmoil, finding themselves unable to avoid a decision which they knew would have disastrous consequences. Pharaoh was thus taught an important lesson about God. Pharaoh had said, *"Who is God that I should listen to Him?"* (5:2), meaning to say, "I shall do as I please and nobody will influence me otherwise." By depriving Pharaoh of free choice, the illusion of his own authority was shattered, and God's absolute power over man demonstrated.

DARKNESS: GOD CREATED DAY AND NIGHT

The Egyptians believed that day and night were created by different gods. The fact that there are distinct periods of light and dark, they argued, suggests the existence of two authorities, each with their own times of jurisdiction.

This heresy was dispelled by the plague of *Darkness*, where at *the same time* the Egyptians were suffering from darkness, the Jews enjoyed light.

SLAYING OF THE FIRSTBORN: EGYPT IS PUNISHED

An unusual feature of this plague was that the Jewish People were required to make a special "sign" to distinguish them from the Egyptians: *"You shall touch the lintel and the two doorposts with blood....*

Not one of you shall go out from the entrance of his house until morning" (Shemos 12:22).

Why, all of a sudden, was it necessary to make a distinction between Jew and Egyptian? The Jews did not suffer from many of the previous plagues and yet we do not find that they were required to make a special sign?

In all previous cases, the primary purpose of these outstanding miracles was, as we have shown, to teach the Egyptians about God. The Jewish people, however, already believed in God (*"the people believed"*—4:21), and there was no need for them to be taught a lesson of faith. Therefore, the plagues were not directed towards them.

With the *Slaying of the Firstborn*, however, the goal was clearly one of punishment rather than education. (Once a person is dead he can no longer learn.) The Egyptians had simply failed to take heed of the previous nine miracles, and refused to accede to God's wishes that the Jewish people should be freed, so more harsh measures had proven necessary.

With the purpose of the plague redefined, the distinction between Jew and Egyptian was framed somewhat differently. When it came to awareness of God, the Jews' simple faith vastly surpassed the polytheistic beliefs of the Egyptians; but in terms of

It is a distinct possibility that Rabbi Yosi Haglili does not argue with Rabbi Eliezer and Rabbi Akiva. The latter discuss subdivisions of the plagues whereas Rabbi Yosi refers to the general scheme of ten plagues, with which they also concur (Likutei Ta'amim u'Minhagim).

With how many plagues were they struck by the "finger" [in Egypt]? Ten plagues.

So you must now say that since in Egypt they were struck by *ten* plagues [from a single "finger"], at the sea they must have been struck by *fifty* plagues [from a whole "hand"]!

RABBI ELIEZER SAYS:

FROM WHERE DO YOU DERIVE that each plague which the Holy One, blessed be He, brought upon the Egyptians in Egypt [and at the sea] consisted of *four* plagues?

=== CLASSIC QUESTIONS ===

● **Why did the Egyptian sorcerers refer to the plagues as the "finger" of God?**

MIDRASH: They said, "God is only striking us with one finger. If He would strike us with an entire hand we would be destroyed immediately!" (*Midrash Seichel Tov*).

ABARBANEL: While the expression, "finger of God" was said by the sorcerers only in reaction to the Third Plague, the Plague of Lice, it apparently expressed their impression of all the plagues.

● **How is the notion of 50, 200 or 250 plagues to be reconciled with our Sages' teaching: "Ten miracles were enacted for our fathers in Egypt *and ten by the sea*** (*Avos d'Rabbi Noson* 33; *Avos* 5:4)?

RAMBAM: The plagues which, according to our tradition, afflicted the Egyptians by the sea were more numerous than those which occurred in Egypt, *but they were of the same basic ten types* with various subdivisions.

=== TORAS MENACHEM ===

culpability for sins, the Jews were not too different from their Egyptian neighbors. In fact, the mystics taught that the Jews had reached an all-time national spiritual low point and were on the brink of total and irreversible corruption (see p. 156).

So if this plague was coming to punish the sinful, *who could say that a Jew was better than an Egyptian?*

Thus, it now proved crucial for the Jewish people to make a sign on the doorposts, and not leave their houses until the morning. For when the prosecuting angel comes to the streets or to unmarked houses, he will punish *anybody* for their sins.

Why was this seemingly minor "sign" sufficient to save the Jewish people if they were indeed guilty? Is it rational or fair that one sinful nation should be punished while another is saved?

The answer is no, it is not rational at all. But that, precisely, is the point. God's commitment to the Jewish people is *irrational,* it defies and transcends logic. He simply loves us, like a parent loves a child, no matter what that child may do.

But to evoke that love and to remind Him of it, we too needed to demonstrate our irrational commitment to God. In Egypt, this took two forms of expression: a.) The blood of circumcision, a *mitzvah* normally carried out on a child *before* he can make a rational, informed decision; and, b.) the blood of the Paschal Lamb, which required the ultimate irrational commitment from the Jewish people: to endanger their lives by slaughtering a lamb, the deity of Egypt, merely to perform a religious ritual.

Love evokes love. The Jewish people's irrational commitment to God, despite their low standing,

שֶׁנֶּאֱמַר: "יְשַׁלַּח־בָּם חֲרוֹן אַפּוֹ עֶבְרָה

וָזַעַם וְצָרָה מִשְׁלַחַת מַלְאֲכֵי רָעִים":

"עֶבְרָה" — אַחַת. "וָזַעַם" — שְׁתַּיִם. "וְצָרָה"

— שָׁלֹשׁ. "מִשְׁלַחַת מַלְאֲכֵי רָעִים" — אַרְבַּע.

אֱמוֹר מֵעַתָּה: בְּמִצְרַיִם לָקוּ **אַרְבָּעִים** מַכּוֹת,

וְעַל הַיָּם לָקוּ **מָאתַיִם** מַכּוֹת:

CLASSIC QUESTIONS

● **Do all texts of the Haggadah include this passage about the plagues which struck the Egyptians at the sea?**

R' AVRAHAM, SON OF THE RAMBAM: My father did not include this passage in his published text of the Haggadah, because he maintained it is not a practice which had spread widely and it is not crucial. Nevertheless, his personal custom was to say it, as was the custom of the earlier sages of the West. For it adds to our intellectual appreciation of the Exodus, and "whoever tells the story of the Exodus at length is praiseworthy" (cited in *Ma'aseh Rokeach*).

LIKUTEI TA'AMIM U'MINHAGIM: This passage likewise appears in many authoritative Haggados, such as those of R' Amram Ga'on, R' Sa'adia Ga'on, *Machzor Vitry, Abarbanel* and *Arizal.*

TORAS MENACHEM
---

aroused a similar sentiment above, and God saved His people whom He loves so dearly.

(Sources: Intro. — *Sichas Shabbos Parshas Bo* 5744; *Blood* — *Sichas Shabbos Parshas Va'era* 5747; *Frogs* — ibid., and *Bo* 5744; *Lice* — *Likutei Sichos* vol. 11, pp. 31-2; *Wild Creatures* — ibid. p. 28; vol. 36, p. 31; *Pestilence* — ibid. vol. 16, p. 156; *Boils* — vol. 36, ibid.; *Hail* — vol. 6, p. 60, note 21; vol. 31, pp. 43-5; *Locusts* — vol. 6, p. 57*ff; Darkness* — *Sefer ha-Ma'amarim* 5663, pp. 83-4; *Slaying of the Firstborn* — *Likutei Sichos*, vol. 3, p. 864*ff*)

בְּמִצְרַיִם לָקוּ ... וְעַל הַיָּם לָקוּ ◈◈ — *In Egypt they were struck... and at the sea they were struck.*

The Biblical command to recall the Exodus, which we fulfil tonight by reading the Haggadah, is to "remember *this day* (*singular*) that you went out of Egypt" (*Shemos* 13:3), i.e., the events of the fifteenth of Nissan, when we actually left Egypt. It does not seem to include the events of the twenty-first of Nissan, when the Egyptians were afflicted with a further barrage of plagues and were finally obliterated at the sea.

On the other hand, the fact that our text of the Haggadah includes this rather lengthy passage about the events at the sea (see *Classic Questions*) indicates that by recounting this story we *do* fulfil the *mitzvah* of recounting the Exodus.

But how could this be the case when the splitting of the sea did not occur on "*the day* that you left Egypt," but almost a week later?

The answer can be gleaned from sources which discuss the *daily* obligation to recall the Exodus. *Tosefta* (*Brachos* 2:1) states that in addition to recalling the Exodus in our daily prayers during the third paragraph of the *Shema*, there is also an obligation to mention the splitting of the Reed Sea, which, in our liturgy, is included in the passage *emes veyatziv* (*Siddur Tehillas Hashem* p. 48). This, explains *Chasdei David* (*Tosefta*, ibid.), is because the splitting of the sea represents the complete fulfillment of the Exodus.

The logic here is not too hard to fathom. Imagine leaving the land of Egypt with the full knowledge that the Egyptians would soon be chasing behind with a near-invincible army (see *Rashi* to *Shemos* 14:5). One

From the verse: "He sent forth against them His fierce anger: fury, indignation, and misfortune, a band of messengers of evil" (*Tehillim* 78:49) :~

"Fury," is one; "indignation," makes two; "misfortune," makes three; "a band of messengers of evil," makes four.

Now we apply the 1:5 ratio of plagues in Egypt to plagues at the Sea. So you must now say that in Egypt they were struck by *forty* plagues [from a single "finger"], and at the sea they were struck by *two hundred* plagues [from a whole "hand"]!

=== CLASSIC QUESTIONS ===

● **What, exactly, was the point of contention between Rabbi Eliezer and Rabbi Akiva?**

Ritva: The literal interpretation is that Rabbi Eliezer understood each plague as having four subcomponents which struck each of the four elements within the target of the plague. Rabbi Akiva added a fifth subcomponent, corresponding to the essential "hylic substance," which is the primordial matter from which the elements are formed (see also *Akeidas Yitzchak, Beshalach*, portal 40).

=== TORAS MENACHEM ===

רַבִּי אֱלִיעֶזֶר אוֹמֵר... רַבִּי עֲקִיבָא אוֹמֵר — *Rabbi Eliezer says... Rabbi Akiva says...*

Overtly, Rabbi Eliezer and Rabbi Akiva appear to be quarreling over something quite trivial. Based on slightly different expositions of a verse in Psalms, Rabbi Eliezer argued that each of the Ten Plagues had four subcategories, whereas Rabbi Akiva maintained that there were five.

Of what *real* significance is this to our understanding of the Exodus from Egypt that it merited inclusion in the Haggadah? And what message does it convey for our daily lives?

In truth, this exchange between these two Rabbinic giants is laden with immense significance and meaning at many different levels. We will approach the notion of four or five sub-plagues from the perspective of *peshat* (literal meaning), *halachah* (legal ramifications), *remez* (allusion), *derash* (Rabbinic exegesis), *sod* (mysticism), and *hora'ah* (practical instruction), and in each instance we will try to detect a common thread in the argument.

Peshat—Literal Meaning.

Jewish philosophers describe physical matter as existing on three levels: 1.) *Outward appearance.*

wouldn't exactly call that freedom! The Israelites might have left the *geographical* boundaries of Egypt, but the *terror* of Egypt remained.

So the final obliteration of the Egyptians at the sea could be perceived as part of the Exodus, because it was the moment when the dream of a full and complete Exodus finally became a reality.

Nevertheless, remembering the events at the sea is not a *vital* component of remembering the Exodus, as can be gleaned from the following law.

We are taught that if a person fails to recite the third paragraph of the *Shema* (which mentions the Exodus) the omission must be compensated for; but if *emes veyatziv* (which mentions the splitting of the Sea) was forgotten, one need not say this passage later, when one remembers its omission (*Alter Rebbe's Shulchan Aruch* 67:1).

Thus, remembering the events at the sea is an important, effective, but non-vital component of the (daily and annual) *mitzvah* to recall the Exodus from Egypt. It is important, because it depicts the full real-ization of the Exodus; but it is not vital because the precise definition of the *mitzvah* is to "remember *this day* when you went out of Egypt."

(Based on *Sefer ha-Ma'amarim Melukat* vol. 4, p. 226)

רַבִּי עֲקִיבָא אוֹמֵר:

מִנַּיִן שֶׁכָּל־מַכָּה וּמַכָּה שֶׁהֵבִיא הַקָּדוֹשׁ בָּרוּךְ הוּא עַל הַמִּצְרִים בְּמִצְרַיִם הָיְתָה שֶׁל **חָמֵשׁ** מַכּוֹת?

שֶׁנֶּאֱמַר: "יְשַׁלַּח־בָּם חֲרוֹן אַפּוֹ עֶבְרָה וָזַעַם וְצָרָה מִשְׁלַחַת מַלְאֲכֵי רָעִים": "חֲרוֹן אַפּוֹ" — אַחַת.

TORAS MENACHEM

2.) *Composite structure.* At this level, even materials which seem simple to the naked eye are found to be inherently complex. Modern chemistry speaks of over a hundred chemical elements, modern physics of a family of subatomic particles, but the medieval philosophers followed another parallel scheme of four fundamental elements: Fire, Water, Air and Earth (see *Chumash Kol Menachem, Synagogue Edition* p. 7). Everything, they argued, is a mixture of these four basic substances, though only one or more may be apparent to us in any given material. For example, plain water would appear to contain just one element (water), but, in fact, like all other physical entities, it will harbor subtle phenomena associated with the other elements too.

3.) *Hylic essence.* All matter that we know possesses attributes of *form* (shape, size, temperature, energy etc.). But when God created the world, He initially brought into being a kind of primordial, lifeless, amorphous matter that had no form at all, and from this He shaped the Four Elements. This primordial matter is what Scripture refers to as the "astounding" (*tohu*) phenomenon present at the beginning of creation (*Bereishis* 1:2). *Ramban,* in his commentary to this passage, clarifies the connection here: If you could see formless matter you would be unable to describe it—since it would have no distinct qualities—so you would be astounded and lost for words.

The philosophers referred to this substance as *hylic* matter, and it represents the essence and core of all physical entities, a kind of element of the elements.

Based on this classic view of matter (which was also employed by the Sages in the *Midrash Rabah* and *Zohar*), *Ritva* explains the dispute between Rabbi Eliezer and Rabbi Akiva. Both Sages agreed

that the plagues penetrated the physical fabric of Egypt more deeply than its mere *outward appearance* (level 1, above)—they struck its *composite* substructure (level 2). The point of dispute was whether the plagues affected the *hylic* core of Egypt. Rabbi Eliezer said no, which meant that there were just four subcomponents of each plague, corresponding to the Four Elements. But Rabbi Akiva said yes, adding a fifth component to the plagues, corresponding to the *hylic* essence of all physical matter.

So, in the context of the story of the Exodus, they were arguing: How corrupting was the impurity of Egypt? It was certainly powerful enough to contaminate something outwardly; and, according to both rabbis, it corrupted the elemental infrastructure of everything under its dominion. But could the impurity of "the most depraved of all nations" (*Rashi* to *Vayikra* 18:3) seep through to the core, and contaminate the *hylic* essence of matter?

Rabbi Akiva maintained that it could, so he understood that a more potent, five-pronged form of plague was required to purge the impurity of Egypt at the very core.

Halachah—Jewish Law

"Rabbi Yehudah says: 'The only way Chametz (leaven) may be eliminated is through burning it.' "The other Sages say: 'One may also crumble it and scatter it into the wind, or cast it into the sea'" (*Mishnah, Pesachim* beg. ch. 2).

If we perceive "eliminating Chametz" as the process of destroying the unique evil of Egypt (of which Chametz is symbolic), then this *Mishnah* would seem to parallel precisely our discussion in the Haggadah between Rabbi Akiva and Rabbi Eliezer.

Rabbi Akiva Says:

From where do you derive that each plague which the Holy One, blessed be He, brought upon the Egyptians in Egypt [and at the sea] consisted of *five* plagues?

From the verse: "He sent forth against them his fierce anger, fury, indignation, and misfortune, a band of messengers of evil": "His fierce anger," is one;

TORAS MENACHEM

Rabbi Yehudah, who maintained that Chametz must be burned, agreed with Rabbi Akiva, that the evil of Egypt had penetrated to the *hylic essence* of matter. Therefore, in his view, the only way to eliminate this evil from the Chametz is to obliterate it *completely*.

The other Sages, however, sympathized with the view of Rabbi Eliezer (in the Haggadah) that the evil of Egypt only contaminated the composite structure of matter and not its very essence. Thus, the other Sages argued that merely by breaking that composite structure, through crumbling the Chametz into tiny pieces and scattering it, the evil has already been eliminated. There is no need to destroy it completely, since the "essence" of the Chametz is, in their view, uncontaminated.

(See original *Sichah* for a number of further halachic ramifications.)

Remez—Allusion

The respective positions of Rabbi Eliezer and Rabbi Akiva are alluded to by the contrasting images portrayed by these two Sages.

The Biblical name Eliezer is derived from the phrase "the God of *my father* came to my aid" (*Shemos* 18:4), stressing the idea of tradition, transmission and continuity of Jewish identity from father to son. Obviously, for this to be viable, some incorruptible core identity must be passed down through each generation so as to sustain an unbroken link. Rabbi Eliezer, *whose very name represents Jewish continuity*, thus maintained that impurity and contamination can never reach the core, the secret of our chain of tradition.

Rabbi Akiva, on the other hand, was a descendant of converts to Judaism (*Seder ha-Doros*), so he appreciated how an entire Jewish personality—including its core identity—could be established without historical prologue. He was thus not bound by Rabbi Eliezer's perception of an inviolable core that is transmitted from generation to generation. On the contrary, the notion of conversion rings home that one *can* acquire a Jewish identity from scratch—and if the core of the soul can be found in a person's lifetime, then it can also be "lost" (or, to be precise, temporarily compromised) through sin.

So Rabbi Akiva maintained that impurity can be effective even against the essence of a soul, and likewise, against the *hylic* essence of matter.

Derash—Rabbinic Exegesis

In a number of source texts, our Sages referred to a scheme of Four Exiles (political regimes) that have oppressed the Jewish people throughout history. The precise definition of these Four Exiles, however, differs from text to text. Most importantly for our discussion, sometimes the Egyptian exile is included as one of the four (*Ein Ya'akov, Megilah* 29a; *Zohar* I 81b, 125a); though very often it is not (e.g. *Bereishis Rabah* 2:4; 16:4; 44:15,17).

But when Egypt is omitted, the intention is not to play down its significance, but, on the contrary, to underscore its far-reaching effects. "*All* the political regimes are associated with *Mitzrayim* (Egypt)," said the Sages, "because they all oppressed (*metzayrim*) the Jews" (*Bereishis Rabah* 16:4). As *Arizal* explained: "*The Egyptian exile is equivalent to them all, or even more... therefore it is not mentioned with them*" (*Likutei Torah*, beg. *Parshas Ki Seitzei*).

If we view the Four Exiles to be four fundamental types or "elements" of oppression, then a parallel emerges here between the two *Midrashic* views (whether or not Egypt is one of the Four Exiles), and the dispute between Rabbi Eliezer and Rabbi Akiva.

"עֶבְרָה" — שְׁתַּיִם. "וָזַעַם" — שָׁלֹשׁ. "וְצָרָה"
— אַרְבַּע. "מִשְׁלַחַת מַלְאֲכֵי רָעִים" — חָמֵשׁ.

אֱמֹר מֵעַתָּה: בְּמִצְרַיִם לָקוּ **חֲמִשִּׁים** מַכּוֹת,
וְעַל הַיָּם לָקוּ **חֲמִשִּׁים וּמָאתַיִם** מַכּוֹת:

=== TORAS MENACHEM ===

If Egypt is just one of the Four Exiles, it means that the impurity of Egypt only reached the level of the Four Elements, the underlying *composite structure* of matter, but no deeper—i.e., the view of Rabbi Eliezer.

The other *Midrashic* view maintains that the impurity of Egypt is the source of all further exiles and is too profound to be listed as one of the four. This is because it contaminated the *hylic* essence which lies at the core of the Four Elements (Exiles)—i.e., the view of Rabbi Akiva.

Sod—Kabbalah

The Kabbalists taught that God's four-letter ineffable name, the Tetragrammaton, visually depicts man's psyche and soul-powers.

The first letter, *yud* (י), is effectively a single point; it has no substantial width or height. It therefore represents our ability to look at the whole rather than the parts, to see or conceive an idea in its entirety. This power of *Chochmah* (conceptual wisdom), represented by the *yud*, is intuitive, holistic, synthesizing, and, to a very great extent, subjective, because it acts as a first point of expression for the innermost recesses of the soul.

Being a mere point or flash of intellect, it seeks articulation, which requires assistance from a completely different soul-address. The faculty of *Binah* (cognition) is represented by the second letter of the Tetragrammaton, *hei* (ה). Spatially, the *hei* has everything the *yud* lacks: it is fully formed in both dimensions of width and height, indicative of the cognitive ability to flesh out a raw idea and explore all its possible ramifications, rationally and objectively. *Binah* absorbs the spark of *Chochmah*, shapes it and refines it. It systematizes, organizes and characterizes, focussing entirely on the parts rather than the whole.

Chochmah and *Binah* are, of course, highly interdependent, which is why the Kabbalah depicts them as the "father" and "mother" of all practical wisdom.

Without the inspirational contribution of *Chochmah*, *Binah* would have no substance to analyze or dissect; and without the sober, careful logic of *Binah*, *Chochmah's* ideas would soon dissipate.

Vav (ו), the third letter of the Tetragrammaton, is a vertical line which, when drawn by a scribe, begins with a *yud,* and is then gradually drawn downwards on the page. This visually depicts the soul's outward journey of communication, beginning with *Chochmah* (*yud*), through *Binah,* taking expression in the rest of the personality, which is largely a process of emotional processing.

The final letter, *hei* (ה), represents *action,* the personal, selfless completion of a job.

So, in all, the Tetragrammaton depicts most of the activities of our conscious lives: imagination, cognition, emotional management and action.

But there is another fascinating aspect to this four-letter image, a more subtle feature which alludes to the underlying human drive of will, belief and the need for fulfillment. And this is represented by the *thorn of the yud.*

When drawn scribally, the *yud* is not merely a shapeless dot; it contains a thorn-like protrusion.

← THORN

Unlike the main body of the *yud,* which, while small, does manage to spread itself across a certain space, the *thorn* is tiny and thin, and merely points to something else. It is as if the *thorn* is saying, "What I represent is too subtle to be depicted visually by a letter, so I am just pointing to something outside and beyond."

The thorn of the *yud,* which points upwards, thus alludes to the transcendent qualities of will and belief which drive all of our activities—mental, emotional and practical—and yet cannot be associated with a certain organ or "place" in our person-

"fury," makes two; "indignation," makes three; "misfortune," makes four; "a band of messengers of evil," makes five.

So you must now say that in Egypt they were struck by *fifty* plagues [from a single "finger"], and at the sea they were struck by *two hundred and fifty* plagues [from a whole "hand"]!

Now we apply the 1:5 ratio of plagues in Egypt to plagues at the sea.

TORAS MENACHEM

alities. These powers are essential, all-encompassing and, much of the time, subconscious.

In the image of the Tetragrammaton we see, once again, a strong contrast between the conscious, composite personality of *four* primary elements, in contrast to a higher *fifth* essential power, indicated by the *thorn of the yud.*

So even at the Kabbalistic level the contrast between Rabbi Eliezer and Rabbi Akiva's view is echoed. Rabbi Eliezer would maintain that the impurity of Egypt only compromised the four letters of the Tetragrammaton—our conscious, composite personalities—whereas Rabbi Akiva would argue that even the *thorn of the yud,* the essence of our souls, was affected.

Hora'ah—Practical Lessons

The general theme of the Exodus is one of liberation. In Egypt, we experienced a national, political liberation, and we have been promised by the prophets that this will occur once again with the coming of Mashiach. As we find ourselves currently between these two great events, leaving Egypt (*Mitzrayim*) takes on a more personal connotation of self-liberation from internal, psychological constraints (*maytzarim*).

This, of course, is the classic conception of the Exodus. But in light of the above discussion, our understanding of this idea is greatly enriched. We can now appreciate that personal liberation occurs on many different levels—four, according to Rabbi Eliezer, and five, according to Rabbi Akiva—because we can suffer from constraints within all four "elements" of our personality. And, in Rabbi Akiva's opinion, even our *hylic* essence, our core soul-identity, can suffer from crippling constraints.

Here are a few examples of the types of mini-Exodus that we need to enact on a day-to-day basis:

a.) *Practical constraints* (corresponding to the final *hei* of the Tetragrammaton): Honesty in business, dealing kindly and respectfully with everyone we come into contact with, giving generously to charity, studying Torah and observing the commandments, both Biblical and Rabbinic.

b.) *Emotional constraints* (corresponding to the *vau* of the Tetragrammaton): Feeling comfortable being a Jew and not embarrassed. Not worrying what our neighbors and peers think of us.

c.) *Cognitive constraints* (corresponding to the first *hei* of the Tetragrammaton): Performing all the commandments out of dedication to God and not merely because they make sense. Not allowing our passion for Jewish life to be dampened by the dictates of reason.

d.) *Self-awareness constraints* (corresponding to the *yud* of the Tetragrammaton): Even if we do all of the above, our actions can sometimes be plagued by an excessive degree of self-consciousness which holds us back from living life to its fullest and dedicating ourselves completely to God. We need to learn from the simplicity of the *yud,* to shed our outer shell of sophistication, to be devoted, humble people.

Even after success in these four areas, Rabbi Akiva would add a fifth: *Don't be sure of yourself!* Things may be going well, and you may be enjoying success in all areas of personal development, but the very essence of your soul (the *thorn of the yud*) might still be in Egypt. Even the great Sage Rabbi Yochanan ben Zakai, who lived a life devoid of sin, wondered if he would merit *Gan Eden* (heaven)—"I don't know which way they will take me," he confessed (*Brachos* 28b)—because he knew that his good behavior on every conscious level was no proof for the spiritual health of his hidden essence.

But God gives us the strength to face even this challenge. With genuine dedication we *can* free ourselves from any trace of internal constraint, however deep-rooted it may be. And what better time to do so than the night of the Exodus itself?

(Based on *Likutei Sichos* vol. 16, p. 87*ff;*
Sichah of 2nd night *of Pesach* 5725)

כַּמָּה מַעֲלוֹת טוֹבוֹת לַמָּקוֹם עָלֵינוּ!

אִלּוּ הוֹצִיאָנוּ מִמִּצְרַיִם

וְלֹא עָשָׂה בָהֶם שְׁפָטִים   דַּיֵּנוּ:

אִלּוּ עָשָׂה בָהֶם שְׁפָטִים

וְלֹא עָשָׂה בֵאלֹהֵיהֶם   דַּיֵּנוּ:

אִלּוּ עָשָׂה בֵאלֹהֵיהֶם

וְלֹא הָרַג אֶת־בְּכוֹרֵיהֶם   דַּיֵּנוּ:

CLASSIC QUESTIONS

● **Why do we now enumerate all the favors that God bestowed upon us?**

SHIBOLEI HA-LEKET: The previous paragraphs described the enormous number of miracles that God performed for the Jews in Egypt and at the sea. Now, we continue this discussion by stating that there are many more miracles which He performed for us, which we have not touched upon.

TORAS MENACHEM

כַּמָּה מַעֲלוֹת טוֹבוֹת לַמָּקוֹם עָלֵינוּ — *How many are the good things that the Almighty has showered upon us.*

While a number of the "good things" mentioned here are directly connected with the Exodus from Egypt, many of them are not. Even if we will argue that the events up to and including the drowning of the Egyptians at the sea were part of the Exodus—since the threat of being recaptured still loomed until that point (see p. 104)—this passage still lists a number of subsequent events which apparently have no direct connection with the Exodus: "*He supplied our needs in the desert for forty years; and fed us the Manna; and He gave us the Shabbos; and He brought us before Mount Sinai; and He gave us the Torah; and He brought us into the land of Israel; and He built for us the Chosen House, to atone for all our sins.*"

What does all this have to do with "*this day* (*singular*) when you went out of Egypt" (*Shemos* 13:3), the fifteenth of Nissan, whose events we are commemorating tonight by reading the Haggadah?

A simple approach would be to argue that the additional points cited here are admittedly unrelated to the main theme of the Haggadah, but it was nevertheless deemed appropriate to make a digression here so as to recount the further chronicles of the Jewish people. In this way, many further remarkable "good things which the Almighty showered upon us" are brought to light.

Such an argument, however, is difficult to accept. For a *brief* digression or parenthetical statement is all well and good, but why would the Haggadah include a substantial passage whose *predominant* theme is something other than the Exodus?

How many are the Good Things that the Almighty has showered upon us!

If He had brought us out of Egypt,

But had not carried out judgments against them

—*It would have been enough for us!*

If He had carried out judgments against them,

But not against their gods

—*It would have been enough for us!*

If He had destroyed their gods,

But had not slain their firstborn

—*It would have been enough for us!*

TORAS MENACHEM

The answer, it seems, is that so long as the Jewish people were in the desert and had not reached their final destination in the Land of Israel, there always remained a concern that Egypt would again win over the Jewish people, thereby reversing and nullifying the effects of the Exodus.

But how could Egypt reclaim the Jewish people if they had been destroyed, to the extent that *"not even one of them remained"* (*Shemos* 14:28)?

Because they were not completely destroyed. First, the *Midrash* teaches that Pharaoh survived the drowning at the sea and was later appointed King of Nineveh (*Pirkei d'Rabbi Eliezer* ch. 43; *Midrash Tehilim* 106:5).

Second, even if the notion of Pharaoh's survival reflects only one particular Rabbinic viewpoint, it is nevertheless quite clear from the universally accepted standpoint of *halachah* that the Egyptian *nation* remained (and only their *army* was destroyed). This is evident from the fact that it was prohibited for the

Jewish people to return to Egypt by the force of Torah Law: *"You may never see them again"* (*Shemos* 14:13), *"so that you do not become influenced by their heresy, and follow their depraved customs"* (*Sefer ha-Mitzvos,* prohibition 46).

As long as the Jewish people had not reached their final, secure destination in the Land of Israel, the possibility remained that they would find themselves *"lost in the area and trapped in the desert"* (ibid. 3), *"not knowing how to get out of it or where to go"* (*Rashi* ibid.). Perhaps, then, they would end up returning to Egypt.

Thus in order to appreciate the Exodus as a complete, irreversible process, the Haggadah deemed it necessary to include all the "good things which the Almighty had showered upon us," throughout the period in the desert, until "He brought us to the Land of Israel." For only when we began to dwell in the safe territory of our own civilized land was it clear that we had left Egypt for good.

(Based on *Sichah* of 2nd night of *Pesach* 5730)

אִלּוּ הָרַג אֶת־בְּכוֹרֵיהֶם

דַּיֵּנוּ:   וְלֹא נָתַן לָנוּ אֶת־מָמוֹנָם

אִלּוּ נָתַן לָנוּ אֶת־מָמוֹנָם

דַּיֵּנוּ:   וְלֹא קָרַע לָנוּ אֶת־הַיָּם

אִלּוּ קָרַע לָנוּ אֶת־הַיָּם

דַּיֵּנוּ:   וְלֹא הֶעֱבִירָנוּ בְתוֹכוֹ בֶּחָרָבָה

אִלּוּ הֶעֱבִירָנוּ בְתוֹכוֹ בֶּחָרָבָה

דַּיֵּנוּ:   וְלֹא שִׁקַּע צָרֵינוּ בְּתוֹכוֹ

CLASSIC QUESTIONS

● *"If He had not split the sea for us it would have been enough"*—surely we would have all been killed?

RASHBAM: God could have saved us in another way.

ABARBANEL: Perhaps God would have made Pharaoh have a change of heart and return to Egypt.

YA'AVETZ: God could have led us around the sea to the other side. Or He might have helped the Jewish people swim to the other side.

LIKUTEI TA'AMIM U'MINHAGIM: If God had not intended to split the sea He would not have instructed the Jewish people to turn back [in order to confuse the enemy] and encamp by the sea, waiting for Pharaoh (*Shemos* 13:18).

He would also not have hardened Pharaoh's heart to chase after the Jewish people. The Torah states explicitly that God did both of these things in order to orchestrate the miracle of the splitting of the sea:

TORAS MENACHEM

☙ דַּיֵּנוּ — *It would have been enough.*

The Previous Lubavitcher Rebbe, Rabbi Yosef Yitzchak Schneerson, regularly interrupted the recital of the Haggadah at his *Seder* to enlighten listeners with Chasidic commentary. When it came to this passage, however, he made a point of not stopping, offering insights either beforehand, or after reading *all* the "good things that the Almighty has bestowed on us."

What message was he trying to send us?

The *Ba'al Shem Tov* taught the following parable:

"There was a King who possessed a beautiful palace that had many chambers, one within the other. Numerous guards prevented people from entering or leaving without the King's permission.

"Among those who desired to enter the King's inner chamber, there were different types of people. One group, of the lower-classes, were immediately terrified by the King's guards and fled from them. *They are not the ones whom God desires.*

"A second group did not fear the outer guards, because they had schemed to bribe the guards with money—*like those who give a coin to charity before*

If He had slain their firstborn,

But had not given us their wealth

—It would have been enough for us!

If He had given us their wealth,

But had not split the sea for us

—It would have been enough for us!

If He had split the sea for us,

But had not led us through it on dry land

—It would have been enough for us!

If He had taken us through it on dry land,

But had not drowned our oppressors in it

—It would have been enough for us!

CLASSIC QUESTIONS

"You should encamp...by the sea. Pharaoh will say about the children of Israel, 'They are trapped...' I will harden Pharaoh's heart and he will pursue them. I will be glorified through wreaking vengeance on Pharaoh and his whole army" (ibid. 14:2-4).

Many of the commentators offer solutions as to how the Jewish people would be saved from the entrapment by the sea. But, in truth, this situation would never had arisen in the first place if God had not intended to make a miracle.

TORAS MENACHEM

prayer. They get past the guards, but something else holds them back from reaching the inner chamber and seeing the King's face. When they enter the palace and see the King's private collections—all the exquisite and most stunning treasures that are found there, the likes of which they have never seen before—they get such pleasure from feasting their eyes that they lose themselves there, forfeiting the great opportunity to see the King himself, in all his glory.

"The most outstanding group was not concerned with their own pleasures, and desired only to see the King in his inner chamber. So even when their eyes feasted on all the magnificent things, the likes of which they had never seen before, it was totally insignificant to them in the face of their will and desire to see the glory of the King Himself (*Ohr ha-Me'ir, Parshas Vayishlach*).

Time and time again we see that people become satisfied or "stuck" with a certain level of Judaism,

similar to the second group in this parable, and fail to take the idea of connecting with God to its full, logical conclusion. It is only natural for a person, at some point, to say: *"Dayenu!* This is enough for me! I've come a long way. I've overcome so many hurdles, both psychological and circumstantial, to reach where I am today. I have truly "left Egypt" in the sense that spirituality is meaningful for me in my everyday life. But I already have enough meaning and inspiration from my Judaism, so I'm reluctant to dedicate myself to a higher level of observance or personal refinement. Actually, I don't think I could cope with any more."

There is an element of truth to this argument because, after all, every person has their natural limit. After any growth spurt it's normal to feel: *dayenu,* this is enough for me.

But even if it's true that you really don't want any more, and you simply can't take any more, the *Ba'al Shem Tov* taught us that if you dig deeper into your

אִלּוּ שָׁקַע צָרֵינוּ בְּתוֹכוֹ

וְלֹא סִפֵּק צָרְכֵּנוּ בַּמִּדְבָּר אַרְבָּעִים שָׁנָה   דַּיֵּנוּ:

אִלּוּ סִפֵּק צָרְכֵּנוּ בַּמִּדְבָּר אַרְבָּעִים שָׁנָה

וְלֹא הֶאֱכִילָנוּ אֶת־הַמָּן   דַּיֵּנוּ:

אִלּוּ הֶאֱכִילָנוּ אֶת־הַמָּן

וְלֹא נָתַן לָנוּ אֶת־הַשַּׁבָּת   דַּיֵּנוּ:

אִלּוּ נָתַן לָנוּ אֶת־הַשַּׁבָּת

וְלֹא קֵרְבָנוּ לִפְנֵי הַר־סִינַי   דַּיֵּנוּ:

אִלּוּ קֵרְבָנוּ לִפְנֵי הַר־סִינַי

וְלֹא נָתַן לָנוּ אֶת־הַתּוֹרָה   דַּיֵּנוּ:

אִלּוּ נָתַן לָנוּ אֶת־הַתּוֹרָה

וְלֹא הִכְנִיסָנוּ לְאֶרֶץ יִשְׂרָאֵל   דַּיֵּנוּ:

= CLASSIC QUESTIONS =

● **How could we have survived if God *"had not supplied our needs in the desert for forty years?"***

ABARBANEL: If God had led us on a more populated route, such as *"through the land of the Philistines"* (*Shemos* 13:17), it would not have been necessary to provide food supernaturally.

LIKUTEI TA'AMIM U'MINHAGIM: The *Talmud* relates that the Jewish people were able to buy food items from

---

TORAS MENACHEM

soul you will find the courage, and the desire, to progress further.

So by not interrupting this passage the Previous Rebbe was effectively saying to us: Even when you feel like saying *dayenu*, don't stop. You *can* dedicate yourself to higher standards of Judaism, even when you already feel happy with your lot, because God planted in your soul a deep-rooted, insatiable desire for more.

(Based on *Sichah* of the 2nd night of Pesach 5716)

If He had drowned our oppressors in it,

But had not supplied our needs in the desert for forty years

—It would have been enough for us!

If He had supplied our needs in the desert for forty years,

But had not fed us the Manna

—It would have been enough for us!

If He had fed us the Manna,

But had not given us the Shabbos

—It would have been enough for us!

If He had given us the Shabbos,

But had not brought us before Mount Sinai

—It would have been enough for us!

If He had brought us before Mount Sinai,

But had not given us the Torah

—It would have been enough for us!

If He had given us the Torah,

But had not brought us into the Land of Israel

—It would have been enough for us!

CLASSIC QUESTIONS

various foreign merchants who were active in the desert (*Yoma* 75b). So if "God had not supplied our needs in the desert for forty years," we would have survived with food that we purchased, and "it would have been enough."

● **What would be the purpose of bringing us to Mount Sinai if God would not have given us the Torah there?**

ABARBANEL: The commandments were said directly by God, unlike the rest of the Torah, which was given through Moshe. The Haggadah is saying that if we would not have heard any of the Torah directly from God, it would have been enough.

AVUDRAHAM: The *Talmud* relates that at Sinai we were freed from the spiritual impurity which had descended on the world when Chava (Eve) sinned (*Shabbos* 146a). This alone would have been enough!

LIKUTEI TA'AMIM U'MINHAGIM: Just being at Sinai was a remarkable experience of Divine revelation, as the verse states, *"God has shown us His glory and His greatness"* (*Devarim* 5:21); *"You revealed Yourself in Your cloud of glory on Mount Sinai"* (*Liturgy, Additional Prayer for Rosh ha-Shanah*).

Alternatively, the Haggadah could be understood as saying that if we had only received the Ten Commandments at Sinai, and not the Tablets or the other commandments, it would have been enough.

אִלּוּ הִכְנִיסָנוּ לְאֶרֶץ יִשְׂרָאֵל

וְלֹא בָנָה לָנוּ אֶת־בֵּית הַבְּחִירָה   דַּיֵּנוּ:

עַל

אַחַת כַּמָּה וְכַמָּה טוֹבָה כְפוּלָה וּמְכֻפֶּלֶת לַמָּקוֹם עָלֵינוּ.

שֶׁהוֹצִיאָנוּ מִמִּצְרַיִם.

וְעָשָׂה בָהֶם שְׁפָטִים.

וְעָשָׂה בֵאלֹהֵיהֶם.

וְהָרַג אֶת־בְּכוֹרֵיהֶם.

וְנָתַן לָנוּ אֶת־מָמוֹנָם.

וְקָרַע לָנוּ אֶת־הַיָּם.

וְהֶעֱבִירָנוּ בְתוֹכוֹ בֶּחָרָבָה.

וְשִׁקַּע צָרֵינוּ בְּתוֹכוֹ.

וְסִפֵּק צָרְכֵּנוּ בַּמִּדְבָּר אַרְבָּעִים שָׁנָה.

TORAS MENACHEM

וְלֹא בָנָה לָנוּ אֶת בֵּית הַבְּחִירָה — *But had not built for us the Chosen House.*

One can appreciate that all of the details listed here, until *"He brought us to the Land of Israel,"* are directly related to the Exodus from Egypt, because so long as the Jewish nation were wandering in the desert the entire process of Exodus remained in jeopardy (see above, p. 111). But why was it necessary to

include in the Haggadah the final point that *"He built for us the Chosen House,"* an event which occurred several hundred years after the Exodus?

One solution might be to suggest that this final line is a parenthetical statement, not directly related to the main theme of the Haggadah. Having mentioned the idea of settling in the Land of Israel, it is only natural to mention the Temple, which is the

If He had brought us into the Land of Israel,
But had not built for us the Chosen House
—*It would have been enough for us!*

How Much More So

*should we be grateful to God for the
doubled and redoubled goodness
that He has bestowed upon us!*

He brought us out of Egypt;

and He carried out judgments against them;

and against their gods;

and He slayed their firstborn;

and He gave us their wealth;

and He split the sea for us;

and He led us through it on dry land;

and He drowned our oppressors in it;

and He supplied our needs in the desert for forty years;

TORAS MENACHEM

focal point of the Land where the *Shechinah* (Divine Presence) rested.

But perhaps we could suggest a more contextually satisfying explanation. Above we argued that entering the Land of Israel brought a significant level of national security that was sorely lacking in the desert, which is why we could say with confidence that the Jewish people had left Egypt for good.

Where, though, was the guarantee that the settlement of the Land would be successful? At what point could it truly be said that the occupation of the Land was irreversible? This, answers the Haggadah, was when "*He built for us the Chosen House,*" because, "*the sanctity of the Temple and Jerusalem is due to the Shechinah, and the Shechinah cannot be displaced*" (*Rambam, Laws of the Chosen House* 6:16).

(Based on *Sichah* of 2nd night of *Pesach* 5730)

וְהֶאֱכִילָנוּ אֶת־הַמָּן.

וְנָתַן לָנוּ אֶת־הַשַּׁבָּת.

וְקֵרְבָנוּ לִפְנֵי הַר־סִינַי.

וְנָתַן לָנוּ אֶת־הַתּוֹרָה.

וְהִכְנִיסָנוּ לְאֶרֶץ יִשְׂרָאֵל.

וּבָנָה לָנוּ אֶת־בֵּית הַבְּחִירָה לְכַפֵּר עַל כָּל־עֲוֹנוֹתֵינוּ:

רַבָּן גַּמְלִיאֵל הָיָה אוֹמֵר:

כָּל־שֶׁלֹּא אָמַר שְׁלֹשָׁה דְבָרִים אֵלּוּ בַּפֶּסַח לֹא יָצָא יְדֵי חוֹבָתוֹ. וְאֵלּוּ הֵן:

פֶּסַח מַצָּה וּמָרוֹר:

CLASSIC QUESTIONS

● **Does one merely have to *mention* Pesach, Matzah and Maror at the Seder?**

RASHBAM: No, one must ex*plain* the reasons for these *miztvos*.

● **If a person fails to explain these three things has he not fulfilled his obligation *at all*?**

RAN: The Haggadah means to say that he has not fulfilled his obligation *properly* (*Pesachim* 116a-b).

RASHBATZ: One must explain the reason for these three *mitzvos* here, otherwise one has not fulfilled one's obligation to recount the Exodus.

Even though some of these ideas were touched upon earlier, during the Four Questions, they must be clarified properly here.

● **Which obligation, exactly, are we speaking about here?**

KIRYAS SEFER: One must explain the reasons for Pesach, Matzah and Maror, in order to fulfill the *mitzvah* of remembering the Exodus properly (*Laws of Chametz and Matzah* 7:5).

RABEINU MANOACH: One must explain the reasons for Pesach, Matzah and Maror in order to fulfill the *mitzvos* of Pesach, Matzah and Maror properly. (*ibid.*).

and He fed us the Manna;

and He gave us the Shabbos;

and He brought us before Mount Sinai;

and He gave us the Torah;

and He brought us into the land of Israel;

and He built the Chosen House

for us, to atone for all our sins.

RABBAN GAMLIEL USED TO SAY:

Whoever has not mentioned the following three things on Pesach has not fulfilled his obligation. They are:

Pesach, Matzah & Maror.

WHAT ARE WE DOING NOW?

This concludes the Haggadah's chronological exposition of the Exodus story (beginning on p. 36) (Rashbatz).

Thus, while the following passage is integral to the Haggadah, and to the mitzvah of recalling the Exodus (see Classic Questions), it is nevertheless not part of the actual chronicle of the Exodus itself (Likutei Sichos vol. 17, p. 79, note 20).

TORAS MENACHEM

פֶּסַח מַצָּה וּמָרוֹר — *Pesach, Matzah and Maror.*

There are three general categories of food: a.) food that is required for normal development, or is vitally needed to sustain life; b.) food that is harmful, and must be excluded or even destroyed; and, c.) food that while not indispensable is a source of additional nourishment and pleasure.

These three categories are alluded to in the three special Pesach foods—Matzah, Maror and Pesach:

a.) Matzah is, of course, unleavened bread and *"bread sustains a man's life"* (Psalms 104:15). In a broader sense, the term "bread" is used for a whole meal, and the entire daily diet (see *Daniel* 5:1; *Rashi* to *Bereishis* 31:54).

b.) Maror—in our context—signifies undesirable things which we need to perceive as bitter, and therefore reject.

c.) The Pesach sacrifice had to be eaten *"al ha-sova,"* when filled to satisfaction (*Rambam, Laws of Pesach Sacrifice* 8:3). It came as a "dessert," a source of additional nourishment and pleasure. For this reason the Pesach had to be eaten sumptuously, *"in a manner of royal festivity"* (*Rashbam* to *Pesachim* 119b).

פֶּסַח שֶׁהָיוּ אֲבוֹתֵינוּ אוֹכְלִים בִּזְמַן שֶׁבֵּית הַמִּקְדָּשׁ קַיָּם עַל־שׁוּם מָה? עַל־שׁוּם שֶׁפָּסַח הַקָּדוֹשׁ בָּרוּךְ הוּא עַל־בָּתֵּי אֲבוֹתֵינוּ בְּמִצְרָיִם. שֶׁנֶּאֱמַר: "וַאֲמַרְתֶּם זֶבַח־פֶּסַח הוּא לַיהֹוָה אֲשֶׁר פָּסַח עַל־בָּתֵּי בְנֵי־יִשְׂרָאֵל בְּמִצְרַיִם בְּנָגְפּוֹ אֶת־מִצְרַיִם וְאֶת־בָּתֵּינוּ הִצִּיל, וַיִּקֹּד הָעָם וַיִּשְׁתַּחֲווּ":

TORAS MENACHEM

Based on the above, we can discern three types of spiritual "food" that need to be given to a child through the process of education:

a.) The first vital need of the child is to receive a daily ration of staple nourishment, that is, Torah and *mitzvos*, which are termed "bread," as the verse states, *"Come and eat bread from My bread"* (*Proverbs* 9:5). The verse alludes to two "breads"—the Written Torah and the Oral Torah; the legal and mystical parts of Torah; and to both Torah and *mitzvos*.

Furthermore, one should be careful that the learning of Torah and the observance of the *mitzvos* are humble and flat, like Matzah, without any trace of *chametz* (leaven) that causes the dough to arrogantly rise, expand, and swell (*Likutei Torah, Tzav* 13c).

b.) At the same time, it is necessary to protect the child against undesirable (bitter) influences from outside—alluded to by the Maror—through discipline and rebuke. But just as nowadays the obligation to eat Maror does not have the same legal force as in Temple times (it is now a Rabbinic and not a Biblical obligation), so too, the contemporary approach to discipline should be softer than in the past. *Matzah,* by contrast, remains a full Biblical requirement to this day, exactly as it was in Temple times, which teaches us that we should continue *with full force* to offer positive reinforcement to our children in their "staple diet" of Torah and *mitzvos*.

c.) If we follow these guidelines in the education of our children (and ourselves) step by step, we will become "satiated" with Torah and *mitzvos*, such that the holiness in the heart of every Jew will come to the surface, engendering a total commitment to God. Then we will learn Torah with even greater dedica-

tion and observe the *mitzvos* with every possible enhancement, doing it all with true joy (*"in a manner of royal festivity"*) as reflected in the Pesach sacrifice.

(communal letter, 11th of *Nissan* 5737)

৪৩ **פֶּסַח** — *Pesach, the Paschal Lamb.*

The birth of the Jewish nation was accompanied by extraordinary difficulties, because Egypt was at that time the mightiest and most advanced country in terms of power, science, etc., yet, also the most depraved in terms of morality and religion.

After centuries of physical and spiritual enslavement in Egypt, the Jews had to undergo a complete transformation—in quite a short period of time—and move to the other extreme, in order to be ready and worthy to receive the Torah at Sinai. There they would attain the highest level, both in the realm of religion—the belief in One God (pure Monotheism) —as well as in relation to man, as expressed in the Ten Commandments, and all this was to be implemented in their actual everyday life and conduct.

Yet, despite the extraordinary difficulties, the Jewish people succeeded in making the radical transition from dismal slavery to sublime freedom. This they achieved by virtue of the fact that, while still in Egypt, they took a stance of "an upraised arm" in their resolute determination to carry out all the Divine imperatives pertaining to the Passover sacrifice. For this sacrifice called for public renunciation of the idolatry of Egypt, at grave peril to their lives.

One of the basic teachings and instructions that follow from the above is that what is true of the birth of the Jewish nation as a whole is also true of the birth of every Jewish child.

*P*esach—the Paschal lamb that our ancestors ate when the Holy Temple stood—is for what reason?

Because God passed over our fathers' houses in Egypt, as the verse states:"You should say,'It is a Pesach-offering to God, because He passed over the houses of the children of Israel in Egypt when He struck the Egyptians, and He spared our households.' Then the people bowed down and prostrated themselves" (*Shemos* 12:27).

TORAS MENACHEM

Jewish parents ought to realize that the upbringing of a Jewish child begins from the moment that the child is born. They should immediately begin preparing the child to be a rightful member of the *"Kingdom of Priests and a holy nation"* (*Shemos* 19:6).

Despite the fact that life in this world is replete with difficulties—though many of them are only imaginary—there is no doubt that when parents take the stance of "an upraised arm" in providing a Torah-true education for their children, they are bound to succeed, just as our ancestors in Egypt succeeded; all the more so since the road has already been paved.

(Communal letter, *Rosh Chodesh Nissan* 5737)

שֶׁפָּסַח הַמָּקוֹם עַל בָּתֵּי אֲבוֹתֵינוּ בְּמִצְרַיִם — *God passed over our fathers' houses in Egypt.*

The festival of Pesach, so named after the *Korban Pesach* (Passover sacrifice), emphasizes the importance of *Chinuch*—the proper rearing of Jewish children. As a matter of fact, one of the underlying motives for the whole Seder is to educate the children. While this can be seen from various passages in the Haggadah, the *Korban Pesach* emphasizes most forcefully the extent to which Jewish education affects not only the child, but also the parents.

If parents fail in their duty to their child, they forfeit the opportunity of "offering the *Korban Pesach*," together with all the things and blessings associated with it, both material and spiritual; specifically the benefit spelled out in the Torah: *"It is a Pesach unto God... and I will pass over you (or I will have mercy on you)... and shall not let the Destroyer (plague) enter your houses to smite"* (*Shemos* 12:11-13 and *Rashi,* ibid). This is God's assurance of mercy and protection even in a world afflicted with ills, physical or

spiritual; the Jew who properly observes the *"Korban Pesach"* is promised that such ills will "pass over" him and his house.

At the time when the children of Israel were in Egypt, the *Korban Pesach* protected their houses against the Destroyer (plague) raging outside. Only the firstborn were threatened then. But in our day and age, when Jews everywhere are still in Exile, in a physical as well as a spiritual Exile, some Jewish parents have unfortunately disregarded the *Korban-Pesach*, the first prerequisite of which, as stated in the Torah, is *"withdraw and take unto yourselves"* (ibid. 21), meaning, *"withdraw from idolatry* (foreign ideologies) *and cleave to mitzvos"* (*Mechilta,* ibid.).

Consequently, the Destroyer finds an open door to these houses, seeking victims to lead astray, God forbid, and not discriminating whether they be firstborn or not, boys or girls. The plague has spread to many Jewish homes, Heaven protect us. This is the result of the failure of some parents to abandon alien ideologies, many of which are antithetical to Judaism.

The sad and tragic effects of such an attitude are not far to see, sad and tragic not only for the neglected children, but also for the neglecting parents.

The festival of Pesach, and especially the *Korban Pesach,* reminds us most emphatically that if Jews desire to secure for themselves and their children the blessing of *"I shall have mercy and pass over (exclude) you"* and of the "Season of Our Liberation" in general—liberation from all existing and potential harm, at a time when the Destroyer roams in the streets and even in the halls of learning—such liberation can be assured only if the parents themselves will reject all "idolatries" and attach themselves to authentic Judaism. They need to give their children a thorough Torah-true Jewish education from infancy,

> THE MIDDLE MATZAH IS LIFTED UP AND SHOWN WHILE THE FOLLOWING PASSAGE IS RECITED.

מַצָּה זוֹ שֶׁאָנוּ אוֹכְלִים עַל־שׁוּם מָה? עַל־שׁוּם שֶׁלֹּא הִסְפִּיק בְּצֵקָם שֶׁל אֲבוֹתֵינוּ לְהַחֲמִיץ עַד שֶׁנִּגְלָה עֲלֵיהֶם מֶלֶךְ מַלְכֵי הַמְּלָכִים הַקָּדוֹשׁ בָּרוּךְ הוּא וּגְאָלָם. שֶׁנֶּאֱמַר: "וַיֹּאפוּ אֶת־הַבָּצֵק אֲשֶׁר הוֹצִיאוּ מִמִּצְרַיִם עֻגֹת

TORAS MENACHEM

the kind of education which is sealed in their body and soul, through the practical fulfillment of the Torah and *mitzvos* in the daily life, in actual practice. Then there is hope and confidence that the parents and their children, all the children, will be together at the Seder-table and celebrate Pesach, the Festival of Our Liberation—liberation in every possible way.

(Communal letter, 11th *Nissan* 5730)

מַצָּה זוֹ — *This Matzah, unleavened bread.*

"Sin lies at the door" (*Bereishis* 4:7), warns the Torah, waiting to jump into our lives. Virtually every person leaves himself an open "doorway" of temptation, through which the negative, the forbidden and the profane may enter.

But just as sin possesses an "entrance door" into our personalities, it also has a metaphorical "exit." "'Make me a single opening of teshuvah (repentance) just as wide as the tip of a needle,' says God, 'and I will make for you an opening as wide as the entrance to the Temple'" (see *Shir ha-Shirim Rabah* 5:3). *Teshuvah* is described as a "small" opening because the genuine resolve to become a better person takes just a brief moment—yet it brings an instantaneous transformation for the good (see *Kidushin* 49b). In one second, even many years of sins which have entered through our gaping front "doorway," can pass out discreetly through a small "exit" opening at the rear.

The notion of sinning with or without subsequent *teshuvah* is alluded to by the two Hebrew letters *hei* and *ches*. The *hei* (ה) has a wide opening below, representing the gaping "entrance doorway" of sin; but it also has a tiny "exit gap" on the upper left, suggestive of the "small opening" of *teshuvah* through which

sins may depart. So the *hei* represents a person who, after succumbing to sin, regathers his composure and returns to God.

The *ches* (ח), by contrast, has an entrance below, but lacks an exit. The sins come in, but they cannot leave. This is a person who resists *teshuvah*.

What is the cause of his resistance?

Matzah provides us with the solution. The Hebrew words for Matzah, and its antithesis, Chametz (leaven), both consist of three letters, (two of which are the same: *mem* and *tzadik*). The only difference between them is the third letter: Matzah (מַצָּה) is spelled with a *hei*, whereas Chametz (חָמֵץ) is spelled with a *ches*.

So in order to crack the resistance to *teshuvah*, we need to stop being like Chametz (*ches*) and start to emulate Matzah (*hei*). When a person is humble and "flat" like Matzah, even if he succumbs momentarily to sin, he will soon admit his error and contemplate *teshuvah*. The sins will "enter" and then "depart."

But someone who has an inflated ego, puffed up like Chametz, will not be so quick to repent. A sense of arrogance and overbearing pride blinds the person's eyes to the possibility that *he* may have done something wrong. Almost effortlessly, he produces a barrage of logical arguments in his defense, arguments which—to his ear—sound eminently reasonable, because, *"(self) love covers up all sins"* (*Prov.* 10:12).

The internal psychological upheaval which *teshuvah* demands can seem daunting at first, but Matzah teaches us that it is really not so difficult—it just requires a *small* opening. Our self-perception can become more fair and objective in just one instant if we choose to be honest with ourselves, and then

> THE MIDDLE MATZAH IS LIFTED UP AND SHOWN WHILE THE FOLLOWING PASSAGE
> IS RECITED.

*T*his Matzah, unleavened bread, that we eat is for what reason? Because the dough of our fathers did not have time to become leavened before the King—the King of kings, the Holy One, blessed be He—revealed Himself to them and redeemed them, as the verse states: "They baked the dough that they had taken out of Egypt into cakes of Matzos, for it had not leavened, since they

---

CLASSIC QUESTIONS

● **Why does the Haggadah suggest here that Matzah was eaten due to circumstantial reasons (because they had to leave in a hurry) when prior to the Exodus the Jews had already been commanded to eat Matzah** (see *Shemos* 12:8)**?**

AVUDRAHAM: Through foreseeing the future, God knew that at the moment of Exodus there would not be time for the dough to rise. Therefore He gave them the *mitzvah of* Matzah in advance, to celebrate the *future* miracle of a speedy departure that was to take place.

ABARBANEL: In fact, we find exactly the same scenario with the Paschal lamb: It was commanded in connection with a future miracle, that God was going to pass over the Jewish houses later that night.

LIKUTEI TORAH: The Torah speaks of two different kinds of Matzah which relate to two specific times:

1.) *Matzah of Obligation.* The commandment to eat Matzah issued prior to the Exodus was a requirement to eat it along with the Paschal lamb and bitter

herbs (*Shemos* 12:8), and this had to be *"before midnight"* (*Zevachim* 5:8).

2.) *Matzah of Revelation.* The Matzah which the Haggadah speaks of here was eaten after *"the King of kings...revealed Himself to them,"* i.e. after midnight, (since *"It was at midnight when God struck every firstborn"*—ibid. 29). Spiritually speaking, this second Matzah was vastly superior as it was associated with a revelation of *"the King of kings."*

At the Seder we eat an obligatory Matzah before midnight, so you might think that we are only commemorating the spiritually inferior *Matzah of Obligation* that was eaten in Egypt before midnight. The Haggadah therefore explains that now, subsequent to the Exodus, our Matzah has both connotations: Even though we eat it before midnight, it also has the higher spiritual caliber of the *Matzah of Revelation* that our ancestors ate after midnight (*Tzav* 13b).

TZEMACH TZEDEK: Ultimately, the *Alter Rebbe's* explanation (in *Likutei Torah*) fails to solve our problem

---

TORAS MENACHEM

God *"will make for you an opening as wide as the entrance to the Temple."*

(Based on *Likutei Sichos* vol. 1, p. 129*ff*)

עַל שׁוּם שֶׁלֹּא הִסְפִּיק בְּצֵקֶת שֶׁל אֲבוֹתֵינוּ 🙠
לְהַחֲמִיץ — *Because the dough of our fathers did not have time to become leavened.*

Remarkably, the Haggadah gives just one reason for "this Matzah that we eat," namely, that our ancestors left Egypt in a hurry and their dough had no time

to rise. By first posing the question, *"This Matzah that we eat is for what reason?"* the Haggadah seems to suggest that this is the one and only reason for this *mitzvah.*

Many commentators have noted that this assertion seems peculiar. There are numerous reasons why we eat Matzah, not just one, so why should the Haggadah single out this one reason in particular? And how could the Haggadah possibly imply that this is the *only* reason, to the exclusion of all others?

מַצּוֹת, כִּי לֹא חָמֵץ, כִּי־גֹרְשׁוּ מִמִּצְרַיִם וְלֹא יָכְלוּ
לְהִתְמַהְמֵהַּ וְגַם־צֵדָה לֹא־עָשׂוּ לָהֶם":

➤ THE BITTER HERBS ARE LIFTED UP AND SHOWN WHILE THE FOLLOWING PASSAGE IS
RECITED.

מָרוֹר זֶה שֶׁאָנוּ אוֹכְלִים עַל־שׁוּם מָה?
עַל שׁוּם שֶׁמֵּרְרוּ הַמִּצְרִים אֶת־חַיֵּי
אֲבוֹתֵינוּ בְּמִצְרָיִם. שֶׁנֶּאֱמַר: "וַיְמָרְרוּ אֶת־חַיֵּיהֶם

CLASSIC QUESTIONS

here. For the *"Matzah that we eat"* is before mid-night, so how could it be *"because the dough of our fathers did not have time to become leavened before the King of kings...revealed Himself etc.,"* an event which occurred *after* midnight?

The Alter Rebbe wishes to argue that, somehow, our ancestors' post-midnight *Matzah of Revelation* has now been incorporated into our pre-midnight

Matzah of Obligation. At the literal level, however, such an interpretation is tenuous. [For how can we honestly say *"this Matzah* that we eat" at *this* time is to commemorate a *different* type of Matzah which was eaten at a *different* time?]

Rather, the most straightforward solution to this problem is that of *Avudraham* (*Ohr ha-Torah, Bo,* p. 307).

TORAS MENACHEM

To appreciate how great the omission seems to be here, let us briefly examine a number of important themes represented by the Matzah we eat today:

a.) It is to commemorate the fact that in Egypt, before the Exodus, the Jewish people were already commanded to eat Matzah on the eve of the fifteenth of Nissan (before the Exodus), as the verse states, *"In the evening you shall eat Matzos"* (Shemos 12:18).

b.) The explanation of the Haggadah, that we eat Matzah to commemorate the Divine revelation of the Exodus (*"the King of kings... revealed Himself"*), which caused the Jewish people to leave in a hurry.

c.) Unlike the Matzah eaten at the time of the Exodus ('b'), which was eaten due to circumstantial necessity (lack of time to bake Chametz), our Matzah is a *mitzvah* which we actively choose to observe.

d.) The Alter Rebbe explains in *Likutei Torah* that in Egypt there were two different types of Matzah: *Matzah of Obligation* and *Matzah of Revelation*. And our Matzah, he writes, combines *both* of these qualities in one.

e.) All our observances have the authority of Sinai, in contrast to the events of the Exodus which occurred before the Giving of the Torah. This endows our Matzah-eating with additional significance that vastly exceeds anything that came to pass in Egypt. For all pre-Sinaitic commands are legally and spiritually insignificant compared to the Sinaitic precepts that superseded them.

f.) The Exodus was a Divine revelation: *"The King of kings, the Holy One blessed be He, revealed Himself to them."* And, as is the case with any new phenomenon, it can take some time to tune into and appreciate what has been uncovered. That is why, for example, we find that there were forty-nine days of Counting the *Omer* between the Exodus and the Giving of the Torah, when the Jewish people absorbed and took to heart the revelations of the Exodus through personal refinement, so as to be fit to receive the Torah.

Now if we bear in mind that: i.) a person observes numerous *mitzvos* throughout the year, and ii.) that

were driven out of Egypt and could not delay, but had also not prepared any provisions" (*Shemos* 12:39).

➤ THE BITTER HERBS ARE LIFTED UP AND SHOWN WHILE THE FOLLOWING PASSAGE IS RECITED.

This Maror, bitter herbs, that we eat is for what reason? Because the Egyptians embittered our ancestors' lives in Egypt, as the verse states: "And they embittered their lives

---

TORAS MENACHEM

these *mitzvos* have a cumulative effect of refining his personality, then it follows that when Pesach comes around every year, each person is *more prepared than ever* to absorb the revelations of the Exodus that resurge on that day. So, in addition to all the above points ('a'–'e'), our Matzah defies any historical precedent since it is the most "prepared for" *mitzvah* of its kind to date.

If we bear in mind all these remarkable qualities of our current observance of Matzah, it seems almost absurd that when discussing "the Matzah *that we eat*" the Haggadah should mention just one of the above points ('b'), and imply that it is to the exclusion of all others! (Even according to the Alter Rebbe's explanation, points 'c,' 'e' and 'f' are still not indicated in the Haggadah [and we are left with the question of the *Tzemach Tzedek*]).

First of all, we need to bear in mind that the current passage is part of the Haggadah's extended narration of the Exodus story. We do not mention Matzah here simply because it is a *mitzvah*, a practice prescribed by Jewish law today, but because by relating the reason (or reasons) behind the *mitzvah* we enhance the miraculous chronicle of the Exodus.

[Thus when the Haggadah asks, "This Matzah that we eat is for what reason?" the inquiry is not, as it may at first seem, "Tell me some of the important reasons for the *mitzvah* of Matzah." Rather, the Haggadah is asking: "Can you elaborate on any particular significance of Matzah which will enhance the miraculous chronicle of the Exodus?".]

A second, crucial point is that the *mitzvah* of chronicling the Exodus tonight is to relate the story *as it happened then*, regardless of any additional layers of significance that may have been added to it subsequently. We are not here to describe the

influence of the Exodus on post-Sinaitic *mitzvos,* or to suggest how our celebrations today are spiritually superior to those experienced by the Jews in Egypt. Our purpose in reciting the Haggadah tonight is to get back to "grass roots" and explain how the Jewish nation was born, i.e. to recount and relive the events of the fifteenth of Nissan 1312 BCE.

[Thus the Haggadah's phrase "This Matzah *that we eat*" is effectively a parenthetical statement. The question here is not "What is the reason for the Matzah that we eat?," but rather, "This Matzah—that we eat—is for what reason?," i.e., how is it significant to the story of the Exodus? (cf. *Likutei Ta'amim u'Minhagim* ibid.)]

In the final analysis, it turns out that the only explanation which answers this question by i.) enhancing the Exodus chronicle; and, ii.) relating specifically to the circumstances surrounding the original Exodus, is that: *"the dough of our fathers did not have time to become leavened before the King of kings, the Holy One, blessed be He, revealed Himself to them and redeemed them."*

(Based on *Ma'amar* of eve of 14 Nissan 5749, s.v. *Matza zu*; *Likutei Sichos* vol. 17, p. 79, note 20).

מָרוֹר זֶה ✦ — *This Maror, bitter herbs.*

Of Rabban Gamliel's "three things" which must be mentioned at the Seder, the first two need little clarification: both Pesach and Matzah clearly convey the theme of Exodus and liberation, as we have shown. But why is Maror, the bitter herbs which remind us of our ancestors' suffering in Egypt, a symbol of freedom? It might well represent what we were liberated *from*, but it does not appear to be *in itself* a food associated with freedom. Why, then, is it highlighted here as one of the key "take-home" messages of tonight's experience?

בַּעֲבֹדָה קָשָׁה בְּחֹמֶר וּבִלְבֵנִים וּבְכָל־עֲבֹדָה בַּשָּׂדֶה,
אֵת כָּל־עֲבֹדָתָם אֲשֶׁר־עָבְדוּ בָהֶם בְּפָרֶךְ":

בְּכָל־דּוֹר וָדוֹר חַיָּב אָדָם לִרְאוֹת אֶת־
עַצְמוֹ כְּאִלּוּ הוּא יָצָא מִמִּצְרַיִם.
שֶׁנֶּאֱמַר: "וְהִגַּדְתָּ לְבִנְךָ בַּיּוֹם הַהוּא

TORAS MENACHEM

In order to appreciate the positive and practically useful message conveyed by the Maror, we need to first understand its position, or "spiritual address," on the Seder plate. Look at the plate on the table in front of you. The egg and vegetable are on the left side, the bone and Charoses are on the right side, and in the middle are two helpings of bitter herbs (Maror and Chazeres). This arrangement follows the Kabbalistic custom of the *Arizal* (Rabbi Yitzchak Luria of Safed, 1534-72).

Jewish mystics always associated the left side with harshness and severity, and the right side with generosity and kindness. The middle was thus seen to represent a mediation between the two opposing thrusts. When severity says, "This person needs to be punished," and kindness says, "No, we must show only love to our fellow creatures," the solution, says the Kabbalah, comes from the "middle" path of empathy, compassion and mercy. Empathy says to the harsh left side, "You are right, this person deserves to be punished. But have mercy on him! He is poor and well-meaning. Empathize with his sorry state and be kind to him even though he doesn't really deserve it."

Compassion is an effective form of mediation because it essentially agrees with severity that punishment is in order, but pleads for positive, kind action based on the circumstances. The middle path, therefore, represents the ability to neutralize or "sweeten" the harshness of the left, steering it toward the positive conclusion of the right.

Maror is a bitter substance that reminds us of suffering and racial persecution. It appears to convey no message of compassion, nor does it suggest the neutralization or sweetening of punishments. So why does it belong in the *middle* of the Seder plate? Maror would seem to be a clear-cut "left" substance, from a Kabbalistic point of view.

A simple explanation might be argued based on the conviction shared by every religious person that nothing is essentially or perpetually negative. Everything that God does He does for the good, and it is only that we, as mortal humans, are not always capable of perceiving the implicit benefits. So even a bitter "Maror" experience is not truly negative. One day we will be able to perceive our difficult moments as necessary growth spurts, or as crucial links in a broader chain of positive events.

However, while this religious conviction is, of course, well-founded, it does not appear to solve our problem. For if everything is essentially good *then there should be no left side at all.* The Kabbalists gave credence to the phenomenon of "left," because while everything is ultimately for the good, momentarily at least we suffer *real* pain. One day we will realize the positive side of the experience, but *now* it is painful.

So we are left with the question: If Maror represents pain and suffering, it surely belongs on the left?

To understand the innovative theology of suffering represented by Maror, we need to examine its basic legal foundation. While the consumption of Maror is a Biblical obligation, *"it is not an independent Biblical commandment in its own right, but one that is contingent on eating the Paschal lamb. For there is just one single commandment: to eat the Paschal lamb together with... Maror"* (Rambam, *Laws of Chametz and Matzah* 7:12). In other words the Maror is a mere accompaniment to the Paschal lamb.

If the Paschal lamb represents liberation, and Maror represents life's difficulties, then the message implicit

with hard labor, with mortar and with bricks and with all kinds of labor in the field, all their work that they made them do was crushing labor" (ibid. 1:14).

QUICK INSIGHT
A person must see himself as if he has been freed, not merely from generic slavery, but from the uniquely harsh slavery of Egypt (see Toras Menachem).

In each and every generation a person must see himself as if he had personally left Egypt, as the verse states: "You shall tell your son on that day,

TORAS MENACHEM

in the above law is that our difficulties should never be perceived in isolation. They are nothing but an "accompaniment" to enhance our subsequent feelings of liberation and happiness, just like the Maror was a "flavor enhancer" to the Paschal lamb.

The "left side" tells us: "right now you feel pain, and *later* this pain will be transformed into joy." But tonight the Maror is placed in the middle, as if to say, "You might feel pain right now, but you are in the process of liberation. It's not that your pain will be *followed* by gain, you are gaining right now. This misery is all part of one big package, which is intended for no other purpose than to uplift and redeem you."

It's certainly not easy, but when viewed in this light, the bitter taste of life's difficulties can be effectively sweetened. We need to keep in mind that setbacks and solutions are not two separate entities but one: the setbacks and hurdles are sent to us by God *for no other reason* than to make the subsequent relief more profound and personally meaningful.

Tonight, on the festival of our liberation, God is granting us the strength and inspiration to perceive all problems as "enhancements" to their solutions, and all pain as a gift from above to motivate us to greater achievements. Life's darker moments may still taste bitter, but by keeping in sharp focus that as we suffer we are in the midst of growth and redemption, it will help to sweeten and neutralize the pain.

(Based on *Sichah* of *Acharon Shel Pesach* 5720)

❧ **בְּכָל דּוֹר וָדוֹר** — *In each and every generation....*

This injunction and demand has been made upon *every generation* of Jews, during the time when the royal house of David had been reigning for

generations, as also in the darkest times of exile and extermination, may the Merciful One spare us.

Likewise is it made upon every Jew and *every day*. Even though he experienced the "release from bondage" yesterday, he is to relive it today, and again tomorrow.

For the meaning of "liberation from Egypt" is the attainment of freedom from obstacles and limitations which the Jew encounters in his way to self-fulfillment, hindering him from reaching his destiny and from accomplishing what he must.

That is why the freedom which he experienced yesterday does not hold good for his position and state of today, and his attainment today will prove inadequate tomorrow.

To get a clearer and better understanding of what has been said above, let us consider an analogy from Nature:

On the level of *plant life*, we would consider a plant completely "free" from all "anxiety" and hindrance, when it has been fully provided with all the things needed for its growth: soil, water, air, etc. Although it cannot move from its place, being "condemned" to remain rooted to its spot all its life—nevertheless it enjoys the fullest freedom of plant life. So long as it remains a plant, it is truly free.

An *animal*, however, even when it is fully provided with its needs in the way of food, water, etc., yet is forcibly confined to one place, such confinement would spell the utmost deprivation for it, and a most dreadful imprisonment, inasmuch as it would be denied that which is *the essential aspect of its being.*

In the case of a human being, inasmuch as man's distinction is that of the intellect, if he would be given

לֵאמֹר, בַּעֲבוּר זֶה עָשָׂה יְהֹוָה לִי בְּצֵאתִי מִמִּצְרָיִם": לֹא אֶת-אֲבוֹתֵינוּ בִּלְבָד גָּאַל הַקָּדוֹשׁ בָּרוּךְ הוּא אֶלָּא

=== CLASSIC QUESTIONS ===

● **How does one "personally leave Egypt"?**

RAMBAM: In each and every generation a person is obligated to display himself as if he is personally now leaving the servitude of Egypt, as the verse states, "*And He brought **us** out from there*" (*Devarim* 6:23). This matter was commanded by God in the Torah: "*Remember that you were a slave*" (ibid. 5:15; 15:15), which means, it is as if you yourself had been a slave and were set free and redeemed.

Therefore, when one dines on this night, he should eat and drink in a reclining position in the manner of free men. Furthermore, every person, man and woman, is required to drink four cups of wine on this night (*Laws of Chametz and Matzah* 7:6-7).

● **How does *Shemos* 13:8 prove that the Exodus phenomenon exists in every generation?**

MAHARSHA: While the verse was said to the generation that actually left Egypt, it nevertheless points to future generations, with the words, "You shall tell your son *on that day.*" Thus the verse is saying, even in the future ("*on that day*") a person must relate that the Exodus was "for me." From here we see that the Exodus is an ongoing phenomenon (*Chiddushei Agados, Pesachim* 16b).

=== TORAS MENACHEM ===

also freedom of movement, yet be excluded from intellectual activity—he would be a prisoner held in the kind of captivity which deprives him of his *essential identity*.

Likewise in the realm of the intellect itself. He who is capable of the highest intellectual advancement, yet is constrained to a life of childlike mentality—surely this is a most painful restraint upon his true self, especially if such a restriction be self-imposed.

When a person dissipates his years, intellect and capacities in pursuit of his physical needs and the gratification of the lower appetites to the exclusion of all else—surely such a self-imposed enchainment is, in many respects, even more dreadful and more tragic in its consequences.

As for Jews, of whom each and every one possesses a Divine soul, a veritable "part" of God above, which even while it is shrouded in the "animal" soul and confined in a clay frame is yet inseparably bound to the *En Sof* (The Infinite)—its impelling quest for true freedom and release from bondage is ceaseless and infinite. It cannot rest in one place. With each day, as the soul progressively rises higher by means of the Torah and *mitzvos* which bring it closer to the *En Sof*, it experiences a deep and innermost feeling that whatever state it had attained the day before has today assumed confines from which it must break loose in order to rise higher still.

(Communal letter, 11th *Nissan* 5718)

בְּכָל דּוֹר וָדוֹר ❧ — *In each and every generation....*

This sentence is cited verbatim from the *Mishnah* (*Pesachim* 116b). However, when the same text appears in *Rambam's Laws of Chametz and Matzah*, it seems to have undergone a substantial metamorphosis (see *Classic Questions*). We will address each of *Rambam's* major innovations, one by one.

Q. *The Haggadah cites the verse, "It is because of this that God did for me" (Shemos 13:8). Why does Rambam cite a different verse, "He brought us out from there" (Devarim 6:23)?*

A. From a transcript in *Rambam's* own handwriting we know that his text of the *Mishnah* did not cite any verse here at all (printed in Kapach (trans.), *Mishnah im Perush Moshe ben Maimon*, Jerusalem 5723). So, at first glance, the choice of a different verse than ours does not appear to represent any real innovation on *Rambam's* part. He did not change his source, but rather, he simply filled in a gap.

Nevertheless, this answer alone cannot suffice. For, in the absence of any scriptural proof from the

saying, 'It is because of this that God did for ME *when 7 left Egypt'"* (ibid. 13:8). *Tt was not only our fathers that the Holy One, blessed be He, redeemed, but He redeemed*

TORAS MENACHEM

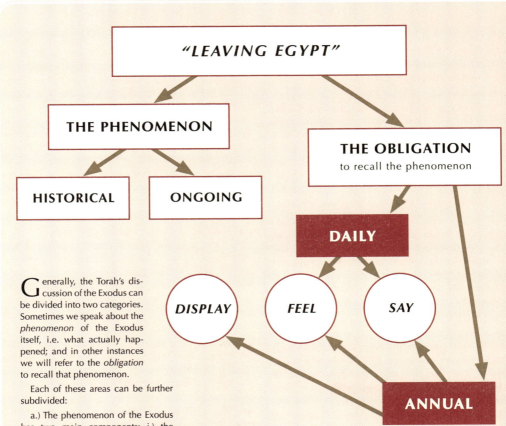

Generally, the Torah's discussion of the Exodus can be divided into two categories. Sometimes we speak about the *phenomenon* of the Exodus itself, i.e. what actually happened; and in other instances we will refer to the *obligation* to recall that phenomenon.

Each of these areas can be further subdivided:

a.) The phenomenon of the Exodus has two main components: i.) the *historical* events, which occurred when the Jews left Egypt; and, ii.) the *ongoing* phenomenon of the Exodus, which renders it, even today, *"a major foundation and powerful support to our Torah and faith"* (*Sefer ha-Chinuch, mitzvah* 21), such that, *"If the Holy One, blessed be He, had not taken our fathers out of Egypt, then we, our children, and our children's* children would still be enslaved to Pharaoh in Egypt" (Haggadah, above, p. 37).

b.) The *obligation* to recall the Exodus phenomenon is multifaceted. First we have a distinction between the *daily* requirement to recall the Exodus (which is achieved through reciting the third paragraph of the *Shema*), and the annual commemoration on the fifteenth of Nissan, the day when the Exodus actually took place.

This annual obligation itself has three components: i.) to *say*— verbally recall the Exodus; ii.) to *feel* (לִרְאוֹת אֶת עַצְמוֹ), i.e. to see oneself as leaving servitude; and, iii.) to *display* (לְהַרְאוֹת) that feeling to others.

אַף אוֹתָנוּ גָּאַל עִמָּהֶם. שֶׁנֶּאֱמַר: "וְאוֹתָנוּ הוֹצִיא מִשָּׁם, לְמַעַן הָבִיא אוֹתָנוּ לָתֶת לָנוּ אֶת־הָאָרֶץ אֲשֶׁר נִשְׁבַּע לַאֲבוֹתֵינוּ":

TORAS MENACHEM

Mishnah, why did *Rambam* not gravitate towards the verse cited in our text? If this is the correct verse then surely *Rambam* should have chosen it too?

Both our text and *Rambam* bring Scriptural support for the same reason: to prove that the Exodus is an ongoing phenomenon, such that *"in every generation,"* a person can *"see himself as if he had personally left Egypt."* Our text understood that this is implicit from the words, "You shall tell your son... 'it is because of this that God did for *me* when *I* left Egypt'" (*Shemos* 13:8). For if every Jew must tell his son that *he* left Egypt, then the Exodus must be happening today too.

However, a closer look at the historical context of this verse reveals a certain problem: Moshe said these words to the generation which actually left Egypt. Where, then, is the proof that it applied to *future* generations too, who had not left Egypt? (See **Maharsha**, cited in *Classic Questions,* for a counter-argument which defends our text.)

Due to this problem, *Rambam* chose to cite another verse: *"You shall say to your son... 'and He brought us out from there'"* (*Devarim* 6:23). This verse was said by Moshe forty years later to the *following generation* who had not been part of the actual Exodus. Thus, the fact that the Torah could require them to say "He brought *us* out from there" proves unequivocally that the Exodus is an ongoing phenomenon.

Q. Does it make any practical difference which verse the principle of ongoing Exodus is derived from?

A. Yes, there is a significant difference. Even once we have proven that the Exodus phenomenon is ongoing, there remains the question: Is it as powerful now as it was then? Are we merely enjoying the liberation of an ordinary slave who is freed, or is our freedom of the same degree as that of the original Exodus?

Only our text stresses this latter notion of an ongoing Exodus of the same original intensity. For only in our verse are we told that in every generation ("on that day"—see *Maharsha*) we stand in the shoes of the father who left Egypt for the first time, saying, *"It is because of this that God did for me when I left Egypt."* We see this from the fact that the verse draws a contrast between the father who left Egypt ("me"), and the son, who did not (only "*I* left Egypt")—and we, the reader, are given the role of the father. The verse thus implies that we are to simulate the experience of the first generation of the Exodus, communicating what had happened to the next generation.

In *Rambam's* verse, however, this point is lacking. (The verse equates father and son, referring to them collectively as "us:" "He brought us out from there.") So according to *Rambam,* there is no proof that in every generation one has to see oneself as leaving the servitude of Egypt itself; rather, one merely has to feel liberated *in general.*

However, according to our text, for a person to fulfil the obligation *"to see himself as if he had personally left Egypt"* it is not sufficient merely to feel that *"you yourself had been a* (generic) *slave and were set free and redeemed,"* as *Rambam* writes. Rather, one must perceive oneself as an *Egyptian* slave who was liberated from the uniquely harsh persecution of Pharaoh (see *Alter Rebbe's Shulchan Aruch, Orach Chaim* 472:7, where this point is indicated).

Q. Why does Rambam cite an additional verse, "Remember that you were a slave"?

A. *Rambam's* first verse "[You shall say to your son]... He brought us out from there" (and, likewise, the verse cited by our Haggadah, *"You shall tell your son.... it is because of this that God did for me"*) only proves: a.) the Exodus is an ongoing phenomenon—

us with them too, as the verse states: "He brought US out from there to bring us to the land which He swore to our fathers, and gave it to us" (Devarim 6:23).

CLASSIC QUESTIONS

● **Must a person "see himself as if he had personally left Egypt" all year round?**

RASHI: "Today you are going out" [of Egypt] (Shemos 13:4)—Each day it should be in your eyes as if you left today (text of Rashi according to Chasam Sofer, Drashos le-Pesach, p. 521).

SEFER CHAREDIM: We must remember every day in our hearts that we were slaves to Pharaoh in Egypt performing harsh labor and that if we would not have been taken out, we would still be there...as the verse states, "He took us out from there," and as the

Haggadah teaches, "In each and every generation a person must see himself as if he personally left Egypt" (ch. 9, par. 24).

AITZ YOSEF: "You redeemed us from Egypt" (daily morning prayers)—as our Sages taught, "In each and every generation a person must see himself as if he personally left Egypt," and as the verse states, "He took us out from there" (Otzar ha-Tefilos, Shacharis).

TANYA: In each and every generation, and likewise each and every day, a person must see himself as if he personally left Egypt (ch. 47).

TORAS MENACHEM

that is occurring to "us" (or "me"); and, b.) we must declare this fact verbally—"You shall say to your son." But there is no proof that we have an obligation to feel and relive that phenomenon, i.e. that "a person must see himself as if he had personally left Egypt." After all, what we utter with our lips and what we inspire ourselves to feel are two separate activities which, from a legal perspective, each require a source in their own right.

Therefore, Rambam cited further Scriptural proof that there is an obligation to "remember that you were a slave," i.e. to take it to heart and to feel it. Thus, when we combine the two verses—that i.) there is a phenomenon of ongoing liberation, and thus ii.) we are obligated to feel it—we reach the conclusion that "this matter was commanded by God in the Torah... it is as if you yourself had been a slave and were set free and redeemed."

Q. If the verse "Remember that you were a slave" (Devarim 5:15) is crucial here, how could the Haggadah omit it?

A. Quite simply because the Haggadah is not a legal compendium. It is not the Haggadah's business to record all of tonight's obligations, never mind provide proofs for them. The purpose of the Haggadah is to

provide us with a formula (text) to recite so that we can properly fulfill the mitzvah of recalling the Exodus.

The main point of the current passage in the Haggadah is to demonstrate the general significance of the Exodus, to the extent that "a person must see himself as if he had personally left Egypt." But the Haggadah is not interested in proving legally how this obligation is incumbent on us, so it only brings Scriptural support for the phenomenon of ongoing Exodus and not for the obligation to relive it.

Rambam's words, on the other hand, were written as part of his legal code, so his task was clearly to provide the reader with a source for each of the evening's religious obligations. Therefore he cited the additional verse, "Remember that you were a slave," which is the scriptural proof that "a person must see himself as if he had personally left Egypt."

Q. According to Rambam, must a person "see himself as if he had personally left Egypt" only on this night (15th of Nissan)? Or does it apply all year?

A. In Jewish law there is an obligation to recall the Exodus verbally every day, which, practically speaking, we fulfil by reciting the third paragraph of the Shema. There is also a further, totally distinct obligation to recall the Exodus on its annual anniversary, the

▶ COVER THE MATZOS AND HOLD THE CUP IN YOUR RIGHT HAND.

לְפִיכָךְ

אֲנַחְנוּ חַיָּבִים לְהוֹדוֹת לְהַלֵּל לְשַׁבֵּחַ
לְפָאֵר לְרוֹמֵם לְהַדֵּר לְבָרֵךְ לְעַלֵּה
וּלְקַלֵּס. לְמִי שֶׁעָשָׂה לַאֲבוֹתֵינוּ
וְלָנוּ אֶת־כָּל־הַנִּסִּים הָאֵלּוּ.

TORAS MENACHEM

night of the fifteenth of Nissan. This latter *mitzvah* is understandably more thorough and elaborate.

In *Rambam's* legal code, the daily obligation is recorded in his *Laws of Reciting the Shema* whereas the details of the annual obligation are written in the *Laws of Chametz and Matzah.* Thus, the fact that the obligation for a person to *"see himself as if he had personally left Egypt"* appears only here in the *Laws of Chametz and Matzah* suggests that *Rambam* understood it to be a unique feature of the annual obligation.

However, in light of the above discussion, such a conclusion is untenable. For, as we have shown, *Rambam* derives the obligation for a person to *"see himself as if he had personally left Egypt,"* from the verse, *"Remember that you were a slave,"* a verse which does *not* refer specifically to the night of the fifteenth. In fact, this expression appears a number of times in a variety of contexts, such as observance of Shabbos (*Devarim* 5:15), and the precept of giving gifts to Jewish slaves upon their release (ibid. 15:15).

So if *Rambam's* scriptural proof is from a verse which is legally applicable the whole year, then the obligation for a person to *"see himself as if he had personally left Egypt"* must apply all year round.

However, this leaves us with the question: If this is a daily obligation, why does it not appear in *Rambam's* *Laws of Reading the Shema*?

The answer, simply, is that *Rambam* mirrored the codification system of the *Mishnah.* And since the *Mishnah* included this law in Tractate *Pesachim,* and not in Tractate *Brachos,* where the daily recalling of the Exodus is codified, *Rambam* was faithful to the same arrangement.

Q. If "a person must see himself as if he had personally left Egypt" all year round, how does this fit in with the rest of the Haggadah which speaks of our annual obligation?

A. The Haggadah states, "A person must see himself *etc.*" as a mere introduction to the following passage, *"therefore* it is our obligation to thank, to laud, to praise, etc." The unique status of this night (15th of Nissan) is the subject of the second passage: "therefore it is *our* obligation (tonight) to thank, etc." So the Haggadah is effectively saying: We see that the precept of recalling the Exodus is so great that all year round "a person must see himself as if he had personally left Egypt," "therefore" certainly on this special night when the Exodus actually occurred, "it is our obligation to thank, to laud, to praise, etc.," in an exemplary manner.

(In fact we find that the author of the Haggadah also included the passage, *"Rabbi Elazar ben Azarya said, 'I am like a seventy-year-old man...'"* which refers *explicitly* to the daily obligation to recall the Exodus, and not the unique obligation of Seder Night. So evi-

► COVER THE MATZOS AND HOLD THE CUP IN YOUR RIGHT HAND.

❧ Therefore ❧

it is our duty to thank, praise, extol, glorify, exalt, honor, bless, ennoble and acclaim He who did all these miracles for our fathers and for us.

═══════════════ TORAS MENACHEM ═══════════════

dently, the Haggadah does not limit itself exclusively to texts which speak of the annual obligation.)

Q. Why does Rambam write that it is as if a person is now leaving "the servitude of Egypt," when the Haggadah states simply that is as if he is leaving "Egypt"?

A. With this turn of phrase, *Rambam* answered a practical problem that a person might have with the whole concept of "feeling" the Exodus from Egypt. Namely, that it is impossible for a contemporary Jew to genuinely recreate the feeling that he just left the geographical boundaries of Egypt. (This is especially true when we consider that the Torah *forbids* a Jew from living in Egypt (*Shemos* 14:13). In order to feel that we have left the country, we would first have to imagine that we are residents there, and how could a religious person be expected to imagine and "feel" himself doing a sin?)

Therefore, *Rambam* clarifies that the Haggadah means we are required to recreate a sensation of liberation, not from the historical land of Egypt, but from the type of harsh *servitude* that was imposed on the Jews in Egypt.

This point was not specified by the *Mishnah* (Haggadah), since the *Mishnah* was written in an intentionally brief and terse style. *Rambam,* however, whose task was to clarify for the reader every fine detail of his religious obligation, deemed it necessary to add a few words to make the *Mishnah's* intention clear.

Q. Rambam writes that a person must "display" himself as if he had personally left Egypt (i.e. show his feeling to others), a principle that is not mentioned

in the Mishnah or Haggadah. What is the basis for this major innovation?

A. At first glance, one might imagine that *Rambam* had a different textual variant of the *Mishnah* from the version which is widespread today. (The difference between "to feel," (לִרְאוֹת אֶת עַצְמוֹ) and "to display" (לְהַרְאוֹת אֶת עַצְמוֹ) is just one letter in Hebrew, and both versions are to be found in various manuscripts of the *Mishnah*).

However, this is clearly not the case. *Rambam's* own printed text of the Haggadah, and likewise a transcript of the *Mishnah* in his own handwriting, both read "to feel" and not "to display."

The notion of our "displaying" the Exodus thus appears to be *Rambam's* own innovation. And while he obviously did not feel authorized to alter the text of the *Mishnah*, he was certainly entitled to compose his *own* legal code as he saw fit, stressing the law that on this night "feeling" alone is not enough; we have to "display" the Exodus too.

Rambam's logic is not too difficult to fathom. As we have shown, a person is required to: a.) *mention* (say), and, b.) *feel* the concept of ongoing Exodus, every day of the year. On the night of the 15th of Nissan, the way in which we are required to *mention* the Exodus verbally is transformed. Unlike during the year when it is sufficient to mention the Exodus *to oneself,* on the night of the 15th: "'*You shall tell your son*' (*Shemos* 13:8).... *One is commanded to tell the story to his children*" (*Rambam, Laws of Chametz and Matzah* 7:2).

In other words, a fundamental innovation of the annual *mitzvah* is that it is insufficient to recount the Exodus to oneself; one must tell the story to others.

הוֹצִיאָנוּ

מֵעַבְדוּת ✻ לְחֵרוּת.

מִיָּגוֹן ✻ לְשִׂמְחָה.

וּמֵאֵבֶל ✻ לְיוֹם טוֹב.

וּמֵאֲפֵלָה ✻ לְאוֹר גָּדוֹל.

וּמִשִּׁעְבּוּד ✻ לִגְאֻלָּה.

וְנֹאמַר לְפָנָיו שִׁירָה חֲדָשָׁה הַלְלוּיָהּ:

TORAS MENACHEM

This is such a crucial point that even *"if one is alone one should ask himself, 'Why is this night different?'"* (ibid. 3), because tonight the story must be broadcast outwards.

Rambam thus reasoned as follows. Since we see that on this night the requirement to *mention* the Exodus verbally has been "upgraded" from a personal recollection to an outward display, it follows that the parallel obligation to *feel* the Exodus must also have been "upgraded," requiring us to display our feelings of liberation to others. For, ultimately, "mentioning" and "feeling" are not two independent activities, but two expressions of our general efforts to recall the Exodus. So if our verbal approach has undergone such a radical transformation, from a personal recollection to a public one, then surely all our efforts to recall the Exodus must take on a public flavor on this night.

Consequently, *Rambam* writes: *"A person must display himself as if he had personally left Egypt. Therefore, when one dines on this night, he should eat and drink in a reclining position in the manner of free men. Furthermore, every person, man and woman, is required to drink four cups of wine on this night"*—

because with all these actions we display, broadcast and make public our inner feeling of liberation.

Q. If this is such an important mitzvah, then why is the requirement to "display" our feelings about the Exodus not mentioned in the Haggadah?

A. As explained above, the Haggadah is not a legal compendium aimed at clarifying all the obligations of this evening, and we find that many important legal requirements—such as the precept of drinking Four Cups of wine—are not mentioned in the Haggadah. So it comes as no surprise that the obligation to "display" a feeling of liberation is not mentioned either.

Q. If the Mishnah only indicates an obligation to "feel" the Exodus, how could Rambam add an obligation to "display it," based on his own logic?

A. *Rambam* did not rule based on logic alone. Rather, he used the above logic to decipher a cryptic statement of the *Talmud*.

After the *Mishnah's* teaching, *"In each and every generation a person must see himself as if he had*

He Took us Out

from SLAVERY ✳ *to* FREEDOM,

from GRIEF ✳ *to* JOYOUSNESS,

and from MOURNING ✳ *to* FESTIVITY,

and from DARKNESS ✳ *to* BRIGHT LIGHT,

and from BONDAGE ✳ *to* REDEMPTION.

So let us declare before Him a new song Halleluyah!

TORAS MENACHEM

personally left Egypt," the *Talmud* adds: *"Rava said, 'One must say, "And He took us out from there."'"*

At first glance, Rava seems to be adding no further insight to the *Mishnah.* Once we have already read out loud, "A person must see himself as if he had personally left Egypt," we have made clear that we consider ourselves to be part of tonight's ongoing Exodus experience. So why did Rava consider it necessary to to add, "And he took *us* out from there," which is essentially saying the same thing?

The only element added by Rava's contribution appears to be the use of the plural, "And he took *us* out from there." But what, precisely, does this teach us? And why did Rava deem it so important?

[As we have shown, there are just two explicitly stated obligations on this evening: a.) to recall the Exodus *verbally,* and, b.) to *feel* as if one is leaving Egypt, so Rava must surely be teaching us a detail relating to, and implicit from, one of these *mitzvos.*]

At first glance, Rava's use of the plural seems to be teaching us a *verbal* obligation ("One must *say...*"). Namely, that when relating the story of the Exodus it is insufficient to say "God took *me* out of Egypt," one must use the plural, "He took *us* out from there."

Such a conclusion, however, is untenable since it would represent a step outside the scriptural definition

of this *mitzvah.* The verse from which we derive tonight's obligation to recount the Exodus story states that one merely has to "tell it to your son," and, for this, use of the singular would clearly suffice ("God took *me* out of Egypt").

The only explanation, therefore, is that Rava is not teaching us a detail pertaining to the *mitzvah* of recalling the Exodus verbally, but to the second requirement of "feeling" that one is leaving Egypt. [The main point is thus not the actual saying of words here, for we are not speaking of an essentially verbal obligation, but rather, what the words suggest to us when we say them.] Rava is teaching us that we must use the plural so as to emphasize the group mentality, that when we go through the emotional process of feeling as if we have left Egypt, we must not keep it to ourselves, but display it to others.

In fact, this is precisely how *Rashbam* (ibid.) interpreted Rava's words: *"This verse, 'And He took us out from there,' indicates that he must display himself as if he had left there."*

So, in the final analysis, the notion that even our efforts to "feel" the Exodus on this night must take outward expression was not the *Rambam's* totally original innovation, but his understanding of the words of Rava.

(Based on *Likutei Sichos* vol. 12, p. 39*ff*)

➤ (SOME PUT THE CUP DOWN ON THE TABLE).

הַלְלוּיָהּ, הַלְלוּ עַבְדֵי יְהֹוָה, הַלְלוּ אֶת־שֵׁם יְהֹוָה: יְהִי שֵׁם יְהֹוָה מְבֹרָךְ, מֵעַתָּה וְעַד־עוֹלָם: מִמִּזְרַח־שֶׁמֶשׁ עַד־מְבוֹאוֹ, מְהֻלָּל שֵׁם יְהֹוָה: רָם עַל־כָּל־גּוֹיִם | יְהֹוָה, עַל הַשָּׁמַיִם כְּבוֹדוֹ: מִי כַּיהֹוָה אֱלֹהֵינוּ, הַמַּגְבִּיהִי לָשָׁבֶת: הַמַּשְׁפִּילִי לִרְאוֹת, בַּשָּׁמַיִם וּבָאָרֶץ: מְקִימִי מֵעָפָר דָּל, מֵאַשְׁפֹּת יָרִים אֶבְיוֹן: לְהוֹשִׁיבִי עִם־נְדִיבִים, עִם נְדִיבֵי עַמּוֹ: מוֹשִׁיבִי עֲקֶרֶת הַבַּיִת אֵם־הַבָּנִים שְׂמֵחָה, הַלְלוּיָהּ:

═══════ CLASSIC QUESTIONS ═══════

● **Why do we recite Hallel in the Haggadah?**

MACHZOR VITRY: Just as the Jewish people said Hallel when they left Egypt, we do the same (see *Pesachim* 117a).

● **Why do we not follow the normal practice of standing for the recitation of Hallel?**

ALTER REBBE'S SHULCHAN ARUCH: Because all the actions of this evening should be indicative of the theme of liberation. Therefore, we do not trouble a person to stand up (*Orach Chaim* 473:48).

● **Why do we not follow the normal practice of making a blessing before Hallel?**

R' TZEMACH GA'ON: Because we do not read the whole of Hallel now. We interrupt it to eat the meal (cited in *Ohr Zeruah* vol. 1, beg. ch. 43).

R' HAI GA'ON: It is not a *mitzvah* to say Hallel at all now. We are merely reciting the *text* of Hallel in our efforts to praise God (ibid.).

● **Why do we split Hallel, and eat the meal in the middle?**

ABARBANEL: Hallel is actually composed of two distinct parts. The first two chapters speak of the Exodus from Egypt and of Sinai, while the remainder relates to the future redemption (see *Pesachim* 118a). In order to emphasize the difference between these two parts, we interrupt them with the meal.

● **How much of the Hallel do we recite now?**

MISHNAH: The School of Shammai says, "Until '*a joyful mother of children*' (end of ch. 113)."

The School of Hillel say, "Until '*the flint into a fountain of water*' (end of ch. 114, overleaf)" (*Pesachim* 116b).

JERUSALEM TALMUD: The School of Shammai said to the School of Hillel: "According to you, we mention the Exodus in Hallel (in chapter 114) before the meal, at an hour when the Jewish people had not even left Egypt!"

The School of Hillel replied: "Even if you were to wait until the rooster's call in the morning you would not even be halfway to the redemption, for the Exodus was in the middle of the day....

"How, then, can we commemorate the redemption at an hour when they had not yet been redeemed? Because since we have in any case begun the *mitzvah* of recalling the Exodus, we may as well finish it" (*Pesachim* 10:5).

➤ (SOME PUT THE CUP DOWN ON THE TABLE).

Halleluyah! Give praise, you servants of God! Praise the name of God! May God's name be blessed from now and forever. From the rising of the sun to its setting, God's name is praised. High above all nations is God, His glory is above the heavens. Who is like God, our God, who is enthroned on high yet looks down low upon heaven and earth? He raises the poor from the dust; from the trash heaps He lifts the needy, to seat them with nobles, with the nobles of His people. He transforms the barren wife into a joyful mother of children. Halleluyah!

TORAS MENACHEM

הַלֵּל — *Hallel.*

In the **Mishnah**, we find a dispute between the School of Shammai and the School of Hillel as to what portion of Hallel ("chapters of praise") is to be read before the meal. The point of contention is Chapter 114, which begins with the words, *"When Israel went out of Egypt..."* (overleaf).

The **Jerusalem Talmud** clarifies the various lines of reasoning. The School of Shammai maintained that this chapter, which celebrates the actual Exodus, should not be read before the meal, since it would be inappropriate to sing praise to God for the Exodus at such an early hour when our ancestors had not yet left Egypt.

The School of Hillel responded that nothing is to be gained by delaying Chapter 114 until after the meal. The actual Exodus occurred well past the time of any of this evening's celebrations—it was in the middle of the following day. So it turns out that even the School of Shammai chose to say Hallel at an inappropriate time!

This is indeed a sharp criticism of the School of Shammai's position. How would they respond?

The confusion over this issue appears to be rooted in Scripture itself, which sends ambivalent messages about the time of the Exodus. On one hand we read, *"God brought you out of Egypt at night"* (*Devarim* 16:1), yet another verse states that the Exodus was *"in the heat of the day"* (*Shemos* 12:51; see *Jerusalem Talmud* ibid.).

Noting this contradiction, the *Babylonian Talmud* suggests that even though the Jews left Egypt during the day, *"the redemption had already begun in the evening"* (*Brachos* 9a), because at that time Pharaoh *"gave them permission to leave"* (*Rashi* ibid.).

Now there has been much written about the thread underlying the various disputes of the Schools of Shammai and Hillel. A number of studies have shown that the School of Shammai always views an entity as it exists *in potential*, whereas the School of Hillel rules that we must consider only the *actual* state of affairs (see Rabbi Yosef Engel, *Beis ha-Otzar* 1:27; 2:2; Rabbi Shlomo Yosef Zevin, *"Le-shitos Beis Shammai u'Veis Hillel"* in *Le-Ohr ha-Halacha*).

Based on this approach we could argue that as soon as Pharaoh had sanctioned the release of the Jews (at midnight), the Exodus had begun *in potential*, even

בְּצֵאת יִשְׂרָאֵל מִמִּצְרָיִם, בֵּית יַעֲקֹב
מֵעַם לֹעֵז: הָיְתָה יְהוּדָה לְקָדְשׁוֹ,
יִשְׂרָאֵל מַמְשְׁלוֹתָיו: הַיָּם רָאָה וַיָּנֹס, הַיַּרְדֵּן יִסֹּב
לְאָחוֹר: הֶהָרִים רָקְדוּ כְאֵילִים, גְּבָעוֹת כִּבְנֵי־צֹאן:
מַה־לְּךָ הַיָּם כִּי תָנוּס, הַיַּרְדֵּן תִּסֹּב לְאָחוֹר: הֶהָרִים
תִּרְקְדוּ כְאֵילִים, גְּבָעוֹת כִּבְנֵי־צֹאן: מִלִּפְנֵי אָדוֹן
חוּלִי אָרֶץ, מִלִּפְנֵי אֱלוֹהַּ יַעֲקֹב: הַהֹפְכִי הַצּוּר
אֲגַם־מָיִם, חַלָּמִישׁ לְמַעְיְנוֹ־מָיִם:

TORAS MENACHEM

though they had not actually left. Therefore, in line with their position that Jewish law focuses on the potential state of affairs, the School of Shammai deemed the Exodus to have begun at this point. In their eyes, the key event that we are to celebrate was the moment when the dream of liberation became a real possibility. The actual departure from Egypt was a consequence that later flowed from that seminal moment.

Since Pharaoh was finally committed to release the Jews straight after the plague of the firstborn, which struck at midnight, the School of Shammai suggested that we should say chapter 114 ("*When Israel went out of Egypt*") at the end of the meal, after eating the Paschal lamb, because the Paschal lamb may only be eaten until midnight.

So, following this logic, the School of Shammai understood that they were praising God for the Exodus at the correct time.

One difficulty with the solution is that it forces us to accept a conclusion which is unprecedented in Rabbinic literature. We have effectively argued that according to the School of Shammai, one must wait until midnight to say Chapter 114, in order for it to be at the correct time. None of the commentators, however, seem to make this point, which means that our solution is, regrettably, a little too innovative.

In order to reach a more satisfactory conclusion, we need to explain why the School of Shammai would delay Chapter 114 only until after eating the Paschal lamb, not until after midnight.

Why should eating the Paschal lamb represent the beginning of the Exodus in potential?

Our Sages taught that the redemption came in the merit of the blood of the Paschal lamb (see p. 75), and that the *mitzvah* of slaughtering the lamb only reached fruition when it was roasted and eaten, since *"the Paschal lamb was only brought in the first instance in order that it would be eaten"* (Pesachim 76b).

So, it turns out that once the Paschal lamb was consumed, the Jewish people already possessed sufficient merit for the redemption to take place, which means that the Exodus had begun *in potential*. The School of Shammai, who always perceived potential as most important, therefore ruled that by delaying Chapter 114 until after the Paschal lamb (eaten at the end of the meal), we would praise God for the Exodus at the time it actually began, in potential at least.

One final point that needs to be clarified is the issue of redundancy. A basic presumption that we follow when studying any source text of the Oral Law is that it contains no superfluous information or unnecessary repetition. Or, speaking in terms relevant

When Israel went out of Egypt,
the House of Ya'akov from a people of
foreign tongue, Yehudah became His sanctu-
ary, Israel His dominions. The sea saw and fled;
the Jordan turned backward. The mountains skipped like
rams, the hills like young lambs. What is with you, O sea, that
you flee? O Jordan, that you turn backward? O mountains, that
you skip like rams? O hills, like young lambs? Before the
Master, who formed the earth. Before the God of
Ya'akov, who turns rock into a pond of water,
the flint into a fountain of water.

TORAS MENACHEM

to our discussion, the *Mishnah* would not record two different cases of the same essential dispute if we could have derived one from the other logically. Thus, in each of the disputes between the Schools of Shammai and Hillel, which follow the same principle of *potential* versus *actual,* it is important that we identify in each case some new angle or insight into the positions of these two schools that we would not have gleaned from any other source. (In the various studies of the Hillel/Shammai debate to date, this issue appears to have been overlooked).

In our case, if we already know that the School of Shammai sees a matter in terms of its *potential,* and that the School of Hillel focuses on the *actual* state of affairs, then what genuinely new information is conveyed by our *Mishnah?* Could an astute student not have fathomed their various positions based on the underlying principles that we already know from elsewhere?

However, there is one significant insight into the School of Shammai's position that we can gather here, and that is the limit to which they were willing to extend the "potential" argument in our case. After all, even before the Jews were exiled in Egypt, Avraham had been given a Divine promise that his children would one day by enslaved and subsequently redeemed (*Bereishis* 15:14), so perhaps the "potential

Exodus" had begun then, when God's promise had already guaranteed it? Even if we look at the time much closer to the actual Exodus, there were many significant developments that could have been heralded as the inception of liberation. For example: a.) some six months before the Exodus, on *Rosh ha-Shanah* of that year, servitude for the Jewish people was abolished (*Rosh ha-Shanah* 11a); b.) then, on the first of Nissan a new month of redemption was declared (see *Shemos Rabah* 15:11).

So, in the final analysis, our *Mishnah* is not redundant, as it enlightens us with the School of Shammai's conceptualization of "potential redemption" in this case. Namely that it began *only* with the *mitzvah* of eating the Paschal lamb, as we have shown.

The final ruling in Jewish law follows the School of Hillel, that we must make our judgment based on the *actual* state of affairs. If we translate this into a practical message, it means that we should never be satisfied with anything less than the *actual* redemption from this final, bitter exile. Our duty is to plead with God that His promises of a brighter future alone, however encouraging, are not enough. We must have the true and final redemption now, speedily in our days!

(Based on *Likutei Sichos* vol. 6, p. 69*ff*)

➤ ALL HOLD THE CUP AT THIS POINT.

בָּרוּךְ אַתָּה יְהֹוָה אֱלֹהֵינוּ מֶלֶךְ הָעוֹלָם, אֲשֶׁר
גְּאָלָנוּ וְגָאַל אֶת־אֲבוֹתֵינוּ מִמִּצְרַיִם
וְהִגִּיעָנוּ הַלַּיְלָה הַזֶּה לֶאֱכָל־בּוֹ מַצָּה וּמָרוֹר. כֵּן יְהֹוָה
אֱלֹהֵינוּ וֵאלֹהֵי אֲבוֹתֵינוּ יַגִּיעֵנוּ לְמוֹעֲדִים וְלִרְגָלִים
אֲחֵרִים הַבָּאִים לִקְרָאתֵנוּ לְשָׁלוֹם שְׂמֵחִים בְּבִנְיַן
עִירֶךָ וְשָׂשִׂים בַּעֲבוֹדָתֶךָ, וְנֹאכַל שָׁם מִן הַזְּבָחִים
וּמִן הַפְּסָחִים (ON SATURDAY NIGHT—מִן הַפְּסָחִים וּמִן הַזְּבָחִים) אֲשֶׁר
יַגִּיעַ דָּמָם עַל קִיר מִזְבַּחֲךָ לְרָצוֹן, וְנוֹדֶה לְּךָ שִׁיר
חָדָשׁ עַל גְּאֻלָּתֵנוּ וְעַל פְּדוּת נַפְשֵׁנוּ: בָּרוּךְ אַתָּה
יְהֹוָה, גָּאַל יִשְׂרָאֵל:

**בָּרוּךְ אַתָּה יְהֹוָה אֱלֹהֵינוּ מֶלֶךְ
הָעוֹלָם, בּוֹרֵא פְּרִי הַגָּפֶן:**

➤ RECLINE TO THE LEFT AND DRINK THE ENTIRE CUP (OR AT LEAST THE
MAJORITY OF IT), PREFERABLY WITHOUT PAUSING.

═══ CLASSIC QUESTIONS ═══

● **Why do we say, "who has redeemed us and redeemed our fathers," mentioning ourselves first, whereas above (p. 133) we said this in the reverse, "for our fathers and for us?"**

CHASAN SOFER: In the above passage the Haggadah refers to "all these miracles" which were witnessed directly by our fathers and not by us, so our fathers are mentioned first. But here, we are speaking about the redemption, which is an ongoing phenomenon that we experience too. Therefore we mention "us"

before "our fathers," to stress that this is not something merely handed down by tradition but a phenomenon that we are experiencing today.

● **Why is the Chagigah sacrifice mentioned before the Pesach-offering?**

ALTER REBBE'S SHULCHAN ARUCH: Because the Chagigah is eaten before the Paschal lamb in order that the latter should be eaten when already satiated (*Orach Chaim* 473:49).

➤ ALL HOLD THE CUP AT THIS POINT.

Blessed are You, God, our God, King of the universe, who has redeemed us and redeemed our fathers from Egypt, and brought us to this night to eat Matzah and Maror. Likewise, God, our God and God of our fathers, bring us, to other high holidays and festivals that will come to us in peace, gladdened in the rebuilding of Your city, and joyful in Your service. Then we shall eat of the [*Chagigah*] sacrifices and of the Pesach-offerings (ON SATURDAY NIGHT—of the Pesach-offerings and of the [*Chagigah*] sacrifices [the next day]), whose blood will be sprinkled on the wall of Your altar for acceptance. We will then thank You with a new song for our redemption and for the liberation of our souls. Blessed are You, God, who redeemed Israel.

Blessed are You, God, our God, King of the universe, who creates the fruit of the vine.

➤ RECLINE TO THE LEFT AND DRINK THE ENTIRE CUP (OR AT LEAST THE MAJORITY OF IT), PREFERABLY WITHOUT PAUSING.

=== CLASSIC QUESTIONS ===

● **Why on Saturday night do we say *"of the Pesach-offerings and of the [Chagigah] sacrifices"* in the reverse order?**

ALTER REBBE'S SHULCHAN ARUCH: Because the *Chagigah* is not offered when Erev Pesach falls on Shabbos, and is delayed until the next day (ibid.).

● **"Song" is usually written in the feminine (*shirah*). Why is the masculine form (*shir*) used in this case?**

TOSFOS: A woman suffers the pain of childbirth. Therefore, all the Songs of Praise chanted throughout history are referred to by the Torah with the feminine term *shirah*, alluding to the fact that the redemption was short-lived and was followed by the further pains of subsequent exile. The future redemption, by contrast, will be a permanent one, not followed by further Exile. So the Haggadah alludes to this distinc-

tion by referring to our future Songs of Praise with the unusual term, *shir* (Pesachim 116b).

● **Why do we need to repeat the blessing, *"who creates the fruit of the vine,"* which was already recited earlier?**

ALTER REBBE'S SHULCHAN ARUCH: Because each of the Four Cups is considered a celebration of freedom and a *mitzvah* in its own right and is thus deserving of its own blessing (ibid. 474:2).

● **Why do we not recite the blessing, *"Who has done miracles..."* (*she'asah nisim*) as we do on *Chanukah* and *Purim*?**

RASHI: Because this blessing, which praises God for the redemption, takes its place (Sefer ha-Ohrah).

MAHARIL: The blessing "...*Who has done miracles...*" was only introduced for holidays of Rabbinic origin.

רָחְצָה

➤ IT IS CUSTOMARY FOR THE HEAD OF THE HOUSEHOLD TO HAVE THE WATER BROUGHT TO HIS SEAT.

➤ WITH A CUP, EACH PERSON WASHES THE RIGHT HAND TWICE, AND THEN WASHES THE LEFT HAND TWICE (SEE P. 23).

➤ MAKE THE FOLLOWING BLESSING:

בָּרוּךְ אַתָּה יְהֹוָה אֱלֹהֵינוּ מֶלֶךְ הָעוֹלָם,
אֲשֶׁר קִדְּשָׁנוּ בְּמִצְוֺתָיו וְצִוָּנוּ עַל נְטִילַת יָדָיִם:

➤ DRY YOUR HANDS AND DO NOT TALK.

מוֹצִיא

➤ HOLD THE TWO WHOLE MATZOS AND THE BROKEN PIECE IN THE MIDDLE WITH BOTH HANDS AND SAY:

בָּרוּךְ אַתָּה יְהֹוָה אֱלֹהֵינוּ מֶלֶךְ הָעוֹלָם,
הַמּוֹצִיא לֶחֶם מִן הָאָרֶץ:

➤ DO NOT BREAK THE MATZAH YET.

Washing the Hands

➤ It is customary for the head of the household to have the water brought to his seat.

➤ With a cup, each person washes the right hand twice, and then washes the left hand twice (see p. 23).

➤ Make the following Blessing:

Blessed are You, God, our God, King of the universe, who has sanctified us with His commandments and commanded us about the washing of the hands.

➤ Dry your hands and do not talk.

Blessing before the Meal

➤ Hold the two whole Matzos and the broken piece in the middle with both hands and say:

Blessed are You, God, our God, King of the universe, who brings forth bread from the earth.

➤ Do not break the Matzah yet.

מַצָּה

➤ LET GO OF THE BOTTOM MATZAH. KEEP HOLDING THE TOP TWO.

➤ SAY THE FOLLOWING BLESSING, HAVING IN MIND THAT IT APPLIES ALSO TO THE *KORECH* ("SANDWICH") AND *AFIKOMAN*:

בָּרוּךְ אַתָּה יְהֹוָה אֱלֹהֵינוּ מֶלֶךְ הָעוֹלָם,
אֲשֶׁר קִדְּשָׁנוּ בְּמִצְוֹתָיו וְצִוָּנוּ עַל אֲכִילַת מַצָּה:

➤ TAKE AT LEAST 0.9OZ FROM EACH OF THE TWO MATZOS THAT YOU ARE HOLDING AND EAT THEM TOGETHER.

➤ EAT ALL THE MATZAH WITHIN 2 MINUTES (OR AT MOST 9), WHILE RECLINING TO THE LEFT.

➤ EVERY ADULT MUST EAT AT LEAST 1.5 OZ OF MATZAH.

➤ MOST PEOPLE DO NOT DIP THIS MATZAH IN SALT.

CLASSIC QUESTIONS

● **Why do we recite the blessing of *hamotzi* before the blessing on the *mitzvah* of Matzah?**

PRI CHADASH: Because of the Talmudic principle that a more commonly observed precept should be observed before a less common one (*Orach Chaim* 475:3).

R' AMRAM GA'ON: First we thank God for "bringing forth bread from the ground" and then we thank Him for the *mitzvah* performed with this bread (*Siddur*).

● **Why is the blessing of *shehecheyanu* (recited when we do a *mitzvah* for the first time each year) not recited here on the Matzah?**

AVUDRAHAM: Because we have just said in the Haggadah that God "*brought us to this night to eat Matzah and Maror*" (p. 141) which is effectively the same as the *shehecheyanu* blessing, "*He has brought us to reach this time.*"

Alternatively, we could argue that the blessing of *shehecheyanu* recited during *kiddush* (to thank God for reaching the festival—p. 13), covers all the precepts of the festival (*Seder tefilos shel chol*, s.v. *kol mitzvah*).

LIKUTEI TA'AMIM U'MINHAGIM: Avudraham's second explanation is very difficult to accept, for according to his logic—that the *shehecheyanu* blessing of *kiddush* applies to the Matzah eaten later on—we should find a clearly stipulated requirement to have this intention in mind when making the *shehecheyanu* blessing. Like, for example, in the case of Purim, the law states that when we make *shehecheyanu* on reading the daytime Megillah we should have in mind that the blessing also applies to the *mitzvos* of giving food gifts (*mishloach manos*) and the festive meal of Purim, carried out later in the day (*Magen Avraham* beg. ch. 692).

Matzah

➤ LET GO OF THE BOTTOM MATZAH. KEEP HOLDING THE TOP TWO.

➤ SAY THE FOLLOWING, HAVING IN MIND THAT IT APPLIES ALSO TO THE *KORECH* ("SANDWICH") AND *AFIKOMAN*:

Blessed are You, God, our God, King of the universe, who has sanctified us with His commandments and commanded us about eating Matzah.

➤ TAKE AT LEAST 0.9OZ FROM EACH OF THE TWO MATZOS THAT YOU ARE HOLDING AND EAT THEM TOGETHER.

➤ EAT ALL THE MATZAH WITHIN 2 MINUTES (OR AT MOST 9), WHILE RECLINING TO THE LEFT.

➤ EVERY ADULT MUST EAT AT LEAST 1.5 OZ OF MATZAH.

➤ MOST PEOPLE DO NOT DIP THIS MATZAH IN SALT.

CLASSIC QUESTIONS

● **On every festival we are required to eat bread in any case. What did the Torah add by commanding us to eat Matzah on this night?**

RAN: In order to fulfil the command to eat bread on a festival, *any* type of Matzah would do. The Torah added an extra commandment to eat Matzah on this night so as to specify *what type* of Matzah we must use. Namely, that it must be made from flour and water only, without any added juice or oil, etc. (*Succah* 12b, s.v. *Rabbi Eliezer*).

LIKUTEI TA'AMIM U'MINHAGIM: In addition to the explanation of *Ran*, it appears that a special commandment to eat Matzah is required, since the obligation to eat bread on a festival is in any case

TORAS MENACHEM

מַצָּה וְשֶׁהֶחֱיָנוּ — *Matzah and Shehecheyanu.*

Avudraham offers two explanations why the blessing of *shehecheyanu*, normally recited when we perform a *mitzvah* for the first time in any given year, is not said here, before eating Matzah.

Avudraham's second explanation—that the *shehecheyanu* blessing made on the festival (during *kiddush*, p. 12) also applies to the Matzah—was disputed in *Likutei Ta'amim u'Minhagim*. For, in another parallel instance (Purim) where an earlier *shehecheyanu*

blessing refers to *mitzvos* performed at a later time, the law requires us to have these *mitzvos* expressly in mind when making the *shehecheyanu* blessing. Therefore, it would seem, if the *shehecheyanu* made earlier in the *Seder* actually referred to the *mitzvah* of Matzah, we would find a similar legal requirement to have the Matzah in mind.

In a letter to the author of *Likutei Ta'amim u'Minhagim*, Rabbi Shlomo Yosef Zevin (1890-1978) posed the following objections.

CLASSIC QUESTIONS

Rabbinic (see *Alter Rebbe's Shulchan Aruch* 529:5. Even those authorities that maintain that eating bread on a festival is a Biblical obligation (*Rabbenu Yehudah* cited in *Rosh to Brachos* ch. 7. par 23; see *Alter Rebbe's Shulchan Aruch* 242:1) would concur that this does not apply to the *first night* of the festival when there is no Biblical obligation to rejoice, as *Shaagas Aryeh* (ch. 68) has shown).

● Why do we make the blessing of *hamotzi* on two and a half *matzos*?

Talmud: The Torah refers to Matzah as *"poor man's bread"* (*Devarim* 16:3). Just as it is the way of a poor man to use a broken loaf of bread, here too we are to use a broken Matzah (*Pesachim* 115b).

Rif: Normally on Shabbos and festivals we make the blessing of *hamotzi* on two whole loaves, to commemorate the double portion of manna that fell in the desert in honor of these special days.

The *Talmud* teaches us here that at the Seder we make an exception to this rule. Our Sages explained that Matzah is referred to as "poor man's bread" to indicate that one of the two loaves should be broken. We thus make the blessing of *hamotzi* on one and a half loaves (*Pesachim* 25b).

Rosh: I do not see why Pesach should be different from all the other festivals of the year, in that we should not have two whole loaves. The Talmud's requirement to have a broken loaf, in my opinion, is *in addition* to the two whole loaves, and not, as *Rif* argues, that the broken loaf replaces one of the whole loaves (*Pesachim* ch. 10, par. 30).

Bach: Our practice is to follow the opinion of the *Rosh* (end of *Orach Chaim* 475; see *Alter Rebbe's Shulchan Aruch,* ibid. 3).

● With which piece do we fulfill the actual *mitzvah* of eating Matzah?

Pri Megadim: There are three opinions:

1.) *Rosh* (cited above), maintained that the blessing of *hamotzi* is on the two whole Matzos, following

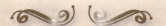

TORAS MENACHEM

1.) We find that the *shehecheyanu* blessing of *kiddush* even applies retroactively to the search for Chametz, which takes place a day beforehand (*Rosh, Pesachim* 1:10; *Tur* ch. 432; *Alter Rebbe's Shuchan Aruch* ibid. 3). Surely, then, it can apply to the *mitzvah* of Matzah which *follows* it?

2.) The comparison between Pesach and Purim does not appear to be a fair one. On Purim we do not make a blessing on the *general* festival itself [since labor is permitted on this day], only on the *specific mitzvah* of reading the Megillah. So it makes sense

that in order for the *shehecheyanu* (made specifically on the Megillah) to apply to the other distinct precepts of that day (food gifts and festive meal), a clear intention is needed to "extend" the *shehecheyanu* beyond its original context.

However, in the case of Pesach, the *shehecheyanu* blessing we make during *kiddush* is on the festival itself. Thus, being that the context of this *shehecheyanu* is a general one, it *implicitly* refers to all the precepts of the festival, such as Matzah and Maror, so no specific intention is required.

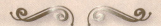

The Alter Rebbe declared: *The Matzah of the first night of Pesach is the "Food of Faith;" the Matzah of the second night is the "Food of Healing."*

His son, the Mitteler Rebbe, explained the precise order. When healing comes before faith, it means that you were sick, God cured you, and you thanked Him. But when faith comes before healing, it means that, because of your faith, you were never sick to start with.

All this applies to both physical and spiritual health, because one is dependent on the other.

CLASSIC QUESTIONS

our usual practice throughout the year, and the *mitzvah* of eating Matzah is carried out with the broken piece.

2.) *Hagahos Maimoniyos* (citing *Smag*) maintained that, to the contrary, *hamotzi* is made on the broken piece, and the *mitzvah* of eating Matzah is fulfilled with the whole piece.

His logic was: i.) When our Sages instructed us to eat a broken loaf in the spirit of "poor man's bread," they were not referring specifically to the *mitzvah* of eating Matzah, but rather, to eating bread generally (i.e. *hamotzi*).

ii.) Since we make *hamotzi* on the broken piece, it would be inappropriate to perform another *mitzvah* with it (because *ayn osin mitzvos chavilos chavilos*, "we do not bundle *mitzvos* together"—*Pesachim* 102b). Therefore, the *mitzvah* of eating Matzah must be performed with the whole piece.

3.) *Rif* (as explained by Ran), maintained that both *hamotzi* and the *mitzvah* of eating Matzah are carried out with the broken piece. First one makes *hamotzi* on one and a half pieces (the broken piece replacing one of the whole loaves used throughout the year), and then fulfils the *mitzvah* of eating

Matzah with the broken piece (*Orach Chaim* 475, *Mishbetzos Zehav* par. 2).

● **Which opinion do we follow?**

PRI MEGADIM: We act in a way that satisfies all opinions. Therefore the Code of Jewish Law ruled that we make the blessing *al achilas Matzah* (on the mitzvah of eating Matzah) while holding the broken piece (to satisfy *Rosh and Rif*) *and* a whole piece (to satisfy *Hagahos Maimonios*). Then we eat the minimum required portion from *both* pieces of Matzah within the minimum required time (ibid).

● **If we are to have in mind the "Sandwich" when making the blessing *al achilas Matzah,* why do we first drop the third Matzah from which the Sandwich is later made?**

LIKUTEI TA'AMIM U'MINHAGIM: 1.) We drop the third Matzah in order to demonstrate that the *main* focus of the blessing is on the top two Matzos.

2.) A more likely explanation is that we drop the third Matzah so that it is not eaten in error at this point, (just as we put the Afikoman aside, so that we do not eat it inadvertently during the meal, as *Siddur Ya'avetz* writes).

TORAS MENACHEM

How, then, can *Likutei Ta'amim u'Minhagim* bring a proof from Purim to Pesach when the two cases are not comparable?

The above distinction between two types of *shehechyanu* is further highlighted by a contrasting minority opinion, cited by *Meiri* (*Megillah* 4a). Interestingly, this view maintains that the *shehecheyanu* blessing on Purim day does indeed apply to the festival of Purim itself (and not specifically to the Megillah).

Following the above logic, we would imagine that, according to this opinion, the *mitzvos* of the day *are* implicit in the (festival) *shehecheyanu* blessing, and that no specific intentions are therefore required.

And this conclusion is, in fact, borne out by the text: nowhere does this minority opinion indicate that when making the *shehecheyanu* blessing one should have the other *mitzvos* of the day in mind.

Based on all of the above, it seems that the parallel between Purim and Pesach suggested in *Likutei Ta'amim u'Minhagim* is imprecise.

This concludes Rabbi Zevin's questions.

In support of what was written in *Likutei Ta'amim u'Minhagim*, the following could be argued.

1.) Rabbi Zevin writes that if the *shehecheyanu* blessing can apply retroactively to the search for Chametz, then it must certainly be capable of extending forward to the *mitzvah* of eating Matzah. This is, of course, true. Nowhere did we argue that the *shehecheyanu* blessing *couldn't* be effective for the subsequent *mitzvah* of Matzah. Our point was that in order for it to be effective the *shehecheyanu* would have to be accompanied by a specific intention, because the precept of eating Matzah is out of the immediate context of the earlier *shehecheyanu* blessing. The fact that no such intention is documented proves that the normative practice is not to "extend" the *shehecheyanu* made at *kiddush* so as to apply to the Matzah (as *Avudraham* wished to argue).

While the search for Chametz is likewise "out of context," we nevertheless do not find a requirement to have it in mind when making the *shehecheyanu* blessing, since it would make no sense to have an "intention"—i.e. an attempt to mentally determine the result—for something that has *already* happened.

2.) Rabbi Zevin also questioned our proof from the case of Purim, based on an elaborate theory. He argues that when the *shehecheyanu* blessing is made on the festival, as it is on Pesach, it implicitly includes all the

מָרוֹר

➤ ALL ADULTS MUST EAT 1.1OZ (OR AT LEAST 0.62OZ) OF MAROR [GRATED HORSERADISH AND/OR ROMAINE LETTUCE].

➤ DIP THE MAROR INTO THE CHAROSES.

➤ SAY THE FOLLOWING BLESSING, HAVING IN MIND THAT IT APPLIES ALSO TO THE BITTER HERBS IN THE KORECH ("SANDWICH").

בָּרוּךְ אַתָּה יְהֹוָה אֱלֹהֵינוּ מֶלֶךְ הָעוֹלָם,
אֲשֶׁר קִדְּשָׁנוּ בְּמִצְוֹתָיו וְצִוָּנוּ עַל אֲכִילַת מָרוֹר:

➤ EAT THE ENTIRE AMOUNT WITHIN 2 MINUTES (OR AT MOST 9).

➤ DO NOT LEAN.

CLASSIC QUESTIONS

● **Why is the Matzah not dipped in salt?**

MAHARIL: To show how much we cherish this *mitzvah*, that we do not wish to change the flavor of the Matzah in any way.

LIKUTEI TORAH: Matzah represents the faith which forms the very foundation of our relationship with God. That faith must be pure and unconditional, without any foreign elements "mixed in" (*Vayikra* 6c).

TORAS MENACHEM

precepts of the festival. But when *shehecheyanu* is made on a specific *mitzvah*, such as on the Megillah, it has no implication beyond that actual *mitzvah*, unless it is "extended" with a conscious intention.

For this theory to represent a genuine challenge it would need to be *consistently* supported by all the important sources relating to this subject. For since it is only a theory (without a textual proof) the only possible indication of its correctness would be if its predictions are consistently ratified.

So if, in our case, we could find an opinion that maintained that: a.) *shehecheyanu* is made on a festival; and, b.) nevertheless, specific intention *is* required for it to apply to subsequent *mitzvos*, then we will have refuted Rabbi Zevin's theory.

And, in fact, such an opinion is clearly documented. *Siddur Ya'avetz* rules that if a person has no Megillah, he must still make the *shehecheyanu* blessing. Obviously, then, *Ya'avetz* maintained that the *shehecheyanu* blessing refers to the *festival* of Purim, and not the *mitzvah* of Megillah (which is not being performed here). Yet, despite that fact that he maintained that the *shehecheyanu* refers to the festival in general, *Ya'avetz* also ruled that when making the blessing *shehecheyanu* one should have intention for the other *mitzvos* performed later in the day.

The theory that a general festival *shehecheyanu* precludes the need for specific intention is therefore refuted, and our proof stands.

(Based on *Igros Kodesh* vol. 15, p. 40)

Bitter Herbs

➤ ALL ADULTS MUST EAT 1.1OZ (OR AT LEAST 0.62OZ) OF MAROR [GRATED HORSERADISH AND/OR ROMAINE LETTUCE].

➤ DIP THE MAROR INTO THE CHAROSES.

➤ SAY THE FOLLOWING BLESSING, HAVING IN MIND THAT IT APPLIES ALSO TO THE BITTER HERBS IN THE KORECH ("SANDWICH").

Blessed are You, God, our God, King of the universe, who has sanctified us with His commandments and commanded us about eating Maror.

➤ EAT THE ENTIRE AMOUNT WITHIN 2 MINUTES (OR AT MOST 9).

➤ DO NOT LEAN.

━━━━━━━━━━ CLASSIC QUESTIONS ━━━━━━━━━━

● **Nowadays, is Maror a Biblical or a Rabbinic requirement?**

RAMBAM: To eat the Maror is not an independent Biblical commandment in its own right, but one that is contingent on eating the Paschal lamb. For there is just one single commandment: to eat the Paschal lamb together with Matzah and Maror. However, the Sages require us to eat Maror on its own on this night, even in the absence of the Paschal lamb (*Laws of Chametz and Matzah* 7:12).

MAHARIL: Currently, Maror is not binding Biblically. Nevertheless we eat it to remind us of Temple times, for when the Temple will be built—speedily in our days—Maror will once again be a Biblically binding precept (*Responsa* no. 158; see also *Alter Rebbe's Shulchan Aruch* 475:15).

━━━━━━━━━━ TORAS MENACHEM ━━━━━━━━━━

✐☙ **מָרוֹר** — *Maror, the Bitter Herbs.*

Chasidic thought stresses that any *mitzvah*, Biblical or Rabbinic, is not merely an obligation, but also a form of empowerment. Whereas secular law issues commands and we are left to gather the strength to observe them, Torah law, by contrast, actually nourishes the soul, granting us the energy and ability to complete the required task. Even more than that, as a *Divine* command a *mitzvah* renders us as agents of a Higher Authority, endowing us with much more power than we could muster on our own.

From this we can understand also the reverse. If a Torah command is, for whatever reason, temporarily suspended, it does not mean that God no longer desires the task to be carried out. It is simply that, in our current condition, we are incapable of this achievement, and God would never burden us with something which is beyond our ability.

What is the significance of the Charoses?

ALTER REBBE'S SHULCHAN ARUCH: Our Sages enacted that a person should have Charoses in front of him when reciting the Haggadah, to remember the mortar with which our ancestors [bonded bricks when they] were enslaved in Egypt.

It is also to remember the "apple tree" as we shall explain....

The Charoses should be made from fruits that the Torah employs as a metaphor for the Jewish people, such as figs, as the verse states, *"The fig tree puts forth her green figs"* (Song. 2:13); and nuts, as the verse states, *"into the garden of nuts"* (ibid. 6:11); and dates, as the verse states, *"I will go up to the palm tree"* (ibid. 7:9); and pomegranates, as the verse states, *"Like a piece of a pomegranate"* (ibid. 6:7); and apples, to remember the fact that *"I roused you under the apple tree [there your mother was in labor with you]"* (ibid. 8:5), namely that God caused the Jewish women to give birth to their children without pain [in Egypt] (*Orach Chaim* 473:20,32).

If we already have Bitter Herbs, to remember servitude in Egypt, why is it necessary to have Charoses too?

MAHARAL: Maror only represents the bitterness of exile *in general*. The harsh labor which was unique to the Egyptian exile was working with mortar (see *Shemos Rabah* 1:27), and this is alluded to by the Charoses (*Gevuras Hashem* ch. 63).

Why do we not make a blessing on the *mitzvah* of dipping in Charoses?

ALTER REBBE'S SHULCHAN ARUCH: While dipping the Charoses is indeed a *mitzvah,* to remember the mortar, nevertheless, we do not make a blessing upon it, since it is secondary to the Maror and covered by the blessing on the Maror (ibid. 475:11).

TORAS MENACHEM

In the case of Maror, we have a rather interesting scenario. In the absence of the Holy Temple the Biblical commandment to eat Maror is no longer in force (see *Classic Questions*). The simple reason for this is because Maror is technically an accompaniment for the Pesach sacrifice, which can no longer be offered.

The Holy Temple, and the sacrifices in particular, are symbols of the general notion of worshipping God and coming closer to him. On the Altar, we saw heaven and earth meet: Each time a sacrifice was offered, a fire came down from above to consume it, teaching us that our efforts to worship God had been warmly accepted. Even the word for "sacrifice" in Hebrew, *korban*, illustrates this point, because it is a derivative of the word *kiruv*, meaning "bringing near." Thus, the message conveyed by God's fiery embrace of the sacrifices was: "Yes, your efforts to come close to Me really are meaningful and effective."

The fact that Maror, bitter herbs, are an intrinsic part of the Pesach sacrifice suggests that we can come close to God and worship Him even through life's more bitter and difficult moments. It goes without saying that when we worship God by observing His commandments we come closer to Him, but are the obstacles and difficulties which get in the way of observance a component of the worship too? Maror teaches us, yes, to offer a *korban* (i.e., to come close to God), life will not always be sweet; it is sometimes necessary to have some bitter herbs too.

Nevertheless, in the absence of the Temple, when the Jewish people's national morale has been eroded through the influence of non-Jewish culture, the Biblical precept of Maror is not currently in force. Our spirits are simply so low in this exile, that we cannot cope with any more misery. Life's difficulties were never the *focus* of worshipping God, but merely an *enhancement* to bring out our true dedication (just as the Maror was a non-crucial accompaniment to the Pesach sacrifice—*Rambam, Laws of the Pesach Sacrifice* 8:2), so these obstacles could be dispensed with if necessary. Thus, while we are in exile God says, "You can't cope any more. I will exempt you from Maror. I will no longer make it difficult for you to worship Me."

But the Sages came along and said, "It's really important for a person to be challenged with obstacles so that his life will prove to be meaningful and rewarding. The Torah says that right now you can't cope with any more difficulties, *but we will give you extra strength!* With the Rabbinic *mitzvah* of Maror, your parched soul will be revitalized such that even in exile you will be able to cope with life's difficulties. And if you *can* cope with problems, God will send them to you, because ultimately they are for your benefit."

So next time you are faced with a problem—thank God. Thank Him for giving you a stimulus for personal growth that will make your life more rewarding. And thank Him for giving us Rabbinic law (which, of course, is mandated by the Torah itself), an extra source of nourishment for our souls to withstand the spiritual confusion and apathy of our day.

(Based on *Sichas Acharon Shel Pesach* 5720)

חֲרוֹסֶת — Charoses.

At first glance, the Charoses, which reminds us of the harsh servitude in Egypt, may appear to be somewhat of a minor precept. We make no blessing on dipping in Charoses because of its secondary importance (see *Classic Questions*), and there is no minimum quantity of Charoses that we must consume (as is the case with Matzah and Bitter Herbs). All this seems to send the message that the Charoses is relatively unimportant.

In truth, however, this *mitzvah* is laden with significance. The lack of any special blessing or a minimum quantity actually points to a *superior* quality in the Charoses.

By way of illustration: *"Through the blessing made on a mitzvah, a sublime radiance (makif) is drawn into the world. Thus, in the case of the head-tefillin the Sefardic and Ashkenazic authorities differ over the question whether an additional blessing is made (Orach Chaim 25:5), since the sublime radiance of the head-tefillin is so lofty that, according to the Sefardim, it cannot be drawn down palpably into this world. Therefore, they maintain that no blessing is made"* (*Torah Ohr, Shemos* 52b).

Likewise, we could argue that no special blessing is made on the Charoses because it, too, represents something extremely sublime.

This is stressed further by the fact that there is no prescribed minimum quantity (*shiur*) of Charoses. In most cases, a *shiur* suggests that Jewish law views the required (or prohibited) substance as consisting of numerous, individual particles that must be combined to have the required effect (*shiur hamitztaref*). The identifying property of the substance is, of course, present in every single particle—in our case, they are all particles of Matzah or Maror—but each particle is not significant enough in its own right. Only when it is combined with a sufficient amount of the same substance does it become prohibited or mandated (see *Mefa'aneach Tzefunos* pp. 185-6).

On the other hand, when there is no minimum quantity it can be an indication that the identifying feature of the substance stands out in even the tiniest particle. For example, Jewish law states that an object of idol worship is forbidden even in the tiniest amount, due to the extreme intensity and severity of this sin which is considered an absolute heresy (*Avodah Zarah* 73b; *Rambam, Laws of Idol Worship* 7:15; 4:7).

So, in our case, the fact that there is no minimum quantity for Charoses suggests that the spiritual potency of Charoses is so great that it shines forth from even a miniscule amount of this substance.

What, then, does the Charoses represent, and why is its message so powerful?

Another unusual feature of the Charoses can be gleaned from a careful reading of the *Alter Rebbe's Shulchan Aruch* (cited in *Classic Questions*). In Chapter 475 he states that *dipping* in the Charoses is a (Rabbinic) *mitzvah*, whereas in chapter 473 he writes that it is a commandment from the Sages to *display* the Charoses on the table when reciting the Haggadah. So it turns out that there are really *two mitzvos* that we do with the Charoses: *displaying* and *dipping*. Why is this the case?

A key to understanding the elusive properties of the Charoses, both its lofty, intense spirituality and its double-mitzvah status, is to be found in the writings of **Maharal**. In *Gevuras Hashem*, Maharal draws a fundamental distinction between the Maror and Charoses, namely, that Maror represents bitterness in general, i.e., the suffering experienced throughout all the exiles, whereas Charoses alludes to the suffering unique to the Egyptian exile in particular.

"All the political regimes are associated with Mitzrayim (Egypt)," said the Sages, "because they all oppressed (*metzayrim*) the Jews" (*Bereishis Rabah* 16:4). I.e., the Egyptian exile was not merely worse than the oppressive regimes that followed; spiritually speaking, Egypt was their source. Or, as we explained above (p. 107), Egypt represents the *essence* of the evil forces that have subjugated us, whereas the other regimes are merely diluted *manifestations* of it, reflecting how the essential evil of Egypt has seeped through and influenced the composite structure of matter.

Charoses has no minimum quantity, because it represents Egypt, the potent, indivisible *essence* of evil. Maror, on the other hand, represents the influence of Egypt on the subsequent four exiles. Thus Maror has a *shiur hamitztaref*: enough particles must be combined to have the required effect, because here we are not speaking of the essence of evil, but rather, how that essence has penetrated and *partially* influenced something else.

Likewise, we can also appreciate why Charoses has two distinct legal elements: *displaying* Charoses represents the essence of evil (Egypt) itself; *dipping* the Maror in Charoses represents how that essence influences and manifests itself in the subsequent exiles.

For every evil force there must be an equal and opposite positive force, since *"God made one corresponding to the other"* (*Koheles* 7:14). So if the evil which oppresses the Jewish people is comprised of both *essence* and *manifestations*, it follows that

כּוֹרֵךְ

➤ TAKE A PIECE FROM THE THIRD MATZAH (1.1OZ, OR AT LEAST 0.62 OZ) AND THE SAME AMOUNT OF MAROR [HORSERADISH AND/OR ROMAINE LETTUCE].

➤ DIP THE BITTER HERBS IN CHAROSES.

➤ MAKE A SANDWICH, AND SAY THE FOLLOWING:

זֵכֶר לְמִקְדָּשׁ כְּהִלֵּל. כֵּן עָשָׂה הִלֵּל בִּזְמַן שֶׁבֵּית הַמִּקְדָּשׁ הָיָה קַיָּם הָיָה כּוֹרֵךְ (פֶּסַח) מַצָּה וּמָרוֹר וְאוֹכֵל בְּיַחַד. לְקַיֵּם מַה שֶׁנֶּאֱמַר: "עַל מַצּוֹת וּמְרוֹרִים יֹאכְלֻהוּ":

➤ EAT THE WHOLE SANDWICH WITHIN 2 MINUTES (OR AT MOST 9), WHILE RECLINING TO THE LEFT.

TORAS MENACHEM

the same is true with regard to the power which God charged the Jewish soul to withstand all the exiles—this too must have an *essence* and *manifestations*.

In fact, this appears to be the message of another highly significant passage of *Maharal*:

"*People ask: What was the benefit of the Exodus to us, since we are now subjugated by other regimes? What difference does it make if the Egyptians or somebody else is persecuting us?*

"*This is a foolish question. For when the Jewish people came out of Egypt a tangible, positive change occurred to them, rendering them intrinsically free. The Jew now possesses an essential quality which means that he deserves to be free by virtue of who he is, and an essential quality is never lost due to something circumstantial, such as a subsequent exile*" (*Gevuras Hashem* ch. 61).

In other words, in Egypt, even the essence of the Jewish identity was compromised by the equally

potent, essential evil of Egypt. But with the Exodus, we were permanently redeemed from this predicament. The current exile can only endanger the "Jewishness" (manifestations) of the Jew, such as one's level of observance, but there is an essential quality that always remains intact within the soul.

And this is the second allusion within the Charoses, that it represents the Jewish people ("*Charoses should be made from fruits that the Torah employs as a metaphor for the Jewish people,*" and it is "*to remember the fact that God caused the Jewish women to give birth to their children without pain*"). For while we may still be in exile, our core Jewish identity always remains intact. Our task is merely one of "dipping" in the Charoses, to ensure that our essential Jewish consciousness penetrates every area of thought, speech and deed.

(Based on *Likutei Sichos* vol. 32, p. 44*ff*; *Sichas Acharon Shel Pesach 5746*)

"Sandwich"

WHAT ARE WE DOING NOW?

The first half of the Seder celebrates the Exodus from Egypt; and the second half, the final redemption. Since we mention here the Holy Temple, which is to be rebuilt in the future, it follows that the "second half" of the Seder begins here (Sichas Shabbos Parshas Korach 5744, par. 21).

➤ TAKE A PIECE FROM THE THIRD MATZAH (1.1OZ, OR AT LEAST 0.62 OZ) AND THE SAME AMOUNT OF MAROR [HORSERADISH AND/OR ROMAINE LETTUCE].

➤ DIP THE BITTER HERBS IN CHAROSES.

➤ MAKE A SANDWICH, AND SAY THE FOLLOWING:

In remembrance of the Temple, we do as Hillel did at the time when the Holy Temple was standing: He would combine (Paschal-lamb,) Matzah and Maror and eat them together, to fulfil the verse, "They shall eat it together with Matzos and Maror" (Bamidbar 9:11).

➤ EAT THE WHOLE SANDWICH WITHIN 2 MINUTES (OR AT MOST 9), WHILE RECLINING TO THE LEFT.

CLASSIC QUESTIONS

● **Why do we eat the Sandwich?**

ALTER REBBE'S SHULCHAN ARUCH:

[a. *Eating a Sandwich alone is problematic in the current era, according to all opinions.*]

In the current era, if a person were to make a sandwich of the required quantity of Matzah with the required quantity of Maror, chew them together and eat them, he would not fulfil his obligation [to eat Matzah]. For the flavor of the Maror, which is a Rabbinic requirement, would neutralize the flavor of the Matzah, which is a Biblical requirement.

[b. *Eating a Sandwich alone is acceptable in Temple times, according to all opinions.*]

However, in Temple times, when Maror was a Biblical requirement, one could fulfil the *mitzvos* of Matzah and Maror together. For Biblical commandments do not neutralize each other, since they are all the commandments of God and thus share an equal status.

TORAS MENACHEM

כֵּן עָשָׂה הִלֵּל בִּזְמַן שֶׁבֵּית הַמִּקְדָּשׁ הָיָה קַיָם ◊◊
— *This is what Hillel did at the time when the Holy Temple was standing.*

At first glance, our efforts to remember and re-enact the practice of Temple times on Seder night appear to be somewhat inconsistent. Here, for example, we eagerly do *"what Hillel did at the time when the Holy Temple was standing"* and actually eat a "sandwich." On the other hand, when it comes to remembering the Paschal lamb eaten in Temple times, we go to the opposite extreme. We refuse categorically to eat *any* meat in the sandwich *"even the meat of a calf or chicken which cannot be used for the Pesach sacri-*

CLASSIC QUESTIONS

[c. Eating a Sandwich alone was obligatory in Temple times, according to Hillel.]

Furthermore, according to the view of Hillel the Elder, a person did not fulfil his obligation unless he made a sandwich of the required amount of Paschal lamb, Matzah and Maror, and ate them together, in accordance with the verse, *"They shall eat it together with Matzos and Maror"* (Bamidbar 9:11).

[d. Eating a Sandwich alone is problematic in the current era, even according to Hillel.]

However, even according to Hillel, if a person would make a sandwich in the current era of (Rabbinic) Maror and (Biblical) Matzah and eat them together, he would not fulfil his obligation, for the Maror would neutralize the flavor of the Matzah. Therefore [even according to Hillel] in the current era a person is required to eat the prescribed quantity of Matzah *on its own* without Maror, so as to fulfil the Biblical requirement of Matzah.

[e. Eating Maror alone is problematic in the current era, according to Hillel.]

Nevertheless, according to Hillel, a person does not fulfil his obligation to eat Maror unless he eats it in a sandwich together with a *further* prescribed quantity of Matzah. This is because the Sages enacted the requirement of Maror in the current era as a reminder of the Biblical *mitzvah* of Temple times, and, according to Hillel, in Temple times the Biblical Mitzvah of Maror could only be fulfilled when sandwiched together with Matzah. Consequently, a sandwich with Matzah is required now too.

[f. Eating Maror in a sandwich is problematic in the current era, according to the other Sages.]

Hillel's colleagues, however, disagreed with him, maintaining that there is no requirement of a sandwich at all—neither Biblically, during Temple times, nor Rabbinically, in the current era. Thus, in their opinion, if a person would first eat the prescribed

TORAS MENACHEM

fice" (Alter Rebbe's Shulchan Aruch, Orach Chaim 476:3). And even the zeroa (shankbone), which we display to remember the Paschal lamb, *"is not eaten on this night... for eating it on this night would resemble the prohibition of eating a sacrifice outside its prescribed location"* (ibid. 473:21).

So where do we draw the line between our desire to remember and re-enact Temple practice, on the one hand, and our fear of imitating Temple practice too much, on the other?

In Parshas Bechukosai we read: *"I will remember My covenant with Ya'akov, and My covenant with Yitzchak too. I will also remember My covenant with Avraham"* (Vayikra 26:42). Toras Kohanim (cited by Rashi ibid.) addresses the question why the word "remember" is mentioned here twice, in reference to Avraham and Ya'akov, but is not repeated a third time in reference to Yitzchak.

"Why is 'remembrance' not said in connection with Yitzchak? Because Yitzchak's ashes are visible before Me, heaped up and lying on the altar."

From this a clear definition emerges: It is only possible to "remember" something that is not present. If the thing itself is "visible before Me," or at least the key, defining element of that thing ("the ashes of Yitzchak"), then a "remembrance" is unnecessary. (In fact, it is impossible.)

While there were many detailed elements to the Paschal lamb ritual, many of which would disqualify the offering if performed incorrectly, we nevertheless

find that the key element of this *mitzvah* was eating the lamb: *"From the outset, it is only brought in order that it should be eaten"* (Rambam, Laws of the Pesach Sacrifice 7:8).

So if we were to eat ordinary roasted lamb in our sandwich on Seder night in the current era, even though it would not be a sacrifice at all, we would nevertheless be enacting the key element of this ritual, the *eating* of meat. For this reason our Sages were concerned that such an act "*would resemble the prohibition of eating a sacrifice outside its prescribed location,"* because it does contain the key element of the Paschal lamb ritual, namely eating meat.

On the other hand, eating a sandwich of just Matzah and Maror without any meat could be considered a "remembrance" because the key element of this ritual—the Paschal lamb—is missing here.

Our attempts to remember and reenact Temple ritual are not mere nostalgia, or looking backwards, they have a positive side too.

a.) Chasidic thought explains that when we carry out a ritual "in remembrance of the Temple" we elicit a form of spiritual irradiation which is somewhat reminiscent of the real Temple practice itself (see Likutei Sichos vol. 32, p. 20).

b.) Reenacting Temple ritual is part of our efforts to prepare for the coming of Mashiach and the rebuilding of the Temple. As Rashi suggests: *"Even after you go into exile, make yourselves distinctive with My commandments... so that they will not be new to*

CLASSIC QUESTIONS

amount of Matzah on its own, and then a sandwich of the prescribed amounts of Maror and Matzah, he would not fulfil his obligation of Maror. For, according to them, the Matzah in the sandwich would be purposeless, not being a requirement of religious law, and it would therefore neutralize the flavor of the Maror in the sandwich when they are chewed together.

[g. *No consensus was reached. In order to fulfil the mitzvah of Maror, we follow both opinions.*]

No final consensus was reached in this matter, neither in favor of Hillel nor his colleagues.

Therefore, in order to satisfy both opinions:

A person must first eat the prescribed amount of Matzah on its own, without Maror, making the blessing *al achilas Matzah*. With this prescribed amount he fulfils the Biblical requirement to eat Matzah, even according to Hillel.

Then he must eat the prescribed amount of Maror on its own, without Matzah, making the blessing *al achilas Maror*, for with this he satisfies the view of Hillel's colleagues.

Afterwards, he makes a sandwich of the prescribed amounts of Matzah and Maror, and eats them together, to remember the practice of Temple times in accordance with Hillel (*Orach Chaim* 475:16-18).

TORAS MENACHEM

you when you return" (commentary to *Devarim* 11:18, from *Sifri*).

In fact, from the *Talmud* it appears that we make "a remembrance of Temple times" not merely in *patient* expectation of the rebuilding of the Temple, but rather, as a *proactive* attempt to bring the redemption.

"*From where do we derive the principle of performing acts in memory of the Temple? R' Yochanan said: From the verse '...She is Zion, there is none that seek her'* (Jer. 30:17). *'There is none that seek her'—this implies that she should be sought*" (*Succah* 41a).

Here we see that re-enacting Temple practice expresses our yearning to actively "seek" our return to Zion. In fact, in his commentary on the above Talmudic passage, the Maggid of Mezritch suggests that these emotions should be constant and unfaltering.

"'*She should be sought'—this teaches us a general principle that every day of a person's life, indeed every moment, he must 'seek'*" (*Likutei Amarim* 64a; *Ohr Torah* 79c).

(Based on second *Sichah* of *Shabbos Bereishis* 5748, par. 30; *Sichah* of 13 *Tishrei* 5740, par. 53; *Likutei Sichos* vol. 34, p. 203).

❀ הָיָה כּוֹרֵךְ פֶּסַח מַצָּה וּמָרוֹר וְאוֹכֵל בְּיַחַד — He would combine Paschal-lamb, Matzah and Maror and eat them together.

In the **Alter Rebbe's Shulchan Aruch** we find an intricate and detailed explanation why in the current era it is necessary to eat Maror twice, once in a sandwich with Matzah, and once on its own.

Central to the argument is a unanimously agreed rule that "if a person would make a sandwich in the current era of (Rabbinic) Maror and (Biblical) Matzah and eat them together, he would not fulfil his obligation, *for the Maror would neutralize the flavor of the Matzah.*"

By contrast, "When Maror was a Biblical requirement, one could fulfil the *mitzvos* of Matzah and Maror together. *For Biblical commandments do not neutralize each other, since they are all the commandments of God and thus share an equal status.*"

The logic here is somewhat difficult to understand. For, at the end of the day, the human tongue experiences the same taste, regardless of whether Maror is Rabbinic or Biblical, and the bitter herbs will inevitably change the taste of plain Matzah. When both *mitzvos* are Biblical, the law is totally unconcerned if the physical taste of Matzah is drowned out, and "one could fulfil the *mitzvos* of Matzah and Maror together." But, remarkably, when the legal status of Maror changes to a Rabbinic precept, flavor suddenly becomes a legally decisive factor: "*he would not fulfil his obligation, for the Maror would neutralize the flavor of the Matzah.*"

So we are left confused: Is the taste of the Maror significant, or not?

In many instances, conflicting statements of the law can be reconciled by clarifying whether the halachic incumbency of a particular *mitzvah* is on the person (*gavra*), or the entity which is used to fulfil the *mitzvah* (*cheftza*). In our case: Does the law require the *actual person* to taste the Matzah? Or does the *Matzah itself* need to *possess* taste, regardless of whether somebody actually experiences that taste or not?

The solution is not too difficult to fathom. We are taught that "if a person swallowed Matzah" without tasting it at all, "he has fulfilled his obligation" (*Pesachim* 115b), indicating that the person's taste experience is not legally decisive here.

On the other hand, "*While a person does not have to taste the Matzah in his mouth... nevertheless, the* **Matzah itself** *must possess the taste of Matzah, and*

שֻׁלְחָן עוֹרֵךְ

➤ IT IS CUSTOMARY TO BEGIN BY EATING EGG IN SALT WATER.

➤ ENJOY A GOOD FESTIVE MEAL BUT LEAVE SOME ROOM FOR THE *AFIKOMAN*.

➤ MANY HAVE THE CUSTOM NOT TO BRING ANY MATZAH INTO CONTACT WITH WATER.

➤ SOME ARE CAREFUL TO LEAN THROUGHOUT THE MEAL.

TORAS MENACHEM

not be flavored by another ingredient" (*Alter Rebbe's Shulchan Aruch, Orach Chaim* 461:12).

So, clearly, when we say that "the taste of Matzah" is a crucial clause in this *mitzvah,* we are speaking of a quality in the Matzah itself (*cheftza*), and not the experience of the person eating it (*gavra*).

Thus, returning to our original discussion, when the law states that "*the Maror would neutralize the flavor of the Matzah,*" the point is not, as we had first assumed, that the flavor of Matzah would no longer be perceptible to the human tongue. For, as we have shown, the *gavra* is not the law's concern in this instance. Rather, the question is whether a valid flavor is present in the Matzah *itself.*

But if the tongue is not our test of flavor, then what will be?

The answer is that *the law will decide.* Just as the law proclaims a cracker of flour and water to have the status of "Matzah," it too will decide what is a legally valid flavor and what is not. As far as the tongue is concerned, two flavors may taste exactly the same, but from the point of view of the law, one flavor may be valid and the other invalid.

In our case, Rabbinic Maror is a *legally foreign* flavor to Biblical Matzah. Therefore "*the Maror would neutralize*" not merely the physical taste, but, more importantly, the legality of the Matzah's flavor.

On the other hand, a legally valid flavor would never compromise another flavor of equal legal

validity (even if the tongue considers them to clash), so, "*Biblical commandments do not neutralize each other.*" Consequently, "when Maror was a Biblical requirement, one could fulfil the *mitzvos* of Matzah and Maror together... since they are all the commandments of God and thus share an equal (legal) status" [see *Ran, Meiri* and *Milchamos Hashem* to *Pesachim* 115a].

What is the *inner* reason why taste is only important to the Matzah itself, and not to the person eating it?

Earlier we read: "*This Matzah that we eat is for what reason? Because the dough of our fathers did not have time to become leavened before the King—the King of kings, the Holy One, blessed be He—revealed Himself to them and redeemed them*" (p. 122).

Tzror Hamor explains the need for this extreme urgency:

"*The Jewish people were living in Egypt for an extended period, during which time they were strongly influenced by the surrounding culture.... If God, in His kindness, would not have shattered the forces of impurity and taken the Jewish people out at that moment, their "dough" would have fermented—i.e. they would have been irreversibly overpowered, as in the Talmudic analogy, "We want to do Your will, but the yeast in the dough is holding us back"* (*Brachos* 17a). *The dough was on the verge of "fermenting" within the blink of an eye... and if the Jewish people had remained in Egypt for just a*

Festive Meal

> ➤ IT IS CUSTOMARY TO BEGIN BY EATING EGG IN SALT WATER.

> ➤ ENJOY A GOOD FESTIVE MEAL BUT LEAVE SOME ROOM FOR THE *AFIKOMAN*.

> ➤ MANY HAVE THE CUSTOM NOT TO BRING ANY MATZAH INTO CONTACT WITH WATER.

> ➤ SOME ARE CAREFUL TO LEAN THROUGHOUT THE MEAL.

TORAS MENACHEM

moment longer, they would have been trapped there forever" (commentary to *Shemos* 12:40).

The purpose of the Exodus was thus to free the Jewish people from the corrupting, spiritually noxious influence ("impurity") of Egypt. But while the Exodus released the Jews from any external negative influence, they nevertheless took a bit of Egypt along within them, in that they had internalized Egyptian values and impurity. Nevertheless, after seven weeks, they managed to rid themselves of this too—as *Zohar Chadash* explains:

"The Jewish people were drenched in forty-nine powers of impurity which God freed them from, and granted them instead forty-nine gates of spiritual understanding.... This is why we count the days and the weeks from the second day of Pesach until the festival of Shavuos... because on each day we were relieved of a further force of impurity, and granted a corresponding force of purity" (*Zohar Chadash* II, 39a).

Piecing all this information together, a number of important points emerge:

1.) God did not take us out of Egypt because we were spiritually prepared for redemption. On the contrary, He took us out because of our pitiful state.

2.) The purpose of the Exodus was to rid the Jewish people of spiritual impurity.

3.) This only achieved fruition seven weeks later, at the time when the Torah was given.

4.) The Exodus thus granted us the *potential* to rid ourselves of impurity, something that we only fully appreciated and internalized seven weeks later.

With this in mind, we could gain a deeper insight into the two laws of Matzah discussed above:

a.) that Matzah must have its natural taste; and,

b.) that the Matzah itself (*cheftza*) must *possess* the taste, and not that the person (*gavra*) should actually taste it.

Matzah—bread that had no time to rise—brings to light that the Exodus was an emergency act of God which we did not appreciate at the time. Therefore, the law does not require us to taste the Matzah, because at the time of the redemption the Jewish people did not yet "taste" or appreciate what God had just done. That would take another seven weeks.

Nevertheless, whatever was internalized seven weeks later was already given to the Jewish people *in potential* at the moment of the Exodus. This is reflected in the idea that the Matzah must *possess* taste, for even if the immense impact of freedom from impurity could not be appreciated at the time of the Exodus, it had to *be there* so that later on the Jewish people could gradually embrace it with their minds and with their hearts.

After all, true spirituality has always been something of an "acquired taste."

(Based on *Likutei Sichos* vol. 26, p. 44, 48)

צָפוּן

➤ THE AFIKOMAN SHOULD BE EATEN BEFORE HALACHIC MIDNIGHT.

➤ EVERYBODY SHOULD EAT A DOUBLE PORTION OF MATZAH (A TOTAL OF AT LEAST 1.24OZ): ONE PORTION TO REMEMBER THE PASCHAL LAMB AND ANOTHER PORTION TO REMEMBER THE MATZAH EATEN WITH THE PASCHAL LAMB.

➤ IF THIS IS TOO DIFFICULT, EAT A SINGLE PORTION OF MATZAH (AT LEAST 0.62OZ).

➤ EAT ALL THE MATZAH WITHIN 2 MINUTES (OR AT MOST 9), WHILE RECLINING TO THE LEFT.

➤ DO NOT EAT OR DRINK AFTER EATING THE *AFIKOMAN* (EXCEPT WATER ETC.).

CLASSIC QUESTIONS

● Why do we eat the Afikoman? And why are we not allowed to eat anything after it?

TALMUD: Rabbi Yehudah said in the name of Shmuel: "We do not serve any dessert after the Matzah" (*Pesachim* 119b).

RASHI: The *Talmud* is referring here to a requirement to eat Matzah at the end of the festive meal, in remembrance of Temple times when Matzah was eaten at the end of the meal, together with the Paschal lamb. For this we use the Matzah which was broken [at the beginning of the Seder].

This Matzah at the end of the meal [is not eaten to fulfil a mere Rabbinic precept or custom. Rather,] we eat it to fulfil our Biblical obligation [to eat Matzah on this night].

[I.e., the Rabbis instructed us not to fulfil our Biblical obligation with the Matzah that we eat before the meal, so that we can fulfil the *mitzvah* at the end of the meal, as they did in Temple times.

However, this begs the question: Why do we make the blessing on the *mitzvah* of eating Matzah (*al achilas Matzah*) before the meal if we only fulfil this *mitzvah* after the meal?]

We are forced to make the blessing on the first Matzah, even though it is not used to fulfil our obligation...for after we have already filled our stomachs with Matzah how could we then make a blessing on it later on?

Thus, when we make the blessing it refers to *both* the Matzah eaten at the beginning of the meal and at the end of the meal (ibid.).

RASHBAM: [According to *Rashi's* explanation] we can understand the *Talmud's* ruling that *"we do not serve any dessert after the Matzah."* For since we fulfil a Biblical obligation with this final Matzah, we want its taste to remain in our mouths (ibid.).

ROSH: If the Afikoman was really eaten to remember the Matzah eaten with the Paschal lamb, as *Rashi* and *Rashbam* argue, then why is it not eaten with Maror and Charoses too, as in Temple times?

Due to this problem, I maintain that the Afikoman is not eaten to fulfil the Biblical obligation to eat Matzah, as *Rashi* argues. Rather, it is [a Rabbinic requirement] as a remembrance of the Paschal lamb itself, which was eaten at the end of the meal when satiated.

And since it commemorates the Paschal lamb, we give it the same law (*"We do not serve any dessert after the Paschal lamb"*) and refrain from eating afterwards (*Pesachim* ch. 10, par. 34).

BACH: [In response to *Rosh's* question on *Rashi* and *Rashbam*, the following could be argued.]

In the current era, Matzah remains a Biblical obligation. Therefore, the Sages were insistent that we perform this Mitzvah in the same fashion that it was done in Biblical times, i.e. at the end of the meal,

Eat the Afikoman

➤ THE AFIKOMAN SHOULD BE EATEN BEFORE HALACHIC MIDNIGHT.

➤ EVERYBODY SHOULD EAT A DOUBLE PORTION OF MATZAH (A TOTAL OF AT LEAST 1.24OZ): ONE PORTION TO REMEMBER THE PASCHAL LAMB AND ANOTHER PORTION TO REMEMBER THE MATZAH EATEN WITH THE PASCHAL LAMB.

➤ IF THIS IS TOO DIFFICULT, EAT A SINGLE PORTION OF MATZAH (AT LEAST 0.62OZ).

➤ EAT ALL THE MATZAH WITHIN 2 MINUTES (OR AT MOST 9), WHILE RECLINING TO THE LEFT.

➤ DO NOT EAT OR DRINK AFTER EATING THE *AFIKOMAN* (EXCEPT WATER ETC.).

── CLASSIC QUESTIONS ──

when satiated. However, Maror in the current era is only a Rabbinic precept, so the Sages did not have the same insistence.

Our custom is to eat twice the prescribed quantity of Matzah for the Afikoman, so as to satisfy both the opinions of *Rosh* and *Rashbam*. In order to avoid entering into the dispute a person should not suffice with just one (commentary to Tur ch. 477).

── TORAS MENACHEM ──

צָפוּן — *The Afikoman.*

The Afikoman is eaten at the end of the meal, just as the Paschal lamb itself was eaten *"when satiated"* (*Pesachim* 70a), and not earlier on when the person was still hungry. One of the reasons why the Paschal lamb was eaten when a person was already satiated was to demonstrate that this act is performed solely

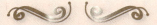

THE REBBE MAHARASH TAUGHT that the Afikoman is called "Tzafun" because it grants us the power to eliminate the Yetzer Hara (Evil Inclination) which is also called Tzafon: "I will remove the Tzafuni far off from you" (Joel 2:20).

The Afikoman has no taste. This teaches us that we should not attempt to reason with the Yetzer Hara, to "taste" its arguments in order to refute them. The best approach is to be unrelenting and uncompromising: I will do the right thing! There is simply no other option!

➤ (ACCORDING TO SOME, ELIYAHU'S CUP OF WINE IS NOW POURED.)

➤ THE THIRD CUP OF WINE IS POURED.

שִׁיר הַמַּעֲלוֹת, בְּשׁוּב יְהֹוָה אֶת־שִׁיבַת צִיּוֹן, הָיִינוּ
כְּחֹלְמִים: אָז יִמָּלֵא שְׂחוֹק פִּינוּ וּלְשׁוֹנֵנוּ רִנָּה,
אָז יֹאמְרוּ בַגּוֹיִם הִגְדִּיל יְהֹוָה לַעֲשׂוֹת עִם־אֵלֶּה: הִגְדִּיל
יְהֹוָה לַעֲשׂוֹת עִמָּנוּ, הָיִינוּ שְׂמֵחִים: שׁוּבָה יְהֹוָה אֶת־
שְׁבִיתֵנוּ, כַּאֲפִיקִים בַּנֶּגֶב: הַזֹּרְעִים בְּדִמְעָה בְּרִנָּה יִקְצֹרוּ:
הָלוֹךְ יֵלֵךְ וּבָכֹה נֹשֵׂא מֶשֶׁךְ־הַזָּרַע, בֹּא־יָבֹא בְרִנָּה נֹשֵׂא
אֲלֻמֹּתָיו:

תְּהִלַּת יְהֹוָה יְדַבֶּר־פִּי, וִיבָרֵךְ כָּל־בָּשָׂר שֵׁם קָדְשׁוֹ לְעוֹלָם
וָעֶד: וַאֲנַחְנוּ נְבָרֵךְ יָהּ מֵעַתָּה וְעַד־עוֹלָם, הַלְלוּיָהּ: הוֹדוּ
לַיהֹוָה כִּי טוֹב, כִּי לְעוֹלָם חַסְדּוֹ: מִי יְמַלֵּל גְּבוּרוֹת יְהֹוָה,
יַשְׁמִיעַ כָּל־תְּהִלָּתוֹ:

TORAS MENACHEM

for the sake of a *mitzvah* and not to satisfy any physical need (see *Meiri* to *Nazir* 23a).

Thus, the message of this precept, and likewise the message of the Afikoman which replaces it today, is that tonight we are being granted the strength to serve God in a pure and dedicated fashion where physical needs and urges no longer get in the way. The body is now "satiated" so we can worship God undisturbed.

Of course, most people will admit that reaching such a level seems far beyond anything in sight. But in *Tanya* the *Alter Rebbe* argues that, practically speaking, it is largely a question of attitude whether we allow our body to hamper our spirituality, or not:

"*While the body remains abhorrent and odious... nevertheless, let his soul be more precious to him than his ignoble body, so that he does not allow his sorry physical state to interfere with or disturb his joy in spiritual matters. This is what it means to 'leave Egypt'*" (*Tanya*, ch. 31).

So even if we cannot eliminate our physical urges that draw us away from a spiritual life, we can certainly choose to focus intensely on the spiritual, and ignore any distractions as much as possible. And tonight, we are granted the energy to carry out this mission the whole year, so that we can worship God with the utmost dedication, as if our body was already "satiated" in all its needs.

Grace after Meals

➤ (ACCORDING TO SOME, ELIYAHU'S CUP OF WINE IS NOW POURED.)

➤ THE THIRD CUP OF WINE IS POURED.

A SONG OF ASCENTS. When God will return the exiles of Zion, we will be like dreamers. Then our mouth will be filled with laughter, and our tongue with glad song. Then will declare among the nations: God has done great things for them. God has done great things for us, we were gladdened. O God, restore our exiles as springs in the Negev. Those who sow in tears will reap in glad song. He who bears a measure of seed goes along weeping, but he will return with exultation, bearing his sheaves.

My mouth will utter the praise of God, and all flesh will bless His holy name forever and ever. And we will bless God from now and forever—Halleluyah! Thank God, for He is good, for His kindness is everlasting. Who can express the mighty acts of God? Who can declare all His praise?

TORAS MENACHEM

Like the body, the soul too can become "satiated." The myriads of worlds above are an elaborate mesh of many different types of spiritual irradiation, and at some point on its journey upwards the soul can simply say, "I've had enough. This level of spirituality is sufficient for me."

On Pesach, however we are taught that *"the King of kings, the Holy One, blessed be He, revealed Himself to them and redeemed them"* (p. 123). So tonight we are inspired not to allow the soul to be "satiated" by anything less than the "King of kings" Himself.

At this point you may be wondering: Who, exactly, are we talking to here? On the one hand we are giving advice to a person whose physical needs and urges are drawing him away from God. And yet, on the other hand, we have just addressed someone whose only problem is that his soul has not yet reached the most transcendent of all heights. Surely, these are two different messages for two very different personalities?

Logically speaking, perhaps, that may be true, but tonight is not a time of order and logic. "Pesach" means to pass over and "leap," suggesting that we are currently being granted the power to break beyond the limitations of conventional spirituality. So even if you don't feel too holy, and physical things still matter to you immensely, aim high and think big. "Leap" for something spiritually ambitious, and do not feel chained any longer by your physical side, for tonight we are leaving Egypt.

(Based on *Sichah* of the 2nd Night of Pesach 5711)

➤ (IF THERE ARE LESS THAN THREE MEN SKIP TO בָּרוּךְ אַתָּה ה' BELOW.)

➤ THE LEADER SAYS:

רַבּוֹתַי נְבָרֵךְ:

➤ EVERYONE RESPONDS:

יְהִי שֵׁם יְהֹוָה מְבֹרָךְ מֵעַתָּה וְעַד־עוֹלָם:

➤ THE LEADER SAYS:

בִּרְשׁוּת מָרָנָן וְרַבָּנָן וְרַבּוֹתַי נְבָרֵךְ [אֱלֹהֵינוּ IF TEN MEN ARE PRESENT] שֶׁאָכַלְנוּ מִשֶּׁלּוֹ:

➤ EVERYONE RESPONDS:

בָּרוּךְ [אֱלֹהֵינוּ IF TEN MEN ARE PRESENT] שֶׁאָכַלְנוּ מִשֶּׁלּוֹ וּבְטוּבוֹ חָיִינוּ:

➤ THE LEADER CONCLUDES:

בָּרוּךְ [אֱלֹהֵינוּ IF TEN MEN ARE PRESENT] שֶׁאָכַלְנוּ מִשֶּׁלּוֹ וּבְטוּבוֹ חָיִינוּ:

➤ IF TEN MEN ARE PRESENT THE LEADER SAYS:

בָּרוּךְ הוּא וּבָרוּךְ שְׁמוֹ:

בָּרוּךְ אַתָּה יְהֹוָה אֱלֹהֵינוּ מֶלֶךְ הָעוֹלָם, הַזָּן אֶת־הָעוֹלָם כֻּלּוֹ בְּטוּבוֹ בְּחֵן בְּחֶסֶד וּבְרַחֲמִים, הוּא־נוֹתֵן לֶחֶם לְכָל־בָּשָׂר כִּי לְעוֹלָם חַסְדּוֹ: וּבְטוּבוֹ הַגָּדוֹל תָּמִיד לֹא חָסַר לָנוּ וְאַל יֶחְסַר־לָנוּ מָזוֹן לְעוֹלָם וָעֶד: בַּעֲבוּר שְׁמוֹ הַגָּדוֹל, כִּי הוּא אֵל זָן וּמְפַרְנֵס לַכֹּל וּמֵטִיב לַכֹּל וּמֵכִין מָזוֹן לְכָל־בְּרִיּוֹתָיו אֲשֶׁר בָּרָא: בָּרוּךְ אַתָּה יְהֹוָה, הַזָּן אֶת הַכֹּל:

➤ (IF THERE ARE LESS THAN THREE MEN SKIP TO "BLESSED ARE YOU".)

➤ THE LEADER SAYS:

Gentlemen, let us say the blessings!

➤ EVERYONE RESPONDS:

May the name of God be blessed from now and forever.

➤ THE LEADER SAYS (IF TEN MEN ARE PRESENT ADD THE BRACKETS):

With the permission of the masters, teachers and gentlemen, let us bless He (our God) of whose bounty we have eaten.

➤ EVERYONE RESPONDS:

Blessed be He (our God) of Whose we have eaten and through Whose goodness we live.

➤ THE LEADER CONCLUDES:

Blessed be He (our God) of Whose we have eaten and through Whose goodness we live.

➤ IF TEN MEN ARE PRESENT THE LEADER SAYS:

Blessed be He and blessed be His Name!

BLESSED ARE You, God, our God, King of the universe, who feeds the whole world in His goodness, with grace, with kindness and with mercy. He gives food to all flesh, for His kindness is eternal. Through His great goodness, we have never lacked food, and may we never lack it for eternity. For the sake of His great name, because He is God who feeds and sustains all, does good to all, and prepares food for all His creatures that He has created. Blessed are You God, who provides food for all.

נוֹדֶה לְךָ יְהֹוָה אֱלֹהֵינוּ עַל שֶׁהִנְחַלְתָּ לַאֲבוֹתֵינוּ אֶרֶץ חֶמְדָּה טוֹבָה וּרְחָבָה, וְעַל שֶׁהוֹצֵאתָנוּ יְהֹוָה אֱלֹהֵינוּ מֵאֶרֶץ מִצְרַיִם וּפְדִיתָנוּ מִבֵּית עֲבָדִים, וְעַל־בְּרִיתְךָ שֶׁחָתַמְתָּ בִּבְשָׂרֵנוּ וְעַל תּוֹרָתְךָ שֶׁלִּמַּדְתָּנוּ וְעַל חֻקֶּיךָ שֶׁהוֹדַעְתָּנוּ וְעַל חַיִּים חֵן וָחֶסֶד שֶׁחוֹנַנְתָּנוּ, וְעַל אֲכִילַת מָזוֹן שָׁאַתָּה זָן וּמְפַרְנֵס אוֹתָנוּ תָּמִיד בְּכָל־יוֹם וּבְכָל־עֵת וּבְכָל־שָׁעָה:

וְעַל הַכֹּל יְהֹוָה אֱלֹהֵינוּ אֲנַחְנוּ מוֹדִים לָךְ וּמְבָרְכִים אוֹתָךְ, יִתְבָּרַךְ שִׁמְךָ בְּפִי כָל־ חַי תָּמִיד לְעוֹלָם וָעֶד, כַּכָּתוּב, וְאָכַלְתָּ וְשָׂבָעְתָּ וּבֵרַכְתָּ אֶת־יְהֹוָה אֱלֹהֶיךָ עַל־הָאָרֶץ הַטּוֹבָה אֲשֶׁר נָתַן־לָךְ: בָּרוּךְ אַתָּה יְהֹוָה, עַל־הָאָרֶץ וְעַל־הַמָּזוֹן:

רַחֶם יְהֹוָה אֱלֹהֵינוּ עַל־יִשְׂרָאֵל עַמֶּךָ וְעַל־ יְרוּשָׁלַיִם עִירֶךָ וְעַל־צִיּוֹן מִשְׁכַּן כְּבוֹדֶךָ וְעַל־מַלְכוּת בֵּית דָּוִד מְשִׁיחֶךָ, וְעַל־הַבַּיִת הַגָּדוֹל וְהַקָּדוֹשׁ שֶׁנִּקְרָא שִׁמְךָ עָלָיו: אֱלֹהֵינוּ אָבִינוּ רְעֵנוּ, זוּנֵנוּ פַרְנְסֵנוּ וְכַלְכְּלֵנוּ וְהַרְוִיחֵנוּ וְהַרְוַח לָנוּ יְהֹוָה

WE THANK YOU, God, our God, for having given as a heritage to our forefathers a desirable, good and spacious land; for having brought us out, God, our God, from the land of Egypt and redeemed us from the house of bondage; for Your covenant which You have sealed in our flesh; for Your Torah which You have taught us; for Your laws which You have made known to us; for the life, grace and kindness which You have bestowed upon us; and for the food we eat with which You constantly nourish and sustain us every day, in every season, and at every hour.

FOR ALL THIS, God, our God, we thank You and bless You. May Your Name be blessed by the mouth of every living being, constantly and for eternity—as the verse states: "You shall eat and be satisfied, then you shall bless God, your God, for the good land which He has given you." Blessed are You, God, for the land and for the sustenance.

HAVE MERCY, God, our God, upon Israel, Your people; upon Jerusalem, Your city; upon Zion, the resting place of Your glory; upon the monarchy of the house of David, Your anointed; and upon the great and holy House which is called by Your name. Our God, our Father, our Shepherd! Sustain us, support us, nourish us and relieve us! O God, our God,

אֱלֹהֵינוּ מְהֵרָה מִכָּל־צָרוֹתֵינוּ: וְנָא אַל־תַּצְרִיכֵנוּ
יְהֹוָה אֱלֹהֵינוּ לֹא לִידֵי מַתְּנַת בָּשָׂר וָדָם וְלֹא לִידֵי
הַלְוָאָתָם, כִּי אִם לְיָדְךָ הַמְּלֵאָה הַפְּתוּחָה הַקְּדוֹשָׁה
וְהָרְחָבָה, שֶׁלֹּא נֵבוֹשׁ וְלֹא נִכָּלֵם לְעוֹלָם וָעֶד:

▶ **On Shabbos Add:**

רְצֵה וְהַחֲלִיצֵנוּ יְהֹוָה אֱלֹהֵינוּ בְּמִצְוֹתֶיךָ
וּבְמִצְוַת יוֹם הַשְּׁבִיעִי הַשַּׁבָּת הַגָּדוֹל
וְהַקָּדוֹשׁ הַזֶּה. כִּי יוֹם זֶה גָּדוֹל וְקָדוֹשׁ הוּא לְפָנֶיךָ,
לִשְׁבָּת־בּוֹ וְלָנוּחַ־בּוֹ בְּאַהֲבָה כְּמִצְוַת רְצוֹנֶךָ. וּבִרְצוֹנְךָ
הָנִיחַ לָנוּ יְהֹוָה אֱלֹהֵינוּ שֶׁלֹּא תְהֵא צָרָה וְיָגוֹן וַאֲנָחָה
בְּיוֹם מְנוּחָתֵנוּ. וְהַרְאֵנוּ יְהֹוָה אֱלֹהֵינוּ בְּנֶחָמַת צִיּוֹן
עִירֶךָ, וּבְבִנְיַן יְרוּשָׁלַיִם עִיר קָדְשֶׁךָ, כִּי אַתָּה הוּא
בַּעַל הַיְשׁוּעוֹת וּבַעַל הַנֶּחָמוֹת:

אֱלֹהֵינוּ וֵאלֹהֵי אֲבוֹתֵינוּ יַעֲלֶה וְיָבֹא,
וְיַגִּיעַ וְיֵרָאֶה וְיֵרָצֶה, וְיִשָּׁמַע
וְיִפָּקֵד וְיִזָּכֵר, זִכְרוֹנֵנוּ וּפִקְדוֹנֵנוּ, וְזִכְרוֹן אֲבוֹתֵינוּ,
וְזִכְרוֹן מָשִׁיחַ בֶּן־דָּוִד עַבְדֶּךָ, וְזִכְרוֹן יְרוּשָׁלַיִם

grant us speedy relief from all our misfortunes! O God, our God, please do not make us needful of the gifts of human hands nor of their loans, but of Your full, open, holy and generous hand, so that we will not be shamed nor humiliated forever and ever.

➤ On Shabbos Add:

MAY IT PLEASE You, God, our God, to fortify us through Your commandments, and through the commandment of the seventh day, this great and holy Shabbos. For this day is great and holy before You, to cease from work on it, and to rest on it, with love, according to the commandment of Your will. In Your will, God, our God, grant us tranquility, that there shall be no trouble, sorrow or grief on the day of our rest. And let us see, God, our God, the consolation of Zion, Your city, and the rebuilding of Jerusalem, Your holy city, for You are one who works salvations and consolations.

OUR GOD, and God of our fathers, may the remembrance and recollection of us, the remembrance of our fathers, the remembrance of Mashiach the son of David Your servant, the remembrance of Jerusalem Your holy city, and the remembrance of all Your people the House of Israel,

עִיר קָדְשֶׁךָ, וְזִכְרוֹן כָּל־עַמְּךָ בֵּית יִשְׂרָאֵל לְפָנֶיךָ, לִפְלֵיטָה לְטוֹבָה, לְחֵן וּלְחֶסֶד וּלְרַחֲמִים לְחַיִּים וּלְשָׁלוֹם, בְּיוֹם חַג הַמַּצּוֹת הַזֶּה. זָכְרֵנוּ יְהֹוָה אֱלֹהֵינוּ בּוֹ לְטוֹבָה, וּפָקְדֵנוּ בוֹ לִבְרָכָה, וְהוֹשִׁיעֵנוּ בוֹ לְחַיִּים: וּבִדְבַר יְשׁוּעָה וְרַחֲמִים חוּס וְחָנֵּנוּ וְרַחֵם עָלֵינוּ וְהוֹשִׁיעֵנוּ, כִּי אֵלֶיךָ עֵינֵינוּ, כִּי אֵל (מֶלֶךְ) חַנּוּן וְרַחוּם אָתָּה:

וּבְנֵה יְרוּשָׁלַיִם עִיר הַקֹּדֶשׁ בִּמְהֵרָה בְיָמֵינוּ. בָּרוּךְ אַתָּה יְהֹוָה בֹּנֵה בְרַחֲמָיו יְרוּשָׁלָיִם. אָמֵן:

בָּרוּךְ אַתָּה יְהֹוָה אֱלֹהֵינוּ מֶלֶךְ הָעוֹלָם, הָאֵל, אָבִינוּ מַלְכֵּנוּ, אַדִּירֵנוּ בּוֹרְאֵנוּ גּוֹאֲלֵנוּ יוֹצְרֵנוּ, קְדוֹשֵׁנוּ קְדוֹשׁ יַעֲקֹב רוֹעֵנוּ רוֹעֵה יִשְׂרָאֵל הַמֶּלֶךְ הַטּוֹב וְהַמֵּטִיב לַכֹּל שֶׁבְּכָל יוֹם וָיוֹם, הוּא הֵיטִיב, הוּא מֵטִיב, הוּא יֵיטִיב לָנוּ, הוּא גְמָלָנוּ הוּא גוֹמְלֵנוּ הוּא יִגְמְלֵנוּ לָעַד, לְחֵן וּלְחֶסֶד וּלְרַחֲמִים, וּלְרֶוַח הַצָּלָה וְהַצְלָחָה, בְּרָכָה

rise, come, reach, be noted, favored, heard, recalled and remembered before You, for deliverance, well-being, grace, lovingkindness, mercy, life and peace, on this day of the Festival of Matzos. Remember us on it, God, our God, for good; Call us to Mind on it for blessing; Save us on it for life. With the promise of deliverance and compassion, save us and be gracious to us; have mercy upon us and save us. For our eyes are turned to You, for You, God, are a gracious and merciful King.

REBUILD JERUSALEM the holy city speedily in our days. Blessed are You, God, who in His mercy rebuilds Jerusalem. Amen.

BLESSED ARE YOU, God, our God, King of the universe: God our Father, our King; our Sovereign, our Creator, our Redeemer, our Maker; our Holy One, the Holy One of Ya'akov, our Shepherd, the Shepherd of Israel, the King who is good and does good to all, each day. He has done good, He does good, and He will do good for us. He has bestowed, He bestows, and He will forever bestow upon us with grace, kindness and mercy; relief, salvation and success; blessing and salvation; consolation, sustenance and

וִישׁוּעָה, נֶחָמָה פַּרְנָסָה וְכַלְכָּלָה וְרַחֲמִים וְחַיִּים

וְשָׁלוֹם וְכָל־טוֹב, וּמִכָּל־טוּב לְעוֹלָם אַל יְחַסְּרֵנוּ:

הָרַחֲמָן הוּא יִמְלֹךְ עָלֵינוּ לְעוֹלָם וָעֶד:

הָרַחֲמָן הוּא יִתְבָּרַךְ בַּשָּׁמַיִם וּבָאָרֶץ:

הָרַחֲמָן הוּא יִשְׁתַּבַּח לְדוֹר דּוֹרִים וְיִתְפָּאַר בָּנוּ לָעַד

וּלְנֵצַח נְצָחִים וְיִתְהַדַּר בָּנוּ לָעַד וּלְעוֹלְמֵי עוֹלָמִים:

הָרַחֲמָן הוּא יְפַרְנְסֵנוּ בְּכָבוֹד: הָרַחֲמָן הוּא יִשְׁבּוֹר

עֻלֵּנוּ מֵעַל צַוָּארֵנוּ וְהוּא יוֹלִיכֵנוּ קוֹמְמִיּוּת לְאַרְצֵנוּ:

הָרַחֲמָן הוּא יִשְׁלַח לָנוּ בְּרָכָה מְרֻבָּה בַּבַּיִת הַזֶּה

וְעַל שֻׁלְחָן זֶה שֶׁאָכַלְנוּ עָלָיו: הָרַחֲמָן הוּא יִשְׁלַח

לָנוּ אֶת־אֵלִיָּהוּ הַנָּבִיא זָכוּר לַטּוֹב, וִיבַשֶּׂר־לָנוּ

בְּשׂוֹרוֹת טוֹבוֹת יְשׁוּעוֹת וְנֶחָמוֹת:

➤ THOSE EATING AT THEIR OWN TABLE SAY THE FOLLOWING (INCLUDING WORDS THAT APPLY).

הָרַחֲמָן הוּא יְבָרֵךְ אוֹתִי (וְאָבִי וְאִמִּי) (וְאֶת־

אִשְׁתִּי / בַּעְלִי וְאֶת־זַרְעִי) וְאֶת־כָּל־אֲשֶׁר לִי.

➤ GUESTS RECITE THE FOLLOWING (CHILDREN AT THEIR PARENTS' TABLE ADD PARENTHESES).

הָרַחֲמָן, הוּא יְבָרֵךְ אֶת (אָבִי מוֹרִי) בַּעַל הַבַּיִת הַזֶּה,

וְאֶת (אִמִּי מוֹרָתִי) אִשְׁתּוֹ בַּעֲלַת הַבַּיִת הַזֶּה, אוֹתָם

וְאֶת־בֵּיתָם וְאֶת־זַרְעָם וְאֶת־כָּל־אֲשֶׁר לָהֶם,

nourishment; compassion, life, peace and all goodness; and may He never let us lack any good.

*M*AY THE MERCIFUL ONE reign over us forever and ever. May the Merciful One be blessed in heaven and on earth. May the Merciful One be praised for generations, and be glorified through us eternally, and honored through us forever. May the Merciful One sustain us in honor. May the Merciful One break the oppressive yoke from our neck and may He lead us upright to our land. May the Merciful One send us abundant blessing into this house and upon this table at which we have eaten. May the Merciful One send us the Prophet Eliyahu, may he be remembered for good who will bring us good tidings, salvation and comfort.

➤ THOSE EATING AT THEIR OWN TABLE SAY THE FOLLOWING (INCLUDING WORDS THAT APPLY).

May the Merciful One bless me (and my father and mother) (and my wife / husband and my children) and all that belongs to me.

➤ GUESTS RECITE THE FOLLOWING (CHILDREN AT THEIR PARENTS' TABLE ADD PARENTHESES).

May the Merciful One bless (my father, my teacher) the master of this house, and (my mother, my teacher), the lady of this house; them and their household, their children and all that belongs to them.

➤ **ALL CONTINUE:**

אוֹתָנוּ וְאֶת־כָּל־אֲשֶׁר לָנוּ: כְּמוֹ שֶׁנִּתְבָּרְכוּ אֶת־ אֲבוֹתֵינוּ אַבְרָהָם יִצְחָק וְיַעֲקֹב בַּכֹּל מִכֹּל כֹּל, כֵּן יְבָרֵךְ אוֹתָנוּ כֻּלָּנוּ יַחַד בִּבְרָכָה שְׁלֵמָה, וְנֹאמַר אָמֵן:

בַּמָּרוֹם יְלַמְּדוּ עֲלֵיהֶם וְעָלֵינוּ זְכוּת שֶׁתְּהֵא לְמִשְׁמֶרֶת שָׁלוֹם, וְנִשָּׂא בְרָכָה מֵאֵת יְהֹוָה וּצְדָקָה מֵאֱלֹהֵי יִשְׁעֵנוּ, וְנִמְצָא חֵן וְשֵׂכֶל טוֹב בְּעֵינֵי אֱלֹהִים וְאָדָם:

➤ **ON SHABBOS ADD:**

הָרַחֲמָן הוּא יַנְחִילֵנוּ יוֹם שֶׁכֻּלּוֹ שַׁבָּת וּמְנוּחָה לְחַיֵּי הָעוֹלָמִים:

הָרַחֲמָן הוּא יַנְחִילֵנוּ יוֹם שֶׁכֻּלּוֹ טוֹב (יוֹם שֶׁכֻּלּוֹ אָרוּךְ, יוֹם שֶׁצַּדִּיקִים יוֹשְׁבִים וְעַטְרוֹתֵיהֶם בְּרָאשֵׁיהֶם וְנֶהֱנִים מִזִּיו הַשְּׁכִינָה, וִיהִי חֶלְקֵנוּ עִמָּהֶם:)

הָרַחֲמָן הוּא יְזַכֵּנוּ לִימוֹת הַמָּשִׁיחַ וּלְחַיֵּי הָעוֹלָם הַבָּא. מִגְדֹּל יְשׁוּעוֹת מַלְכּוֹ

➤ All Continue:

Ours, and all that is ours, just as our forefathers, Avraham, Yitzchak, and Ya'akov, were blessed in everything, through everything, and with everything, so may He bless all of us together with a perfect blessing. And let us say, Amen.

On high, may there be pleaded for them and for us such merit so as to make a sure guarantee of peace. May we obtain a blessing from God, and just kindness from the God of our salvation, and may we find grace and good understanding in the eyes of God and man.

➤ On Shabbos Add:

May the Merciful One bring us to inherit the day that will be entirely Shabbos and rest for eternal life.

May the Merciful One bring us to inherit that day which is entirely good, (that everlasting day, the day when the righteous sit with crowns on their heads, enjoying the radiance of the Divine presence, and may our portion be with them)!

May the Merciful One merit us with the days of Mashiach and life in the World to Come. "He is a tower of salvation for His king, and bestows

וְעֹשֶׂה־חֶסֶד לִמְשִׁיחוֹ לְדָוִד וּלְזַרְעוֹ עַד־עוֹלָם: עֹשֶׂה שָׁלוֹם בִּמְרוֹמָיו הוּא יַעֲשֶׂה שָׁלוֹם עָלֵינוּ וְעַל כָּל־יִשְׂרָאֵל וְאִמְרוּ אָמֵן:

יְראוּ אֶת־יְהוָֹה קְדֹשָׁיו, כִּי־אֵין מַחְסוֹר לִירֵאָיו: כְּפִירִים רָשׁוּ וְרָעֵבוּ, וְדֹרְשֵׁי יְהוָֹה לֹא־יַחְסְרוּ כָל־טוֹב: הוֹדוּ לַיהוָֹה כִּי־טוֹב, כִּי לְעוֹלָם חַסְדּוֹ: פּוֹתֵחַ אֶת־יָדֶךָ, וּמַשְׂבִּיעַ לְכָל־חַי רָצוֹן: בָּרוּךְ הַגֶּבֶר אֲשֶׁר יִבְטַח בַּיהוָֹה, וְהָיָה יְהוָֹה מִבְטַחוֹ: נַעַר הָיִיתִי גַּם־זָקַנְתִּי, וְלֹא־רָאִיתִי צַדִּיק נֶעֱזָב, וְזַרְעוֹ מְבַקֶּשׁ־לָחֶם: יְהוָֹה עֹז לְעַמּוֹ יִתֵּן, יְהוָֹה יְבָרֵךְ אֶת־עַמּוֹ בַשָּׁלוֹם:

➤ HOLD THE CUP IN YOUR RIGHT HAND.

בָּרוּךְ אַתָּה יְהוָֹה אֱלֹהֵינוּ מֶלֶךְ הָעוֹלָם, בּוֹרֵא פְּרִי הַגָּפֶן:

➤ RECLINE TO THE LEFT AND DRINK THE CUP (AS BEFORE).

➤ THE CUP OF ELIYAHU IS POURED. THE FOURTH CUP OF WINE IS POURED.

=== CLASSIC QUESTIONS ===

● **Why do we pour Eliyahu's cup?**

R' MOSHE CHAGIZ: Our Sages taught that God rewarded Eliyahu the prophet with the merit of visiting and testifying to every Jewish circumcision, since he zealously defended this *mitzvah* in his lifetime (see *Pirkei d'Rabbi Eliezer* ch. 29). Since an uncircumcised person is forbidden to eat from the Paschal lamb (*Shemos* 12:48), we invite Eliyahu to "testify" that we are all circumcised (*Bircas Eliyahu*).

VILNA GA'ON: The *Talmud* debates the question whether we should drink a Fifth Cup of wine (*Pesachim* 118a), but since no final consensus was reached in this matter, we will have to wait until Eliyahu comes to rule on the law, based on the tradition that he will clarify all unresolved disputes.

We therefore pour a cup of wine but do not drink it, referring to it as "the Cup of Eliyahu" (cited in *Ta'amei ha-Minhagim, inyanei Pesach* par. 551).

ALTER REBBE'S SHULCHAN ARUCH: Some places have the custom not to lock the rooms where they sleep on the night of Pesach because it is *"a night which God had been keeping in mind for generations to take the Jewish people out"* (cf. *Shemos* 12:42) of this exile. Thus if Eliyahu will come he will find an open door, and we will be able to go out and greet him quickly. This is what we believe, and it is a belief which will be greatly rewarded....It is customary in these countries to pour another cup of wine, besides those poured by the participants, which is referred to as the cup of Eliyahu the prophet (*Orach Chaim* 480:5).

kindness on His anointed, to David and his seed forever."
He who makes peace in His heights, may He grant peace
for us and for all Israel. and say, Amen.

F EAR GOD, you His holy ones, for those who fear Him
lack nothing. Young lions are in need and go hungry,
but those who seek God shall not lack any good. Give thanks to
God for He is good, for His kindness endures forever. You open
Your hand and satisfy the desire of every living thing. Blessed
is the man who trusts in God, and God will become his trust. I
was a youth and also have aged, and I have not seen a righteous
man forsaken, with his children begging for bread. God will give
might to His nation. God will bless His nation with peace.

> HOLD THE CUP IN YOUR RIGHT HAND.

Blessed are You, God, our God, King of the universe, who creates the fruit of the vine.

> RECLINE TO THE LEFT AND DRINK THE CUP (AS BEFORE).

> THE CUP OF ELIYAHU IS POURED. THE FOURTH CUP OF WINE IS POURED.

WHAT ARE WE DOING NOW?
The second half of the Seder focuses on the final redemption. Thus the Third Cup of wine, made on the blessing after the meal, alludes to the festive meal which God will make for the righteous in the future, when King David will bless on the cup (*Likutei Sichos* vol. 36, p. 212).

===== CLASSIC QUESTIONS =====

LIKUTEI TA'AMIM U'MINHAGIM: The explanation of R' Moshe Chagiz is difficult to accept, for if Eliyahu's cup was directly connected to the Pesach sacrifice, one would expect the cup to be poured earlier, some time before eating the Afikoman (which replaces the Pesach sacrifice).

===== TORAS MENACHEM =====

כּוֹס שֶׁל אֵלִיָּהוּ — *Eliyahu's Cup.*

The **Vilna Ga'on** suggested that Eliyahu's cup is poured due to a halachic doubt which arises from the *Talmud*, that perhaps five cups of wine are required and not four. It is named after Eliyahu, since we are promised that, in the future, Eliyahu will determine which reading of the Talmud is the correct one.

The **Alter Rebbe,** however, clearly rejected this notion, suggesting instead that Eliyahu's cup is poured as an act of faith in the imminent coming of the redemption, to be announced by Eliyahu. (He perceived the Fifth Cup as a totally separate matter, addressing it in a different chapter (481) of his *Shulchan Aruch,* where he states that it is a precept generally not practiced today.)

If one reflects on the *Alter Rebbe's* position here, one cannot help but remark upon two glaring ironies.

First, whereas the Vilna Gaon saw this custom as an expression of *doubt*—that we are unclear as to the correct law—the Alter Rebbe perceived it as an expression of *certainty,* that we believe with perfect faith in Mashiach's coming. In fact, our expectations are so ripe that we even pour a cup for Eliyahu and leave all the doors open so as to make a speedy exit!

➤ THE FRONT DOOR OF THE HOUSE IS OPENED.

שְׁפֹךְ חֲמָתְךָ אֶל־הַגּוֹיִם
אֲשֶׁר לֹא־יְדָעוּךָ, וְעַל
מַמְלָכוֹת אֲשֶׁר בְּשִׁמְךָ לֹא
קָרָאוּ: כִּי אָכַל אֶת־יַעֲקֹב,
וְאֶת־נָוֵהוּ הֵשַׁמּוּ:

TORAS MENACHEM

The second irony is a striking discordance between the source texts of Jewish law and the normative practice observed today. The Fifth Cup, which has a clear Talmudic precedent and is documented as something actually observed by primary medieval authorities, is nevertheless not a feature of contemporary practice. Meanwhile Eliyahu's cup, which has no precedent in the Talmud or early authorities, has become a universal practice observed by all Jews.

Of course there is nothing terribly disturbing here. One practice simply became less widespread while another (remarkably similar) custom emerged and gained popularity. But what is the *inner* reason why we see an almost reciprocal relationship here, that as the Fifth Cup gradually stepped into the background, Eliyahu's cup rose to the forefront of mainstream Judaism?

This "switching of the cups" represents the crossing of two diametrically opposed historical currents. On the one hand we find a general decline in man's spiritual and intellectual caliber as the generations pass. *"If the earlier scholars were like angels,"* remarks the Talmud, *"then we are like men. And if the earlier scholars were like men, we are like donkeys"* (Shabbos 112b). In another instance, the Talmud

dismisses the notion of spiritual "progress" as being utterly inconceivable: *"Is it credible that the generations have improved"* (Yevamos 39b)?

Nevertheless, the decline in scholarship and general clarity of mind has enabled other qualities to foster and develop—most notably, our absolute faith in God and unbending dedication to Him. For when it comes to simple, unquestioning faith, knowledge tends to hinder, not help, because the sophisticated mind has difficulty accepting things that do not sit well with its established rules and norms. So as the generations have become gradually less cerebral, we have become more passionate, deeply loyal and intuitively drawn to God.

But this is not, God forbid, because we are foolish or naive. Rather, as the "left-brain" qualities of carefully honed logic and precise, analytical deduction have diminished, it has allowed our "right-brain" faculties of soul-intuition and holistic vision to come to the fore. The sober, analytical mind tends to split the whole into its elemental parts, understanding and grasping them well, but it tends to pay the price of losing an overall picture and "feel" of the concept.

So as "right-brainers," we latter generations tend to take our holistic intuition to its logical conclu-

➤ THE FRONT DOOR OF THE HOUSE IS OPENED.

POUR OUT YOUR ANGER UPON THE NATIONS THAT DO NOT RECOGNIZE YOU, AND UPON THE KINGDOMS THAT DO NOT CALL UPON YOUR NAME. FOR THEY HAVE DEVOURED YA'AKOV AND LAID WASTE HIS DWELLING PLACE (PSALMS 79:6-7).

═══════════ CLASSIC QUESTIONS ═══════════

● **Why do we say *"Pour out your anger, etc."*?**

AVUDRAHAM: The Four Cups of wine are symbolic of the "Four Cups of punishment" which God is destined to "pour out" on the wicked nations. Thus, as we pour the fourth and final cup, we say to God: "With this cup we complete the *mitzvah*. Now do what You have promised us and pour out those Four Cups of punishment on the wicked nations!" (See also *Ran, Pesachim* 19a; *Bachaye* to *Shemos* 6:8.)

═══════════ TORAS MENACHEM ═══════════

sion—that there is a single, unifying force behind all the diverse elements of this world. Consequently, we excel in the intuitive awareness of One God. Our grasp of God's Instruction Manual, the Torah, may be relatively poor, but our religious dedication and gutsy feel for Judaism is impressive. And unlike the left-brain personality which is at peace with reality, we yearn to change the world. Our rich imagination cannot help but picture a brighter future which we pursue impetuously. No wonder, then, that as "latter-generation" Jews, the anticipation for Mashiach is more keenly felt in our hearts.

The Fifth Cup is a culmination and perfection of the Four Cups that preceded it. It therefore represents the kind of advanced, highly refined Judaism that was typical in the earlier generations—which is

the inner reason why this precept enjoyed popularity in the past. Eliyahu's Cup, on the other hand, represents the belief in Mashiach, which is one of our outstanding qualities. So as latter-generation Jews we proudly invite Eliyahu to our Seder and outwardly display our faith that he will come to announce the redemption, this very night.

(Based on *Likutei Sichos* vol. 27, p. 52*ff*; *Sichah* of 2nd Night of Pesach 5723; *Hemshech Ayin Beis* vol. 2, p. 717)

שְׁפוֹךְ חֲמָתְךָ אֶל הַגּוֹיִם אֲשֶׁר לֹא יְדָעוּךְ — *Pour out Your anger upon the nations that do not recognize You.*

While the second half of the Seder in general focuses on the future redemption (see p. 180), it is here for the first time that the Haggadah speaks overtly about

שְׁפָךְ-עֲלֵיהֶם זַעְמֶךָ,
וַחֲרוֹן אַפְּךָ יַשִּׂיגֵם:

תִּרְדֹּף בְּאַף וְתַשְׁמִידֵם
מִתַּחַת שְׁמֵי יְהֹוָה:

➤ THE DOOR MAY NOW BE CLOSED.

TORAS MENACHEM

the Messianic Era, when God will punish the wicked nations who persecuted the Jewish people during their exile.

However, this does not mean to say that *all* the nations will be punished. The verse states, "Pour out Your anger upon the nations *that do not recognize You*," indicating that those who *do* recognize God, and have not "devoured Ya'akov," will be spared. Rather, instead, *"I will transform the nations... that they may all call upon the name of God, to serve him with one accord"* (Zeph. 3:9); *"And they shall bring all your brothers for an offering to God from all nations...*

just as the people of Israel bring an offering in a clean utensil to the House of God" (Isaiah 66:20).

Nowadays this would seem to apply to a large portion of the world's inhabitants. Whereas in previous generations, most Jews lived in countries which opposed the practice of Judaism, this is not the case in our days when most of us live among nations which allow freedom of religion.

This is especially true since the collapse of the Soviet Union in the early Nineties, when we witnessed a significant change for the good, as restrictions on

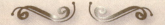

"My Father the Rebbe once told me," related Rabbi Yosef Yitzchak of Lubavitch, *"that during the Seder you should think to yourself, 'I want to be a mentch (a person of integrity),' and God will help. This applies especially at the time when the doors are opened.*

"Don't ask for material success," he concluded, *"but for spiritual growth!"*

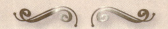

POUR OUT YOUR INDIGNATION UPON THEM, AND LET YOUR FIERCE ANGER OVERTAKE THEM (PSALMS 69:25).

PURSUE THEM WITH WRATH, AND DESTROY THEM FROM BENEATH THE HEAVENS OF GOD (LAMENTATIONS 3:66).

➤ THE DOOR MAY NOW BE CLOSED.

TORAS MENACHEM

Torah observance were lifted and Jews were permitted to emigrate much more freely. In fact, Russia actually helped Jews to travel to the Holy Land, which gave us a little taste of how the nations will help the Jews to leave exile with the true and complete redemption.

In addition to the direct assistance to Jews from the nations, we also see so many instances where non-Jews themselves perform acts of goodness and kindness. In the past, it was largely the Jewish people (*"the smallest of all the nations,"* Devarim 7:7) who actively addressed the task of making a *"home for God below"* (*Tanchuma, Naso* 15), while most of the nations behaved cruelly to one other. Their main pursuit was personal gain, be it through conquering other countries, or other means.

But in recent years we now see that large segments of the global population are preparing and assisting the way to the redemption. Primarily, this has been in the areas of charity and education, which are the two foundations of a civilized world. For example, in the area of charity, international humanitarian aid has also become a norm, and America, for example, has used its immense power to help and rescue people in distant regions of the world, despite the fact that American citizens receive no direct benefit from these efforts.

While for the Jewish people such activities would

not be considered out of character, as we have always been guided by the ethical values of Torah and *mitzvos* in the areas of charity and education etc., it represents a major change of heart for the nations, when one considers the *modus operandi* for most of the history of the world, since antiquity.

Unfortunately, however, Jews in general have failed to take sufficient notice of this fundamental shift in the conduct the world. If only people would open their eyes they would see the prelude of the Messianic Era unfolding.

(Based on *Sichas Shabbos Parshas Metzorah* 5746 & 5749; *Mishpatim* 5744; *Acharei-Kedoshim* 5751)

פּוֹתְחִין הַדֶּלֶת— *We open the door.*

Our Sages taught that whatever God tells the Jewish people to do, He does too (*Shemos Rabah* 30:9). So if God has told us to open the door, then He, too, must be opening up heavenly doors for every one of us—*"on this night, the treasure houses of dew are opened"* (*Pirkei d'Rabbi Eliezer* ch. 32).

Simply put, this means that every person, regardless of how he or she has behaved throughout the year, can, at this moment, leap to great spiritual heights. Because that is what this festival is all about; the very word "Pesach" means "leap."

(Based on *Likutei Sichos* vol. 4, p. 1298)

הַלֵּל

לֹא לָנוּ יְהֹוָה לֹא־לָנוּ, כִּי לְשִׁמְךָ תֵּן כָּבוֹד, עַל־חַסְדְּךָ עַל־אֲמִתֶּךָ: לָמָּה יֹאמְרוּ הַגּוֹיִם, אַיֵּה־נָא אֱלֹהֵיהֶם: וֵאלֹהֵינוּ בַשָּׁמָיִם, כֹּל אֲשֶׁר־חָפֵץ עָשָׂה: עֲצַבֵּיהֶם כֶּסֶף וְזָהָב, מַעֲשֵׂה יְדֵי אָדָם: פֶּה־לָהֶם וְלֹא יְדַבֵּרוּ, עֵינַיִם לָהֶם וְלֹא יִרְאוּ: אָזְנַיִם לָהֶם וְלֹא יִשְׁמָעוּ, אַף לָהֶם וְלֹא יְרִיחוּן: יְדֵיהֶם וְלֹא יְמִישׁוּן, רַגְלֵיהֶם וְלֹא יְהַלֵּכוּ, לֹא־יֶהְגּוּ בִּגְרוֹנָם: כְּמוֹהֶם יִהְיוּ עֹשֵׂיהֶם, כֹּל אֲשֶׁר־בֹּטֵחַ בָּהֶם: יִשְׂרָאֵל בְּטַח בַּיהֹוָה, עֶזְרָם וּמָגִנָּם הוּא: בֵּית אַהֲרֹן בִּטְחוּ בַיהֹוָה, עֶזְרָם וּמָגִנָּם הוּא: יִרְאֵי יְהֹוָה בִּטְחוּ בַיהֹוָה, עֶזְרָם וּמָגִנָּם הוּא:

CLASSIC QUESTIONS

● **Why are these chapters of Hallel said now?** (see also above, p. 136)

ABARBANEL: In my opinion, this entire section of Hallel refers to the future redemption. Thus, these chapters speak in the future tense, whereas the chapters of Hallel that we read before the meal are in the past tense. The Sages instituted that we say this section on the night of Pesach after the meal, since the future redemption is intrinsically connected with the Exodus from Egypt.

● **What does the heading *Nirtzah*, "Acceptance," refer to?** (see p. 189)

SHALOH: This is not actually a heading of part of the Haggadah text. It simply means that after following all the previous steps of the Seder, we hope that our efforts will be found pleasing and "accepted" above in heaven.

Hallel

NOT FOR OUR SAKE, *God, not for our sake, but for Your Name's sake give glory, for the sake of Your kindness and Your truth. Why should the nations say, "Where is their God?" Our God is in heaven; He has done whatever He has desired. Their idols are silver and gold, the work of human hands. They have mouths, but they do not speak; they have eyes, but they do not see; they have ears, but they do not hear; they have a nose, but they do not smell; hands, but they do not feel; feet, but they do not walk; they make no sound with their throat. Those who make them will become like them, whoever trusts in them. Israel, trust in God! He is their help and their shield. House of Aharon, trust in God! He is their help and their shield. Those who fear God, trust in God! He is their help and their shield.*

TORAS MENACHEM

☙ הַלֵּל— *Hallel.*

The recital of these chapters of Hallel at this point prompts two questions.

a.) The first two chapters of Hallel were said before the meal. Why, then, does the *siman* (heading) "Hallel" appear here in the Haggadah, and not earlier when we *began* the Hallel? b.) We only say Hallel on a miracle that has already occurred, not on one that is promised in the future [see *Jerusalem Talmud, Pesachim*

10:6]. So if these chapters of Hallel refer to the future redemption—as **Abarbanel** writes—how could we recite Hallel on the future redemption *now*?

A possible solution is to be found in the commentaries which address a different question: why is no blessing made on the recital of Hallel in the Haggadah? *Rav Hai Gaon* answers that no blessing is made because, *"It is not a mitzvah to say Hallel at all now. We are merely reciting the text of Hallel in our efforts to praise God"* (see p. 136).

יְהֹוָה זְכָרָנוּ יְבָרֵךְ, יְבָרֵךְ אֶת־בֵּית יִשְׂרָאֵל, יְבָרֵךְ אֶת־בֵּית אַהֲרֹן: יְבָרֵךְ יִרְאֵי יְהֹוָה, הַקְּטַנִּים עִם־הַגְּדֹלִים: יֹסֵף יְהֹוָה עֲלֵיכֶם, עֲלֵיכֶם וְעַל־בְּנֵיכֶם: בְּרוּכִים אַתֶּם לַיהֹוָה, עֹשֵׂה שָׁמַיִם וָאָרֶץ: הַשָּׁמַיִם שָׁמַיִם לַיהֹוָה, וְהָאָרֶץ נָתַן לִבְנֵי־אָדָם: לֹא הַמֵּתִים יְהַלְלוּ־יָהּ, וְלֹא כָּל־יֹרְדֵי דוּמָה: וַאֲנַחְנוּ נְבָרֵךְ יָהּ מֵעַתָּה וְעַד־עוֹלָם, הַלְלוּיָהּ:

אָהַבְתִּי כִּי־יִשְׁמַע יְהֹוָה אֶת־קוֹלִי תַּחֲנוּנָי: כִּי־הִטָּה אָזְנוֹ לִי, וּבְיָמַי אֶקְרָא: אֲפָפוּנִי חֶבְלֵי־מָוֶת וּמְצָרֵי שְׁאוֹל מְצָאוּנִי, צָרָה וְיָגוֹן אֶמְצָא: וּבְשֵׁם־יְהֹוָה אֶקְרָא, אָנָּה יְהֹוָה מַלְּטָה נַפְשִׁי: חַנּוּן יְהֹוָה וְצַדִּיק, וֵאלֹהֵינוּ מְרַחֵם:

TORAS MENACHEM

So, if we are not doing the *mitzvah* of Hallel, but merely reciting its *text*, i.e., we are just reading the Book of Psalms, then surely the concern about saying Hallel on a future miracle does not apply?

However, while this appears to be a possible solution, we are still left without an explanation according to the other authorities that maintain that we do perform the *mitzvah* of Hallel tonight. In fact, taking a close look at the *Alter Rebbe's Shulchan Aruch* reveals that he ruled in favor of this latter view, that reciting Hallel in the Haggadah is a *mitzvah*.

Again, the *Alter Rebbe* does not address this matter directly, but we can elucidate his opinion from another passage.

"While there is a requirement to stand when saying Hallel, nevertheless, Hallel on this night may even be said seated because all the actions of this evening should be indicative of the theme of liberation. Therefore, we do not trouble a person to stand up" (*Orach Chaim* 473:48).

Now, if, in the *Alter Rebbe's* opinion, Hallel was not a *mitzvah*, what would be objectionable about reciting some Psalms sitting down? Clearly, the *Alter Rebbe* did deem this to be a *mitzvah*, forcing him to give an explanation why the legal requirement to stand does not apply in this case.

So we are left with our original questions: How can Hallel be said on a future event, the miracle of the final redemption? And why does the heading "Hallel"

*G*OD, *who has remembered us, will bless. He will bless the House of Israel; He will bless the House of Aharon; He will bless those who fear God, the small with the great. May God add upon you—upon you and upon your children. You are blessed by God, the Maker of heaven and earth. The heavens are the heavens of God, but the earth He has given to mankind. The dead cannot praise God, nor can those who descend into silence. But we will bless God, from now and for evermore. Halleluyah!*

I LOVE GOD, *because He hears my voice and my prayers. For He has inclined His ear to me, so all my days I will call upon Him. The cords of death surrounded me, and the pains of the grave came upon me. Trouble and sorrow I encountered. Then I called the name of God: Please, God, deliver my soul! God is gracious and just, and our God is compassionate.*

TORAS MENACHEM

appear here, and not at the beginning of this *mitzvah*, before the meal?

The explanation would appear to be that the two chapters said before the meal are not recited to fulfil the *mitzvah* of Hallel, but merely as part of "*Magid,*" the *mitzvah* of recalling the Exodus. I.e., just as the Jewish people said Hallel when they left Egypt, we too say Hallel on this night to recall their experience (see p. 136). So we can understand why the heading "Hallel" does not appear before the meal, since those chapters are essentially part of the section entitled "*Maggid.*"

And even though the Haggadah places the heading

"*Hallel*" here, it would also seem that the next few chapters are not part of the *mitzvah* of Hallel, since they speak about the future.

Rather, the only section which could be described as Hallel proper is Chapter 136 (below, p. 193), which is referred to by the Talmud as *Hallel ha-Gadol,* "the Great Hallel" (*Pesachim* 118a), and the subsequent passage, beginning *Nishmas* ("The soul...," p. 197).

In fact, if we follow a process of elimination, this must be the case, since neither *Hallel ha-Gadol* nor *Nishmas* have any heading before them, so the heading "Hallel" here must apply to them.

(Based on *Sichah* of 2nd Night of Pesach 5723)

שֹׁמֵר פְּתָאיִם* יְהֹוָה, דַּלּוֹתִי וְלִי יְהוֹשִׁיעַ: שׁוּבִי נַפְשִׁי לִמְנוּחָיְכִי, כִּי־יְהֹוָה גָּמַל עָלָיְכִי: כִּי חִלַּצְתָּ נַפְשִׁי מִמָּוֶת, אֶת־עֵינִי מִן־דִּמְעָה, אֶת־רַגְלִי מִדֶּחִי: אֶתְהַלֵּךְ לִפְנֵי יְהֹוָה, בְּאַרְצוֹת הַחַיִּים: הֶאֱמַנְתִּי כִּי אֲדַבֵּר, אֲנִי עָנִיתִי מְאֹד: אֲנִי אָמַרְתִּי בְחָפְזִי, כָּל־הָאָדָם כֹּזֵב:

מָה־אָשִׁיב לַיהֹוָה, כָּל־תַּגְמוּלוֹהִי עָלָי: כּוֹס־יְשׁוּעוֹת אֶשָּׂא, וּבְשֵׁם יְהֹוָה אֶקְרָא: נְדָרַי לַיהֹוָה אֲשַׁלֵּם, נֶגְדָה־נָּא לְכָל־עַמּוֹ: יָקָר בְּעֵינֵי יְהֹוָה, הַמָּוְתָה לַחֲסִידָיו: אָנָּה יְהֹוָה כִּי־אֲנִי עַבְדֶּךָ, אֲנִי עַבְדְּךָ בֶּן־אֲמָתֶךָ, פִּתַּחְתָּ לְמוֹסֵרָי: לְךָ אֶזְבַּח זֶבַח תּוֹדָה, וּבְשֵׁם יְהֹוָה אֶקְרָא: נְדָרַי לַיהֹוָה אֲשַׁלֵּם, נֶגְדָה־נָּא לְכָל־עַמּוֹ: בְּחַצְרוֹת בֵּית יְהֹוָה בְּתוֹכֵכִי יְרוּשָׁלָיִם, הַלְלוּיָהּ:

הַלְלוּ אֶת־יְהֹוָה כָּל־גּוֹיִם, שַׁבְּחוּהוּ כָּל־הָאֻמִּים: כִּי גָבַר עָלֵינוּ חַסְדּוֹ, וֶאֱמֶת־יְהֹוָה לְעוֹלָם, הַלְלוּיָהּ:

* הָאָלֶ"ף נֶעְלָם וְהַחִירִיק נִקְרָאת תַּחַת הַיּוֹ"ד

God protects the simple. I was brought low and He saved me. Return to your rest, O my soul, for God has dealt kindly with you. For You have delivered my soul from death, my eyes from tears, my feet from stumbling. I will walk before God in the land of the living. I kept faith even when I said, "I am greatly afflicted." It was in my haste I said, "All men are false."

WHAT COULD I REPAY GOD for all His kindness to me? I will raise the cup of salvation and call upon the name of God. I will pay my vows to God now in the presence of all His people. Precious in the eyes of God is the death of His pious ones. I thank you, God, for I am Your servant. I am Your servant the son of Your handmaiden, You have loosened my bonds. To You I will bring a thanksgiving sacrifice, and I will call upon the Name of God. I will pay my vows to God in the presence of all His people, in the courtyards of the House of God, in the midst of Jerusalem. Halleluyah!

PRAISE GOD, all you nations! Praise Him, all you peoples! For His kindness to us was great, and the truth of God endures forever. Halleluyah!

➤ AFTER EACH OF THE FOLLOWING FOUR LINES IS CHANTED BY THE LEADER, ALL
OTHERS RESPOND OUT LOUD: הוֹדוּ לַיהוָה כִּי טוֹב כִּי לְעוֹלָם חַסְדּוֹ.

הוֹדוּ לַיהוָה כִּי טוֹב,   כִּי לְעוֹלָם חַסְדּוֹ:

יֹאמַר־נָא יִשְׂרָאֵל,   כִּי לְעוֹלָם חַסְדּוֹ:

יֹאמְרוּ נָא בֵית־אַהֲרֹן,   כִּי לְעוֹלָם חַסְדּוֹ:

יֹאמְרוּ נָא יִרְאֵי יְהוָה,   כִּי לְעוֹלָם חַסְדּוֹ:

מִן־הַמֵּצַר קָרָאתִי יָּה, עָנָנִי בַמֶּרְחָב
יָּה: יְהוָה לִי לֹא אִירָא, מַה־
יַּעֲשֶׂה לִי אָדָם: יְהוָה לִי בְּעֹזְרָי, וַאֲנִי אֶרְאֶה
בְשֹׂנְאָי: טוֹב לַחֲסוֹת בַּיהוָה מִבְּטֹחַ בָּאָדָם:
טוֹב לַחֲסוֹת בַּיהוָה מִבְּטֹחַ בִּנְדִיבִים: כָּל־
גּוֹיִם סְבָבוּנִי, בְּשֵׁם יְהוָה כִּי אֲמִילַם: סַבּוּנִי
גַם־סְבָבוּנִי, בְּשֵׁם יְהוָה כִּי אֲמִילַם: סַבּוּנִי
כִדְבֹרִים דֹּעֲכוּ כְּאֵשׁ קוֹצִים, בְּשֵׁם יְהוָה כִּי

===== TORAS MENACHEM =====

בֵּין שְׁלִישִׁי לִרְבִיעִי לֹא יִשְׁתֶּה — *One may not
drink between the Third and Fourth Cups.*

When reciting this section of the Haggadah, the
Previous Lubavitcher Rebbe, Rabbi Yosef Yitzchak,
made a point of not stopping to offer commentary, as
was his custom during the earlier part of the Seder.

Since all of the Rebbe's actions were spiritually
attuned, based on Torah sources, perhaps the following explanation could be offered.

The *Mishnah* states, "One may not drink [wine]
between the Third and Fourth Cups" (Pesachim 117b).
Wine, which is rich in flavor, alludes to the idea of
offering commentary to "flavor" and enrich our experience of reciting the Haggadah. The fact that the
Mishnah forbids wine between the Third and Fourth
Cups hints to the idea of not offering commentary at
this junction.

However, this does not, of course, suggest in any
way that these chapters are devoid of additional

➤ AFTER EACH OF THE FOLLOWING FOUR LINES IS CHANTED BY THE LEADER, ALL OTHERS RESPOND OUT LOUD: "THANK GOD, FOR HE IS GOOD, FOR HIS KINDNESS IS EVERLASTING."

THANK GOD, for He is good, for His kindness is everlasting.

LET ISRAEL SAY, "For His kindness is everlasting."

LET THE HOUSE of Aharon say, "For His kindness is everlasting."

LET THOSE who fear God say, "For His kindness is everlasting."

OUT OF THE STRAITS I called upon God; God answered me with expansiveness. God is with me, I will not fear. What can man do to me? God is for me, through my helpers, therefore, I can look upon those who hate me. It is better to rely on God, than to trust in man. It is better to rely on God, than to trust in princes. All nations surrounded me, but in the name of God, I cut them down. They surrounded me, they also encompassed me, but in the name of God I cut them down. They surrounded me like bees, but they were quenched like a fire of thorns, for in the name of God

---

TORAS MENACHEM

meaning; to the contrary, their significance is so lofty that it cannot truly be captured by the mortal intellect. So the Rebbe's silence was, in fact, indicative of a transcendent quality of the current text.

(Based on *Sichah* of the 2nd Night of Pesach 5715)

Another insight into the rule that "*one may not drink between the Third and Fourth Cups*" could be gleaned from the general theme of the second half of the Seder, around which these two cups are focused. As **Abarbanel** stresses (p. 180), the theme of

the Fourth Cup, on which we say the current chapters of Hallel (praise), is that of the final redemption. But we find that even the Third Cup (recited over Grace after Meals) is focused on the future, for the festive meal concludes with the Afikoman, eaten to remind us of the Pesach sacrifice that will once again be eaten when the Temple is rebuilt.

The only difference is that the Third Cup reminds us of *eating* in the future era, whereas the Fourth Cup alludes to the more spiritual pursuit of *singing praise* to God, after Mashiach comes.

אֱמִילָם: דָּחֹה דְחִיתַנִי לִנְפֹּל, וַיהוָה עֲזָרָנִי:
עָזִּי וְזִמְרָת יָהּ, וַיְהִי־לִי לִישׁוּעָה: קוֹל רִנָּה
וִישׁוּעָה בְּאָהֳלֵי צַדִּיקִים, יְמִין יְהוָה עֹשָׂה
חָיִל: יְמִין יְהוָה רוֹמֵמָה, יְמִין יְהוָה עֹשָׂה חָיִל:
לֹא־אָמוּת כִּי־אֶחְיֶה, וַאֲסַפֵּר מַעֲשֵׂי יָהּ: יַסֹּר
יִסְּרַנִּי יָּהּ, וְלַמָּוֶת לֹא נְתָנָנִי: פִּתְחוּ־לִי שַׁעֲרֵי־
צֶדֶק, אָבֹא־בָם אוֹדֶה יָהּ: זֶה־הַשַּׁעַר לַיהוָה,
צַדִּיקִים יָבֹאוּ בוֹ:

אוֹדְךָ כִּי עֲנִיתָנִי, וַתְּהִי־לִי לִישׁוּעָה:
(REPEAT) **אֶבֶן** מָאֲסוּ הַבּוֹנִים, הָיְתָה לְרֹאשׁ
פִּנָּה: (REPEAT) **מֵאֵת** יְהוָה הָיְתָה זֹּאת, הִיא
נִפְלָאת* בְּעֵינֵינוּ: (REPEAT) **זֶה־הַיּוֹם** עָשָׂה
יְהוָה, נָגִילָה וְנִשְׂמְחָה בוֹ: (REPEAT)

* הא' נעלם

TORAS MENACHEM

Therefore, we might suggest that the Third Cup represents the festive meal which God is destined to serve the righteous in the future (*Pesachim* 119b); whereas the Fourth Cup is symbolic of the World-to-Come where "*there will be no eating or drinking. Rather the righteous will simply sit and enjoy the radiance of the Divine Presence*" (*Brachos* 17a).

So now we can appreciate why "*one may not drink between the Third and Fourth Cups,*" because the verses of praise recited now are reminiscent of the time when "*there will be no eating or drinking.*"

If we probe even deeper, there is a further signifi-cance to be found here. Generally speaking, there are two "styles" of worshipping God: either through *elevating* the physical world around us, utilizing it for a good and holy purpose; or by yearning to *escape* the trappings of the physical world, which ultimately act as a barrier between ourselves and God.

These two different approaches parallel the contrast between the *tzadik* (righteous man) and the *ba'al teshuvah* (penitent). The *tzadik* already lives a life of holiness, so the most effective way he could come even

I cut them down. You pushed me again and again to make me fall, but God helped me. God is my strength and song; He has been my salvation. The voice of joy and salvation is in the tents of the righteous, "God's right hand does valiantly! God's right hand is exalted! God's right hand makes war!" I shall not die, but live and tell the works of God. God has chastised me, but He did not give me over to death. Open for me the gates of righteousness. I will go into them and give thanks to God. This is the gate of God; the righteous will enter it.

I THANK YOU for You have answered me, and You have become my salvation (REPEAT). THE STONE which the builders rejected has become the main cornerstone (REPEAT). THIS WAS INDEED from God, it is marvelous in our eyes (REPEAT). THIS IS THE DAY which God has made, let us be glad and rejoice on it (REPEAT).

TORAS MENACHEM

closer to God is through *escaping* his physical existence. The *ba'al teshuvah*, on the other hand, is unique in that he retroactively *elevates* all of his prior worldly involvement at the moment he returns to God.

Since both these approaches are important, they will continue in the future era, albeit in a superior form. Thus, we find that there will be both a festive *meal* for the righteous, i.e. the elevation of the physical, as well as a time when we will *escape* the confines of our physical existence, because *"there will be no eating or drinking."*

But, most importantly, to reach true perfection, both approaches must converge into a single, unified path. And this is the inner meaning of the idea that *"one may not drink between the Third and Fourth Cups,"* namely, that the theme of these two Cups (*elevation* and *escape*) will merge, to the extent that

there will be nothing "between" them. Thus, we are promised that *"Mashiach will bring the righteous to teshuvah"* (*Zohar*, as cited in *Likutei Torah* 92b), inspiring the "escape"-orientated approach of the righteous, to learn from, and take on board, the advantage of "elevation" shared by the *ba'al teshuvah*.

Of course, this does not mean that the righteous will actually sin and then repent. It is simply that the righteous will learn to reach the unparalleled passion for Jewish observance that the *ba'al teshuvah* possesses. For, after *teshuvah*, a person *"thirsts for God with more intensity than the souls of the righteous"* (*Tanya* ch. 7). This is because *"his soul had been, up until now, in a land of drought and death's shadow"* (ibid), and when a person flees from the threat of death he does so with every fiber of his being.

(Based on *Likutei Sichos* vol. 36, p. 210ff)

➤ THE FOLLOWING IS SAID RESPONSIVELY.

אָנָּא יְהֹוָה הוֹשִׁיעָה נָּא:

אָנָּא יְהֹוָה הוֹשִׁיעָה נָּא:

אָנָּא יְהֹוָה הַצְלִיחָה נָא:

אָנָּא יְהֹוָה הַצְלִיחָה נָא:

בָּרוּךְ הַבָּא בְּשֵׁם יְהֹוָה, בֵּרַכְנוּכֶם מִבֵּית יְהֹוָה (REPEAT): אֵל יְהֹוָה וַיָּאֶר לָנוּ, אִסְרוּ־ חַג בַּעֲבֹתִים עַד־קַרְנוֹת הַמִּזְבֵּחַ (REPEAT): אֵלִי אַתָּה וְאוֹדֶךָּ, אֱלֹהַי אֲרוֹמְמֶךָּ (REPEAT): הוֹדוּ לַיהֹוָה כִּי־טוֹב, כִּי לְעוֹלָם חַסְדּוֹ (REPEAT):

יְהַלְלוּךָ יְהֹוָה אֱלֹהֵינוּ (על) כָּל־מַעֲשֶׂיךָ וַחֲסִידֶיךָ צַדִּיקִים עוֹשֵׂי רְצוֹנֶךָ, וְכָל־עַמְּךָ בֵּית יִשְׂרָאֵל בְּרִנָּה יוֹדוּ וִיבָרְכוּ וִישַׁבְּחוּ וִיפָאֲרוּ וִירוֹמְמוּ וְיַעֲרִיצוּ וְיַקְדִּישׁוּ וְיַמְלִיכוּ אֶת־שִׁמְךָ מַלְכֵּנוּ. כִּי לְךָ טוֹב לְהוֹדוֹת וּלְשִׁמְךָ נָאֶה לְזַמֵּר כִּי מֵעוֹלָם וְעַד עוֹלָם אַתָּה אֵל:

➤ THE FOLLOWING IS SAID RESPONSIVELY.

Please save us, God!

Please save us, God!

Please grant us success, God!

Please grant us success, God!

BLESSED IS HE who comes in the name of God; we bless you out of the House of God (REPEAT). God is God, Who has shown us light; bind the festival sacrifice with cords to the horns of the altar. (REPEAT). You are my God and I will thank You; my God, I will exalt You. (REPEAT). Give thanks to God, for He is good, for His kindness endures forever. (REPEAT)

MAY ALL YOUR WORKS praise You, God, our God, with your pious ones, the righteous, who do Your will. May all Your people, the House of Israel, give joyful thanks, bless, praise, glorify, exalt, adore, sanctify and proclaim the sovereignty of Your name, our King. For it is good to give You thanks, and befitting to sing to Your Name, because forever and for eternity You are God.

הוֹדוּ לַיהֹוָה כִּי־טוֹב,   כִּי לְעוֹלָם חַסְדּוֹ:

הוֹדוּ לֵאלֹהֵי הָאֱלֹהִים,   כִּי לְעוֹלָם חַסְדּוֹ:

הוֹדוּ לַאֲדֹנֵי הָאֲדֹנִים,   כִּי לְעוֹלָם חַסְדּוֹ:

לְעֹשֵׂה נִפְלָאוֹת גְּדֹלוֹת לְבַדּוֹ,   כִּי לְעוֹלָם חַסְדּוֹ:

לְעֹשֵׂה הַשָּׁמַיִם בִּתְבוּנָה,   כִּי לְעוֹלָם חַסְדּוֹ:

לְרוֹקַע הָאָרֶץ עַל־הַמָּיִם,   כִּי לְעוֹלָם חַסְדּוֹ:

לְעֹשֵׂה אוֹרִים גְּדֹלִים,   כִּי לְעוֹלָם חַסְדּוֹ:

אֶת־הַשֶּׁמֶשׁ לְמֶמְשֶׁלֶת בַּיּוֹם,   כִּי לְעוֹלָם חַסְדּוֹ:

אֶת־הַיָּרֵחַ וְכוֹכָבִים לְמֶמְשְׁלוֹת בַּלָּיְלָה,   כִּי לְעוֹלָם חַסְדּוֹ:

לְמַכֵּה מִצְרַיִם בִּבְכוֹרֵיהֶם,   כִּי לְעוֹלָם חַסְדּוֹ:

וַיּוֹצֵא יִשְׂרָאֵל מִתּוֹכָם,   כִּי לְעוֹלָם חַסְדּוֹ:

בְּיָד חֲזָקָה וּבִזְרוֹעַ נְטוּיָה,   כִּי לְעוֹלָם חַסְדּוֹ:

לְגֹזֵר יַם־סוּף לִגְזָרִים,   כִּי לְעוֹלָם חַסְדּוֹ:

GIVE THANKS TO GOD, FOR HE IS GOOD

—for His kindness is everlasting;

GIVE THANKS TO THE GOD OF GODS

—for His kindness is everlasting;

GIVE THANKS TO THE MASTER OF MASTERS

—for His kindness is everlasting;

WHO ALONE DOES GREAT WONDERS

—for His kindness is everlasting;

WHO MADE THE HEAVENS WITH UNDERSTANDING

—for His kindness is everlasting;

WHO STRETCHED OUT THE EARTH OVER THE WATERS

—for His kindness is everlasting;

WHO MADE THE GREAT LIGHTS

—for His kindness is everlasting;

THE SUN, TO RULE BY DAY

—for His kindness is everlasting;

THE MOON AND STARS, TO RULE BY NIGHT

—for His kindness is everlasting;

WHO STRUCK EGYPT THROUGH THEIR FIRSTBORN

—for His kindness is everlasting;

AND BROUGHT ISRAEL OUT FROM AMONG THEM

—for His kindness is everlasting;

WITH A STRONG HAND AND AN OUTSTRETCHED ARM

—for His kindness is everlasting;

WHO SPLIT THE SEA OF REEDS INTO PARTS

—for His kindness is everlasting;

QUICK INSIGHT

This Psalm is known as Hallel ha-Gadol ("the Great Hallel"), since it praises God for giving "food to all flesh," which, says the Talmud, is "a great thing" (Pesachim 118a).

Or because it contains 26 verses of praise, corresponding to the numerical value of God's essential Name, Havayah, and, "Great is Havayah and exceedingly praised, מְהֻלָּל" (Tola'as Ya'akov).

וְהֶעֱבִיר יִשְׂרָאֵל בְּתוֹכוֹ,   כִּי לְעוֹלָם חַסְדּוֹ:

וְנִעֵר פַּרְעֹה וְחֵילוֹ בְיַם־סוּף,   כִּי לְעוֹלָם חַסְדּוֹ:

לְמוֹלִיךְ עַמּוֹ בַּמִּדְבָּר,   כִּי לְעוֹלָם חַסְדּוֹ:

לְמַכֵּה מְלָכִים גְּדֹלִים,   כִּי לְעוֹלָם חַסְדּוֹ:

וַיַּהֲרֹג מְלָכִים אַדִּירִים,   כִּי לְעוֹלָם חַסְדּוֹ:

לְסִיחוֹן מֶלֶךְ הָאֱמֹרִי,   כִּי לְעוֹלָם חַסְדּוֹ:

וּלְעוֹג מֶלֶךְ הַבָּשָׁן,   כִּי לְעוֹלָם חַסְדּוֹ:

וְנָתַן אַרְצָם לְנַחֲלָה,   כִּי לְעוֹלָם חַסְדּוֹ:

נַחֲלָה לְיִשְׂרָאֵל עַבְדּוֹ,   כִּי לְעוֹלָם חַסְדּוֹ:

שֶׁבְּשִׁפְלֵנוּ זָכַר לָנוּ,   כִּי לְעוֹלָם חַסְדּוֹ:

וַיִּפְרְקֵנוּ מִצָּרֵינוּ,   כִּי לְעוֹלָם חַסְדּוֹ:

נוֹתֵן לֶחֶם לְכָל־בָּשָׂר,   כִּי לְעוֹלָם חַסְדּוֹ:

הוֹדוּ לְאֵל הַשָּׁמָיִם,   כִּי לְעוֹלָם חַסְדּוֹ:

And led Israel right through it

> —for His kindness is everlasting;

And cast Pharaoh and his army into the Reed Sea

> —for His kindness is everlasting;

Who led His people through the desert

> —for His kindness is everlasting;

Who struck great kings

> —for His kindness is everlasting;

And slew mighty kings

> —for His kindness is everlasting;

Sichon, king of the Emori

> —for His kindness is everlasting;

And Og, king of Bashan

> —for His kindness is everlasting;

And gave their land as an inheritance

> —for His kindness is everlasting;

An inheritance to Israel, His servant

> —for His kindness is everlasting;

Who remembered us in our lowliness

> —for His kindness is everlasting;

And delivered us from our oppressors

> —for His kindness is everlasting;

Who gives food to all flesh

> —for His kindness is everlasting;

Give thanks to the God of the heavens

> —for His kindness is everlasting;

נִשְׁמַת כָּל־חַי

תְּבָרֵךְ אֶת־שִׁמְךָ יְהֹוָה אֱלֹהֵינוּ, וְרוּחַ כָּל־בָּשָׂר
תְּפָאֵר וּתְרוֹמֵם זִכְרְךָ מַלְכֵּנוּ תָּמִיד. מִן־הָעוֹלָם
וְעַד־הָעוֹלָם אַתָּה אֵל, וּמִבַּלְעָדֶיךָ אֵין לָנוּ מֶלֶךְ
גּוֹאֵל וּמוֹשִׁיעַ פּוֹדֶה וּמַצִּיל וּמְפַרְנֵס וּמְרַחֵם
בְּכָל־עֵת צָרָה וְצוּקָה, אֵין לָנוּ מֶלֶךְ אֶלָּא אָתָּה:
אֱלֹהֵי הָרִאשׁוֹנִים וְהָאַחֲרוֹנִים, אֱלוֹהַּ כָּל־בְּרִיּוֹת,
אֲדוֹן כָּל־תּוֹלָדוֹת, הַמְהֻלָּל בְּרֹב הַתִּשְׁבָּחוֹת,
הַמְנַהֵג עוֹלָמוֹ בְּחֶסֶד וּבְרִיּוֹתָיו בְּרַחֲמִים.
וַיהֹוָה לֹא־יָנוּם וְלֹא יִישָׁן, הַמְעוֹרֵר יְשֵׁנִים
וְהַמֵּקִיץ נִרְדָּמִים וְהַמֵּשִׂיחַ אִלְּמִים וְהַמַּתִּיר
אֲסוּרִים וְהַסּוֹמֵךְ נוֹפְלִים וְהַזּוֹקֵף כְּפוּפִים,
לְךָ לְבַדְּךָ אֲנַחְנוּ מוֹדִים. אִלּוּ פִינוּ מָלֵא שִׁירָה
כַיָּם וּלְשׁוֹנֵנוּ רִנָּה כַּהֲמוֹן גַּלָּיו, וְשִׂפְתוֹתֵינוּ
שֶׁבַח כְּמֶרְחֲבֵי רָקִיעַ וְעֵינֵינוּ מְאִירוֹת כַּשֶּׁמֶשׁ
וְכַיָּרֵחַ, וְיָדֵינוּ פְרוּשׂוֹת כְּנִשְׁרֵי שָׁמָיִם וְרַגְלֵינוּ
קַלּוֹת כָּאַיָּלוֹת: אֵין אֲנַחְנוּ מַסְפִּיקִים לְהוֹדוֹת

The Soul
of every living thing

SHALL BLESS YOUR NAME, GOD, OUR GOD.
And the spirit of all flesh will glorify and exalt Your
remembrance at all times, our King. From eternity
to eternity You are God, and besides You we have no
king, redeemer, savior, deliverer, liberator, sustainer and
source of mercy in every time of trouble and distress.
We have no King but You. God of the first and of the
last, God of all creatures, Master of all events, who is
extolled with many praises; Who guides His world
with kindness and His creatures with compassion. God
neither slumbers nor sleeps. He arouses the sleepers
and wakens the slumberers, gives speech to the dumb,
releases the bound, supports the fallen and straightens
the bent. To You alone we give thanks. Even if our
mouths were filled with song like the sea, and our
tongues with melody like the multitudes of its waves,
and our lips with praise like the breadth of the sky; and
our eyes shining like the sun and the moon, and our
hands spread out like the eagles of the skies, and our feet
as swift as deer—we still could not sufficiently thank

לְךָ יְהֹוָה אֱלֹהֵינוּ וֵאלֹהֵי אֲבוֹתֵינוּ וּלְבָרֵךְ אֶת־
שְׁמֶךָ, עַל־אַחַת מֵאֶלֶף אֶלֶף אַלְפֵי אֲלָפִים וְרִבֵּי
רְבָבוֹת פְּעָמִים הַטּוֹבוֹת שֶׁעָשִׂיתָ עִם אֲבוֹתֵינוּ
וְעִמָּנוּ: מִמִּצְרַיִם גְּאַלְתָּנוּ יְהֹוָה אֱלֹהֵינוּ, וּמִבֵּית
עֲבָדִים פְּדִיתָנוּ. בְּרָעָב זַנְתָּנוּ וּבְשָׂבָע כִּלְכַּלְתָּנוּ,
מֵחֶרֶב הִצַּלְתָּנוּ וּמִדֶּבֶר מִלַּטְתָּנוּ, וּמֵחֳלָיִם רָעִים
וְנֶאֱמָנִים דִּלִּיתָנוּ: עַד־הֵנָּה עֲזָרוּנוּ רַחֲמֶיךָ וְלֹא־
עֲזָבוּנוּ חֲסָדֶיךָ, וְאַל־תִּטְּשֵׁנוּ יְהֹוָה אֱלֹהֵינוּ
לָנֶצַח: עַל־כֵּן אֵבָרִים שֶׁפִּלַּגְתָּ בָּנוּ וְרוּחַ וּנְשָׁמָה
שֶׁנָּפַחְתָּ בְּאַפֵּינוּ וְלָשׁוֹן אֲשֶׁר שַׂמְתָּ בְּפִינוּ:
הֵן הֵם יוֹדוּ וִיבָרְכוּ וִישַׁבְּחוּ וִיפָאֲרוּ וִירוֹמְמוּ
וְיַעֲרִיצוּ וְיַקְדִּישׁוּ וְיַמְלִיכוּ אֶת־שִׁמְךָ מַלְכֵּנוּ:
כִּי כָל־פֶּה לְךָ יוֹדֶה וְכָל־לָשׁוֹן לְךָ תִשָּׁבַע, וְכָל־
בֶּרֶךְ לְךָ תִכְרַע וְכָל־קוֹמָה לְפָנֶיךָ תִשְׁתַּחֲוֶה.
וְכָל לְבָבוֹת יִירָאוּךְ וְכָל־קֶרֶב וּכְלָיוֹת יְזַמְּרוּ
לִשְׁמֶךָ, כַּדָּבָר שֶׁכָּתוּב: כָּל עַצְמוֹתַי תֹּאמַרְנָה,
יְהֹוָה מִי כָמוֹךָ, מַצִּיל עָנִי מֵחָזָק מִמֶּנּוּ וְעָנִי
וְאֶבְיוֹן מִגֹּזְלוֹ: מִי יִדְמֶה־לָּךְ וּמִי יִשְׁוֶה־לָּךְ וּמִי
יַעֲרָךְ־לָךְ, הָאֵל הַגָּדוֹל הַגִּבּוֹר וְהַנּוֹרָא אֵל עֶלְיוֹן

You God, our God, and God of our fathers, or bless Your name properly for even one of the thousand thousands of millions, and many myriads of favors which You have done for our fathers and us. You have redeemed us from Egypt, God, our God, and You have freed us from the house of bondage. You have fed us during famine and nourished us in plenty. You have saved us from the sword, rescued us from pestilence, and raised us from foul and lingering diseases. Until now Your mercies have helped us, and Your kindnesses have not forsaken us; and, God our God, You will never abandon us. Therefore, the limbs which You have set within us, the spirit and soul which You breathed into our nostrils, and the tongue which You have placed in our mouth—they shall all, thank, bless, praise, adore, exalt, glorify, sanctify and proclaim the sovereignty of Your Name, our King. For to You every mouth will offer thanks, every tongue will swear by You, every knee will bend to You, all who stand upright will bow down before You, all hearts will fear You, and every innermost part will sing praise to Your name, as the verse states: "All my bones will say, 'God, who is like You, who saves the poor from one stronger than him, the poor and the needy from one who would rob him!'" Who can be likened to You, who can be equaled to You, who can be compared to You? The great, mighty, awesome God; the Supreme God, owner of

קֹנֵה שָׁמַיִם וָאָרֶץ: נְהַלֶּלְךָ וּנְשַׁבֵּחֲךָ וּנְפָאֶרְךָ
וּנְבָרֵךְ אֶת־שֵׁם קָדְשֶׁךָ. כָּאָמוּר: לְדָוִד, בָּרְכִי
נַפְשִׁי אֶת־יְהֹוָה, וְכָל־קְרָבַי אֶת־שֵׁם קָדְשׁוֹ:

הָאֵל בְּתַעֲצֻמוֹת עֻזֶּךָ. הַגָּדוֹל בִּכְבוֹד
שְׁמֶךָ. הַגִּבּוֹר לָנֶצַח וְהַנּוֹרָא בְּנוֹרְאוֹתֶיךָ.
הַמֶּלֶךְ הַיּוֹשֵׁב עַל כִּסֵּא רָם וְנִשָּׂא:

שׁוֹכֵן עַד מָרוֹם וְקָדוֹשׁ שְׁמוֹ. וְכָתוּב: רַנְּנוּ
צַדִּיקִים בַּיהֹוָה, לַיְשָׁרִים נָאוָה תְהִלָּה: בְּפִי יְשָׁרִים
תִּתְהַלָּל. וּבְדִבְרֵי צַדִּיקִים תִּתְבָּרַךְ. וּבִלְשׁוֹן
חֲסִידִים תִּתְרוֹמָם. וּבְקֶרֶב קְדוֹשִׁים תִּתְקַדָּשׁ:

וּבְמַקְהֲלוֹת רִבְבוֹת עַמְּךָ בֵּית יִשְׂרָאֵל
בְּרִנָּה יִתְפָּאַר שִׁמְךָ מַלְכֵּנוּ בְּכָל־דּוֹר וָדוֹר.
שֶׁכֵּן חוֹבַת כָּל־הַיְצוּרִים, לְפָנֶיךָ יְהֹוָה אֱלֹהֵינוּ
וֵאלֹהֵי אֲבוֹתֵינוּ לְהוֹדוֹת לְהַלֵּל לְשַׁבֵּחַ לְפָאֵר
לְרוֹמֵם לְהַדֵּר לְבָרֵךְ לְעַלֵּה וּלְקַלֵּס, עַל כָּל־דִּבְרֵי
שִׁירוֹת וְתִשְׁבָּחוֹת דָּוִד בֶּן־יִשַׁי עַבְדְּךָ מְשִׁיחֶךָ:

heaven and earth. We will acclaim You, praise You and glorify You, and we will bless Your holy name, as the verse states: "A Psalm by David. Bless God, my soul, and all that is within me His holy name."

You are God in the power of Your strength; great in the honor of Your name, mighty forever, and awesome in terror of Your deeds; the King who sits upon a lofty and exalted throne.

Dwelling for eternity, high and holy is His name, as the verse states: "You righteous, rejoice in God; it befits the upright to offer praise." By the mouth of the upright You are praised, by the words of the righteous You are blessed, by the tongue of the pious You are exalted, and among the holy ones You are sanctified.

In the assemblies of the multitudes of Your people, the House of Israel, shall Your Name, our King, be glorified with song in every generation. For such is the obligation of all creatures before You, God, our God and God of our fathers: to thank, to laud, to praise, to glorify, to exalt, to adore, to bless, to extol and to honor You, beyond all the words of songs and praises of David son of Yishai, Your anointed servant.

יִשְׁתַּבַּח שִׁמְךָ לָעַד מַלְכֵּנוּ הָאֵל הַמֶּלֶךְ הַגָּדוֹל וְהַקָּדוֹשׁ בַּשָּׁמַיִם וּבָאָרֶץ. כִּי לְךָ נָאֶה יְהֹוָה אֱלֹהֵינוּ וֵאלֹהֵי אֲבוֹתֵינוּ: שִׁיר וּשְׁבָחָה הַלֵּל וְזִמְרָה עֹז וּמֶמְשָׁלָה נֶצַח גְּדֻלָּה וּגְבוּרָה תְּהִלָּה וְתִפְאֶרֶת קְדֻשָּׁה וּמַלְכוּת. בְּרָכוֹת וְהוֹדָאוֹת מֵעַתָּה וְעַד עוֹלָם: בָּרוּךְ אַתָּה יְהֹוָה, אֵל מֶלֶךְ גָּדוֹל בַּתִּשְׁבָּחוֹת, אֵל הַהוֹדָאוֹת, אֲדוֹן הַנִּפְלָאוֹת, הַבּוֹחֵר בְּשִׁירֵי זִמְרָה, מֶלֶךְ אֵל חֵי הָעוֹלָמִים:

> HOLD THE CUP IN YOUR RIGHT HAND.

בָּרוּךְ אַתָּה יְהֹוָה אֱלֹהֵינוּ מֶלֶךְ הָעוֹלָם, בּוֹרֵא פְּרִי הַגָּפֶן:

> RECLINE TO THE LEFT AND DRINK THE CUP (AS BEFORE).

> AFTER DRINKING THE FOURTH CUP, RECITE THE FOLLOWING BLESSING:

בָּרוּךְ אַתָּה יְהֹוָה אֱלֹהֵינוּ מֶלֶךְ הָעוֹלָם, עַל־הַגֶּפֶן וְעַל־פְּרִי הַגֶּפֶן וְעַל תְּנוּבַת הַשָּׂדֶה וְעַל־אֶרֶץ חֶמְדָּה טוֹבָה וּרְחָבָה שֶׁרָצִיתָ וְהִנְחַלְתָּ לַאֲבוֹתֵינוּ לֶאֱכוֹל מִפִּרְיָהּ וְלִשְׂבּוֹעַ מִטּוּבָהּ. רַחֶם־נָא יְהֹוָה אֱלֹהֵינוּ עַל־יִשְׂרָאֵל עַמֶּךָ וְעַל־יְרוּשָׁלַיִם עִירֶךָ וְעַל־צִיּוֹן מִשְׁכַּן כְּבוֹדֶךָ וְעַל־מִזְבְּחֶךָ וְעַל־הֵיכָלֶךָ, וּבְנֵה יְרוּשָׁלַיִם עִיר הַקֹּדֶשׁ בִּמְהֵרָה בְיָמֵינוּ וְהַעֲלֵנוּ לְתוֹכָהּ,

MAY YOUR NAME be praised forever, our King, the great and holy God and King, in heaven and on earth. For You, God, our God and God of our fathers, befit song and praise, accolade and hymn, strength and dominion, victory, fame and might, glory, splendor, holiness and sovereignty; blessings and thanksgivings from now to eternity. Blessed are You, God, Almighty King, great in praises, God of thanksgivings, Master of wonders, who chooses songs of praise; King, God, life of all worlds.

➤ HOLD THE CUP IN YOUR RIGHT HAND.

Blessed are You, God, our God, King of the universe, who creates the fruit of the vine.

➤ RECLINE TO THE LEFT AND DRINK THE CUP (AS BEFORE).

➤ AFTER DRINKING THE FOURTH CUP, RECITE THE FOLLOWING BLESSING:

BLESSED ARE YOU, GOD OUR GOD, KING OF THE UNIVERSE, for the vine and the fruit of the vine, for the produce of the field, and for the precious, good and ample land that You have favored and given as an inheritance to our ancestors, to eat of its fruit and be sated by its goodness. Have mercy please, God our God, on Israel Your people, on Jerusalem Your city, on Zion the abode of Your glory, on Your altar and on Your Temple. Rebuild Jerusalem, the holy city, speedily in our days. Bring us up into it, and let us rejoice in its reconstruction. Let us eat of its fruits

וְשַׂמְּחֵנוּ בְּבִנְיָנָהּ וְנֹאכַל מִפִּרְיָהּ וְנִשְׂבַּע מִטּוּבָהּ, וּנְבָרֶכְךָ עָלֶיהָ בִּקְדֻשָּׁה וּבְטָהֳרָה, (—ON SHABBOS ADD וּרְצֵה וְהַחֲלִיצֵנוּ בְּיוֹם הַשַּׁבָּת הַזֶּה) וְשַׂמְּחֵנוּ בְּיוֹם חַג הַמַּצּוֹת הַזֶּה. כִּי אַתָּה יְהֹוָה טוֹב וּמֵטִיב לַכֹּל וְנוֹדֶה לְּךָ עַל־הָאָרֶץ וְעַל־פְּרִי הַגָּפֶן: בָּרוּךְ אַתָּה יְהֹוָה עַל־הָאָרֶץ וְעַל־פְּרִי הַגָּפֶן:

נִרְצָה

חֲסַל סִדּוּר פֶּסַח כְּהִלְכָתוֹ, כְּכָל־מִשְׁפָּטוֹ וְחֻקָּתוֹ, כַּאֲשֶׁר זָכִינוּ לְסַדֵּר אוֹתוֹ, כֵּן נִזְכֶּה לַעֲשׂוֹתוֹ: זָךְ שׁוֹכֵן מְעוֹנָה, קוֹמֵם קְהַל עֲדַת מִי מָנָה, בְּקָרוֹב נַהֵל נִטְעֵי כַנָּה, פְּדוּיִם לְצִיּוֹן בְּרִנָּה:

and be sated in its goodness we will bless You over it in holiness and purity; (ON SHABBOS ADD—May it please You to strengthen us on this Shabbos day) and bring us joy on this day of the Festival of Matzos. For You, God, are good and do good to all, and we thank You for the Land and for the fruit of the vine. Blessed are You, God, for the Land and for the fruit of the vine.

Acceptance

OUR PESACH SERVICE is now completed in correct form with all its regulations and precepts. Just as we have had the privilege to celebrate it tonight, so may we merit to celebrate it in the future. O Pure One, who dwells in heaven, raise up the gathering of Your innumerable people! Soon, lead them "the plants of Your vine," as free ones to Zion in song.

לְשָׁנָה הַבָּאָה בִּירוּשָׁלָיִם

Next Year

➤ ON THE FIRST NIGHT RECITE THE FOLLOWING. (ON THE SECOND NIGHT, TURN TO P. 210)

וּבְכֵן וַיְהִי בַּחֲצִי הַלַּיְלָה:

אָז רוֹב נִסִּים הִפְלֵאתָ   בַּלַּיְלָה.

בְּרֹאשׁ אַשְׁמוּרוֹת זֶה   הַלַּיְלָה.

גֵּר צֶדֶק נִצַּחְתּוֹ כְּנֶחֱלַק לוֹ   לַיְלָה.

וַיְהִי בַּחֲצִי הַלַּיְלָה:

TORAS MENACHEM

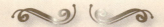 **הַחֲזָרַת הַיַּיִן מִכּוֹסוֹ שֶׁל אֵלִיָּהוּ לְהַבַּקְבּוּק** — *Returning the wine from the Cup of Eliyahu to the bottle.*

At first glance, pouring the wine back from Eliyahu's cup may not seem to have any real significance at all. Since the Seder is now complete, and this wine was not consumed, returning it to the bottle could be perceived as just part of clearing off the table.

In Lubavitch, however, it was always a custom of the Rebbe himself to return the wine to the bottle, so evidently, there must be some important spiritual significance to this act.

Eliyahu's wine is poured twice at the Seder. It is poured *out* of the bottle before we say the words, *"Pour out your anger upon the nations"* (p. 179); and

then it is returned *back* to the bottle after saying the words, *"Next year in Jerusalem."*

These two statements represent two general phases in the unfolding of the Messianic process. Initially, the world is resistant to the redemption, such that many nations oppose it and it is necessary for God to "pour out His anger" on them.

But, ultimately, Judaism is a religion of peace. It was never our dream to destroy others who oppose the message of true monotheism, but rather, to win them over so that they too could join us in worshipping the one, true God. So the prophets promised us thousands of years ago that when we will eventually return to Jerusalem, all the nations will join us and assist us in our holy work.

THE ALTER REBBE omitted from the text of his Haggadah the passage beginning, "The order of Pesach is now concluded," because, according to Chabad, Pesach never ends. Its influence extends continuously.

The truth is that a glimmer of every festival shines forth at least some part of the day, but Pesach's influence—the feeding of our faith—reaches us the whole of each day.

➤ On the First Night Recite the following. (On the Second Night, turn to p. 211)

IT CAME TO PASS AT MIDNIGHT

A host of miracles You performed   at night;

In the early watches of   this night;

You gave the righteous convert Avraham

victory when you divided the   night;

IT CAME TO PASS AT MIDNIGHT.

TORAS MENACHEM

What will prompt the transformation from hostility to friendship on the part of the nations? The Kabbalah explains that the physical world itself, and all its inhabitants, will have become more *receptive* to genuine spirituality. In fact, the Kabbalah deems this receptiveness as being so important that it sees the whole scheme of Torah and *mitzvos* as being focused towards this goal.

Why are all the commandments so physically orientated, revolving around rituals performed with material objects? Because, answers the Kabbalah, one of the main objectives of these *mitzvos* is to render *physical matter itself* more receptive to spirituality. By performing acts of worship with them, we not only inspire ourselves in a very tangible way, but,

more importantly, each *mitzvah* renders the world a bit more attuned to its Creator.

The culmination of all this activity, over a period of thousands of years, we believe, will be that the world itself and all its inhabitants will come to worship the one God—not because God will make a new world order, but simply because physical matter will have become more receptive to Him after so many centuries of hard work.

So, after saying the words *"next year in Jerusalem,"* we pour the wine back into the bottle, i.e. back into its *receptacle*, alluding to the perfection of the Messianic Era when it will no longer be necessary for God to "pour out His anger" on the nations, because they will all be *receptive* to Him.

(Based on *Sichas Shabbos Parshas Metzorah* 5749, note 78)

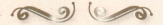

When we say "Next year in Jerusalem" it does not suggest, God forbid, that we do not imagine that Mashiach will come until next year.

Rather, we expect that Mashiach will come NOW, and then, next year, when we celebrate Pesach we will ALREADY be in Jerusalem.

דָּנְתָּ מֶלֶךְ גְּרָר בַּחֲלוֹם | הַלָּיְלָה.
הִפְחַדְתָּ אֲרַמִּי בְּאֶמֶשׁ | לַיְלָה.
וַיָּשַׂר יִשְׂרָאֵל לְמַלְאָךְ וַיּוּכַל לוֹ | לַיְלָה.

וַיְהִי בַּחֲצִי הַלַּיְלָה:

זֶרַע בְּכוֹרֵי פַתְרוֹס מָחַצְתָּ בַּחֲצִי | הַלָּיְלָה.
חֵילָם לֹא מָצְאוּ בְּקוּמָם | בַּלַּיְלָה.
טִיסַת נְגִיד חֲרֹשֶׁת סִלִּיתָ בְּכוֹכְבֵי | לַיְלָה.

וַיְהִי בַּחֲצִי הַלַּיְלָה:

יָעַץ מְחָרֵף לְנוֹפֵף אִוּוּי, הוֹבַשְׁתָּ פְגָרָיו | בַּלַּיְלָה.
כָּרַע בֵּל וּמַצָּבוֹ בְּאִישׁוֹן | לַיְלָה.
לְאִישׁ חֲמוּדוֹת נִגְלָה רָז חֲזוֹת | לַיְלָה.

וַיְהִי בַּחֲצִי הַלַּיְלָה:

מִשְׁתַּכֵּר בִּכְלֵי קֹדֶשׁ נֶהֱרַג בּוֹ | בַּלַּיְלָה.
נוֹשַׁע מִבּוֹר אֲרָיוֹת פּוֹתֵר בְּעֲתוּתֵי | לַיְלָה.
שִׂנְאָה נָטַר אֲגָגִי וְכָתַב סְפָרִים | לַיְלָה.

וַיְהִי בַּחֲצִי הַלַּיְלָה:

עוֹרַרְתָּ נִצְחֲךָ עָלָיו בְּנֶדֶד שְׁנַת | לַיְלָה.
פּוּרָה תִדְרוֹךְ לְשׁוֹמֵר מַה | מִלַּיְלָה.

Grar's king Avimelech, You judged in a dream   by night;

You frightened Lavan in the dark   of night;

Yisra'el overcame an angel and won   by night;

IT CAME TO PASS AT MIDNIGHT.

You crushed Egypt's firstborn at   midnight;

Their strength they found not when they rose   at night;

You swept away the prince of Charoshes'
army with the stars of   the night;

IT CAME TO PASS AT MIDNIGHT.

Sancheriv, the blasphemer, You disgraced   by night;

Babylon's idol fell in the dark   of night;

Daniel was shown secret visions   at night;

IT CAME TO PASS AT MIDNIGHT.

The one who drank from the Temple's vessel,
was killed that   night;

The one saved from the lion's den interpreted
the visions   of night;

The hateful Agagite wrote letters   at night;

IT CAME TO PASS AT MIDNIGHT.

You began to defeat him in the king's sleepless   night;

Trample the winepress and aid those who ask:
What of   the night?

צָרַח כַּשׁוֹמֵר וְשָׂח אָתָא בֹקֶר וְגַם לָיְלָה.

וַיְהִי בַּחֲצִי הַלָּיְלָה:

קָרֵב יוֹם אֲשֶׁר הוּא לֹא־יוֹם וְלֹא לָיְלָה,

רָם הוֹדַע כִּי לְךָ הַיּוֹם אַף־לְךָ הַלָּיְלָה,

שׁוֹמְרִים הַפְקֵד לְעִירְךָ כָּל־הַיּוֹם וְכָל הַלָּיְלָה,

תָּאִיר כְּאוֹר יוֹם חֶשְׁכַּת לָיְלָה,

וַיְהִי בַּחֲצִי הַלָּיְלָה:

➤ ON THE SECOND NIGHT RECITE THE FOLLOWING. (ON THE FIRST NIGHT, turn to P. 214)

וּבְכֵן וַאֲמַרְתֶּם זֶבַח פֶּסַח:

אֹמֶץ גְּבוּרוֹתֶיךָ הִפְלֵאתָ בַּפֶּסַח,

בְּרֹאשׁ כָּל־מוֹעֲדוֹת נִשֵּׂאתָ פֶּסַח,

גִּלִּיתָ לְאֶזְרָחִי חֲצוֹת לֵיל פֶּסַח,

וַאֲמַרְתֶּם זֶבַח פֶּסַח:

דְּלָתָיו דָּפַקְתָּ כְּחֹם הַיּוֹם בַּפֶּסַח,

הִסְעִיד נוֹצְצִים עֻגוֹת מַצּוֹת בַּפֶּסַח,

וְאֶל־הַבָּקָר רָץ זֵכֶר לְשׁוֹר עֵרֶךְ פֶּסַח,

וַאֲמַרְתֶּם זֶבַח פֶּסַח:

זֹעֲמוּ סְדוֹמִים וְלֹהֲטוּ בָּאֵשׁ בַּפֶּסַח

The watchman responds: Morning comes after   night;

IT CAME TO PASS AT MIDNIGHT.

Hasten the eternal day which is not day   nor night;
Exalted One, proclaim that Yours are day and   night;
Set guards over Your city all day and   night;
Brighten as day the darkness of   the night;

IT CAME TO PASS AT MIDNIGHT.

➤   On the Second Night Recite the following. (On the First Night, turn to p. 215)

AND YOU WILL SAY: "IT IS A PESACH OFFERING"

You displayed Your wondrous powers on   Pesach;
Chief of all festivals did You make   Pesach;
To Avraham you revealed midnight of   Pesach;

And you will say, "It is a Pesach offering."

To his door You came at noon on   Pesach;
With Matzos He served angels on   Pesach;
"He ran for the ox," recalling Yosef on   Pesach;

And you will say, "It is a Pesach offering."

The men of Sodom were burned in anger on   Pesach;

חִלַּץ לוֹט מֵהֶם וּמַצּוֹת אָפָה בְּקֵץ   פֶּסַח

טִאטֵאתָ אַדְמַת מֹף וְנֹף בְּעָבְרְךָ   בְּפֶסַח

<u>וַאֲמַרְתֶּם זֶבַח פֶּסַח:</u>

יָהּ, רֹאשׁ כָּל־אוֹן מָחַצְתָּ בְּלֵיל שִׁמּוּר   פֶּסַח

כַּבִּיר, עַל בֵּן בְּכוֹר פָּסַחְתָּ בְּדַם   פֶּסַח

לְבִלְתִּי תֵּת מַשְׁחִית לָבֹא בִפְתָחַי   בְּפֶסַח

<u>וַאֲמַרְתֶּם זֶבַח פֶּסַח:</u>

מְסֻגֶּרֶת סֻגָּרָה בְּעִתּוֹתֵי   פֶּסַח

נִשְׁמְדָה מִדְיָן בִּצְלִיל שְׂעוֹרֵי עֹמֶר   פֶּסַח

שֹׂרְפוּ מִשְׁמַנֵּי פוּל וְלוּד בִּיקַד יְקוֹד   פֶּסַח

<u>וַאֲמַרְתֶּם זֶבַח פֶּסַח:</u>

עוֹד הַיּוֹם בְּנֹב לַעֲמוֹד עַד גָּעָה עוֹנַת   פֶּסַח

פַּס יָד כָּתְבָה לְקַעֲקֵעַ צוּל   בְּפֶסַח

צָפֹה הַצָּפִית עָרוֹךְ הַשֻּׁלְחָן   בְּפֶסַח

<u>וַאֲמַרְתֶּם זֶבַח פֶּסַח:</u>

קָהָל כִּנְּסָה הֲדַסָּה צוֹם לְשַׁלֵּשׁ   בְּפֶסַח

רֹאשׁ מִבֵּית רָשָׁע מָחַצְתָּ בְּעֵץ חֲמִשִּׁים   בְּפֶסַח

שְׁתֵּי אֵלֶּה רֶגַע תָּבִיא לְעוּצִית   בְּפֶסַח

תָּעֹז יָדְךָ וְתָרוּם יְמִינְךָ כְּלֵיל הִתְקַדֶּשׁ חַג פֶּסַח

<u>וַאֲמַרְתֶּם זֶבַח פֶּסַח:</u>

Lot was saved, he baked Matzos at the end of   Pesach;

You swept and destroyed Egypt when passing on   Pesach;

And you will say, "It is a Pesach offering."

God, You crushed every Egyptian on the night of   Pesach;

But your firstborn You passed over on   Pesach;

So that no evil destroyed Israel's homes on   Pesach;

And you will say, "It is a Pesach offering."

The well-locked city of Jericho fell on   Pesach;

Midian was destroyed through a barley-cake
from the Omer of   Pesach;

Assyria's mighty armies were consumed by fire on   Pesach;

And you will say, "It is a Pesach offering."

Sancheiriv would have held his ground at
Nov if it were not for the siege on   Pesach;

A hand inscribed Babylon's fate on   Pesach;

Babylon's festive table was destroyed on   Pesach;

And you will say, "It is a Pesach offering."

Esther called a three-day public fast on   Pesach;

You hung the evil Haman on the gallows on   Pesach;

You will punish Edom doubly on   Pesach;

May Your right hand be strong on the festival of   Pesach

And you will say, "It is a Pesach offering."

➤ ON BOTH NIGHTS SAY THE FOLLOWING

כִּי לוֹ נָאֶה, כִּי לוֹ יָאֶה:

אַדִּיר בִּמְלוּכָה, בָּחוּר כַּהֲלָכָה,
גְּדוּדָיו יֹאמְרוּ לוֹ:
לְךָ וּלְךָ, לְךָ כִּי לְךָ, לְךָ אַף־לְךָ, לְךָ יְיָ הַמַּמְלָכָה,

כִּי לוֹ נָאֶה, כִּי לוֹ יָאֶה:

דָּגוּל בִּמְלוּכָה, הָדוּר כַּהֲלָכָה,
וָתִיקָיו יֹאמְרוּ לוֹ:
לְךָ וּלְךָ, לְךָ כִּי לְךָ, לְךָ אַף־לְךָ, לְךָ יְיָ הַמַּמְלָכָה,

כִּי לוֹ נָאֶה, כִּי לוֹ יָאֶה:

זַכַּאי בִּמְלוּכָה, חָסִין כַּהֲלָכָה,
טַפְסְרָיו יֹאמְרוּ לוֹ:
לְךָ וּלְךָ, לְךָ כִּי לְךָ, לְךָ אַף־לְךָ, לְךָ יְיָ הַמַּמְלָכָה:

כִּי לוֹ נָאֶה, כִּי לוֹ יָאֶה:

יָחִיד בִּמְלוּכָה, כַּבִּיר כַּהֲלָכָה,
לִמּוּדָיו יֹאמְרוּ לוֹ:
לְךָ וּלְךָ, לְךָ כִּי לְךָ, לְךָ אַף־לְךָ, לְךָ יְיָ הַמַּמְלָכָה:

כִּי לוֹ נָאֶה, כִּי לוֹ יָאֶה:

➤ On both nights say the following

TO HIM PRAISE IS FITTING!
TO HIM PRAISE IS DUE!

Powerful in kingship! Truly chosen!

His troops sing to Him: "To You! To You!
To You because of You! To You and only
to You! To You, God, is the Kingship!"

To Him praise is fitting! To Him praise is due!

Famous in kingship! Truly glorious!

His faithful sing to Him: "To You! To You!
To You because of You! To You and only
to You! To You, God, is the Kingship!"

To Him praise is fitting! To Him praise is due!

Guiltless in kingship! Truly strong!

His angels sing to Him: "To You! To You!
To You because of You! To You and only to
You! To You, God, is the Kingship!"

To Him praise is fitting! To Him praise is due!

Alone in kingship! Truly powerful!

His scholars sing to Him: "To You! To You!
To You because of You! To You and only to
You! To You, God, is the Kingship!"

To Him praise is fitting! To Him praise is due!

מוֹשֵׁל בִּמְלוּכָה, נוֹרָא כַּהֲלָכָה,
סְבִיבָיו יֹאמְרוּ לוֹ:
לְךָ וּלְךָ, לְךָ כִּי לְךָ, לְךָ אַף־לְךָ, לְךָ יְיָ הַמַּמְלָכָה:
כִּי לוֹ נָאֶה, כִּי לוֹ יָאֶה:

עָנָו בִּמְלוּכָה, פּוֹדֶה כַּהֲלָכָה,
צַדִּיקָיו יֹאמְרוּ לוֹ:
לְךָ וּלְךָ, לְךָ כִּי לְךָ, לְךָ אַף־לְךָ, לְךָ יְיָ הַמַּמְלָכָה:
כִּי לוֹ נָאֶה, כִּי לוֹ יָאֶה:

קָדוֹשׁ בִּמְלוּכָה, רַחוּם כַּהֲלָכָה,
שִׁנְאַנָּיו יֹאמְרוּ לוֹ:
לְךָ וּלְךָ, לְךָ כִּי לְךָ, לְךָ אַף־לְךָ, לְךָ יְיָ הַמַּמְלָכָה:
כִּי לוֹ נָאֶה, כִּי לוֹ יָאֶה:

תַּקִּיף בִּמְלוּכָה, תּוֹמֵךְ כַּהֲלָכָה,
תְּמִימָיו יֹאמְרוּ לוֹ:
לְךָ וּלְךָ, לְךָ כִּי לְךָ, לְךָ אַף־לְךָ, לְךָ יְיָ הַמַּמְלָכָה:
כִּי לוֹ נָאֶה, כִּי לוֹ יָאֶה:

Commanding in kingship! Truly revered!

His near ones sing to Him: "To You! To You!
To You because of You! To You and only to
You! To You, God, is the Kingship!"

To Him praise is fitting! To Him praise is due!

Humble in kingship! Truly redeeming!

His righteous sing to Him: "To You! To You!
To You because of You! To You and only to
You! To You, God, is the Kingship!"

To Him praise is fitting! To Him praise is due!

Holy in kingship! Truly merciful!

His angels sing to Him: "To You! To You!
To You because of You! To You and only to
You! To You, God, is the Kingship!"

To Him praise is fitting! To Him praise is due!

Forceful in kingship! Lawfully supporting!

His innocent sing to Him: "To You! To You!
To You because of You! To You and only to
You! To You, God, is the Kingship!"

To Him praise is fitting! To Him praise is due!

אַדִּיר הוּא

יִבְנֶה בֵיתוֹ בְּקָרוֹב.

בִּמְהֵרָה בִּמְהֵרָה, בְּיָמֵינוּ בְּקָרוֹב:

אֵל בְּנֵה, אֵל בְּנֵה, בְּנֵה בֵיתְךָ בְּקָרוֹב:

בָּחוּר הוּא, גָּדוֹל הוּא, דָּגוּל הוּא,

יִבְנֶה בֵיתוֹ בְּקָרוֹב, בִּמְהֵרָה בִּמְהֵרָה, בְּיָמֵינוּ בְּקָרוֹב:

אֵל בְּנֵה, אֵל בְּנֵה, בְּנֵה בֵיתְךָ בְּקָרוֹב:

הָדוּר הוּא, וָתִיק הוּא, זַכַּאי הוּא, חָסִיד הוּא,

יִבְנֶה בֵיתוֹ בְּקָרוֹב, בִּמְהֵרָה בִּמְהֵרָה, בְּיָמֵינוּ בְּקָרוֹב:

אֵל בְּנֵה, אֵל בְּנֵה, בְּנֵה בֵיתְךָ בְּקָרוֹב:

טָהוֹר הוּא, יָחִיד הוּא, כַּבִּיר הוּא, לָמוּד הוּא,

מֶלֶךְ הוּא, נוֹרָא הוּא, סַגִּיב הוּא, עִזּוּז הוּא,

פּוֹדֶה הוּא, צַדִּיק הוּא,

יִבְנֶה בֵיתוֹ בְּקָרוֹב, בִּמְהֵרָה בִּמְהֵרָה, בְּיָמֵינוּ בְּקָרוֹב:

אֵל בְּנֵה, אֵל בְּנֵה, בְּנֵה בֵיתְךָ בְּקָרוֹב:

קָדוֹשׁ הוּא, רַחוּם הוּא, שַׁדַּי הוּא, תַּקִּיף הוּא,

יִבְנֶה בֵיתוֹ בְּקָרוֹב, בִּמְהֵרָה בִּמְהֵרָה, בְּיָמֵינוּ בְּקָרוֹב:

אֵל בְּנֵה, אֵל בְּנֵה, בְּנֵה בֵיתְךָ בְּקָרוֹב:

HE IS POWERFUL!

May He build His temple soon. Speedily!
Speedily! Soon in our days! O God, build it!
O God, build it! Build Your temple soon!

He is chosen! He is great! He is famous!

May He build His temple soon. Speedily!
Speedily! Soon in our days! O God, build it! O
God, build it! Build Your temple soon!

He is brilliant! He is faithful! He is innocent! He is kind!

May He build His temple soon. Speedily!
Speedily! Soon in our days! O God, build it!
O God, build it! Build Your temple soon!

He is pure! He is one! He is powerful! He is wise! He is king! He is awesome! He is almighty! He is bold! He is the savior! He is righteous!

May He build His temple soon. Speedily!
Speedily! Soon in our days! O God, build it!
O God, build it! Build Your temple soon!

He is holy! He is merciful! He is God! He is strong!

May He build His temple soon. Speedily!
Speedily! Soon in our days! O God, build it!
O God, build it! Build Your temple soon!

אֶחָד מִי יוֹדֵעַ?

אֶחָד אֲנִי יוֹדֵעַ:
אֶחָד אֱלֹהֵינוּ שֶׁבַּשָּׁמַיִם וּבָאָרֶץ:

שְׁנַיִם מִי יוֹדֵעַ? שְׁנַיִם אֲנִי יוֹדֵעַ: שְׁנֵי לֻחוֹת
הַבְּרִית, אֶחָד אֱלֹהֵינוּ שֶׁבַּשָּׁמַיִם וּבָאָרֶץ:

שְׁלֹשָׁה מִי יוֹדֵעַ? שְׁלֹשָׁה אֲנִי יוֹדֵעַ: שְׁלֹשָׁה אָבוֹת,
שְׁנֵי לֻחוֹת הַבְּרִית, אֶחָד אֱלֹהֵינוּ שֶׁבַּשָּׁמַיִם וּבָאָרֶץ:

אַרְבַּע מִי יוֹדֵעַ? אַרְבַּע אֲנִי יוֹדֵעַ: אַרְבַּע
אִמָּהוֹת, שְׁלֹשָׁה אָבוֹת, שְׁנֵי לֻחוֹת הַבְּרִית,
אֶחָד אֱלֹהֵינוּ שֶׁבַּשָּׁמַיִם וּבָאָרֶץ:

חֲמִשָּׁה מִי יוֹדֵעַ? חֲמִשָּׁה אֲנִי יוֹדֵעַ: חֲמִשָּׁה
חֻמְשֵׁי תוֹרָה, אַרְבַּע אִמָּהוֹת, שְׁלֹשָׁה אָבוֹת, שְׁנֵי
לֻחוֹת הַבְּרִית, אֶחָד אֱלֹהֵינוּ שֶׁבַּשָּׁמַיִם וּבָאָרֶץ:

שִׁשָּׁה מִי יוֹדֵעַ? שִׁשָּׁה אֲנִי יוֹדֵעַ: שִׁשָּׁה
סִדְרֵי מִשְׁנָה, חֲמִשָּׁה חֻמְשֵׁי תוֹרָה, אַרְבַּע
אִמָּהוֹת, שְׁלֹשָׁה אָבוֹת, שְׁנֵי לֻחוֹת הַבְּרִית,
אֶחָד אֱלֹהֵינוּ שֶׁבַּשָּׁמַיִם וּבָאָרֶץ:

WHO KNOWS ONE?
I KNOW ONE!

One is our God in heaven and earth.

WHO KNOWS TWO? I know two!
Two are the Tablets of the Covenant; One
is our God in heaven and earth.

WHO KNOWS THREE? I know three! Three
are the Fathers of Israel; Two are the Tablets of the
Covenant; One is our God in heaven and earth.

WHO KNOWS FOUR? I know four! Four
are the Mothers of Israel; Three are the Fathers
of Israel; Two are the Tablets of the Covenant;
One is our God in heaven and earth.

WHO KNOWS FIVE? I know five! Five are the
books of the Torah; Four are the Mothers of Israel;
Three are the Fathers of Israel; Two are the Tablets of
the Covenant; One is our God in heaven and earth.

WHO KNOWS SIX? I know six! Six are the
orders of the Mishnah; Five are the books of the
Torah; Four are the Mothers of Israel; Three are
the Fathers of Israel; Two are the Tablets of the
Covenant; One is our God in heaven and earth.

שִׁבְעָה מִי יוֹדֵעַ? שִׁבְעָה אֲנִי יוֹדֵעַ: שִׁבְעָה יְמֵי שַׁבַּתָּא, שִׁשָּׁה סִדְרֵי מִשְׁנָה, חֲמִשָּׁה חֻמְשֵׁי תוֹרָה, אַרְבַּע אִמָּהוֹת, שְׁלשָׁה אָבוֹת, שְׁנֵי לֻחוֹת הַבְּרִית, אֶחָד אֱלֹהֵינוּ שֶׁבַּשָּׁמַיִם וּבָאָרֶץ:

שְׁמוֹנָה מִי יוֹדֵעַ? שְׁמוֹנָה אֲנִי יוֹדֵעַ: שְׁמוֹנָה יְמֵי מִילָה, שִׁבְעָה יְמֵי שַׁבַּתָּא, שִׁשָּׁה סִדְרֵי מִשְׁנָה, חֲמִשָּׁה חֻמְשֵׁי תוֹרָה, אַרְבַּע אִמָּהוֹת, שְׁלשָׁה אָבוֹת, שְׁנֵי לֻחוֹת הַבְּרִית, אֶחָד אֱלֹהֵינוּ שֶׁבַּשָּׁמַיִם וּבָאָרֶץ:

תִּשְׁעָה מִי יוֹדֵעַ? תִּשְׁעָה אֲנִי יוֹדֵעַ: תִּשְׁעָה יַרְחֵי לֵדָה, שְׁמוֹנָה יְמֵי מִילָה, שִׁבְעָה יְמֵי שַׁבַּתָּא, שִׁשָּׁה סִדְרֵי מִשְׁנָה, חֲמִשָּׁה חֻמְשֵׁי תוֹרָה, אַרְבַּע אִמָּהוֹת, שְׁלשָׁה אָבוֹת, שְׁנֵי לֻחוֹת הַבְּרִית, אֶחָד אֱלֹהֵינוּ שֶׁבַּשָּׁמַיִם וּבָאָרֶץ:

עֲשָׂרָה מִי יוֹדֵעַ? עֲשָׂרָה אֲנִי יוֹדֵעַ: עֲשָׂרָה דִבְּרַיָּא, תִּשְׁעָה יַרְחֵי לֵדָה, שְׁמוֹנָה יְמֵי מִילָה, שִׁבְעָה יְמֵי שַׁבַּתָּא, שִׁשָּׁה סִדְרֵי מִשְׁנָה, חֲמִשָּׁה חֻמְשֵׁי תוֹרָה, אַרְבַּע אִמָּהוֹת, שְׁלשָׁה אָבוֹת, שְׁנֵי לֻחוֹת הַבְּרִית, אֶחָד אֱלֹהֵינוּ שֶׁבַּשָּׁמַיִם וּבָאָרֶץ:

WHO KNOWS SEVEN? I know seven! Seven are the days of the week; Six are the orders of the Mishnah; Five are the books of the Torah; Four are the Mothers of Israel; Three are the Fathers of Israel; Two are the Tablets of the Covenant; One is our God in heaven and earth.

WHO KNOWS EIGHT? I know eight! Eight are the days to circumcision; Seven are the days of the week; Six are the orders of the Mishnah; Five are the books of the Torah; Four are the Mothers of Israel; Three are the Fathers of Israel; Two are the Tablets of the Covenant; One is our God in heaven and earth.

WHO KNOWS NINE? I know nine! Nine are the months to childbirth; Eight are the days to circumcision; Seven are the days of the week; Six are the orders of the Mishnah; Five are the books of the Torah; Four are the Mothers of Israel; Three are the Fathers of Israel; Two are the Tablets of the Covenant; One is our God in heaven and earth.

WHO KNOWS TEN? I know ten! Ten are the commandments; Nine are the months to childbirth; Eight are the days to circumcision; Seven are the days of the week; Six are the orders of the Mishnah; Five are the books of the Torah; Four are the Mothers of Israel; Three are the Fathers of Israel; Two are the Tablets of the Covenant; One is our God in heaven and earth.

אַחַד עָשָׂר מִי יוֹדֵעַ? אַחַד עָשָׂר אֲנִי יוֹדֵעַ:
אַחַד עָשָׂר כּוֹכְבַיָּא, עֲשָׂרָה דִבְּרַיָּא, תִּשְׁעָה
יַרְחֵי לֵדָה, שְׁמוֹנָה יְמֵי מִילָה, שִׁבְעָה יְמֵי
שַׁבַּתָּא, שִׁשָּׁה סִדְרֵי מִשְׁנָה, חֲמִשָּׁה חֻמְשֵׁי
תוֹרָה, אַרְבַּע אִמָּהוֹת, שְׁלֹשָׁה אָבוֹת, שְׁנֵי
לֻחוֹת הַבְּרִית, אֶחָד אֱלֹהֵינוּ שֶׁבַּשָּׁמַיִם וּבָאָרֶץ:

שְׁנֵים עָשָׂר מִי יוֹדֵעַ? שְׁנֵים עָשָׂר אֲנִי
יוֹדֵעַ: שְׁנֵים עָשָׂר שִׁבְטַיָּא, אַחַד עָשָׂר
כּוֹכְבַיָּא, עֲשָׂרָה דִבְּרַיָּא, תִּשְׁעָה יַרְחֵי לֵדָה,
שְׁמוֹנָה יְמֵי מִילָה, שִׁבְעָה יְמֵי שַׁבַּתָּא,
שִׁשָּׁה סִדְרֵי מִשְׁנָה, חֲמִשָּׁה חֻמְשֵׁי תוֹרָה,
אַרְבַּע אִמָּהוֹת, שְׁלֹשָׁה אָבוֹת, שְׁנֵי לֻחוֹת
הַבְּרִית, אֶחָד אֱלֹהֵינוּ שֶׁבַּשָּׁמַיִם וּבָאָרֶץ:

שְׁלֹשָׁה עָשָׂר מִי יוֹדֵעַ? שְׁלֹשָׁה עָשָׂר אֲנִי יוֹדֵעַ:
שְׁלֹשָׁה עָשָׂר מִדַּיָּא, שְׁנֵים עָשָׂר שִׁבְטַיָּא, אַחַד
עָשָׂר כּוֹכְבַיָּא, עֲשָׂרָה דִבְּרַיָּא, תִּשְׁעָה יַרְחֵי
לֵדָה, שְׁמוֹנָה יְמֵי מִילָה, שִׁבְעָה יְמֵי שַׁבַּתָּא,
שִׁשָּׁה סִדְרֵי מִשְׁנָה, חֲמִשָּׁה חֻמְשֵׁי תוֹרָה,
אַרְבַּע אִמָּהוֹת, שְׁלֹשָׁה אָבוֹת, שְׁנֵי לֻחוֹת
הַבְּרִית, אֶחָד אֱלֹהֵינוּ שֶׁבַּשָּׁמַיִם וּבָאָרֶץ:

WHO KNOWS ELEVEN? I know eleven!
Eleven are the stars in Yosef's dream; Ten are the commandments; Nine are the months to childbirth; Eight are the days to circumcision; Seven are the days of the week; Six are the orders of the Mishnah; Five are the books of the Torah; Four are the Mothers of Israel; Three are the Fathers of Israel; Two are the Tablets of the Covenant; One is our God in heaven and earth.

WHO KNOWS TWELVE? I know twelve!
Twelve are the tribes of Israel; Eleven are the stars in Yosef's dream; Ten are the commandments; Nine are the months to childbirth; Eight are the days to circumcision; Seven are the days of the week; Six are the orders of the Mishnah; Five are the books of the Torah; Four are the Mothers of Israel; Three are the Fathers of Israel; Two are the Tablets of the Covenant; One is our God in heaven and earth.

WHO KNOWS THIRTEEN? I know thirteen!
Thirteen are the attributes of God; Twelve are the tribes of Israel; Eleven are the stars in Yosef's dream; Ten are the commandments; Nine are the months to childbirth; Eight are the days to circumcision; Seven are the days of the week; Six are the orders of the Mishnah; Five are the books of the Torah; Four are the Mothers of Israel; Three are the Fathers of Israel; Two are the Tablets of the Covenant; One is our God in heaven and earth.

חַד גַּדְיָא

חַד גַּדְיָא. חַד גַּדְיָא, דְּזַבִּין אַבָּא
בִּתְרֵי זוּזֵי, חַד גַּדְיָא, חַד גַּדְיָא:

וְאָתָא שׁוּנְרָא, וְאָכְלָה לְגַדְיָא, דְּזַבִּין אַבָּא
בִּתְרֵי זוּזֵי, חַד גַּדְיָא, חַד גַּדְיָא:

וְאָתָא כַלְבָּא, וְנָשַׁךְ לְשׁוּנְרָא, דְּאָכְלָה לְגַדְיָא,
דְּזַבִּין אַבָּא בִּתְרֵי זוּזֵי, חַד גַּדְיָא, חַד גַּדְיָא:

וְאָתָא חוּטְרָא, וְהִכָּה לְכַלְבָּא,
דְּנָשַׁךְ לְשׁוּנְרָא, דְּאָכְלָה לְגַדְיָא, דְּזַבִּין
אַבָּא בִּתְרֵי זוּזֵי, חַד גַּדְיָא, חַד גַּדְיָא:

וְאָתָא נוּרָא, וְשָׂרַף לְחוּטְרָא, דְּהִכָּה לְכַלְבָּא,
דְּנָשַׁךְ לְשׁוּנְרָא, דְּאָכְלָה לְגַדְיָא, דְּזַבִּין
אַבָּא בִּתְרֵי זוּזֵי, חַד גַּדְיָא, חַד גַּדְיָא:

וְאָתָא מַיָּא, וְכָבָה לְנוּרָא, דְּשָׂרַף לְחוּטְרָא,
דְּהִכָּה לְכַלְבָּא, דְּנָשַׁךְ לְשׁוּנְרָא, דְּאָכְלָה לְגַדְיָא,
דְּזַבִּין אַבָּא בִּתְרֵי זוּזֵי, חַד גַּדְיָא, חַד גַּדְיָא:

וְאָתָא תוֹרָא, וְשָׁתָה לְמַיָּא, דְּכָבָה לְנוּרָא, דְּשָׂרַף
לְחוּטְרָא, דְּהִכָּה לְכַלְבָּא, דְּנָשַׁךְ לְשׁוּנְרָא, דְּאָכְלָה
לְגַדְיָא, דְּזַבִּין אַבָּא בִּתְרֵי זוּזֵי, חַד גַּדְיָא, חַד גַּדְיָא:

ONE KID

One kid, one kid that Father bought
for two zuzim; One kid, one kid.

The cat came and ate the kid that father
bought for two zuzim; One kid, one kid.

The dog came and bit the cat that
ate the kid that father bought for
two zuzim; One kid, one kid.

The stick came and beat the dog that bit
the cat that ate the kid that father bought
for two zuzim; One kid, one kid.

The fire came and burned the stick that beat
the dog that bit the cat that ate the kid that
father bought for two zuzim; One kid, one kid.

The water came and quenched the fire
that burned the stick that beat the dog
that bit the cat that ate the kid that father
bought for two zuzim; One kid, one kid.

The ox came and drank the water that quenched
the fire that burned the stick that beat the
dog that bit the cat that ate the kid that father
bought for two zuzim; One kid, one kid.

וְאָתָא הַשׁוֹחֵט, וְשָׁחַט לְתוֹרָא, דְּשָׁתָה
לְמַיָּא, דְּכָבָה לְנוּרָא, דְּשָׂרַף לְחוּטְרָא, דְּהִכָּה
לְכַלְבָּא, דְּנָשַׁךְ לְשׁוּנְרָא, דְּאָכְלָה לְגַדְיָא,
דְּזַבִּין אַבָּא בִּתְרֵי זוּזֵי, חַד גַּדְיָא, חַד גַּדְיָא:

וְאָתָא מַלְאַךְ הַמָּוֶת, וְשָׁחַט לְשׁוֹחֵט, דְּשָׁחַט לְתוֹרָא,
דְּשָׁתָה לְמַיָּא, דְּכָבָה לְנוּרָא, דְּשָׂרַף לְחוּטְרָא,
דְּהִכָּה לְכַלְבָּא, דְּנָשַׁךְ לְשׁוּנְרָא, דְּאָכְלָה לְגַדְיָא,
דְּזַבִּין אַבָּא בִּתְרֵי זוּזֵי, חַד גַּדְיָא, חַד גַּדְיָא:

וְאָתָא הַקָּדוֹשׁ בָּרוּךְ הוּא, וְשָׁחַט לְמַלְאַךְ
הַמָּוֶת, דְּשָׁחַט לְשׁוֹחֵט, דְּשָׁחַט לְתוֹרָא, דְּשָׁתָה
לְמַיָּא, דְּכָבָה לְנוּרָא, דְּשָׂרַף לְחוּטְרָא, דְּהִכָּה
לְכַלְבָּא, דְּנָשַׁךְ לְשׁוּנְרָא, דְּאָכְלָה לְגַדְיָא,
דְּזַבִּין אַבָּא בִּתְרֵי זוּזֵי, חַד גַּדְיָא, חַד גַּדְיָא:

TORAS MENACHEM

וְאָתָא הַקָּדוֹשׁ בָּרוּךְ הוּא וְשָׁחַט לְמַלְאַךְ הַמָּוֶת
— *The Holy One, blessed be He, came and slaughtered the Angel of Death.*

The Talmud teaches that the Angel of Death is none other than Evil Inclination (which first "goes down" to incriminate and then "rises" to prosecute—*Bava Basra* 16a). So the "slaughtering" of the Angel of Death depicted here in the Haggadah alludes to *"the future, when the Holy one, blessed be He, will take the Evil Inclination and slaughter it"* (*Succah* 52a).

The final extermination of man's darker side, which has been responsible for all the world's ills, seems, at first glance, to be a long-awaited triumph of justice. But, if we think about it more closely, there appears to be a serious miscarriage of justice here. After all, the

Evil Inclination is a tool made by God Himself, placed in this world to give man free choice and the rewards that come from exercising that choice correctly. The Evil Inclination does not function, God forbid, outside the orbit of Divine providence and it is a loyal servant of its Creator, no less than the heavenly angels. So why should it be punished and "slaughtered" for carrying out its appointed mission?

To answer this question, the *Ba'al Shem Tov* cited a teaching of the Talmud, which speaks of the prohibition against slaughtering an animal on Shabbos. Which of the thirty-nine categories of prohibited labor does such an act violate? The Talmud offers various answers, one of which is that the slaughterer is guilty of the labor of "dyeing" (since the blood stains the animal when it is slaughtered—*Shabbos* 75a).

The slaughterer came and killed the ox that drank the water that quenched the fire that burned the stick that beat the dog that bit the cat that ate the kid that father bought for two zuzim; One kid, one kid.

The Angel of Death came and slew the slaughterer that killed the ox that drank the water that quenched the fire that burned the stick that beat the dog that bit the cat that ate the kid that father bought for two zuzim; One kid, one kid.

The Holy One, blessed be He, came and slaughtered the Angel of Death that slew the slaughterer that killed the ox that drank the water that quenched the fire that burned the stick that beat the dog that bit the cat that ate the kid that father bought for two zuzim; One kid, one kid.

TORAS MENACHEM

In Hebrew, the term *tzavuah* (dyed) also connotes insincerity and duplicity. Thus the *Ba'al Shem Tov* expounded: For what is the Evil Inclination guilty that he will be slaughtered in the future? Not for tempting man to sin, but for doing so *dishonestly*.

If the Evil Inclination would merely have said, "Why don't you disobey God? Why don't you anger him?" that would have been transparent and fair. But instead, he makes us imagine that by sinning *we are doing the right thing*. He says to us, "If you work on Shabbos, and are not so careful to be scrupulous in business you will have more money to give to charity." So, ultimately, his punishment will come, not for

actually promoting sin, which is his job, but for the way in which he did it, through "unfair advertising."

Ultimately, however, even the slaughtering of the Evil Inclination will not be a punishment, in the simple sense of the word. In Judaism, ritually slaughtering an animal is not perceived as something purely negative, a mere end to a life, but as a spiritual "ascent" that allows the animal to be used for a holy purpose. So when we say that the Evil Inclination will be slaughtered, it means that our animal side, the source of our strongest passions, will be elevated and "realigned" to more noble pursuits, and be used only for things good and holy.

(Based on *Sichah* of 10th *Shevat* 5719; *Shabbos Parshas Ki Sisa* 5747)

☙☙ Bibliography

Abarbanel—Rabbi Don Yitzchak Abarbanel (1437–1508), famous Jewish philosopher and leader of Spanish Jewry. Authored an extensive, running commentary on the entire Bible. His commentary to the Haggadah is entitled *Zevach Pesach*.

Akeidas Yitzchak—Lengthy philosophical-homiletic commentary on the Pentateuch by Rabbi Yitzchak ben Moshe Arama (1420 – 1494), one of the leading rabbis of fifteenth-century Spain.

Alshich—Rabbi Moshe Alshich (1508–c1600), Rabbi and preacher in Tzefas, Israel and author of a popular commentary on the Bible, often cited in Chasidic discourses.

Alter Rebbe—Rabbi Shneur Zalman of Liadi (1745–1812), the first Rebbe and founder of the Chabad Movement. His monumental works include the *Tanya*, and his *Shulchan Aruch*.

Alter Rebbe's Shulchan Aruch—or *Shulchan Aruch ha-Rav*. Major recodification of the *Shulchan Aruch* by Rabbi Shneur Zalman of Liadi (the Alter Rebbe), which includes reasons for the laws. First section printed in Shklov in 1814.

Alter Rebbe's Siddur—Liturgical rite of the *Arizal*, with the Alter Rebbe's alterations and grammatical adjustments. The Alter Rebbe combed through over sixty editions of *Siddur Arizal* before deciding on the correct version of the text.

Amram Ga'on—R. Amram ben Sheshna Gaon (d. c875). Head of the academy of Sura in Babylonia during the ninth century. Compiled standard text for the daily prayers, adding halachic decisions and commentary on customs.

Arizal—Rabbi Yitzchak Luria (1534–1572), leading Kabbalist who influenced the Kabbalistic thought of subsequent generations. His teachings have been accepted as the final word on Kabbalistic thought.

Avos d'Rabbi Nasan—Minor tractate by R. Nasan of Babylonia; a commentary on *Avos*.

Avudraham—Primary text of commentary to the prayers by Rabbi David ben Yosef Avudraham, l4th century halachist and liturgist.

Ba'al Haturim—Commentary on the Torah by Rabbi Ya'akov Meir ben Asher (1268–1340), author of the *Tur*, analyzing the significance of word usage.

Ba'al Shem Tov—Rabbi Yisra'el ben Eliezer (1698–1760), founder of the Chasidic movement. Emphasized the virtues of pure devotion to God, the significance of prayer, love of God, and love of one's fellow Jew.

Bach—"*Bayis Chadash*," a legal commentary on the *Tur* by R' Yoel Sirkis (1561–1640).

Bachaye—Rabbi Bachaye ben Asher (1263–1340) of Saragossa, Spain. Author of a popular Torah commentary which incorporates literal, allegorical and Kabbalistic interpretations.

Beis ha-Otzar—Highly original encyclopedic work which seeks to analyze the conceptual principles underlying Talmudic law, by Rabbi Yosef Engel (1859–1920) of Poland.

Beis Yosef—Halachic commentary by R' Yosef Caro (1488–1575) on the *Tur*. He was also the author of the *Shulchan Aruch* and *Kesef Mishneh*, a commentary on *Rambam's* code.

Bereishis Rabah—The section of *Midrash Rabah* on the Book of Genesis. (See "*Midrash Rabah*")

Bereishis—The Book of Genesis.

Brachos—Talmudic tractate in Order of Zeraim (Agriculture).

Chagigah—Talmudic tractate in Order of Mo'ed (Festivals).

Chasam Sofer—Rabbi Moshe Sofer (Schreiber) (1762–1839), Rabbi and Rosh Yeshiva in Hungary, and one of the most influential halachic authorities. His works include *Toras Moshe* on the Torah, gloss to the Talmud, gloss to the *Shulchan Aruch* and responsa.

Chasan Sofer—Rabbi Shmuel Eherenfeld (1835–1883), Chief Rabbi of Mattersdorf, Austria and grandson of the *Chasam Sofer*. Author of responsa and commentary on the Haggadah entitled *Pedus Nafsheinu*.

Chida—Rabbi Chaim Yosef David Azulai (1724–1806), halachist, Kabbalist, historian and bibliographer. Rabbi of Cairo, and later Livorno, Italy. Author of numerous works, including a commentary on the Haggadah entitled *Simchas ha-Regel*.

Chiddushei Aggados—See *Maharsha*.

Chizkuni—Commentary on the Torah by Rabbi Chizkiyah ben Manoach, thirteenth century scholar from Provence, France.

Chok Ya'akov—Major commentary to *Shulchan Aruch*, Laws of Pesach by Rabbi Ya'akov Back (Bechofen) Reischer (1661–1733), a prominent European Rabbi who served communities in Prague, Galicia, Germany and France.

Chulin—Talmudic tractate in Order of Kodashim (Offerings).

Darkei Moshe—Commentary to the *Tur* by Rabbi Moshe Isserles (c1520–1572). See *Rema*.

Derech Mitzvosecha—Compendium of fundamental Chasidic discourses on many *mitzvos* of the Torah by the third Lubavitcher Rebbe, Rabbi Menachem Mendel of Lubavitch (the *"Tzemach Tzedek"*). Also known as *"Ta'amei Hamitzvos."* First published in 1911, in Poltova, Ukraine.

Devarim Rabah—The section of *Midrash Rabah* on the Book of Deuteronomy. See *Midrash Rabah*.

Devarim—The Book of Deuteronomy.

Eitz Chaim—Primary Kabbalistic teachings of the Arizal (Rabbi Yitzchak Luria, 1534–1572) received orally and later recorded by his foremost disciple Rabbi Chaim Vital (1543–1620). Credited with resolving all prior disputes among the Kabbalists. First printed in 1782.

Eitz Yosef—Commentary to Ein Ya'akov, the homiletic passages of the Talmud, and to *Midrash* alongside his *Anaf Yosef* and *Yad Yosef,* by Rabbi Chanoch Zundel of Bialystok (d. 1867).

Gevuras Hashem—Discussion of the Exodus from Egypt and the Pesach Haggadah by Rabbi Yehudah Loewe of Prague (1526–1609). See *Maharal*.

Hagahos Maimonios—Commentary on the *Mishneh Torah* by an unnamed disciple of Rabbi Meir ben Boruch ha-Kohen (c1215–1293), the *Maharam* of Rotenburg, teacher of the *Rosh* and *Mordechai*.

Hai Ga'on—R' Hai ben Sherira Gaon (939–1038), theologian, rabbi and scholar who served as leader of the Talmudic academy of Pumbedisa. He wrote extensively on philosophical, linguistic and liturgical issues.

Ha-Melech bi-Mesibo—Insights shared by the Lubavitcher Rebbe, Rabbi Menachem Mendel Schneersohn, during festival meals from 1953–1970. Published by Kehos Publication Society in 1993. 2 volumes.

Hayom Yom—Handbook of Chasidic insights following the calendar, compiled by the Lubavitcher Rebbe, Rabbi Menachem Mendel Schneersohn. First printed in 1942.

Hisvaduyos—43 volumes of public talks of the Lubavitcher Rebbe, Rabbi Menachem Mendel Schneersohn, delivered from 1981–1992, translated into Hebrew. Published by *Va'ad Hanachos be-Lahak*.

Ibn Ezra—R' Avraham ibn Ezra (1080–1164). Born in Spain, he was the author of a classic commentary to Tanach, and was also a prominent grammarian and poet.

Igeres Hakodesh—Fourth part of *Tanya* consisting of a collection of letters written by the *Alter Rebbe* to his disciples and various Chasidic communities. See *Tanya*.

Igeres ha-Teshuvah—Third section of *Tanya*, discussing the concept of *teshuvah* according to talmudic and Kabbalistic sources. See *Tanya*.

Igros Kodesh—Correspondence of the Lubavitcher Rebbe, Rabbi Menachem Mendel Schneersohn, from 1928–1973. Kehos Publication Society (1987–2006). 28 volumes.

Igros Melech—Communal letters addressed to the global Jewish community on various occasions from 1950–1992 by the Lubavitcher Rebbe, Rabbi Menachem Mendel Schneersohn. Kehos Publication Society (1992). 2 volumes.

Imrei Shefer—commentary on the Haggadah by Rabbi Naftali Tzvi Yehuda Berlin (1817–1893), Rosh Yeshiva in Volozhin, Russia. Commonly known as the *Netziv*.

Iyun Ya'akov—Commentary to the homiletic passages of the *Talmud* by Rabbi Ya'akov Back (Bechofen) Reischer (1661–1733), which appears in standard editions of *Ein Ya'akov*. See also *Chok Ya'akov*.

Jerusalem Talmud—See *Talmud*.

Keser Shem Tov (Gaguine)—Comprehensive work tracing the sources of Sefardic customs by Rabbi Shem Tov Gaguine (1885–1954), leader of the Spanish and Portuguese Jews' Congregations of England.

Kesubos—Talmudic tractate in Order of Nashim (Women).

Kiryas Sefer—Commentary to the *Rambam's Mishneh Torah* by Rabbi Moshe Trani (1500–1580), head of the *Beis Din* of *Tzefas* after the passing of Rabbi Yosef Caro.

Kocho d'Rabbi Eliezer b'Rashbi—Kabbalistic treatise by Rabbi Yeshayahu Asher Zelig Margolis of Jerusalem (1894–1969).

Kolbo—Important compendium of Jewish ritual and civil laws by an unknown author. Attributed by some to Rabbi Aharon ben Ya'akov ha-Cohen of Narbonne, France (13th–14th c.), author of *Orchos Chaim.*

Le'ohr ha-Halacha—A compendium of articles on subjects of halachic interest by R' Shlomo Yosef Zevin (1890–1978), editor of *Encylopedia Talmudis*. Published in 1955.

Likutei Levi Yitzchak—Kabbalistic commentary to the Zohar by Rabbi Levi Yitzchak Schneersohn (1878–1944), Chief Rabbi of the Ukrainian city of Yekaterinoslav (Dnepropetrovsk) from 1907–1939, and father of the Lubavitcher Rebbe, Rabbi Menachem Mendel Schneersohn. First published in New York in 1971.

Likutei Sichos—39 volume work of the Lubavitcher Rebbe, Rabbi Menachem Mendel Schneersohn, analyzing all parts of the Torah in an original manner and bringing them into harmony with one another. Published by *Va'ad le-Hafatzas Sichos* (Kehos) from 1962 to 2001.

Likutei Ta'amim u'Minhagim—Commentary to the Haggadah by Rabbi Menachem Mendel Schneersohn tracing the sources for general and Chasidic customs observed at the Seder, the textual precedents of the Chabad Nusach and insights into the Haggadah. First published in New York, 1946.

Likutei Torah—Fundamental Chasidic discourses on Leviticus, Numbers, and Deuteronomy by Rabbi Shneur Zalman of Liadi, author of *Shulchan Aruch* and *Tanya*. See *Alter Rebbe.*

Ma'amarei Admor ha-Emtzoie—Chasidic discourses of the Mitteler Rebbe, Rabbi Dov Ber of Lubavitch. Published by Kehos Publication Society in 19 volumes from 1985–1991.

Ma'aseh Rokeach—Commentary to *Rambam's Mishneh Torah* by Rabbi Mas'ud Chai ben Aharon Rokeach (1689–1768).

Ma'asei Nisim—Commentary to Haggadah by Rabbi Ya'akov Lorberbaum (1760–1832), author of *Nesivos ha-Mishpat.*

Machzor Vitry—Liturgical comments and rulings, as well as many Piyutim by Rabbi Simcha of Vitry, France (d.1105), a student of *Rashi.*

Magen Avraham—Primary commentary on *Shulchan Aruch Orach Chaim*, by Rabbi Avraham Gombiner (1634–1682) of Kalisch, Poland. The *Alter Rebbe* relied heavily on his rulings when writing his *Shulchan Aruch.*

Maggid of Mezritch—Rabbi Dovber (c1704–1772). Primary disciple and successor of the Baal Shem Tov and one of the most important propagators of Chasidus.

Maharal—Rabbi Yehudah Loewe of Prague, (1526–1609). Chief Rabbi in Moravia, Posen, and Prague, a direct descendent of King David. Author of numerous works in many fields of Torah. There is a tradition that the *Tanya* was significantly influenced by *Maharal.*

Maharil—R' Ya'akov ben Moshe ha-Levi Moelin (c1365–1427) of Germany. Leading Ashkenazic halachic authority of his times. His rulings are often incorporated in the *Rema's* glosses to *Shulchan Aruch.*

Maharsha—*Moreinu HaRav Shmuel Eliezer Halevi Eidels* of Ostroh, Poland (1555–1632), Rosh Yeshiva and Rabbi in a number of the leading communities of Poland. Author of important commentaries on the Talmud, divided into halachic and aggadic sections.

Maharzu—Commentary to the *Midrash Rabah* by Rabbi Ze'ev Wolf Einhorn (19th century.).

Malbim—*Meir Leibush ben Yechiel Michel* (1809–1879), Rabbi in Germany, Romania, and Russia. Author of popular Bible commentary which connects the Oral and Written traditions.

Mechilta—Halachic Midrash of the Tannaic period on the Book of Exodus.

Mefa'ane'ach Tzefunos—Compendium of insights into the conceptual framework of Rabbi Yosef Rosen, the Rogatchover Gaon (1858–1936), detailing and explaining his terminology and method, by Rabbi Menachem Kasher (1895–1983). Published in Jerusalem, 1976.

Megilah—Talmudic tractate in Order of Mo'ed (Festivals).

Meiri—Extensive commentary to the Talmud by Rabbi Menachem ha-Meiri (c1249–c1306).

Midrash—Compilation of exegetical teachings of the Tannaic period divided into Aggadic Midrash and Halachic Midrash.

Midrash Lekach Tov—(also known as *Pesikta Zutrasa*). Midrashic anthology arranged by R' Toviah Hagadol (1036–1108) of Greece and Bulgaria.

Midrash Rabah—A major collection of homilies and commentaries on the Torah, ascribed to Rabbi Oshiah Rabah (c 3rd century), perhaps assembled during the early Geonic period. First printed in Constantinople 1512.

Midrash Tehilim—Agadic teachings of the Sages arranged according to the verses of the book of Psalms. Also known as *Midrash Shocher Tov.*

Minchas Chinuch—Scholarly supercommentary to Sefer ha-Chinuch by Rabbi Yosef Babad (1800–1875), Rabbi of Tarnipol, Poland.

Mishnah—Fundamental collection of the legal pronouncements and discussion of the Tanna'im, compiled by Rabbi Yehudah ha-Nassi early in the third century. The Mishnah is the basic text of the Oral Law.

Mishnas Chasidim—Kabbalistic work on the teachings of the Arizal by Rabbi Refa'el Emanuel Chai Riki (1687–1743), one of the greatest Kabbalists of Italy and later in Safed, Israel.

Mitteler Rebbe—Rabbi Dov Ber Schneuri (1773–1827), son of Rabbi Schneur Zalman of Liadi; second Lubavitcher Rebbe.

Ohr haChaim—Commentary on the Torah by Talmudic and Kabbalist scholar Rabbi Chaim ben Attar (1696–1743).

Ohr ha-Meir—Chassidic commentary on Torah by Rabbi Ze'ev Wolf of Zhitomir (c1730–c1795), one of the leading disciples of the *Maggid of Mezritch.*

Ohr ha-Torah—Extensive exposition of Chabad Chasidic thought by the third Lubavitcher Rebbe, Rabbi Menachem Mendel (the Tzemach Tzedek, 1789–1866). Printed in New York between 1951 and 1983 in 48 volumes.

Ohr Torah—Anthology of Chasidic commentaries by Rabbi Dovber, the Maggid of Mezritch. First published in Koretz in 1781.

Ohr Zarua—a Halachic compendium by Rabbi Yitzchak ben Moshe of Vienna (c1180–c1250), a student of the Tosafists in Ashkenaz and teacher of Maharam of Rotenburg. The author does not give merely the halachic decisions, but also quotes the Talmud, explains the subject matter, and develops the law from it. The halachic decisions of the *Ohr Zarua* are cited frequently by later authorities.

Orach Chaim—First of the four sections of the *Tur* and *Shulchan Aruch*, dealing with laws that follow a time cycle.

Orchos Chaim—a comprehensive work on Halachah and Minhag by Rabbi Aharon ben Ya'akov haCohen of Narbonne, France (13th and 14th centuries).

Pesach Me'ubin—The laws of searching for chametz and the Seder night by Rabbi Chaim ben Yisrael Benveniste (1603–1673) of Izmir, Turkey. Collected from his responsa *Kneses haGedolah.*

Pesachim—Tractate of Talmud in the Order of Mo'ed (Festivals).

Pirkei d'Rabbi Eliezer—Midrashic work by the school of Eliezer ben Hyrcanus (1st–2nd centuries). First published in Constantinople in 1514.

Pirush ha-Mishnayos—commentary to Mishna by the Rambam. (see: Rambam)

Pnei Moshe—Running commentary to the *Jerusalem Talmud*, by Rabbi Moshe Margulies of Amsterdam and Zamut. (1710–1781).

Pri Chadash—Commentary to the *Shulchan Aruch* by R' Chizkiyah de Silva (1659–1698).

Pri Etz Chaim—Kabbalistic work of the *Arizal* written by his student R' Chaim Vital.

Pri Megadim—Supercommentary by Rabbi Yosef Teomim (1727–1792), Rabbi in Frankfurt, Germany on the main commentaries of the Shulchan Aruch; Magen Avraham, Taz and Shach.

R' Avraham, son of the Rambam—(1186–1237) succeeded his father as official leader (Nagid) and Chief Rabbi of Egyptian Jewry.

R' Moshe Chagiz—(1672–1762), great Talmudic scholar and fierce opponent of the Sabbatean movement. Author of many works, both halachic and polemic in nature.

Ra'avad—Rabbi Avraham ben David of Posquieres (c 1120–c 1197), Talmudist, halachist, and Kabbalist. Author of critical notes on *Rambam's* Mishneh Torah and numerous other works.

Ra'avan—Rabbi Eliezer ben Nathan (c 1090 – 1170). Author of Sefer [Piskei] haRa'avan. His main work is entitled Even Ha'Ezer. This work is comprised of responsa, halacha, customs, and a commentary on parts of the Talmud.

Rabbi Yosef Yitzchok of Lubavitch—see Rebbe Rayatz

Rabeinu Bachaye—see Bachaye

Rabeinu Manoach—commentary to Rambam by Rabbi Manoach ben Yaakov (13th–14th centuries), of Narbonne, France.

Ralbag—"Gersonides," Rabbi Levi ben Gershom (1288–1344). Author of rationalistic commentary to the Bible.

Rambam—"Maimonides," Rabbi Moshe ben Maimon (1135–1204), leading Torah scholar of the Middle Ages. His major works are *Sefer ha-Mitzvos, Commentary to the Mishnah, Mishneh Torah (Yad Hachazakah),* a comprehensive code of Jewish law, *Moreh Nevuchim,* "Guide for the Perplexed," a primary work of Jewish philosophy.

Ramban—"Nachmanides" (1194–1270), Rabbi Moshe ben Nachman of Gerona, Spain, one of the leading Torah scholars of the Middle Ages; author of a major commentary to the Torah and numerous other works.

Ran—Rabbenu Nissim (1308–1376). Authored an important commentary to the Talmud, published in most major editions.

Rashbam—Rabbi Shmuel ben Meir, Talmud and Torah Commentator, who supplemented his grandfather Rashi's commentary to the Talmud (c 1085–1174). Brother of *Rabeinu Tam.*

Rashba—Rabbi Shlomo ibn Aderes (1235–1310), Rabbi of Barcelona, known for his Talmudic commentary and many responsa.

Rashbatz—Rabbi Shimon ben Tzemach of Duran (c1361–1444). Left Spain in the aftermath of the 1391 massacres and moved to Algiers, where he later became Chief Rabbi. Author of the halachic treatise *Tashbetz, Magen Avos* on Pirkei Avos, and *Yavin Shmuah* which includes his commentary to the Haggadah.

Rashi—Rabbi Shlomo Yitzchaki (1040–1105), author of basic commentary on the Bible and Talmud. According to Chasidic tradition, his commentary to the Torah contains allusions to Kabbalistic concepts.

Rebbe Maharash—Rabbi Shmuel of Lubavitch (1834–1882). Youngest son and successor of the Tzemach Tzedek . Fourth Rebbe of Chabad.

Rebbe Rashab—Rabbi Sholom Dovber Schneersohn of Lubavitch (1860–1920). He was the grandson of the Tzemach Tzedek and the fifth Rebbe in the Chabad dynasty.

Rebbe Rayatz—Rabbi Yosef Yitzchak Schneersohn of Lubavitch (1880–1950). Son of the *Rebbe Rashab* and sixth Rebbe of Chabad. Unflinching, fearless leader in Communist Russia where he was arrested for spreading Judaism. Established large network of Jewish day schools in the United States, and pioneered the process of spreading Jewish observance to the Jewish masses worldwide.

Ri ben Yakar—Rabbi Yehuda Ben Yakar (1150–1225) teacher of the *Ramban.* Wrote a commentary on the Haggadah which can be found at the end of his work *Perush HaTefillot Ve'Habrachot,* also known as *Ma'ayan Ganim.*

Rif—R' Yitzchak al-Fasi, Talmudist and Codifier (1013–1103).

Ritva—R' Yom Tov Ibn Asevili (1248–1330), Talmudic Commentator and Halachist.

Rogatchover Ga'on—Rabbi Yosef Rosen, (1858–1936), the 'genius from Rogatchov' who later became Rabbi of Dvinsk. Authored numerous responsa, a commentary to *Rambam* and a commentary on the Torah entitled *Tzafnas Pane'ach.*

Rosh—R' Asher ben Yechiel, Talmudic commentator and author of halachic compendium arranged on the tractates of the *Talmud* (c 1250–1328).

Rosh Hashanah—Talmudic tractate in Order of Mo'ed (Festivals).

Sa'adiah Ga'on—(882–942) Author of works in many areas of Torah, including the philosophical work, Emunos v'Deos.

Sanhedrin—Tractate of Talmud in Order of Nezikin (Damages).

Seder ha-Doros—A chronology of events and personalities from creation until 1696, based on Rabbinic sources, by Rabbi Yechiel Heilprin (1660–1746), Lithuanian rabbi, Kabbalist, and chronicler. First published in 1769.

Sefer Charedim—by Rabbi Elazar ben Mordechai Azkari (1531–1600), a Kabbalist and great expounder of the Torah. Author of the Yedid Nefesh prayer.

Sefer ha-Mamarim—Collected Chasidic discourses by the Rebbes of Chabad.

Sefer ha-Chinuch—Compendium of basic explanations on the 613 *mitzvos* by an unknown Spanish author of the 13th century. Ascribed by some to Rabbi Aharon Halevi, a student of *Rashba*.

Sefer ha-Ma'amarim Melukat—Chasidic discourses of the Lubavitcher Rebbe, Rabbi Menachem Mendel Schneersohn, in six volumes, published by Vaad le-Hafatzas Sichos (Kehos) between 1987 and 1992.

Sefer ha-Minhagim Chabad—authoritative collection of Chabad customs compiled by Rabbi Menachem Ze'ev ha-Levi Greenglass and Rabbi Yehuda Leib Groner (Kehos 1966).

Sefer ha-Mitzvos—Codification of the commandments and their basic sources by Rambam.

Sefer ha-Sichos—Public addresses of the Lubavitcher Rebbe, Rabbi Menachem Mendel Schneersohn, from the years 1986–92, published by Vaad le-Hafatzas Sichos (Kehos) in 12 volumes.

Sforno—Commentary on the Torah by Rabbi Ovadiah Sforno of Rome and Bologna, Italy (1470–1550).

Sha'arei Ohrah, Sha'arei Teshuvah—Chasidic discourses by Rabbi Dovber of Lubavitch the Mitteler Rebbe (1773–1827). First published in Zhitomir in 1864.

Shabbos—Talmudic tractate in Order of Mo'ed (Festivals).

Shaloh—*Shenei Luchos Habris* ("The Two Tablets of the Covenant"), an encyclopedic compilation of ritual, ethics, and mysticism by Rabbi Yeshayah Hurwitz (1560–1630). There is a tradition that the *Tanya* was significantly influenced by the Shaloh.

Shemos—The Book of Exodus.

Shemos Rabah—The section of Midrash Rabah on the Book of Exodus. See "*Midrash Rabah.*"

Shibolei haLeket—Commentary to the Haggadah by Rabbi Tzidkayah ben Avraham HaRofeh Anav, Rome, Italy (1230–1300).

Shulchan Aruch—Universally accepted Code of Jewish Law encompassing all areas of practical halachah, by Rabbi Yosef Caro (1488–1575).

Sichos Kodesh—50 volumes of public addresses by the Lubavitcher Rebbe, Rabbi Menachem Mendel Schneersohn, delivered from 1950–1981 in Yiddish. Published in 1985-7.

Siddur Kol Ya'akov—A Siddur with meditations of the Arizal by Rabbi Ya'akov Koppel (d. 1786), a student of the Ba'al Shem Tov.

Siddur Tehillas Hashem—See Alter Rebbe's Siddur.

Siddur—Set order of daily prayers, including core passages composed by the Biblical prophets and Sages of the Second Temple era to which later texts were appended.

Sifri—Halachic Midrash on the books of Bamidbar and Devarim.

Simchas ha-Regel—see Chida.

Ta'amei ha-Minhagim—A collection of sources and reasons for Jewish customs and traditions by Rabbi Avraham Yitzchok Sperling. First published in Lvov, 1896.

Ta'anis—Talmudic tractate in Order of Mo'ed (Festivals).

Talmud—Comprehensive term for the *Mishnah* and *Gemara* as joined in the two compilations known as Babylonian Talmud (6th century) and Jerusalem Talmud (5th century).

Tanya—Primary chasidic text authored by Rabbi Shneur Zalman of Liadi. See *Alter Rebbe.*

Terumas ha-Deshen—Halachic Responsa by Rabbi Yisroel ben Pesachya Isserlein (1390–1460), Chief Rabbi of Wiener Neustadt, Austria and student of *Maharil*. An important source of the practices of the Ashkenazi Jews, it was drawn upon extensively by *Rema* in his gloss to *Shulchan Aruch*.

Tola'as Ya'akov—an important Kabbalistic exposition of the prayer ritual by Meir Ibn Gabbai of Spain (1480–1543). Published posthumously in 1560 by his son-in-law.

Torah Ohr—Fundamental Chasidic discourses on Genesis and Exodus by Rabbi Shneur Zalman of Liadi. *See* Alter Rebbe.

Toras Shmuel—Chasidic discourses of Rabbi Shmuel of Lubavitch (1834–1882), the *Rebbe Maharash*. Published by Kehos Publication Society from 1945 to 2007 in 16 volumes.

Tosefta—Tannaitic collection of Braisos, paralleling the Mishnah. Compiled by the Tanna Rabbi Chiya together with Rabbi Oshiya around the end of the second century CE.

Tosfos—Talmudic commentary of the French, German and English rabbis of the 12th and 13th centuries.

Tur—Code of Jewish law composed by R' Yaakov, son of the Rosh (c1275–c1340).

Tur Barekes—a Kabbalistic commentary to the *Shulchan Aruch* by Rabeinu Chaim ha-Kohen, a student of Rabbi Chaim Vital.

Turei Zahav (Taz)—a major commentary to the *Shulchan Aruch* by R' David ben Shmuel Ha'Levi, Rabbi of Ostroh, Ukraine and later in Lemberg (1586–1667).

Tzafnas Pane'ach—Highly original commentary to *Rambam's Mishneh Torah* by Rabbi Yosef Rosen. See Rogatchover Gaon.

Tzemach Ga'on—appointed Gaon c895, often cited in Rishonim.

Tzemach Tzedek—Rabbi Menachem Mendel Schneersohn of Lubavitch (1789–1866), commonly known as *Tzemach Tzedek* after the name of his halachic responsa. A grandson of the Alter Rebbe, he succeeded his father-in-law, the Mitteler Rebbe, as third Rebbe of the Chabad dynasty.

Tzror Hamor—Commentary to the Torah by R' Avraham Saba (1440–1508) of Spain, Portugal, and Morocco.

Vayikra—The Book of Leviticus.

Vilna Ga'on—R' Eliyahu ben Shlomo of Vilna (1720–1797), famed Lithuanian Talmudist, Kabbalist, grammarian, and mathematician.

Ya'avetz – Rabbi Ya'akov ben Tzvi Emden (1698–1776) of Altona, Germany, son of the *Chacham Tzvi*.

Yalkut Shimoni—Comprehensive Midrashic anthology, covering the entire Bible, attributed to Rabbi Shimon HaDarshan of Frankfurt (13th century).

Zohar—Primary text of Kabbalah, compiled by Rabbi Shimon ben Yochai and his disciples in the form of a commentary on the Torah. First published in the late 13th century by Rabbi Moshe de Leon (c1250–1305), in Spain.

✍ Chabad Haggados and Pesach anthologies

In Hebrew:

Haggadah Shel Pesach B'Ohr ha-Chasidus (Heichal Menachem, New York 1996). A collection of insights on the Haggadah from Chabad and other Chasidic sources.

Hilchos Leil ha-Seder mi-Shulchan Aruch Admur ha-Zakein—(Rabbi Chaim Eliezer Ashkenazi, Montreal 2005–7, 2 vols.) An exhaustive analysis of chapters 472-486 of the *Alter Rebbe's Shulchan Aruch*, which contain the laws relevant to the Seder.

Ispashtusa de'Moshe al ha-Rambam—(Rabbi Joseph Hecht, Ramat Bet Shemesh, 2004). An exhaustive compendium of Halachic teachings of all the Chabad Rebbeim on Rambam's discussion of the Pesach laws and the Haggadah.

Kuntres Biuray ha-Haggadah—(*Machon Ohr ha-Chasidus*, New York, 2006). A selections of insights into the Haggadah adapted from the Rebbe's teachings into Hebrew.

Mayan Chai, Haggadah Shel Pesach—(Kehos 1994). Insights from the Rebbe on the Haggadah, adapted for children.

Mi-Shulchan ha-Seder—An anthology of insights offered by the Previous Lubavitcher Rebbe at his Seder from 1946–9. Printed in the journal *B'Ohr ha-Chasidus* (Heichal Menachem, New York, 2002, issue 5).

Otzar Minhagei Chabad—(Rabbi Yehoshua Mondshine, Kehos 1996. 2 vols.). A compendium of all extant primary sources that relate to the Chabad festival customs.

Sha'arei Haggadah—(appended to *Likutei Ta'amim u'Minhagim,* Heichal Menachem Edition, Jerusalem 5759). A selection of the Rebbe's insights on the Haggadah, condensed and rewritten in Hebrew. The insights are largely drawn from the *Biurim* in the Rebbe's Haggadah, though they are supplemented with additional material.

Sha'arei Mo'adim, Chag ha-Pesach—(Heichal Menachem, Jerusalem 1997. 2 vols.) An anthology of the Rebbe's talks on Pesach themes, drawing from both edited and unedited sources, translated into Hebrew.

Sha'arei Shalom—Scholarly commentary to *Likutei Ta'amim u'Minhagim* by Rabbi Shalom Spalter (Morristown, New Jersey 2005).

Shulchan ha-Melech—(Machon Oholei Shem, Lubavitch, Kfar Chabad, 1992). An anthology of the Rebbe's commentaries on the *Alter Rebbe's Shulchan Aruch* (see bibliography). Vol. 2 is dedicated to festival laws.

Sipur Shel Chag, Chag ha-Pesach—(Rabbi Menachem Zigelboim, Kfar Chabad 2004). An anthology of stories relating to Pesach and the Seder from Chabad sources.

In English:

At Our Rebbe's Seder Table—(Rabbi Eli Touger, Kehos 1994). This was the first Haggadah to include comprehensive directions in English within the Haggadah itself that conform to current Chabad practice. (In *Likutei Ta'amim u'Minhagim* the reader must refer to footnotes). There is also a wide selection of insights drawn from an impressive array of sources, though they are quite brief.

Haggadah for Pesach—(Kehos 1996, 8th edition) a translation of the Haggadah and selected insights from *Likutei Ta'amim u'Minhagim* by Rabbi Jacob Immanuel Schochet.

Haggadah for Pesach, Annotated Edition—(Kehos 2005), the basic Haggadah with Schochet's translation with clear instructions that reflect current Chabad practice. No commentary is included.

Haggadah for Pesach in the light of Chasidus—(Rabbi Y. Green, Kfar Chabad 1995). This is probably the best anthology of insights to the Haggadah from all the Chabad Rebbeim, though, in English translation they remain somewhat obtuse. Includes a comprehensive guide to the laws and customs of the Seder.

Ki Yishalcha Bincha—(Rabbi Moshe Bogomilsky, New York 1999). An original commentary to the Haggadah, in question and answer format, drawing on both Chabad sources and a vast array of other classical material.

The Passover Haggadah—(Kehos 1999). The basic Haggadah with Schochet's translation, to which Chasidic commentary written by Rabbi Yanki Tauber is appended.

The Rebbe's Haggadah in Q & A for Youth—(Rabbi Zalman Shanowitz, 2007). A very accessible rendition of *Likutei Ta'amim u'Minhagim* into English, aimed at a non-scholarly audience.

לעילוי נשמות
ר' דוד וזוגתו **לאה סלאגער**
ר' **דוד** וזוגתו **רינה עטר**
זכרונם לברכה
תהיינה נשמותיהם צרורות בצרור החיים

נדפס ע"י
ר' דוד שיחי' **סלאגער**
וזוגתו מרת **לארא** תחי'
ובנותיהם:
חנה ושרה מלכה

ולזכות
ר' ראובן שיחי' **סלאגער**
וזוגתו מרת **מרים** תחי'

לעיילוי נשמות

החסיד ר' **אברהם** וזוגתו **זעלדא פייגלין**

הרה"ג הרה"ח ר' **מרדכי זאב** הכהן גוטניק

הרה"ג הרה"ח ר' **אשר** וזוגתו **חי'ה בתי'ה אברמסאן**

הרה"ג הרה"ח ר' **דוד ארי'ה** הכהן יארמוש

זכרונם לברכה

תהיינה נשמותיהם צרורות בצרור החיים

❧

ולזכות

הרה"ג הרה"ת ר' **שלום דובער** שיחי' הכהן גוטניק

ראב"ד דק"ק מעלבורן יע"א

וזוגתו מרת **דבורה** תחי'

❧

מרת **שרה נחמה** תחי' יארמוש

❧

נדפס ע"י

הרה"ח הרה"ת ר' **מאיר** שיחי' הכהן גוטניק

וזוגתו מרת **שיינדל טעמא** תחי'

בניהם ובנותיהם:

הרה"ת **שמואל מרדכי זאב** הכהן וזוגתו מרת **פייגא דינה**,

וילדיהם שיינא אסתר שפרה ודוד ארי'ה

חנה ובעלה הרה"ת **צבי אלימלך שפירא**

וילדיהם חי' מושקא, מנחם מענדל ודוד ארי'ה

מנוחה רחל ובעלה הרה"ת **יוסף יצחק באָרבער**

וילדיהם איטא וחי' מושקא

זעלדא ובעלה הרה"ת **מיכאל אלעזר לערנער** ובתם חי' מושקא

מנחם מענדל הכהן, **סימא אסתר**, **שפרינצא לאה**, **יוסף יצחק** הכהן,

אברהם שלמה הכהן, **חי'ה בתי'ה**, ו**דוד ארי'ה** הכהן

שיחיו לאורך ימים ושנים טובות

מוקדש

לחיזוק התקשרות

לכבוד קדושת אדוננו מורנו ורבנו

נשיא דורנו

ISBN 978-1-934152-13-3

ממצרים שנאמר והגדת לבנך ביום ההוא כ